# Certified in Production and Inventory Management

# Material and Capacity Requirements Planning Reprints

**Articles selected by the
Material and Capacity Requirements Planning Committee
of the APICS Curricula and Certification Council**

©1991 The American Production and Inventory Control Society, Inc.
International Standard Book Number: 1-55822-042-9
Library of Congress Number: 91-71925

Stock No. 05002, 6/91, 5000

# Table of Contents

## Basic Techniques and Applications

## Communications to Top Management

## Implementation and Project Management

## The Relation of MRP to Zero Inventory Practices

## Repetitive, Process, and Make-to-Order Applications

## Interfaces to Other Production and Inventory Control Functions

## Interfaces to Engineering Functions

## Interfaces to Purchasing and Financial Functions

## Special Topics

# Preface

The "knowledge explosion" so frequently mentioned these days is fast upon those of us in manufacturing. This phenomenon is nowhere more clearly felt than in the creation of a new edition of the APICS Material and Capacity Requirements Planning Reprints. As a society dedicated to furthering the understanding of manufacturing excellence, the American Production and Inventory Control Society has both contributed to the explosion of information and, hopefully, cast some light on the important issues.

These articles are drawn largely from APICS periodicals and conferences. They were assembled by the MRP/CRP Subcommittee of the Curricula and Certification Council. The objectives of this compilation were simple:

1.      Supplement the primary texts of the MRP/CRP Certification Study Guide with relevant articles to help prepare the test candidate for the MRP/CRP certification test. There is no reason to include in this book subjects that are better covered in the textbooks. However, those areas of the certification examination outside the standard texts can be addressed (for example, training, implementation, and communication to senior management).

2.      Furnish material that will help APICS members stay abreast of current and practical approaches to MRP/CRP. This may include material that is not yet sufficiently well-defined to be considered part of the MRP/CRP "body of knowledge." Therefore, the material in these reprints may extend beyond the current boundaries of the certification exam itself.

3.      Select both the best of the current material (to meet the interest in zero inventory and computer integrated manufacturing as they relate to MRP/CRP, for example), while retaining important and still-relevant articles from the past.

4.      Select articles that will relate to the actual practitioners of production and inventory management. The reprints should be thought of as a "job aid" for the APICS professional. Therefore, case studies, and practical experiences were included.

The titles have been grouped into nine specific areas to simplify the test candidate's search for knowledge. The topical arrangement is also valuable to the practitioner who just wants information on a subject. We acknowledge that many worthy articles may not have been included and that a few divergences of opinion remain among some of those authors who were included. This is healthy.

It is our earnest wish that this volume inform the inquirer, support the test candidate, fortify the project manager, and sharpen the practitioner's skill.

**The MRP/CRP Committee**

Paul J. Rosa, Jr., CFPIM, (Chairperson); George P. Adams, CPIM; Richard J. Bruun, CPIM; Merle L. Ehlers, CFPIM; Donald N. Frank, CFPIM; Kenneth L. Trask, CFPIM; Nancy Ann Varney, CPIM; Richard Westphal, CFPIM.

Reprinted from APICS 1984 *Conference Proceedings*.

# "40 DAYS TO THE DUE DATE" BY WILLY MAKEIT: THE ROLE OF CAPACITY MANAGEMENT IN MRP II

Lloyd Andreas, CPIM*
IBM Corporation

## INTRODUCTION

Capacity is nothing more than a constraint on a manufacturing facility. In far too many cases, the impact of this constraint is not recognized or properly planned for. The pressures to sell more, produce more, and ship more product are constantly with us. In a growth environment, these are valid objectives. Management can and should be involved in a continuing process of planning these objectives and analyzing the requirements for resources needed to achieve the plans. The purpose of this paper is to present those areas of the planning process where capacity constraints need to be evaluated and to outline some of the techniques used in these evaluations.

## CONTRASTING "CAPACITY" AND "LOAD"

The APICS Dictionary defines capacity as "the highest reasonable output rate which can be achieved with the current product specifications, product mix, work force, plant and equipment". Capacity in the manufacturing environment is a measure of output, usually expressed as the number of hours of production available over a specific time period such as a shift, day, week, or month. Facilities producing only a few products requiring equal resources per unit may define capacity in terms of units of production per period. In both cases, this rate of output must be achievable over extended periods, and it must be reasonable. If overstated or understated, plans may be implemented that either cannot be met or result in poor utilization of resources.

Capacity must be available to handle the load imposed by the manufacturing plans. "Load" is the amount of work scheduled to be done by a manufacturing facility. It is typically expressed as hours or units of production. Simply stated, load is work input to a resource. The capacity of the resource determines how much time is required to complete the work. The implication of these definitions is basic, yet often ignored: a manufacturing plan that exceeds capacity will not be achieved!

## FACTORS AFFECTING CAPACITY

Capacity is rarely constant over time. A major function of management is to change capacity as required to meet the short, medium, and long-range plans of the company. To accomplish this, the requirements for capacity must be known, together with the available capacity. The required capacity can be derived from the business plans, production plans, master schedule, and the material requirements plan. Available capacity must be defined for a facility or each specific resource. There are many factors which affect capacity that can be planned. Other factors impacting capacity cannot be planned, but must be monitored continuously. Planned factors include:

| | |
|---|---|
| Land and space | Tooling |
| Labor force | Days worked per week |
| Facilities | Shifts worked per day |
| Machines | Overtime |
| Technology changes | Subcontracting |
| Manufacturing/Process changes | Alternate routings |
| Learning curves | Preventive maintenance |
| | Number of setups |

Monitored factors include:

| | |
|---|---|
| Unplanned orders | Absenteeism |
| Scrap and rework | Labor performance |
| Material shortages | Machine breakdowns |
| Excessive tooling problems | |

The consequences of not planning or monitoring these factors carefully results in poor capacity plans and manufacturing schedules, usually evidenced by the following problems:

| | |
|---|---|
| Bottlenecks | Late orders or shortages |
| Low productivity | Higher labor cost |
| Higher WIP investment | Extended lead times |
| Long progress meetings | Poor labor relations |

The net effect of poor capacity management, however, is a decrease in profits and lowered return on investment!

## CAPACITY MANAGEMENT AS A SYSTEM

Within the framework of MRP II, capacity management plays a vital role. By validating the feasibility of the manufacturing plans with respect to capacity in each stage of the planning process, major problems can be anticipated and avoided. This does not imply that capacity problems will not occur on a regular basis; they usually will. Through the use of effective capacity management techniques, however, these problems can be minimized and dealt with in an efficient manner.

Figure 1 outlines the major elements of capacity management and their place in MRP II. Each of these "subsystems" is employed at a different level of planning or execution. Only the first three will be discussed in this paper, even though all should be included either on a manual or automated basis to achieve the greatest benefit from an MRP II system.

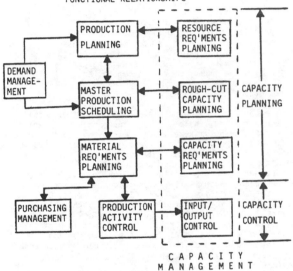

CAPACITY MANAGEMENT IN MRP II
FUNCTIONAL RELATIONSHIPS

Figure 1

## RESOURCE REQUIREMENTS PLANNING

The objective of Resource Requirements Planning (RRP) is to identify the aggregate level of major resources required to meet the Production Plan. The Production Plan is top management's operating lever; used to control the level of inventory or backlog, the stabilization of the work force, and the long-range direction of the business. These plans are reviewed and updated on a monthly or quarterly basis, with data aggregated at the product family level in monthly or quarterly time periods. Resource definition at this level is also an aggregation, with the critical groups of key resources being included in a resource profile. For example, rather than including each machining operation in the profile, the machining hours might be expressed as a total for a unit of the product family, weighted according to the average mix of the family's production. Other resource constraints which could be specified in the profile include labor hours, critical material, cubic feet of warehouse space, and transportation requirements. The construction of resource profiles requires experience and judgement together with analysis of the detailed routings for the items in a product family.

By extending the production plan quantities over the resource profiles, top management is presented with a picture of the requirements for critical resources throughout the planning horizon. This visibility allows management to adjust the plan or to procure additional resources with sufficient lead time, rather than "reacting" to severe resource limitations later.

## ROUGH-CUT CAPACITY PLANNING

The Master Production Schedule is the implementation of the Production Plan. Where the Production Plan involved product families, covered a long (1-5 years) horizon, and planned in monthly or quarterly increments, the master schedule is much more detailed. The planning horizon is shorter, usually covering a period somewhat longer than the longest cumulative lead time of any product. The production quantities, timing, and mix of specific products is defined in the master schedule. With this increased level of detail, a more comprehensive capacity analysis can be made.

Resource profiles can be constructed for each master scheduled item, similar to the profiles used in RRP, but having a finer breakdown of resource groupings and the timing of their need relative to the master scheduled item. A resource profile can be generated using bill of material explosion logic and accessing the routing for the master scheduled item and each of its manufactured components at all levels of the product structure. Work centers in which the operations are performed can be grouped together under a "resource ID". As each routing is accessed, the scheduling of a standard lot size is simulated, and resource profile records created which specify the resource ID, quantity, and timing offset relative to the master scheduled item.

Rough-cut Capacity Planning (RCCP) can now be used to verify that the master schedule is realistic in terms of capacity. The master schedule quantities are extended over the resource profiles, producing a time-phased analysis of the requirements for critical resources over the master schedule horizon. Again, management is provided with enough lead time to adjust the master schedule or change the capacity without having a negative impact on current operations.

## CAPACITY REQUIREMENTS PLANNING

Through each of the planning stages, the amount of detail has been increasing, while the time increments of planning and the planning horizon have been decreasing. In the short to medium-range horizon, plans are being made and executed through material requirements planning (mrp), capacity requirements planning (CRP), production activity control (PAC) and Input/Output Control. Although major capacity problems have been resolved during the higher level planning process, the day-to-day capacity problems will still exist. CRP is the tool used to identify those problems and to validate the material plan generated by mrp. CRP determines the amount of specific labor and machine resources required to meet the material plan over the short to medium-range horizon. It is a detailed simulation of the time-phased load on each work center which will be generated by planned and released (open) manufacturing orders.

## INPUT TO CRP --- ORDER STATUS

Capacity requirements planning must deal with both planned and open orders to be most effective. If only one type or the other is used in CRP, an incomplete load picture will result. Exclusion of open orders distorts the analysis of capacity requirements in the near term. If planned or firm planned orders are not included, the load picture will become increasingly distorted from the present time through all future planning periods.

The open order data required by CRP includes:

- Order due date
- Order quantity remaining to be completed
- Operation status

Planned and firm planned orders should specify:

- Planned order release date
- Order due date
- Order quantity

## INPUT TO CRP --- ROUTING DATA

CRP uses the standard routing for planned orders of an item and the specific routing for open orders currently in work-in-process. Routing data required by CRP includes:

- Operation sequence. The order in which the operations will be performed.

- Planned work center. The work center in which the operation will be performed. For open orders, the actual work center should be specified if the operation has been started.

- Performance standards. These include the standard setup time, run time per unit, operation yield, and the time required to move the order to the operation from the previous operation.

- Tool requirements. Tooling required by an operation can be noted in the routing so that it can be included in a time-phased capacity plan.

The status of each operation on a released order must be known. This status should be continuously updated through feedback from the shop floor, and should specify whether or not the order has arrived at the operation, is being worked at the operation, or if the operation has been completed. If the operation is currently in process, the quantity yet to be completed must be specified.

## CRP INPUT --- WORK CENTER DATA

The following information must be available for each work center:

- Rated capacity
- Primary scheduling constraint
- Performance standards
- Capacity allocation method
- Planned queue time

CRP determines the requirements for capacity by scheduling the operations of each order through the individual work centers. This requirement for capacity is then compared to the "available" capacity to identify potential overloads or underloads. A distinction must be made between "theoretical" capacity, "demonstrated" capacity, and "rated" capacity. If a machining center has 2 machines, and the company works one 8-hour shift, the "theoretical" capacity of the work center is 16 hours per day. By evaluating historical work center performance, it is found that over an extended period of time an average of only 10 standard hours of work per day have been produced by the work center. This is sometimes used as a measure of "demonstrated" capacity, but it can be misleading. The historical average really represents output of the work center. Actual or average output may not be a realistic measure of capacity because it is dependent not only on the capacity of the work center, but also on the input of work to the work center. If work does not exist at a work center, there will be no output. "Demonstrated" capacity should be evaluated over periods when a backlog of work was available at the work center.

"Rated" capacity can be calculated for use by CRP, and should approximate the demonstrated capacity. Figure 2 is used to illustrate the first step in these calculations.

### CALCULATING WORK CENTER CAPACITY

WORK CENTER: W016   EFFICIENCY: 90%   UTILIZATION: 80%

SCHEDULING CONSTRAINT: LABOR   PLANNED QUEUE: 3 DAYS

| --SHIFT--<br>NO. HOURS | NO. OF<br>EMPLOYEES | NO. OF<br>MACHINES | SHIFT<br>CAPACITY | |
|---|---|---|---|---|
| 1 | 8 | 6 | 6 | 48 HOURS |
| 2 | 8 | 4 | 6 | 32 " |
| 3 | 0 | 0 | 6 | 0 " |

"THEORETICAL" AVAILABLE CAP'Y   80 HOURS/DAY

Figure 2

The primary scheduling constraint in this work center is labor. Even though 6 machines are always available, an operator is needed full-time to run one machine. Only four machines are used on the second shift, and none on the last.

Producing 80 standard hours of work in this work center over any length of time is an unrealistic expectation. To determine an achievable rated capacity, performance factors must be applied. The first factor is efficiency.

$$\text{EFFICIENCY} = \frac{\text{STANDARD HOURS EARNED}}{\text{DIRECT LABOR HOURS}}$$

Efficiency can be monitored through feedback from the shop floor. Efficiency for both the current production period and an average over time can be maintained. In calculating rated capacity, however, a "planned" efficiency is typically used. This technique allows management to use efficiency as a policy variable, and to plan increases (or decreases) in efficiency.

A second factor which should be applied to available capacity is utilization.

$$\text{UTILIZATION} = \frac{\text{DIRECT LABOR HOURS}}{\text{ATTENDANCE HOURS}}$$

A common mistake in determining utilization based on historical data is the inclusion of time when no work was available. If a work center sits idle because of lack of work, its utilization will be lowered. In reality, its capacity was not affected. In the calculation of rated capacity, "planned" utilization should be used, taking into account the time allotted to breaks, rework, maintenance, and other activities resulting in a loss of production.

If the primary constraint in a work center is machine time rather than labor, then the direct labor hours and attendance hours should be replaced by the machine hours used in direct production and the available machine hours in the formulas for efficiency and utilization.

Applying efficiency and utilization to the "theoretical" capacity yields the rated capacity which is used by CRP. Using the data from Figure 2:

| | | |
|---|---|---|
| AVAILABLE CAPACITY | = | 80 HOURS/DAY |
| X EFFICIENCY (90%) | | .90 |
| | | 72 HOURS/DAY |
| X UTILIZATION (80%) | | .80 |
| = RATED CAPACITY | | 57.6 HOURS/DAY |

Two more data elements associated with work centers are required by CRP in order to schedule each operation: the capacity allocation method and the planned queue time.

In the example being used, 57.6 daily hours of capacity are available in work center W016. The capacity allocation method specifies how much of that capacity, on the average, will be allocated to a single order for CRP scheduling purposes. The amount of capacity actually used by an order on the shop floor will vary based on the order's priority. CRP has to make an assumption as to the number of hours that will be spent working on a single job in each work center.

Average daily scheduling hours is a very effective approach for most machine-oriented work centers, and some assembly centers. This method allocates the rated daily capacity equally to the largest number of orders that can be run concurrently in the work center, assuming one order per machine or employee. In the example from Figure 2, based on a labor constraint, 6 orders can be run on the first shift. Dividing the rated daily capacity of 57.6 hours by the largest number of concurrent jobs (6) yields average daily scheduling hours of 9.6 . Using this method, an operation scheduled through this work center having 19.2 hours of work to be completed would require 2 days of operation time to be scheduled.

In work centers where multiple people or machines are normally assigned to a single order, scheduling may be more realistic using a specific number of resources per job. This method calculates daily scheduling hours by multiplying the resources/job times the sum of the active shift lengths. Efficiency and utilization are then applied. Again using the example in Figure 2, with a capacity allocation of 2 people per job:

| | | | |
|---|---|---|---|
| | SHIFT 1 | = | 8 HOURS |
| | SHIFT 2 | = | 8 HOURS |
| | TOTAL SHIFT LENGTHS | = | 16 HOURS |
| X | RESOURCES PER JOB | | 2 |
| | | | 32 |
| X | EFFICIENCY (90%) | | .90 |
| | | | 28.8 |
| X | UTILIZATION (80%) | | .80 |
| = | DAILY SCHEDULING HOURS | | 23 |

The result of these calculations should always be checked to ensure that it does not exceed the rated daily capacity.

A third method of capacity allocation for CRP scheduling is the use of the sum of the rated shift lengths. This approach is similar to the average daily scheduling hours technique in that it assumes that an order will be run on only one machine or worked on by only one person. If the number of people or machines is the same on all active shifts it will yield the same result. In calculating this number, the sum of the active shift lengths is multiplied by the work center efficiency and utilization. In the previous example, the result would be 11.5 daily scheduling hours.

The objective of using daily scheduling hours in CRP is to smooth the load in a realistic manner based on how each work center usually works on jobs. It is not "finite" loading, but merely an attempt to apply some limits to CRP's infinite loading techniques. This subject will be addressed further in the discussion about scheduling rules.

The last element of work center data required by CRP is the planned queue time, normally expressed in days. Simply stated, the queue is the backlog of work present at a work center, waiting for work to be started. The amount of time that an order waits in the queue is the queue time. This time will vary in actual practice. The actual queue time of an order is a function of the work center capacity and the priority of the order. From a CRP perspective, priorities are not considered in scheduling and the actual queue time for any order is not known. CRP therefore uses a planned queue time. Even though current queue times and average queue times can be updated for each work center by constant feedback from the shop floor, these values should not be used by CRP. Planned queue time can be used as a management policy variable to aid in controlling queues and lead times. Planned queue time is the "average" length of time that management wants any order to sit in a queue at a work center.

## CRP INPUT --- SCHEDULING RULES

In addition to the data discussed previously, CRP requires a set of scheduling rules. Two major approaches to scheduling orders are most often used in automated CRP systems; forward scheduling and backward scheduling. Both methods have advantages and disadvantages. Before addressing the detail of each method, a few misconceptions regarding CRP should be discussed.

CRP uses infinite loading techniques. CRP is not a "finite" scheduling system, but does use limits in its scheduling process. Obviously, if capacity were truly infinite, queues would not exist and an order would be completed in the time required to make one piece, even if millions of pieces were required. Infinite loading refers to the approach in which CRP schedules individual orders without regard to order priority, other orders planned or in process, or the load generated on any work center by other orders. Almost every aspect of the planning and execution of MRP II systems is centered around "due dates". To be effective as a planning tool, CRP should provide a picture of capacity requirements that:

- Is aligned to order due dates
- Has no "past due" load
- Is based on work being performed according to standard move, queue, setup, and run times.

In effect, CRP should answer the question: "If all planned and open orders are to be completed by their due dates, assuming current status and planned work standards, what capacity is required by each work center over the time span from today until the end of the planning horizon?". CRP's scheduling and loading process determines the amount and timing of these requirements.

In forward scheduling (Figure 3), each order is scheduled beginning "today" or, if not yet started, on its future planned start date. Using the order status, routing, and work center data, CRP schedules move, queue, setup and run time for each operation. Setup and run time for an operation is accumulated for the work center in which the operation is performed. The duration of the setup and run time in days is based on the capacity allocation method specified for the work center.

A major problem exists when CRP uses a forward scheduling technique: the load of orders ahead of or behind schedule is not aligned to the order due dates. If all orders were be-

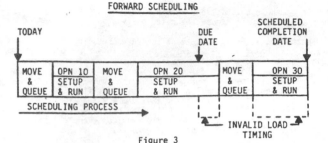

FORWARD SCHEDULING

Figure 3

hind schedule as in Figure 3, a load picture might result which shows no overloaded or underloaded work centers. To meet the due dates, however, all work scheduled later than the due dates would have to be performed prior to those dates, resulting in severe actual overloads. In the example, the load from all 3 operations would have to occur earlier than shown if the due date is to be met. CRP ignores due dates when forward scheduling, resulting in the projected load being shown in earlier or later time periods than it will probably occur for orders ahead of or behind schedule.

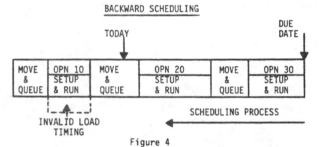

BACKWARD SCHEDULING

Figure 4

Backward scheduling is similar to forward scheduling, except that it begins scheduling an order on the order due date, schedules the last operation first, then each preceding operation, as shown in Figure 4. This is the reason backward scheduling is usually recommended for CRP; all load is aligned to the due dates of the orders. As illustrated in Figure 4, however, backward scheduling also has some drawbacks. Orders that are behind schedule, or planned for release with inadequate lead time, may have some of their work scheduled prior to "today"; in the past. Contrary to continuing beliefs and efforts, work cannot be done on an order "yesterday". To meet the due date in the example, operation 10 will have to start today, resulting in a shift in timing of the later operations. A distorted picture of projected load can easily be developed using backward scheduling, although there is an advantage to this approach. The identification of "past due load" can assist management in evaluating short-term capacity problems.

QUEUE ADJUSTMENT

The problems associated with forward and backward scheduling can be resolved through the use of queue adjustment. These techniques are based on the concept that actual queue time is a function of priority. Orders ahead of schedule have a lower priority and will tend to spend more time in queues. Orders behind schedule will be expedited, spending less time in queues. Priorities are developed for released orders by the production activity control system, using forward or backward scheduling techniques similar to CRP. As mentioned previously, the objective of CRP is to schedule all orders so that 1) all load is aligned to order due dates, and 2) no load is scheduled in the past. Queue adjustment is used to accomplish these objectives. To use queue adjustment, orders must be scheduled twice. The order is first scheduled in either a forward or backward manner to determine the following:

Scheduled queue time. This is the sum of the planned queue time for all operations that are not completed or in process.

Days off schedule. This value represents the number of days the order is ahead of or behind schedule. In forward scheduling, it is the difference between the order due date and the forward scheduled completion date. In backward scheduling, it is the

difference between the backward scheduled start date of the first non-completed operation and "today". This value may be negative.

Total slack. The total slack is the sum of the scheduled queue time and the days off schedule. It is the amount of time that an order can actually sit in queues and still meet the due date based on using standard setup and run time.

Queue adjustment factor. This is defined as the total slack divided by the scheduled queue time. It can be viewed as a percent of planned queue time that the order can actually incur and still meet the due date.

Figure 5 is an example of queue adjustment calculations for several orders which have been forward scheduled.

| ORDER NO. | DUE DATE | SCHEDULED COMPLETION | DAYS OFF SCHEDULE | SCHEDULED QUEUE | TOTAL SLACK | Q ADJ. FACTOR |
|---|---|---|---|---|---|---|
| 1 | 12/18 | 1/14 | -20 | 15 | -5 | * |
| 2 | 11/30 | 12/04 | -4 | 10 | +6 | .60 |
| 3 | 11/28 | 11/28 | 0 | 12 | +12 | 1.00 |
| 4 | 12/20 | 12/16 | +4 | 8 | +12 | 1.50 |
| 5 | 12/14 | 11/20 | +18 | 14 | +32 | 2.29 |

Figure 5

In scheduling the orders a second time, the planned queue at each operation is multiplied by the order's queue adjustment factor. This results in scheduled queues being expanded or compressed so that the order fits between "today" ( or its future release date) and its due date. If total slack is negative, as in order no. 1 of Figure 5, the order cannot be expected to complete on time without special handling. Such an order should be forward scheduled without scheduling any queue time, and flagged for management attention.

Using the queue adjustment factor in CRP scheduling will compress or expand planned queues by a constant factor. Another queue adjustment technique may be used based on the days off schedule.

If an order is ahead of schedule (orders no. 4 and 5 in Fig. 5), the days ahead of schedule can be added to the planned queue for the first operation not started. Scheduling would use the planned queue for successive operations. For those orders behind schedule, no queue time would be scheduled by CRP until the days behind schedule are recovered. For example, if order no. 2 has 4 operations remaining, with planned queue times of 3 days for the first operation and 2 days for the second, no queue time would be scheduled for the first operation and only 1 day for the second. The third and fourth operations would be scheduled with the planned queue time for each.

Through the use of queue adjustment techniques in CRP, a more realistic picture of projected load on each work center can be constructed. These techniques can be applied using either a forward or backward scheduling method, and consider to some degree the priority of each order.

Figure 6 illustrates the effect of queue adjustment on an order that is in process and behind schedule. Figure 7 shows the same effect on an order that is ahead of schedule. The result of forward scheduling, backward scheduling, and the application of queue adjustment using both a factor and the days off schedule is shown in each example.

QUEUE ADJUSTMENT --- ORDER BEHIND SCHEDULE

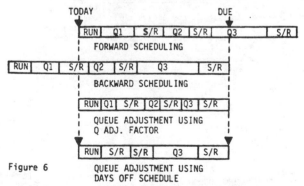

Figure 6

QUEUE ADJUSTMENT USING DAYS OFF SCHEDULE

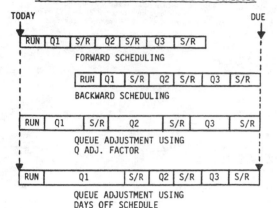

QUEUE ADJUSTMENT --- ORDER AHEAD OF SCHEDULE

Figure 7

OUTPUT OF CAPACITY REQUIREMENTS PLANNING

At the completion of CRP's scheduling process, the time-phased load calculated for each work center can be presented in various numerical and graphical formats. The potential overload and underload conditions at each work center can be easily identified, as shown in Figure 8.

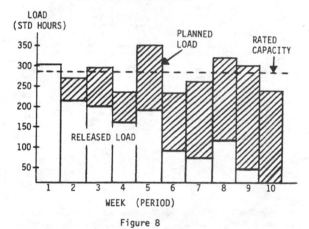

LOAD PROFILE
WORK CENTER: WO16

Figure 8

In addition to showing a summarized load profile, CRP should also present the detail that makes up the load. This data should be available in a report or through online inquiries,

and for each work center should identify by time period each order and operation that was scheduled. By having available the order status, operation load data, work center capacity, performance and queue data, management is in a position to answer the questions:

- Which orders (and operations) make up the load ?
- Where are the orders currently ?
- Which orders can be pulled up quickly, or deferred ?
- Where are the bottlenecks ?
- Are order due dates valid and realistic ?
- Are planned queue times realistic ?
- How much load is "past due" ?
- Is overall capacity available to meet the materials plan ?

If an effective job of managing capacity has been done at the higher levels of planning (Resource Requirements Planning and Rough-cut Capacity Planning), the problems identified through CRP should be minor, and should not prevent the materials plan from being achieved. The overload/underload conditions discovered using CRP can usually be resolved by "fine-tuning". Only in rare instances should changes be required in the master schedule or production plans.

CHANGING CAPACITY

Capacity or resource problems encountered at any level of planning can easily be resolved by changing the production plan or the master schedule. In fact, changing the timing or the levels of production is a fundamental part of the planning process. The role of capacity management is to verify that these plans are realistic. The point remains, however, that the master schedule and production plans are put in place to meet the overall business plans of the company. If capacity constraints prevent that, then capacity must be increased (or decreased). Common approaches used to vary capacity, based on the lead time available, include:

LONG RANGE (PRODUCTION PLANNING/RRP)
    Change land or facilities
    Change capital equipment
    Change work force level or skills

MEDIUM RANGE (MASTER SCHEDULING/ROUGH-CUT)
    Change make/buy decisions    Reallocate work force
    Plan alternate routings    Change work force level
    Subcontract (long periods)    Add additional tooling

SHORT RANGE (MRP/CRP/Input-Output Control)
    Schedule overtime    Select alternate routings
    Subcontract (short periods)    Reallocate work force

SUMMARY

MRP II systems allow a company to plan for the future in an intelligent manner; to resolve major crises before they happen, rather than reacting after they occur or at a point in time when corrective action becomes counter-productive. Capacity management plays a vital role in MRP II, providing all levels of management with visibility into the future and a better understanding of what is required to meet the short, medium, and long-range plans of the business.

About the author

Lloyd Andreas is currently a product planner in the Industrial Sector Product Planning Department of IBM in Atlanta, Georgia. In this position, he is responsible for defining and validating the functional content of IBM's MAPICS manufacturing software. A graduate of California Lutheran College, Lloyd has been with IBM for fifteen years. He has worked with a wide range of manufacturing clients in previous positions in Sales, Systems Engineering, and as a Manufacturing Industry Specialist. Lloyd has made numerous presentations on manufacturing topics at local seminars and national conferences sponsored by IBM. He has attained APICS certification at the Fellow level, and has conducted certification workshops on mrp and production activity control for the Atlanta chapter. In addition, Lloyd serves on the Inventory Management Committee of the APICS Curricula and Certification Council.

Reprinted from APICS 1979 *Conference Proceedings.*

CAPACITY MANAGEMENT

James T. Clark
IBM Corporation
Manufacturing Industry Education
Poughkeepsie, N.Y.

Capacity management is receiving attention today that rivals the attention given to materials management during the MRP crusade of a decade ago.

And for good reasons:

o   Capacity, like inventory, represents one of the largest manageable assets of a manufacturing company.

o   Many MRP systems today still are not successful because of inadequate capacity management in the production plan and in the master schedule.

o   Problems in the operational capacity management system downstream from MRP are diminishing MRP's effectiveness because of an inability to execute MRP reschedules.

o   The economic climate and lack of government policy and direction on such key issues as incentive tax credits and energy have discouraged capital expansion in the United States.  (It is interesting to note that even though we are entering a recessionary period, many manufacturers will continue to be confronted with capacity problems.  Consumer spending and housing will be effected more than other economic areas, but manufacturers of capital equipment will be buffered by two facts:  prior to the downturn earlier this year, capital spending had lagged dramatically the unprecedented 51 months of sustained growth in the U.S. economy and inventory to sales ratios had also failed to stay in step with this growth.)

o   And . . . .the payoff for good capacity management is substantial.

This paper will address the following areas:

A.   Capacity management . . . .the payoff.

B.   Capacity management . . . .a closed loop system, and its relationship to priority management.

C.   Capacity management techniques in the various capacity management systems.

A.   CAPACITY MANAGEMENT . . . . THE PAYOFF

Figure 1. is a DuPont chart of a manufacturing company.  The top portion of the tree diagram starts with the balance sheet items on the far right.  These are split into current assets and depreciated plant and equipment, or net fixed assets.  The bottom portion of the chart represents the income statement.

Examination of the chart establishes inventory as the largest manageable asset of this company; specifically 40.7% of all assets.  Accounts receivable are 28.8% and net fixed assets are 25.0%.

Net fixed assets relate to capacity.  Obviously office buildings, furniture, etc. do not represent capacity but there is one capacity item that is not on the balance sheet:  the direct labor force.  If somehow this could be quantified on the balance sheet and combined with plant, equipment and tooling, then productive capacity might prove to be the largest manageable asset of many manufacturing companies.

You will also notice that it is the depreciated fixed assets that have been referred to.  If this company had to increase capacity to increase output, that capacity would certainly not be purchased at a depreciated amount.  Based on this, one can easily argue that capacity is related to the replacement cost of plant and equipment and this might elevate capacity to the largest manageable asset.

The data outside the boxes, associated with the dotted lines on the DuPont chart resulted from a simulation assuming:  1% increase in output (net sales) accompanied by a 1% increase in accounts receivables and a 1% increase in inventory.  (Good inventory management might easily produce additional sales with no increase in inventory, so assuming an inventory increase presents a conservative position).  Additionally the simulation assumes that an increase in output is accomplished with the same plant, equipment, burden and labor force.  Consequently net fixed assets is unchanged.  Cost of sales has been increased only by a 1% increase in material costs, assumed here to be 50% of cost of sales.

Figure 2.  Is a plot of the ROI (or return on total assets, which is calculated by multiplying profit margin by total asset turns) for a range of assumed output increases.

This contrasts sharply with Figure 3. which is a plot of the result of inventory reduction simulations.  The inventory simulations were based on assumptions of 16% inventory carry costs.  A reasonable range for small increments of inventory change ranges from 10% or 11% up to 16% for carry cost.  This is predominantly the cost of money.

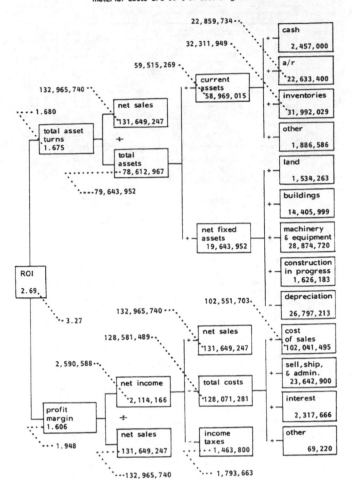

Simulation....1 % increase in output (sales) assuming a 1 % increase in a/r, inventory, and material costs and assuming material costs are 50 % of cost of goods sold

Figure 1.

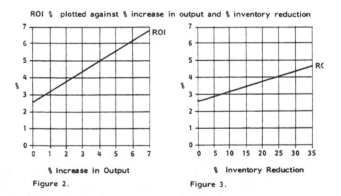

ROI % plotted against % increase in output and % inventory reduction

Figure 2.

Figure 3.

Other simulations were also conducted on purchased material cost reductions, reductions in selling, shipping and administrative costs, and a reduction in accounts receivable collection period (interest 10%).

A recap of these simulations presents some interesting comparisons in Figures 4.  The financial impact on the company demonstrated by increases in output is truly dramatic.

| | To increase earnings per share by 10¢ | To gain an additional 1 % in ROI |
|---|---|---|
| Reduce inventory by | 7.6 % | 17.6 % |
| or..Decrease material costs by | 2.6 % | 8.9 % |
| or..Increase output by | .5 % | 1.8 % |
| or..Decrease collection period by | 10 days | 24.3 days |
| or..Decrease ship., sell., and admin. costs by | 1.6 % | 5.6 % |

Figure 4.

Output is related to capacity management, and hence the need for better capacity management systems is clearly emphasized.

There is also a legitimate argument that concludes that better inventory management will produce increased output. This emphasizes a need to relate both inventory and capacity management (or priority and capacity management) because in fact, one cannot successfully exist without the other.

B. CAPACITY MANAGEMENT . . . . A CLOSED LOOP SYSTEM, AND ITS RELATIONSHIP TO PRIORITY MANAGEMENT.

Figure 5. is a variation of the often illustrated and often discussed 'closed loop' manufacturing system. It forms the basis for any discussion of priority and capacity management.

The development of the discussion of capacity management systems is predicted by the following:

a. No matter now complex we attempt to make a discussion of manufacturing systems, a fundamental fact exists. The fact is that manufacturing systems are a series of scheduling systems.

b. All scheduling systems must be accompanied by some priority management system.

c. All priority management systems must be accompanied by some capacity management system.

d. Schedules change and therefore priority and capacity management systems change. They are dynamic.

e. There are multiple priority and capacity management systems. Their time horizons vary as well as their level of detail.

f. Manufacturing systems must support management in the following critical endeavors:

1. Develop and manage a valid and realistic master schedule

2. Plan priorities

3. Plan capacities

4. Control priorities

5. Control capacities

The first schedule . . . the company's formal business plan.

It is assumed that the company has a formal business plan. (Unfortunately this is not a valid assumption for far too many companies today). The business plan is not a glib 'make a profit' statement nor is it volumes of detail. It is a page or two stating the basic direction of the business. It spells out the kind of business the company is in, the products it will design, manufacture, and market, and the market place to be served. It depicts an orderly growth in gross sales, net profits and earnings per share. It presents assumptions on technology, the economy and relationships with customers, the government and society. It will ultimately be supported by more detailed targets, objectives and strategies. It has priority and capacity constraints.

The next level of scheduling is related to the production plan or long range production plan. The production plan defines the product groups or product lines. It can also specify families or models. It must be general enough to allow for longer range planning, forecasts and estimates, but must have enough detail to support the gross sales and net profit dollars of the business plan. It is often expressed in assembly rates per time period or units of build per time period.

The production plan horizon is coincident with the formal business planning horizon. It is typically around five years, but extends even further for some companies.

The master production schedule or master schedule is the scheduling system one level below the production plan. The master production schedule horizon varies by company, but it is common to see schedules covering from one to two and sometimes three years. It is completely supportive of the production plan but differs in its level of detail and the frequency of its re-evaluation and change. The level of detail includes specific identification of 'finished' goods or master scheduled items, and implies a unique

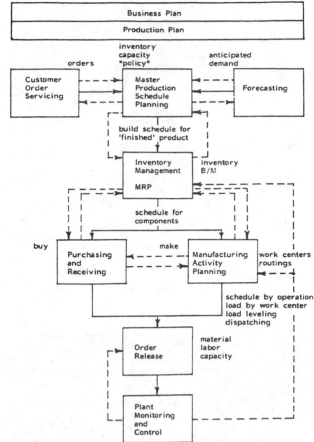

Figure 5.

manufacturing or planning bill of material for the item. ('Finished' items may be actual final assembled items, high level buildable options, modular-non buildable options, spare parts, etc.) Simply stated the master schedule is a schedule for 'finished' product: part number, quantity and due date.

The MRP system, or inventory management system, is downstream from the master schedule. MRP has been discussed and examined in detail for over a decade now. A review of the simple mechanics of MRP establishes that at a minimum the output of MRP is simply a part number, quantity and due date. It is a schedule for components. Dependent components are defined as demand items which support the building of the master scheduled items such as raw materials, purchased and fabricated parts, subassemblies, etc.

The recent emphasis on the priority planning and priority control aspects of MRP is evidence that MRP is finally being understood and accepted as a scheduling system.

The order schedule of MRP feeds both the 'make' system (Manufacturing Activity Planning) and the 'buy' system (Purchasing and Receiving). The Manufacturing Activity Planning system includes scheduling orders by operation, loading standard hours into work centers, load leveling and dispatching. These activities represent a major part of the operationsal level capacity management system.

Figures 6, 7 and 8 should assist in this review of scheduling systems.

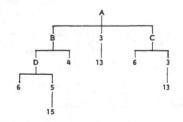

Figure 6.

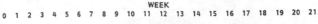

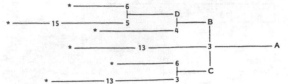

Figure 7.

1200 5 's due in week 11 (shop calendar day 450)
Lead time = 25 days
order release = day 425

| ROUTING OPERATION | WORK CENTER | STANDARD HOURS | START DATE | DUE DATE |
|---|---|---|---|---|
| | | | ORDER RELEASE | 425 |
| 10 | A | 3.4 | 428 | 429 |
| 20 | B | 1.6 | 432 | 434 |
| 30 | C | 2.7 | 437 | 438 |
| 40 | D | 5.8 | 441 | 442 |
| 50 | E | 6.5 | 445 | 446 |
| 60 | F | 7.6 | 449 | 450 |

For scheduling:

Assume 3 day queue and move between operations and round standard hours up to the nearest 8 hour day.

Figure 8.

All of these scheduling systems must be accompanied by priority management systems. Priorities in the business plan and production plan are typically related to the business direction, profitability and other major financial measurements such as return on assets, return on equity, earnings per share, etc. Business segments, major customers, markets and market share are among some additional considerations.

The master schedule priority system must reflect the business plan and production plan priorities. The master schedule by contrast though is the first schedule that defines specific products and it is the first schedule that is apt to be reflected in functional and operation level managements' performance plan objectives. It is an agreed to estimate of the build schedule by manufacturing. It represents in many cases, a compromise among the conflicting objectives of marketing, manufacturing and finance.

Company policy and practices in the business plan and production plan are often major determinants in priority setting in the master schedule. An example would be sequencing customer orders in the backlog, or sequencing allocation of finished goods inventory to customer orders. The master schedule also demands written, understood and abided by policy on who can change the master schedule, on what product and in what portion of the schedule horizon. This last item implies the establishment of time fences for products or product lines, and this may even vary by market or customer.

The resultant master schedule then becomes the driver for the operational level material planning and capacity planning systems.

Assuming that the master schedule is valid and realistic (reflects objectives and priorities of the production plan and is attainable) then MRP establishes a specific priority system. It is a natural due date (need date) driven priority system based on the comparison and ranking of valid order due dates. MRP establishes order priorities for both manufacturing and purchasing.

In short lead time manufacturing (for example, 5 days or less cumulative lead time) or manufacturing with very few operations, order due dates are adequate for priority management. Longer lead times with many manufacturing operations however, require one more level of detail in priority management.

This is provided by the operation scheduling system. Operation scheduling, as in Figure 8, provides the ability to establish and compare valid operation due dates. This is the basis for priorities by operation by work center. This operation priority overcomes the short comings of simply comparing order due dates by factoring in the work accomplished and work remaining on an order.

The operations scheduling system is divided into three subsystems: capacity requirements planning, completion time estimating and operation sequencing. These scheduling systems present a starting point for the development of priority and capacity management systems. This is summarized in Figure 10.

Priority management includes both priority planning and priority control. The initial flow through a manufacturing system is depicted by the solid lines in Figure 5. This establishes the priority plan. Changes originating in the business plan, production plan or customers orders and forecasting must be reflected down through the system. Changes originating from within the plant via plant monitoring and control such as scrap, machine down, worker absent, etc. and changes from vendors via Purchasing

and Receiving must also be fed back through the system. Engineering changes, inventory adjustments and other changes to the basic data of the business are also part of the feedback. Change and feedback are depicted by the dashed lines. All schedules must be kept valid and this then is the basis for priority control.

Priority control is particularly critical in the close-in portions of the horizon. Released orders dominate here and the operation priorities derived simply from due dates in capacity requirements planning must often be adjusted to reflect the unanticipated realities of the plant. User factors based on user judgement are therefore included in the completion time estimating and operation sequencing systems.

C. CAPACITY MANAGEMENT TECHNIQUES IN THE VARIOUS CAPACITY MANAGEMENT SYSTEMS

Capacity management is also represented by a series of systems varying in horizons, level of detail, and techniques. Various techniques are defined, but at a minimum, all capacity management systems should be supported by some type of input/output monitoring and control, even if it is a relatively simple manual system.

Capacity planning in the business plan, production plan, and master schedule is supported by resource requirements planning. The approach here is to identify a manageable number of typical products, groups of products or families. Products within groups or families should be related to similar resource utilization. The resources identified should also be a manageable number and should obviously be the critical resources. Critical resources cover a wide range of items such as cash, critical labor skill, long lead time components, expensive parts, engineering design time, warehouse cubeage, etc.

Resource requirements planning is often referred to by its techniques, such as load profile simulations, bills of labor, etc. Some advanced resource requirements systems include accommodation of learning curves (particularly appropriate in the integrated circuit business) and product life cycles. The business plan and production plan capacity systems can also be supported by econometric models.

The operational level capacity requirements planning system is fundamentally a scheduling by operation and loading by work center system. It is referred to as 'infinite' loading for the simple reason that capacity is not a constraint in the loading of work centers. The eventual load is however, compared to available capacity to pinpoint potential underload and overload problems. Important considerations in this system is the cumulative load to capacity measurement and the distribution of that load. If cumulative load is equal to or less than cumulative capacity, an evenly distributed load (no extensive periods of continuous overload) can probably be leveled.* If there are extensive periods of overload then the ability to level is minimized or eliminated all together. If these overloads are in the current periods of the horizon then an overloaded or front end loaded master schedule is often the cause.**

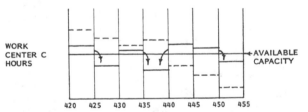

Figure 9.

The capacity planning flow follows the same solid lines of the priority planning flow in Figure 5. The dashed lines of feedback are the basis for capacity control. If there is an unresolvable overload in the capacity requirements planning system then feedback to the MRP system and possibly to the master schedule is in order.

It is advantageous, of course, to solve problems within the bounds of the operational level system (MRP and CRP). This then insulate the master schedule from change. If, however, problems cannot be resolved in the operational system (and if no additional capacity is available) then the master schedule must absolutely be changed.

Completion time estimating operates in a much shorter horizon than all of the previous systems. It is the first system that is constrained by capacity in the scheduling operation. Since this system is a finite loading system order priorities are a major consideration. (High priority orders are loaded first). The system gets its name from the fact that orders that are delayed because of capacity constraints are identified with their delay and anticipated completion time. Additionally, the overloaded work centers that contributed to the delay are identified.

The completion time estimating systems horizon is at least as long as the order lead time of released orders. Since it deals primarily with released orders it is particularly dependent on feedback and user priority factors. This is also true of the lowest level detail system, operation sequencing.

*This is illustrated by the solid lines and arrows in Figure 9.
**This is illustrated by the dashed lines in Figure 9.

| SCHEDULING SYSTEM | SCHEDULE FOR | HORIZON | DETAIL | PRIORITY SYSTEM | CAPACITY SYSTEM |
|---|---|---|---|---|---|
| Business plan | Business, business segments, major product lines | 5 - 7 years | Varies monthly to quarterly into future, units & dollars | Business direction, financial measurements, major customers, markets, etc. | Resource requirements planning (load profile simulations, bills of labor, etc.) input/output mgmt. |
| Production plan | Product groups, models, families | 5 - 7 years | Varies monthly to quarterly into future, units & dollars | Must support business plan and direction, financial measurements, key customers, markets, etc. | Resource requirements planning (load profile simulations, bills of labor, etc.) input/output mgmt. |
| Master schedule | Specific 'finished' products with specific B/M | 1 - 3 years (product dependent) | Weekly units & dollars | Finished product date, priorities, backlog mgmt., customers, etc. | Resource requirements planning (load profile simulations, bills of labor, etc.) input/output mgmt. |
| MRP schedule | Specific components | 1 - 3 years (product dependent) | Specific day date or week date by component part no. | Order priorities by specific day or week | MRP has no capacity calculation. It relies on the Master schedule and the operational capacity requirements planning system. |
| Operations schedule (Mfg. Activity Plng.) | | | | | |
| a. Capacity requirements planning | Specific operations/work center/component | 1 - 3 years | Weekly bucket load hours | Operational priorities derived from order due | 'Infinite' loading weekly bucket load vs. available capacity & cumulative load vs. cumulative available capacity, input/output mgmt. |
| b. Completion time estimating | Specific operations/work center/component | 4 - 6 months & min. of released horizon | Weekly bucket load hours | Operation priorities derived from order due dates & user factors | 'Finite' loading to weekly buckets with compl. time estimate in days |
| c. Operation sequencing | Specific operations/work center/component | 5 - 10 days | Daily or shift load hours | Operation due dates and user factors | 'Finite' facility loading (machine, tool, worker) |

Figure 10.

Operation sequencing is very short term and ranges anywhere from two to five days or even up to 10 days. (Normally a few additional days beyond the MRP replanning interval). It, too is a 'finite' loader and in addition to the work center loading of operation sequencing, it accommodates tooling, workers or other related facilities.

This system is a simulation of a job shop and since this simulation is based on calculating queues and set-up and run standards, it must be driven by operation priorities. Operation priorities are order date driven but are subject to modification by user factors.

A good example would be a high priority on an operation which is a split operation when the other part of the split is in progress.

Solutions to capacity problems in this system which provides daily or shift work-to lists includes: operation splitting, grouping for set up, overlapping, alternate routings, alternate work centers, etc.

'Finite' loading systems tend to lead to much discussion and disagreement. The fact is that factories and work centers have 'finite' capacities and this is particularly apparent in the shorter range systems. The informal systems that have been effectively used over the years recognize this and therefore any formal systems we devise must also account for this fact.

## SUMMARY

The details of the many systems defined here goes well beyond the scope of this paper. Fortunately today, more material is becoming available on the subject. The short list of references included is only a sample and by no means a complete list.

The reader is challenged to go well beyond this general overview that hopefully puts the many levels of priority and capacity management systems in perspective.

REFERENCES

'Master Production Schedule Planning Guide', IBM Publication GE20-0518.
'Capacity Planning and Operation Sequencing System-Extended', IBM Publication GH12-5119.
'Hot List', R. D. Garwood, Inc., January/February 1978, March-June 1978:
    'The Making and Remaking of a Master Schedule'.
'Hot List', R. D. Garwood, Inc., September-December 1978:
    'Capacity Planning'
'Communications Oriented Production Information and Control System-Master Production Schedule Planning', IBM Publication G320-1976.
'Communications Oriented Production Information and Control System-Manufacturing Activity Planning & Order Release', IBM Publication G320-1978

James T. Clark

Biography

Mr. Clark is a Senior Instructor in IBM's Manufacturing Industry Education Center in Poughkeepsie, New York. He has eight years of marketing experience and ten years of manufacturing education experience in IBM.

Mr. Clark teaches manufacturing courses and consults with IBM customer executives throughout the United States. He has taught in Europe, Japan and Canada. He is the co-author and co-producer of IBM's Material Requirements Planning (MRP) Video Course which is currently in use worldwide.

He has been presenting to APICS Chapters across the United States for the last six years. In the last two years alone, he participated in 35 APICS activities.

CAPACITY MANAGEMENT
PART TWO

AN EXPANSION OF 'CAPACITY MANAGEMENT'
FROM THE 1979 APICS
ANNUAL CONFERENCE PROCEEDINGS

James T. Clark
IBM Corporation
Manufacturing Industry Education
Poughkeepsie, N.Y.

This paper is an expansion of the paper "Capacity Management" included in the APICS 22nd Annual Conference Proceedings (Page 191). If this paper is not available to the reader, one will be mailed by the author on request.

The initial paper addressed three capacity management topics: The financial payoff, a closed loop capacity management system and its relationship to priority management, and an outline of various capacity management techniques.

The major principle that was developed was that manufacturing companies are driven by a series of schedules ranging from the long range formal business plan to the detailed short range operation sequence or dispatch list. A derivation of this principle suggests there must be a series of priority systems and a series of capacity systems associated with each of the many scheduling systems.

This is recapped in figure 10 of the 1979 proceedings.

(Please note that the schedules listed and the corresponding diagram of a closed loop system in the 1979 Capacity Management paper imply that the final assembly schedule and master production schedule are synonymous. This is often the case in manufacturing build to order as well as make to stock products.

It is necessary however, in some manufacturing environments to separate the final assembly schedule from the master production schedule. The obvious example of this is assembled to order products that depend on a customer order dictating a mix of options for specific end-product configurations.

The scheduling system mattrix would then include the final assembly schedule between the production plan and the master schedule. In the closed loop flow: customer order servicing would be input to the final assembly schedule, forcasting would be input to the master production schedule for option forecasts and there would be two way communication between the final assembly schedule and the master production schedule. The master production schedule would continue to feed MRP.)

The objective of this paper is to expand on the details of the series of capacity management systems.

The following topics will be addressed:

A. Resource Requirements Planning and Rough Cut Capacity Planning

B. Input/Output Monitoring and Control

C. Manufacturing Activity Planning

. Capacity Requirements Planning
. Completion Time Estimating
. Operation Sequencing

In the heirarchy of capacity management systems that support the heirarchy of scheduling systems a number of techniques and approaches have been employed.

It is impossible to identify a single specific technique with a specific level of schedule or level of planning and control for all manufacturers. One manufacturer for example, might use a detailed operations schedule and weekly bucket loading system for capacity management as it relates to the production plan. Another manufacturer might find this impractical because of the data and data processing volumes, and utilize resource load profile simulations. A consumer packaged goods manufacturer might use linear programming to optimize production schedules while this technique would be totally impractical in a job shop.

The definition of short, medium and long range vary by manufacturer and even by product as does the definition of the level of detail relative to the elements of time, product, capacity, etc.

In addition, the proliferation of terminology is overwhelming. Consider: Resource planning, load profile simulations, bills of resources, bills of labor, infinite loading, rough cut capacity planning, job shop simulations, etc.

To minimize this confusion, Figure 1 introduces the terminology of this paper as well as a relative placement of the capacity systems on the axes of planning horizon length and level of detail.

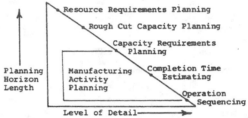

figure 1.

A. Resource Requirements Planning and Rough Cut Capacity Planning

Resource requirements planning, or simply resource planning, has been defined as the process of determining long range resource or capacity needs. The resource planning horizon is at least as long as the lead time to acquire the resource. The resource should also include sufficient additional time to determine if the need will exist for a long enough period to justify capital commitments.

Rough cut capacity planning has been defined as an analysis of the master schedule to assist in evaluating capacity requirements for critical manufacturing facilities. It falls between resource requirements planning and detailed operational level capacity requirements planning (CRP). Rough cut capacity planning is by definition less detailed than capacity requirements planning and is generally done less frequently.

The major distinction between resource requirements planning and rough cut capacity planning is that the former is associated with the business plan and production plan while the latter is associated with the master production schedule. This implies differences in horizons, level of detail, frequency of evaluation, etc.

Capacity management approaches can vary from econometric models to load profile simulations to long range runs of CRP. The exact same technique might be used for both resource requirements planning and rough cut capacity planning, or the same technique but at different levels of detail, or entirely different techniques.

The technique of product load profile simulations is presented here. It presumes that the operational level CRP system involves too much detailed data, too detailed a forecast and too much data processing to be practical for long-range planning.

The steps involved in resource requirements planning include:
a. Defining a typical product structure.
b. Defining the resources that must be considered
c. Determining the "product load profile" for each typical product, that is, how much load is imposed on the resources by a single unit of an end product.

d. Extending these product load profiles by the quantity called for in the production plan or master schedule, and thus determining the total load or "resource requirement", on each of the production facilities and other resources.
e. Simulating the effect of different production plans or master schedules in order to make the best possible use of resources.

Figure 2. Depicts a typical product structure.

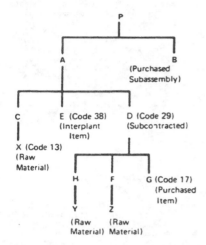

figure 2.

Product P is generally a product group to take advantage of the improved accuracy of aggregate forecasting. Product groups also decrease the amount of data to be considered and processed. The product group must be developed not only to allow aggregate forecasting but must group products that utilize similar resources.

Product P could be a group of machines including a statistical mix of options, it could be a single unique product or it could be an 'average' product that is never really built.

The next step is to identify critical resources consumed in the manufacture of P. Figure 2 specifies certain critical materials which are offset over lead time in Figure 3.

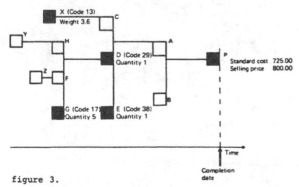

figure 3.

Critical labor is identified and offset over the lead time of product P in figure 4. This is often referred to as a bill of labor.

Other critical resources could include design engineering time, long lead time components, warehouse cubeage, cash, quality assurance, very expensive components, final assembly and test cells, etc. The objective is to include the truly critical resources but to keep the list to a manageable number.

Multiple individual resource profiles make up the product resource profile of Product P. This is depicted in Figure 5.

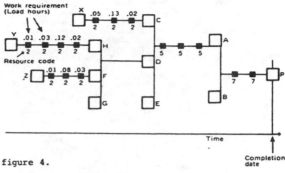

figure 4.

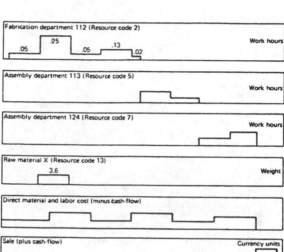

figure 5.

Figure 6. Demonstrates how the profiles are extended by the quantity in the production plan or the master schedule. The calculated total requirements profile could now be modified by other factors such as learning curves or be used to derive the profiles of related resources.

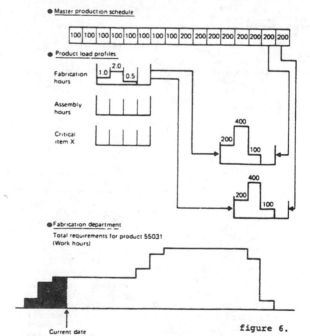

figure 6.

The advantages of the product load profile approach are:

a. It overcomes the data and data processing impracticalities often associated with using the CRP System for long range planning.
b. Its simplicity and speed of processing allows extensive simulation. The result is the ability to develop the probable results of many different possible courses of action. A simulation might indicate for example, that a product group forecast could vary by up to 15% before a major capital formation commitment was shifted into a different fiscal reporting period.
c. A completely computerized bill of material, MRP, routing and scheduling system is not necessary (although the availability of any of this data would obviously be helpful).
d. It allows for the identification of the specific "typical" finished product that created load problems (this may not be practical within the detailed CRP operational system).

The disadvantages include:

a. It is primarily a planning system and does not accomodate measurement and control.
b. The profiles are developed for the manufacture of one unit of the typical product so lot sizing assumptions must be made. A one for one lot sizing approach would usually produce a smoother load than the eventual load produced by the operational level MRP and CRP systems. This is not a serious deficiency for long range planning but could create some problems if the technique were employed in the nearer term. Capacity requirements for set-up would also have to be estimated. Another approach involves using current data from the operational level lot sizes and loads.
c. Available inventories and committed capacities are not considered. This problem is similar to the lot sizing problem and is of minimum consequence for long range planning. Utilizing the approach in the short range, again demands caution.
d. It is not exact. This is more a statement of fact than a disadvantage. The technique is not intended to be exact. If the user realizes this, then there should not be a problem.

B. Input/Output Monitoring and Control

Input/output monitoring and control can be utilized to support various levels of management in manufacturing. Input/output monitoring and control is as useful in production planning and master production scheduling as it is in supporting the management of individual work centers. The examples used here are oriented to a work center since this is the simplest form of input/output monitoring and control. As simple as it is, though, its use is ignored in far too many factories.

A sample input/output report is illustrated in Figure 7.

INPUT/OUTPUT

| | PERIOD | 1 | 2 | 3 | 4 | 5 | 6 |
|---|---|---|---|---|---|---|---|
| INPUT | PLAN | 500 | 500 | 500 | 550 | 550 | 550 |
| | ACTUAL | 450 | 520 | 580 | 540 | | |
| | DEVIATION | -50 | +20 | +80 | -10 | | |
| | CUM. DEVIATION | -50 | -30 | +50 | +40 | | |

| | PERIOD | 1 | 2 | 3 | 4 | 5 | 6 |
|---|---|---|---|---|---|---|---|
| OUTPUT | PLAN | 500 | 500 | 500 | 550 | 550 | 550 |
| | ACTUAL | 470 | 480 | 530 | 550 | | |
| | DEVIATION | -30 | -20 | +30 | - | | |
| | CUM. DEVIATION | -30 | -50 | -20 | -20 | | |

figure 7.

It is important to understand the data elements in input/output monitoring and control.

a. Planned input is the most critical element and the most challenging to manage. Input must be managed. It is not simply taken blindly from a CRP computer report.
b. Actual input as well as actual output are measured values. Accurate and timely shop reporting is essential. Actual output establishes the true available capacity of a work center.

c. The planned output is an estimate into the near future from the work center foreman. It is based on his knowledge of machine and worker capability and availability, job characteristics and mix, and anticipated input.

Actual input and output will have some variability so the cumulative deviation is monitored as well as period deviations. This provides the first indication of whether a work center has an input or an output problem. Cumulative deviation is monitored relative to a specified band or tolerance. Action should be taken when the tolerance is exceeded.

Problems in input force the examination of upstream work centers or in the case of gateway or primary work centers the examination of the order release system and MRP system. The gateway work centers are easier to control in terms of input, particularly if a machine load report and MRP system are available. Order release dates must be managed to insure a steady and realistic flow into the gateway work centers. The order release system is extremely important because it provides a unique opportunity to manage gateway work center input. In fact, it also represents the last opportunity.

The input to secondary or intermediate work centers and to final assembly are more difficult to control because input load is coming from multiple sources. The availability of machine load reports and planned orders from MRP will also support this effort.

Some operation scheduling systems, utilizing combinations of forward and backward scheduling, have been used to accomodate bottleneck work centers, but the discussion of this is beyond the scope of this paper.

In some manufacturing environments the uncoupling of the final assembly schedule from the master schedule is a method of managing input to final assembly. Inventories of assemblies just below the final assembly are justified to maintain controlled input to a high volume final assembly line.

Problems in output are problems with capacity (unless of course they are the direct result of input problems) and the solution of the output problem is an effective capacity planning system. A realistic production plan and master schedule, should be developed with support from resource requirements planning and rough cut capacity planning. The master schedule is input to the MRP and CRP systems and the managed output of CRP develops capacity requirements. Capacity requirements essentially define output requirements. This obviously doesn't eliminate all output problems but hopefully it will minimize them. The short and intermediate range solutions to output problems such as alternate work centers, overtime, subcontract, buy vs. make, etc. will continue to support output management.

The monitoring portion of input/output monitoring and control is relatively simple to implement. It remains for management to provide the dimension of control. Input/output monitoring and control can be completely manual because computerized MRP and CRP is not a prerequisite. Readily available data from any current MRP and CRP systems, would of course, be helpful.

There is no legitimate reason why input/output monitoring and control is not a part of every factory's operation.

C. Manufacturing Activity Planning

Manufacturing Activity Planning, as depicted in the closed loop manufacturing system in the 1979 paper, is down stream from MRP and is the operational level or detail level capacity management system. This system is extremely critical to many interrupted flow manufacturers (job shop or discrete manufacturing) but of minimum importance in continuous flow manufacturing.

Manufacturing Activity Planning is subdivided into capacity requirements planning, completion time estimating and operation sequencing. Figure 8 below, as well as Figure 10 in the 1979 paper, put these systems in perspective.

| MANUFACTURING ACTIVITY PLANNING | | | |
|---|---|---|---|
| | Level of Detail | Planning Horizon | Objective |
| Capacity Requirements Planning | Week | Months | Develop feasible capacity and material plans |
| Completion Time Estimating | Day | Weeks | Measure performance against due dates |
| Operation Sequencing | Hour | Days | Develop detail shop operating plan |

figure 8.

It is essential to understand and accept the following premises before pursuing the details of these capacity management systems.

   a. Interrupted flow manufacturing is characterized
      by the presence of work in process inventory,
      or queues.
   b. The fundamental challenges of this type of
      manufacturing involve deciding on what in the
      queue to work on next and determining if capa-
      city is available to work on it. (priority
      and capacity management).
   c. Capacity requirements planning and other short-
      er term detailed capacity management systems
      essentially involve scheduling by operation and
      loading by work center.
   d. The capacity requirements planning system can
      only be as good as the scheduling system.
   e. Scheduling orders and operations demands an
      understanding of manufacturing lead time.
   f. Manufacturing lead time in job shop or discrete
      manufacturing (interrupted flow) is made up of
      set-up and run and interoperation time.
   g. Interoperation time consists of queue for work,
      queue for move (wait time) and move time. In
      interrupted flow manufacturing this typically
      represents 80%-90% of manufacturing lead time.
   h. Queue time is the major ingredient in inter-
      operation time and can easily represent 95% of
      interoperation time (or 75%-85% of manufactur-
      ing lead time).

Assuming that these premises are acceptable then a fundamental conclusion emerges that strongly suggests that capacity requirements planning demands the under- standing of, the monitoring of, and the management of work in process inventories and queues.

The following details on capacity requirements planning, completion time estimating and operation sequencing develop progressively increasing refine- ments in the understanding of and the management of queues.

Capacity Requirements Planning

Capacity requirements planning consists of order scheduling and work center loading. This is often referred to as infinite loading since capacity is not considered in the scheduling or the loading.

Figure 9 is a simple example of scheduling an order by individual operations. The top portion of Figure 9 is input from MRP and includes the part number, quantity, due date and average lead time. The operation schedules are derived by backward scheduling from the due date using a simple scheduling algorithm.

1200 5's due in week 11 (shop calendar day 450)
Lead time = 25 days
order release = day 425

| ROUTING OPERATION | WORK CENTER | STANDARD HOURS | START DATE | DUE DATE |
|---|---|---|---|---|
| | | | ORDER RELEASE | 425 |
| 10 | A | 3.4 | 428 | 429 |
| 20 | B | 9.6 | 432 | 434 |
| 30 | C | 2.7 | 437 | 438 |
| 40 | D | 5.8 | 441 | 442 |
| 50 | E | 6.5 | 445 | 446 |
| 60 | F | 7.6 | 449 | 450 |

For scheduling:

Assume 3 day queue and move between operations and round standard hours up to the nearest 8 hour day.

figure 9.

A feasible schedule must be developed before the loading step can proceed. Figures 10 illustrate vari- ous scheduling situations.

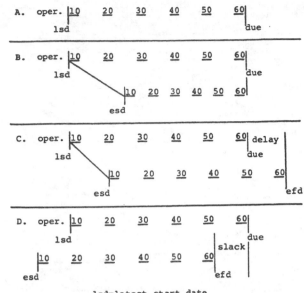

lsd=latest start date
esd=earliest start date
efd=earliest finish date
due=due date

figure 10.

Figure 10A is another way to view Figure 9 and it assumes the order can and will be started on the latest start date.

Figure 10B illustrates a situation where the ear- liest the order can be started is later than the latest start date. This could be caused by material avail- ability for example. Since the available time is less than the lead time, the interoperation times have been compressed to meet the due date.

Figure 10C is a similar situation showing the delay that would result if interoperation times were not compressed. This decision may have been made in the initial schedule with the intent of compressing interoperation time after order release (expediting) or to simply be late on the order.

Figure 10D illustrates an early start date that is earlier in time than the latest start date and there- fore slack is developed. This situation provides an option of starting on the earliest or latest start dates.

These many scheduling possibilities would obvious- ly result in different work center loadings from a timing standpoint. Another key point is that a work center cannot be loaded in the past, so feasible start dates must be developed through logical scheduling.

Capacity requirements of all operations are accum- ulated for each work center in a given time period based on the results of order scheduling. Figure 11 displays the loads in weekly time buckets for work center C.

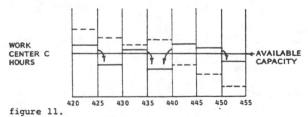

figure 11.

Load profiles can be developed for both early start dates and late start dates. In addition cumula- tive load should be presented and related to cumulative capacity over some specified horizon.

The load is compared to available capacity to pinpoint potential underload and overload problems. Another important consideration is the cumulative load to capacity measurement and the distribution of that load. If cumulative load is equal to or less than cumulative capacity, an evenly distributed load can probably be leveled. (Solid load lines and arrows in Figure 11). If there are extensive periods of overload or a "moving wave" of current period overloads (dashed load lines in Figure 11) then the ability to level is minimized or eliminated all together.

Capacity requirements planning has a quantity accuracy as good as the standards and a timing accuracy as good as the schedule. Industrial engineering techniques and data collection have long been utilized to define and adjust standards. Unfortunately not enough attention has been given to scheduling, and in particular queue times which is the largest time element in scheduling.

Figures 9 and 10A illustrates a schedule that assumes the same average interoperation time (primarily queue) for all operations and all work centers. This simplifying assumption can probably be tolerated in the longer range, but it can have serious consequences in the timing of load in the near term.

Another important point is that average lead time based on average queue time assumptions tend to be self fulfilling prophecies. (Assuming queues and lead time are not totally out of control). If MRP uses an average planning lead time then it will schedule order due dates and release dates with this average time. Since the planned lead time assumes queues and allows for them, execution to the planned schedule will develop the same queues. This is supported by one of the laws of queue, or backlog, which states that once a queue has been built it will tend to remain at a fixed level unless there are significant changes in personnel, equipment or the health of the business.

Breaking into this loop by reducing queues and lead times is a major challenge, and it also represents a very significant potential for overall improvement in a manufacturing business. The result can be a better competitive position via shorter lead times, less WIP inventory investment, more effective capacity utilizations, less scrap, fewer E.C. problems, etc.

A first step then toward improved capacity management is to evaluate queues by individual work center. This will support more accurate scheduling as well as pinpointing those work centers that have too little or too much queue.

The data gathered in input/output monitoring and control (Figure 7) can be utilized along with the value of the starting queue (prior to period 1) to develop a period by period measurement of queue. If the starting queue were 300 standard hours the queues for periods 1 through 4 would be as illustrated in Figure 12.

figure 12.

|  | QUEUE | | | |
|---|---|---|---|---|
| Period | 1 | 2 | 3 | 4 |
| Planned Q | 300 | 300 | 300 | 300 |
| Actual Q | 280 | 320 | 370 | 360 |
| Deviation | -20 | +20 | +70 | +60 |

Figure 13 is a plot of the distribution of queue values in four different work centers.

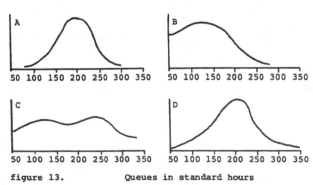

figure 13.          Queues in standard hours

Work center A has an average queue of about 200 hours and over the period of our data has never had a queue less than 80 hours. Clearly we could reduce the queue by almost 80 hours and still in all probability never run out of work in that work center.

Work center B however has a high incidence of idle time because of a frequent occurance of zero queue. Work center C shows a wide range of data and an indication that queues may be out of control

Work center D appears to represent the best situation, but even this distribution could be improved upon. Figure 14, progressing from a to b to c shows this improvement.

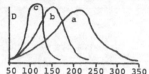

figure 14.          50 100 150 200 250 300 350

Queues can be viewed in a statistical sense like safety stock in finished goods inventory. The variability of input and output is similiar to the variability of demand (vs. forecast). The ability to manage and decrease this variability through input/output monitoring and control can result in more stable queues and decreased queues with all the associated benefits.

The evaluation of queues by work center will give the ability to introduce more accurate average queue times per work center in the scheduling algorithm. It will also draw managements' attention to work centers with queues that are too large or too small and to work centers with too great a variability in input and/or output.

Completion Time Estimating

Completion time estimating is the scheduling and loading system in the medium range. The previous level, capacity requirements planning, highlights potential capacity problems, while completion time estimating shows which individual orders are affected. This is the first system to consider finite capacity availability.

Each order is loaded considering latest start dates in priority sequence to the finite capacities of each time period for each work center. The order is loaded beginning with the first operation. If capacity is available, the operation is loaded. If capacity is not available, the operation is delayed until capacity is found. If an order is available, it can be pulled early to take advantage of any available capacity. In the event of delays interoperation time can be reduced.

The sequence of scheduling and loading of orders is dictated by order priorities initially determined in capacity requirements planning. These priorities can then be modified by other factors such as delay, slack, the amount of interoperation compression and external priorities.

Completion time estimating must also consider the results of operation sequencing which is the short range scheduling system

Completion time estimating develops an estimate of order completion time for orders based on the priority of the order and availability of capacity. Additionally, an individual order's contribution to any bottleneck conditions will be detailed.

Operation Sequencing

Operation sequencing is the short range scheduling and loading system and like completion time estimating, considers finite capacity availability. Completion time estimating and capacity requirements planning took into account only the total capacity within a time period without considering the sequence of operations. In contrast, operation sequencing considers the capacity and operation sequence each shift and computes a queue of operations for each machine.

Essentially, operation sequencing is a job shop simulation. It calculates a workable sequence of operations for each single machine considering the existing situation. This involves considering the capacity and the existing load of each individual machine, as well as operation due dates.

More advanced considerations could include alternate routings and operations, alternate work centers, operation splitting, overlapping, time critical operations and grouping related operations.

The objective of operation sequencing is to sequence the operations in a queue, therefore an operation priority must be established to determine the ranking of the operations. Some elements considered include operation in process, successive operations on the same order in the same work center, splits for this operation in process, operation belongs to high priority order and user specified priorities.

The scheduling techniques of developing a prioritized queue of operations for each machine significantly increases the probability of meeting schedules and maximizing capacity utilization.

The operation sequencing system should help manage release of orders into the shop and provide a priority controlled leveling of loads and a realistic dispatch list.

Supporting these three subsystems of Manufacturing Activity Planning is three levels of increasing refinement of queue management. This increased ability to manage queues was defined earlier as a critical prerequisite to better capacity management. This is detailed in Figure 15.

The capacity requirements planning system utilizes average queue time in its scheduling. This should be an average queue time by specific work center.

Standards, of course, are used for set-up and run times for all levels of manufacturing activity planning. An average move time is depicted for capacity requirements planning but the move time matrix shown for completion time estimating and operation sequencing could easily be used.

Completion time estimating introduces a logical refinement of queue times. It recognizes that some orders have longer than average queue times while others have shorter than average queue times in a given work center. The degree of "longer" and "shorter" is arbitrary and in our example there is four levels of detail. This approach demands rigorous record keeping and data collection because it is based on the measurement of actual queue time experienced by all orders and the relationship of the queue time to order priority. Completion time estimating is dependant on order priorities so the presence of priorities is assumed. The priority groups could be determined by simply stratifying the range of priorities.

The table indicates that orders in priority group 4 in work center B had an average queue time of 38 hours This data from past intermediate range history will be used as projections for queue times for scheduling in the future intermediate range of completion time estimating. The single average queue time for this work center in capacity requirements planning could have been 22 hours.

This approach is identical for queue for move (wait) and the move time matrix is used for transit time.

The final refinement is the actual calculation of expected queue time in the operation sequencing function. Since a queue prioritized by operation exists for a work center, it is a simple matter to calculate specific operation and order queue times in a work center. The expected queue time for any operation is simply the total of the standard set-up and run times for all preceeding operations in the queue. The fourth operation in queue in the operation sequencing example will wait 15 hours, which is the sum of the standard set-up and run time of the preceding three operations. The estimate of queue for move is still a refined average because we assume no standards exist for transit time.

Summary

The capacity management systems defined here represent a wide range of systems to support a range of schedules from the formal business plan down to the dispatch list. These systems represent a natural sequence starting with gross and rough cut planning over long horizons and evolving down to very detailed job shop simulations over very short horizons. An essential element of this is the increasing levels of refinement in the understanding of and the management of work-in process inventories and queue times.

Clearly these approaches do not apply to all manufacturers. The systems described here, for example, would be more appropriate for interrupted flow manufacturing. Even within interrupted flow manufacturing, the classical build to order job shop might utilize some refined techniques that are beyond the needs of a build to forecast manufacturer. There is even a greater contrast in capacity management approaches when interrupted flow manufacturing is compared with process or continuous flow manufacturing.

Regardless of the industry, better capacity management should be a high priority for all manufacturers. The rewards are immense. Better capacity management will result in higher productivity, lower costs and shorter lead times, all of which are essential in an increasingly competitive world marketplace and in a U. S. economy that is plagued with productivity problems. Indeed, better capacity management may be the key to survival for many manufacturing enterprises.

OPERATION LEAD TIME

| | HORIZON | QUEUE (WORK) | SET-UP | RUN | QUEUE (MOVE) | MOVE |
|---|---|---|---|---|---|---|
| CAPACITY REQUIREMENTS PLANNING | 'LONG' RANGE (MONTHS) | AVERAGE | STANDARDS | | AVERAGE | AVERAGE |
| COMPLETION TIME ESTIMATING | INTERMEDIATE RANGE (WEEKS) | REFINED AVERAGE — PRIORITY/WORK CENTER (A B C D): 1: 12 16 14 10; 2: 17 19 19 13; 3: 21 26 22 17; 4: 29 38 34 20 | STANDARDS | | REFINED AVERAGE — PRIORITY/WORK CENTER (A B C D): 1: 1 5 3 2; 2: 3 8 6 3; 3: 4 10 8 6; 4: 7 12 11 8 | REFINED AVERAGE — FROM/TO (A B C D): A: - 2 1 4; B: 2 - 1 6; C: 1 3 - 2; D: 4 5 1 - |
| OPERATION SEQUENCING | SHORT RANGE (HOURS) | CALCULATED — OPERATION SEQUENCE / STANDARDS / QUEUE: 1: 6 0; 2: 4 6; 3: 5 10; 4: 3 15 | STANDARDS | | REFINED AVERAGE — PRIORITY/WORK CENTER (A B C D): 1: 1 5 3 2; 2: 3 8 6 3; 3: 4 10 8 6; 4: 7 12 11 8 | REFINED AVERAGE — FROM/TO (A B C D): A: - 2 1 4; B: 2 - 1 6; C: 1 3 - 2; D: 4 5 1 - |

figure 15.

REFERENCES

'Master Production Schedule Planning Guide', IBM
Publication GE20-0518
'Capacity Planning and Operation Sequencing System-
Extended', IBM Publication GH12-5119
'Hot List', R. D. Garwood, Inc., January/February 1978,
March-June 1978:
    'The making and Remaking of a Master Schedule'
'Hot List', R. D. Garwood, Inc., September-December
1978:
    'Capacity Planning'
'Communications Oriented Production Information and
Control System-Master Production Schedule Planning',
IBM Publication G320-1976.
'Communications Oriented Production Information and
Control System-Manufacturing Activity Planning &
Order Release', IBM Publication G320-1978
'Asset Management and Long Term Capacity Aquisition
Planning', Frank O. Sunderland, 1979 APICS Annual
Conference Proceedings.
'Manufacturing Scheduling', R. L. Lankford, A Paper
presented at the University of Wisconsin, 1973.
'Short Term Planning of Manufacturing Capacity',
R. L. Lankford, 1978 APICS Annual Conference
Proceedings
'Master Production Scheduling-Principles and Practices',
William L. Berry, Thomas E. Vollmann and D. Clay
Whybark, APICS, 1979

Biography

Mr. Clark is a Senior Instructor in IBM's Manufacturing
Industry Education Center in Poughkeepsie, New York.
He has eight years of marketing experience and eleven
years of manufacturing education experience in IBM.

Mr. Clark teaches manufacturing courses and consults
with IBM customer executives throughout the United
States. He has taught in Europe, Japan and Canada. He
is the co-author and co-producer of IBM's Material
Requirements Planning (MRP) Video Course which is
currently in use worldwide.

He has been presenting to APICS Chapters across the
United States for the last seven years. He was a topic
coordinator and speaker in the 1977 and 1979 APICS
Annual Conference and a speaker in the NCPDM National
Conference in 1976 and 1980.

Reprinted from *Production and Inventory Management*, Second Quarter, 1983.

# INVENTORY-BASED PRODUCTION CONTROL SYSTEMS: A HISTORICAL ANALYSIS

James P. Gilbert, CPIM
*Western Illinois University*     *Macomb, IL*

Richard J. Schonberger
*University of Nebraska-Lincoln*     *Lincoln, NB*

For the student of production and operations management, the historical development of inventory-based production control systems can be most fascinating. This article presents the flow of events which led to the development of material requirements planning (MRP). As we shall see, the development of MRP is the logical extension of the work of many people.

It is not the intention here to re-describe the contributions of great leaders in management theory such as Taylor, Gilbreth, Gantt, Emerson, Mayo, Tippett, or Henry Ford. These contributors to management theory are most important and their works have been described in detail by business historians. The historical review presented here will look at the events leading to the "discovery" of material requirements planning.

## EARLY PRODUCTION CONTROL TECHNIQUES

The history of inventory-based production control systems, leading to the development of MRP, dates back to at least 1744. George Plossl relates that it was in 1744 that the first bill of material was illustrated in an advertisement for a Franklin Stove [9]. Plossl states that ". . . the ad listed the bill of materials, giving the quantities of each component and showing how to make the assembly using sketches of its component parts" [9, p. 1].

It has been suggested by Evan Scheele, William Westerman, and Robert Wimmert that the first complete production control system was applied in a manufacturing plant at the Watertown Arsenal in the 1880s [12]. Production control sophistication has come a long way from that late-19th-century beginning.

Early in the twentieth century, one of the first significant events leading to the development of MRP occurred: the development of production lot sizing rules. In 1915, F.W. Harris first established the economic order quantity (EOQ) lot sizing technique [4]. This rule stated that the economic run length of lot size should be directly proportional to the square root of the rate of sales and the cost of changing from one run to the next, and inversely proportional to the square root of the cost of stocking.

During the period between 1920 and 1940, forecasting became important. As products became more complex and customer order backlogs dwindled, there was a much greater need for accurate projections of sales [9]. Manufacturers were starting to recognize the need for more flexible production control techniques.

In 1934, a major step forward in production planning was taken. R.H. Wilson developed the statistical re-order point. In a *Harvard Business Review* article, Wilson discussed the effect of ordering points on inventory, cost, and safety stock. The ideal ordering point was defined for each stock item as ". . . the least number of units on the shelves when a restocking order is started, which will prevent the item from running out of stock more often than is desirable for efficient operation" [19, p. 117]. This definition has been restated mathematically as: re-order point (ROP) equals demand (D) through the leadtime (LT) plus safety stock (SS) or $ROP = DLT + SS$.

Wilson combined the Harris economic order quantity formula with his ideal ordering point to develop an overall inventory planning technique that would become a "cult" for the next twenty-plus years. Wilson stated that the use of EOQ and ROP would cut inventory by 15 percent, stockouts by 20 percent, and stock reorders by 34 percent [19].

By 1942, most of the documents (paperwork) necessary for movement of a production order through a plant were available (see Table 1). Law-rence Bethel, Walter Tann, Franklin Atwater, and Edward Rung described the detailed design and use of production planning and control documents in an early production control textbook [1]. In the early 1940s, Henry Kaiser (famous bridge and ship builder) popularized the term "expediter." The expediter has been portrayed as an ". . . action-oriented go-getter who made a vital contribution of meeting production schedules" [10, p. 3]. In MRP systems today, the expediter who is "rushing" and "chasing" around after production or purchase orders which are needed in less than normal leadtime is seen as the symbol of the informal system and a person to "get rid of" if the system is to be successful.

During World War II, the manufacturing community addressed itself to war production. In the late 1940s, there were a number of developments which enhanced the field of production control. Punched card processing on unit record equipment was more widely utilized which made an efficient bill of material explosion possible. Widespread use was made of micro and memomotion film analysis for understanding and measuring the work environment. Quality control acceptance sampling plans for both attributes (MIL-STD-105D) and variables (MIL-STD-414) were prepared to determine acceptable quality levels of military production. Work simplification, developed by Allen Morgensen in the 1920s,

---

TABLE 1
Production Planning and Control Documents Available by 1942

| Document | Description |
|---|---|
| Master Schedule | using the forecast information or customers' orders, lists the production requirements of a given product for a division or department of the company. |
| Bills of Material | listed on the operation master (routing sheet). |
| Production Schedules (orders) | sometimes referred to as a "Calendar Schedule" used to authorize production runs. |
| Work or Job Tickets | contained information for each individual operation. This ticket was used by the foreman in assigning work, the workers in reporting work, the timekeepers/accountants for payroll and cost control, and the production schedulers to assist in dispatching. |
| Balance-of-Stores Record (Stock Record) | an inventory card indicating the order quantity, quantity on hand, quantity allocated for future production, and balance available for future use. |
| Stores Requisition | authorized the removal of components from a stockroom. |
| Purchase Requisition | authorized the purchasing department to order a particular raw material, part, or supply. |
| Purchasing Follow-up | a reminder form necessary to maintain a follow-up procedure to ensure deliveries being made as promised. |
| Receiving Slip | used by receiving dock personnel to check incoming materials and supplies. The quantity of goods received is compared with the quantity ordered. |
| Tool or Equipment Requisition | authorized the removal of tools or other production equipment from the toolroom. |
| Bin Tag | materials delivered to a stockroom are tagged with the appropriate part number, description, location, and quantity. |

TABLE 1—Continued
Production Planning and Control Documents Available by 1942

| Document | Description |
|----------|-------------|
| Production Specification Sheet | listed the components of the item being produced along with a description of each component, the operation to be performed, and other engineering information needed by manufacturing. |
| Routing Sheet | called an Operation Master; used for production scheduling, cost accounting, and for production departments. This document also listed the standard time estimates from industrial engineering. |
| Move Tickets | used for controlling the movement of a production order from one department or work station to another. |

Source. Adapted from Lawrence L. Bethel, Walter L. Tann, Franklin S. Atwater, and Edward E. Rung, *Production Control*, New York: McGraw-Hill, Inc., 1942.

saw significant use during the war years. In 1947, Dantzig developed linear programming in support of the U.S. Air Force project known as Project SCOOP (Scientific Computation of Optimum Programs).

The next section looks at production control activities leading to MRP development after World War II.

## PRODUCTION CONTROL DEVELOPMENTS FROM WORLD WAR II TO THE MID-1950s

A direct predecessor to MRP was a technique known as the quarterly ordering system. This production control technique has been used for a long time to plan procurement of materials for machine tools, shipbuilding, aircraft, locomotives, and other heavy products [8, p. 69]. The following description of the Quarterly Ordering System is based on that contained in the 1967 George Plossl and Oliver Wight text [10].

During the period starting shortly after the conclusion of World War II and ending in the mid-1950s, many manufacturing industries were able to develop production plans based solely on firm customer order backlogs. Americans returning to a "normal" life after World War II were clamoring for manufactured goods that were either scarce or unavailable during the war. This strong demand produced order backlogs (12–18 month backlogs were not uncommon) that were longer than most total manufactured products leadtime.

This large pool of demand allowed producer firms to use a tool called the quarterly ordering system. This production planning system utilized three techniques that are still widely used today: (1) final assembly required date, (2) component item "explosion," and (3) backward scheduling. The quarterly ordering system started with a management review of customer order backlogs to determine total demand by product. The required finish date was then set for final assemblies. Once the production planner knew when the final assembly was to be completed, it was a fairly easy job to determine the production start date for sub-assemblies, parts, and raw materials. The start date for these components is simply the final assembly finish date less the component leadtime (time of fabrication). By backward scheduling (taking leadtime into account) from the final assembly to the sub-assemblies to parts to purchased materials, the production planner was able to establish a fairly accurate picture of the total amount of work that was required in any period of time—for each work center as well as for the plant as a whole.

By knowing what machines and other work centers were required to fabricate each of these assemblies and components, the manufacturing manager was able to determine the production level for each work center in the plant. Manufacturing work orders were then written and released by the calculated start date in anticipation of some future final assembly required finish date.

As Plossl and Wight point out, ". . . the backlogs served as a known forecast of requirements, and planning could be done once each quarter . . . with certainty" [10, p. 191]. The quarterly ordering system was fairly effective as long as customer order backlogs remained greater than total manufacturing leadtimes.

The unique backlog situation came to an end in the late 1950s and early 1960s. Forecasting, therefore, again became increasingly important as firms were required to anticipate future demand not covered by backlogs. During this time period, consumers were forgetting about war shortages and clamoring for quicker product delivery. The demand for shorter leadtimes and the presence of smaller backlogs forced manufacturers to alter the way they planned production. Many industries were changing from post-war manufacture-to-order firms to manufacture-to-stock companies. This production strategy switch caused management to look at other production planning techniques.

## PRODUCTION CONTROL DEVELOPMENTS FROM THE MID-1950s TO 1960

The mid 1950s saw the focus of business scholars becoming more generalized as they changed from developing techniques for just manufacturing management to developing techniques for other productive organizations. Production management became the new term that ". . . was to stress the fact the field had become a functional management discipline in itself and not just a set of manufacturing management techniques" [6, p. 13].

Elements of a sound production control system were laid down by J.F. Magee in 1958. Magee listed three basic elements necessary for an effective production control system [5, p. 165]:

1. A forecast of demand, expressed in units of production capacity;
2. A production plan or preliminary budget which establishes the inventory and production budget; and
3. A control procedure for deciding how fast to restore inventories to budget levels when errors in the demand forecast cause inventories to exceed or fall below budget.

### Systems With Time-Phasing Characteristics

During 1957 and 1958, several production control systems were established which had some MRP characteristics but were not inventory-based techniques. Two systems were developed which improved the planning and control of projects. The first was designed in 1957 by the Catalytic Construction Company and was entitled the Critical Path Method (CPM). This CPM technique was credited with helping to save both time and money on a plant construction project that Catalytic Construction was building for the Du Pont Corporation [14, p. 252].

A short time later (1958), a second critical path project management technique was developed by the consulting firm of Booz, Allen, and Hamilton along with the U.S. Navy Special Projects Office [14, p. 252]. This network-based system was called the Program Evaluation and Review Technique (PERT) and assisted research managers during the construction of the Polaris missile project.

These two techniques simulate a project's critical path as well as develop the earliest event start dates for each project activity. This is similar to MRP's simulation capabilities, i.e., MRP simulates planned order need dates and work-center loads.

A production planning technique called product line-control (PLC) was being used by the U.S. Navy (PLC was developed by G. Fouch at the Goodyear Company in 1941). This technique had some time-phasing characteristics and is commonly referred to today as the line-of-balance scheduling method. The product-line control scheduling technique is a method suitable for controlling limited-quantity, large-scale production.

This scheduling method is similar to MRP in some respects. Like MRP, PLC sets a future delivery date for an end item. Once the due date is established, the components are scheduled using the backward scheduling method (as in MRP) in order to arrive at the start date for each component item all the way back to raw materials or purchased parts.

The second step in PLC scheduling is to develop a daily delivery schedule which shows the cumulative number of end items to be delivered plotted against the cumulative delivery schedule. This is also similar to MRP in that production planning is checking daily the delivery performance against the delivery plan for this particular end item.

Product-line control scheduling also watches the progress of each component. This process is also similar to MRP. A comparison is made, usually daily, between actual production output for each component and the desired production output. The component schedule is adjusted daily to the expected delivery level to assure on-time delivery of the end item. This schedule is commonly referred to today as the line-of-balance (LOB). Any component below the LOB is in a behind schedule condition and management attention is needed.

Although this PLC scheduling technique has some of the aspects of MRP, PLC is not good enough for most manufacturers because it lacks several significant factors: (1) PLC lacks the ability to foresee future demand on common components from other items, (2) PLC is closed-ended, i.e., it applies to a limited quantity delivered over a limited time period, and (3) PLC is not able to de-expedite, i.e., if a significant bottleneck occurs it is very difficult for management to physically locate all other production orders for the affected end item and to change the operational due dates to some future period. Thus, PLC does not have the capability to slow down this job (de-expedite) or free-up productive capacity for other jobs. Only MRP has these capabilities.

### The ROP/Shortage List System

Richard J. Schonberger discusses a production control system that was popular during the 1950s and 1960s (and is still used by many firms) called the ROP/shortage list system [13]. This system was developed as a manual system in the 1950s using unit-record equipment. As business computers developed in the 1960s, the ROP/shortage list system was converted to computerized data processing methods.

Firms adopting the ROP/shortage list system use a combination of production control techniques, specifically, reorder point (ROP) and bill-of-material (BOM) explosion. Schonberger states that ". . . in the ROP/ shortage list system, ROP provides for routine replenishment of parts, and shortage lists (developed through a BOM explosion) try to compensate for the ROP failures" (parentheses added) [13, p. 107].

There are a couple of major problems which users of this system must be aware of. First, ROP systems cause excess inventory as all components are replaced as stock levels fall below the ROP "trigger" point, whether the inventory is needed for future production or not. Second, the shortage list which is developed as an integral part of this production control system requires that the informal mechanism referred to as expediting be employed. Expediting is expensive for the manufacturer because it leads to disruption on the shop floor, i.e., rush jobs, extra set-ups, and unstable priorities. For a detailed discussion of the ROP/shortage list system, the reader is referred to Schonberger [13].

### Formal and Informal Systems

By 1960, Scheele et al. had begun classifying production control activities as "Formal" and "Informal." Formal production control was defined as ". . . centralizing the coordination of the various functions of Production Control in order to establish and sustain the best method known at any given time . . . it means that a systematic paperwork procedure takes the place of people physically following each step in the process" [12, p. 7]. The formal production planning priority system has been referred to by practitioners as the "push" system, as decisions to release orders to the production floor or to purchasing are made in the inventory control system [18]. MRP is a formal production planning and control system and, thus, a push system.

The informal production control system, referred to as the "pull" system, was defined by Scheele et al. as ". . . one in which the first-line supervision, or the manager, does everything—plans, requisitions materials and tools, determines when each job shall be done, determines what shall be done, what equipment to use and who shall do the job, and then personally watches each job to be assured that it is being run exactly as he wishes it run" [12, p. 7]. The informal system is still used, fully or partially, by many manufacturers today. Decisions are made in the factory itself as to what will be produced and when. The pull system stages (accumulates) material in order to find out the real shortages. These shortages are then expedited through the shop [18].

### Corrective Action in Production Control

Scheele et al. recognized the need to take corrective action on the production floor when off-standard performance was occurring [12].

These authors suggested that off-standard production performances may be caused by external or internal factors, such as [12, pp. 238–41]

External Factors
1. The changes in the priority of the orders.
2. The delays in receiving the material into the facility.

Internal Factors
1. The customer, knowing that his order might be delivered late, tells the salesman that he requires the order one week before he actually needs it.
2. The salesman, having been disappointed on delivery dates before, writes the order out for delivery several days before the date specified by the customer.
3. The sales office introduces an additional "safety factor."
4. The production control department, knowing that the shop is falling behind schedule, subtracts several more days off the shipping date and places the order in the shop as a "rush" job.

It was recommended by Scheele et al. that production control take corrective action three ways: (1) use schedule flexibility, (2) use schedule modification, and (3) use capacity modification [12]. Unfortunately, for most manufacturers it was physically impossible to perform all three suggested modifications at the same time. There were simply too many jobs running across too many work stations with too little time and too few people to make the corrections to the schedule manually. The only real alternative was to expedite the work.

The first business computer, IBM's 650, came into use in 1954. The relatively high efficiency of computers using magnetic tape and internal core memory was an important advance over the punched-card (unit record) era. Manufacturing companies rapidly converted their BOM explosion and inventory transaction processes from punched cards to tape. But the stage was not yet set for MRP because tape systems were cumbersome and computer processing costs needed to come down. The costs did drop, and file handling became streamlined via substitution of disk storage with random access for magnetic tape.

By the end of 1960, most of the production control techniques, methods, tools, documents and formulas were in place, and computer power was available. What was needed was someone to pull these things together in such a manner as to develop an efficient and effective production planning and inventory control system. Three such men came forward to assist in this effort: Oliver W. Wight, George W. Plossl, and Joseph A. Orlicky. Much of the next section is devoted to the work of these three men.

### THE SIXTIES: THE DECADE OF MRP DEVELOPMENT

In the early 1960s, the field of production planning and inventory control was ready for MRP. The techniques and documentation were all known and the state of development of the computer was advanced with the availability of random-access magnetic disk computer file storage. In the book entitled *Material Requirements Planning by Computer: A Special Report*, George Plossl and Oliver Wight stated that ". . . requirements planning approaches have been known to practitioners for many years . . . it was extremely tedious to calculate requirements manually for components of complex assemblies; it was virtually impossible to re-explode requirements frequently enough as schedules changed using a manual system. . . . With the advent of the computer, (material) requirements planning became a practical inventory control technique" (parentheses added) [11, p. 3].

Many "firsts" occurred during the sixties. The first batch MRP system was developed at The American Bosch Company of Springfield, Massachusetts [7]. This system was actually running on a bi-weekly basis in 1959. In 1961–1962, the first continuous net change MRP system was installed. This net change MRP system was designed at the J.I. Case Company in Racine, Wisconsin, under the leadership of Dr. Joseph A. Orlicky who was the director of production control [7].

In 1965, the objectives for manufacturing management in profit-seeking firms were set down by G.R. Gedye [3]. These objectives were restated by Plossl and Wight [10] and have now become famous quotes in the literature on MRP (see Table 2).

---

TABLE 2
Objectives of Manufacturing Management of Profit Seeking Firms

| G.R. Gedye*<br>Three Main Objectives | Plossl and Wight†<br>Three Major Objectives |
|---|---|
| 1. To use the plant to the best advantage and minimize idle time | Efficient (low-cost) plant operation |
| 2. To give good delivery to customers and to honor promises | Maximum customer service |
| 3. To keep the work-in-progress and finished stock at a minimum consistent with objectives 1 and 2 | Minimum inventory investment |

*G.R. Gedye, Scientific Method In Production Management, London, England: Oxford University Press, 1965, p. 147.

†George W. Plossl and Oliver W. Wight, Production and Inventory Control: Principles and Techniques, Englewood Cliffs, N.J.: Prentice-Hall, Inc., 1967. p. 1.

---

The defining of the principles of independent and dependent demand was a seminal event in the historic development of material requirements planning. In 1965, Orlicky, now at IBM, proposed the independent/dependent demand principle. This principle states that ". . . the order point should be used only on independent demand items, while MRP should be used for dependent demand items" [18, p. 31].

A second important event occurred in 1965. Martin K. Starr expounded his concept of modular production [15]. Modular production allows for the stocking of semi-finished items below the level of finished goods inventory. The master production schedule is then able to plan at the modular level which assists greatly in the computerization of MRP as, among other things, there are a smaller number of items to forecast, master schedule, and explode. Thus, far less computer processing time is needed.

Plossl relates that the earliest literature on MRP was produced by computer software and hardware suppliers, e.g., IBM and UNIVAC [19]. The literature was supplied by these firms as an aid in selling computers; thus the literature ". . . covered the mechanics of MRP very well but had little useful information on solving the problems of applying the technique" [9, p. 2].

The first textbook to address MRP directly was written in 1967 by Plossl and Wight. Sixteen pages of Chapter 5 were devoted to requirements planning. It was not until the mid-1970s that most texts authored by academics started to discuss MRP in any significant way.

It was not until the second half of 1968 that the first two articles on MRP were published. Wight wrote an article entitled "To Order Point or Not to Order Point" for Production and Inventory Management in the 3rd quarter of 1968 [17]. In November of the same year, Romeyn Everdell had published an article in Modern Material Handling entitled "Time Phasing: The Most Potent Tool Yet for Slashing Inventories" [2].

During the 1960s, then, MRP was developing into a manufacturing production planning and control technique of tremendous productivity potential. For the dependent demand manufacturer, MRP was a tool that could cut operating costs, reduce work-in-process inventories, and improve customer delivery performance at the same time. To the managers of the "fire fighter" era this must have seemed like a miracle. Orlicky best summarizes the 1960s as follows [7, p. 4]:

It is now a matter of record that among manufacturing companies that pioneered inventory management computer applications in the 1960s, the most significant results were achieved not by those who chose to improve, refine, and speed up existing procedures, but by those who undertook a fundamental overhaul of their systems. The result was abandonment of techniques proven unsatisfactory and a substitution of new, radically different approaches that the availability of computers made possible.

## THE SEVENTIES AND THE MRP CRUSADE

The need to disseminate information about material requirements planning was evident early in 1971. The American Production and Inventory Control Society (APICS), which was formed in 1957, played a major role in "spreading the word" about MRP to all areas of the U.S. APICS published a special report in 1971 entitled Material Requirements Planning By Computer [11]. This report showed clearly how MRP systems were developed and how the system could be installed in manufacturing facilities. Successful MRP users discussed the practical application of the system and allowed copies of their actual system print-outs to be published as a guide for other firms to follow.

At the suggestion of Wight and Plossl, APICS set out on a decade long (1971–1979) information campaign called "The MRP Crusade." This crusade, chaired by Jim Burlingame, was a special effort to put MRP into proper perspective [9]. MRP was discussed at local, regional, and national APICS meetings. Many materials managers gave freely of their time and energy to educate production control managers across the nation on the benefits and pitfalls of MRP installation. The success of the MRP crusade is a tribute to the unselfishness of American materials managers.

It was not until the latter half of the 1970s that published articles about MRP became frequent. Plossl estimated that by mid-1971 only 25 articles had been published about MRP [9].

## THE EIGHTIES: GROWTH OF MRP

This article set out to develop the flow of events leading to the development of the material requirements planning system. There has been a logical progression of events since the illustration of the Franklin stove in 1744 to the installation of MRP in many manufacturing firms. Inventory-based production control systems have played (and are playing) an important role in the pursuit of efficient plant operations, maximum customer service, and minimum inventory investment in manufacturing plants.

Many people helped in the progression of events leading to MRP. Certainly the role of APICS during the 1970s cannot be overstated. Now that MRP is developed, the 1980s look to be a decade of continued system growth. The term MRP II is a sign of this growth. MRP II refers to Manufacturing Resource Planning which is a ". . . method for the effective planning of all the resources of a manufacturing company" [16, p. 16].

As users of MRP gain a better understanding of both system strengths and weaknesses, growth through improved system performance is a natural result. It is hoped that this look at the historical development of inventory-based production control systems will help in this understanding and, thus, in the growth and improvement of system performance.

# REFERENCES

1. Bethel, Lawrence L., Walter L. Tann, Franklin S. Atwater, and Edward E. Rung. *Production Control*. New York: McGraw-Hill Book Company, Inc., 1942.
2. Everdell, Romeyn. "Time Phasing: The Most Potent Tool Yet for Slashing Inventories." *Modern Materials Handling*, November, 1968.
3. Gedye, G.R. *Scientific Method In Production Management*. London, England: Oxford University Press, 1965.
4. Harris, F.W. *Operations and Cost* (Factory Management Series), Chapter IV, Chicago, Ill.: A.W. Shaw Company, 1915.
5. Magee, J.F. *Production Planning and Inventory Control*. New York: McGraw-Hill, Inc., 1958.
6. Meredith, Jack R., and Thomas E. Gibbs. *The Management of Operations*. New York: John Wiley and Sons, 1980.
7. Orlicky, Joseph A. *Material Requirements Planning: The New Way of Life in Production and Inventory Management*. New York: McGraw-Hill, Inc., 1975.
8. Plossl, George W. *Manufacturing Control: The Last Frontier for Profits*. Reston, Virginia: Reston Publishing Company, Inc., 1973.
9. Plossl, George W. "MRP Yesterday, Today, and Tomorrow." *Production and Inventory Control*, 21, No. 3 (1980), 1–10.
10. Plossl, George W., and Oliver W. Wight. *Production and Inventory Control: Principles and Techniques*. Englewood Cliffs, N.J.: Prentice-Hall, Inc., 1967.
11. Plossl, George W., and Oliver W. Wight. *Materials Requirements Planning By Computer: A Special Report*. Washington, D.C: American Production and Inventory Control Society, Inc., 1971.
12. Scheele, Evan D., William L. Westerman, and Robert J. Wimmert. *Principles and Design of Production Control Systems*. Englewood Cliffs, N.J.: Prentice-Hall, Inc., 1960.
13. Schonberger, Richard J. "The ROP/Shortage List System." *Production and Inventory Management*, 21, No. 4 (1980), 106–17.
14. Schonberger, Richard J. *Operations Management: Planning and Control of Operations and Operating Resources*. Dallas: Business Publications, Inc., 1981.
15. Starr, Martin K. "Modular Production—A New Concept." *Harvard Business Review*, Vol. 43 (1965), 131–40.
16. Wallace, Thomas F. (Ed.). *APICS Dictionary*, 4th ed. Washington, D.C.: American Production and Inventory Control Society, Inc., 1980.
17. Wight, Oliver W. "To Order Point or Not To Order Point." *Production and Inventory Management*, 3rd Qtr. 1968.
18. Wight, Oliver W. *Production and Inventory Management in the Computer Age*. Boston, Mass.: Cahners Books, 1974.
19. Wilson R.H. "A Scientific Routine For Stock Control." *Harvard Business Review*, Vol. XIII, No. 1 (October 1934), 116–28.

**About the Authors—**

*JAMES P. GILBERT*, CPIM, is Assistant Professor of Operations Management at Western Illinois University. He received his B.S. in Industrial Relations and Economics in 1967 from Bowling Green State University, an M.B.A. in Operations Management from Western Illinois University, and is completing a Ph.D. in POM from the University of Nebraska-Lincoln.

His industrial experience includes both staff and line foreman positions and a position as Production Planning and Inventory Control Section Manager for the DeVilbiss Corporation of Toledo, Ohio. He is a member of APICS, AIDS, and the Academy of Management.

*RICHARD J. SCHONBERGER* is Professor of Operations Management and Management Information Systems at the University of Nebraska-Lincoln. Professor Schonberger was employed as an Industrial Engineer for eight years prior to taking a Ph.D. at the University of Nebraska.

He has conducted workshops in MRP and Japanese management systems for the local APICS Chapter. He has published many articles in the POM area and is author of a textbook entitled *Operations Management: Planning and Control of Operations and Operating Resources*.

Reprinted from *Production and Inventory Management*, Third Quarter, 1984.

# INVENTORY PLANNING AT BLACK & DECKER

John J. Kanet, Ph.D., CPIM*

*University of Erlangen       Nuremberg, West Germany*

Whenever one hears an APICS discussion of "Class A" MRP users, invariably the name Black & Decker is mentioned. Black & Decker's MRP system has been highly acclaimed—and justifiably so! But what is it about Black & Decker's system that has made it so good? In this paper, the author attempts to answer this question by providing an overview of Black & Decker's MRP system. The paper is not meant to be an exhaustive account of B&D's procedures; however, enough attention is given to certain details to show some of the nuances of the system as well as to demonstrate the problem-solving style at Black & Decker.

## BACKGROUND

The Black & Decker Manufacturing Company is the largest manufacturer of power tools in the world. It is an international corporation with annual sales well over $1 billion, more than half of which goes to markets outside the United States. It manufactures a variety of products to serve three distinct markets—home users, industrial, and construction. Some typical products include drills, circular saws, sabre saws, die grinders, portable sanders and grinders, lawn mowers, hedge trimmers, and vacuum cleaners.

With a number of plants throughout the world, the largest is located in Hampstead, MD. Though the largest, the Hampstead plant is typical in terms of facility design. Tools are produced in lots or batches and with the proper set up, most of the plant's products can be produced on any one of a number of different assembly lines. Several additional lines are reserved for unusually bulky products and continuously running products. Approximately 120 major product groups are assembled at Hampstead. Tools and accessories generate 20,000 different inventory items including 10,000 manufactured parts, 7000 purchased parts, and 3000 raw materials.

Black & Decker's Hampstead plant represents an excellent example of repetitive manufacturing. Its products and technology are ready-made for material requirements planning and there is little wonder as to why Black & Decker has been a pioneer in the development of MRP-based manufacturing logistics systems. The MRP system known as PACE was first implemented in 1967. It is a net-change system with transactions batched for daily update. The measure of time is weeks with a rolling horizon of 1 year. Order action is taken weekly and components are divided into 4 categories: manufactured parts, purchased parts, raw materials, and miscellaneous supply items. Material requirements are "pegged" and a sophisticated allocation system exists to match the issue of material to the correct parent manufacturing order. A large number of inquiry capabilities into the data base are possible, resulting in CRT display or printed copy.

## PLANNED ACTION AND CONSTANT EVALUATION

There is no "black magic" at Black & Decker. Their success in production and inventory management is the simple result of clear thinking about what they want their inventory system to do, and then designing it to accomplish those objectives. They see inventory management comprised of four key activities which are perhaps quite simple to state but difficult to carry out. These key activities are:

1) Maintaining a Sound Material Plan—
A sound material plan constitutes the cornerstone of the inventory planning function. It must be responsive to the master schedule and sympathetic to the capabilities of the production facilities.

2) Executing the Plan—
Though not usually thought to be an inventory management function, executing the material plan is recognized at Black & Decker as the best method to control inventory levels.

3) Inventory Reduction Analysis—
This activity involves special projects for the reduction of inventory levels.

4) Maintaining Record Integrity—
For many firms record accuracy turns out to be the "Achilles heel" of their inventory management system. At Black & Decker record accuracy is recognized as a fundamental system requirement and a well-conceived program exists for maintaining record integrity.

Black & Decker's inventory planning system can be characterized as one of planned action and constant evaluation. Indeed, its name—PACE—stands as the acronym for that description. Having introduced the four key activities of the PACE system let us now examine each in more detail.

## MAINTAINING A SOUND MATERIAL PLAN

A major portion of the inventory control activity falls under the category of creating and maintaining the material plan. Given a master schedule, the inventory planning and control system responds with three major activities:

1. Order planning
2. Order re-planning
3. Engineering change analysis

The premise is that when each of these activities are done well, the groundwork is laid to make inventory management a simple task.

### Order Planning

Each week all inventory items are input to an inventory analysis program. The program examines each item to determine if a planned order resides in the current or past due weeks.[1] If one does, the item is placed on an exception report and a copy of the inventory status of the part is printed and made available for planner action. It is necessary to search the past due since some activity within the last week, such as an unplanned issue or a reschedule of a higher level component, could have driven a planned order for an item into the past due.

A number of methods exist for calculating the suggested order quantity for the inventory item. However, each method is essentially a variation of one of three basic themes. These are lot-for-lot order quantity, production lot size, and part-period-balancing. All categories of parts have provisions for adding a scrap factor (contained in the part master file) to the calculated order quantity; however, it has been customary to use this only for manufactured items.

Lot-for-lot ordering strategy is generally used when the holding cost is high compared to set-up cost and when the item appears at a high level in the bill of material. Examples of parts where this kind of order strategy is used are motor parts like armatures and fields, and other major sub-assemblies. The high piece cost is an apparent reason for holding these lot sizes low. Another reason is the limited capacity for producing such parts. The large labor content in an armature, for instance, requires that its production on the shop floor be coordinated closely with the assembly of the final product. Lot-for-lot order strategy is also used for very expensive lower level parts when the demand for the item is very sparse.

The second order quantity logic works as follows. In each item master file there is a space reserved to hold a production lot size quantity for that inventory item. When this quantity is other than 0 and when the part is coded with the proper code, planned orders for that item are calculated in multiples of the production lot size quantity. Table 1 demonstrates this action. Shown in the table are 2 possible inventory plans for a hypothetical part which has a 4 week lead time and 100 units on hand.

---

[1] In actuality, manufactured parts are considered for replenishment when a planned order enters the fourth week from the current week. This is done to provide time for dispatching the order as well as to provide some buffer of manufacturing orders so as to control the release of orders to the factory floor and enable the development of a "short-range schedule." For ease of illustration, this technicality is ignored in the balance of this paper.

# TABLE 1
## Lot-For-Lot vs. Production Lot Size Order Logic

### Example 1A: Lot-for-Lot Order Logic

| Period | 1 | 2 | 3 | 4 | 5 | 6 | 7 | 8 | 9 | 10 | 11 | 12 ... |
|---|---|---|---|---|---|---|---|---|---|---|---|---|
| Requirements | | | | | 200 | 200 | 200 | 65 | 200 | 200 | | 65 |
| Orders | | | | | | | | | | | | |
| Available | 100 | 100 | 100 | 100 | −100 | −300 | −500 | −565 | −765 | −965 | −965 | −1030 |
| Planned Orders | 100 | 200 | 200 | 65 | 200 | 200 | | 65 | | | | |

### Example 1B: Production Lot Size Order Logic (PLS = 300)

| Period | 1 | 2 | 3 | 4 | 5 | 6 | 7 | 8 | 9 | 10 | 11 | 12 ... |
|---|---|---|---|---|---|---|---|---|---|---|---|---|
| Requirements | | | | | 200 | 200 | 200 | 65 | 200 | 200 | | 65 |
| Orders | | | | | | | | | | | | |
| Available | 100 | 100 | 100 | 100 | −100 | −300 | −500 | −565 | −765 | −965 | −965 | −1030 |
| Planned Orders | 300 | | 300 | | 300 | 300 | | | | | | |

Note the size and location of planned orders. With no production lot size, the location of the planned orders tends to echo the raw requirements through the lead time offset. The lower part of Table 1 shows the effect on planned orders when the item's master file contains a production lot size (PLS) of 300 and the part has the proper order code. Remembering that one item's planned orders explode to produce lower level requirements, the two different effects on the item's raw materials can be envisioned. Notice that even though only 100 items are needed in week 5, the planned order to cover the first requirement is still 300. This would be true even if the availability in week 5 were only −1 part. (Assuming 199 on hand.) This fact provides further evidence of the wisdom in limiting higher level parts to lot-for-lot order code.

The actual quantity of the production lot size is at the discretion of the inventory planner. Although there are exceptions, the production lot size is usually set to a rounded economic order quantity. Each quarter, or more frequently at the prerogative of the inventory control manager, economic order quantities are calculated for each inventory item. The economic order quantity (EOQ) is determined from the formula

$$EOQ = \sqrt{2AS/ci},$$

where

A = projected annual usage,
S = fixed costs per order (set up + order cost),
c = material and labor cost per part, and
i = holding cost rate per annum.

It is significant to note that A represents projected annual usage—not past annual usage. An item's projected usage is determined by multiplying the item's next 9 months requirements by the factor 4/3. This procedure adjusts for the fact that an item's requirements tend to "dry up" near the end of the one year planning horizon because of lead time offsetting from the master schedule. An item's EOQ serves only as a benchmark. If the inventory planner feels that the assumptions of the EOQ model are reasonably met, then she will likely set the production lot size quantity to the EOQ after rounding to nearest container quantity.

The third basic order logic—part-period-balancing (PPB) is limited to parts with high set up costs and relatively lumpy demand and is reserved for parts at low levels in the bill of material. Further, the planned orders are not dynamically calculated with the part-period-formula. This is done to avoid the possible wild fluctuations of requirements on the lower level materials. To assure that some reservation is made for material, the planner assigns a production lot size to the item. Considerable judgement is required since this lot size must be a best estimate of what the part-period lot size is likely to be. Consequently, each time an order is placed the production lot size is reviewed. A final security measure is to check that the raw material will indeed be available before actually releasing a PPB-calculated order.

A final technique used in ordering parts is family group analysis. A relatively few, but nonetheless significant, number of parts are manufactured with nearly the same tooling set up as one or more other parts. Each member of such a group is chained to the others through mutual membership in a family group. The family group membership number is part of the item master record. When any member of the group becomes due to be ordered, the inventory status record along with the records of all members of that group are presented to the planner. The planner then examines all records to determine the appropriate order action.

## Order Replanning

Besides the planning of replenishment orders for inventory items, a second major inventory planning activity is the rescheduling of existing orders. Each week the inventory analysis program searches for two possible error conditions with respect to an item's open orders. The first condition called "out-of-phase low (late)" occurs when a negative availability exists in the same week, or in any week prior to the due date of an order. Table 2 demonstrates two such out of phase conditions. The first example in Table 2 is out-of-phase "low" because the ordered quantity is insufficient to cover demand in the periods up to and including the period of the order. The appropriate planner action is to increase the order quantity or issue a new order for 300 items due week 4. The second example in Table 2 is out-of-phase "late" because the quantity ordered is sufficient but the due date is not. The appropriate planner action would be to reschedule the order for 5500 to week 4.

The second error condition is called "out of phase high (early)". A manufactured part is out of phase "high" when either the entire order quantity for a given week is in excess, or when a portion of the order quantity is in excess with the restriction that the carrying cost of the excess is greater than the item's set-up cost. Table 3 illustrates these two conditions. Example 3A is out of phase "early" because the entire order in week 4 is

# TABLE 2
## Examples of Out-Of-Phase Low (Late)

### Example 2A

| Period | 1 | 2 | 3 | 4 | 5 | 6 | ... |
|---|---|---|---|---|---|---|---|
| Requirements | | | | 5500 | | | |
| Orders | | | | 5200 | | | |
| Available | | | | −300 | −300 | −300 | |

### Example 2B

| Period | 1 | 2 | 3 | 4 | 5 | 6 | ... |
|---|---|---|---|---|---|---|---|
| Requirements | | | | 5500 | | | |
| Orders | | | | | | 5500 | |
| Available | | | | −5500 | −5500 | | |

in excess of the demand through week 4. The order should be rescheduled to week 5. Such a move seems trivial, but the rescheduling of all such orders assures that the most accurate due dates are used in the priority calculation of the shop floor control system. Example 3B is out of phase "high" because the holding cost of the 5000 excess exceeds the set up cost; i.e.,

$$\text{holding cost} = \underset{\substack{\text{quantity} \\ \text{in excess}}}{5000} \times \underset{\substack{\text{piece} \\ \text{cost}}}{1.25} \times \underset{\substack{\text{holding} \\ \text{cost/week}}}{.0071} \times \underset{\substack{\text{number of} \\ \text{weeks held}}}{2} = \$88.75$$

Purchased materials are considered out of phase high when the holding cost of any excess exceeds a fixed dollar amount. This dollar amount is at the discretion of the inventory control manager. It is a policy variable representing the maximum amount that management is currently willing to pay to avoid rescheduling a vendor.

An essential aspect of the design of the system is that orders are not automatically rescheduled by the computer. For example, in Table 3 Example 3B the suggested action is to reduce the order to 500. As with the ordering of parts, the computer only suggests a certain action. The planner makes the final decision.

## TABLE 3
### Examples of Out-Of-Phase High (Early)

Example 3A

| Period | 1 | 2 | 3 | 4 | 5 | 6 | ... |
|---|---|---|---|---|---|---|---|
| Requirements | | | | | 5500 | | |
| Orders | | | 5500 | | | | |
| Available | | | 5500 | | | | |

Example 3B

(Set-up Cost = $25.00)
(Piece Cost = $1.25)
(Holding Cost = 37% per annum)

| Period | 1 | 2 | 3 | 4 | 5 | 6 | ... |
|---|---|---|---|---|---|---|---|
| Requirements | | | 500 | | 5000 | | |
| Orders | | | 5500 | | | | |
| Available | | | 5000 | 5000 | | | |

### Engineering Change Analysis

When an engineering change notice (ECN) affects a product's bill of materials, the ECN subsystem of PACE provides a means for setting the date when such a change becomes effective. These "time fences" provide for efficient balancing of inventory items prior to making the change in the product's structure. It is a complicated system in itself. Nonetheless, it is a critical activity for the effective control of inventory.

## EXECUTING THE PLAN

### A Task with No Substitute

The importance given by Black & Decker to efficiently carrying out the material plan cannot be overstated. At B&D, building to schedule is recognized as the most important activity for the control of inventory. Building to schedule is a demanding task, one that requires near-perfection, but as one Black & Decker manager has put it ". . . a task for which there is no substitute."

### The Stretch for the Finish

Three to four weeks prior to the planned assembly of a product, a manufacturing assembly order is released. The release of this order triggers the issue of storeroom orders for the unit's components, thus allocating that material for the assembly lot. This activity is the "stretch for the finish" in the manufacturing cycle. With the release of the assembly order, a series of reports are generated. One report entitled "Materials Status Report" displays the exact status of all materials required for this assembly lot. Typically, some parts could already be in the storeroom. Others could be on the receiving dock or in-process. If the material is not yet received, the supporting manufacturing or purchase order number is displayed. A second set of reports entitled "Assembly Expedite Report" is produced for manufactured parts and for each buyer/planner group responsible for purchased parts. These reports list all products with assembly orders that have a supporting order for material which is not yet received. These reports form the basis for directing expediting effort and for communication of delivery information to the assembly planning group.

### Starts on Time—A Key Measure

A performance indicator designed to measure the effectiveness in executing the material plan is the percent of assembly starts on time. This weekly indicator is given by the ratio:

$$\frac{\text{number of products scheduled to start this week that did}}{\text{total number of products scheduled to start this week.}}$$

Figure 1 illustrates the conceptual relation of starts on time to inventory and labor efficiency. Each curve represents a given level of assembly starts on time. Note that as starts on time improve, the inventory level required to achieve a given level of labor efficiency becomes less. Likewise, as starts on time improve the labor costs necessary to operate at a given inventory level are less. In effect, a higher percentage of starts on time permits more efficient *combinations* of labor cost and inventory.

Efficient deployment of a large pool of assembly laborers demands that *all* components for an assembly be available on time. A naive solution to the problem would be to schedule material far enough ahead of the assembly date to guarantee parts availability. When the value of even one weeks worth of assembly material is in the millions of dollars, the impracticality of this type of solution becomes apparent. Clearly, at Black & Decker, building to schedule is a task for which there is no substitute.

## INVENTORY REDUCTION ANALYSIS

In theory, an MRP-driven inventory control system could operate with no inventory. This would happen if all items were ordered lot-for-lot and nothing were delivered early or late. But perfect execution (nothing early

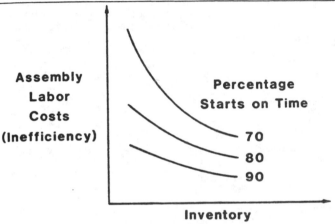

## FIGURE 1
The effect of percentage starts on time to labor costs and inventory

or late) would not be sufficient to achieve this ideal. A sudden change in the master schedule or the bill of materials file could leave a number of completed component orders with little or no usage in the foreseeable future.

With many companies, marketing and engineering change is a way of life. Black & Decker is no exception. Because of this, special efforts are needed to monitor and control the "excess" inventory caused by the accommodation of marketing and engineering changes. Black & Decker employs a number of analyses aimed at reducing this type of inventory. These special inventory reduction analyses include:

1. Excess and obsolete inventory analysis
2. Storeroom valuation analysis
3. A-B-C analysis

### Excess and Obsolete Inventory Analysis

Not all engineering changes can be implemented on a "use up stock" basis. This is a major reason for the existence of "obsolete inventory". Obsolete inventory is defined as any inventory item which is not a member of some bill of material. Excess inventory is defined as inventory on hand, but with no demand within the 52-week horizon. An excess and obsolete inventory analysis report provides inventory valuation listings of such items by category (manufactured, purchased, raw material). These reports are continually analyzed by the responsible inventory control group. This analysis results in action such as reworking the items into some other part, selling the material back to suppliers, or scrapping the material.

Another special report is the surplus inventory report. This report captures inventory items that technically can be overlooked by the excess or obsolete inventory reports, and provides some means of estimating the throughput rate of slow moving inventory. This report only lists items whose on hand balance is in excess of the upcoming 52 week demand. The dollar balance for each part is projected for each of the next eight quarters. In this projection open orders are not netted, but items with open orders are flagged for immediate action. The dollar balances are extended and summarized by category.

### Storeroom Valuation Analysis

Another major report used by Black & Decker to reduce inventory is the weekly storeroom valuation report. Here, the on hand balance for each inventory item is valuated and displayed in descending dollar sequence by category. The results are extended and summarized by A-B-C classification within category. This report is used to monitor and detect changes in the makeup of inventory.

### A-B-C Analysis

Each quarter, or more frequently at the prerogative of the inventory control manager, a set of A-B-C reports is generated. One set of reports sorts the parts by category and lists the parts within category in descending annual-usage-dollar volume. Each category of parts is examined and A-B-C classification break points are determined. Roughly the top 20% of the line items comprising 80% of the annual-usage-dollars are designated as A parts. The bottom 50% of the items comprising 20% of the annual-usage-dollars are classified as C parts. The remainder are designated B parts. Additionally, bulky parts, parts requiring special handling, or parts with a short shelf life (such as some plastic raw materials) are categorized as A parts regardless of annual-usage-dollars. These lists are made available to the individual inventory planners responsible for each commodity. They enable the planner to judge the appropriate degree of control to exercise on a given item.

Black & Decker maintains an aggressive and ongoing profit improvement program. A significant staff of manufacturing, purchasing, and development engineers exist to support this program. When the A-B-C analysis is run, another series of reports is generated. One set of reports lists purchased parts and raw materials by class code. (A class code is used to link similar parts to the same group; e.g., ball bearings, chucks, etc.) Another set of reports lists manufactured parts by key machine group. All of the reports are in descending annual-usage-dollar sequence. These reports are of great value in channeling the efforts of the profit improvement program. For example, the manufacturing engineering group responsible for the machining of die castings has a listing of all the die cast parts that are machined. This report is used to determine which parts might provide the greatest payback to any investment in process redesign.

### MAINTAINING RECORD INTEGRITY

Without accurate records any inventory management system is doomed to failure. In recognition of this, Black & Decker places considerable effort toward maintaining an accurate data base.

Rather than closing down operations to perform an annual physical inventory count, Black & Decker maintains an ongoing continuous cycle counting effort. It is beyond the scope of this paper to describe this procedure in any detail; however, it is important to communicate the role of this activity in the total effort to control inventories. Black & Decker maintains a team of employees whose full-time job is to conduct the inventory count. It is the duty of the correct count team to not only correct record errors, but also to investigate the source of such errors and to initiate changes in the system design that will enhance record accuracy.

Another duty of the correct count team is to conduct an on-going storeroom location audit. Over the course of time every storeroom location is examined and the actual contents of that location is compared with the storeroom's location record file. This activity uncovers "lost" components, i.e., components which are mis-located within the storeroom. A "lost" component probably represents the worst of all worlds for the inventory planner—the item is known to be on hand but not available for use—

and the error is not discovered until it is time to use the item. The location audit helps to ameliorate these kinds of problems and acts to compliment the correct count activity.

At Black & Decker the on-hand inventory records are not the only records under surveillance. Each week the inventory planner conducts what is known as a past-due analysis. The past-due analysis consists of an examination of certain files of each inventory item. These files are requirements, allocations, and orders for that item. Items that have a requirement, allocation, or order residing in any week that is six weeks or more into the past-due are listed for examination. The six week parameter is a variable subject to management discretion. Through such analysis these files are purged of data that is not authentic. Without "pegged" files this analysis could not be performed. This is one reason why PACE has been able to successfully operate on a net change basis and avoid costly regenerations of requirements.

### SUMMARY

Figure 2 serves to summarize the major inventory planning activities at Black & Decker. Black & Decker's approach to inventory management is straight-forward. It consists of four key activities for inventory management; namely:

1. maintaining a sound material plan
2. executing the plan
3. inventory reduction analysis
4. maintaining record integrity

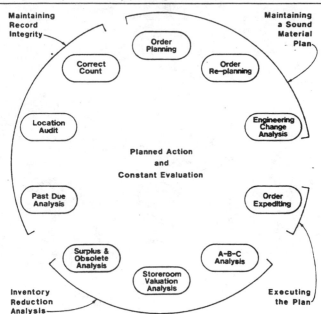

**FIGURE 2**
Summary of inventory planning activities at Black & Decker

Given this framework, all inventory activities can be seen to be serving one or more of these objectives. Order planning, order re-planning, and ECN analysis are viewed as activities necessary for the creation and maintenance of a sound inventory plan. This level of activity attempts to combine the best of applicable inventory models, computerized information systems, and human judgement. The goal of this set of activities is to produce a plan that optimizes cost with a high responsiveness to change. Continual effort is made to improve all aspects of the inventory planning system.

Order expediting and related activities are the means of assuring effective execution of the plan. The importance of this activity cannot be underestimated. The various special inventory analyses represent the overt efforts to analyze and reduce inventories. Analysis of the past due and the storeroom correct count activities are done to maintain and improve record integrity. For any part of the system to be effective, a high degree of record accuracy is essential.

Performing all four of these functions well, and in harmony, is the goal at Black & Decker. The acronym PACE is well chosen as the name for Black & Decker's inventory planning system. It is indeed one of "planned action and constant evaluation".

**About the Author—**

*JOHN J. KANET, CPIM* is an Associate Professor of Business Analysis and Research at Texas A&M University where he teaches graduate and undergraduate courses in operations management. His special interests are in the area of production and inventory management.

Prior to entering the academic profession, Dr. Kanet spent eight years with the Black and Decker Manufacturing Company. While at B&D he held various positions in production engineering and materials management. His most recent position was Manufactured and Purchased Materials Manager at Black & Decker's largest plant in Hampstead, Maryland.

Professor Kanet holds a B.S. degree in mechanical engineering from Lehigh University and an M.B.A. from Loyola College (Baltimore). His Ph.D. degree is from the Pennsylvania State University where he concentrated in operations management. He is a member of Beta Gamma Sigma and Sigma Iota Epsilon honorary business fraternities and is active in professional societies including the American Institute for Decision Sciences, the American Production and Inventory Control Society, the Institute of Management Sciences and the Operations Management Association. He has written numerous journal articles on various topics in production and inventory management. He is certified by APICS as a Fellow and has addressed various APICS groups at chapter meetings, seminars, and national conferences. For 1984–85, he is a Senior Fulbright Scholar at the University of Erlangen/Nuremberg, West Germany.

Reprinted from *Production and Inventory Management*, Third Quarter, 1978.

# PRIORITY FIXATION VERSUS THROUGHPUT PLANNING

*Presented at the APICS International Conference, 1977*

Hal Mather & George Plossl
*Mather & Plossl, Inc.*    *Atlanta, GA*

**Hal Mather:**

## INTRODUCTION

There are two essential elements in every manufacturing control system. These are priority (what to make, when) and capacity, (volume flowing per time period). Most people in manufacturing control concentrate on priorities to the exclusion of capacity. In many plants, capacity desired and available are reviewed annually, plans made to solve any mismatches, and once that is over, concentration switches to getting the right things made at the right time. This is a natural approach as pressures are hourly or daily for information on customers' orders, checking whether vendors' deliveries will be on time, reacting to line shortages, etc. But these two sides of a manufacturing control program are interrelated and one cannot be successful when disregarding the other.

The performance of formal priority systems to date (material requirements planning and shop floor control) is proof of this. So far these techniques are not approaching anywhere near their potential in the bulk of applications. The major reason is that capacity is not getting its share of attention. They must *both* be managed for a successful manufacturing control program.

There are five basic functions in all manufacturing control programs, shown in Figure 1. The first of these is the need for a master production schedule, specifying the total amount of product that is needed to be made over a given time period. It is called a game plan; it is a set of numbers formulating the strategy that the whole plant will be trying to achieve.

The next two functions, capacity planning and control, answer the question "Is the volume of material flowing adequate to support the master production schedule?" Visualize a manufacturing plant as a refinery. These two techniques together are planning and controlling the diameter of pipelines feeding product through work centers and from

FIGURE 1

## BASIC FUNCTIONS

MASTER SCHEDULING — GAME PLAN

CAPACITY PLANNING
AND CONTROL — GET ENOUGH

PRIORITY PLANNING — GET RIGHT
AND CONTROL THINGS

vendors. They ensure the diameters are adequate to handle the volume of product to be made in the plant, defined as the master production schedule.

The next two functions, priority planning and control, answer the question, "Are we getting the right items?" Here is where the flow of product through work centers or from vendors must be sequenced correctly to get the first items first, second items second, etc. Here is where manufacturing control people concentrate their attention, on the sequencing or priority problem. However, if capacity is inadequate in any of the pipelines in a plant or at vendors, it is impossible to get the right priority on jobs.

"Are we getting the right stuff?" is the wrong question to ask unless we are sure we are getting enough. Few of us are getting enough! That means fewer still are getting the right ones!

### PRIORITY FIXATION

The oldest technique in manufacturing control systems is expediting. It is still running the bulk of industry to ensure parts get made when needed. An expediter's role is to go out and locate missing or late parts and prioritize these through the plant. Even with the new techniques of material requirements planning and shop floor control, expediting is not out of favor. Recently I saw some new advertising for "Hot stickers", in beautiful colors, shaped like flames, containing special wording, etc. However, these hot stickers have been made more modern. Now they get stuck on computer generated paper instead of being stuck on hand-written paper.

The interest in material requirements planning and its emphasis in industry to the exclusion of most other techniques is relatively understandable. It was only logical that the expediter's process, our most successful technique, would be formalized first. MRP identifies shortages systematically and provides a better "when" system. In the early days of MRP, weekly time buckets were used and the system usually replanned weekly. This seemed adequate for a while, but then concern started to grow over priority changes within the week. Hence a lot of interest has developed in the technique called "Net Change MRP". Its great contribution to the field is that many times it requires less computer time to perform the same job as a regenerative program because it only processes exceptions. The practitioner's interest, however, was not in saving the computer resource, but freeing up enough of that resource to be able to prioritize his jobs more often; hence daily net change or at least twice a week net change. This provided more priority information, more up-to-date.

But now concern has switched from running the process more often to looking at the time increment that is being used. The early net change programs still used weekly time buckets; hence the priority system was relatively coarse providing information only in five day increments. But what if the demand was on Monday and replenishment on Friday of the same week. (We all know that early in the week to purchasing means any time up until noon on Friday.) This obviously was untenable and a more definitive time increment was needed.

This has caused bucketless MRP, or one day bucketing systems, to be in vogue to provide priority information to the day of the week. The only question now is, "Is the demand in the morning or the afternoon?" I expect the next generation of MRP programs to be not only date responsive but also time of the day. And the real big question is "How well do we know what we intend doing in the future to the day, and how good is much of the data we are using, eg. lead times, shrinkage factors, lot-sizes, etc. to support this level of precision?"

And heard like a voice in the wilderness from the users is the plea to reduce the amount of information they are getting. "MRP means More Reams of Paper" is heard fairly often and users have difficulty reacting to all the exceptions on a timely basis. Hence a suggestion has been made to allow the computer to reschedule open orders automatically. Another suggestion has been to apply dampening rules to the exception messages. For example, if the expedite is two days or less don't report that, and if the delay is five days or less don't print that either. So from weekly regeneration of weekly buckets has evolved daily net change with daily buckets and, applying these over-rides, changes either get made automatically without full cognizance of the effects these changes are making or dampening rules blunt the precision of these techniques to provide information on weekly changes only. Is this progress?

And in the bulk of cases, making changes to priorities more often will not improve the situation at the plant. Priority is not the major problem in most situations.

From this level of expertise interest is now swinging to the need to execute priorities in the plant, hence shop floor control. This is a series of techniques to provide a list to the foreman showing the sequence in which work should be performed to make the master schedule happen. Here, people are choosing up sides. One group says, "The foreman should be constrained and must follow the lists exactly the way they are shown", and the other side says, "Don't do that, let him be flexible, let him cherry pick". But the major problem at the moment is the list *cannot* be followed. The production control man goes out to the foreman and says, "Work on the top job for me would you Joe," and Joe says, "Where is it? When you get it here I'll work on it." Obviously the P.C. man recovers quickly and says, "O.K. Joe, if you can't do that one, how about working on the second one?" And Joe says, "Where have you been, I finished that job three days ago." But maybe the most important problem of all is that there are too many urgent priorities and too many changes to these priorities for anybody in a plant to consider the list a valid plan. How about vendors; can they, or are they, willing to react to changes on a daily basis? If they are not, what good is changing the plan daily if materials will not be received in matched sets to make products?

## WHERE DO PRIORITIES COME FROM?

The priority system starts from a set of numbers defined as a master production schedule. This is a statement of what, how much, and when something will be made, relatively high up in a bill of materials. A master schedule typically has a one-year horizon, although many companies have much longer horizons than this, and a few have shorter. The definition of products put into the master production schedule is usually for specific items, either finished goods or an intermediate level lower down in the bill of material. MRP takes this information and converts the overall plan into detail plans. A typical example is shown in Figure 2. The master production schedule explodes through bills of material, calculates requirements at the first level, and nets against inventory, both on-hand and on order. Lot-sizes are calculated or applied where justified and lead times offset to generate the next level requirements, etc. MRP's role is to provide exception reporting wherever a mismatch of timing between demand and supply exists. It is a priority system and typical messages are "expedite, delay, launch a new order, cancel an existing order, etc." MRP provides what is called order priority.

To get order priority into operational priority at the foreman level, these orders must be broken down finer. MRP or order priority provides the need date to the scheduling system. Scheduling rules take the total

FIGURE 2

## MASTER PRODUCTION SCHEDULE

| WEEK NO. | 40 | 41 | 42 | 43 | 44 | 45 | 46 | 47 |
|---|---|---|---|---|---|---|---|---|
| WILL MAKE | | 20 | | 30 | | 25 | | 35 |

## MAJOR ASSEMBLY

| | | | | | | | | |
|---|---|---|---|---|---|---|---|---|
| REQUIRE | | | 20 | | 30 | | 25 | | 35 |
| HAVE NOW | 10 | | | | | | | |
| WILL GET | | | 10 | | | | | |
| NEED | | | | | 30 | | 25 | | 35 |
| START | | | | 30 | | 25 | | 35 | |

## SUB ASSEMBLY

| | | | | | | | |
|---|---|---|---|---|---|---|---|
| REQUIRE | | | 30 | | 25 | | 35 | |
| HAVE NOW | | | | | | | | |
| WILL GET | | | 30 | | | | | |
| NEED | | | | | 25 | | 35 | |
| START | | | 60 | | | | | |

lead time for an order and break it into smaller segments, as shown in Figure 3. Using the setup and run times for a job, move and queue times for work centers, etc., due dates can be calculated for each operation.

FIGURE 3

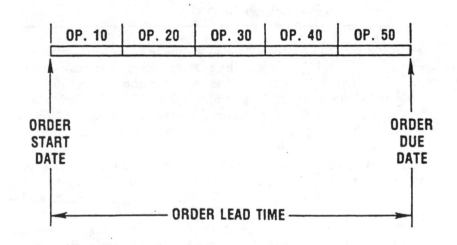

| OP. 10 | OP. 20 | OP. 30 | OP. 40 | OP. 50 |

ORDER START DATE

ORDER DUE DATE

← ORDER LEAD TIME →

These estimated operation dates are now used to create a priority list for each foreman, as shown in Figure 4. Priorities can be calculated using techniques such as critical ratio, queue ratio, etc., to rank jobs in their desired sequence. As changes occur to the master production schedule, engineering changes are implemented to the bills of material, inventory adjustments are made to the on-hand inventories, scrap or late delivery occurs to the open orders, etc., then these priorities are up-dated, first of all through MRP and then through the scheduling system into a priority change at the foreman or vendor level. The priority system is a date driven system.

---

FIGURE 4

---

## DAILY DISPATCH LIST
### WORK CENTER 103

DATE: 10-3                                                    CAPACITY: 298

| PART | | ORDER | | | PRIOR | |
|---|---|---|---|---|---|---|
| NUMBER | DESCRIPTION | NO. | QUANT | HRS | RANK | GOES TO |
| 117175 | SLEEVE | 841A | 1500 | 22 | 1 | 106-1 |
| 276112 | GEAR | 920E | 300 | 13 | 2 | 110-2 |
| 523153 | HOUSING | 663B | 120 | 8 | 3 | 106-4 |
| 319181 | FRAME | 717C | 165 | 10 | 26 | 108-2 |

TOTAL HRS IN 103 = 287

---

If these data are analyzed in more detail, estimates, forecasts, guesses, and averages are found throughout the system, which obviously affect the quality of information generated. The master production schedule is the starting set of numbers for the planning system. The detailed priority list that a foreman gets is the execution phase of that plan linked to the master schedule through bills of material and MRP, and through scheduling rules to operational priorities.

There are some problems with this flow of information. The first of these is the tendency within industry to make the master production schedule anything but a realistic plan. It is usually well over-stated and hence provides far too many priorities to foremen for them to execute. Another problem with the master production schedule is that it is often too dynamic. Dynamic changes at the top of bills of material obviously ripple throughout the whole planning system and result in rather dramatic changes in priority on the plant floor which may or may not be achievable. A master production schedule often contains elements of forecast. These are frequently placed in arbitrary time buckets, especially if the forecast is for monthly quantities and the master schedule is in weekly time increments.

The bills of material used in the plan are usually today's bills of materials. Future changes to existing products and new products engineers are designing are not in this planning program and will affect today's decisions as these changes get implemented. The system uses lot-sizes at each level in the BoM to cover net requirements and explodes these lot-sizes to calculate requirements at the next lower level. Frequently these lot-sizes are over-ridden when releasing work for short term reasons. This means that the priorities used for lower level materials that are already made were wrong, even though calculated precisely. Many other factors such as scrap, rework, inventory adjustments, unplanned requirements from sales or engineering, etc. are all going to impact and affect the priority system to a greater or lesser degree. Hence precision of planning in the priority system has to be balanced against the quality of information available.

## THROUGHPUT PLANNING'S ROLE

Another critical parameter for timing is the one labeled "Lead time". The lead time for a part is the length of time from knowing it is required until it is ready, complete for use at the next level of manufacture. However, it is not the lead time for individual parts that is important to the priority system but the stacked lead time from initiating procurement of materials all the way through the various processing steps up to the master production schedule. This stacked lead time has a major effect on the priority system. The longer this lead time is, the more time there is for change, either with the master production schedule or with the other sets of data used in the system. As these changes are made, the system will attempt to reflect these changes in priorities but maybe it will be too late to react. The earlier comments about bills of material that change obviously are more severe the longer the stacked lead time. It provides the engineers more time to change their minds on the product design. Lead times are critical to the priority system but very little is being done to control and manage lead times to a minimum.

A company several years ago was a classic example of the problems of long lead times. I gave a presentation to the shop foremen and schedulers in this plant regarding inventories, customer service, productivity and their roles in improving these. Just a few minutes after my presentation started a foreman stood up and wondered why I was wasting his time. When I explained that I thought he had something to do with getting products made on time, efficiently, with low inventories, he agreed that was true, but suggested I go and talk to the purchasing department. He said the purchasing people were the ones who had all the wrong material in the plant and hence he could not make what customers needed. They were the ones that were causing most of the problems.

This is a typical feeling among many plant people. They have the opinion "give me the materials and I can make anything the customer wants". They also feel victims of purchasing departments not having needed materials. They feel they can react with materials on hand to provide a given customer what he needs, but if the materials are not available they cannot get a customer out of trouble. A little analysis and digging on my part found the following conditions in this company's planning system. Their bill of materials was relatively simple with few levels in it; however, their stacked lead time was as shown on Figure 5. They procured castings with 13 weeks lead time which at that period in the economic cycle was far better than most other people buying castings. Their purchasing department was doing an *excellent* job of getting reasonably short lead times for product. These castings were then machined with very tight tolerances and a significant number of operations. 16 weeks was the lead time in the planning system for machining castings. After the machining was done the castings were sent to a secondary department where they were welded together and subsequent machining performed. The tolerances again were very tight and several operations were necessary to make sure these castings were perfectly balanced. This again took 16 weeks of processing time, or at least that was in the system. The last stage of making the product was assembly and test, and the system was told this took 4 weeks because everything had to be 100% tested under some rather stringent conditions.

---

FIGURE 5

---

STACKED LEAD TIME EXAMPLE

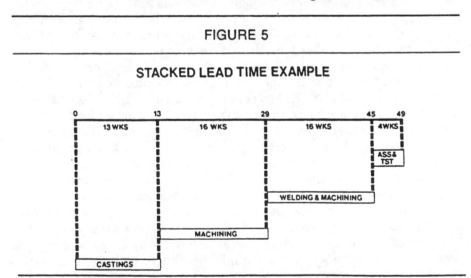

As you can see, this put the quantity in the master production schedule 49 weeks in the future, triggering purchasing people to order castings now. There is no chance of getting the right material procured with a master production schedule quantity that far out. No matter how precisely the priorities are calculated they will be invalid, both for vendors and the plant, as changes occur when that number gets closer to the current time period. In this plant there was plenty of material around, including castings, but they were all the wrong ones. Inventories of material were high at the same time as customer service was low. And with priorities shifting fast, the efficiency in the plant was poor because of broken set ups, confusion, expediting and the rest of the activities that occur when a plant goes out of control.

Capacity control was the missing link. Their actual capacity was adequate to make all the product customers required. However, their effective capacity, making what was needed in matched sets to suit a customer order, was inadequate. They were making many things not required because of the invalid priority system.

This tendency of lead times to cause effective capacity to be well below actual capacity must be solved. Many plants have multi-level bills of material with cumulative lead times that are very long. It is not valid to plan priorities this way. Replanning more often won't solve the problem, neither will doing it with more precision. The only way to attack this problem is to cut lead times down to a bare minimum.

The technique of throughput planning (input/output control) can reduce them dramatically. The emphasis in plants must be changed to volumes flowing, making sure the pipeline diameters are large enough. When volumes are planned and controlled adequately then lead times can be reduced to provide valid priorities. Only this way will effective capacity and actual capacity be in step. It is also the ultimate test of the realism of the master production schedule. It provides feedback as to whether the actual throughput is adequate to support the master production schedule or not. Decisions can be made to increase the actual throughput where necessary or decrease the MPS to suit the actual throughput available. The priority system can now be valid. This way we can really make progress.


George Plossl:

Priority planning and control is certainly important in manufacturing but it is only one-half of the total job. Control of priority depends on managing lead times. This, to many people, is a strange and incomprehensible term; they don't believe lead times can be managed. Far too many people believe that they need a system capable of responding more quickly and precisely, changing the planned lead time to match the actual lead times being experienced. Among the greatest needs in manufacturing control today is a better understanding of lead time—its management and its true role in manufacturing control.

Lead time is viewed differently by the two material ordering techniques. The order point approach assumes some average lead time required for replenishment of the item. It recognizes that demand will often exceed the planned average over this lead time and that the lead time itself might be longer; hence, it needs safety stock to compensate. In effect it uses excess inventory to cover the likelihood that actual demand over the real lead time may be in excess of the planned quantity. It depends on expediting when the safety stock is not available or when the quantity required over the actual lead time exceeds the planned maximum.

Material requirements planning, on the other hand, assumes controlled lead times. It makes a rigorous calculation of requirements and plans a replenishment, scheduling an item as needed to support its parent's schedules. It plans the release of the item at the beginning of some average lead time. During this lead time, however, it recognizes that requirements will change, machines will break down and other failures will interrupt the flow of replenishment orders. MRP assumes that actual lead times can be managed (i.e., compressed or extended) as needed to meet the latest and best due date assigned by the MRP program.

Unfortunately, too few managers and practitioners recognize that managing lead time requires sound planning and effective control of capacity. The missing link in most modern systems is capacity planning and input/output control.

---

FIGURE 6

---

## 2 LEAD TIMES

- WORK CENTER LEAD TIME
  PLANNED-AVERAGE
  ACTUAL-AVERAGE

- ORDER LEAD TIME
  PLANNED-AVERAGE
  ACTUAL-SPECIFIC

---

Figure 6 identifies two types of lead time. Each work center, because of its work-in-process queues, requires some average lead time to complete a new order arriving at the work center; this depends on how many other orders are there ahead of it, in other words, on the level of work-in-process. This work-center-average lead time can be controlled only when the input of work to the work center matches its output so that backlogs are kept constant. Managing this average lead time, then, requires managing capacity. To run a sound system, the objective must be to have the actual average lead time to get work through the work center match as closely as possible the planned average lead time.

Each order in the queue at a work center has a priority which determines its position in the queue and sets the length of time it remains there. Orders can experience literally no queue, for example, when the general manager issues an edict that he wants some order out as soon as possible. On the other hand, all other orders with lower priority will then spend more time sitting in the work-in-process queue.

To plan priorities in an MRP program, we need a planned average order lead time which will be the sum of the setup time, running time, move time and queue time in each of the work centers through which it is processed, as shown in Figure 7. Subtracting this average order lead time from the due date, MRP sets a start date suggesting when the order should be released. In operation, however, the objective *is not* to get the actual order lead times to match the planned average. Actual lead time must be "managed" to complete the order on the adjusted due date; the position or ranking of each order in the queue is based on the latest and best priority requirements.

---

FIGURE 7

## ELEMENTS OF LEAD TIME

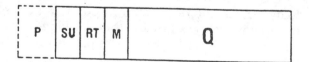

---

Figure 7 also includes an element of paperwork time or preparation time. This would include, for example, writing requisitions, having the purchasing department solicit bids from vendors, review their quotations and place a firm order; it normally is thought to include all work necessary preparatory to releasing the order to the vendor. In manufacturing in-house, this would include preparing shop packets, getting tools ready and otherwise completing all work needed prior to release of the order. In well-designed ordering techniques, however, the "forward visibility" of the release date for the order provides adequate time in which to accomplish this paperwork. It is, therefore, unnecessary to build allowances for paperwork time into planned lead times. The real advantage of this is in reducing the total manufacturing cycle time within which material is being committed and capacity being assigned to specific items associated with some end product. Two weeks of paperwork time at each of nine levels of a bill of material will lengthen the horizon of the master schedule, directing that some material and capacity be committed to specific items, up to eighteen weeks farther out into the future than is necessary. The validity of the whole manufacturing plan can be improved by shortening the cumulative or stacked lead times; eliminating the paperwork element makes a significant contribution to this.

Obviously, since the queue time represents 90–95% of the total lead time of most manufactured and purchased items, this is the element which must be controlled. It is absolutely ridiculous that castings, bearings, forgings, chain, steel, chemicals and most products made from these are thought to require lead times of many weeks when the time actually required to process a normal batch of any of these is a few hours.

Only a very few items made in industry require more than a few manufacturing hours to produce a normal quantity; why is it that most lead times are expressed in weeks and many stated in months? The reason is a basic misunderstanding of the truth about lead time. Most people think that planned lead times must be adjusted to match the actual time experienced. They believe the system is then told "the truth about lead time". Nothing could be further from the real truth.

To understand the truth about lead time and how it can be managed, we must identify the basic problems to be solved. The first problem is inadequate capacity. Obviously, if the capacity of a work center is not able to handle the volume of work flowing to it, backlogs ahead of such work centers will grow and the lead times required for orders to get through the work center will become increasingly long and more variable. In the past, we attempted to use machine loading to determine whether or not the capacity of a work center was adequate. Figure 8 shows a typical machine load diagram. Most material control people would concentrate on the load during the first few weeks and would

FIGURE 8

# TYPICAL
# WORK CENTER LOAD REPORT

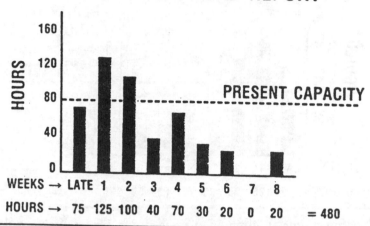

| WEEKS → | LATE | 1 | 2 | 3 | 4 | 5 | 6 | 7 | 8 | |
|---------|------|-----|-----|----|----|----|----|---|----|--------|
| HOURS → | 75 | 125 | 100 | 40 | 70 | 30 | 20 | 0 | 20 | = 480 |

conclude that the capacity of the work center was inadequate, pointing to the late orders together with the heavy load in the first two weeks. They would bring pressure to bear on manufacturing foremen and superintendents to increase the output of the work center to "get back on schedule".

Line operations people, however, looking at the total load over the eight weeks illustrated, would be most reluctant to increase capacity "to run out of work sooner" seeing that the total load over the eight weeks is not sufficient to keep the work center busy at its present output rate of eighty standard hours per week. Material control people have an answer to this objection, of course. They point out that the total load shown over the eight-week horizon is *based only on released orders* and that more orders will be released in this period. Those with MRP programs developing a planned order profile well out into the future and with computerized scheduling and loading techniques can calculate this planned load in addition to the released load as indicated by the open bars in Figure 9. This is the classical capacity requirements planning technique.

Now it would seem clear that the work center capacity is truly inadequate; the 800 total standard hours in the load is far in excess of the 640 hours the center is capable of handling. However, two factors must not be overlooked. First, if all of the orders in the load were to be completed, the work center would be out of work at the end of Week 8. The erratic flow of work to this work center, indicated by the varying lengths of the bars, makes it imperative to have a substantial queue

FIGURE 9

## CAPACITY
## REQUIREMENTS PLAN

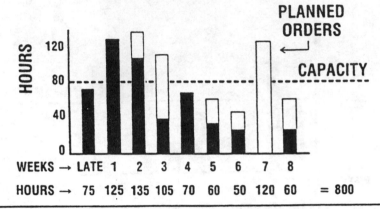

PLANNED
ORDERS

CAPACITY

| WEEKS → | LATE | 1 | 2 | 3 | 4 | 5 | 6 | 7 | 8 | |
|---|---|---|---|---|---|---|---|---|---|---|
| HOURS → | 75 | 125 | 135 | 105 | 70 | 60 | 50 | 120 | 60 | = 800 |

ahead of the center at all times to avoid down time which would really cut into its effective capacity. If this "standard queue" is set at two weeks' work (160 hours), the net load to be handled will be only 640 hours, matching the available capacity of the work center. Load and capacity are different as illustrated in Figure 10. Machine loading and the classical capacity requirements planning techniques assume that they are the same. They are not!

FIGURE 10

## LOAD vs. CAPACITY

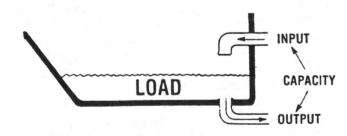

INPUT

CAPACITY

LOAD

OUTPUT

The second factor to be considered is that unplanned occurrences will place additional requirements on capacity above those shown in the formal plan represented in Figure 9. These include scrap, rework, methods changes, design changes, new product introductions and record errors, all of which require capacity. These are not in the present formal plan. Classical capacity requirements planning is highly precise but its real accuracy is subject to considerable question. It resembles counting individual snowflakes and then attempting to calculate how deep a snow drift they might form.

Although many practitioners criticize the rough-cut approaches, they are considerably easier and may, in fact, be far more practical and yield more useful results than the full, formal, detailed calculations. Figure 11 shows a bill of labor for a product family (it could also be a typical product in a family) listing the important work centers together with the standard hours required to produce *all of the components in the product family* together with capacity requirements for some critical purchased materials. The unit of measure in this bill of labor is "standard hours" for internal work. Various units of measure meaningful to the vendor in determining his capacity needs have been used for purchased items.

This bill of labor has two uses: first, to evaluate the realism of the master production schedule and, second, to develop planned levels of capacity required to support the master schedule in specific and critical work centers. Figure 12 shows a rough-cut plan developed for one month for all of the product families in the master schedule. Figure 13

---

## FIGURE 11

---

## BILL OF LABOR

### PRODUCT FAMILY #1

| WORK CENTER | STD. HRS PER 1000 UNITS |
|---|---|
| 110 | 10 |
| 108 | 8 |
| 105 | 14 |
| 104 | 28 |
| 103 | 9 |
| 101 | 17 |
| VENDORS — CASTINGS | 250 MOLDS |
| CHEMICALS | 400 GALLONS |
| FASTENERS | 4500 PIECES |
| STEEL | 520 LBS |

---

FIGURE 12

# ROUGH-CUT CAPACITY PLAN

| WORK CTRS | FAMILIES #1 | #2 | #3 | #4 | #5 | #6 | TOTAL MONTH #1 |
|---|---|---|---|---|---|---|---|
| MPS UNITS | 5570 | 3120 | 830 | 6120 | 2220 | 4610 | |
| 110 | 56 | | | | | | 330 |
| 108 | 45 | | | | | | 200 |
| 106 | | | | | | | 150 |
| 105 | 78 | | | | | | 650 |
| 104 | 156 | | | | | | 1,450 |
| 103 | 50 | | | | | | 290 |
| 102 | | | | | | | 460 |
| 101 | 95 | | | | | | 1,010 |
| 100 | | | | | | | 370 |
| CASTINGS | 1,395 | | | | | | 6,200 |
| CHEMICALS | 2,230 | | | | | | 8,320 |
| FASTENERS | 25,100 | | | | | | 97,960 |
| STEEL | 2,900 | | | | | | 15,520 |

FIGURE 13

# SUMMARY ROUGH-CUT CAPACITY PLAN

| WORK CTRS | PRESENT CAPACITY | REQUIRED CAPACITY — STD. HRS. MO. #1 | MO. #2 | MO. #3 | MO. #4 |
|---|---|---|---|---|---|
| 110 | 320 | 330 | | | |
| 108 | 230 | 200 | | | |
| 106 | 170 | 150 | | | |
| 105 | 500 | 650 | | | |
| 104 | 1.500 | 1.450 | | | |
| 103 | 310 | 290 | | | |
| 102 | 440 | 460 | | | |
| 101 | 960 | 1,010 | | | |
| 100 | 370 | 370 | | | |
| CASTINGS | 5.900 | 6.200 | | | |
| CHEMICALS | 8.450 | 8.320 | | | |
| FASTENERS | 98.000 | 97,960 | | | |
| STEEL | 12,000 | 15,520 | | | |

summarizes the results for all products in the master schedule over the full planning horizon. Even when the master schedule is expressed in weeks, rough-cut capacity plans are frequently set up in months.

People who are detail-minded have several criticisms of this approach. First, there is no time-phasing; the hours required to make the product are assumed to be needed in the same time frame in which the product appears in the master schedule. This obviously will not be the case; work in a given bill of labor may extend over several weeks. However, the purpose is to develop an estimate over a long time period of the *average capacity needed;* offsetting work to recognize lead times is an unnecessary refinement. A second criticism is that there is no "netting" out of quantities of components already in inventory. This factor, like lead time offsetting, is usually negligible unless a significant reduction is planned for component inventories. Then it may be necessary to reduce the summarized capacity figures to allow the master schedule to "draw capacity out of the inventory" instead of supplying it in the work centers. A third criticism of the rough-cut approach is that it neglects the effects of changes in the mix of products within and among the families. Again, this is usually not a significant factor but, if it should be, adjustments can be made to recognize it. The ease of developing and modifying the data more than makes up for these deficiencies in most companies.

The basic purpose of the summary rough-cut plan is to evaluate whether or not the master schedule is realistic. This requires a comparison of needed and available capacity, shown in the column headed "Present Capacity". These data are best obtained by using *actual production rates of good pieces in the recent past.* Last week's output is your plant capacity whether you think it should be more or not. Some companies average output over the last four weeks to compensate for factors like holidays, serious production problems of a temporary nature and other intermittent effects.

Viewing the rough-cut approaches in proper perspective, it is obvious that there is no excuse for delaying capacity planning and control. Even companies which do not yet have full routings and well-engineered standards can utilize simple bills of labor and input/output control to insure that backlogs on the plant floor are well-managed and that lead times are kept under control.

The second major problem in controlling lead time is that good ordering techniques do not release work at a level rate. Figure 14 shows the erratic way in which work can come out of a sound MRP program. The ordering technique is following its own rules regarding due dates, lead times and release times. In one time-period, several orders will be suggested for issue and will total a very significant load. In another, there may be hardly any work released by the system. This tendency must be overcome if work-in-process levels are to be controlled. There are so few work centers that can handle a very erratic load that it is useless to talk about them. Every effort must be made in the starting or gateway centers as well as in secondary centers to level or smooth the flow of work into and through these operations.

The proper approach in starting operations uses MRP or time-phased order points to rank the items in a priority sequence. A scheduler then selects items from the top of the ranked list until the total of work released equals or is close to the planned input rate to his work centers. He thus smooths out the release of work. In some periods he withholds issuing orders which would exceed the planned input rate; in others he "reaches ahead" into the system and draws out early orders which would otherwise not yet be released in order to feed his work center at a level rate. There is only one alternative to doing this—accepting erratic backlogs and erratic lead times in critical work centers.

For secondary or downstream work centers it is not so easy to smooth out the flow. Simply measuring the input, however, and keeping track of cumulative deviations from the planned average will indicate whether or not a work center is being overloaded or is starving. In some cases a careful adjustment of the mix of orders into starting operations will help to get work to flow better through downstream work centers. This is relatively easy for "semi-process" flow operations such as the production of pharmaceuticals, chemicals and many hard goods products where materials follow the same operation sequences.

---

## FIGURE 14

---

# WORK PROJECTION

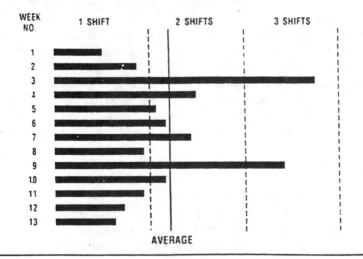

The basic principle of input/output control, known for a long time, is that the input should be less than or equal to the output—never more! The prime objective is to keep backlogs in work centers under control and not let them grow or become highly erratic.

The third major problem is one of a basic understanding of the nature of lead time and its influence in ordering techniques. We have called it the Lead Time Syndrome. To illustrate this, we have developed a game which can be played by four teams of people representing companies buying a variety of materials from a game leader representing one of their suppliers.

Orders are placed via small cards; the color indicates the customer company and the number of the card indicates the week delivery is desired. Each card represents a batch of material. The vendor could be supplying any one of a wide variety of commodities such as castings, forgings, glass bottles, chemicals, etc. sold in a number of different items to each customer.

There are two basic rules: the vendor must quote honest lead times based on his capacity and total backlog of orders, and customers must place orders covering their requirements over the vendor's quoted lead times. Each customer's real requirements are one order per period over the duration of the game. The vendor has capacity as the game begins to produce four orders per week, which is adequate to cover his customers' total needs. The vendor has been quoting three weeks lead time; as a result he has twelve orders in his backlog, three from each customer. A typical run of the game is illustrated on the attached tabulation entitled "Vendor Tally Sheet", Figure 15. In Week 1, with three weeks quoted

---

## FIGURE 15

---

# VENDOR TALLY SHEET

| WEEK NO | CAPAC | NEW ORD | SHPD | BACK LOG | QUOT LT | WEEK NO | CAPAC | NEW ORD | SHPD | BACK LOG | QUOT LT. |
|---|---|---|---|---|---|---|---|---|---|---|---|
| START | 4 | - | - | 12 | 3 | 18 | | | | | |
| 1 | 4 | 4 | 4 | 12 | 3 | 19 | | | | | |
| 2 | 4 | 4 | 4 | 12 | 3 | 20 | | | | | |
| 3 | 4 | 5 | 4 | 13 | 4 | 21 | | | | | |
| 4 | 4 | 8 | 4 | 17 | 5 | 22 | | | | | |
| 5 | 4 | 8 | 4 | 21 | 8 | 23 | | | | | |
| 6 | 4 | 16 | 4 | 33 | 12 | 24 | | | | | |
| 7 | 4 | 20 | 4 | 49 | 16 | 25 | | | | | |
| 8 | 4 | 20 | 4 | 65 | 20 | 26 | | | | | |
| 9 | 4 | 20 | 4 | 81 | 25 | 27 | | | | | |
| 10 | 5 | 24 | 5 | 100 | 25 | 28 | | | | | |
| 11 | 5 | 4 | 5 | 99 | 25 | 29 | | | | | |
| 12 | 5 | 4 | 5 | 98 | 20 | 30 | | | | | |
| 13 | 5 | -16 | 5 | 77 | 15 | 31 | | | | | |
| 14 | 5 | -16 | 5 | 56 | 11 | 32 | | | | | |
| 15 | 5 | -12 | 5 | 39 | 7 | 33 | | | | | |
| 16 | 5 | -12 | 5 | 22 | 4 | 34 | | | | | |
| 17 | 3 | -8 | 3 | 11 | | 35 | | | | | |

lead-time, the vendor receives four orders, ships four orders, maintains his backlog of twelve orders and continues to quote three weeks lead-time. In Week 2 the same things happen again. In Week 3, however, we introduce *one additional order* from one customer allowing the normal three weeks delivery. The vendor receives five new orders, ships four, sees his backlog increase to thirteen orders and, therefore, "to be honest", quotes four weeks lead time.

In Week 4, each customer must now cover his normal week's needs *plus an additional week's requirements*. The vendor receives eight new orders, ships only four and sees his backlog increase to seventeen which is still beyond his capacity to handle. He, therefore, quotes five weeks lead time.

Because of the increase in lead time, each customer must again release one additional order to cover requirements. The vendor again receives eight orders, ships four, sees his backlog rise to twenty-one and still has more orders than he can deliver in the quoted lead time. Seeing how the incoming order rate has increased and, faced with the continuing overload in the backlog, the vendor tries to "get ahead of it" by jumping his lead time to eight weeks.

Just to cover real requirements of one order per week over the longer lead time, each customer must now issue four orders, three to cover the increased lead time and one for the regular week's business. The vendor's incoming order rate jumps to sixteen, he ships his usual four and his backlog is now at thirty-three orders, still one excess! (Whether he knows it or not the vendor will never catch up to this one extra order simply by increasing his lead times since the customers respond with additional orders).

Following the same logic the vendor goes through successive lead time increases to sixteen, twenty and twenty-five weeks by Week 9. His order backlog now has increased to eighty-one orders and he has seen a remarkable increase in incoming new orders. He is now confident he can justify investing in additional capacity so he plans to add twenty-five percent in Week 10 and raise his output to five orders per week.

Believing the "good business" he's enjoying will continue to bring in a heavy flow of new orders, he decides to hold twenty-five weeks lead time in Week 10, although his capacity now is adequate to clean up his backlog of one hundred orders in twenty weeks. The excess backlog has finally disappeared! Since the vendor has not increased his lead time, each customer needs to place only one order, a normal week's requirement, so the vendor receives only four orders. He ships five and his backlog drops (for the first time) to ninety-nine orders. Thinking that this one week drop-off in orders is purely a temporary situation, the vendor holds his twenty-five week quoted lead time in Week 11.

Each customer again places only one order, he ships five and his backlog drops to ninety-eight. Becoming somewhat concerned that he is "losing his share of the market", the vendor decides to "offer his customers better service" and drops his lead time to twenty weeks in Week 12.

Each customer now recognizes that he has orders placed with the vendor too far out into the future and cancels orders for the excess. With his shipments for Week 13, the vendor sees his backlog slump to seventy-seven total orders, panics and cuts his lead time to fifteen weeks. Again the cut in lead time shuts off new orders and cancels more; with his shipments his order backlog is reduced by another twenty-one orders to a total of fifty-six. In Week 14, the vendor reduces his quoted lead time to eleven weeks.

It takes only three weeks more for the vendor's backlog to be reduced close to the original total, permitting him to quote in Week 16 an "honest" three-week lead time. By now the new order rate over the last few weeks indicates that a "depression" has hit his business. The obvious action indicated is to reduce capacity dramatically so the vendor now cuts capacity to three orders per week. In a very few weeks, this will start the cycle all over again.

This game shows clearly the fallacy of assuming that a gap between planned and actual lead times can be closed by changing the planned numbers. What is not so evident is that this approach, so commonly used in industry throughout the world, leads inevitably to the vicious cycle illustrated in Figure 16. When delivery dates are missed, orders are not received on time and it is too easy to assume that the basic problem

---

## FIGURE 16

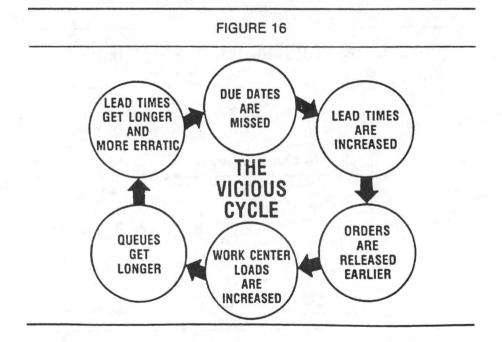

LEAD TIMES GET LONGER AND MORE ERRATIC

DUE DATES ARE MISSED

LEAD TIMES ARE INCREASED

THE VICIOUS CYCLE

QUEUES GET LONGER

WORK CENTER LOADS ARE INCREASED

ORDERS ARE RELEASED EARLIER

---

is that lead times are too short and must be lengthened. Increasing the lead times, of course, only generates more orders to go into the plant to increase the queues, lengthen the lead times and make them more erratic. The true result is aggravating the basic disease.

We must learn to recognize the truth about lead time—it will be what you say it is, occasionally plus a little more. When actual lead times do exceed the planned figures because of an increase in input or because of a lack of capacity caused by machine breakdowns, interrupted production or any other reason, it must be recognized that this difference between planned and actual can be removed only by changing the capacity. Lead time management is capacity management not simply priority planning and control.

It is time that practitioners recognized that lead times have several roles in controlling manufacturing. Most people know that lead time is a vital parameter in ordering techniques like MRP and order point. Many see clearly that it determines the level of work-in-process and the resultant capital investment. This is shown clearly in Figure 17. With shorter lead times, materials are held in process for less time and the investment is lowered proportionately.

Figure 17, however, illustrates clearly another role of lead time, not well understood. The primary strategy of manufacturing control is,

---

FIGURE 17

---

# WORK IN PROCESS vs. LEAD TIME

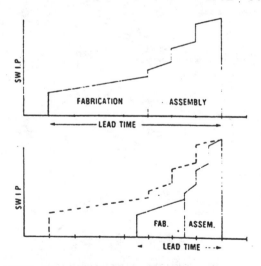

"Never commit materials or capacity to a specific item until the last possible moment". Stated simply, "Keep it moving!" This is possible, of course, only if lead times are short and work doesn't wait long periods in queues.

Another important role of lead time, also not clear to most people in manufacturing or to those who view its activities, is its influence on the validity of the whole manufacturing plan. One of the most ridiculous statements ever made in our field was that a company could live with infinite queues if they had a sound priority planning and control system. We're not just referring to the choice of the word "infinite" either. As is clearly shown in Figure 18, the longer the lead times (based upon longer queues) the earlier materials will have to be committed and capacity assigned to individual items. As queues grow and lead times lengthen, this commitment will have to be made far in advance to satisfy some quantity in a future master schedule time period. How can a priority plan be valid when based on long lead times? The only thing known for certain is that changes will be made many times before the actual completion date arrives and material and capacity will have been assigned to more wrong items. A company can live with changing demands on its facilities and with the upsets that it will inevitably experience only if lead times are short. Only then will a priority plan have any validity. Control of lead times requires planning and controlling capacity, not simply planning and controlling priorities.

FIGURE 18

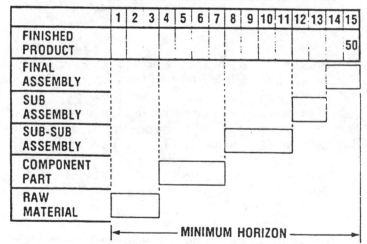

MASTER PRODUCTION SCHEDULE

The need for education in these concepts is enormous. Not only do we have to get understanding among practitioners in material control and manufacturing line people, we must also convince marketing and purchasing people that long lead times are not better but, in fact, are much worse if their objectives are to be met. We must also convince top management that lead time is one of their primary "handles" on the whole operation and that extending lead times or tolerating long lead times is sure to develop inefficiency, upset and extra cost. Add to this the need for educating editors of technical journals and newspapers, economists, college professors and government analysts so that these people understand fully the effects of the lead time syndrome on the basic statistics relating to manufacturing. The two most common sets of data used to analyze the health of a business or of our overall economy are Incoming Order Rates and Order Backlogs or Bookings Totals. Both figures, as shown by our lead time syndrome game, are distorted immensely by changes in lead times introduced by "amateurs" who do not understand their full influence. The benefits in manufacturing and improved control from a clear understanding of lead time and sound management of this important variable are literally enormous.

---

**About the Authors—**

*HAL MATHER* is currently President, Mather & Plossl, Inc., Management Counselors and Educators in the area of Manufacturing Control. Prior to this he was Materials Manager at Gilbarco, Inc., manufacturers of gasoline pumps and related service station equipment. His formal education was in mechanical engineering, and he has held positions of Project Engineer, Quality Control Manager, Production and Inventory Control Manager and Administrator of Manufacturing Systems.

Hal is a frequent speaker at professional society meetings, seminars and universities. He is co-author of a booklet, "The Master Production Schedule", as well as the author of several articles in the field of manufacturing control.

He has been certified at the Fellow level by the American Production and Inventory Control Society and is a member of that Society's National Advisory Planning Council.

MR. PLOSSL is Chairman of the Board of Mather & Plossl, Inc., a Management Education and Counseling firm with clients throughout the United States and in Europe and Africa. Formerly he was Plant Manager of the Stanley Strapping Systems Division of the Stanley Works with plants in New Britain, Connecticut, and Pittsburg, California. Prior to that he held the position of Materials Manager of its Stanley Tools Division.

He received AB, BS and MS Degrees in Mechanical Engineering from Columbia University. He is a Registered Professional Engineer in Massachusetts. Mr. Plossl has taught production control and industrial management college courses and is a frequent speaker at meetings of APICS, other technical societies and leading universities.

He has written many articles on production and inventory management. With O. W. Wight, he is co-author of "PRODUCTION AND IN-VENTORY CONTROL: Principles and Techniques", Prentice-Hall, 1967. He is author of "MANUFACTURING CONTROL: The Last Frontier for Profits", Reston Publishing Company, 1973. He was Chapter Editor of the APICS Production and Inventory Control Handbook and editor of the 3rd edition of the APICS Bibliography. His latest book, co-authored with H. F. Mather, is "THE MASTER PRODUCTION SCHEDULE; Managements' Handle on the Business", 1975.

Listed in Who's Who in the Southeast, Mr. Plossl has been active in professional organizations, holding offices and directorships in APICS, AIIE and other technical societies. He has been certified at the Fellow level with the American Production and Inventory Control Society. He was Chairman of APICS Curriculum and Certification Program Council and a member of the National Advisory Planning Council.

Reprinted from *Production and Inventory Management*, Fourth Quarter, 1972.

## STRUCTURING THE BILL OF MATERIAL FOR MRP

Joseph A. Orlicky
George W. Plossl
Oliver W. Wight

### INTRODUCTION

An important distinction between Order Point systems and Material Requirements Planning systems lies in the fact that the order point/order quantity approach is *part based* whereas MRP is *product-oriented*. Order Point views each inventory item independently of all the others, whereas MRP looks at the product and the relationships of its components, using bills of material as the basis for planning.

MRP puts the bill of material to a whole new use. Under MRP, the bill acquires a new function, in addition to serving as part of the product specs. It becomes a framework on which the whole planning system hangs.

Often, however, the bill of material furnished by the engineering department is not necessarily *usable* for material requirements planning. As a key input to an MRP system, the bill of material must be accurate and up to date if MRP outputs are to be valid. But in addition it must be unambiguous and so structured as to *lend* itself to MRP. The mere existence of a bill of material is no guarantee that MRP will actually work.

To understand the reason for this, we must remember that the bill of material is basically an engineering document. Historically, the function of the bill of material has been to define the product from the design point of view and from the design point of view only. But now, because we want to use the bill of material for purposes of material planning, we must re-define the product from the manufacturing and planning point of view. Proper product definition is crucial to a planning system such as MRP, which directly depends on it—*unlike* an order point system.

People usually think of bills of material, and of MRP as being applicable only in hard goods manufacturing. But businesses that *mix* component materials, *sew* them together, *package* them, etc., can also use material requirements planning to advantage. Companies in the garment industry, pharmaceutical houses, batch chemical manufacturers, and others, all have bills of material except they call them by different names—material lists, formulations, specifications, etc.

With MRP, the prime input to the whole system is the master production schedule. The product must be defined in such a way as to make it possible to put a valid master schedule together in terms of bill of material numbers; i.e., assembly numbers. If the overall plan of production—and that is what the master schedule is—cannot be stated in terms of bills of material, it is not possible to do material requirements planning successfully.

The master schedule and the structure of the bill of material must be thought of together, when an MRP system is being developed. The bills of material and the master schedule must *fit together* like lock and key. If these are not compatible, nothing turns. Neither is there any guarantee that an MRP system can function properly just because the bill may already have been organized and loaded onto a computer file under a *Bill of Material Processor* program. This type of software will load practically anything onto a disc file, including straight engineering parts lists—which are not much good for purposes of material requirements planning. The functions of a bill processor are merely to organize, maintain, and retrieve bill of material data. A Bill of Material Processor is not designed to *structure* the bill. It assumes that the bill is already properly structured to serve the user's needs.

The intent of the discussion that follows is to clarify the subject of bill of material *structuring*, so that it will not be confused with bill of material *file organization* under a bill processor.

In most instances, companies planning to implement MRP will be wise to review their bills of material, to determine whether certain changes in the structure of this file data may have to be made, and of what kind. In reviewing the bill for this purpose, the following seven-point checklist will help in spotting its structural deficiencies:

1. *The bill should lend itself to the forecasting of optional product features.* This capability is essential for purposes of material requirements planning.

2. *The bill should permit the master schedule to be stated in the fewest possible number of end items.* These end items will be products or major assemblies, as the case may be, but in either case they must be stated in terms of bill of material numbers.
3. *The bill should lend itself to the planning of subassembly priorities.* Orders for subassemblies have to be released at the right time, and with valid due dates.
4. *The bill should permit easy order entry.* It should be possible to take a customer order that describes the product either in terms of a model number, or as a configuration of optional features, and translate it into the language that the MRP system understands: bill of material numbers.
5. *The bill should be usable for purposes of final assembly scheduling.* Apart from MRP, the final assembly scheduling system needs to know, specifically, which assemblies (assembly numbers) are required to build individual units of the end product.
6. *The bill should provide the basis for product costing.*
7. *The bill should lend itself to efficient computer file storage and file maintenance.*

When, in a given case, these yardsticks are applied to the existing bill of material, it will usually be found that some, but not all, of the above requirements can be satisfied. If that is the case, changes in bill of material structure are called for. This can and should be done. While the bill still must serve its primary purpose of providing product specifications, it should not be regarded as a sacrosanct document that must not be tampered with. The bill may have to be modified, or *restructured*, as required for purposes of material requirements planning. This can be done without affecting the integrity of the specs.

The severity of the bill of material structure problem varies from company to company, depending on the complexity of product and nature of the business. The term "bill of material structuring" covers a variety of *types* of changes to the bill, and several different techniques for effecting these changes.

The topics that make up the subject of bill of material structuring, as reviewed in this article, can be categorized as follows:

1. *Assignment of identities*
   (a) Elimination of ambiguity
   (b) Levels of manufacture
2. *Modular bill of material*
   (a) Disentangling product option combinations
   (b) Segregating common from unique parts.
3. *Pseudo-bills of material*

### IDENTIFICATION OF MATERIALS AND THEIR RELATIONSHIPS

There are several principles involved here. First, the requirement that each individual item of inventory covered by the MRP system be uniquely identified. This includes raw materials and subassemblies.

The assignment of subassembly identities tends to be somewhat arbitrary. Between the design engineer, the industrial engineer, the cost accountant and the inventory planner, each might prefer to assign them differently. The question is: When do unique subassembly numbers have to be assigned? In reality, it is not the design of the product but the way it is being manufactured; i.e., assembled, that dictates the assignment of subassembly identities.

The unit of work, or task, is the key here. If a number of components are assembled at a bench and then are forwarded as a completed task, to storage or to another bench for further assembly, a subassembly number is required so that orders for these subassemblies can be generated and their priorities planned. An MRP system will do this, but only for items with individual identities.

Some engineering departments are stingy in assigning new part numbers, and we often see the classic example of this in a raw casting that has the same part number as the finished casting. This may suit the engineer, but it is difficult to see how an automated inventory system such as MRP is supposed to distinguish between the two types of items that must be planned and controlled separately.

The second requirement is that an identifying number define the *contents* of the item uniquely, unambiguously. Thus the same subassembly number must not be used to define two or more different sets of components. This sometimes happens when the original design of a product subsequently becomes subject to variation. Instead of creating a new bill with its own unique identity, the old one is specified with instructons to substitute, remove, and add certain components. This shortcut method, called "add and delete," represents a vulnerable procedure, undesirable for MRP. We will come back to it in a later example.

The third requirement is that the bill of material should reflect the way material flows in and out of stock. "Stock" here does not necessarily mean "stockroom" but rather a *state of completion*. Thus when a piece part is finished or a subassembly is completed, it is considered to be "on hand"; i.e., in stock, until withdrawn and associated with an order for a higher level item as its component. An MRP system is constructed in such a way that it assumes that each inventory item flows into and out of stock at its respective level in the product structure. MRP also assumes that the bill of material accurately reflects this flow.

Thus the bill of material is expected to specify not only the *composition* of a product but also the *process stages* in that product's manufacture. The bill must define the product structure, in terms of so-called *levels of manufacture*, each of which represents the completion of a step in the buildup of the product.

A schematic representation of product structure is shown in Figure 1. The structure defines the relationship among the various items that make up the product in terms of levels, as well as the parent item/component item relationships. These things are vital for material requirements planning because they establish, in conjunction with lead times, the precise *timing* of requirements, order releases, and order priorities.

The product represented by Figure 1 has four levels of manufacture. The end product is designated, by convention, as being at level zero, its immediate components as being at level one, etc. The parent/component relationships depicted in the example indicate that "A" is the parent of component "C" (also of "B" and "1"). Item "C," in turn, is the parent of component "3," etc. Thus "A" is the only item that is not also a component.

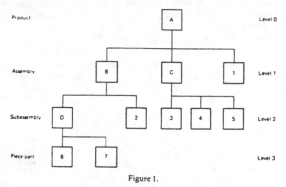

Figure 1.

Items "B," "C" and "D" are both parents (of their components at the next lower level) and components (of their parent items at the next higher level). Items "1" through "7" are components but never parents.

This would be true if all of the piece parts were purchased. If item "6," however, is manufactured from raw material "X," then it becomes a parent in relationship to this component material. Thus the distinction between parent item and component item appears not only in assembly but also in the conversion of material for a single part from one stage of manufacture to another.

This also applies to semi-finished items that are stocked (in the sense described earlier) and that are to be controlled by the MRP system. The raw material, the semi-finished item, and the finished item must be uniquely identified; i.e., must have different part numbers.

People are sometimes reluctant to assign different identities to semi-finished and finished items, where the conversion to the finished stage is of minor nature. A good example is a die casting that is machined and then painted one of four different colors, as shown in Figure 2. The four varieties of painted casting will have to be assigned separate identities if they are to be ordered, and their order priorities planned, by the MRP system.

This is an example of a situation where item identity (of the painted casting) would normally not exist, but would have to be established pre-requisite to MRP, because otherwise such items would fall outside the scope of the system and loss of control would result.

Another example of an item identity problem that is almost the opposite is the transient subassembly, sometimes called a "blow-through" or "phantom." Assemblies of this type never see a stockroom, because they are immediately consumed in the assembly of their parent items. An example of this is a subassembly built on a feeder line that flows directly into the main assembly line. Here the subassembly normally carries a separate identity.

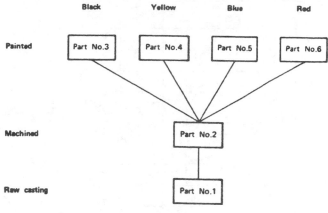

Figure 2.

Because it is recognized in the bill of material, the MRP system would treat it the same as any other subassembly.

This may be undesirable, because if this kind of item is to be planned under an MRP system, we must remember that the logic of MRP assumes that each component item goes in and out of stock. That is the way the basic time-phased record is designed and updated. So the question arises as to how to handle such subassemblies within an MRP system. MRP users have worked out techniques to deal with this situation. People often wonder whether this type of assembly should be identified in the bill at all. The phantom does not require separate identity in the bill of material, provided there is never

1. An over-run
2. A service part demand
3. A customer return.

Otherwise, it must be separately identified in the bill and item records (stock status) must be maintained. This is so because over-runs, service demand, and returns create a need to stock material, and to control it. But then the MRP user would have to report all transactions for the phantom sub-assemblies, so that the system can post these and keep the records up to date. This seems like unnecessary effort and paperwork in the case of order releases and order completions.

Fortunately, there is no need to do this. A technique called the "phantom bill" eliminates the need for posting such transactions for these items. (This technique is used, for instance, by the Black & Decker Manufacturing Company, a skilled MRP user.) Using this technique, it is possible to have your cake and eat it. While transactions of the type mentioned do not have to be reported and posted, the MRP system will pick up and use any phantom items that may happen to be on hand. Service part requirements can also be entered into the record and will be correctly handled by the system. But otherwise MRP will, in effect, bypass the phantom item's record and go from its parent item to its components directly.

To describe the application of this technique, let's assume that assembly "A" has a transient subassembly "B" as one of its components, and part "C" is a component of "B." Thus, for purposes of illustration, item "B," the phantom, is envisioned as being sandwiched between "A," its parent, and "C," its component.

To implement this technique, the phantom item is treated as follows:
1. Lead time is specified as zero
2. Lot sizing is discrete (lot for lot)
3. The bill of material (or the item record) is coded, so that the system can recognize that it is a phantom and apply special treatment.

The special treatment referred to above means departing from regular procedure, or record update logic, when processing the phantom record. The difference between the procedures can best be described through examples.

In Figure 3, inventory status data for items "A" (top), "B" (middle), and

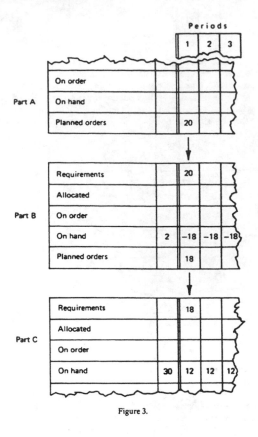

Figure 3.

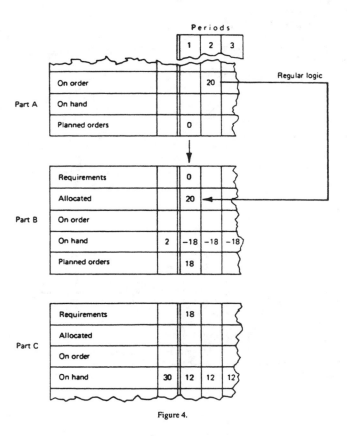

Figure 4.

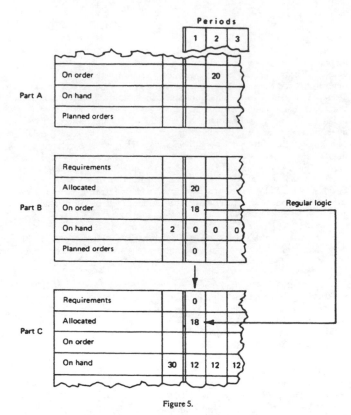

Figure 5.

"C" (bottom) are shown. Note that the zero lead time offset on the item in the middle places the planned order release for 18 pieces in the same period as the net requirement. This, in turn, corresponds to the requirement for 18 "C"s in the same period.

Following the release of the planned order for "A," the update procedure for item record "B" will vary, depending on whether it is coded as a phantom. In the absence of such a code, regular logic applies. The regularly updated records of "A" and "B" are shown in Figure 4. Record "C" continues unchanged. Following the release of the planned order for "B," item record "C" is updated, as shown in Figure 5.

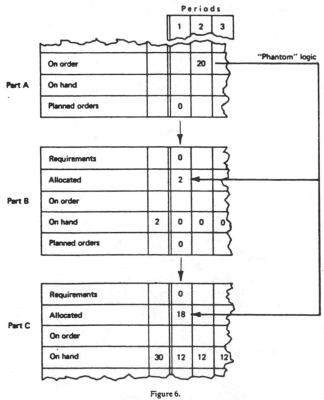

Figure 6.

Had item "B" been coded as a phantom, all three records would have been updated in one step, as shown in Figure 6, as a result of the planned order release of item "A." Note that the release of planned order "A," which normally would reduce only the corresponding requirement "B" (as in Figure 4), in this case reduces also the requirement for "C," *as though "C" were a direct component of "A."*

Note also that the two pieces of "B" in stock (perhaps a return from a previous over-run) are applied to the requirement for "A," and that the allocation has been *distributed* between "B" and "C." Upon closer examination of these examples it will be seen that the phantom logic is nothing more than a different treatment of *allocation.* (Zero lead time and discrete lot sizing are assumed. These can, however, be specified for non-phantom sub-assemblies also.) Once this step is carried out, regular logic applies, causing the records to be updated and their data aligned, in the correct manner.

The phantom bill technique, as described above, applies to MRP systems of the Net Change type. In conventional regenerative MRP systems the question of posting or not posting transactions to the phantom record is not crucial, because a planned order release does not update component requirements data. Hence, the problem of rebalancing or realigning the planned order and requirements data of the three records does not arise. Following the planned order release of the phantom's parent, the next regeneration will wash out both the requirement and the planned order release for the phantom item.

The objective of not having to post phantom transactions still remains, however, and it can be achieved by, again, setting lead time to zero, specifying discrete lot sizing, and coding the phantom item so that notices for planned order releases are either suppressed or flagged to be disregarded. The MRP system will function correctly.

The problem then becomes one of component requisitioning (for the phantom parent order) and it must be solved by modifying the requisition generating procedure. When some phantom items are on hand, *two* requisitions will have to be generated:
1. One for the quantity of the phantom on hand
2. One for the balance of the order; for the phantom's components.
In the Figure 6 example, these quantities are 2 and 18, respectively.

## MODULAR BILLS OF MATERIAL

The term "bill of material structuring" is most commonly used in reference to modularizing the bill of material file. The process of modularizing consists of *breaking down* the bills of high-level items (products, end items) and *reorganizing* them into product modules. There are two, somewhat different, objectives in modularizing the bill:
1. To disentangle combinations of optional product features
2. To segregate common from unique, or peculiar, parts.
The first is required to facilitate forecasting, or, in some cases, to make it possible at all under the MRP approach. The second has as its goal to minimize inventory investment in components common to optional units which must be forecast and thus make it necessary to carry safety stock. We will deal separately with each of these two objectives, and the techniques used to achieve them.

The question probably most frequently asked by people interested in MRP is what to do with the bill of material to handle product variations. Under

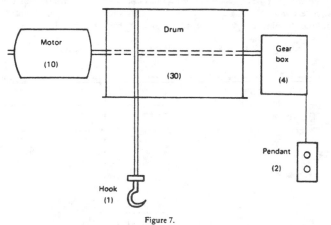

Figure 7.

MRP, these product variations, or optional features, must be forecast at the master schedule level, that is to say, we must be able to forecast end items rather than their individual components, as we do under Order Point. If a product has many optional features, their combinations can be astronomical and forecasting them becomes impossible. Furthermore, if separate bills of material were to be set up for each of the unique end products that it is possible to build, the file would be enormous—too costly to store and maintain. Not only that. A valid master schedule could not even be put together, using such bills, for the MRP system to explode.

The solution to this problem is the modular bill of material. Instead of maintaining bills for individual end products, under this approach the bill of material is restated in terms of the building blocks, or modules, from which the final product is put together. The problem, and its solution, can best be demonstrated on an example. Figure 7 represents a familiar product, a hoist that is used to handle material in a factory.

The hoist manufacturer offers his customers a number of options, in this case 10 motors, 30 drums, 4 gear boxes, and 2 pendants (the hook assembly is standard), from which a customer configures the specific hoist he wants. Figure 8 shows the schematic product structure of this family of hoists. By assembling the optional features in various combinations, it is possible to build 2,400 models; i.e., 2,400 unique configurations.

Assuming we manufacture this product and wish to implement MRP, the question is what to do with the bill of material. We can see clearly how to write a bill of material for each of the 2,400 models, but we certainly would

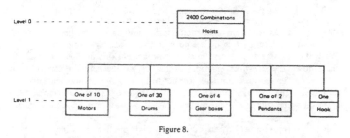

Figure 8.

not want to carry all those bills. Consider this: There is only one variety of hook on this product, but the engineers are probably working on that. If they introduce just one more option—a choice between two hooks, the number of possible configurations will *double* from 2,400 to 4,800—and another 2,400 bills would have to be added to the file.

That is one reason we do not want to set up bills for the end products themselves. But aside from this consideration, with all those bills we would not know how to develop a master schedule showing a quantity of each model needed in specific time periods.

Suppose we produce 100 hoists per month. Which 100 out of 2,400 should we select as a forecast for a particular month? This is clearly an impossible situation. Note that *volume* is part of the problem here. A product family with 100 models is a problem if volume is 20 per month. If volume were 10,000 per month, the forecasting problem would not be nearly as serious.

The solution here is to forecast each of the highest-level *components* (i.e., major assembly units) separately, and not to try to forecast the end products at all. That way, we would forecast each of the ten different motor variations, the thirty drum sizes, the four types of gear box, and the two types of pendant.

Specifically, since we only have one hook assembly and want to make 100 hoists during a month, we will need 100 hooks. This quantity would appear in the master schedule, and a bill of material for this "module" would be required to match the schedule. But we have two types of pendant. From previous sales of this product we know that, let us say, 75 percent of the orders call for type "A" and 25 percent for type "B." Applying these percentages to the pendant option, we could schedule seventy-five "As" and twenty-five "Bs." But here we would probably want some safety stock, because the batch of 100 customer orders in any one month is unlikely to break down exactly 75 and 25 percent.

The proper way to handle safety stock under material requirements planning is to plan it at the master schedule level. Thus, instead of scheduling 75 and 25 percent of the pendants we would deliberately overplan and put, let us say, 90 and 30 into the master schedule. (This would not be done in every period; the unused safety stock is rolled forward.) The same approach would be followed for the motor option, the drum option, and the gear box option.

Each of the options, or *modules*, would have to have a bill of material, for use by the MRP system. Under this approach, the total number of bills of material—and the things to forecast—would be as follows:

| | | | |
|---|---|---|---|
| Motors | 10 | Pendants | 2 |
| Drums | 30 | Hook | 1 |
| Gear Boxes | 4 | Total | 47 |

This total of 47 compares with 2,400 if each product model had a bill of its own. If the engineers add a second variety of hook, this would only add one more bill to the 47, instead of doubling the file.

At this point, the reader may be wondering how this type of problem is being handled in a real-life situation, if the manufacturer *does not* have the bills set up in modular form. Chances are that there would be several bills, for *some* of the 2,400 configurations, and they would be used for everything by adding and subtracting optional components. Quite a few companies use this "add-and-delete" technique as a solution to the problem we have discussed.

This technique solves some but not all of the problems. Its main disadvantages are vulnerability to human error, slowing down Order Entry, but mainly, failure to establish the proper historical data for option forecasting purposes. Under this approach, the company would most likely use order points and safety stock on the "add-and-delete" components. That would be highly undesirable because it would deprive the user of some important benefits of an MRP system.

But suppose we *have* a certain number of bills for end products, and we want to restructure them in a modular fashion, so we can get away from adding and deleting. How do we go about such restructuring, specifically? We will demonstrate this on the next example. For this purpose, we have to scale down the previous example somewhat, so the solution can be seen clearly. Let us assume that the product has only *two* optional features, the motor and the drum, each with only two choices. The customer can then select between motor #1 and motor #2, and between drum "A" and drum "B."

Figure 9 represents the four bills of material: the first combines motor #1 with drum "A," the second one, motor #1 with drum "B," etc. In the product structure, the end product (model) numbers, 12-4010 etc., are considered to be on level zero. The level-one components, A13, C41, etc., may represent assemblies, but their components are not shown on the chart, so as not to make it too busy.

To restructure these bills into modules, we break them down, analyze and compare the use of level-1 items, and group them by use. For example, we see

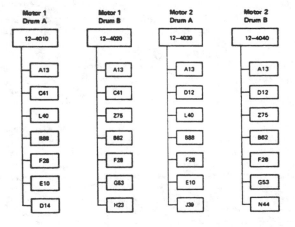

Figure 9.

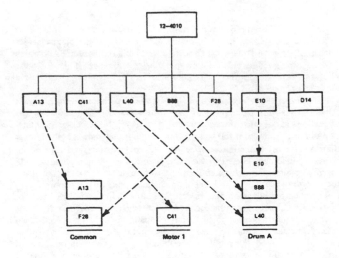

Figure 10.

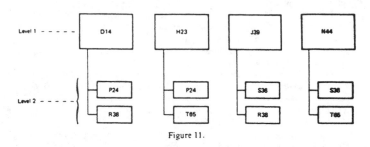

Figure 11.

that the first component in the first bill, A13, is common to all products, and assign it to the *Common* group. The next item, C41, is found in #1-A and #1-B combinations but not in #2-A and #2-B, which indicates that it is *unique to motor option #1*. The item that follows, L40, is *used only with drum option "A."* The remaining component items are similarly examined and assigned to groups. The result is shown in Figure 10.

Note, in Figure 10, that the last level-1 component item, D14, does not fit into any of the groupings. When all of the bills are broken down this way and their level-1 components are grouped by option, items D14, H23, J39, and N44 in our example remain unassigned, because each of them is used only with one or the other of the option *combinations*. Here we must carry the process one step further; i.e., break down these items, as shown in Figure 11, and assign *their* (level-2) components to the groupings by option. The final result is represented by Figure 12, where all of the items involved in our example are grouped into the respective modules.

In our case, we solved the entire problem through the technique of breakdown and group assignment. But if items D14, H23, etc. had not been subassemblies but piece parts, we would not have been able to break them down. In a case like that, the part that is used only with a certain combination of options should, if possible, be redesigned, particularly if it is an expensive item.

Low-cost items of this type need not be re-engineered, because we can

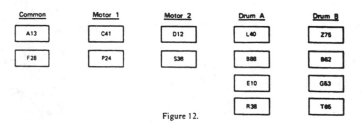

Figure 12.

afford to overplan them and carry some excess inventory. In the modularizing process, such parts can simply be assigned to more than one grouping. For example, item D14 (Figure 9) could be duplicated in both #1 and "A" modules (Figure 12), ensuring that it would never be planned short. Another solution, of course, is to forecast (and over-forecast) the option combinations for purposes of ordering this type of component.

Let us recap what we have done with the example under discussion, up to this point. We have *abolished* the end product numbers and we have done away with their bills of material as unnecessary for purposes of MRP. Where the final product formerly served as the end item in the bill of material, we have now *promoted* level-1 items (and in one case, level-2 items) to end item status.

This procedure established a new, modular *planning bill*, suitable for forecasting, master scheduling, and material requirements planning. The job of restructuring is not finished, however. The former level-1 items, D14, H23, etc., that are excluded from the planning bill cannot simply be abolished. These items will eventually have to be assembled, and the production control system has to be able to place orders for these items, schedule them, and requisition their components. These bills must therefore be retained for the purposes just mentioned.

This represents another technique of bill of material structuring: the establishment of *manufacturing bills*, or *M-bills*, which together constitute the M-bill file. These bills are coded to distinguish them from planning bills, so that the MRP system will, in effect, bypass them. M-bills are not involved in the process of component requirements planning. They are used for purposes of assembly only. M-items are built against the final assembly schedule, usually to customer order (or warehouse order), using the components planned through MRP.

The principle involved here is that in modularizing the bill of material at whatever level, *end product bills (level-0) can be abolished entirely but not any bills formerly on level-1 or lower*. These must be segregated in the M-bill file and retained for purposes of ordering, scheduling, costing, etc. Specifying options in Order Entry (or in scheduling a warehouse order) will call out and reconstruct the proper bills for individual end products, but not for lower level assemblies that have been removed from the planning bill file.

In the example we have been using, the total bill of material file would consist of:

1. *The planning bill file*
   comprising bills shown in Figure 12.
2. *The M-bill file*
   comprising bills for D14, H23, J39, and N44.

The *Production and Inventory Control Handbook** contains an example of bill of material restructuring that illustrates another technique. Namely, *reassigning* components from one bill to another. It is in chapter 17, and the reader is referred to the detailed discussion and illustrations contained there. The example used involves an engine, transmission, intake manifold, carburetor, and flywheel housing. This technique is really another version of modularizing. The difference is that the items being broken out, like the manifold, are *not* being promoted to level-1 status but are reassigned as components of another level-1 item, such as the carburetor.

This will get the right components planned but, because the manifold, for instance, does not *really* get assembled with the carburetor, certain new problems will be created. For example, stock requisitions or service parts orders for the carburetor should not call out manifolds, the cost build-up of the carburetor must not include the manifold, etc. Special procedures would have to be established within the system to handle this. Two bills would have to be maintained for the carburetor. One, a planning bill, with the manifold and another one, an M-bill, without it. But in this case, it would not otherwise be necessary to set up two carburetor bills if the illegitimate components were not assigned to it.

This technique of reassigning components is unnecessarily complicated and vulnerable. The straight modularization technique demonstrated on the previous example is cleaner and gets the job done in a simpler fashion. We mentioned earlier that one reason for modularizing is to disentangle option combinations, for purposes of forecasting and master scheduling. In our

*Production & Inventory Control Handbook. McGraw-Hill. 1970.

example of the hoist, this has been accomplished by establishing the modular planning bill shown in Figure 12. The other objective of modularization, segregating common from unique (optional) parts for purposes of inventory minimization, has not been fully met, however.

In modularizing the bills, we assigned level-1 items to groups, by option. But those items were *assemblies*, and they may contain common components. For example, a subassembly that is only used for motor #1 could have some common parts with another subassembly used for motor #2. Requirements for such common parts will be overstated, if they are included in the safety stock for *both* options. If we want to get at these common parts, we would have to tear the bills apart even further. In some cases it is desirable to do that, but if this technique is carried to its extreme, we might finally end up with a planning bill that has only piece parts in it and no subassemblies. The ultimate module of the product is really the piece part.

The question is this: When we do modularize, how far down the product structure should we go? What we are really doing when we modularize is determining the right level in the bill of material at which to forecast. Whether we should forecast the subassembly itself or just its components—and that is the question here—depends on *when* we need to assemble it.

We have two choices. Either we assemble it as a function of executing the master schedule, through MRP. This means assembling to stock, or *pre-assembling*, before the end product itself is scheduled to be built, which is probably after receipt of a customer order. Or we defer putting this subassembly together until such time when we build the end product. The making of the subassembly then becomes a function of executing the final assembly schedule. The decision between these two alternatives is pretty much dictated by the nature of the product in question, and by the nature of the business. Lead times and the economics of subassembly operations will determine, in each case, whether the item should be pre-assembled or whether it can wait until final product assembly.

Let us take the pendant on the hoist as an example. We can wait and assemble the pendant, and *its* subassemblies, when we built the final hoist to customer or warehouse order. But, on the other hand, we may want to have the pendants in stock when the order comes in, so as not to have to assemble them one at a time. If this is the case, we would have to leave the respective bills alone, even though some common parts will consequently be tied up in the pendant assemblies. The master schedule would then contain pendant bill numbers rather than their component numbers.

In trying to arrive at the answer to the question we are examining here it is helpful to distinguish between the

1. Master production schedule
2. Final assembly schedule

The master schedule represents a *procurement and fabrication schedule*. The final assembly schedule, created later in time, must stay within the constraints of component availability provided by the master schedule through the MRP system. (These schedules may coincide where the product either contains no options, or is small and simple, etc.) Different subassemblies are under the control of these two schedules, and in modularizing bills of material we are, in effect, assigning a given subassembly to either one of these schedules:

1. To the master schedule, by retaining it in the planning bill
2. To the final assembly schedule, by breaking down its bill (i.e., transforming it into an M-bill)

Thus the question of how far down the product structure one should go in modularizing tends to answer itself when the bill for a particular product is analyzed, and when we look at the nature of the various subassemblies in a particular business environment.

To conclude the discussion of modular bills of material, it may be proper to reflect on the objectives of modularization. Besides the specific objectives brought out earlier, there is a broader, more fundamental reason. And that is to maintain flexibility of production with a minimum investment in materials inventory. We want to offer a wide choice of products and to give maximum service to customers, and at the same time keep component inventories down. Modular bills of material are intended to help us do just that.

## PSEUDO-BILLS OF MATERIAL

There is one more problem that is related to the modular bill of material. When the bill is broken down in the process of modularizing, various assemblies are promoted and become end items; i.e., highest-level items with no parent. This tends to create a large number of end items. Because it is the end items that will have to be forecast, and because the master schedule has to be stated in terms of these end items, we could end up with hundreds (or thousands) of end items, too many to work with.

Fortunately, there is a simple solution to this. We certainly want the smallest possible number of things to forecast, and the smallest possible number of end items shown on the master schedule. To accomplish this, we can use the technique of creating "pseudo-bills of material." If we go back to Figure 12, where the newly created end items are grouped by option, there is nothing to stop us from taking any group of such items and creating a pseudo-bill to cover all of them. We have done so in Figure 13, where an artificial parent has been assigned to each group, and a new series of (pseudo) bills has been created.

These new bills, sometimes called *super-bills* or *S-bills*, are an example of *non-engineering part numbers* being introduced into a restructured bill of material. An S-number, such as S-101 in Figure 13, identifies an artificial bill of material for an imaginary item that, in reality, will never be built. The only purpose of the S-number is to facilitate planning. With the S-bills set up, when we forecast drum size, for instance, we forecast S-104 and S-105 only. These pseudo-bill numbers will also represent these options in the master schedule. The MRP system will explode the requirements automatically from

this point on, using the S-bills in the bill of material file.

A total of 47 S-bills (one for each option plus one for common items including the hook) would cover the original (non-simplified) example of the hoist represented in Figures 7 and 8. The 47 compares with 2,400 end product bills, or with several hundred end item (level-1) bills.

In this article, the terms "S-bills," "S-number," and others, are being used for lack of standard terms. The terminology in this whole area is unfortunately entirely non-standard, as the subject has been almost totally neglected in literature. One of very few exceptions is the article by Dave Garwood* in which he described the results of restructuring the bills of material at Fisher Controls Co. In his article, the term "partial parts list" (PPL) corresponds to the S-bill, and the term "Item" to an option or option grouping.

Another pseudo-bill term in current use is the "Kit number" or "K-number." This technique is used by some companies that have a lot of small loose parts on level one in the product structure, as in the example in Figure 14. These are often the fasteners, nuts, and bolts, used to assemble the major assemblies together. If you do not want to deal with all these parts in-

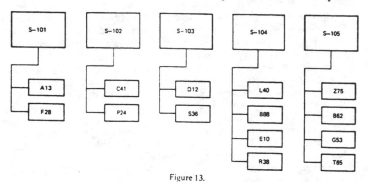

Figure 13.

Figure 14.

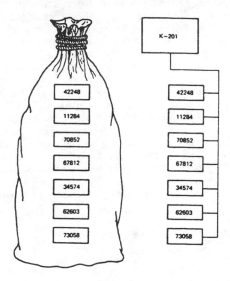

Figure 15.

dividually—and you certainly do not under an MRP system—you can put them into an imaginary bag, as depicted in Figure 15. You can then assign a part number to this bag of parts and treat it, in effect, as an assembly. This means setting up a bill of material for such a kit number (also shown in Figure 15).

The principle is the same as in the case of the S-bill—assigning a single new identity code to individually coded items that constitute a logical grouping, and employing the format of a bill of material to relate the items together for system purposes. The K-bill is another non-engineering part number created in the process of structuring the bill of material. These artificial identity codes have little to do with the design of the product and are not part of the product specs, but are created for more convenient planning, forecasting, and master scheduling.

These newly created bills, along with the M-bills we discussed earlier are sometimes collectively called the *superstructure*. The superstructure, once established, must then be maintained along with the rest of the bill of material file. This is a new job, which means that the cost of file maintenance will normally go up.

* "Stop: Before You Use the Bill Processor," by D. Garwood, *Production & Inventory Management*, Second Quarter 1970.

## CONCLUSION

In the previous sections of this article we have reviewed modularization, which does away with end product bills and creates separate planning bills and manufacturing bills. We have seen how artificial bills are created in the process of restructuring, and for what purpose. We have also touched on the relationship of item identities to material requirements planning, and on the treatment of "phantom" assemblies. All of this goes to show that by making these kinds of changes, we can put the bill to new uses.

There are still other uses that can be assigned to the bill of material. An interesting example of modifying and using the bill of material in a new way is to expand the traditional concept of the bill to include other materials which may not actually be part of the product, but which are consumed in its making. For example, a ball bearing manufacturer has added special grinding wheels to bills of material for ball bearings. In effect, they are saying that a "part" made of a portion of the grinding wheel goes into each bearing assembly. The "quantity per" is the fraction of wheel life to make one bearing. Adding this item to bills of material makes it possible for this company to project requirements for expensive grinding wheels and thus minimize investment in this inventory, as well as to reduce the possibility of a shortage of grinding wheels.

An electrical machinery manufacturer has added electrical specification numbers for power transformers to bills of material. The assembly orders generated from these bills then show not only the parts that go into the assembly but also the proper specifications for final inspection and test.

In conclusion, we want to indicate who does and who does not need to restructure the bill of material, as a pre-condition to successful MRP system operation. Where the product line consists of a fnite, limited number of items (models), modularizing the bill, or any other changes for the sake of bill of material structure may be unnecessary. For example, a company making power tools—a highly successful user of MRP—did not have to restructure bills of material. In their business the bill simply is no problem, because they manufacture only so many varieties of power drill, power saw, etc., in large quantities. Furthermore, the product is relatively simple and small, in terms of the number of different components used per unit of end product. With a product line like that, it is feasible to maintain complete bills for each product model, and forecast and plan by model.

On the other hand, bill of material restructuring is called for where the product line consists of a virtually infinite number of end products, due to complexity of design and wide choice of optional features. Modular bills of material make material requirements planning possible for such diverse products as highway truck trailers, mining machinery, gasoline station pumps, cranes, elevators, office machinery, farm machinery, computers, machine tools, instruments, industrial tractors, and a multitude of others, who have the common problem of an almost endless product variety that makes it otherwise impossible to develop valid master schedules.

The study of how bills of material should be constructed is therefore a vital part of the work of designing and implementing an MRP system. Structuring the bill of material requires some real cooperation from the engineering department, and sometimes this can be a problem. After the bill is restructured, it can no longer "belong" to the engineers exclusively, and that can sometimes be a problem also.

The bill of material can and should be more than just part of product specs. It should also be viewed and used as a *tool for planning*. The resistance by some engineering departments to change in bill of material format, structure, maintenance, etc., cannot really be justified. After all, the engineers create the bill so that, by definition, somebody other than the designer can make the product. The bill of material is, therefore, really made for others, in the first place. And it would seem to follow that it should be structured for the *user's*, not the designer's, convenience.

An ex-engineer friend of ours put it this way: "When I worked as an engineer, I saw the creation of the bill of material as the *last step in the process of design*. But when I later moved into production and inventory control, I began to see it as a *first step in the process of planning*."

Reprinted from *Production and Inventory Management*, Third Quarter, 1973.

## CAPACITY PLANNING AND CONTROL*

George W. Plossl and Oliver W. Wight

### George W. Plossl

When we were invited in 1971 to address the APICS International Conference in St. Louis, Oliver Wight and I selected as our topic, capacity planning and control, with the focus on machine loading. We recognized the need to prepare ourselves more fully to handle this interesting aspect of production control. While it has been around a long time, machine loading has not been well understood and is rarely, if ever, well done. During the year, we visited many companies and talked with many people who had experience using this technique. This research culminated in a two-day conference in September at Lake Sunapee to which we invited a small group to review our conclusions.

We regret that this work was not completed in time to have our presentation included in the Conference Proceedings, but we believed it more important to verify our conclusions and present the latest thinking on the subject rather than to meet a publishing deadline. We wish to thank the people who gave so freely of their time and experience to help us assimilate their knowledge gained from actually using scheduling and loading techniques. While emphasizing that we assume full responsibility for the conclusions presented, we want particularly to express our appreciation to the following men: James Burlingame, Twin Disc Incorporated; Dr. Joseph A. Orlicky, IBM Corporation; Thomas Putnam, Markem Corporation; Alex Willis, IBM Corporation; and, of course, our associates, Walt Goddard and Ernie Theisen.

There is a great deal of confusion in the meaning of the terms "Capacity" and "Load." While both are simple in concept, successful application appears to be extremely difficult in the real world; part of the problem is confusion in meaning. Figure 1 uses a bathtub to illustrate the difference. The

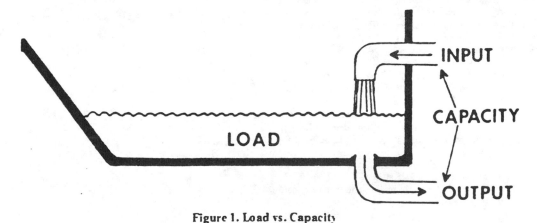

Figure 1. Load vs. Capacity

*This article was presented at the APICS International Conference in St. Louis, Missouri on November 4, 1971.

"Load" is the level of water in the tub; the "Capacity" (input or output) is the rate at which the water is flowing. These are closely related concepts but quite different in meaning.

Almost every company has tried machine loading but few succeed in really making it work. Production control people are about equally divided between the "haves" and the "have nots" and both groups appear to be equally dissatisfied. Often, in speaking to APICS and other groups, we will ask the group, "How many of you have a machine load program?" and usually between 40 and 50 percent raise their hands. Our next question is, "How many of the rest of you would like to have one?" This brings the balance of the hands up. Our third question is, "Of those having such a program, how many find that it is really being used?" and usually one or two will raise their hands. The obvious question, then, is, "Well, what do the rest of you want it for?" While it is the second oldest production control technique (only expediting has been around longer) available since Henry Gantt showed us how to make bar charts about 1903, it has had little effective use.

On the other hand, not too many companies have really tried capacity planning. Recently, however, because of the availability of computer programs, there has been a rapid growth in interest in capacity planning and more companies are attempting it now. This will be covered in more detail later.

Let's review some definitions starting with "Infinite Loading." This is really "loading to infinite capacity" and, shown in Figure 2, begins with a schedule of work orders.

The schedule is based on calculations or estimates of the elements of lead time shown in Figure 3.

Setup and running time are frequently covered by labor standards; preparation and move times can be estimated along with want-to-move times, but some rule of thumb is generally used to provide queue times. Some sophisticated scheduling systems may also include inspection time, calibration, or similar operations following completion of actual work on the product.

Infinite loading is usually based on backward scheduling, starting with the date wanted as shown in Figure 4. The total lead time calculated for operation 50 is deducted from the date wanted and this establishes the start time for this operation in its work center. In like manner, the lead times for opera-

```
Schedule Work Orders
Load Work Centers
Update - Remove Finished
Add New
```

Figure 2. Infinite Loading

```
Preparation
Setup
Running Time
Move Time
Queue Time
```

Figure 3. Elements of Lead Time

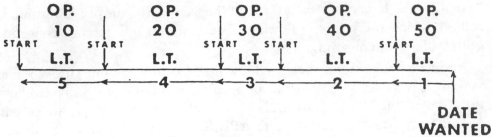

Figure 4. Backward Scheduling

tions 40, 30, 20, and 10 are deducted successively to set start dates in the work centers involved. These starting dates determine the time periods in which it is assumed the load will hit the individual work centers. As shown in Figure 2, the second step in infinite loading is to total up the load from all jobs in each time period for the individual work centers. Updating an infinite load is simple; completed jobs are removed and new jobs added as they are released.

Finite Loading, really "loading to finite capacity," is not simple and requires considerably more work. As shown in Figure 5, it also starts with a schedule of work orders determined in the same way as for infinite loading.

> Schedule Work Orders
> Set Priorities - Components
> Set Work Center Capacities
> Load Work Centers - in
>     priority sequence
> Reschedule overloads
> Update - Start Over

Figure 5. Finite Loading

Before finite loading can begin, however, priorities must be set on individual orders. Obviously, the highest priority orders should get first claim on available capacity in each work center. The next step is to set limiting capacities for each work center. This is usually done with two values: "standard" capacity and "maximum" capacity, the latter including overtime or an added shift. The jobs are then loaded into the individual work centers in priority sequence. As soon as a work center is filled to its limiting capacity, additional jobs are rescheduled either earlier or later until they find available capacity. Because of the requirement to load based on priority, a finite load cannot be updated using the same add-and-deduct approach as an infinite load. The only way to revise a finite load is to start over, rearranging jobs in the new priority sequence and reloading.

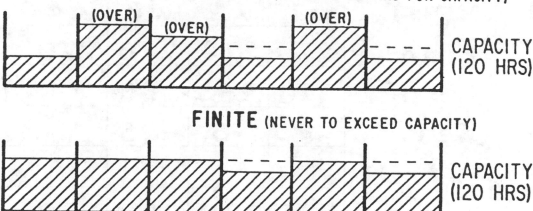

**INFINITE** (WITHOUT REGARD FOR CAPACITY)

(OVER)    (OVER)    (OVER)

CAPACITY
(120 HRS)

**FINITE** (NEVER TO EXCEED CAPACITY)

CAPACITY
(120 HRS)

Figure 6. Loading Methods

Figure 6 illustrates the difference between finite and infinite loads. The infinite load shows both overloads and underloads because the jobs were loaded in without regard to capacity limitations. It identifies and measures these overloads in addition to showing the time periods in which they will occur. The detailed load information gives the specific jobs involved so that overloads can be analyzed. The finite load, in contrast, does not permit overloads; it reschedules jobs to earlier or later time periods. It will show underloads, however, when the full nominal capacity is not utilized.

Finite loading is supposed to develop realistic schedule dates based on priorities assigned and the capacity limitations assumed for the various work centers. It is interesting to note that if the Master Schedule covering the finished products to be assembled could be handled properly, the infinite load picture in Figure 6 would look like the finite load. In effect, then, infinite loading measures the inability to schedule properly at the end product level.

Capacity planning answers the question, "How much is enough?" showing the output required to meet the total demand forecast and also bring the total inventory to planned levels. Obviously, if the inventory is to be reduced, the factory must produce less than is shipped and vice versa. The equation in

$$I_S + P - S = I_E$$

Where: $I_S$ = total inventory at start of planning period

$I_E$ = total inventory at end of planning period

P = total production

S = total shipments

Figure 7.

| INPUT | w1 | w2 | w3 | w4 |
|---|---|---|---|---|
| plan | 270 | 270 | 270 | 270 |
| actual | 270 | 265 | 250 | |
| dev. | | -5 | -25 | |
| OUTPUT | | | | |
| plan | 300 | 300 | 300 | 270 |
| actual | 305 | 260 | 280 | |
| dev. | +5 | -35 | -55 | |

Figure 8. Input/Output

Figure 7 is used to calculate capacity needed.

A form of capacity plan more useful for individual work centers is shown in Figure 8. Here, planned rates of both input and output are shown for future weekly periods. In this particular example, output is planned to exceed input by 30 hours each week and for three weeks to reduce the level of work-in-process inventory now in this work center. Actual data for both input and output rates are posted to the plan as they develop. Deviations are calculated for input and output and these are most useful figures. Applying these simple concepts, though, has given many people serious problems.

### Oliver W. Wight

Last year, in an attempt to solve some of the problems with standard scheduling and loading techniques, I wrote a paper on a technique we've had great success with called "Input/Output Control." The concept is simple: First, for a given work center, you plan your capacity requirements; then you average these to give the foreman a level, realistic production rate; then actual production in standard hours is measured against this planned rate. This planned rate, of course, would be the "output" required. Output is simply the number of standard hours completed by the work center.

I suggested also that we should plan the input rate to a work center and measure that also; that is, measure the standard hours of work coming into that work center as well as going out. Now the reasoning behind planning both the input and the output was very simple: lead time in practically any company is a function of backlog. Backlog, obviously, is a function of the input/output relationship. If output is higher than input, the backlog will drop and the lead time will be reduced. If input is higher than output, the backlog will increase and the lead time will increase. Input/Output Control was designed to focus attention on this vital relationship.

In my article on Input/Output Control, I mentioned that, particularly for starting work centers, there is no reason—and we have done this in practice many times—why the actual input from the inventory system or the scheduling system couldn't be smoothed out. If, for example, a production rate of a screw machine work center is planned at 240 hours per week, there's no reason why planners can't smooth out the release of work rather than releasing 600 hours one week and 150 the next. If the input isn't smoothed out, larger backlogs or queues will be needed in the work center to absorb the fluctuation. I also mentioned that if backlogs started to build up in the shop, it would be better to hold work back rather than keep feeding it in. I probably should have mentioned that this would be a temporary expedient since the real cure for a backlog problem is to get the output or capacity and, if you can't get it, ultimately you will have to change the Master Schedule. So the idea behind the input/output concept was to focus our attention on the *production rates that caused backlogs and lead time problems* when they get out of control as opposed to focusing on the backlogs themselves. The I/O technique in application has proven to be very satisfactory. In retrospect, however, I do wish I had put a little less attention on leveling input to a starting work center because I think this diverted many people's attention from the real significance of Input/Output Control.

There has been a great deal of confusion in the minds of practitioners about all three of the "Capacity Planning" techniques we've discussed. The debate over infinite loading vs. finite loading has raged for years with the "infinite loaders" claiming finite loading wasn't a valid technique and vice versa. In practice, both sides have been proven partially correct; *neither technique* has been used very satisfactorily! Recognizing, then, that there has been some misunderstanding, let's look at the *apparent problems* with these three techniques:

1. **Infinite Capacity Is Not Infinite**

    The opponents of the infinite loading concept have objected to it because they recognize that you simply can't load work into a plant without regard for its capacity and assume that the plant is going to respond. In fact, if production control simply accepts orders and actually loads the plant to infinite capacity, they are doing little more than passing the buck. On the other hand, proponents of infinite loading have hastened to point out some serious problems involved with finite loading. Their most vehement objection has been:

2. **Finite: Deliveries Will Be Extended**

    Obviously, if each order comes along and is fit into the capacity available and nothing is ever done to increase capacity when an increase is required, customer service is likely to be very poor indeed. Many people have pointed out a problem with the third technique:

### 3. I/O Control: Difficult to Control Input

It takes quite a bit of effort to identify all of the items the inventory system is likely to feed into a given starting work center and then to smooth out this flow. Beyond that, of course, the problems involved in smoothing out the flow of input to downstream work centers are virtually insurmountable.

Before discussing these *apparent* problems any further, let's go back to infinite loading and try to understand some of the real problems that have existed with this technique in practice a little better.

Even where practitioners using the infinite loading technique have tried not to abuse it and have tried to load their shop as realistically as possible, they have run into serious difficulties. The typical machine load report almost always shows a large backlog in the past due period. It is not only large, but it's almost always *unbelievable*. In one company, for example, 60 percent of the entire load is past due in the fabrication department, yet the plant superintendent points out that the factory is really "on schedule" since assemblies are going out the door on time.

What causes this situation? Obviously, if the machine load report says that most of the work is past due and it really isn't, little credibility will be given to this report. Its value as a capacity plan will be seriously impaired.

Really, what we see here is due to a breakdown in the "priority planning" system. By priority planning, we mean the system that puts "due dates" on orders. It tells us what material we want and when. Usually the inventory system, in most companies, does the "priority planning." This problem of establishing *and maintaining* proper priorities is a very serious one. As a matter of fact, in most companies, the "formal system" simply doesn't do it well. Nevertheless, the priority problems vary from company to company. Let us think of companies in four general categories from the point of view of *priority complexity:*

### 1. One Piece. Make to Order Shop

This could be a shop that makes and sells forgings. The customer sends in an order and *he* establishes the order priority. Production control tries to fit it into the load somewhere and then acknowledges a delivery date. This becomes the priority. In this kind of company, the date due is the customer promise date. This isn't to say that the customer doesn't sometimes change this due date by requesting a reschedule. But even when he does, *it's easy to see that the due date is changed!* In the more complex types of businesses, from a priority point of view, one of the great difficulties is knowing that the priority really has changed.

In the second type of company, the priority problem becomes much more complex:

## 2. Assembled Product, Made to Order

In this type of company, *priorities are dependent.* Any change in the assembly schedule will mean changing the required dates for all components. Another type of rescheduling must take place when any one of the components going into a sub-assembly or assembly must be rescheduled because the original lot was scrapped, for example. There is no sense in bringing through all of the other parts when the assembly can't be put together. This is what we meant about the difficulty of recognizing a priority change. In most companies, if one part is scrapped, the original due dates remain on all other parts even though it's obvious that it would be far better to use available capacity to make some parts that could be put together into an assembly and shipped.

The third type of company has a comewhat different priority problem:

## 3. One Piece Product, Made to Stock

Here the problem is to update priorities, *after* shop and purchase orders have been released. A stock replenishment order, for example, is released when a reorder point is tripped. This reorder point has built into it some kind of estimate of future demand over lead time. Obviously, the due date placed on this replenishment order will be determined based on that lead time. Whenever the forecast of demand over lead time isn't exactly right — and it's not likely to be very often — the due date on the replenishment order should be updated. In practice, particularly with manual systems, this was very difficult to do and, as a consequence, most companies tried to pretend that the original due date they put on the order was going to be valid throughout the entire lead time. The natural result was that many items went out of stock *and then* the expediting started! And many other orders were "late" but not needed.

The fourth type of company combines the problems of companies 2 and 3:

## 4. Assembled Product: Made to Stock

Obviously, the stock replenishment due dates have to be kept up to date and this has to be related to the components going into the assembly. Once again, if any one of the components is scrapped and can't possibly be completed by the required due date, the other components going into the assembly should be rescheduled to give them valid priorities.

With the manual system that companies had for years, keeping priorities valid was virtually impossible in all but the one piece, make to order type of company. The amount of calculation and recalculation simply wasn't practical. So the *Formal System* usually didn't attempt it. But somehow someone had to find out about at least some of the changed priorities in order to keep the factory operating and the bulk of the shipments going out the door. This became the expediter's main task. Even though priorities weren't officially updated, he found out about some of the material that was *really* needed when the items showed up on shortage lists and backorder lists.

The expediters in a company making an assembled product, for example, usually pulled the parts required to make an assembly out of the stockroom; "staged" (or "accumulated") them; made up shortage lists; and expedited the missing parts. Of course, this *Informal System* always found the shortages too late to do anything about them without generating chaos in the factory, in the purchasing department, and with vendors. As a result, expediting is a dirty word in most companies. But it's also a necessity when the formal priority planning system simply doesn't work.

The four categories of companies listed above are intended to be representative rather than all inclusive. There are companies that don't make assembled products, for example, that do have the dependent priority problem. Consider a company making mechanic's hand tools. They make a forging, process it through some preliminary operations, and then put it into semi-finished inventory. When they wish to make a given size of box wrench, for example, they will draw the proper forging out of inventory and run it through the finishing operation. One semi-finished forging could make a number of different wrench sizes. Note that while this isn't a classical assembled product, the demand on the semi-finished forging *is dependent*.

In fact, a "bill of material" for this particular type of product would look "upside down" as compared with a normal bill of material for an assembled product. An assembled product is made up of a number of parts. The semi-finished item can be finished to make a number of different items.

The practitioner should recognize that even though he doesn't have an assembled product, he may very well have the dependent priority type of problem. The breakdown of the formal priority planning system is indicated when expediters must spend a large part of their time trying to find out *what the real priorities are*.

The inability of most formal priority planning systems to keep priorities properly updated has been one of the most significant causes of machine load reports that simply aren't credible to shop people. One of the reliable features of the informal priority system is that it *expedites and never unexpedites!* Figure 9 attempts to show this graphically. The vertical line represents the original due date put on eight different shop or purchase orders. The expediter has discovered that four of these shop orders are needed sooner than originally planned. But he has not been able to determine that a number of these orders should be rescheduled to a later date. After all, expediting takes a lot of time and effort. There is none left over for unexpediting.

The result is a system that says, "Work on all the orders to meet the original dates unless they're needed sooner." Of course, this means plenty of late orders that aren't really needed. *The consequence is a machine load report that's badly overstated in the early time periods!* It usually shows a

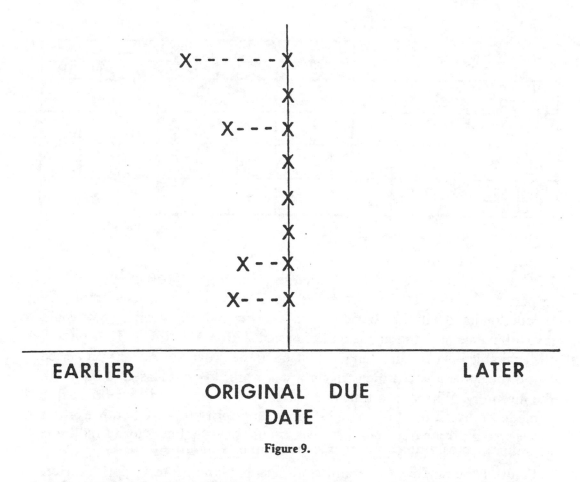

EARLIER                                    LATER
ORIGINAL   DUE
DATE

Figure 9.

large past due load because jobs that are not needed have not been rescheduled. The result: Nobody believes the machine load report.

We can conclude, then, that capacity planning is not going to be very effective until priority planning is effective. If there are many "late" jobs around that are not really needed, capacity plans will always be overstated and they won't be credible to the users. *A prerequisite to an effective capacity planning system is an effective priority planning system.*

The function of the priority planning system is to put the proper due dates on orders and to maintain those due dates so that they are correct. Until this can be done successfully, capacity planning will not be able to generate credible information.

**George W. Plossl**

Successful scheduling and loading requires accurate priorities for individual jobs; these priorities are set by the ordering system. There are two basic systems: the Order Point/Order Quantity System and Material Requirements Planning. Figure 10 illustrates how the order point system works to set priorities. Item Y2L has a forecast of 200 per period with an order point set at 300, a lot size of 600, and a lead time of 1 period. There are 700 on

O.P. = 300          O.Q. 600          L.T. = 1

| Y 2 L | | PERIOD | | | | | | | |
|---|---|---|---|---|---|---|---|---|---|
| | | 1 | 2 | 3 | 4 | 5 | 6 | 7 | 8 |
| PROJECTED REQUIREMENTS | | 200 | 200 | 200 | 200 | 200 | 200 | 200 | 200 |
| SCHEDULED RECEIPTS | | | 600 | | | | 600 | | |
| ON HAND | 700 | 500 | 900 | 700 | 500 | 300 | 700 | 500 | 300 |
| PLANNED ORDER RELEASE | | | | | | 600 | | | 600 |

Figure 10.

hand at the start of the planning period and a quantity of 600 is on order, due in period 2. If the 200 forecast for period 1 are actually used, the projected balance on hand will then be 500. Using another 200 and receiving 600 would give a balance on hand at the end of period 2 of 900. Using 200 per period, the available balance on hand would drop to the order point of 300 in period 5 and the system would then trigger a new order to be released to replenish the inventory. With a lead time of 1 period, the order would be scheduled to come in in period 6. This would establish its priority relative to other orders in the system; those due in earlier weeks would have higher priority and those due later would be lower.

Figure 11 shows how Material Requirements Planning sets priorities. Here the data shows rather lumpy demand in the 8 periods because the Y3L is required in a variety of assemblies at higher levels. The quantities shown are calculated from the Master Production Schedules to make the end product assemblies. The order quantity is 350 and the lead time is 2 periods with a quantity of 400 pieces on hand to start the planning period. Using the projected requirements, the on hand figure would drop to 300 in period 1, 150 in period 2, and would show a negative balance of 120 in period 4. In require-

O.Q. = 350          L.T. = 2

| Y 3 L | | PERIOD | | | | | | | |
|---|---|---|---|---|---|---|---|---|---|
| | | 1 | 2 | 3 | 4 | 5 | 6 | 7 | 8 |
| PROJECTED REQUIREMENTS | | 100 | 150 | 120 | 150 | 100 | 90 | 110 | 120 |
| SCHEDULED RECEIPTS | | | | | 350 | | | 350 | |
| ON HAND | 400 | 300 | 150 | 30 | -120 / 230 | 130 | 40 | -70 / 280 | 160 |
| PLANNED ORDER RELEASE | | | 350 | | | 350 | | | |

Figure 11.

70                                      © **American Production & Inventory Control Society**

ments planning, this is the period in which we need more material and 350 would be scheduled to be received in period 4. This would establish priority on this item relative to other items also on order. The release date would be indicated by backing off 2 periods (lead time); the first order should be released in period 2.

Because of basic differences between the two systems, significantly different priorities can be developed. At the 1970 APICS International Conference in Cincinnati, Dr. J.A. Orlicky used an example to illustrate how uniform demand for finished products results in very lumpy demand for components. His data are shown in Figure 12. The demand for each of the four end products is uniform in each week. Their inventories are replenished by running the lot sizes indicated on the "Production" line. The sub-assemblies then have demands for 14 and 35 in alternate time periods as shown in the center section. The part common to both sub-assemblies has extremely lumpy demand; although its average demand is 17, individual period demands vary from 65 maximum to 0 minimum.

The order point system would plan replenishment of this item as shown in the upper section of Figure 13. The demand would be forecast at the average of 17 and actual demand would reduce the available balance week by week until it had dropped below the order point of 85. The system would then say, "Start a new order and schedule it in at the end of its planned lead time of four weeks."

Contrasted to this, the bottom section of Figure 13 shows how requirements planning would handle this. The requirements would be calculated as shown and the available figure projected into the future indicating that the inventory on hand would be used up in the last week shown. This would then

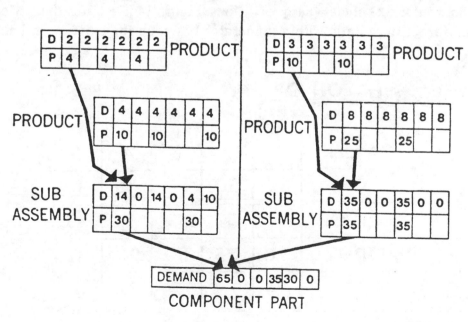

Figure 12.

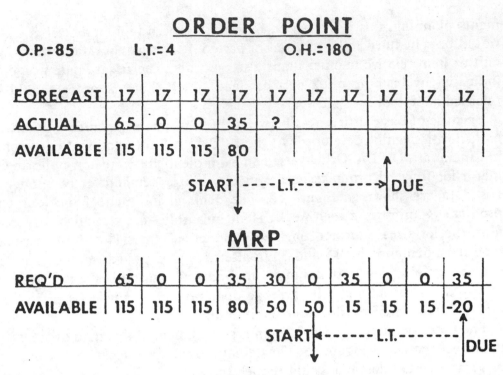

# ORDER POINT

O.P.=85          L.T.=4                    O.H.=180

| | | | | | | | | | | |
|---|---|---|---|---|---|---|---|---|---|---|
| FORECAST | 17 | 17 | 17 | 17 | 17 | 17 | 17 | 17 | 17 | 17 |
| ACTUAL | 65 | 0 | 0 | 35 | ? | | | | | |
| AVAILABLE | 115 | 115 | 115 | 80 | | | | | | |

START | - - - - L.T. - - - - - - - - - | DUE

## MRP

| | | | | | | | | | | |
|---|---|---|---|---|---|---|---|---|---|---|
| REQ'D | 65 | 0 | 0 | 35 | 30 | 0 | 35 | 0 | 0 | 35 |
| AVAILABLE | 115 | 115 | 115 | 80 | 50 | 50 | 15 | 15 | 15 | -20 |

START | < - - - - - - L.T. - - - - - - - | DUE

Figure 13.

be the due date for a new order which would be scheduled to start the lead time of four weeks earlier. Notice the two weeks difference in priorities for this item between the two systems.

Many practitioners feel they can overcome this problem by installing a dynamic priority system such as Critical Ratio. Let's examine how Critical Ratio would work under these conditions. Figure 14 illustrates the basic formula for Critical Ratio with a numerator based on the balance on hand of

$$CR = \frac{OH/OP}{LTR/LT}$$
          O.P.=85
          L.T.= 4

| WEEK | 1 | 2 | 3 | 4 | 5 |
|---|---|---|---|---|---|
| OH | 80 | 50 | 50 | 15 | 15 |
| OH/OP | .94 | .59 | .59 | .18 | .18 |
| LTR/LT | 1.0 | .75 | .50 | .25 | .12 |
| CR | .94 | .79 | 1.2 | .72 | 1.5 |

Figure 14. Critical Ratio

parts remaining in stock and a denominator reflecting how the replenishment order is moving through the plant. When the order point system triggered an order, the On Hand balance was 80 compared to the order point of 85 so the numerator ratio is 0.94. Since work had not been started, the full lead time remains and the lead time ratio is 1. The Critical Ratio is then 0.94 and the system says: "You are essentially on time." Critical Ratios between 0.95 and 1.05 indicate "on time"; for smaller ratios, expediting is indicated and for larger ratios, slack time is available and the job can be set aside.

In week 2, an additional quantity of 30 has been used so the On Hand figure is now 50 and the On Hand/Order Point ratio 0.59. Assuming the job progressed normally through the plant (since it was not being expedited), the lead time remaining is three weeks and this ratio is 0.75. The Critical Ratio is 0.79 which says, "Expedite, you are behind schedule." In week 3, no more parts were used so the numerator remains 0.59. Assuming that a normal week's work was accomplished, the lead time ratio would drop to 0.5 and the Critical Ratio would rise to 1.2, indicating that the job is no longer critical and saying, in effect, "You did it, fellows, you got back on schedule. In fact, you are now ahead and can relax." In week 4, however, an additional quantity of 35 was issued, dropping the numerator to 0.18. Since no extra effort was being put on the job, perhaps only one week's work was finished and the lead time ratio would be 0.25, indicating a Critical Ratio of 0.72. This says in effect, "Get on the ball again because this job is now urgently needed." At the end of week 5, with no more parts being used, the numerator remains unchanged. Whatever work is done to reduce the remaining lead time might drop the denominator to 0.12 and the system could easily again indicate slack time available. In this kind of environment with lumpy demand, Critical Ratio behaves like a yo-yo.

Obviously, there is no way to cope with use of the wrong ordering system through fancy scheduling, priority systems, loading, or any other technique. Using the wrong ordering system, the wrong due dates will be established. With incorrect dates, the schedule, the priorities, and the projection of when the load will hit individual work centers will be fiction.

In such an environment, the informal system usually takes over and the real priorities are set by the "hot list" based upon known shortages at assembly. The number of jobs *apparently* past due invariably rises, but the factory people know most of these are not really needed and pay attention only to the informal system priorities. The credibility gap widens until the formal system is ignored or discarded. I know one company with 93 full-time expediters working to five different priority systems—one indicates jobs needed 10 days hence, one 5 days hence, one tomorrow, and one (called the "drop dead" list) covers items without which the assembly line will shut down within the hour. Guess what the fifth priority system is? That's right—when there are no higher priority jobs to do, work to the "date wanted" on the order. Only 8 percent of the orders come through on the original wanted date. No wonder the credibility gap exists.

Effective scheduling and loading requires the elements shown in Figure 15.

| Plan | Control |
|------|---------|
| Priorities | Capacity |
| Capacity | Priorities |

Figure 15.

There must be a priority planning system that works; this means using the proper ordering system for independent and dependent demand items. There must be a capacity plan to insure that adequate capacity is available to handle the work. There must be a control system to see that capacity is adjusted to meet changes in both customer requirements and in the factory's output. And there must be a priority control system to respond to changes, adjusting priorities to bring the proper jobs through in the right sequence. No machine load or scheduling system will work when based on the wrong priorities. Let's now take a closer look at infinite loading and how it works.

### Oliver W. Wight

Remember that there are two fundamental ways to go about loading; one is to show the load in the time period when it's scheduled *regardless* of the available capacity (infinite capacity loading), and the other is to load to "finite capacity" which means, of course, that even though the load may be scheduled in a given time period, if capacity isn't available in this time period, the load will be moved to another time period.

Whoever coined the term "loading to infinite capacity" really did the field of production and inventory control a disservice. When you think about it, it's pretty obvious that a company *should start* by doing some kind of "infinite loading." Certainly finite loading doesn't even show them the capacity they *need!* It just assumes that this capacity is absolutely inflexible. The first step is to find out what capacity is needed. You must start with "infinite loading" rather than "finite loading."

Let's review the steps in scheduling and loading. Figure 16 shows a typical shop order. Note that this shop order is due on calendar day 412. We're working with a shop calendar that shows only the working days to facilitate scheduling. Note that the standard hours for each operation have been calculated based on the quantity on the shop order; in this case, 300 pieces. Assume also that we're working with some scheduling rules. In this case, our scheduling rules allow two days for inspection and two days "transit time" between operations in different departments. The job is due to be completed on day 412; it has to be out of the polishing operation on day 410. This company works on eight-hour shift so two days will have to be allowed for the polishing operation. Since two days are allowed between operatons in different departments, the job must be completed out of grinding on day 406. In this manner, the job can be "Back Scheduled" to determine when each operation must be finished (and/or started) and a "schedule date" can be assigned to each operation.

| Part No. B-4848 | | | Shop Order No. 50043  Quant. 300  Due: 412 | | | |
|---|---|---|---|---|---|---|
| Oper. | Dept. | Mach. | Description | Setup | Per Piece | |
| 10 | 08 | 1322 | Cut off | .5 | .010 | |
| 20 | 32 | 1600 | Rough turn | 1.5 | .030 | |
| 30 | 17 | 8660 | Heat treat | | | |
| 40 | 32 | 1204 | Finish turn | 3.3 | .048 | |
| 50 | 32 | 1204 | Drill, ream | 1.2 | .035 | |
| 60 | 12 | 1466 | Mill slots | 1.8 | .025 | |
| 70 | 03 | 1742 | Grind | .6 | .010 | |
| 80 | 22 | 1003 | Polish | .3 | .029 | |
| 90 | 11 | | Inspect | | | |
| | | | | | | |

| Release | | |
|---|---|---|
| Std. Hrs. | Start | Finish |
| 3.5 | | |
| 10.5 | | |
| | | |
| 17.7 | | |
| 11.7 | | |
| 9.3 | | |
| 3.6 | | |
| 9.0 | | |
| | | |
| | | |
| 65.3 | | |

Figure 16.

| | | WEEKLY LOAD IN STANDARD HOURS | | | | | | |
|---|---|---|---|---|---|---|---|---|
| DEPT. | MACH. | 376 380 | 381 385 | 386 390 | 391 395 | 396 400 | 401 405 | 406 410 |
| 03 | 1742 | | | | | | | |
| 08 | 1322 | | | | | | | |
| 12 | 1466 | | | | | | | |
| 22 | 1003 | | | | | | | 9 |
| 32 | 1204 | | | | | | | |
| | 1600 | | | | | | | |

Figure 17.

Note that nine standard hours of polishing work will then be required in work center 1003 and must be completed by day 410. Figure 17 shows the weekly load report in standard hours. The nine hours have been loaded in the proper work center in the proper week. By doing this with all of the shop orders, an "infinite capacity load" would be developed.

As we've pointed out. *it's essential that we know what capacity is needed* and only this kind of approach will do that. We frankly think that *the biggest problem with infinite capacity loading is the name!* If we had been astute enough to give it a name that properly described the function, this technique would have had far better acceptability and more intelligent use. My nomination for a more descriptive term is *CAPACITY REQUIREMENTS PLANNING.*

We have Material Requirements Planning (MRP) that tells us what material we need and when we need it. Capacity Requirements Planning should tell us what capacity we need and when we need it. How is Capacity Requirements Planning different from infinite loading? Since I have coined the term, allow me to define it. Capacity Requirements Planning uses exactly the same logic as the old "infinite loading" with one minor difference. In addition to picking up the released orders or "load," it also picks up the *planned orders* from MRP. These planned orders *are not real shop orders.* MRP simply generates a part number, a quantity, and a time period when an order is to be released. MRP uses these planned orders to generate lower level material requirements. But they can also be run against the routing file, each planned order can be back-scheduled and a forecast of capacity requirements can thus be developed.

Capacity Requirements Planning is certainly an essential function in any production and inventory control system. But let's stop using that emotion-laden word "Infinite" right now! Nobody can really load a plant to infinite capacity! But certainly we do need to have an idea of capacity requirements before we start trying to load the plant to a given capacity.

Remember Figure 15 that showed the four basic elements in a production and inventory control system:

Plan Priorities / Plan Capacities / Control Capacities / Control Priorities

The inventory control system (usually MRP) is the priority planning function. Capacity Requirements Planning is the capacity planning function. Dispatching is the priority control function in the shop. But how about *capacity control?*

We frankly don't believe that the typical machine load report was ever designed to be a "control system." A control system has four fundamental elements to it:

A NORM / TOLERANCE / FEEDBACK / ACTION

The wall thermostat is our favorite example of a control system. The temperature is set to the desired level, then the actual temperature is monitored via a feedback system. Whenever the actual has deviated from the norm—or "Plan"—by a predetermined amount (tolerance), action is taken to get the temperature restored to the norm.

Think of the typical machine load report. Is there a norm? Where is there a plan that's practical? A plan that you can hold people responsible for executing. Certainly when you have tremendous variations in the amount of load in a work center each week, *there's no way* you can hold the foreman responsible for working to that production level. It simply isn't practical in most factories to have dramatic fluctuations in capacity. Manpower and machine capacity are limited and it is most economical to hold them as stable as possible from one week to the next.

By the same token, where is the comparison of "actual" with "plan" in the typical machine load report? Very seldom does the load report show the output from the work center involved and if output is shown, it's usually only shown for one week. Obviously, output for one week is hardly representative of the ability of that work center to meet the capacity plan. Actual output should be compared with planned output for a number of weeks.

Certainly two essentials that ought to be involved in any kind of "capacity control" or "output control" system are:

A practical plan

Feedback to compare "actual" with the plan.

| | | | |
|---|---|---|---|
| 1. | 284 | 6. | 286 |
| 2. | 61 | 7. | 50 |
| 3. | 321 | 8. | 147 |
| 4. | 139 | 9. | 695 |
| 5. | 531 | 10. | 176 |

Figure 18. Capacity Requirements

Let's look briefly at a Capacity Requirements Plan. When all of the hours by work center, by time period, are accumulated, the result would look something like Figure 18. This shows capacity requirements for 10 weeks for a given work center in standard hours. Note that there is a random variation from week to week.

How can this random variation be smoothed out? The most practical way is simply to *add it up and average it out*. The minute you get a week out into the future, your prediction of how many hours are going to be at what work center at what time is an approximation at best. The average weekly capacity requirement from Figure 18 would be 270 hours per week.

| | W1 | W2 | W3 | W4 | W5 |
|---|---|---|---|---|---|
| PLANNED | 270 | 270 | 270 | 270 | 270 |
| ACTUAL | 250 | 220 | 190 | | |
| DEVIATION | -20 | -70 | -150 | | |

Figure 19. Output Control

could be set up in an "Output Control" report. Remember that we're trying to show a "norm"—a realistic attainable plan that people can be held responsible for attaining. Below the *plan*, the *actual* standard hours of output are shown. Below that, of course, we show the deviation.

It would be a good idea, in practice, to determine a tolerance. How far away from the planned can the actual be allowed to drift? We've seen companies use this kind of report. By pre-determining what the tolerance was, the foreman coming into the weekly production meeting knew whether or not they were going to be required to work overtime or do something else to increase capacity. They were told, for example, "If the cumulative deviation is more than 50 hours off the plan, the burden is on *you* to get extra capacity—quick!" Setting the tolerance *in advance* saved a lot of debates in production meetings.

Infinite loading is dead; it has been replaced by *Capacity Requirements Planning*. There is nothing wrong with the technique *if it used properly!* We certainly need to plan capacity well out into the future. The term Capacity Requirements Planning—by definition—implies that we are using planned orders out of MRP as well as actual released orders. Then the leveled planned production rate is just the average of the weekly capacity requirements usually planned out three to four months in advance. This sets the production rate against which the actual output will be measured. Many people spend a lot of time trying to figure out what their capacity is when the actual current capacity is very easy to determine by looking at labor variance reports and other already existing reports that show the number of standard hours worth of work produced.

Note that the report I showed you, the Output Report, is really part of the technique that we called Input/Output Control. Let's think a little more about the real significance of this technique.

### George W. Plossl

The traditional approach to developing a production and inventory control system has been to first design and install an ordering system—a set of procedures to trigger orders for both purchased and manufactured parts. This has been generally called "Inventory Control." The next step is to release immediately to vendors or to the factory the orders triggered by this system. Next comes an attempt to control the sequence in which these orders are worked on by activities in the plant under the general heading of "Production Control."

A popular technique among manufacturing people is to watch the backlogs in a machine load and attempt to use them as a tool for adjusting capacity. Unfortunately, this rarely works. Increasingly popular are shop floor control systems using dynamic priority techniques and data collection equipment. The basic idea seems to be that if we know where each job is, we can get it through when we need it. This, unfortunately, doesn't seem to be very effective either. In fact, both approaches are nothing but a massive assult on the symptoms while the basic diseases of poor priority information and/or inadequate capacity go unchecked.

We now have two fine ordering systems and a basic principle to tell us when to use each of them. The independent/dependent demand principle clearly identifies where the order point/order quantity system should be applied and where to use Material Requirements Planning. With both systems, however, we still need dependable lead times and this means that queues or backlogs of work-in-process must be under control.

There are three reasons why queues (and lead times) are out of control:

1. Inadequate Capacity—if you are not making enough in total, then something must wait, queues grow and lead times get longer and more erratic.

2. Erratic Input—no ordering system releases work at a level rate matching the capacity of the plant. When the lumps and bunches of work triggered by either of the basic ordering systems hit the shop, it is obvious that all cannot move steadily through the plant. Backlogs and queues will increase and lead time will get longer and more erratic.

3. Inflated Lead Times—it is now well recognized that we can't "make it easy" for the plant or for the ordering system by simply allowing more time to get jobs finished. Increasing planned lead times triggers more orders and dumps more load into the plant without regard to its ability to hadle it. Longer queues and erratic lead times result.

Lead times will never be controlled and a plant will never be on schedule unless it controls capacity. The Input/Output approach is the first available tool which has been successfully used in controlling capacity. Unlike the typical machine load shown in Figure 20, Input/Output measures and

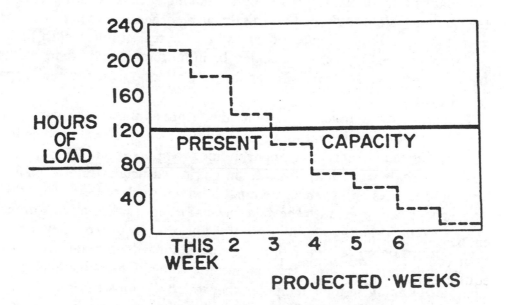

Figure 20. Typical Machine Load Pattern

attempts to control the *through-put*, the flow in and out, rather than the backlogs. Production control people look at the present overloads on the machine load in Figure 20 and tell the foreman, "You're in trouble." The foreman looks at the future underloads on the machine load and says, "You better believe it." They're thinking of something entirely different.

Recently, I sat with a plant manager, his manufacturing superintendent, and his production control manager looking at a report issued weekly for each major work center in the plant. This report showed standard machine hours of actual input, actual output, total backlogs and the past due portion of the backlog in each work center. The manufacturing superintendent said his people looked only at the backlog figures. I asked why they didn't use the actual output information and he said, "Notice how steady and level these figures are. They don't tell us much." I also asked why they did not use the input figures and he said, "Look how they jump up and down. What does that really tell you? We've run out of work before and there is no indication in these input figures we won't run out again. We use the backlog figures which are the only data giving us any *forward visibility at work* in the plant." Could you argue with him? With future *planned* capacity data lacking, what else could he do?

The biggest hangup on applying the Input/Output Control approach seems to be the difficulty of seeing how to control input in secondary work centers. Input can really be controlled only at starting operations and at assembly or sub-assembly areas where we have control of the orders released from the planning system to the plant. However, *average rates* of work input can be planned and *actual rates measured* at all work centers. This gives very valuable information as illustrated in Figure 21. Against a planned average rate of 210 standard hours per week, actual output has fallen short by a cumulative total of 300 standard hours. Looking at the output figures only, a logical conclusion would be that this department needs more capacity. However, the input figures make it obvious that the real problem must lie in the departments feeding this work center. Its input total is more than 300 hours behind the plan. Measuring input focuses attention on the real capacity problem areas.

Extending the planned figures into the future as shown in Figure 21 gives manufacturing people that forward visibility which is so vital to them in controlling capacity. Another company decided to apply Input/Output Controls and immediately ran into difficulty in getting sufficient data to plan input and output rates and to measure input at major work centers. They decided to go ahead, however, with the data they had. They ranked all new orders released by the inventory planning system in priority sequence. They completed the routings on all orders, estimating time standards in major work centers where they were missing. Using an infinite capacity machine load program they had running on their computer, they tested what load these orders would place on each work center. Since they had no formal scheduling system, they ignored the time delay from starting an operation in one work center and

(ALL FIGURES IN STANDARD HOURS)

| WEEK ENDING | 505 | 512 | 519 | 526 |
|---|---|---|---|---|
| PLANNED INPUT | 210 | 210 | 210 | 210 |
| ACTUAL INPUT | 110 | 150 | 140 | 130 |
| CUMULATIVE DEVIATION | -100 | -160 | -230 | -310 |

| PLANNED OUTPUT | 210 | 210 | 210 | 210 |
|---|---|---|---|---|
| ACTUAL OUTPUT | 140 | 120 | 160 | 120 |
| CUMULATIVE DEVIATION | -70 | -160 | -210 | -300 |

**Figure 21. Input/Output Control**

having it reach a subsequent work center some days or weeks later. They assumed each job hit each work center immediately when it was released, just as if all were starting operations.

From payroll data, they logged the actual hours of output in each of the major work centers and carried a weighted running average. When the scheduled orders to be released exceeded this average actual output in any work center, they rescheduled some orders to minimize such overloads. Their objective was to *put into each work center less work than it was turning out.* In a period of six weeks, the work-in-process was reduced almost 40 percent, lead times came down proportionately and their ability to get needed jobs through the plant increased rather dramatically.

The real use of Input/Output Control techniques is, of course, to measure actual versus planned data as a basis for control. Control of all priorities and inventory levels depends on controlling capacity. Among the elements of the effective production control system shown in Figure 15, the key is controlling capacity. With adequate capacity, even if you can't level out the input, you can manage long queues of work and long average lead times *if you have a priority planning system that works.* Without adequate capacity, you can only hope to minimize the pain or isolate it.

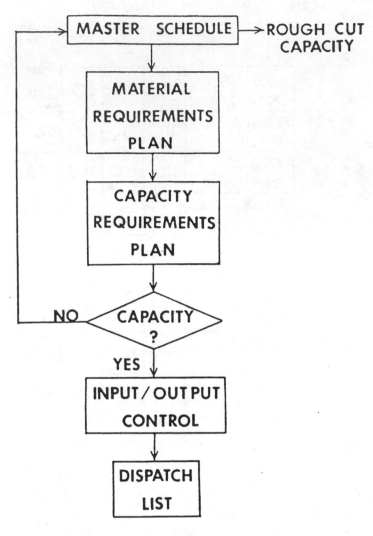

**Figure 22.**

Oliver W. Wight

We've talked about planning and controlling priorities and capacities. Let's see how the techniques we have discussed fit into this overall format.

Priority planning— the *Material Requirements Planning* technique will be used in most companies.

Capacity planning—this is where we need to use *Capacity Requirements Planning.*

Capacity control —Input/Output Control.

Priority control —Dispatching in the shop, follow-up in Purchasing.

Figure 22 shows the overall relationship of the elements in a production and inventory control system. Starting with a Master Production Schedule, it goes into a Material Requirements Plan; the Capacity Requirements Plan can then be developed from both released orders and planned orders. Then a decision is indicated. Can the plant meet the capacity requirements?

Obviously, they should try to meet these if this is at all practical and economical. If the capacity requirements look reasonable, Input/Output Control could be set up as a capacity control device. A Dispatch List — probably issued to the shop daily — would be used to communicate priorities to the shop floor as they are revised by the Material Requirements Plan. Looking at this schematic, you recognize that it illustrates the functions of planning and controlling priorities and capacities. The Material Requirements Plan is *priority planning*. Capacity Requirements Planning is *capacity planning*. The Input/Output technique is used for *controlling capacity* and the Dispatch List is used for *controlling priorities*.

*Note that if capacity is not available, the Master* Schedule *must be changed!* There are really two alternatives when capacity requirements are in excess of actual capacity:

> Change capacity.
> Change the schedule.

Note by the way, that a rough cut at capacity requirements might be made as part of the Master Scheduling function. In other words, before going through the detail of the actual Material Requirements Plan and the Capacity Requirements Plan, some long range determination of requirements against resources might be calculated. This is a rough cut just to make sure that the Master Schedule is in the ball park before going through the detailed calculations.

This schematic is anything but theory. There are companies that have Material Requirements Planning, Capacity Requirements Planning, Input/Output Control, and Dispatching working. And very successfully, I might add. Once these techniques are functioning properly, an entirely different approach to running a manufacturing company emerges. With a formal system like this *that works*, decisions are put into their proper perspective ahead of time. Let me give you an example.

One company that I've worked with has all of the techniques mentioned above working successfully. The results from using these techniques have impressed me. But the thing that's impressed *them* more than anything else is their ability to spot problems ahead of time and make good, strategic decisions.

The Director of Manufacturing for this company told me some years ago that he'd be pleased the day he could answer some of the questions put to him honestly. For example, when the President says, "We've got to get a new product out the door in much less than the standard lead time, *can we really do it?*" Without the kind of system that will generate this kind of information, the only course open is to say, "Yes," and try.

Let me show you how this company handles this type of problem today. This past September, the President said he wanted a particular product introduced into the schedule immediately and available for shipment

November 1st. The Director of Manufacturing had the load profile for this new product calculated on the computer and superimposed on top of his current Capacity Requirements Plan. He could see immediately that an impossible backlog would have resulted in front of one of his numerically controlled work centers. There wasn't any chance of getting this work subcontracted for a great many reasons including lack of available capacity in the immediate geographical area. The detailed backup report for the capacity plan showed the actual parts that were causing the capacity requirements. Looking at some of these parts, he traced these to the assemblies they went into. Then he went to the President and showed him that if one of the products that was declining in sales could be removed from the Master Schedule for November, there would be enough capacity available to make the new product. The President readily agreed and this plan was implemented. I might also add that the new product was introduced in November on schedule and everyone was very pleased.

In the past, this Director of Manufacturing pointed out to me that he would have added the new product without being able to determine ahead of time what some of the alternate plans were. And he probably would have been criticized severely if the product that had the declining sales had experienced longer delivery times! Since he had the information available to call it to the attention of the President ahead of time, this was anticipated, and when it materialized, people understood that this was the cost of launching a new product in considerably less than standard lead time.

One manufacturing executive made a very astute observation on this. He said, "You know, a manufacturing executive without the proper information can never say 'No.' All he can do is say 'Yes' and try to meet impossible plans and then be criticized afterwards because something else suffered!" But what a new ball game. The ability to point out ahead of time what the alternatives are, what the consequences are, and to pick out ahead of time what will suffer and recognize why this choice was made. In the next five years, I hope to see the emphasis change from developing systems to learning to use systems to manage. Many managements are going to have an entirely new world to work in when they have the alternatives in front of them *ahead of time*.

Let's come back to our overall schematic of production and inventory control. One point should come through loud and clear:

Lesson #1: WORK LOAD ON A PLANT WILL BE LEVELED VIA THE MASTER SCHEDULE.

The first job is to *get* the needed capacity, if possible and practical. When capacity is not available, the Master Schedule must be revised. Large lumps of capacity requirements will be smoothed out in the Master Schedule.

We have talked a lot about the Master Schedule. Perhaps a couple of words about the types of Master Schedule that different companies might use would be in order. In a company operating strictly off backlog, the Master

Schedule would be primarily customer orders. Most companies don't have the luxury of having enough backlog to work from. They need to forecast what orders they're going to have to manufacture. Under these circumstances, the forecast must be "bled out" constantly as actual demand materializes. The short term Master Schedule consists of actual customer orders, the middle term Master Schedule is a combination of forecast and actual, and the long term consists of forecast only.

The Master Schedule in different types of companies can take many different forms. In a company manufacturing stocked finished goods, the Master Schedule would be the production plan that tells the total number of units that they're going to make for a particular type of product. This could then be allocated for various part numbers as a production forecast and that would be used to create a Material Requirements Plan and Capacity Requirements Plan. In a foundry, the Master Schedule might be expressed in very general terms showing the number of molds to be made per day per work center.

Every company has one or more Master Schedules, even though they may not explicitly recognize this! The Master Schedule drives MRP which drives the rest of the production and inventory management system. It is also the key to better management strategy.

Lesson #2: THE MASTER SCHEDULE CAN BE USED TO SIMULATE AND SHOW THE CONSEQUENCES AND IMPLICATIONS OF VARIOUS POLICY DECISIONS.

When a new product is to be introduced, when production is to be increased or decreased, the Master Schedule will be the point of entry to show the consequences of this change in plan. It's the very guts of production and inventory control. Therefore, if the company doesn't explicitly recognize that they have to have a Master Schedule, their chances of being able to control the production and inventory function are very slim indeed. Back in the days of the informal system, few companies had a recognizable Master Schedule. In the days of formal systems, every company should.

But as we look back at our schematic in Figure 22 again, there's something disturbing. *What became of Finite Loading?* We seem to have handled the four fundamental functions of production and inventory control without even touching on Finite Loading!

**George W. Plossl**

Let's take a more detailed look at finite loading. As discussed earlier, jobs must be loaded in priority sequence, since we want the highest priority jobs to have first claim on available capacity. When priorities change, we must rerun the whole finite loading program. The problem is further complicated by "dependent priorities." Components going into an assembly should have a priority dependent upon the status of other components. It is obvious that there is no need to rush one part through if it will just wait for others before the assembly can be completed.

Load data is really a forecast of when work will hit the work center involved and, like all forecasts, will be less accurate for periods farther out in the future; in other words, for longer lead times. It's certainly optimistic, at the least, to say, "Job 123 will hit this work center 15 weeks from now," and really believe it. With all these problems, few companies have attempted finite loading. It is a good question *if any of them has succeeded*.

The two best known computer programs for finite loading are the PICS Capacity Planning and the CLASS program; both put out by IBM. In Business English, the PICS program says, "If you know all the products you are going to manufacture in the next year, if you have a complete bill of material for each of them, if you have routings and standards for each manufactured item in this bill of material and if you have accurate stock status and open order files, then the computer can calculate for you the load on each work center in each time period over the planning horizon and, in addition, can rearrange this load to meet capacity limitations. Figure 23 shows the steps in the PICS Capacity Planning program. Using the Material Requirements Planning program (RPS), the computer translates a Master Production Schedule into planned orders for components; it then schedules both planned and released orders and develops an infinite load profile for each work center. If the user elects to do finite loading, the computer will then reschedule orders with low priority which hit work centers having inadequate capacity. The program will show which orders were rescheduled, how many hours of load are involved and the specific work centers affected. The user must then analyze the rescheduled orders to determine the effects on the end product Master Schedule and decide whether he can live with these or if he must make other changes. The user can assign job priorities or the system will use the Earliest Start Dates or the Latest Start Dates developed by the

CAPACITY PLANNING

MASTER PRODUCTION SCHEDULE

PLANNED ORDERS - COMPONENTS

SCHEDULE ALL ORDERS

INFINITE LOAD

OR

FINITE LOAD

ANALYZE ORDERS RESCHEDULED

REVISE MASTER SCHEDULE

REPEAT

Figure 23. PICS

scheduling portion of the package. The user must define capacity available in each work center; he has an option of putting in a table showing a planned level and a maximum level of capacity. The difference might be working Saturdays or other overtime periods or transferring a number of men between work centers. The program does not handle unplanned loads such as scrap and rework, machine breakdowns, operator training, and other capacity-wasting activities.

There has been considerable publicity given to another IBM program called called CLASS. CLASS stands for Capacity Loading And Scheduling System, a classic finite loading program developed by Werner Kraus for IBM in Germany. The sequence of activities followed is shown in Figure 24. Unlike PICS capacity planning, CLASS starts with individual work orders and does not require a Material Requirements Planning program to generate them. It does need to know how these orders relate in a product structure since it uses this information to tie the priorities of components to that of the final assembly. The first step is to schedule the work orders and the next to develop an infinite load showing how each work center would be affected if the schedule were followed. The user then adjusts work center capacities as best he can to meet the loads.

Based on user-established priorities on the assemblies, the system develops a finite load attempting to schedule the parts in assembly priority sequence to match available capacity in each work center. The user must then analyze how assemblies were rescheduled to see if he can live with this. If he cannot, he must make other decisions about capacity or priorities and start over. CLASS has an interesting feature in that it simulates the progress of each job through the plant to see if it will be affected by *future overloads*. If jobs #1 and #2 are competing for capacity in one work center, but #1 will be delayed at a subsequent work center, job #2 is given first claim on capacity. Both PICS Capacity Planning and CLASS are truly elegant computer programs and are beautifully designed. They both require massive amounts of computer time because of the tremendous number of calculations involved.

The basic requirements for success with finite loading would appear to be

SCHEDULE WORK ORDERS

INFINITE LOAD

ADJUST WORK CENTER CAPACITIES

SET PRIORITIES — ASSEMBLIES

FINITE LOAD

RESCHEDULE ASSEMBLIES

UP-DATE — START OVER

Figure 24. CLASS

a well-ordered environment, few Master Schedule changes, tight discipline on data accuracy *and a priority plan that is valid*. It is hard to imagine an operation where the work of finite loading programs would be justified by improved results over simpler, more effective techniques. Oliver Wight and I have wondered for a long time if finite loading will ever be a practical technique.

## Oliver W. Wight

Finite loading is certainly an excellent example of "barking up the wrong tree." When a company finite loads the individual shop orders, there's bound to be one predictable result. Some orders won't be able to be completed on time. Obviously, if these orders can't be completed on time, the Master Schedule must be changed. But, as we pointed out before, Capacity Requirements Planning will quickly identify a capacity requirement that can't be met and that the Master Schedule must be changed. Why bother with all the sophistication of finite loading? If ever a technique fell in the general category of "using 300 horsepower to blow the horn," finite loading is it.

Beyond being an over-sophisticated technique, it simply isn't valid. If finite loading were to be done correctly, it would result in endless iteration. Consider a company where they have dependent priorities—parts that go into assemblies, for example. If one part can't be fit into the capacity and its due date has to be extended, then the Master Schedule should be changed for the assemblies using this part. *But when this Master Schedule is changed, the finite load that caused the schedule change is no longer valid.* Some of the load that kept the part in question from being made on time was probably being generated by other parts going into the same assemblies. The minute the Master Schedule is pushed out, some of this load will be pushed out. Now we must finite load again, but, once again, something probably won't be completed on time. Back to the Master Schedule! This, again, will generate the need to recalculate the finite load. If done properly, finite loading would be an endless iteration. One of the companies, using the IBM CLASS program on an IBM 360 Model 40 (certainly not a small computer!) requires *35 hours* to make their computation. When we called to their attention the fact that it's important in most companies to have a daily dispatch list, they pointed out that while they were anxious to do this, they had yet to figure out how to squeeze 35 hours of computer time into a 24-hour day!

But what if we don't change the Master Schedule? Suppose we don't reschedule all of the other parts that go into the assembly. Well, this is certainly a waste of capacity. If any one item can't be made, it's usually necessary to make some other item, particularly if it's important to meet a monthly shipping budget of some kind. When this is true, it's essential to change the Master Schedule and thus reschedule all the parts that aren't needed so that capacity will be available to make the parts that are needed.

One point comes through very clearly: *Overloads will be resolved via the*

*Master Schedule.* Load leveling is going to take place in the Master Schedule. The only load leveling left to be handled will be minor weekly variations in load that are usually not very significant or controllable!

Finite loading, then, was a great way to attack the symptoms, but, in practice, it doesn't work very well. Let's look at the *problems with finite loading:*

### 1. Assumes Predictable Job Arrival.

Going through the precise detail of determining when each job will be at each work center and leveling out this work load assumes that we can predict when jobs will arrive at work centers in the future. The folly of this is obvious to anybody who has ever worked in a factory.

### 2. Component Priorities Are Usually Dependent.

The literature of production and inventory control, be it the order point/ order quantity literature or the literature on scheduling has been obsessed with methods for handling individual independent items. In the real world, most items simply aren't independent. They are parts that go into assemblies, they are raw materials that go into a product. These priorities cannot be looked at independently as so many people have tried to do with order point type systems which apply only to independent priority items. By the same token, *they cannot be scheduled independently.* A new revision in the schedule of any of these items will affect all of the other items that are related to it. This gets to be a complex problem and we have to focus our attention on what's important and what isn't important. In a company that makes an assembled product, for example, optimizing the schedule of any one component is an exercise in triviality. The important thing is to get all of the components together at the right time to make the product. Having any one of them without the rest of them is valueless. And, as we pointed out above, the computations involved in a genuine finite loading exercise where there are dependent demand components would result in endless iteration.

One of the difficulties, of course, is that at the end of each one of these iterations, the Master Schedule would have to be revised. This would require human intervention before the program could continue in its operation. This probably wouldn't be practical. Therefore, some people have suggested that the Master Schedule should be revised automatically by the computer. *Don't do it!* There is a major problem with finite loading:

### 3. Automatic Master Scheduling Is Risky.

As was pointed out, the Master Schedule drives the entire production and inventory control system. A lot of considerations go into the Master Schedule. It's attempting to deal with the real world where some large customers of a company may get preferential treatment in practice, where things like a dock strike may cause an export order to have a higher priority than it normally has and where an order for a new customer who was sold based on the company's ability to give service might have to be given preference. These are the normal day-to-day things that have to be addressed in the real world factory. To try to capture all of that logic in a computer program may intrigue the theoretician. The practitioner recognizes how futile—and silly—it is.

The name of the game is to plan capacity requirements and see if we have this capacity. If we don't, get the capacity or change the Master Schedule. Probably the greatest reason for not using finite loading in most situations is:

## 4. There Are Easier, Better Ways To Do The Job.

Finite loading assumes a very stable environment where a lot of logic can be captured in a computer program and executed. It is filled with pretentious precision as it tries to predict which jobs will arrive at what time at what operation in a factory. Yet, in practice, the company that does finite loading only learns what they could have learned by way of much simpler techniques: when there is a capacity requirement in excess of available capacity, it must be met — or the Master Schedule must be changed.

If this is true, why has finite loading even gained credence? To be sure, it is not something that *most practitioners* view as logical. But a few do.

Well, let's take a look at one prime example. It has often been stated that there are "200 users of the IBM CLASS program in Europe." First, we have to define users. What this really means is that there are 200 people who have accepted a free program from IBM. Then we are likely to hear that there are 30 companies that are actually "running" it, but this usually means that these 30 companies have the program running on the computer. Whether or not anybody uses the output is questionable. As we tried to pin it down further, we find that there are a few companies who are actually supposed to be running their factories this way. The only one that has had much written about it actually makes magnets. Fundamentally, a one-piece product without many dependent priorities and a very simple manufacturing environment. Questionable that they really need finite loading. The fact that is worked under these circumstances is interesting, but not particularly signifiant.

We also hear that there are "a number of companies" using it in the United States. We've tried to track this down and have learned some very interesting things. At one company, for example, the Manufacturing Vice President and Data Processing people speak very highly of finite loading. They are located in a corporate office in Chicago. It works there. Unfortunately, when you get down to the plant in Moline, you find that it does not work.

How can we determine whether finite loading works or doesn't work? First, we've got to understand what the function of finite loading really is. It isn't a capacity planning technique; it certainly isn't a capacity control technique; it isn't a priority control technique either. *It's really a priority planning technique.* It takes the priorities generated by the Material Requirements Plan and attempts to revise them in order to level out the work load. Perhaps a more appropriate name for it would be something like "Order Release Planning," since it addresses the problem of releasing orders into starting work centers in an attempt to level work load.

How do you determine if finite loading is actually working, then? The test is simple: *Does the company using it actually run to the priority list generated by the finite loading system?* This is the only way you can determine if finite loading is working. If they are not running to this priority list, *finite loading does not work.*

I went to a company recently, for example, where they were using the IBM PICS Infinite Loading and Finite Loading packages. They claimed great results from the finite loading system. I was skeptical. Looking at the priority list generated by the finite loading reports confirmed my skepticism. They certainly were not following it. In fact, they worked to a hot list and then crossed the jobs off the weekly computer generated priority list as they were done in the sequence dictated by the hot list.

They did get some lead time reductions, however. They mistakenly attributed this to finite loading! In calculating the infinite load—a prerequisite to finite loading in the IBM package—they had to develop some scheduling rules. The result of using these scheduling rules was to come up with shorter planning lead times than they had been using. Shortening the lead times reduced the input to the factory. Reducing the input dropped the backlogs. Dropping the backlogs cut the lead time. Now normally this would result in a *temporary reduction in lead time* because, in most companies, since they're used to working with the informal capacity planning system, the minute visual backlogs decrease, the output tends to drop off. But this company's production control manager, who is a pretty clever guy, had come up with a capacity control device very similar to Input/Output Control. He took the infinite load report, *discounted 40 percent of the backlog in the current period,* and then averaged that load out over the next 12 weeks. He then set this as a production plan and got the foremen working to this plan. The result: Having reduced input and controlled output, backlogs stayed down, lead time decreased. Finite loading had nothing whatsoever to do with the excellent results these people attained.

People often ask us how IBM could have presented the Finite Loading package in PICS if it isn't a legitimate technique. The answer is—it was an honest mistake. Finite loading looked good. We've got to remember that a lot of the computer people tend to favor the sophisticated. As Townsend said, "These people are complicators—not simplifiers." While blanket indictments like that are never fair, it certainly is true that data processing and systems people generally have favored the sophisticated approaches. The people who develop application programs for computer companies are usually systems people, not practitioners. It's hardly surprising that they would pick up something like finite loading, especially since the reaction of most practitioners to "Infinite Loading" was negative!

Our research this year, our discussions with a lot of people, indicates to us that *not one responsible professional we have talked with believes that finite loading is a valid scheduling and loading technique in a machine shop!*

I hasten to add that George and I both are very much in favor of the IBM PICS package. We favor standardization rather than reinventing the wheel. We applaud IBM for their outstanding contributions with these packages, such as the RPS or Material Requirements Planning portion of PICS. We have a number of clients who have used it and used it successfully. We are very much in favor of the infinite loading or "Capacity Requirements Planning" part of their capacity planning module in PICS, but we feel obligated to tell other practitioners that we simply cannot endorse finite loading as a valid production and inventory control technique.

Does that mean that finite loading will die? Hardly. There is a latent appeal to finite loading and the chances are that it will be with us for some time to come. There are three basic reasons for its appeal:

### 1. It's the Apparent Alternative to Infinite Loading.

Probably the biggest reason that finite loading was ever invented is because of that inappropriate term, "Infinite Loading." If the two choices are infinite loading and finite loading, obviously any man in his right mind is going to take the alternative of finite loading because infinite loading, by definition, just doesn't make sense. When we understand how a production and inventory control system fits together, we recognize that the actual "Finite Loading" is going to take place via the Master Schedule, not by some sophisticated detailed scheduling and loading algorithm.

Perhaps a more insidious reason for wanting to use finite loading was the basic misunderstanding of the relationship of the elements of production and inventory control because finite loading was an:

### 2. Apparent Way to Reschedule the Backlog.

Where there is a large amount of past due work in a machine load report, it's apparent that there's a need to reschedule. So it often looks to top people like the way to handle this is finite loading. Rescheduling that load will get that backlog out of there and put the load out in a realistic time frame. Unfortunately, they don't see how the pieces of the system fit together. Rescheduling the load in front of screw machine, for example, will only result in having to change the Master Schedule because screw machine parts won't be coming out as scheduled. They should have determined ahead of time what the capacity requirements were, and if they couldn't meet these capacity requirements, then the Master Schedule should have been changed ahead of time rather than after a large backlog had built up. So, finite loading seems like a way to reschedule the backlog when, in fact, that backlog is only really going to be rescheduled by changing the Master Schedule. Why not do it directly? Why go through all the nonsense of finite loading?

In the company I mentioned above where they were supposed to have finite loading working, they had to discount the infinite load report by a substantial amount in order to set up their actual capacity plan. Why did they have these large backlogs in the infinite load report? For a very simple reason —they had a Master Schedule that was feeding the Material Requirements Planning system and this Master Schedule was no longer valid. There was a lot of work in there that was late and had never been rescheduled, never put out in the time periods when it was really going to be produced. The result— a large past due backlog. *Finite loading for them was a mirage; it was an attempt to reschedule that backlog.* What a great way to assault the symptoms. The real disease was in the Master Schedule.

Of course, in the twilight of the age of naive sophistication, as I have chosen to call the early years of computer application, we cannot fail to recognize that finite loading has an appeal:

### 3. It Is Sophisticated.

You must remember that many people believe that the more sophisticated approach is the better one. This, of course, is nonsense. It usually results in getting systems so complicated that no flesh and blood mortals can use them intelligently and these systems soon crash down around the designer's ears. They never seem to recognize that if people don't understand systems, they won't use them intelligently.

Many of you know how I have been on the warpath against sophistication. How strongly I feel that this is one of the biggest single reasons for systems failure in most companies. *Sophistication as an end in itself is an immature preoccupation.* So often the man who develops a sophisticated technique doesn't really understand the problem. To express this, I have formulated "Wight's 7th Law: *WHENEVER PEOPLE DO NOT UNDERSTAND FUNDAMENTAL RELATIONSHIPS, THEIR SOLUTIONS TO BASIC PROBLEMS WILL BE OVER-SOPHISTICATED."*

Certainly finite loading falls into that category!

Finite loading violates another principle that is fundamental in designing systems: *SYSTEMS ARE TO SUPPORT PEOPLE, NOT TO SUPPLANT THEM.*

Finite loading attempts to build too much logic into the computer system. Most of it is trivial logic that doesn't really matter in the real world. Thus, the natural result is for people to throw up their hands and either obey it blindly or ignore it completely. People can understand the *intent* of systems; if the systems are "transparent," they can use them quite intelligently. The systems designer who feels that he is doing something smart by sophisticating the system has a lot to learn—the hard way! This is not to say that Capacity Requirements Planning and Input/Output Control give us precise control over a factory. It's very questionable that we ever will have precise scheduling and loading in the real world of factories. The objective is to come up with a system that's better than what we've got today. Many people tend to take the attitude that until they can solve all of the problems, they aren't very interested in solving any of them. It's well to remember:

## *BEST IS THE ENEMY OF BETTER.*

We suspect that finite loading will be around for a long time. Many people will try to do it just to prove that it can be done. There's no question that it can be done, the question is whether it's a worthwhile, practical technique. Everest is there—must we, therefore, climb Everest? It certainly is not a responsible business attitude to want to try to do things just for the sake of doing them when they have no practical value and there are better ways, simpler ways, of doing the same thing.

Let's review then, the apparent problems with the three techniques we've talked about:

1. **Infinite: Capacity Is Not Infinite.**
   Of course, it isn't, but the purpose of Infinite Loading—or better, Capacity Requirements Planning—is to determine what capacity is really needed.

2. **Finite: Extending Deliveries.**
   That's right. Loading to finite capacity will extend deliveries. As a result, the Master Schedule will have to be changed. But we don't need to go through all the gyrations of the sophisticated finite loading computation to determine that.

3. **Input/Output Control: Difficult to Control Input.**
   Controlling input is fine. But *controlling output* is the real important thing. Undoubtedly, too much emphasis was put on the subject of controlling input in some of the things that have been written on Input/Output Control. Perhaps a better name for it would have been Output/Input Control since *it is the only practical tool that we have seen for controlling capacity.* Planning what the input level should be and monitoring the total number of hours going into the downstream work center can give us valuable information. But the prime function of Input/Output Control is *capacity control.* It serves a purpose that no standard

94                                      © **American Production & Inventory Control Society**

production control technique really addressed.

Let's evaluate, then, the opinions we've arrived at about scheduling and loading techniques:

### 1. Infinite: Function Is "Capacity Requirements Planning."

The technique we used to call Infinite Loading should be called Capacity Requirements Planning and it should pick up the *planned orders* out of Material Requirements Planning to extend the planning horizon rather than just try to measure backlog. Obviously, no plant can be loaded to infinite capacity. This is a planning technique, not a loading technique.

### 2. Finite:

A. WORKS FOR ONE WORK CENTER.
B. MISGUIDED SOPHISTICATION IN A MACHINE SHOP.
C. LOAD LEVELED BY MASTER SCHEDULE.

There's no question but that one starting work center—or, as I've called them before, "gateway work centers" (indicating the first *significant* work center in the sequence) can be finite loaded. Work can't be precisely controlled going into all the subsequent work centers. There are too many other things that affect the flow of work into downstream work centers. A detailed finite load can be planned on paper. It certainly isn't going to work out that way in a factory.

Finite loading will tell us that certain items aren't going to be finished on time. The result: The Master Schedule must be changed. Actually, if the Capacity Requirements Plan is used, it can show us where capacity requirements exceed available capacity and where the Master Schedule needs to be changed without going through all the details and sophisticated calculation of finite loading. Remember that the load eventually will have to be leveled by changing the Master Schedule.

### 3. Input/Output: Function Is Capacity Control.

Input/Output Control is an excellent technique. People have used it and had very good results. The fact that it focuses attention on backlog and, consequently, lead time, is one of its greatest attributes. But, in essence, it's a capacity control device. It's a way to monitor the capacity plan to see if the production rates required to meet the Master Schedule are actually being attained.

We've spent a good deal of time in the past year gathering information, visiting companies, learning more about Finite Loading. We went into this with an open mind. Certainly the last thing we want to do is tell people that a technique isn't practical and later have it proved to be practical. We hate to take a negative stand on anything. It's much easier to just ignore it and make believe it doesn't exist, but we felt a responsibility. A lot of people have asked us about Finite Loading. A lot of people have asked us to take a stand to help them to understand it better. We have done our homework, in our opinion, and we have taken our stand. We don't believe that Finite Loading is a valid technique for scheduling and loading a machine shop. Certainly this doesn't say that any company that wishes to support pure research shouldn't pursue Finite Loading. For companies that cannot indulge in this luxury, the mirage of Finite Loading should be avoided.

### George W. Plossl

To summarize, we've been discussing Input/Output Control, Infinite and Finite Loading. We have concluded that Input/Output might more accurately be called Output/Input Control and that Infinite Loading is really Capacity Requirements Planning. We seriously question that finite loading is a valid technique. The best that can be said for it is that it may be a fine-tuning device for very special applications.

We have worked hard to dispel some of the fog surrounding this important area of production management. Production and inventory control is obviously no longer a collection of loosely related techniques. There are underlying principles and sound techniques for applying these principles. It is now possible to see how a plant can be kept on schedule with a priority planning system that works. Capacity Requirements Planning, control of output and a dynamic priority control system to respond to real world changes.

Keeping on schedule requires three basic actions:
1. Load leveling via the Master Schedule. You must smooth out the peaks and valleys as much as possible and scheduling only what you're capable of producing.
2. Some jobs must be started early. You must reach ahead either through the Master Schedule or by individual starting operations and release some jobs *before* the planning system says it is necessary. The plant must be fed at a level rate with a balanced mix of work.
3. You need a two-way priority system which recognizes jobs needed later as well as those needed earlier. Tom Putnam of Marken Corporation at our Sunapee conference stated this very clearly. He said, "You must push out the orders you don't need."

Jim Burlingame of Twin Disc in his article, "Finite Capacity:" in the 2nd Quarter, 1970 issue of the APICS Journal, *Production and Inventory Management*, stated the basic fact as well as it can be said, "The answer to a capacity problem is not to retard the job but to find a way to do it." The vital need is for adequate capacity, not sophisticated computer finite loading and scheduling programs.

MULTI-PLANT MRP

Stanley C. Plzak, CPIM
Mercury Marine

William A. Thurwachter, CPIM, PE
Arthur Andersen & Co.

The objectives of this paper are to:

- Define the integrated multi-plant operations planning and control environment.
- Outline specific operating characteristics.
- Identify system design alternatives that support multi-plant operations planning and control.
- Outline the approach as is being installed at Mercury Marine.

This paper is the result of specific installed application experience as well as numerous discussions with respected consulting sources in the manufacturing industry.

## INTRODUCTION

Multi-plant operations planning and control is a subject which has very little support in current literature. A great deal has been published on the "Closed-Loop" approach for planning and controlling operations, but the literature typically focuses on the independent, or self-contained operating unit-- one plant.

Recently, there have been numerous articles outlining the benefits of using material requirements planning concepts to support the distribution function. Specifically, these articles address maintaining the supply/demand relationships throughout the distribution network to manage finished goods inventory flows from the plant to the customer. Distribution Requirements Planning, as it is labeled, can support a multi-level inventory network with perhaps, central stores, distribution centers and local warehouses. Normally, one production source is recognized for the finished item.

What has been recognized in distribution, but not yet universally addressed in production are the multiple pockets of inventory within an integrated operating organization. Our attention in production materials management has been focused towards the self-contained operating unit. And why not? The literature and available manufacturing software are targeted at the single plant environment.

This paper, however, deals with the management concerns and system design considerations when dealing in a complex multi-level manufacturing inventory environment. This paper does not attempt to identify or defend the strategic considerations for developing an interdependent manufacturing network, but it does identify and support design approaches to plan and control the material flow.

## MULTI-PLANT ENVIRONMENT

Generally speaking, there are two ways to organize multi-plant operations. The first is a product orientation where each plant within a company is organized to support the product(s) manufactured at that location. The majority of the manufacturing technology required to produce the product is available under one roof. The product approach allows the plant to be set up as a self-contained profit center with the local autonomy to plan and control the operation. The reporting relationship to the corporate entity is typically financial alone. However, central marketing and purchasing support may be controlled through corporate as well. The product organization approach does not eliminate but normally reduces any schedule dependency between plants within the company. This is the organization structure that is the target of today's technical literature and software.

The second organizational approach is by manufacturing process. Under this approach plants are structured and managed by various production disciplines such as assembly, forging, casting, machining, fabrication, etc. Products within the process organization cross many plant boundaries to become end items. The plants within the process network are all dependent on the final assembly schedules. In effect, they are captive vendors under the control of the corporation. Under these circumstances, the plants are more effectively managed as cost centers. The production planning as well as marketing functions are all central. The commitment of each plant's resource is not a local decision. Rather, the decision should be communicated through the formal "closed-loop" requirements planning approach. It is this organization, the process structure, that this paper addresses. Multi-plant operations planning and control supports tightly integrated production facilities which have strong schedule dependencies on one another.

In reality, there are numerous organizations that fall within these two extremes. The amount of interplant schedule dependency and some inventory planning considerations will determine the approach for developing the necessary support systems.

## MULTI-PLANT OPERATING CHARACTERISTICS

PLANNING APPROACH - When applying MRP concepts to a multi-plant environment, it pays to remember how a business is planned as a self-contained operating unit. Planning begins at the top with production planning and master scheduling and is then communicated to the shop and vendors in one planning cycle.

It was not too many years ago when practitioners discussed the merits of conversational MRP--material planners intervening at each planning level to deal with each level's exceptions before continuing the planning process. Since that period, we have learned how to control the stability of the plan at all levels, using the master schedule. You won't hear many people today discussing the merits of conversational MRP.

Nevertheless, the immediate temptation in a multi-plant environment is to stop the planning cycle at the plant boundary and pass the demand as an order to the master scheduling function in the next plant. This is conversational planning. With captive plants, dependent on the end item master schedule, stopping the planning process delays the communication of the formal plan. The objective in multi-plant MRP is to be able to communicate the current master schedule throughout the plant network and to the vendors in one planning cycle.

To emphasize this point, consider a multi-plant network three levels deep consisting of assembly, machining and casting plants in that order. If our network is running on a weekly regeneration stopping at each plant boundary, we have added two weeks of delay in reporting the impact of master schedule changes to vendors supplying the casting plant. This delay is increased if the machining plant must perform any operations on component part inserts for the casting plant. Placing the machining plant as a supplier to the casting plant for inserts in effect makes the conversational planning structure four levels deep.

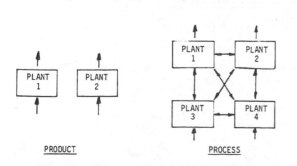

PRODUCT          PROCESS

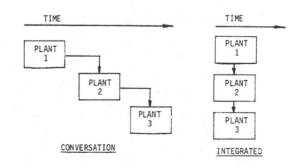

CONVERSATION          INTEGRATED

Routing the production of a product to and from the same plant introduces another subtle problem for conversational planning. The schedules in the plant that perform the preliminary operations and then subsequent operations after the product returns as an assembly will never be in phase within the plant. They will be out of phase by the number of plants and planning cycles between the first contact with the material, and its eventual return. Conversational MRP not only delays the communication of true priorities, it can confuse relative priorities as well. This approach is an excellent example of why users complain that the "system" cannot keep up with the business. This planning approach places the plants at the bottom of the network, multiple weeks behind real priorities and effectively decoupled from the master schedule.

Introducing the element of net change processing to presumably allow more planning cycles within the same time period will reduce the communication time from the top of the network to the bottom. However, under conversational mode between plants, the delay still exists as well as improper schedule synchronization in plants where the material departs and returns.

The prudent approach to planning in a tightly integrated multi-plant network is straight through, top to bottom, one planning cycle. Effectively, this deals with the entire organization as if it were a self-contained unit for the purposes of planning and maintaining valid priorities. The typical reaction to this approach from plant management in dependent plants is the loss of control over the commitment of their capacity.

First, the plant manager is not responsible for the commitment of his capacity; it is committed through the master schedule in the end item assembly plants by corporate management. Second, this reaction from a plant manager suggests that he has been accused of poor resource utilization in the past, more often than not, resulting from a poorly managed master schedule at the top. Third, the dependent plant is probably being treated as a profit center which is a further incongruity given his captive vendor status.

Nevertheless, on an exception basis, there may be specific parts, or groups of parts, which utilize a specific resource that should be master scheduled in a dependent plant.

This would be necessary to stabilize schedules in dependent plants where there is little flexibility. Any end item changes would have to be proceeded by an analysis of the inflexible dependent plant schedules. Remember, master schedule really means manual schedule, so for these types of parts we want heavy analyst control. But it comes with a cost. We have inserted a conversation point in the planning process. This slows the communication to all planning levels below.

INVENTORY PLANNING - Traditional MRP systems can support multiple stocking locations for a part. With discipline used in assigning location identification--multiple warehouses (plants) can be supported. However, when analyzing the supply/demand pattern for a part, normally the sum of the inventory, in all locations, is considered available for netting. This is without regard for geographic location, or the intended use for the inventory. Logically mixing production stocks with service inventories intended for automated picking is a poor planning approach.

To overcome this shortcoming, the following information must be maintained by plant:

- Inventory
- Gross Requirements (Demands)
- Released and planned open orders (Supply)
- Part Source
- Part Netting Sequence

With this setup, MRP now plans by item within plant and plans orders depending on the part source within the plant. Part sources for a plant can be make, buy, or _interplant_. MRP must generate interplant orders to transfer demand from a use location to a supply location. This also explains the need for assigning a planning sequence within an item. Use locations must be planned before supply locations. This ensures all demand has been netted and transferred to the supply source before scheduling the supply.

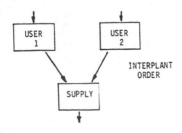

INTERPLANT ORDER

Following an approach like this allows for the formal recognition of the intransit lead time for interplant orders. Consequently, an intransit order can be netted as a time phased scheduled receipt. When plant locations are many transportation days apart, it is important to handle intransit inventory as a scheduled receipt, especially when considering production order availability checking.

This approach of identifying and planning for inventory by part/plant allows for production lot size considerations in the supplying locations as well as interplant lot size and safety stock considerations in the using locations.

Planning inventory flows by location sets up the system to support integrated planning as well as local accountability. In a multi-plant environment, responsibility for a part should be set up by plant. This would cover:

- material planner
- buyer/expeditor
- inventory accuracy
- lead time maintenance
- order policies
- schedule maintenance

Local accountability and control is absolutely necessary to maintain the reliability of the information. This also identifies the need for local materials management expertise in order for the formal system to perform beyond the perimeter of the central (corporate) materials management group.

MULTIPLE SOURCES & STATUS - MRP is a discrete planning tool. It must be provided with the necessary information to plan the correct order type (manufacturing, interplant, or purchase) and to place the demand against the correct source (within the plant, between plants, or a vendor). Normally, MRP systems are developed to support single part status, make or buy, and that implies single source (within the plant, or a vendor).

With multi-plant planning, the status of the part can vary by plant. A purchased part in one plant may be manufactured by another plant, as well as used in a third plant, but sourced from another which would give it an interplant status.

The source for a part will vary by plant as well. It is not uncommon, and in fact desirable, to have purchase items dual sourced. Applying the scheduled release concept to each vendor for the part requires allocating the demand between the sources. This splits the schedule for the part to the vendors and allows for schedule maintenance on any replanning for the part within the affected plant.

With the ability to recognize and plan multiple sources by part/plant, demand can be partitioned between purchased and manufactured, purchase and interplant, interplant and manufactured, multiple vendors and multiple plants. This capability works well for subcontracting work normally manufactured completely in one facility when demand exceeds local resources.

With the addition of one more concept, we have a very complete multiple source/status working model, source date effectivity. Sources can be defined over the planning horizon as effective from a date, to a date with a percent split of the planned demand. This will support phasing out a vendor and phasing in the manufacturing of a part. Vendor splits on dual sourced parts can be proportioned, or demand can be shifted from one vendor to another over the planning horizon.

INTRANSIT SUPPORT - Intransit inventory has traditionally been considered available for netting with the same status as on hand material. With multi-plant inventory transfers, the intransit quantity should be viewed as a scheduled receipt. This makes the material available to the receiving plant on the due date into stores.

For on hand balance maintenance, stock issues and stock receipts track the flow of inventory through stores. With the interplant order to transfer stock between locations, two additional transactions are required, dock ship and dock receipt. This means material sent from the supply plant is first a stock issue, dock ship, dock receipt and finally a stock receipt.

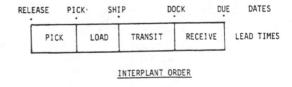

INTERPLANT ORDER

This moves material from the supply plant stockroom, to staged for shipping, shipped to intransit, dock receipt to inspection and then counted into stock. In this case, there are four reporting points to control the movement of interplant material. Count discrepancies will occur. How should they be treated?

1. The supplying plant cannot ship more than was issued.

2. The ordering plant cannot receive at the dock more than was shipped.

3. The ordering plant will be able to count and accept any amount into stock. However, if the ordering plant's stock count disagrees with the dock receipt amount, the discrepancy will be used to adjust the dock receipt quantity, dock shipment quantity and the supply plant stockroom issue. No adjustment should be made to the supply plant's on hand balance, but the part should be scheduled for cycle count to check the accuracy of the stock balance. The automatic count reconciliation should be posted to history to support the stockroom audit trail.

Handling interplant count reconcilations this way focuses the attention for stockroom record accuracy where it should be. Not on the shipping receiving docks, but at the controlled stores access locations.

Inserting an order relationship between two plants introduces a problem if the material is not moved as a discrete lot (the order quantity). The problem exists when parts produced by the supplying plant are shipped as completed only to be issued to the floor on receipt at the ordering plant. This is flow scheduling. Traditional MRP would schedule the source order to be complete prior to the shipment of any material. In an integrated environment, the preferred flow of material may involve shipping production as it is completed by the supply location for immediate consumption in the use location. This requires the scheduled orders to be overlapped between the two plants in order to maintain valid priorities. This is similar to operation overlap in shop floor scheduling and can be labeled order overlap in material planning.

This has typically been accomplished with a lead time adjust factor in the product structure record. But that approach does not readily support the interplant transfer. Rather, the solution to planning the overlap comes through balancing the scheduled demand rates in the using plant with the demonstrated production rates from the supplying plant.

## SYSTEMS ARCHITECTURE

Early attempts to support multi-plant MRP followed two basic approaches: (1) separate data bases, one system for each plant or (2) one data base for all plants that effectively ignored the characteristics attributed to multi-plant planning and control.

Separate data bases require treating supply plants like vendors (placing purchase orders) and use plants like customers (receiving purchase orders). Schedule changes between locations must be communicated externally from the system adding to the planning delay. Separate data bases results in conversational MRP and its characteristic poor response.

Combining all plants in one planning system with a single set of gross requirements, orders and inventory balances for a part allowed for establishing the overall material plan, but prevented local control and priority maintenance.

There are a number of alternatives that can effectively support the multi-plant operating characteristics outlined in this paper.

## SUPPLIER/USER PART SUFFIX

This approach is extremely flexible and supports the data relationships necessary in multi-plant planning and control. The key to the data is structured as follows:

part number/supplier/user

The material flow network is structured in the bill of material file while the item master contains a record for each part/supplier/user combination. This approach uses the traditional manufacturing data base structure with a single bill of material and item master file. But with the addition of the suffix to the data base key, the entire multi-plant network structure can be superimposed on the manufacturing bill to direct the planning process.

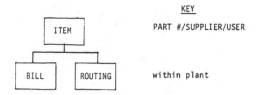

KEY

PART #/SUPPLIER/USER

within plant

This approach results in deep bills of material, for each plant transfer requires a structure relationship. If an item is manufactured in multiple locations, a set of bills is required for each location, with the appropriate supplier/user suffix. Structuring bills in this manner requires some special logic to retrieve a bill from the system to resemble the engineer's view, effectively dropping the suffix and compressing the absolute number of levels.

The advantage to this approach is it can be supported by traditional MRP logic and provide:

● Bill of material effectivity control by plant.
● Source effectivity by plant.
● Planning demand splits by source.

The major disadvantages appear to be:

● The unfavorable impact on processing time given the large files.
● The engineer's reaction to the bill of material configuration which includes all the levels identifying the interplant transfers.

## ROUTING FILE

An intermediate step which accommodates a number of the multi-plant operating considerations focuses on the routing file. Using this approach normally assumes that no lot sizing or inventory netting is necessary between plant boundaries. Rather, a lot which begins in one plant remains in process as it is shipped to the next plant.

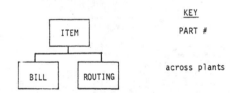

KEY

PART #

across plants

This approach still allows for central planning and local control but assumes the production activities in the company are predominantly "lot for lot". The plants involved are most likely treated as cost centers, so an inventory transfer of in process material will have to be identified.

Inventory netting for a part is performed across all plants. As long as all locations are close together, or inventory is typically used or supplied in only one location, the routing file approach does not introduce an operating problem.

The mechanics necessary to support this approach require assigning each work center to a plant and then developing the operation scheduling logic to properly plan for the interplant transfer. Depending on the circumstances, the operation the material is used on may be coded on the bill so that pick lists can be properly prepared by plant to marshal the material from adjacent stores.

The major disadvantage of this approach is the formal planning mechanism does not directly control the replenishment of stock by location. Consequently, an inventory dispatch function is necessary to logistically maneuver stock to its point of use.

## PLANT/SOURCE SEGMENT

Without trying to reinvent the wheel, but nevertheless attempt to develop the data relationships necessary to support multi-plant MRP, the plant/source segment scheme was developed. This is the approach presently being installed at Mercury Marine.

The functional structure of the data base for engineering is traditional in that each manufactured part has a bill of material. Each part in the system has an item master that includes skeletal information about the part, like description and unit of measure. However, subordinate to the item master is a plant segment which contains plant inventory planning and control data. This data includes on hand balances, intransit data, planning lead times, order policy rules, MRP planning sequence, cycle count schedules, issue control codes, etc. Subordinate to the plant segment is the source segment. This segment identifies the part status within a plant: make, buy, or interplant; and the source for this plant. In addition, the source segment indicates the percent of the total demand to be allocated to each source and the date effective time horizon.

KEY

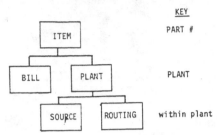

PART #

PLANT

within plant

Perhaps the chief advantage of this approach over the Supplier/User suffix is that the bill file retains its traditional parent/component relationships. This keeps engineering file volumes down as well as the number of item master records. This will have a favorable impact on data processing efficiency.

A disadvantage is that only one structure relationship exists for a manufacturing assembly. Bill of material date effectivity control is a shared responsibility if simultaneous manufacturing of an assembly is occurring. On the other hand, this supports configuration control of the structure across plants.

Perhaps a subtle point, but this approach requires a part number definition at each plant boundary, whereas the routing file approach does not require redefinition as long as the lot integrity is maintained.

SUMMARY

Understanding how to plan and control complex manufacturing environments grows each year. Applying the formal concepts of "closed-loop" operations planning and control to the inter-dependent multi-plant environment can properly guide the system development and management approach.

- Top down planning and feedback control.
- Controlling company resource commitment through responsible production planning and master scheduling.
- Local control and accountability.

All the techniques discussed in the systems architecture section support the single company planning cycle necessary to maintain the integrity of the priority control system. Perhaps the general solution to controlling multi-plant operations planning and control is a combination of the Plant/Source segment and routing file approach. This would allow lot sizing at plant boundaries when necessary or continuous flow between plants under a lot-for-lot situation. This combination would maintain the integrity of the manufacturing bill of material by eliminating the need to establish part number identification of what may appear to be artificial control points.

BIOGRAPHY

Stanley C. Plzak is the Material Control Manager - Manufacturing for Mercury Marine, Fond du Lac, Wisconsin. Formerly, Plzak was a Senior Systems Analyst at Mercury Marine involved with the design and implementation of manufacturing systems. Prior to joining Mercury, he was involved in distribution planning and inventory control at Baxter Travenol Inc., Deerfield, Illinois. He holds a B.S.E.E. from the University of Wisconsin (Madison), and an M.B.A. from the University of Wisconsin (Oshkosh). Plzak is certified at the Fellow level by APICS.

* * * *

William A. Thurwachter is a management consultant in the Administrative Services division of Arthur Andersen & Co.- Milwaukee office. He received his B.S. in Mechanical Engineering and his M.B.A. from the University of Wisconsin (Madison). Thurwachter is a member of APICS and is an active speaker for the local chapter as well as supporting his firm's internal education programs as a faculty member. He is a certified fellow and is registered as a Professional Engineer in the state of Wisconsin.

Reprinted from APICS *Planning and Control Seminar Proceedings,* 1982.

### USING THE MRP OUTPUT
### John F. Proud
### Xerox Computer Services

## Material Planning - A Real Challenge

Obtaining the material needed to produce the product is a problem that many manufacturing companies face every day. To further complicate the issue, the right material must be obtained in the right quantity and at the right time.

As members within the material organizations perform their various functions, several manufacturing problems arise and must be addressed on a daily basis. But all too often, we find ourselves attacking symptom of these manufacturing problems instead of the true problem. Take for example low inventory turns. Many companies attempt to attack this sympton by ordering the inventory be cut 10% across the board; shut down the receiving dock is the word that bounces off the factory walls. And what about part shortages? To solve what is perceived to be the problem, pick lists are released to the stockroom early which allows the pickers to pull parts early thereby identifying which parts are short and need expediting.

What a wonderful life! -- Chasing parts around the shop floor just so some scheduled due dates can be met. All that energy spent trying to solve common symptoms of manufacturing problems. Doesn't it make more sense to identify what the real problems are and then expend our energies on solving them so we can move on to the numerous meaningful tasks which lie ahead.

Let's step back for a minute and look at the causes of these problems. There are several, but a few major ones are listed below:

- No visibility into what is needed, when it is needed, and in what quantity.

- Credibility gap with our vendors (both outside and inside) -- they react when we start expediting.

- Working on the wrong priorities -- too busy fire fighting to solve real problems.

- Lack of disciplines within our own shop that lead to using incomplete or inaccurate data to make decisions.

- Don't have the proper tools to do the job right or just don't understand how and when to use the tools.

## The Need for a Better Planning Method

If the manufacturing problem causes can be identified, surely we should be able to define some potential solutions to the problems. If the problem is caused by lack of visibility, one solution would be to obtain the visibility into what and how much material along with when it is required. This can be done by successfully implementing a Material Requirements Planning (MRP) system. If a credibility gap exists between us and our vendors, let's look for ways to bridge the gap and establish good, solid communication channels. Again, the MRP system projects future needs which can be shared with our vendors. The discipline or record accuracy problems need to be addressed so as to provide the decision makers information required to make good, solid decisions.

These problems can be solved. Many companies have been sold on MRP concepts for long time. The logic used seems to be sound. It briefly states that the demand required to build the company's products should be equally offset by a supply of the material required to produce them. In other words the objective of Material Requirements Planning is to maintain a balance between the requirements (demand) and replenishments (supply).

Data Processing has successfully written the logic that can be used by a computer to generate valuable MRP reports. These reports inform the planners what action needs to be taken to balance the planning system. Now, you say, we're getting somewhere -- a savior for the material planning professional (Figure 1). *LAST PAGE

If you study the figure, it can be seen that the system plan is in balance. Now, what is the next step? Yes, that's right -- I asked, now what do we do? The system's plan can be in perfect balance on paper; the shop may be a different story. Management truly is looking for a saviour, and many firms believe MRP is just that. But, how many organizations have truly been saved? Not many, to say the least! Again, the MRP logic seems sound - so what's the problem?

## Pitfalls of MRP Installation

Many companies have installed a Material Requirements Planning system. In relation to the number who have tried, few have successfully implemented it. There is a difference. Installing the system means that Data Processing has it operating on the computer; implementing means the material planning function is using the output to schedule the priorities of the company. The successful implementor has avoided

the five common pitfalls which can lead to failure:

1. People just don't understand what MRP is and what it can do
   Lack of orientation into the working of MRP and the use of the output.

2. False sense of security
   Computer does the arithmetic; people make it happen.

3. Poor lot sizing policies
   Attempts made to bring everything in too soon because of lot sizes at higher assembly levels asking for all the material.

4. Overstated Master Schedule
   Allowing the sales forecast to directly drive requirements down into priority planning system.

5. Inaccurate data being used to generate decision making information
   Bills-of-material, on hand balances, and open order statuses are not properly monitored or maintained to assure credible input.

These five failure points would seem to be logical and easy to understand. But getting everyone in the company, including direct and indirect users to understand, is a hard thing to accomplish. Everyone installing or thinking of installing a MRP system should pay careful attention to these pitfalls and do whatever is necessary to avoid them. Concentration and effort must be directed at the things that will make the system work for the people.

## Requirements for Success

To be a successful MRP user, five key functions need to be understood and in place (see Figure 2). It would not appear that each point would require much explanation. It is the lack of understanding one or more of these functional areas which cause MRP installation to go astray. Things can be in place ( accurate records, sound logic, meaningful policies) but, if the company's demand is an unrealistic Master Schedule, the resulting output will be an overloaded factory which will be unsuccessful in meeting the plan. By the same token, if a realistic plan is input into Material Requirements Planning and the input records used are inaccurate, there is no way the computer can generate an accurate priority plan. This plan is the main planning tool for the material organization and must state both realistic and accurate information. The inventory management policies that are loaded into the system are as important since they impact the order recommendations.

Of course, it goes without saying that the logic used by the computer must be sound and error free. It also needs to be pointed out that the conversion of data into planning information should be done in a user friendly manner. To say it another way, the output needs to be easy to understand and use.

With these four areas defined, the fifth and most important requirement for success -- PEOPLE -- needs to be discussed. This is where most companies fall down. What is needed is people (planners, schedulers, and management) who truly understand the information available and how to use it! Questions, such as "When should we reschedule?", "When can the plan be trusted?", and "When should action be taken to check out an input?" need to be answered. The list is long. Any planner can handle the easy action messages such as "Order material this week." The tough ones -- "The vendor cannot deliver on time, what do we do?" -- are the real test of a good planner. Solving these problems using MRP is where the real payback is obtained.

## Understanding the Tool — MRP

Before we can address using the output for material requirements planning, we need to understand how it is created and the proper time to use it. Figure 3 is the Manufacturing Closed Loop separated into by time zones: short, intermediate, and long range.

In the future zone such tools as Production Planning, Resource Requirements Planning and Rough-Cut Capacity Planning are of the greatest value. Short term, our interest lies more with Shop Floor and Input/Output Control. Material Requirements Planning, coupled with Master Production Scheduling (MPS), are the tools commonly used to set the priority plan across zones 1 and 2. As we will see later, MRP will formulate the plan across these zones and then direct the planner's attention to the immediate action necessary.

## REQUIREMENTS FOR SUCCESS

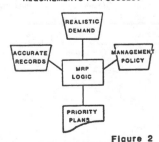

**Figure 2**

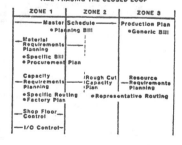

TIME-PHASING THE CLOSED LOOP

**Figure 3**

With an understanding of when MRP is of value to us, let's turn our attention to the report format and review the processing logic used. This logic is not difficult. The basic function is to create a plan that balances the requirements against replenishments. Figure 4 is a general flow chart showing the interfaces in the MRP application

**MRP PROCESSING LOGIC**

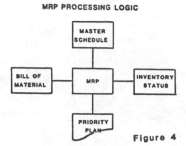

**Figure 4**

As was discussed above, the successful MRP system has - a realistic Master Schedule as its statement of demand. This input is extending by the bill-of-material quantities through a technique known as the explosion process. The result provides us with the gross requirements for each component required to build the product.

Once the gross requirements are known, the netting process takes place. During this phase the gross requirements are matched against the on hand balance as well as the on order status. By taking these two elements into consideration, net requirements can be determined. At this point the computer needs to ask two questions: (1) Is there a net need? and (2) Do any timing problems exist? The answer may require planning action to be taken.

**MRP FORMAT**

PART NUMBER Assembly
LEAD TIME 4 Weeks
LOT SIZE 15
SAFETY STOCK None
SERVICE REQUIREMENTS None

| | | PERIODS | | | | | | | |
|---|---|---|---|---|---|---|---|---|---|
| | 0 | 1 | 2 | 3 | 4 | 5 | 6 | 7 | 8 |
| PROJECTED GROSS REQUIREMENTS | | | 15 | | 15 | | 15 | | |
| SCHEDULED RECEIPTS | | | 12 | | 12 | | | | |
| PROJECTED AVAILABLE BALANCE ON HAND = 10 | 10 | 10 | 7 | 7 | 4 | 4 | -11 | -11 | -11 |
| PLANNED ORDER RELEASE | | | 15 | | | | | | |

PART NUMBER Component
LEAD TIME 7 Weeks
LOT SIZE 25
SAFETY STOCK 5
SERVICE REQUIREMENTS 40/Per 8

| | | PERIODS | | | | | | | |
|---|---|---|---|---|---|---|---|---|---|
| | 0 | 1 | 2 | 3 | 4 | 5 | 6 | 7 | 8 |
| PROJECTED GROSS REQUIREMENTS | | | 30 | | | | 15 | | 40 |
| SCHEDULED RECEIPTS | 8 | | 25 | | 25 | | 25 | | |
| PROJECTED AVAILABLE BALANCE ON HAND = 9 | 12 | 12 | -18 | 7 | 7 | 32 | 17 | 42 | -2 |
| PLANNED ORDER RELEASE | | 25 | | | | | | | |

**Figure 5**

Figure 5 is an example of a manually prepared MRP report for two parts, one an assembly and the other a component that goes into the assembly. The assembly planning sheet is pretty straight forward. It is a stocked part with a four (4) week lead time and has a fixed lot size of 15 units. The first line shows the gross requirements for the assembly to be 15 units every other week starting with week 2. The second line displays the scheduled receipts. It can be seen that two orders (manufacturing orders) are scheduled to be received in week 2 and week 4. Both orders are for twelve units which differs from the presently recommended lot size of fifteen. This is certainly permissible in MRP. The lot size policy is used for recommendations and can be overridden, if necessary.

The net available line is calculated by MRP and displays the projected inventory balance minus safety stock. As long as this line remains positive, no replenishing action is necessary. When a negative quantity is encountered (eg. period 6) or the positive quantity exceeds the inventory policy established, an out-of-balance condition is detected. It is at this point the MRP system reacts by generating computer planned orders or reschedule messages. These system controlled orders (computer planned) make up the data which appears on the last line.

Since the system recognized a net need of 11 units in period 6, a computer planned order was released for 15 (minimum lot size) in period 2 (offsetting for planned lead time) to bring the system back into balance. This computer planned order will now be used to create gross requirement for the lower level parts. In our example two components are required for each assembly. Therefore, the order for 15 is multiplied by 2 giving a projected gross requirement of 30. In addition to this requirement, the figure shows two additional gross requirements for the component. The 15 required in period 6 were created as a result of the explosion from another assembly. The 40 appearing in period 8 reflect a service demand which has been placed on the component. One of the powers of an MRP system is that pulls all the requirements for a component part together so the entire planning for all requirements is done once.

Since the component has a starting balance of 9 units, five of which are tagged as safety stock, the starting net available is determined by taking the 9 on hand minus the 5 safety stock plus the scheduled receipt of 8 (past due). The netting logic is the same as used on the assembly above, but the required action is quite different.

**Planner Messages**

The MRP system is designed to balance the plan on paper and recommend planner action which needs to be taken. It is vital that the user of an MRP system analyze these recommendations and take the appropriate action necessary. MRP logic generates computer planned orders (CPO) to balance the system when necessary. In order to balance the real world (requirements against replenishments), computer generated orders need to be converted into manufacturing and purchase orders. This action is required as CPO's approach the current time period (see the CPO for 25 in period 1). To call the planner's attention to this required action, a planned order message is generated.

Reschedules are certainly not uncommon in the manufacturing environment. The figure shows three scheduled receipts where a reschedule message would be generated. The scheduled receipt in period 3 is really required in period 2 to satisfy the projected shortage. The two scheduled receipts in period 5 and 7 can be moved out because they are not needed until future time periods.

Another exception message is to highlight past dues. The scheduled receipt of 8 in the past due column indicates that an order has not arrived in the stockroom on its due date. This exception requires some action to put the plan back into balance. Not uncommon to MRP system users is when a planned order release falls in a past due column. Assume for a minute if this component had an 8 week lead time instead of 7. The computer planned order (planned release date) would fall past due or in essence cut off one week's lead time to secure the material. The planner message would be "inadequate lead time".

The cancel exception message is used to suggest dropping a replenishment. This would happen if the spares requirement in period 8 were taken out. The system would recognize the fact that the scheduled receipt for 25 in period 7 is no longer required since the balance at the end of period 6 is sufficient to cover all remaining requirements through the planning horizon.

**Exceptions Using Sensitivity**

These planner exceptions or action messages are a key part of the MRP system output. They must be used in order to get the expected payback from the system. If the volume of action messages overpowers the planner, much of the action required may not get done. To assist the planner in focusing their attention on the items with the greatest payback, sensitivity logic can be built into the system.

Sensitivity logic can be applied to both reschedule in and out messages. It can be by direct time or percentage of lead time. In any case it should be handled carefully and controlled by the planner. The general objective of using any sensitivity logic is to decrease the number of insignificant exception messages.

An example of using sensitivity would be to screen and <u>not</u> report any action that requests the planner to reschedule orders for short durations of time (ie. one day). The moving of the order for one day could cause disruption to the vendor or shop and certainly would not be good use of the planner's time. This time duration can be fixed as shown or variable by using a percentage of lead time.

A reschedule-in message is generated following a negative net available position. However, when the scheduled receipt is planned within a few days of an anticipated shortage, a reschedule-in message may not be desired.

If no requirements exist for a scheduled receipt, a reschedule-out message is generated. A search can be made to determine if the scheduled receipt would be consumed within a resaonable amount of time (fixed days or percentage of lead time).

Another way to limit the exception messages is to code selected orders as "non-movable." This coding would notify the system not to report exceptions against the order. An example would be to order more material than required for strike protection.

**Material Planning Zones**

The material planner is a key resource and their time must be effectively used. Material planning information can effectively be used in three planning zones: past, present, and future. The primary planning zone is identified as the present zone which normally covers the product's end-to-end lead time. It is within this zone that the MRP output is most effective (see Figure 6).

Within the present planning zone is the exception window . This window identifies the length of time when ordering action will be considered. It could be used to place sensitivity on reschedule messages, although this is not common. The exception window is normally defined to cover the time between MRP runs. This becomes extremely important in a regenerative system.

**MATERIAL PLANNING ZONES**

| | TODAY | | |
|---|---|---|---|
| PART SHORTAGES | EXCEPTIONS | MRP | POTENTIAL EXCESS |
| PAST | EXCEPTIONS | PRESENT | FUTURE |

**Figure 6**

Beyond the planning horizon is the future time zone. What the planner wants to control this zone is potential excess stock. Zone one is for past due requirements and replenishments. MRP does a good job highlighting past due requirements with its pegging capability. To further assist the planner in working the past due receipts, a part shortage report is necessary. This report identifies the part which is short, the order which requires it, and all purchasing or manufacturing data associated with the short part.

## MRP Output

The payback from implementing any MRP system is determined by what the material planner does with the output. This output can be displayed in two basic formats: horizontal by buckets and vertical by date. In both cases general part data is commonly displayed across the top of the page. Information such as part number, description, stocking location, planner, buyer, value classification, lead time, order policy, order multiples, safety stock and cost arm the planner with valuable facts to aid in the decision making process.

The main body of the bucket report (See Figure 7) is a matrix that has weekly information. The data presented is similar to what we saw in the manual report -- gross requirements, scheduled receipts, net available, and planned order releases. Figure 7 is a sample MRP report for a Base Assembly, part number 2100-2002. This is stocked part that has a lead time of 4 weeks and fixed lot size of 400. Currently there are 445 units in stock and no safety stock has been planned.

### MRP BUCKET REPORT

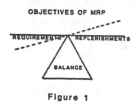

**Figure 7**

The report shows a positive projected net available until week 3/29 when it turns negative and continues to go negative; this identifies a net need. The MRP system reacted by placing a computer planned order for 400 in the current period (offsetting for 4 weeks lead time). An action message "ORDER" has been generated to alert the planner as to the recommended action. The planner should release a manufacturing order this week with a due date of 3/29.

### MRP VERTICAL REPORT

**Figure 8**

Figure 8 displays the MRP information in a vertical format by date. This type of system is generally called a bucketless MRP system. The report can be divided into three sections. The left hand side of the report contains the part information required by the planner to aid in making decisions. The remainder of the report contains the replenishment and requirement data. If the report were separated by the order date, all replenishments for the part would be to the left of the order date while the requirements are to the right.

These requirements and replenishments are sequenced by date with a running net available on the far right hand side of the page. Depending on this projected availability, the system recommends the action required on an exception report. This exception report is used as the primary planning report with the vertical detail available on an as needed basis (eg. on a CRT output device).

In addition to the traditional MRP output, reports which extend the quantities by dollars can be extremely valuable. Simply by extending the purchasing data, a cash flow projection can be generated. By dollarizing the projected inventory balances, we can analyze our future inventory investment today. And by extending the firm and planned production orders, we can project for the production cost over the entire planning horizon.

## Expected Results

The beginning of this paper identified some symptoms of common manufacturing problems. If an MRP system is successfully implemented, the available information will permit the planner to attack some of the true problems, and not just the symptoms.

If the planners really do the job, the company can realize a reduction in inventory by properly timing the receipt of material. The cost of this material can be reduced by negotiating long term contracts with several scheduled delivery dates. Improvement in productivity can be a reality by having the labor force work on the proper priorities, with better throughput, resulting in more output.

Finally, customer service levels can be raised, staging material to find shortages discontinued, and obsolete material reduced. There truly exists an excellent opportunity to increase the company profits by using the MRP output the way it was designed to be used. The MRP system allows for the information to be available. The payback comes when the company commences using Material Requirements Planning to run the business the way it has always wanted to run it.

### OBJECTIVES OF MRP

**Figure 1**

### BIBLIOGRAPHY OF JOHN F. PROUD, CPIM*

John is currently the Customer Education Manager for Xerox Computer Services, a division of Xerox Corporation. Xerox Computer Services is a recognized leader in providing industry with manufacturing, distribution and financial systems. Its success is based on proven software, state-of-the-art concepts, consulting, implementation, and education.

Prior to his present education assignment, John spent several years with three other Xerox divisions. Initially, he was with Xerox Data Systems where he functioned as a production control specialist and manufacturing control analyst. He then joined Xerox Computer Services as the western region manufacturing consultant. After spending two years supporting sales and assisting XCS clients successfully solve business problems, John transferred to Arista Education and Consulting where he assumed the responsibilities of a senior business consultant and instructor. In addition to these Xerox assignments, he has been a systems analyst as well as the Manager, Systems and Programming.

John obtained his Bachelor of Science degree in mathematics from California State Polytechnic University and his Master of Science degree from West Coast University, specializing in Management Sciences. He has been involved in a variety of master scheduling, material and capacity management, and shop floor control seminars sponsored by APICS. He is certified in Production and Inventory Management at the Fellow Level as well as being recognized as an Assistant Professor at California State University, Fullerton.

Reprinted from APICS 1981 *Conference Proceedings*.

RESOURCE REQUIREMENTS PLANNING AND CAPACITY REQUIREMENTS
PLANNING -- THE CASE FOR EACH AND BOTH

F. John Sari
Richard C. Ling, Inc.

## Introduction

The need for effective computer-supported capacity planning
and control tools has existed since the earliest implementations of Material Requirements Planning (mrp*). In fact,
one of the basic tools now in use - Capacity Requirements
Planning (CRP) - has been in use (unfortunately, in very
few firms) just as long as mrp.

> *Mrp or mrp will be used throughout to
> distinguish Material Requirements Planning (mrp)
> from Manufacturing Resource Planning (MRP).

There has been a natural evolution of these capacity tools
which roughly parallels our 1970's progress in basic top-
down manufacturing planning. Using the 1980 APICS Dictionary definitions, this top-down hierarchy of capacity
oriented tools proceeds as follows:

LONG-RANGE RESOURCE PLANNING-A planning activity for long
term capacity decisions, based on the production plan and
perhaps on even more gross data (e.g., sales per year) beyond the time horizon for the production plan. This
activity is to plan long term capacity needs out to the
time period necessary to acquire gross capacity additions
such as a major factory expansion.

RESOURCE REQUIREMENTS PLANNING-The process of converting
the production plan and/or the master production schedule
into the impact on key resources, such as man hours, machine
hours, storage, standard cost dollars, shipping dollars,
inventory levels, etc. Product load profiles or bills of
resources could be used to accomplish this. The purpose of
this is to evaluate the plan prior to attempting to implement it. Sometimes referred to as a rough-cut check on
capacity. Capacity requirements planning is a detailed
review of capacity requirements. Syn: rough-cut capacity
planning, rough-cut resource planning. (cf. closed-loop MRP).

CAPACITY REQUIREMENTS PLANNING (CRP)-The function of establishing, measuring, and adjusting limits or levels of
capacity that are consistent with a production plan. The
term capacity requirements planning in this context is the
process of determining how much labor and machine resources
are required to accomplish the tasks of production. Open
shop orders, and planned orders in the MRP system, are input
to CRP which "translates" these orders into hours of work
by work center by time period. (cf. resource requirements
planning, infinite loading, closed-loop MRP).

INPUT/OUTPUT CONTROL-A technique for capacity control where
actual output from a work center is compared with the planned output developed by CRP. The input is also monitored
to see if it corresponds with plans so that work centers
will not be expected to generate output when jobs are not
available to work on. (cf. capacity control, closed-loop
MRP).

RRP is the more recently formalized capacity planning tool.
The need for RRP came, and good RRP mechanics came into use,
in the late 70's as the APICS community and P & I/C professionals formalized the front-end processed to mrp - Production Planning and the MPS. In terms of acceptance and use
in practice, our experience shows the use of RRP to be
growing faster than CRP.

We frequently see confusion on the uses of RRP and CRP because a certain amount of overlap exists in practice. This
article will discuss environments in which RRP and CRP work
well, factors influencing your choice(s), and their respective strengths and weaknesses.

RRP is a gross, pre-mrp analysis. It is a means to evaluate a proposed Production Plan and/or a MPS prior to plan
acceptance. RRP is accomplished by extending (exploding)
load profiles or bills of labor by these plans. The load
profiles typically define only critical capacities required.
This minimizes computational requirements yet is effective
because overall factory output is usually dictated by the
performance of a very few work centers or critical resources.

Figure 1 is a summary comparison of RRP vs. CRP.

**RRP vs. CRP**

| | RESOURCE RQMTS. PLANNING | CAPACITY RQMTS. PLANNING |
|---|---|---|
| WHAT? | PROJECT GROSS CAPACITY RQMTS FOR CRITICAL CAPACITIES OR KEY RESOURCES | PROJECT NET CAPACITY RQMTS FOR EACH WORK CENTER |
| HOW? | EXPLODE PROD PLAN OR MPS THROUGH LOAD PROFILES | EXPLODE MRP PLANNED ORDER RECEIPTS THROUGH DETAILED ROUTINGS, COMBINE WITH CURRENT WIP STATUS FROM SHOP FLOOR CONTROL |
| WHEN? | AS REQUIRED FOR SIMULATION | ANNUAL & QTRLY. BUDGET DEVELOPMENT; WEEKLY |
| WHY? | 1) PRE MRP EVALUATION OF PRODUCTION PLAN &/OR MPS  2) INTERMEDIATE TO LONG-RANGE PLANNING | 1) POST-MRP DETAILED ANALYSES, SHORT TERM VIEWS  2) PERIODIC CHECK OF ALL WORK CENTERS |
| PRECISION? | AGGREGATE OR GROSS - KEY RESOURCES ONLY | DETAILED - CONSIDERS ON-HAND, LOT SIZING, WIP COMPLETIONS. VOLUMINOUS DATA. |
| COST? | MUCH LESS THAN CRP | USUALLY EXCEEDS MRP |
| PLANNING HORIZON? | NO PRACTICAL LIMIT | MRP HORIZON LESS LEAD TIME OFFSETTING |
| IMPLEMENTATION TIME? | SHORT | REQUIRES MPS, MRP, AND WIP STATUS OF SFC |
| WHO USES? | VIRTUALLY ALL MANUFACTURERS MANY MANUALLY | 10% OF MANUFACTURERS |

Figure 1

RRP is a gross hours analysis for two basic reasons:

1. In constructing load profiles, all hours or
capacities required per Production Plan or
MPS unit are included.

2. Since RRP is a pre-mrp analysis, its load
projections do not reflect on-hand component
balances or completed work-in-process.

CRP, on the other hand, is a net, post-mrp analysis. Essentially, it takes the plans projected by MPS and mrp at all
levels, extends and back-schedules them through the standard
routings and accumulates this planned load for each active
work center. The current actual or scheduled load from the
WIP status information of Shop Floor Control is then included. These two sets of information are consolidated
into the total projected load by work-center.

CRP is a net hours analysis since mrp does net available
on-hand and on-order inventory and CRP includes only the
remaining portion of work-in-process. For example, if only
the last operation is required to complete a given shop
order, that is all CRP includes.

This understanding of the mechanics of RRP and CRP helps to
explain their respective strengths and weaknesses.

## RRP Strengths

1. Since Material Requirements Planning assumes capacity is
available and CRP is a post-mrp analysis, RRP is the only
available tool which permits advance testing of the Production Plan and the MPS. This reasonability of gross hours
leads to a certain level of assurance that the rest of the
down-stream planning process makes sense.

2. Since RRP utilizes load profiles which identify only a
few key resources, it doesn't require massive supporting
data. Many firms effectively rough-cut plan manually.
Others implement simple, computer-aided solutions which
don't require heavy integration or interface with existing
systems.

3. The computational ease of RRP makes it much simpler to
quickly evaluate a wide variety of "what if" situations.

4. RRP's planning horizon is unlimited.

## RRP Weaknesses

1. RRP cannot be used to evaluate the short-term. As a
gross analysis insensitive to both available inventories
and WIP, its close-in projections will always overstate
the load.

2. RRP profiles assume standard lot sizing will always be
used in the factory. On balance that's correct, but
day-by-day practices will vary.

3. Because RRP is somewhat imprecise, it can lack credibility.

## CRP Strengths

1. CRP is a valid short-term capacity planning tool. Since CRP does factor in on-hand, on-order and WIP inventories, its short-term loads can accurately depict current factory status. Thus, it can identify the need for overtime, alternate routings, etc., in the weeks just ahead.

2. CRP projects loads on all active work centers. Periodically, it must be used to insure that today's minor work center doesn't become tomorrow's bottleneck.

3. CRP can be useful in developing RRP load profiles. The mrp/CRP process, assuming no on-hand and on-order inventory, can be used to project gross hours required by work center. This data can then be summarized and used to update the critical resource and load profile data of RRP.

## CRP Weaknesses

1. CRP is expensive. It probably consumes more computer capacity than any other single step within MRP. In order to calculate projected hours, it must extend the complete planned order projection for each active mrp component through every routing step.

2. CRP outputs are voluminous. It's normal outputs are hard to use as effective management tools unless good exception oriented analyses have been incorporated.

3. CRP requires current, accurate standard routings and work center standards. A large, accurate data base must exist in order for CRP to work.

4. CRP's 5-decimal precision appears so precise that it can also lack credibility, particularly in the intermediate-to-long term. It suffers from the same weakness as a statistical forecast -- the farther out one goes, the less comfortable one gets.

5. CRP's planning horizon is limited to mrp's planning horizon less cumulative lead time offset.

As one reviews these respective strengths and weaknesses of RRP and CRP, it's interesting to note how one is strong where the other is weak. The two tools very much complement each other in many important respects.

## Factors Favoring RRP or CRP

Certain characteristics of the manufacturing environment or product tend to favor one tool or the other. Some considerations:

### 1. Type of manufacturer and facility.

Flow-like manufacturers frequently rely exclusively on RRP. Examples would include integrated manufacturing processes, process industries, or many assembly line situations. Because there is a defined flow, that which starts will flow to the finish. Very little beyond loading to process capacity is needed. RRP profiles accomodate this very well.

Discrete manufacturers, particularly those with common use equipment and facilities, usually don't rely exclusively on RRP. The actual lead time for a manufactured item can vary substantially because of queuing and contention. The load profiles of RRP do assume a manufacturing flow and do not depict well the effects of this contention for common work centers, particularly for lower-level component items. Even though CRP, particularly infinite loading CRP, suffers from the same problem, it does provide additional visibility into the situation.

### 2. Levels of manufacture in the product.

The shallower the bill of material for the product, the less one is exposed to the lead time and standard lot sizing assumptions built into RRP profiles.

### 3. Lower-level independent demand.

Manufacturers with significant spare parts businesses, direct sales of lower-level items, interplant component supply situations, etc., may utilize CRP to reflect this lower level demand. Typically, these items are forecast individually and the forecast becomes an input to mrp. Mrp then projects a replenishment plan for the item which covers these independent requirements as well as dependent requirements calculated from upper-level build plans. CRP load projections thus include capacities required to cover both requirement streams.

Unless these segments of the business are substantial, many firms do not routinely include such items in their Production Plan and MPS. If they are not included, RRP load projections cannot reflect the required capacities. When there is significant lower-level demand, companies do identify these segments of their business for Production Planning and RRP purposes. This is especially true with service parts due to the high margins they generate.

### 4. Part Number Precision

The following excerpt from REPORT, Richard C. Ling, Inc., September, 1980, discussed this issue.

"Recently, we encountered Firm A which manufactured long-lived, major capital equipment. Depending on the unit, the equipment was either engineered-to-order with many custom components or primarily assembled-to-order from standard components. Over the years, Firm A had also developed a very significant spare or service parts business. Significant amounts of productive capacity (30-50%) were used to manufacture service parts. The company had been utilizing MRP and CRP for years. Unfortunately CRP did a decent job of projecting only about 60% of the capacities required!"

"CRP did a good job for standard master scheduled options (and their components) which were forecast and planned. It also did a good job for volume service parts which were forecast, planned, and stocked. CRP did no job at all, however, for the camshaft which didn't get engineered until 3 months into a 4 month specification process. CRP also blew it on the flywheel just ordered for service which wasn't too surprising since the item was last made 18 years ago! CRP requires the following to work:

1. A replenishment plan by part number, quantity and date due created by mrp because of MPS planning, service forecast, etc.

2. A current standard routing.

3. Current work center standards."

"If you, like Firm A, cannot accurately forecast and plan for most or all of your business by part number, quantity and date, don't bet all your marbles on CRP. Firm A knew that the new equipment ordered would require a camshaft and could effectively profile the capacity required in RRP. They could not through CRP, however, plan enough in advance for the specific capacity required until engineering specs were complete and they had a part number, routing and associated work center data. Firm A was reasonably sure that 100 fly wheels would be ordered as spare parts per year and could profile that general capacity in RRP also. There was absolutely no way Firm A could forecast specific service part requirements by part number for CRP with any acceptable degree of accuracy."

"CRP was effective for Firm A only out through the firm order horizon. Beyond that, RRP was the preferred tool since it could comprehend more of that 40% of capacity which could not be forecast and planned by specific part number."

## Other RRP Considerations

### 1. Computerization Requirements

Data volume and planning frequency will ultimately dictate the amount of computer support required for RRP. If there are a lot of MPS items to profile, many critical capacities or frequent requirements to evaluate "what if" situations computer help becomes a must.

Because of the relatively small amount of data required for RRP, however, this planning can frequently be accomplished without large-scale computer support. Personal computers and time-sharing implementations have been successful for several firms.

The amount of data manipulation is frequently reduced by development of typical product or average product load profiles. This simplification is very helpful when the need is to evaluate loads at the Production Plan family level. These families usually are composed of many specific, but similar, MPS items. When used, the technique does require periodic reviews of the mix of items used to construct the average or typical profile.

## 2. RRP Profile Capabilities
The degree of precision of RRP is a frequent issue, part of which will dictate the sophistication required in the load profile itself. For example, manufacturers with long manufacturing lead times usually demand the ability to time-phase RRP loads with some form of lead time offset facility. Forms of lead time offsets can also be used to project simultaneous loads on different critical capacities. This may be important to discrete manufacturers with common use facilities.

Often, it is necessary to project loads both forward and backward in time. For example, companies which MPS at levels below the end item may choose to project forward loads for final assembly.

Simpler RRP implementations don't utilize time-phased loads. Gross hours are merely projected in the Production Plan or MPS period. This is most valid when lead times are short. It may also be a legitimate assumption because loads will tend to wash over time in a reasonably balanced factory.

## 3. Degree of RRP Precision
The following excerpt from REPORT, September, 1980, further expands the degree of precision issue mentioned above:

"Frequently, it is necessary to determine both the planning level at which you must perform RRP as well as the degree of precision you require. In many firms, profiles by Production Planning families get it done. If the products within the family are similar and require like processes, profile and evaluate RRP at family levels. What you really want to evaluate is the impact of the overall rates of production by family on critical resources. If, however, specific item mix within the family can hurt you, consider profiling a level below the product family for MPS items."

"Recently we've seen interesting RRP approaches in-use by manufacturers who master schedule product at levels below the salable end item. This is, of course, common amongst firms who produce a wide variety of end item configurations from a smaller number of options, features, attachments, etc."

"For RRP analytical purposes, some master scheduled items can be assumed to flow through manufacturing on a fairly steady basis. This might be true, for instance, for common parts sets on a volume product. Other MPS items, like stocked manufactured or purchased subassemblies and components will be built or procured periodically as stock lots and not on a steady basis. Because of this difference in replenishment _timing_ (steady versus sporadic), you might have to profile these items separately and develop RRP projections from the MPS."

"Similarly, load profiles must be prepared with some lot size assumption in order to reflect setup properly. One lot size assumption may be necessary for steady, repetitive MPS options. Another, very different assumption would be appropriate for a truly "sold-to-order" option which is manufactured one-for-one upon receipt of customer order."

"Under such circumstances, we now see firms 'disentangling' or modularizing load profiles in order to better reflect timing of loads and/or varying lot size practices."

"The level of profile precision required is, again, a function of your product and processes. More often than not, it's a good idea to provide for profile capabilities at both Production Plan and MPS levels. A flexible RRP facility can easily provide both."

## 4. Consider RRP Early in an MRP Implementation
It is difficult to demonstrate tangible results during the early stages of an mrp implementation. There usually are long duration efforts to educate, improve records accuracy, audit bills of material, etc. Because CRP can't come on stream before MPS/mrp, this capacity planning tool is a long way off.

RRP, however, because it's simpler forms do not require substantial computer development or heavy interfaces, can be addressed early. In conjunction with Production Planning, RRP can be used to demonstrate some very substantial, early improvements.

## 5. RRP and Lower-Level Demand
As mentioned above, it may be absolutely required to include service parts and other lower-level demands in RRP planning. Techniques such as grouping like parts into families associated with typical load profiles can be used. This reduces the data volume and still provides a gross measure of capacities required.

An alternative approach is to relate critical capacities required to dollar volumes of these lower-level demands. Although subject to mix variation, this does provide a gross capacity allocation which must be considered.

## 6. RRP and Capacity Booking
RRP is frequently used by make and assemble-to-order firms as an aid when customer promising. If the MPS/mrp process has provided the materials required, RRP can be used to determine the availability of capacity required to convert the product to shippable form.

One client company of ours fabricates primary metals. Their MPS/mrp process provides stocks of an intermediate product. When customers order finished material, the task is to determine availability of the needed finishing capacities. This normal 6-8 week finishing process will vary with backlog. By converting incoming orders to hours required in critical capacities, an up-to-date hours 'available-to-promise' is maintained.

## RRP and CRP Assist Each Other
RRP profiles have proven to be of real use to many confirmed CRP users, particularly in heavy job shop environments. With many levels in the bill of material and common use machinery, it is cumbersome to analyze an under/over load and know which MPS items could be changed to resolve it. RRP profiles automatically provide this needed visibility.

As noted previously, a periodic, non-netted mrp/CRP is an excellent tool for two purposes:

1. to monitor and maintain RRP profile and critical resource data

2. to monitor all work centers, not just critical ones.

Even though the CRP process is used, gross hours are generated very much like the normal RRP process.

## Conclusion
All manufacturers, regardless of product or process, require an appropriate RRP mechanism. Many, but not all, also require more detailed CRP capabilities. Those with both RRP and CRP in their bag of tools are well equipped to plan capacity.

## ABOUT THE AUTHOR

F. John Sari is Executive Vice-President of Richard C. Ling, Inc.

Formerly, John was Vice-President, Consulting Services for Arista Manufacturing Systems, A Xerox Company, and was responsible for the consulting and project activities of the firm. In this capacity, he also conducted many training courses for the public as well as Arista clients.

John is a Mathematics graduate of Wayne State University in Detroit. Upon graduation, he joined General Electric Co. and participated in GE's three-year rotational Manufacturing Management Training Program. Mr. Sari accepted a GE position as Supervisor-Production and Inventory Control upon completion of the MMP program.

John is an active speaker at APICS seminars and events. He holds a Fellow certification in inventory management. He is a Past-President of the Piedmont Triad Chapter of APICS.

Reprinted from APICS 1980 *Conference Proceedings*.

PERFORMANCE MEASUREMENT

David W. Buker, CPIM
President
David W. Buker, Inc.

### INTRODUCTION

Many of you have implemented a "Closed Loop MRP (Manufacturing Resource Planning - MRP II) System" or are thinking about implementing such a system in your company. A basic management question that applies to all of us, no matter where we are in our system's development efforts, is, "What level of performance are you getting with your system?".

Ollie Wight in his 1977 Newsletter introduced the concept of Class A, B, C or D MRP users. He indicated that there are different classes of users based on different levels of performance. The performance rating chart below defines a Class A, B, C and D user, states a numerical performance measurement, and indicates the system's characteristics for each class of user.

## CLASS A, B, C, D USERS

| CLASSIFICATION | PERFORMANCE | CHARACTERISTICS |
|:---:|:---:|:---|
| A | 90% | COMPLETE CLOSED LOOP SYSTEM. TOP MANAGEMENT USES THE FORMAL SYSTEM TO RUN THE BUSINESS. ALL ELEMENTS AVERAGE 80% TO 100%. |
| B | 80% | FORMAL SYSTEM IN PLACE BUT ALL ELEMENTS ARE NOT WORKING EFFECTIVELY. TOP MANAGEMENT APPROVES BUT DOES NOT PARTICIPATE. ELEMENTS AVERAGE 80% TO 90%. |
| C | 70% | MRP IS ORDER LAUNCHING RATHER THAN PLANNING PRIORITIES. FORMAL AND INFORMAL SYSTEM ELEMENTS ARE NOT TIED TOGETHER. SOME SUB-SYSTEMS NOT IN PLACE. ELEMENTS AVERAGE 65% TO 75%. |
| D | 50% | FORMAL SYSTEM NOT WORKING, OR NOT IN PLACE. POOR DATA INTEGRITY. LITTLE MANAGEMENT INVOLVEMENT. LITTLE USER CONFIDENCE IN SYSTEM. ELEMENTS ARE 50% OR BELOW. |

What class user are you? How do you know? How do you evaluate your performance? How do you know how well or how poorly, you're doing? How do you evaluate, motivate and reward your people? How do you identify problem performance areas and prioritize them for management attention and action? How do you pinpoint the real cause of these problems for correction? How can you systematically monitor and improve your performance?

The answer to these questions is a set of performance measurements. A good set of performance measurements will enable you to evaluate your performance, identify problem areas and responsibilities, prioritize problems for management attention and action, and enable you to monitor and improve your performance. A systematic review of performance allows you to continually monitor your performance, to identify and diagnose developing problems early enough, and within reasonable tolerance limits, to avoid crisis management. Measurements are a management tool for monitoring and improving performance.

Measurements are an integral part of the management process. Setting objectives, goals, tolerance limits; developing action plans, allocating resources, assigning responsibilities, implementing plans and measuring performance for feedback and corrective action, are all part of the management process that has been used successfully in all areas of the business for years. A definitive set of performance measurements helps management to "close the loop" in the management process and will help you to improve your performance.

These performance measurements should be easily understood, clearly defined, yet comprehensive enough to include the functions that effect performance.

I have developed a Key Measurement and supporting Detail Measurements for each functional area involved in a Manufacturing Resource Planning System. If the Key Measurement is okay, the detail measurements do not have to be made. However, if the key measurement is not okay, the more detail measurements should be made to find out specifically where the problem is and what corrective action is required. This paper will outline only the Key Measurements for each function in a Manufacturing Resource Planning System.

### MANUFACTURING RESOURCE PLANNING SYSTEM

First, let's take a brief look at the Manufacturing Resource Planning System to set-up the functions of the business, the levels of management, the check points and the accountabilities for our discussion on Performance Measurement.

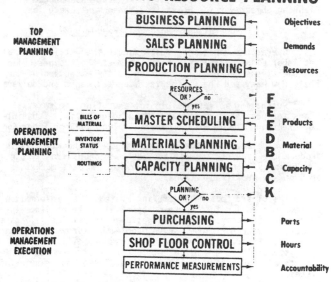

The MRP II System provides a formal system for communicating management's objectives. It starts with Business Planning and ends with Performance Measurement, checking the performance to the Business Plan. It has performance measurements for each function for accountability. It has checkpoints at the levels of management. It has a feedback loop. It has interaction planning and execution. It is a management system that management can use to effectively run the business.

The functions in the MRP II System can be divided into three subsections representing the three levels of management planning and execution.

The three levels of management planning and execution are:

- Top Management Planning
- Operations Management Planning
- Operations Management Execution

## Top Management Planning

Top Management must determine its market, product, and profit objectives in the Business Plan. The Sales Plan forecasts the customer demand for the products in the marketplace. The Production Plan allocates the manufacturing resources to the products to be produced to meet the customer demand.

The Top Management Plan is the responsibility of General Management including Marketing, Engineering, Manufacturing and Financial Executives. It is the What, How Much and When at the market, product, and profit level. It is the definition of Top Management objectives for Operations Management Planning.

## Operations Management Planning

Operations Management Planning takes Top Management objectives and translates them into Operating Plans. Operations Management must plan the detail material and labor requirements to meet the Business Plan.

Operations Management plans the detail product production with the Master Schedule. The Master Schedule is exploded into Materials Plans and Capacity Plans to produce the product to meet the Business Plan.

The Operations Management Plan is the What, How Much and When in manufacturing orders and purchase orders at the parts level. It is the definition of the Operations Management Planning objectives for Operations Management Execution.

## Operations Management Execution

Operations Management must execute the detail material and labor plans established above to meet the Business Plan. The Operations Management Execution is the execution of the What, How Many and When in parts, standard hours and dollars.

Purchasing is responsible for executing the material plans for purchased materials. Manufacturing is responsible for executing the labor and material plans in Shop Floor Control.

The objective of Operations Management Execution is to produce the product, to meet the customer needs, to execute the Business Plan and to achieve Top Management's market, product and profit objectives.

The Closed Loop Manufacturing System is an information system. It does not do anything by itself. It provides information for management to manage; plan priorities, allocate resources, make decisions, solve problems, improve performance. There are different degrees of expertise or skill in using the system. There are different levels of performance in effectively managing a business with a Closed Loop Manufactuing System.

## PERFORMANCE MEASUREMENT

The first step in Performance Measurement is to establish the performance objectives. The performance objectives are the key accountabilities for management that will be measured for performance.

Performance Measurement can be started today. You do not need a new computer or new computer reports. The majority of information that is required for Performance Measurement is available in most companies. What is needed is management that understands the importance, that will set performance objectives, and that will begin to make Performance Measurement part of the Closed Loop Management Process.

The Manufacturing Performance Measurement Summary can be used as a scorecard to record your own performance by functional area as you read through the Performance Measurement section. Rate your performance for each functional area, calculate your total and average performance and determine your class of performance. You can determine whether you are a Class A, B, C or D user. You can identify problem areas for corrective action. You can begin to continuously monitor and improve your performance. Are you interested? Then let's get started.

## Business Plan

The objective of the Business Plan is to develop the market, product, and financial plans for the company. The Business Plan is top management's strategic plan of What, How Much, and When for markets, products, and profit to meet the company's overall business objectives. The Business Plan should state dollars of Income, dollars of Investment and a rate of Return on Investment.

The key measurement for the Business Plan is Return on Investment (ROI). The Return on Investment calculates the Income earned from the Investment required to support the product and market opportunities. Return on Investment is a method for evaluating the success of present markets and produc of the business as well as evaluating the potential of the new markets and products. The Return on Investment Performance is

## MANUFACTURING PERFORMANCE MEASUREMENT SUMMARY

COMPANY_____  BY_____  DATE_____

| | FUNCTIONAL AREA | RESPONSIBILITY | PERFORMANCE OBJECTIVE | PERFORMANCE MEASUREMENT |
|---|---|---|---|---|
| TOP MANAGEMENT PLANNING | BUSINESS PLAN | GENERAL MANAGER | RETURN ON INVESTMENT | |
| | SALES PLAN | SALES | SALES PERFORMANCE | |
| | PRODUCTION PLAN | MANUFACTURING | PRODUCTION PERFORMANCE | |
| OPERATIONS MGMT. PLANNING | MASTER SCHEDULE | MATERIALS | MPS PERFORMANCE | |
| | MATERIALS PLAN | MATERIALS | RELEASE RELIABILITY | |
| | CAPACITY PLAN | MANUFACTURING | CAPACITY PERFORMANCE | |
| DATA BASE | BILLS OF MATERIAL | ENGINEERING | BILL OF MATERIAL ACCURACY | |
| | INVENTORY CONTROL | MATERIALS | INVENTORY ACCURACY | |
| | ROUTINGS | MANUFACTURING | ROUTING ACCURACY | |
| OPERATIONS MGMT. EXECUTION | PURCHASING | PURCHASING | SCHEDULE PERFORMANCE | |
| | SHOP FLOOR CONTROL | MANUFACTURING | SCHEDULE PERFORMANCE | |
| | DELIVERY PERFORMANCE | GENERAL MANAGER | SCHEDULE PERFORMANCE | |
| PERFORMANCE SUMMARY | | CLASS | AVERAGE | TOTAL |
| | | | | |

actual return on investment as a percent of planned return on investment.

$$\text{ROI Performance} = \frac{\text{Actual ROI}}{\text{Planned ROI}} \times 100 = \%$$

A Class A Business Plan performance meets its income, investment and Return on Investment objectives within ± 5% tolerance limit for a 95% Business Plan Performance.

## Sales Plan

The objective of the Sales Plan is to develop a plan of orders received and/or shipments for the company's products and then bring the orders in to plan. The Sales Plan should be stated in dollars and units by month and for the year. The Sales Plan is the What, How Much and When of the products required to meet the customer demand.

The key measurement for the Sales Plan is Sales Plan Performance. Sales develops the Sales Plan and it is their responsibility to bring the orders in to meet the plan. Sales Plan Performance is the number of units booked as a percent of the units planned.

$$\frac{\text{Sales Plan}}{\text{Performance}} = \frac{\text{Units Booked}}{\text{Units Planned}} \times 100 = \%$$

Class A Sales Plan Performance is booking units to plan within ± 5% tolerance limit for a 95% Sales Plan Performance.

## Production Plan

The objective of the Production Plan is to determine the production rates required to meet the Sales Plan and maintain a desired level of finished inventory to provide satisfactory customer service. The Production Plan is the What, How Much and When for production rates and levels of output.

The key measurement is the Production Plan Performance. Once the Production Plan has been established, it is manufacturing's responsibility to produce the Production Plan. The Production Plan Performance is the actual production as a percent of planned production.

$$\frac{\text{Production Plan}}{\text{Performance}} = \frac{\text{Actual Production}}{\text{Planned Production}} \times 100 = \%$$

Class A Production Plan Performance is meeting the Production Plan within a ± 5% tolerance limit for a 95% Production Plan Performance.

## Master Schedule

The objective of the Master Schedule is to determine the product mix to be produced within the production rates of the Production Plan. The Master Production Schedule is the bridge between sales and manufacturing. It is the What, How Much and When at the product, model, feature, or option level for scheduling the manufacturing resources to meet the Sales Plan.

The key measurement is the Master Schedule Performance. The Master Schedule is the schedule of the detail product mix to be produced to meet the Sales Plan. The Master Schedule Performance is the actual MPS produced as a percent of the planned MPS by model, feature, and option.

$$\frac{\text{Master}}{\text{Schedule Performance}} = \frac{\text{Actual MPS}}{\text{Planned MPS}} \times 100 = \%$$

A Class A Master Schedule is producing the product mix within ± 5% tolerance limit for a 95% Master Production Schedule Performance.

## Materials Plan

The objective of the Materials Plan is to determine the time phased requirements for parts required to produce the product and to maintain part priorities for production. It is the What, How Much and When of production at the parts level.

The key measurement is Release Reliability. Release Reliability indicates whether the orders are being released to production or purchasing with sufficient lead time so that the parts can be completed or delivered by the due date for production. Release Reliability is the number of orders released on time as a percent of the total number of orders released.

$$\text{Release Reliability} = \frac{\text{On Time Orders Released}}{\text{Total Orders Released}} \times 100 = \%$$

A Class A Materials Plan Performance releases orders with sufficient lead time within a ± 5% tolerance limit for a 95% Release Reliability Performance.

## Capacity Plan

The objective of the Capacity Plan is to plan the capacity and the labor required to produce the product. It is the What, How Much and When of the capacity and labor required to produce the plan.

The key measurement is Capacity Plan Performance. The capacity plan should be developed by work center, department, and plant to determine the capacity required to meet the plan. The Capacity Plan Performance is the number of capacity hours produced as a percent of the capacity hours required by work center, department, and plant.

$$\frac{\text{Capacity Plan}}{\text{Review}} = \frac{\text{Capacity Hours Produced}}{\text{Capacity Hours Required}} \times 100 = \%$$

A Class A Capacity Plan Performance is meeting capacity plans within a ± 5% tolerance limit for a 95% Capacity Plan Performance.

## Bills of Material

The objective of the Bill of Material is to specify the parts and materials; the quantity of the parts and materials; and the assembly or process relationships required to produce the product.

The key measurement is Bill of Material Accuracy. Bill of Material Accuracy indicates whether the bill of material represents the product as it is being produced. Bill of Material Accuracy is the number of parts on the bill of material that are in agreement with actual production as a percent of the total number of parts.

$$\frac{\text{Bill of Material}}{\text{Accuracy}} = \frac{\text{Parts in Agreement}}{\text{Total Number of Parts}} \times 100 = \%$$

Class A Bill of Material Performance is maintaining the bill of material accuracy within a ± 1% tolerance limit for a 99% Bill of Material Accuracy Performance.

## Inventory Control

The objective of Inventory Control is to maintain accurate and timely inventory status information. It is the What and How Much that is on hand in inventory and that is available to produce the product.

The key measurement is Inventory Accuracy. Inventory Accuracy indicates the accuracy of the on hand inventory record as compared to the physical inventory. Inventory accuracy is the number of parts where the physical count equals the inventory record as a percent of the total number of parts counted.

$$\text{Inventory Accuracy} = \frac{\text{Number of Parts Correct}}{\text{Number of Parts Counted}} \times 100 = \%$$

Class A Inventory Control Performance is maintaining inventory accuracy within a ± 5% tolerance limit for a 95% Inventory Accuracy Performance.

## Routings

The objective of the Routing is to specify the operations to be performance to produce the product. Routings are the responsibility of Manufacturing; Manufacturing Engineering or Industrial Engineering. The routing should specify the operations or sequences, the machine or work center, the tooling or fixtures, and the set up and run hours for each operation. It is the What, and How Much of the operations and standard hours required to produce the product.

The key measurement is Routing Accuracy. Routing Accuracy indicates whether the Routing represents the operations as they are being performance in the shop. Routing Accuracy is the number of operations that are in agreement with the actual operations.

$$\frac{\text{Routing}}{\text{Accuracy}} = \frac{\text{Operations in Agreement}}{\text{Number of Operations}} \times 100 = \%$$

Class A Routing Accuracy is maintaining Routing Accuracy within a ± 5% tolerance limit for a 95% Routing Accuracy.

## Purchasing

The objective of Purchasing is to deliver the purchased materials on the due date to meet the plan. It is the detailed What, How Much and When for purchased materials to execute the plan.

The key measurement is Schedule Performance. Schedule Performance indicates whether the vendors are delivering the purchased parts on schedule. Schedule Performance is the number of purchased parts delivered as a percent on the purchased parts scheduled.

$$\frac{\text{Purchasing Schedule}}{\text{Performance}} = \frac{\text{Parts Delivered}}{\text{Parts Scheduled}} \times 100 = \%$$

Class A Purchasing Performance delivers purchased material to scnedule within a ± 5% tolerance limit for a 95% Purchasing Performance.

## Shop Floor Control

The objective of Shop Floor Control is to deliver the manufactured parts on the due date to meet the production plan. It is a detailed execution of the What, How Much and When of labor and material on the shop floor.

The key measurement is Schedule Performance. Schedule Performance indicates whether the manufacturing parts are being completed on time in the shop. It is the number of manufacturing parts completed as a percent of the manufacturing parts scheduled.

$$\frac{\text{Manufacturing Schedule}}{\text{Performance}} = \frac{\text{Parts Completed}}{\text{Parts Scheduled}} \times 100 = \%$$

Class A Shop Floor Control Performance meets manufacturing schedules within a ± 5% tolerance limit for a 95% Shop Floor Control Performance.

## Delivery Performance

The objective of the Delivery Performance is to build the product on time, ship the product on time, and deliver the produc to the customer when it was promised. It is the delivery of the What, How Much and When in units to meet the Sales Plan.

The key measurement is of Schedule Performance. Delivery Schedule Performance indicates whether the product was delivered to the customer when it was promised. If the customer delivery was promised from the Sales Plan and manufacturing produced the Production Plan, the product will be available for delivery to the customer when it was promised. Delivery Schedule Performance is units delivered as a percent of units promised.

$$\frac{\text{Delivery Schedule}}{\text{Performance}} = \frac{\text{Units Delivered}}{\text{Units Promised}} \times 100 = \%$$

Class A Delivery Performance promises and delivers the product on time within a ± 5% tolerance limit for a 95% Delivery Performance.

## CONCLUSION

Performance Measurement is an important part of the management process. Setting objectives, goals and tolerance limits, sets up the acceptable performance levels. Performance Measurement is a necessary step in achieving these performance levels. It sets up the measurements, the accountabilities, the method of tracking the results. The formal measurements and accountabilities help management pinpoint problems and responsibilities. It slows down the fabled stores, the finger-pointing, the one-liners, and the old alibis. Management begins to examine cause and effect relationships more closely to improve performance. Management can monitor performance and measure the improvements and the results. It matures the management process and the management team.

If a company is to develop this maturity in the management process, to achieve these results, to become a Class A User, it will take a team effort. It will take a Class A Management Team that is committed to managing the resources of the business in a new way:

A new communication system
    THE CLOSED LOOP MRP II SYSTEM

A new method of management
    THE CLOSED LOOP MANAGEMENT PROCESS

A new set of accountabilities
    PERFORMANCE MEASUREMENT

A new set of values
    INDIVIDUAL RESPONSIBILITY

A new quality of life
    INDIVIDUAL SELF-ESTEEM

A new level of performance
    CLASS A USER

My challenge to you is this -- begin that new way today -- begin to set objectives, to measure performance, to practice Closed Loop Management, to develop a Closed Loop MRP II System, to achieve the results, to join the unique group of Class A Users.

## BIOGRAPHY

David W. Buker is President of his own education and counseling firm. Prior to forming his own company he was responsible for development and conduct of Manufacturing Industry Client Education for the Professional Education Division of Arthur Andersen & Co.

Mr. Buker has 20 years management experience in manufacturing including positions as Director of Production Planning and Processing, Director of Materials, and Assistant to the President with responsibilities for Materials Management, Manufacturing Systems, Manufacturing Planning and Strategic Business and Profit Planning for such firms as Hyster Company, Barber-Greene and Dresser Industries.

Mr. Buker has a BA with honors from Wheaton College and an MBA from the University of Chicago's Executive Program. He was the developer of the Materials Management Certification Program. He is a Certified Practitioner in Inventory Management at the fellow level. He is the author of an article on Performance Measurement, published with Oliver W. Wight. He has been a long term member and officer in APICS, IMMS, AMMS, NAPM, ASM. He is a frequent speaker and educator on manufacturing management at regional and national conferences.

Reprinted from APICS 1982 *Conference Proceedings.*

SELLING TOP MANAGEMENT—UNDERSTANDING THE FINANCIAL
IMPACT OF MANUFACTURING SYSTEMS

James T. Clark
IBM Corporation
Poughkeepsie, New York

The objectives of this paper are to assist the reader in
his efforts to:

. Better understand the motivations, the goals and
  objectives, of top management

. Relate the goals of production and inventory management to these goals

. Justify production and inventory management systems

THE GOALS AND OBJECTIVES OF TOP MANAGEMENT

Tell me how a man is measured and I will tell you how to
sell to him.

The simplest and most direct approach to gaining an
understanding of the goals and objectives of top management
is to read the manager's written performance plan. A
properly developed performance plan should define in very
specific numbers and schedules what that person is being
measured against. It should also prioritize multiple objectives giving specific weighting factors to individual
objectives.

However direct and accurate this approach might be, it
is not likely to happen.

It is often possible though, through interview and
discussion, to get a reasonably accurate general description (without confidential data) and ranking of a managers
objectives. It then becomes your responsibility to present
your eventual proposal or results in terms that are easily
translated by that manager to his specific objectives and
measurements.

Another excellent source of information is the formal
business plan. This assumes that there is a formal business
plan and that you have access to it. Unfortunately, formal
business plans are still relatively scarce in industry.
Again, an alternative is intelligent questioning of top
management for useful information.

The business plan should define the business you
intend to be in, the products you intend to sell, and the
marketplace you intend to serve. It should also define
major strategies and priorities. Strategy examples
include: being the low cost and high volume producer; or
having the highest service level or shortest lead time; or
to service only a unique small portion of the marketplace.

The business plan should provide measureable objec-
tives/targets (quantity and date) for key items such as net
sales, net profit, return on investment, return on equity,
market share, etc.

Additionally, statements of policies, practices or
responsibilities relative to employees, the community or
society in general can influence top managements evaluation
of your proposal.

The full employment objective and strategy shared by
government, management, workers and owners in Japan is an
excellent example of a significant influence in justifying
and selling projects or ideas.

In well managed companies, the objectives of all
managers (and employees) should reflect and support the
business plan objectives.

Top management of course, tends to get a grade or
score that is very close to (or exactly the same as) the
'company score'.

The 'company score' is best defined in the company's
Annual Report.

The objectives of the next two sections of this paper
are to provide an introduction to and a basic understanding
of, the company Annual Report or Financial Report. It is
presented in layman's terms. A basic understanding of the
Financial Report is defined as 'What does the Financial
Report tell you?'.

If you are a CPA or are otherwise financially trained,
then skip this portion of the paper.

The Annual Report is the summarized set of company
books that is shared with the stockholders. (Assuming a
public company) There is a second set of books that is
shared with the government. (This is legal) Differences

in these sets of books, for example, could involve depreciation schedules. A third set of books may, or may not be
as well defined. This is the set of books for the decision
makers. This is the most important set of books in justification and selling to top management. Hopefully these
books or something equivalent, are available, at least in
part, to employees of the business.

Access to the detailed facts of the business could make
this portion of the paper seem too general or broad. The
logic, evaluations and comments however, still apply. You
should then read this section and consider how you can
enhance and expand it with your knowledge of more detailed
facts.

AN INTRODUCTION TO A FINANCIAL REPORT

The ABC Manufacturing Company is a durable goods
manufacturer. It stocks subassemblies and is vertically
integrated (it does some fabrication). It manufactures in
an interrupted flow (discrete manufacturing).

ABC's balance sheet consists of Assets (Figure 1) and
Liabilities and Stockholders' Equity which represents
claims against these assets (Figure 2). The asset side and
the liability side of the balance sheet are, as the name
implies, always in balance.

CONSOLIDATED BALANCE SHEET
ABC MANUFACTURING COMPANY

| ASSETS    In Millions of Dollars - December 31, 1981 | | % of Total |
|---|---|---|
| CURRENT ASSETS | | |
| Cash | $ 1.1 | 1.0 |
| Short-Term Investments-At Cost (Appx Mkt) | 2.5 | 2.2 |
| Receivables, Less Allowances of $0.7 Million | 25.6 | 22.5 |
| Inventories | 35.9 | 31.6 |
| Other Current Assets | 3.6 | 3.2 |
| Total Current Assets | 68.7 | 60.5 |
| PROPERTY, PLANT AND EQUIPMENT, AT COST | | |
| Land | 1.1 | 1.0 |
| Buildings | 12.3 | 10.8 |
| Machinery and Equipment | 40.4 | 35.6 |
| Construction in Progress | 5.0 | 4.4 |
| | 58.8 | 51.8 |
| Less Accumulated Depreciation | 22.0 | 19.4 |
| Net Property, Plant and Equipment | 36.8 | 32.4 |
| Investments | 3.9 | 3.4 |
| Prepaid Expenses and Deferred Charges | 1.3 | 1.1 |
| Other Assets | 2.9 | 2.6 |
| Total Assets | $113.6 | |

(Figure 1)

LIABILITIES AND STOCKHOLDERS' EQUITY
In Millions of Dollars - December 31, 1981

| CURRENT LIABILITIES | | % of Total |
|---|---|---|
| Short Term Borrowings and Current Maturities | | |
| of Long Term Debt | $ 9.5 | 8.4 |
| Accounts Payable | 15.2 | 13.4 |
| Accrued Expenses | 6.8 | 6.0 |
| Income Taxes | 4.0 | 3.5 |
| Total Current Liabilities | 35.5 | 31.3 |
| LONG TERM DEBT | 23.9 | 21.0 |
| STOCKHOLDERS' EQUITY | | |
| Preferred Stock of $2.50 Par Value Per Share. | | |
| Authorized 22,000 Shares, Issued - None | - | - |
| Common Stock of $1 Par Value Per Share | | |
| Authorized 15,000,000 Shares, | | |
| Issued 9,700,000 | 9.7 | |
| Additional Paid-In Capital | 13.5 | |
| Retained Earnings | 31.0 | |
| Total Stockholders' Equity | 54.2 | 47.7 |
| Total Liabilities and Stockholders' Equity | $113.6 | |

(Figure 2)

Assets are listed in order of decreasing liquidity from
top to bottom. In other words, items at the top of the list
can be converted to cash sooner and more easily than items
further down the list. Current Assets are expected to be
converted into cash within one year. Property, Plant
and equipment, or fixed assets, as well as certain other
investments are not expected to be converted to cash within
one year.

Liabilities are listed from top to bottom in order of maturity. Items at the top of the list are expected to be paid off sooner. Current liabilities are expected to be paid within one year. Stockholders' equity is considered permanent capital since it is not paid off like payables or debt. It represents what would be left for the stockholders if the company's assets were liquidated at their balance sheet (or book) value (this is highly unlikely if the company did, in fact, go out of business). The entire liabilities and stockholders' equity side of the balance sheet is referred to as the financial structure of the company. It details how the company's assets are financed.

The capital structure (permanent financing) of the company is represented by long term debt and stockholders' equity. It does not include short term (current) liabilities. The capital structure is a part of the financial structure.

The income statement (Figure 3) is often referred to as the 'P&L' or earnings report. The net profit or loss is simply the difference between the incoming dollars for product sold and the outgoing dollars necessary to cover the costs of running the business.

CONSOLIDATED STATEMENTS OF INCOME AND RETAINED EARNINGS
ABC MANUFACTURING COMPANY

| In Millions of Dollars - Year Ended December 31, 1981 | | % of Sales |
|---|---|---|
| NET SALES | $200.00 | |
| | | |
| COSTS AND EXPENSES | | |
| Cost of Sales | 148.6 | 74.3 |
| Selling, General and Administrative Expenses | 34.4 | 17.2 |
| Interest Expense | 3.0 | 1.5 |
| Depreciation | 2.8 | 1.4 |
| Other (Income) Expense | 1.0 | .5 |
| | 189.8 | 94.9 |
| | | |
| INCOME BEFORE INCOME TAXES | 10.2 | 5.1 |
| PROVISION FOR INCOME TAXES | 4.6 | 2.3 |
| NET INCOME | 5.6 | 2.8 |
| | | |
| RETAINED EARNINGS BEGINNING OF YEAR | 27.3 | |
| LESS CASH DIVIDENDS DECLARED | 1.9 | |
| RETAINED EARNINGS AT END OF YEAR | $31.0 | |
| | | |
| NET INCOME PER COMMON SHARE | $ .58 | |
| DIVIDEND PER COMMON SHARE | $ .20 | |

(Figure 3)

The income statement summarizes the activities of an entire fiscal year. The balance sheet represents the financial position of the company on a single specific date.

The additional columns: % of Total Assets, % of Total Liabilities and Stockholders' Equity, and % of Sales, are not normally a part of the financial report. This % decomposition is included for the reader's convenience and discussion further on.

Following is a brief definition of the items detailed in the Financial Report:

Cash - Money in the cash drawer and money deposited in banks.

Short Term Investments - Temporary investment of idle cash, readily marketable and usually with minimum price fluctuation.

Receivables - Amount due from customers for product shipped, adjusted for bad debt allowances.

Inventories - Raw material, work in process and finished goods.

Property, Plant and Equipment (Fixed Assets) - Assets not intended for sale which are employed in the manufacture and distribution of products. These assets include land, buildings, machinery and equipment and construction in progress. They are valued at cost minus accumulated depreciation with the exception of land, which is not depreciated.

Accumulated Depreciation - Decline in useful value of fixed assets due to use, wear, passage of time, obsolescence, etc.

Prepaid Expenses and Deferred Charges - Prepaid expenses are expenses paid before they are actually due such as paying insurance premiums or rentals in advance. The asset listed is the amount which is paid but should not be expensed until sometime after the date of the balance

sheet. Deferred charges allow the spreading of large one time expenditures over future time periods. (Assuming benefits from the expenditures will occur over future time periods.

Short Term Borrowings and Current Maturities of Long Term Debt - Amount which must be paid within the year to banks or other lenders.

Accounts Payable - Amount which must be paid to vendors for purchased goods.

Accrued Expenses - Amount owed for expenses incurred up to the date of the balance sheet which have yet to be paid for, such as salaries, wages, fees, pensions, etc.

Income Taxes - A special category of accrued expenses reported separately because of the relative importance and size of the amount.

Long Term Debt - Debts due beyond one year from the balance sheet date. Examples include notes, mortgage bonds, lease obligations, sinking fund debentures, etc.

Stockholders' Equity - The net worth of the company after subtracting all liabilities.

Preferred Stock and Common Stock (Capital Stock) - Shares in the company owned by stockholders and represented by stock certificates. Preferred stock has preference over common relative to dividends and the distribution of assets in the event of liquidation.

Additional paid in Capital (often referred to as Capital Surplus) - The amount paid in by stockholders for stock purchases which is in excess of the par value (legal value) of the stock.

Retained Earnings (often referred to as earned surplus) - Net profits less dividend payments. This is reported as an accumulated amount from the origin of the business. The accumulation prior to the current year has been reinvested in the business. These funds are not available for current use. The current year retained earnings reported at the bottom of the income statement were available during the year. (Specifically for the ABC Manufacturing Company that would be $5.6 million of net income less $1.9 million in dividend payments or $3.7 million. This $3.7 million has been added to the accumulated retained earnings of the previous years financial statement of $27.3 million resulting in an accumulated retained earnings of $31.0 million at the end of 1981.)

Net Sales - Money received for goods or services provided adjusted for returned goods and price reductions or discounts.

Cost of Sales - Material, labor and burden costs associated with the procurement of raw material and the factory costs to manufacture products.

Selling, General and Administrative Expenses - 'Non-Manufacturing' costs such as office payroll and expenses, executive salaries, salesmen's salaries and commissions, advertising, etc.

Interest Expense - Interest paid during the year to lenders for the use of their money.

Depreciation - Current expense for decline in the useful value of fixed assets.

Net Income (Net Profit) - All income less all costs and expenses.

Cash Dividends - The payout to the stockholders which is declared by the board of directors. It is stated and paid quarterly (at the option of the board) as a per share amount. The total annual amount for ABC Manufacturing was $.20 per share.

Net Income per Common Share - Calculated by dividing net income by the average number of shares outstanding during the year.

It is important to understand that this is a sample financial statement. Many companies have variations and it is essential to gather as much additional information as possible. Some examples of variations are: including physical distribution costs in cost of sales or selling expenses or reporting it separately. Including R&D expenses in cost of sales or general and administrative or reporting it separately.

The first place to look for additional information is in the 'Notes to Consolidated Financial Statements'. An example would be the costing practice applied to inventory and the detailing of the total inventories into finished goods, work in process and raw material. Even with this additional information caution must be exercised because the financial manager's definition of work in process inventory often differs from the manufacturing manager's definition.

Notes cover a wide range of items such as stock option plans, litigation, details of long term debt, and detail sales, profit and asset information by industry segment and geographic area.

Public companies must also file a form 10-K with the Securities and Exchange Commission. This contains additional financial details. Most companies make this available, on request, to stockholders without charge.

## WHAT DOES THE FINANCIAL REPORT TELL YOU?

ABC Manufacturing Company's financial report displays long lists of specific numbers. Inventories are $35.9 million, net income is $5.6 million, receivables are $25.6 million and stockholders equity is $54.2 million. So what! What does this tell you? Even the % numbers supplied, such as selling, general and administrative at 17.2% of sales tells you little or nothing.

These numbers tell us something; they have value, only if they can be related, compared, or trended relative to other numbers.

The following portion of this paper will develop some basic types of financial ratios where multiple specific items in the financial statement are related to one another, where a company is compared with other companies in a similar business, and where the same item is trended over a period of time.

There are four basic types of financial ratios:
. Liquidity ratios which relate to the company's ability to meet its maturing short term obligations
. Activity ratios which relate to the effectiveness of asset utilization
. Profitability ratios which relate to net profits generated on sales and investments.
. Leverage ratios which relate to debt vs equity financing.

In the development of these measurements, particular attention will be paid to areas of current concern. Working capital is one of these. The concern is really with net working capital but unfortunately the words are often improperly interchanged. Working capital is defined as short term assets. Net working capital is defined as current assets minus current liabilities. 'Working Capital Management' includes both current assets and current liabilities.

Working Capital Management is important because:
. Financial managers spend the largest portion of their time in this area.
. Current assets generally represent more than 50% of a company's assets (current assets are 60.5% of ABC Manufacturing's total assets)
. Small firms have limited access to long term capital markets and must rely on the short term which increases current liabilities
. Interest rate uncertainty is also forcing some companies to increase current rather than long term debt.

Net working capital problems plague many companies today. Some of these companies (Automotive provides an example) have significant potential liquidity problems because current assets can barely cover current liabilities.

Proposals that impact this balance unfavorably in todays questionable economy will surely be rejected in many companies, regardless of the long term benefits.

ABC Manufacturing Company has $33.2 million in net working capital. Is that good or bad? Who knows? Liquidity ratios answer these questions.

## LIQUIDITY RATIOS

The current ratio is calculated by dividing current assets by current liabilities. A ratio of 2.0 or better (with few exceptions) indicates a healthy net working capital.

$$\text{Current Ratio} = \frac{\text{Current Assets}}{\text{Current Liabilities}} = \frac{\$68.7 \text{ Million}}{\$35.5 \text{ Million}} = 1.9$$

Generally companies that have small inventories and easily collected receivables can operate more safely than companies with large inventories and extensive credit sales.

The inventories portion of current assets is particularly questionable relative to the ability to sell it quickly and at book value. The quick ratio excludes the inventories in the current ratio calculation, recognizing the importance of the company's ability to pay off short term obligations without relying on the sales of inventory. A safe quick ratio is 1.0 or greater.

$$\frac{\text{Quick Ratio}}{\text{(Or Acid Test)}} = \frac{\text{Current Assets-Inventories}}{\text{Current Liabilities}} = \frac{\$32.8 \text{ Mil}}{\$35.5 \text{ Mil}} = 0.9$$

## ACTIVITY RATIOS

Activity ratios relate sales to many different assets giving multiple measurements of the effectiveness of asset utilization.

$$\text{Inventory Turnover} = \frac{\text{Sales}}{\text{Inventory}} = \frac{\$200.0 \text{ Million}}{\$35.9 \text{ Million}} = 5.6 \text{ times}$$
(Sales)

A problem with the sales to inventory ratio is that sales are at market prices and inventory is at cost. An additional calculation of inventory turnover involves cost of sales:

$$\text{Inventory Turnover} = \frac{\text{Cost of Sales}}{\text{Inventory}} = \frac{\$148.6 \text{ Mil}}{\$35.9 \text{ Mil}} = 4.1 \text{ times}$$
(Cost of Sales)

Another potential problem is that sales occur over the entire year and the inventory asset represents one point in time. The best possible inventory turnover calculation would utilize average inventory and cost of sales. It is also possible to measure inventory turnover for individual inventories such as raw material, work in process and finished goods.

A use of the inventory turns ratio is to compare your company's inventory turnover with other companies in your industry utilizing the key business ratios published by Dun & Bradstreet, Inc. But, be cautious in your conclusions. Differing company strategies for example, can render these comparisons useless.

The best and safest use of the inventory turnover number is to plot it (trend it) over a number of years and use this as a basis for intelligent questioning in identifying or confirming problems.

Caution again is advised because of possible changes in the business, business strategy or inventory costing policy over the time period you are analyzing trend data.

Another activity ratio is collection period which is a measure of accounts receivable turnover. It is calculated by dividing receivables by sales per day. The resulting collection period represents the average amount of time between sales and receipt of payment. It is also defined as the average number of days of sales that is represented by accounts receivable.

$$\text{Sales Per Day} = \frac{\$200.0 \text{ Million}}{365 \text{ Days}} = \$.548 \text{ Million}$$

$$\text{Collection Period} = \frac{\text{Receivables}}{\text{Sales Per Day}} = \frac{\$25.6 \text{ Mil}}{\$.548/\text{Day}} = 46.7 \text{ days}$$

This collection period should be compared with the company's selling terms to see if, on the average, customers are paying their bills on time. Trend data should be related to credit policy changes, billing changes, shipping changes etc.

The aging of receivables (30,60,90 days & over) is also important. Large amounts of older receivables which may be from a relatively small number of customers, can cause an unhealthy skew in the aging. Unfortunately, aging information is normally not provided in financial reports.

Fixed asset turnover, particularly when trend data is plotted, is an excellent indicator of capacity utilization.

$$\text{Fixed Assets Turnover} = \frac{\text{Sales}}{\text{Net Fixed Assets}} = \frac{\$200.0 \text{ Mil}}{\$36.8 \text{ Mil}} = 5.4 \text{ Times}$$

Total asset turnover is an overall measurement of the company's effectiveness in utilizing all its assets.

$$\text{Total Asset Turnover} = \frac{\text{Sales}}{\text{Total Assets}} = \frac{\$200.0 \text{ Mil}}{\$113.6 \text{ Mil}} = 1.76 \text{ Times}$$

In other words, ABC Manufacturing Company generated $1.76 in sales for every $1.00 of assets.

## PROFITABILITY RATIOS

Profit is the 'bottom line' of the business score card. The profitability ratios therefore, give a good measurement of the net result of the overall management of the business.

Profit margin, the profit for every $1.00 of sales, is calculated by dividing after tax net income by sales

$$\text{Profit Margin} = \frac{\text{Net Profit After Taxes}}{\text{Sales}} = \frac{\$5.6 \text{ Mil}}{\$200.0 \text{ Mil}} = 2.8\%$$

114

or $.028 profit per $1.00 of sales. The ABC Manufacturing Company is making a little less than three cents for every sales dollar.

Is that good or bad? Again, it is a function of the type of business and business strategies. After tax profits can range from less than a penny per sales dollar for a super market to over fifteen cents for a computer manufacturer. How do you compare management effectiveness?

This leads us to the return on total assets (return on investment) often called ROI.

$$\text{Return on Total Assets} = \frac{\text{Net Profit After Taxes}}{\text{Total Assets}} = \frac{\$ 5.6 \text{ Mil}}{\$113.6 \text{ Mil}} = 4.9\%$$

This can also be calculated by multiplying total asset turns by profit margin.

$$\text{Return on Total Assets} = \text{Profit Margin} \times \text{Total Asset Turns}$$
$$= 2.8\% \times 1.76$$
$$\text{ROI} = 4.9\%$$

The ROI measurement is the equalizer. It is the result of the management of all the items on the income statement and the asset side of the balance sheet.

Return on equity (net worth) is the critical measurement for the stockholders. ROE measures the return on the stockholders' investment

$$\text{Return on Equity} = \frac{\text{Net Profit After Taxes}}{\text{Total Stockholders' Equity}} = \frac{\$ 5.6 \text{ Mil}}{\$54.2 \text{ Mil}} = 10.3\%$$

ROE can also be calculated by dividing ROI by the total stockholder's portion of total liabilities and stockholders' equity. The decomposition of the balance sheet (Figure 2) provides 47.7% or .477 for total stockholders' equity

$$\text{ROE} = \frac{\text{ROI}}{\text{Equity } \%} = \frac{4.9}{.477} = 10.3\%$$

## LEVERAGE RATIOS

Debt ratio provides the relationship between the two major categories of items on the liabilities and stockholders's equity side of the balance sheet. The debt ratio relates the total funds provided by creditors/lenders to the funds provided by owners/stockholders.

The decomposition %'s of liabilities and stockholders' equity (Figure 2) show a 47.7% contribution by owners and a 52.3% contribution by creditors.

The debt ratio is specifically defined as the % of total funds that have been provided by creditors. ABC Manufacturing has a debt ratio of 52.3% or .523.

Since total funds supplied equals total assets (the balancing act of the balance sheet) the debt ratio calculation is normally portrayed as:

$$\text{Debt Ratio} = \frac{\text{Total Debt}}{\text{Total Assets}} = \frac{\$ 59.4 \text{ Million}}{\$113.6 \text{ Million}} = 52.3\%$$

Relating back to the return on equity calculation in the preceding section on profitability ratios, you see that the ROE calculation can now be written:

$$\text{ROE} = \frac{\text{ROI}}{(1-\text{Debt Ratio})} = \frac{4.9}{(1-.523)} = 10.3\%$$

This demonstrates vividly why the debt ratio is referred to as leverage. As the debt ratio increases the ROE increases relative to ROI, giving an earnings leverage to the stockholders/owners.

There is a favorable leverage only as long as the company earns more on borrowed funds than it pays in interest. Leverage is a two edged sword however, and if the company earns less on borrowed funds than it pays in interest, the leverage can be just as dramatic, but in an unfavorable direction.

A highly leveraged company (50% to 60% or more) might find it difficult to borrow funds since creditors already share the largest portion of risk. A high debt ratio allows a smaller number of owners to control the business. It might encourage irresponsible speculative activity though, because success brings significantly high returns, but failure means only a moderate loss to the owners.

Production and inventory management practitioners should understand the debt ratio in their business. Projects and proposals are both users and hopefully, future suppliers of funds.

## SUMMARY OF FINANCIAL REPORT ANALYSIS

An understanding of the financial report of your business should allow you to better appreciate the concerns and the motivators of top management (it is after all, their score card).

More importantly, it should help you present and discuss your proposals in a language and fashion that top management can easily relate to.

For example: A proposal for an inventory management system (MRP) has potential impact on:

- Total Asset Turns - VIA
  1. Improved inventory turnover
  2. Improved fixed asset turnover due to better utilization of capacity
  3. Increased sales due to better service
  4. Increased receivables turns (reduction in collection period) due to more complete order shipment and more on time shipments

- Profit Margins - VIA
  1. Reduced cost of sales due to decreased carrying costs, reduced factory burden (expeditors, production control) and reduced material cost (improved vendor communications and scheduling and less vendor associated expediting costs)
  2. Reduced selling, general and administrative expenses due to decreased office and marketing costs and reduced physical distribution costs.

- Source of Funds
  1. Funds released from inventory investment are available for other business purposes.

These improvements in both profit margins and total asset turns provide a multiplication effect in the improvement of ROI and ROE.

In using financial report data, always keep in mind the qualifications and limitations previously mentioned. Also recognize that these represent only a partial list.

The best approach is to use trend data of all the %'s, ratios and other financial measurements presented - and - then use this to ask intelligent questions. The management of the many items displayed in the financial report (not to mention voluminous supporting detailed data) and the complex interrelationship of these items suggests prudence in its use.

But - Properly understood - the financial reports are an extremely valuable source of meaningful data to aid in selling to top management.

## FINANCIAL SIMULATIONS USING THE FINANCIAL REPORT

This section describes how to use portions of the financial report to develop simple, yet powerful financial simulations. The simulations are not detailed enough for complete justification. Their value is in ease of use, ease of understanding, and most importantly, getting managements' attention.

The technique is called the DuPont Analysis. It uses the income statement and the asset half of the balance sheet. The DuPont Analysis for ABC Manufacturing is illustrated in Figure 4. It is an after tax model of ROI.

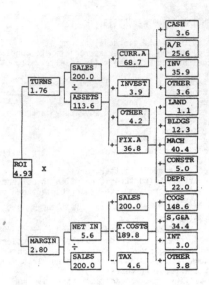

(Figure 4)

The upper half of the diagram is a flow (from right to left) of the assets which are listed in order (current assets followed by fixed assets). Sales are divided by the total assets giving total asset turns of 1.76. The box labeled 'Assets' represents total assets of $113.6 million. The box labeled 'Turns' represents total asset turns of 1.76.

The lower portion of the diagram is the income statement. This flows from the details on the right to the net income of $5.6 million division by sales of $200.0 million for a profit margin of 2.80%.

The result of the multiplication of total asset turns by profit margin is an ROI (Return On Total Assets) of 4.93%. Return on Equity (ROE) could be presented in a box to the left of ROI. You will recall that ROE is ROI divided by (1-Debt Ratio).

This model could be easily expanded to include more details on the right hand side. Receivables (A/R) could be aged; inventories could be split into finished, raw, and work in process; and cost of sales (COGS) could be split into material, labor and burden. Seperate connecting flows could be developed for individual product lines and/or divisions.

The model illustrated can be developed from any annual report with just the income statement and asset half of the balance sheet.

The model, in a simple graphic fashion, shows a number of financial ratios and, most importantly, their relationships.

ROI is again identified as the equalizer. A super market with a profit margin of only 0.9% but with total asset turns of 14.4 (primarily due to inventory turns) can have the same respectable 13% after tax ROI as the computer manufacturer with a profit margin of 11.8% and total asset turns of 1.1.

The model also emphasizes the potential impact that production and inventory management has on the profitability of the company.

Manufacturing company executives, almost without exception, have ROI as one of their major measurements. In viewing the model now from left to right, it essentially defines business managers as managers of margins and managers of turns. Turns management can also be defined as asset management. The obvious largest manageable asset of the ABC Manufacturing Company is inventory.

There is another important asset that is not as easily identified on the balance sheet. That asset is (in production and inventory management terms) capacity. Clearly the capacity asset is not all of the net fixed assets, but in many companies it is a major portion of it.

If management would accurately define manufacturing capacity, it might emerge as the largest manageable asset of the company. Factory buildings, not offices and research centers, would make up the buildings asset. Production machines and tooling, not automobiles and office equipment, would be the machinery and equipment asset. Additionally, the direct labor force would be defined as a dollar value.

Depreciation is a critical element in this development of a dollar asset value of capacity. The depreciated (net fixed) assets of ABC are $36.8 million. The value before depreciation though is $58.8 million. What value should be used? Unfortunately depreciation (particularly older plants) tends to diminish the relative importance of these assets. The value that should be used is the replace cost. The replace cost is reported to the SEC (Securities and Exchange Commission) by public companies for its fixed assets.

The replace cost of ABC's manufacturing capacity could be significant. It is what ABC would have to pay if it had to replace that capacity today.

Inventory and capacity will now be defined as the largest manageable assets of the ABC Manufacturing Company relative to maximizing the turns portion of the DuPont model.

An examination of the income statement, particularly cost of sales (cost of goods sold - COGS) and selling, general and administrative expenses would also identify inventory and capacity as the key items in maximizing the margin portion of the model.

The simulations that follow deal with inventory and capacity management. Other simulations, particularly A/R collection period reductions, are also important, but will not be dealt with here.

All simulations apply a 46% tax rate to the increased earnings. The tax rate in the original model is 45.1%

The inventory simulation of Figure 5 demonstrates a simple use of the DuPont Analysis. Inventory has been reduced 10% assuming an inventory carrying cost of 30%. Carrying cost saving has been subtracted from cost of sales.

The changes in the income statement and balance sheet (asset side) are immediately apparent. The additional output of inventory turns would be a simple addition to the model.

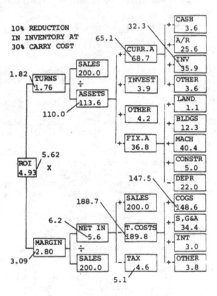

(Figure 5)

[Author's Note: The computerization of such a model is a relatively simple task with the availability of easy to use financial programming languages. One of my P&IC practitioner students in the Dutchess Community College (Poughkeepsie, NY) APICS Certification Classes put this model on his personal home computer in two evenings.]

Adding the liability and stockholders' equity side of the balance sheet to the model would permit the output of all the measurements and ratios previously discussed.

Another interesting use of this particular inventory reduction model is illustrated in Figure 6.

EFFECT OF INVENTORY CARRY COST

| Inventory Carry Cost | 10% Inventory Reduction ROI (4.93%) | EPS ($1.00) |
|---|---|---|
| 24% | 5.51% | $1.08 |
| 30% | 5.62% | $1.10 |
| 36% | 5.72% | $1.12 |

(Figure 6)

There seems to be a continuing debate about carrying cost. Are they too high? too low? One study reported shocking differences between the carrying cost used by the companies in the study to their actual carrying cost. Figure 6 summarizes the results of multiple simulations to evaluate the sensitivity of the model (the company) to the carrying cost variable. Management can then decide if it is worth determining their true inventory carry costs.

A simulation on material costs decrease is illustrated in Figure 7.

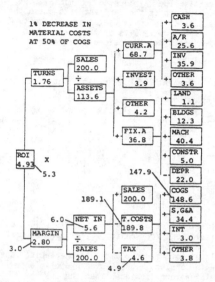

(Figure 7)

The model assumes that material costs are 50% of cost of sales. This equates to 37% of the sales dollar. This has significant leverage on ROI which has been increased by over 7% assuming a 1% decrease in material costs. MRP and purchasing systems should be viewed very favorably based on these results.

The model in Figure 8 could be referred to as a 'Productivity Increase' model. The simulation is evaluating a 2% increase in factory output (sales) assuming no increase in labor costs or increase in plant assets. In other words, better production and inventory control has permitted ABC Manufacturing to produce 2% more product with the same factory and work force.

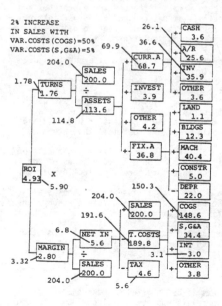

(Figure 8)

Material costs and sales commissions are increased in the model by 2%. Material is assumed to be 50% of cost of sales. Sales commissions are 5% of S,G&A expenses.

Please note that S,G&A has increased (to 34.43) but it does not show in the illustration due to truncating.

A/R has been increased by 2% (collection period was held constant) and the increase is assumed to be financed at 18%. Inventory has also been increased by 2% and a 30% carrying cost has been applied.

This is a very conservative simulation. If the ABC Manufacturing Company implemented good manufacturing systems, they could conceivably produce 2% more sales and have less inventory. If there were no inventory increase, total asset turns would increase to 1.97, margins to 3.39% and ROI to 6.1%. The tax rate on the increase in before tax earnings is 46%.

These simulations were run independently so there is no compounding from one simulation to the next. It would be a simple matter to change multiple items at one time. (For example: an inventory reduction, increase in output, and a material cost reduction)

The advantage of running the simulation with changes in only one item (variable) like A/R or inventory or material cost is to allow you to judge how sensitive the model is to that variable. This helps identify the variable with the most leverage on ROI.

The results of multiple independent simulations are summarized in figure 9.

| | FOR AN ADDITIONAL | |
| --- | --- | --- |
| | 1 % ROI | 20¢ EPS |
| Reduce Inventory (30% Carry Cost) | 14.6% | 20.0% |
| or Reduce Collection Period | 14 Days | 20 Days |
| or Reduce S,G&A Expenses | 6.1% | 6.0% |
| or Reduce Material cost (50%of COGS) | 2.8% | 2.9% |
| or Increase Productivity | 2.1% | 1.0% |
|     Var. Costs (COGS) = 50% | | |
|     Var. Costs (S,G&A) = 5% | | |

(Figure 9)

The significant profit impact of the 'Increased Productivity' simulation might be misleading. Based on the numbers, 'Increasing Productivity' would have a higher priority than 'Reduce Inventory'. The inventory system however, might be the means by which productivity is increased.

The advantage of running the simulation with multiple variables changed is to allow you to simulate what is realistically going to happen with the implementation of good production and inventory management systems. (For example: An inventory reduction accompanied by a reduction in material costs and administrative expenses).

If management has a reasonably good understanding of how production and inventory management systems effect virtually every part of their business, then they should accept proposals and justification data based on savings from many parts of the business. This also permits you to be conservative in using this model. Specifically: very small reductions in inventory and material costs accompanied by a small increase in productivity might compound to produce a yield equivalent to or even greater than a very large inventory reduction. The relative size of these improvements of course, are easily quantified in the model.

## JUSTIFICATION AND CAPITAL BUDGETING

The justification of production and inventory management systems will be viewed by management the same as any other major expenditure. The process of planning expenditures whose returns extend into the future (beyond one year) is defined as capital budgeting.

The production and inventory control practioner must have an appreciation for the capital budgeting process and how management will probably view proposals relative to this process. Capital budgeting is a very broad and complex subject however, and clearly beyond the scope of this paper.

Methods for evaluating and ranking proposals, as part of the capital budgeting process, will be covered here. Three commonly used approaches are:
- Payback
- Net Present Value
- Internal Rate of Return

## PAYBACK

Payback involves the calculation of the number of years to return the initial investment. Figure 10 is an example of ranking two proposals using payback. Assume both projects require an investment of $150,000.

| Year | Net Cash Flow Project I | Project II |
|------|------|------|
| 1 | $80,000 | $20,000 |
| 2 | 70,000 | 40,000 |
| 3 | 40,000 | 60,000 |
| 4 | 10,000 | 80,000 |
| 5 | | 100,000 |

(Figure 10)

The payback on Project I is two years and on Project II it is almost three and a half years. The obvious drawback of the payback method is that it ignores the net cash flow beyond the payback period.

Managers in the business that have short horizons in their performance plans (typically yearly measurements and bonuses) will favor the payback method because the projects with faster payback produce higher profits in the short run.

Longer range production and inventory management projects (MRP is a good example) must be sold to a level of management that has longer range objectives and measurements.

Another approach is to split up large projects into smaller sub-projects and then evaluate these smaller sub-projects. Inventory accuracy or bill of material sub-projects of MRP typically provide paybacks of a year or less. It is important to insure that sub-projects can be integrated and that they are implemented in the proper sequence.

Many companies are currently putting more emphasis on payback (regardless of its shortcomings) because of business conditions, cash flow problems, and high interest rates.

Payback is also often used as a risk measurement in combination with other methods for evaluating projects. (The shorter the payback the less the risk.)

Another disadvantage of the payback method is that it fails to consider the time value of money. In the net cash flow of the project, a dollar five years from now is worth less than a dollar today because of the interest factor. Discounted cash flow techniques accomodate the interest factor.

## NET PRESENT VALUE

The net present value method calculates the present value of future returns minus the cost of the investment. Future returns are discounted at the company's cost of capital. Discounting is the opposite of compounding, as in compound interest in a savings account. $1.00 one year in the future is worth approximately $.87 today discounted at 15%. That is the reverse of investing $.87 today at 15% interest which will be worth $1.00 a year from now.

Projects I and II are evaluated in Figure 11 using the net present value method.

### NET PRESENT VALUE - DISCOUNTING AT 15%

| | PROJECT I | | | PROJECT II | | |
|------|------|------|------|------|------|------|
| Year | Net Cash Flow x | Discount Factor = | Present Value | Net Cash Flow x | Discount Factor = | Present Value |
| 1 | $80,000 | .87 | $69,600 | $ 20,000 | .87 | $17,400 |
| 2 | 70,000 | .76 | 53,200 | 40,000 | .76 | 30,400 |
| 3 | 40,000 | .66 | 26,400 | 60,000 | .66 | 39,600 |
| 4 | 10,000 | .57 | 5,700 | 80,000 | .57 | 45,600 |
| 5 | | .50 | | 100,000 | .50 | 50,000 |
| | | | $154,900 | | | $183,000 |
| | Less | 150,000 | | Less | 150,000 | |
| | NPV | $ 4,900 | | NPV | $ 33,000 | |

(Figure 11)

Projects I and II are both acceptable because they have positive net present values. Project II is ranked considerably higher and would be selected over Project I (particularly if they both represented alternate solutions to the same problem.)

The Discount Factor is calculated:

$$\text{Discount Factor} = \frac{1}{(1+C)^y}$$

C is the Cost of Capital (as a decimal) and y is the number of years in the future.

$$\text{Discount Factor For 4 Years} = \frac{1}{(1+.15)^4} = .57$$

## INTERNAL RATE OF RETURN

The internal rate of return is defined as the interest rate that causes the net present value to equal zero.

Since NPV=Present Value (discounted) - Initial Cost, the internal rate of return is the interest rate where the present value (discounted) is equal to the initial cost.

Figure 12 is a table of results of trial and error calculations for Project II's internal rate of return.

| | | 18% | | 20% | | 22% | |
|------|------|------|------|------|------|------|------|
| Year | Net Cash Flow | Disc. Fact. | Present Value | Disc. Fact. | Present Value | Disc. Fact. | Present Value |
| 1 | $20,000 | .85 | $ 17,000 | .83 | $ 16,600 | .82 | $ 16,400 |
| 2 | 40,000 | .72 | 28,800 | .69 | 27,600 | .67 | 26,800 |
| 3 | 60,000 | .61 | 36,600 | .58 | 34,800 | .55 | 33,000 |
| 4 | 80,000 | .52 | 41,600 | .48 | 38,400 | .45 | 36,000 |
| 5 | 100,000 | .44 | 44,000 | .40 | 40,000 | .37 | 37,000 |
| Present Value | | | $168,000 | | $157,400 | | $149,200 |
| Less | 150,000 | | 150,000 | | 150,000 | | 150,000 |
| NPV | | | $+18,000 | | $+ 7,400 | | $- 800 |

(Figure 12)

The internal rate of return for Project II is just under 22%. Similar calculations for Project I yield an internal rate of return of just under 17%.

The internal rate of return equates to the capital cost % that would make the project a break-even proposition. If the internal rate of return is higher than the cost of capital, the project is profitable.

The internal rate of return calculations, like the net present value calculations, rank Project II above Project I. A list of all projects competing for capital, in sequence of decreasing internal rate of return (or net present value) is a natural input to the capital budgeting process.

Theoretically, all projects on the list that are profitable should be accepted by management. There are a number of reasons however, why management may elect not to do so. Capital rationing exists if a limit has been set on the size of the capital budget. That means that even if your project is a profitable one it may not gain approval because of a low ranking.

In proposing and selling to top management you should be aware of capital rationing and the evaluation approach and how your proposal is likely to relate to that approach. The intent here is to simply introduce the approaches and not go into the details of net present value vs. internal rate of return. It is left to the reader to gain additional knowledge if this is important.

The estimate of future cash flows, of course, is the critical input for the calculation of net present value, internal rate of return and payback.

The DuPont Model, or other models of the income statement allow for the development of estimated income statements into the future. Input to these models would include changes to costs of sales, depreciation costs, taxes, etc. Review the income statement in Figure 3 and imagine how you could project it out into the future with data from your proposal.

The DuPont Model since it includes the asset half of the balance sheet, would also permit projections of the assets, and of course inventory turns, collection period, total asset turns and ROI.

The addition of the liabilities and stockholders' equity side of the balance sheet, with future assumptions relative to the financial structure of the business, would complete the basic model of the financial reports.

At a minimum, simple manual projections of just the income statement, can prove valuable in supplying the cash flow estimates for proposal (project) evaluation.

## ACCURACY

Management that is being asked to make company commitments if your proposal is approved, will obviously be concerned with the accuracy and validity of the data and assumptions in the proposal.

Data representing the current view of the company should be verified by financial management. This includes the financial report data and all the additional detailed data that supports the financial reports as well as carry cost %, depreciation schedules, interest cost, etc.

If the current data is not completely accurate then the assumptions and estimates of future cash flows and savings will probably not be accepted. Even with complete accuracy of the current data, there will be challenges regarding the future.

Documented references of other companies' successes (particularly those from a similar industry) can help support your assumptions. Your own personal successful experiences as well as those of others in the business, particularly top level managers (including work experience in other companies) can also increase credibility.

If your company employs any risk analysis techniques, this should be included in your proposal.

Another excellent technique is to utilize simulations to develop the probable results of many possible courses of action. The carry cost simulation of figure 6 is a simple, but effective example.

Developing computer models of the income statement, the DuPont flow, or all the financial reports can easily permit simulation. Multiple simulations across a range of any of your assumed data, such as inventory reduction, carry cost, increase in sales,etc., can provide significant support in helping management evaluate your proposal.

## SUMMARY

Successful production and inventory management practitioners, particularly those who will be future managers and general managers, will possess skills and knowledge well beyond just the P&IC field. They will be skilled in personnel, communications, motivation, planning and finance. Financial knowledge will be essential.

This paper can be best described as a brief and very basic introduction to only a small part of the world of financial management. It was intended for readers with little or no financial background. Its purpose was to acquaint the reader with some of the financial measurements of the business as well as emphasize the impact of production and inventory management on these measurements. Additionally, it introduced a powerful simulation tool (and there are many), the DuPont analysis. Methods for evaluating and ranking proposals, as a part of the capital budgeting process were also covered.

The overall objective was to assist the reader in selling to management through a better understanding of the goals and objectives of top management.

Another objective, which was not previously stated, was to motivate the reader to look further, to study more, and to understand better the sometimes complex and confusing, but always interesting, challenging, and absolutely essential field of financial management.

I hope it has been useful to you.

References:
'How to Read a Financial Report'
Merrill Lynch, Pierce, Fenner & Smith Inc.

'Essentials of Managerial Finance'
Third Edition
J. Fred Weston, Eugene F. Brigham
The Dryden Press, Hinsdale, Illinois

## BIOGRAPHY

Mr. Clark is a Senior Industrial Sector Representative in IBM's Industrial Sector Education Center in Poughkeepsie, New York. He has eight years of marketing experience and thirteen years of manufacturing education experience in IBM.

Mr. Clark teaches manufacturing courses and consults with IBM customer executives throughout the United States. He has taught in Europe, Japan and Canada. He is the co-author and co-producer of IBM's Material Requirements Planning (MRP) Video course which is currently in use worldwide.

He has been presenting to APICS Chapters in the United States and Canada for the past ten years. He has spoken at numerous APICS International Conferences.

Reprinted from *Production and Inventory Management*, Second Quarter, 1988.

# MRP 96: TIME TO RETHINK MANUFACTURING LOGISTICS

JOHN J. KANET

*Department of Management, 101 Sirrine Hall, Clemson University, Clemson, SC 29634*

Old computers go into museums, but old software goes into production every night.

*Anonymous*

Some 20 years ago a few leading American manufacturing companies like Black & Decker and Twin Disc began to implement the first versions of net-change material requirements planning (MRP) systems. Since then, the growth in popularity of MRP-based manufacturing logistics has been phenomenal. During this period APICS launched its national MRP crusade and watched its membership rolls swell to over 61,000 members. Today there are over 16,000 APICS "certified practitioners" or "fellows" of production and inventory management, each of whom has a demonstrated knowledge of the MRP methodology. In 1975, Orlicky [10] estimated that 700 U.S. companies had MRP-based software systems. Today there are probably at least that many consulting firms and software houses "homilizing" the virtues of MRP.

MRP is the underlying approach to manufacturing planning currently being taken by giants like IBM (with their COPICS and MAPICS software packages) and Arthur Andersen (with their Mac-Pac). A survey by Zais [17] identified 16 companies who in 1984 sold $400 million altogether in MRP software to 17,000 clients. MRP is *big business* in the field of production and inventory management, yet there is a rising tide of disappointment with the MRP-based methods and growing evidence that MRP may well *not* be "the" way to go in manufacturing. One indicator of this is the seemingly unceasing cavalcade of MRP-related buzzwords and acronyms. We have seen MRP, closed-loop MRP, MRP II, CRP, RRP, BRP, MRP 8, JRP, . . . , ad nauseum.

At a recent national conference of operations executives and university professors of operations management, a distinguished speaker, tongue in cheek, referred to the current version as "MRP 95." A few seconds later, he corrected himself with "No, MRP 96!" I interpret his remark as being indicative of a general breakdown in confidence all of us in manufacturing are beginning to have with the MRP-based manufacturing logistics framework. Something is fundamentally awry with the substance when it requires so much sloganeering.

## MRP-Based Manufacturing Logistics

Figure 1 illustrates what is meant here by the term "MRP-based manufacturing logistics." Central to this approach is an MRP component inventory planning system, surrounded by other logistics modules such as master scheduling, capacity planning, shop scheduling and control, and the like. Typically, the approach takes a set of forecasted customer orders and develops a master schedule of production. The master scheduling task is often aided by a "rough-cut" capacity planning module. The MRP "explosion logic" then orchestrates the release of production orders based on planned lead times and predetermined lot sizes. Planned order releases from the MRP inventory system are used to conduct "machine load" analyses for capacity planning. As orders are released to the production system, the factory scheduling module uses the MRP due date as a means for providing priority to orders as sequenced through the factory in competition for limited resources.

## The Record

U.S. manufacturing has embraced MRP because it held the promise for reducing inventory and improving customer service, yet I see little evidence of any widespread major improvement along these lines. Consider Figure 2, which shows inventory turns for the U.S. manufacturing sector over the period 1948–1986. Viewing aggregate figures like these has the advantage of not being fooled by improvements in one industry that may be coming out of the "hide" of some other industry group (such as I fear might be the case as we rush to implement the new just-in-time philosophy). There may be a trend of improvement since the MRP crusade of the early 70s, but a better explanation of changes in inventory is simply the cyclical nature of the economy. In examining Figure 2, we see that, without fail, every low point in inventory turns oc-

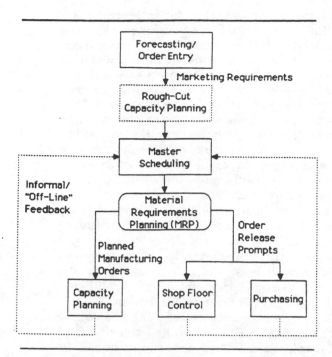

**FIGURE 1: MRP-based logistics system architecture**

curred at the bottom of an economic recession. As the economy recovers, so does inventory turns. Whether or not there has been any significant underlying improvement in inventory turns in recent years is a point for statisticians to debate. I would attribute a major portion of the improvement in inventory turns in the last three years primarily to the steadiness in the U.S. economy and not necessarily to any inherent improvement in manufacturing logistics. But let us be generous and claim that MRP has caused American manufacturers to increase their inventory turns—back to the level experienced in 1950!

### The Potential

Maybe eight inventory turns is simply the best that U.S. manufacturing can muster; my research in manufacturing logistics leads me to a different conclusion. The potential exists for an *order of magnitude improvement* in inventory turns for U.S. manufacturing. My experience with surveying a large variety of manufacturers indicates that the typical manufacturing order in the U.S. (a) has about 10 operations and (b) spends about 10 times more time unproductively waiting within the manufacturing system than in actual machine time. Consider what would happen if we lived in a world of perfect coordination (the world of just-

in-time). Then all the unproductive interoperation times could be eliminated, and each operation of a production order could overlap so as to run simultaneously. The resulting improvement in inventory turns would be on the order of magnitude $10 \times 10$. Can anyone imagine U.S. manufacturing inventory turns being between 700 and 800? Clearly this is an upper bound on what could be possible with perfect coordination, but as long as we stay with the MRP-based approach to manufacturing logistics we will never come close.

### So What's the Matter with MRP?

For at least ten years now, we have been hearing more and more reasons why the MRP-based approach has not reduced inventories or improved customer service of the U.S. manufacturing sector. First we were told that the reason MRP didn't work was because our computer records were not accurate. So we fixed them; MRP still didn't work. Then we were told that our master schedules were not "realistic." So we started making them realistic, but that did not work. Next we were told that we did not have top management involvement; so top management got involved. Finally, we were told that the problem was education. So we trained everyone and spawned the golden age of MRP-based consulting.

I want to be properly understood. There certainly was a data accuracy problem, a problem of unrealistic master schedules, a lack of top management involve-

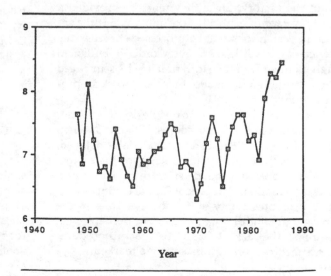

**FIGURE 2: History of U.S. manufacturing inventory turns, 1948–1986**

ment, and a problem of training. But I maintain that all along there also have been fundamental problems in the basic MRP approach—problems which no amount of data accuracy, realism in master schedules, management involvement, or employee training can fix.

## So What's *Really* the Matter with MRP?

There are a number of fundamental flaws in the MRP-based approach to manufacturing logistics. A central weakness is MRP's modus operandi of sequential, independent processing of information. The approach attempts to "divide and conquer" by first planning material at one level and then utilization of manpower and machines at another level. Lot sizing, for example, is done prior to and independent of capacity planning and sequencing/scheduling. The result is production plans which are often found to be infeasible at a point too late in the planning process to afford the system the opportunity to recover. To account for this fundamental weakness, buffers of inventory and planned lead time are embedded everywhere within the system. Sadly enough, even then it is difficult at best to say with any degree of precision whether or not a given master schedule can be feasibly accomplished.

As another example of the inherent weakness of the MRP-based approach, consider the role played by planned lead times in the logistics planning process. Planned lead times are management parameters which are provided *prior* to the planning process. They represent the amount of time budgeted for orders to flow through the factory. Since they must be provided a priori, they cannot explicitly take into account the sequence in which jobs will be processed. Because the sequence is not yet known, every order is budgeted enough planned lead time to permit it to be sequenced first. The result is a tremendous waste of work-in-process inventory.

In MRP-based logistics logic there exist no well-designed formal feedback procedures. When a problem occurs on the shop floor, or a raw material is delayed, there is no well-defined methodology for the system to recover. Procedures that do exist are largely ad hoc, off-line, and manual. The lack of formal feedback procedures promotes safety buffers by everyone in the planning and control organization. But perhaps even more tragic, the lack of formal feedback procedures means a firm can often miss strategic marketing opportunities.

I am reminded of my days as materials manager at Black & Decker. It seemed as though Marketing always had a good reason to want to change the master production schedule—and they always had a well-defined proposal. For example, "If you guys can increase that order of model x33 edger trimmers that is scheduled in seven weeks by 1500, then we'll have a shot at capturing a special order from K-Mart. It means about $30,000 extra in revenues if you guys can do it." The type of answer that really needs to be given would go something like this: "Yes, we can make the schedule change you want, but it can be done only by making the order for model z22 drills, scheduled in six weeks, one week late. Furthermore, the additional out-of-pocket costs for overtime, inventory, and delivery will probably amount to $7200. What would you guys like us to do?" There is no MRP-based logistics planning and control system in existence today that can provide this type of crisp analysis quickly and accurately on a day-in-day-out basis. And as long as we stick with the basic sequential, independent logic of MRP, this type of analysis will never become available.

Aside from a collection of buzzwords and slogans, MRP-based logistics has fostered a whole host of ad hoc functions and methods for handling various aspects of the manufacturing control problem. For example, the activity which IBM calls "order release" in their MRP literature is used to smooth the flow of work into the shop so as to keep work-in-process inventory low. Never mind the fact that since the raw materials for these orders are already available, the real damage to manufacturing inventory is already done! Yet we continue to invent complicated techniques and procedures like work center "input/output analysis" to control work-in-process inventory flows. As long as we hold to the basic MRP logic, the stream of these types of ad hoc recipes and fixes will never end; the flaws in MRP are too basic. There is no sense trying to fix them. It is like trying to make a silk purse out of a sow's ear—we must look to new directions.

## NEW DIRECTIONS FOR MANUFACTURING LOGISTICS

It is one thing to criticize current technology for its shortfalls; it is something else to suggest the shape of something better. I do not claim to have worked out all the details of a new approach for manufacturing logistics, but I have some ideas as to how the search for new approaches might be conducted. I'm 100% confident, at least, in suggesting where *not* to look. We can stop looking into lot sizing, input/output analysis, infinite capacity planning, priority dispatching, queue control, work load balancing, and procedures for reducing system nervousness. They are all band-aids. We can also eliminate JIT because it is not a methodology but rather a philosophy, and we are looking for methodologies here.

### Where to Look

I suggest that, in our search for new methodologies for manufacturing logistics, certain criteria be developed. I would suggest we look to methods which

- Exploit the ever-increasing capability of computers
- Support managerial decision making instead of methods which merely report on or account for it
- Facilitate the insertion of new knowledge as it is discovered
- Are simple, yet not simple-minded.

Seventeen years ago Toffler argued that our society was suffering from what he called "future shock"—the inability to cope with the accelerating changes occurring around us. I would contend that an analogous situation exists in the field of production and inventory management. MRP-based logistics was designed for use on third generation computers of the 1960s whose processing speeds were measured in microseconds. Today, computers are easily 100 times faster, and fifth generation computers, which are just around the corner, promise to be 100 times faster still. Yet the state-of-the-art software that we have in manufacturing logistics does not come close to exploiting this potential.

Probably the single new methodology on the horizon which exploits computer potential and embodies most of the above properties is artificial intelligence (AI). However, I am already hesitant about the "trendiness" of AI. I sense some of the AI gurus to be like the mythological Greek innkeeper Procrustes, who chopped and stretched his guests' legs to fit his beds, or the carpenter whose only tool was a hammer, making all his problems look like nails. But there are a number of aspects of AI which suggest it may hold considerable promise in helping to define the shape of future manufacturing logistics systems. For example, one aspect of AI that has considerable promise in manufacturing logistics is the growing body of knowledge about computer-directed search. Those involved in operations research (OR) have for years known of this under the words "implicit enumeration" or "branch-and-bound." AI researchers have been employing handles like "heuristic" or "constraint-directed" search. Whatever it is called, computer-aided search is likely to be a key ingredient in the design of future production planning and control methods.

## THE CHALLENGE OF CHANGE

Real advances in manufacturing logistics will not come merely by adopting artificial intelligence techniques. What is needed are large doses of the *other* kind of intelligence—the *real* kind. What is important is that we start with a clean slate by first defining what it is that we see to be the objectives of the manufacturing sector of the business, identifying whatever constraints exist, and, perhaps through AI and OR techniques, employing computers to search for satisfactory answers. Somehow, over the years, we have contorted the task of manufacturing logistics by assuming it could be parceled into so many individual activities—inventory planning, production scheduling, capacity planning, as if they were all separable, unrelated functions each having different objectives. We need to get back to the same simple straightforward thinking that people like Henry Gantt used more than half a century ago.

Not too long ago, a nationally recognized consultant told me that, in his opinion, essentially all the principles and techniques for manufacturing control had already been discovered, and that the only remaining task was to get people to just start using them. Unfortunately, this is the mindset that prevails today. I challenge this mindset and say it is time to reassess manufacturing planning and control—starting at the foundation. Obviously this kind of recommendation will strike a controversial nerve, as there is much vested interest in the MRP methodology on the part of managers, consultants, and academics—as there has been considerable effort expended in getting MRP to the level of industrial adoption that it currently enjoys. There is a considerable sunk cost to MRP, not the least of it in emotion. But there exists the possibility for logistics methodologies so much better than MRP that it is only a matter of time until such new methodologies prevail.

## REFERENCES

1. Belt, B., "Men, Spindles and Material Requirements Planning: Enhancing Implementation," *Production and Inventory Management*, Vol. 20, No. 1 (1st Quarter 1979), pp. 54–65.
2. Clark, S. J., Cox, J. F., Jesse, R. R., Jr., and Zmud, R. W., "How to Evaluate Your Material Requirements Planning System," *Production and Inventory Management*, Vol. 23, No. 3 (3rd Quarter 1982), pp. 15–34.
3. Kanet, J. J., "Inventory Planning at Black & Decker," *Production and Inventory Management*, Vol. 25, No. 3 (3rd Quarter 1984), pp. 9–22.
4. ———, "Fifth Generation Manufacturing Resource Planning: The Coming Revolution in Manufacturing Logistics," *American Production and Inventory Control 29th Annual Conference Proceedings* (1986), pp. 10–12.

5. Kanet, J. J. and Adelsberger, H. H., "Expert Systems in Production Scheduling," *European Journal of Operational Research*, Vol. 29, No. 1 (April 1987), pp. 51–59.

6. Kanet, J. J. and Dattero, R., "An Alternative Approach to Manufacturing Logistics," *SETIMS Conference Proceedings* (1986), pp. 84–85.

7. LaForge, R. L. and Sturr, V. L., "MRP Practices in a Random Sample of Manufacturing Firms," *Production and Inventory Management*, Vol. 27, No. 3 (3rd Quarter 1986), pp. 129–137.

8. Mertens, P. and Kanet, J. J., "Expert Systems in Operations Management: An Assessment," *Journal of Operations Management*, Vol. 6, No. 4 (August 1986), pp. 393–404.

9. Miller, J. G. and Sprague, L. G., "Behind the Growth in Material Requirements Planning," *Harvard Business Review*, Vol. 23, No. 5 (September-October 1975), pp. 83–91.

10. Orlicky, J., *Material Requirements Planning*, McGraw-Hill, NY (1975).

11. Plossl, G. W., "MRP Yesterday, Today, and Tomorrow," *Production and Inventory Management*, Vol. 21, No. 3 (3rd Quarter 1980), pp. 1–10.

12. ———, *Production and Inventory Control: Principles and Techniques*, Prentice-Hall, Inc., Englewood Cliffs, NJ (1985).

13. Schroeder, R. G., Anderson, J. C., Tupy, S. E., and White, E. M., "A Study of MRP Benefits and Costs," *Journal of Operations Management*, Vol. 2, No. 1 (October 1981), pp. 1–9.

14. Toffler, A., *Future Shock*, Bantam Books, NY (1970).

15. White, E. M., Anderson, J. C., Schroeder, R. G., and Tupy, S. E., "A Study of the MRP Implementation Process," *Journal of Operations Management*, Vol. 2, No. 3 (May 1982), pp. 145–153.

16. Wight, O. W., *MRP II: Unlocking America's Productivity Potential*, Oliver Wight Limited Publications, Inc., Williston, VT (1983).

17. Zais, A., "IBM Reigns in Dynamic MRP II Marketplace," *Computerworld* (January 27, 1986).

**About the Author—**

*JOHN J. KANET, Burlington Professor of Management, Clemson University, has written numerous articles on a variety of topics in production and inventory management. His current interests include defining the role of manufacturing within the corporate environment and applying artificial intelligence ideas in the design of new manufacturing logistics planning and control systems. A former Fulbright Scholar to West Germany, he is a former materials manager for Black & Decker and is active in APICS, OMA, and ORSA/TIMS.*

Reprinted from *The Oliver Wight Companies Newsletter*, 1985.

## CONTROL OF THE BUSINESS

Where does your company stand in relation to over 1000 MRP/MRP II users? Near the top? In the middle? Hopefully, not at the bottom. We've correlated the data, but only you can make that assessment.

The message this year is control of the business. As you'll see from the survey results, control and competitiveness are tied very closely together.

No surprises! No executive likes to be surprised. Immediately you want to know what happened and why? Good surprises will be rationalized as, "We really did expect it." Bad surprises will be excused as, "Unavoidable." Either way, they usually mean the same thing — something went wrong. When surprises occur often, you are losing control. There's nothing worse.

There's a big difference between being in charge versus being in control. Becoming the boss only brings with it authority. You can direct people, but not necessarily events. You need control to be able to improve deliveries, inventory turns, productivity, costs, quality, and morale. With control, you become an effective manager. You can make the right things happen. Without it, you're just the boss. Anything might happen.

Eliminating surprises by gaining control requires a lot of help. You need accurate and timely data to lay out reliable plans. You need to know the consequences of each alternative to select the best plan. You need to communicate the approved plan so that everyone knows what their job is to carry out the plan. You need to monitor the progress to insure that the plan is being achieved or to initiate corrective action if it's not. In short, you need excellent information to be in control.

Operating a Manufacturing Resource Planning System, MRP II, provides the information to help control the business. Practically all of the companies using MRP II that responded to our MRP/MRP II survey indicated that they had achieved better control. They also reported significant results from having better control.

The objective of the survey was to find out what was happening with MRP and MRP II. In August, we sent it to everyone on our mailing list. Twenty-eight hundred replies were received representing eleven hundred twenty-three companies using MRP and/or MRP II. Whenever there was more than one response from the same company, we consolidated the answers. All of the figures published in this Newsletter reflect a single assessment per company.

To aid you in comparing how you and your company are doing, we have organized the answers to the survey into two categories. First, we show the total representing all companies that replied to the question and, secondly, we show the responses from only those companies that rated themselves as Class A users. This permits you to see how you measure up against the average as well as the best.

You'll be impressed with what you see. In their quest for excellence, many companies are making outstanding progress. It won't simply encourage you, it will stimulate you. Many answers to the survey are noteworthy. One in particular, however, explains how these companies accomplished their results — better control of the business.

### SPECTACULAR RESULTS CAME BACK

An amazing 85% of the companies with MRP/MRP II judge their performance as better than before. Even more amazing is that 80% of the Class A users say it's "enormously better!"

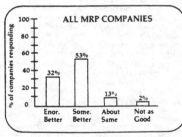
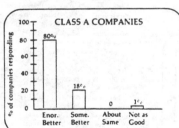

**Better Company Performance**

**CONCLUSION #1:** The success rate of MRP isn't good, it's astronomical. Sometimes the lack of achieving A status is interpreted as failure. Not so. Only 8% of the Class D users indicated that they were not as good as before. The odds are very good that even if you operate it poorly, you will be much better off than you were before.

But how did MRP/MRP II work compared to users' expectations? Sixty-six percent of the MRP users answered that it equaled or exceeded their expectations. The A users were almost unanimous — over 97% indicated that it equaled or exceeded their expectations.

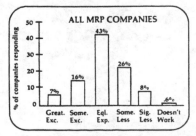
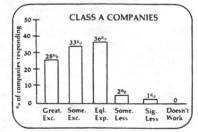

**Met Company's Expectations**

**CONCLUSION #2:** The companies that implement and operate MRP correctly find that the benefits are even greater than what they expected. If there was an error in their assessment, it lies with underestimating the payback, not in overstating it.

However, we wanted to know specific, measurable benefits. Four key indicators of performance for all manufacturing companies are inventory, customer service, productivity, and purchase costs. We asked the MRP/MRP II users for percent improvements in these areas. We have calculated a weighted average for all MRP companies as well as Class A users based on these replies.

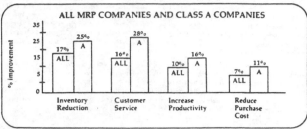

**Measurable Benefits**

**CONCLUSION #3:** "Hard numbers" is how a general manager would evaluate the success of any venture. He's not apt to be impressed with features such as on-line, real-time, better information. The general manager wants to know what you are going to do differently and how this will improve the bottom line. There is a long list of very important activities, each with high potential payback for any one of these important company objectives, ranging from plant layout, revised material handling, robotics, group technology, to CAD/CAM, etc. However, none to my knowledge has produced such impressive improvements in all four areas.

### CONSISTENT COSTS CAME BACK

The average company spent $907,000.00 to implement MRP/MRP II. Surprisingly, there was little difference between an A user, $1,181,000, versus a D user, $1,002,000. Yet, there was a significant difference as to how they invested their money. The A users spent twice as much on education as did the D users.

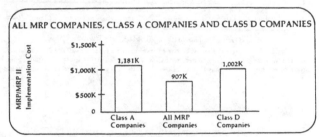

**Approximate Implementation Costs**

**CONCLUSION #4:** These results convert a frequently heard worry, "We can't afford to become a Class A user," into an unfounded myth. That statement comes from somebody who thinks what's needed is better software, a larger computer, more terminals, i.e., more money. The Class A users are not distinguished by spending more money. The major difference between the worst and the best is two words — understanding and attitude. If the general manager has the correct understanding of MRP II and a "can do" attitude to become Class A, you'll succeed.

We then ran an analysis of the reported yearly benefits, question 8, to the costs, question 9. The return on investment reflects a bell shape for the A users, but is badly skewed for the D users.

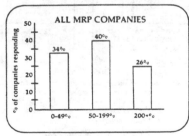
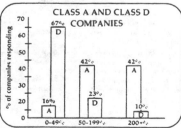

**Return On Investment**

**CONCLUSION #5:** For the A users, the weighted average annual return on investment is an outstanding 200%!

## PREDICTABLE STEPS WERE TAKEN

How was MRP/MRP II implemented? You will see the answers in questions 10 through 15. Significant differences were uncovered. Of interest to everyone, in hindsight, is what would you have done differently? More than half of the companies reported that they needed more education. Even the A users recognized that they didn't do it well enough. Thirty-five percent of them would have done a better job. This contrasts with 64% of the D users indicating that this was a problem. A more dramatic difference existed in terms of top management commitment. Twenty percent of the A users felt that they didn't receive enough, but a whopping 78% of the D users lacked this important ingredient. Encouragingly, 39% of the A users said they would do nothing differently.

We compared the steps followed during implementation and, again, there are some very significant differences. For example, the number of companies who used video for their in-plant education programs was twice the number of those who did not. The A companies aggressively educated their people — as you would expect. Twenty-one percent of the A users educated 100% of their people using video. Eighty-two percent of the A users educated their top management at outside classes versus only 50% of the D users.

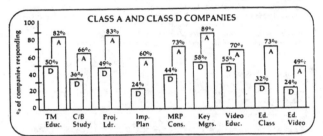

### CLASS A AND CLASS D COMPANIES

During Implementation, What Did Your Division Do?

**CONCLUSION #6:** The answers to the survey confirm what we call the Proven Path. There are a number of prerequisites to become a Class A user. The list is short, but challenging. The good news, however, is that if you follow the path, it leads to a predictable and successful conclusion.

### SIZE OF COMPANY VERSUS SIZE OF RESULTS

We asked for information with respect to the size of the companies responding to the survey. Under 10% of the companies were less than $10,000,000 in terms of dollar volume. All of the other categories were fairly close — in the range of 20% each as you can see on the graph.

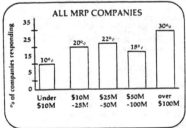
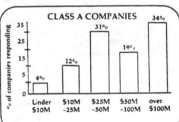

Size of Company

**CONCLUSION #7:** Size and success do not correlate. Some people think that it's easier to implement any new approach in a smaller company. The rationalization is that it takes fewer executives to decide to implement the new approach, fewer people to educate, and fewer old habits to overcome. The results of the survey prove otherwise. It's tough for everybody. But encouragingly, it's just as easy for everybody.

### WHERE ARE YOU GOING?

We were interested in knowing in what areas your use of MRP/MRP II needs improvement. "All areas" was the average answer. The vast majority of A users are satisfied with their current system. A number of users, however, recognize the need to improve their financial interfaces, distribution planning and simulations.

We were also curious as to what other company projects were being considered or actively pursued. The answers indicate that all companies have projects underway. All categories except Kanban showed significant levels of activity. Many of the MRP users are aggressively implementing quality improvement programs and CAD/CAM. Additionally, 50% of the Class A users are cranking up their MRP II efforts to contribute to their Just-In-Time project.

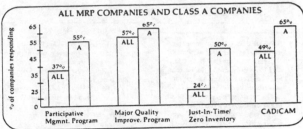

### ALL MRP COMPANIES AND CLASS A COMPANIES

Other Company Projects

**CONCLUSION #8:** The goal to improve any area within a manufacturing company always remains ahead of your current level of performance. To quote our associate, George Bevis, "It's a journey, not a destination." You never get there, you can always improve. The A users are working just as hard as the D users, but more productively.

### THE MOST IMPORTANT FEEDBACK

Not all goals lend themselves to statistical measurements. You can't put a yardstick on the quality of life. Nevertheless, they remain important objectives. We asked the users to assess eight of these. The one that the majority of users rated the highest was "better control of the business." Ninety-nine percent of the A users gained improvement in this area.

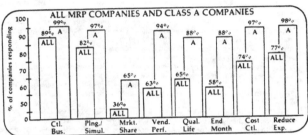

### ALL MRP COMPANIES AND CLASS A COMPANIES

Other Major Benefits

**CONCLUSION #9:** Improved control of the business, in my judgment, is MRP II's most important contribution to manufacturing companies.

### SUMMARY

What did we learn from the survey? Certainly that the potential of MRP II is not conjecture, it's demonstrated. On the other hand, it's not "miracle requirements planning," not a solution by itself. Rather, it provides information for managers. In the hands of an educated executive, this information can help control the business. The right system, accurate data, and people who know how to use them correctly guarantees spectacular results.

The do's and don'ts for implementing MRP II successfully are well known. There is a Proven Path. Follow it and you'll become a Class A MRP II user. Yet, there are executives seeking the "free lunch." They think that buying the hardware, selecting the software, and producing reports should deliver the benefits. But as the Class D users reported, you can't buy the benefits, you have to earn them.

This survey confirms that Pareto's Principle lives — if you stratify any large population, the very best is a small percent. And so it is with the population of MRP II companies. The surprise would be otherwise. Each general manager must decide whether to settle for less payback or to stretch for the maximum payback by becoming an A user.

The Class A MRP II users are achieving great paybacks. Yet, most of them remain unsatisfied. Many of them are actively pursuing a formal Just-In-Time project. As good as they are, they all know that they can be better. They are setting higher goals, not simply remaining content with goals met. They seek new ideas while constantly improving existing procedures, recognizing that both can help them to excel. They understand that it takes an excellent operating system, which MRP II provides, to strive for having all of the resources just when they are needed. They see the challenge within themselves as managers to get the most mileage out of proven systems.

Improvement means rejecting the status quo, raising the highbar of performance, rising to it, and then repeating the cycle. To remain competitive, you need to make this happen. To make this happen, you need control.

# THE RESULTS OF THE SURVEY

**1. Are you currently using MRP or MRP II?**

| | All MRP Companies | Class A Companies |
|---|---|---|
| Only MRP | 35% | 20% |
| MRP and MRP II | 27 | 80 |
| Neither | 38 | — |

The companies that had neither MRP or MRP II were instructed to proceed directly to question #10.

**2. In what areas are you using MRP/MRP II?**

| | All MRP Companies | Class A Companies |
|---|---|---|
| Production Planning | 83% | 93% |
| Master Production Scheduling | 76 | 93 |
| Material Requirements Planning | 95 | 97 |
| Capacity Requirements Planning | 46 | 86 |
| Shop Floor Control | 49 | 80 |
| Input/Output Control | 31 | 68 |
| Vendor Scheduling | 52 | 80 |
| Distribution Resource Planning | 9 | 18 |
| Financial Interface | 38 | 65 |
| Simulations | 19 | 37 |

**3. With MRP/MRP II, is your company's performance better than before MRP?**

| | All MRP Companies | Class A Companies |
|---|---|---|
| Enormously better | 32% | 80% |
| Somewhat better | 53 | 19 |
| About the same | 13 | — |
| Not as good as before | 2 | 1 |

1085 responses; 97% of MRP/MRP II companies.

**4. How has MRP/MRP II worked at your plant?**

| | All MRP Companies | Class A Companies |
|---|---|---|
| Greatly exceeded expectations | 7% | 28% |
| Somewhat exceeded expectations | 16 | 33 |
| Equaled expectations | 43 | 36 |
| Somewhat less than expectations | 25 | 2 |
| Significantly less than expectations | 8 | 1 |
| Doesn't work at all | 1 | — |

1100 responses; 98% of MRP/MRP II companies.

**5. In what areas do you feel your use of MRP/MRP II needs improvement?**

| | Little All | Little A's | Significant All | Significant A's | Major All | Major A's |
|---|---|---|---|---|---|---|
| Production Planning | 40% | 78% | 37% | 17% | 23% | 5% |
| Master Production Scheduling | 36 | 77 | 34 | 16 | 30 | 7 |
| Material Requirements Planning | 60 | 81 | 28 | 15 | 12 | 4 |
| Capacity Requirements Planning | 22 | 59 | 34 | 28 | 44 | 13 |
| Shop Floor Control | 23 | 50 | 33 | 36 | 44 | 14 |
| Input/Output Control | 24 | 52 | 34 | 42 | 42 | 6 |
| Vendor Scheduling | 27 | 46 | 39 | 41 | 34 | 13 |
| Financial Interface | 25 | 35 | 31 | 33 | 44 | 32 |
| Distribution Resource Planning | 31 | 44 | 23 | 26 | 46 | 30 |
| Simulations | 16 | 22 | 27 | 31 | 57 | 47 |

937 responses; 83% of MRP/MRP II companies.

**6. Based on our ABCD Checklist, how does your plant or division rank?**

| | All MRP Companies |
|---|---|
| Class A | 8% |
| Class B | 22 |
| Class C | 24 |
| Class D | 10 |
| Have not answered the checklist | 17 |
| Not aware of the checklist | 19 |

1094 responses; 97% of MRP/MRP II companies.

**7. What have been the major benefits from MRP/MRP II?**

| | None All | None A's | 0-4% All | 0-4% A's | 5-9% All | 5-9% A's | 10-24% All | 10-24% A's | 25-49% All | 25-49% A's | Over 50% All | Over 50% A's |
|---|---|---|---|---|---|---|---|---|---|---|---|---|
| Inventory Reduction | 12% | -% | 9% | 2% | 21% | 10% | 37% | 46% | 17% | 35% | 4% | 7% |
| Improvement in Customer Service | 14 | 2 | 14 | 2 | 22 | 9 | 27 | 38 | 15 | 27 | 8 | 22 |
| Increase in Productivity | 19 | 2 | 18 | 8 | 29 | 28 | 26 | 47 | 7 | 13 | 1 | 2 |
| Reduction in Purchase Costs | 23 | 5 | 25 | 22 | 30 | 34 | 18 | 35 | 3 | 4 | — | 1 |

1019 responses; 91% of MRP/MRP II companies.

| | Significant All | Significant A's | Some All | Some A's | None All | None A's |
|---|---|---|---|---|---|---|
| Better Control of the Business | 39% | 78% | 50% | 21% | 11% | 1% |
| Better Planning/Simulation | 32 | 59 | 50 | 38 | 18 | 3 |
| Improved Market Share | 6 | 19 | 30 | 46 | 64 | 35 |
| Improved Vendor Performances | 9 | 29 | 54 | 65 | 37 | 6 |
| Better Quality of Life for Employees | 17 | 50 | 48 | 38 | 35 | 12 |
| Eliminates the End-of-the-Month Crunch | 18 | 54 | 40 | 34 | 42 | 12 |
| Improved Cost Control | 18 | 40 | 56 | 57 | 26 | 3 |
| Reduced Expediting | 24 | 62 | 53 | 36 | 23 | 2 |

1043 responses; 93% of MRP/MRP II companies.

**8. What would you estimate to be your yearly benefits from MRP/MRP II?**

| | All MRP Companies | Class A Companies |
|---|---|---|
| Under $100K | 25% | 2% |
| 100-249K | 19 | 11 |
| 250-499K | 16 | 26 |
| 500-749K | 12 | 14 |
| 750-999K | 5 | 7 |
| 1M-1.4M | 10 | 14 |
| 1.5-1.9M | 3 | 9 |
| 2.0-2.9M | 5 | 6 |
| 3.0-3.9M | 1 | — |
| 4.0-4.9M | 1 | 1 |
| 5.0-5.9M | — | 1 |
| Over 6M | 3 | 9 |

950 responses; 85% of MRP/MRP II companies.

**9. What were your approximate costs in implementing MRP/MRP II?**

| | All MRP Companies | Class A Companies |
|---|---|---|
| Computer Hardware | $ 257K | $ 394K |
| Computer Software | 176 | 175 |
| Inventory Record Accuracy | 52 | 108 |
| Bill of Material Accuracy | 43 | 52 |
| Routing Accuracy | 29 | 39 |
| Education | 66 | 97 |
| Consulting | 45 | 48 |
| Other Costs | 239 | 268 |
| Total | $907 | $1181 |

579 responses; 52% of MRP/MRP II companies.

**10. In implementing MRP/MRP II, which of the following did your plant or division do?**

| | All MRP Companies | Class A Companies |
|---|---|---|
| Top Mgt. Education | 64% | 82% |
| Formal Cost/Benefit | 46 | 46 |
| Full-Time Project Leader | 68 | 83 |
| Proven Implementation Plan | 43 | 60 |
| MRP Consultant | 51 | 73 |
| Key Mgrs. Educated Outside Classes | 69 | 86 |
| Video-Assisted Education | 62 | 70 |
| Ongoing Educ.- Classes | 47 | 73 |
| Ongoing Educ.- Video | 32 | 49 |

**11. If you sent key managers to outside classes, approximately how many of them did you send?**

| | All MRP Companies | Class A Companies |
|---|---|---|
| Less than 4 | 31% | 13% |
| 5-9 | 32 | 33 |
| 10-24 | 28 | 39 |
| 25-49 | 7 | 12 |
| 50-99 | 1 | 2 |
| Over 100 | 1 | 1 |

943 responses; 84% of MRP/MRP II companies.

**12. If you used video-assisted education for inside education, approximately what percentage of the employees were educated?**

| | All MRP Companies | Class A Companies |
|---|---|---|
| Less than 9% | 13% | 8% |
| 10-49% | 26 | 27 |
| 50-79% | 12 | 9 |
| 80-99% | 10 | 12 |
| 100% | 6 | 15 |
| Did not use video | 33 | 29 |

1123 responses; 100% of MRP/MRP II companies.

**13. If you used video-assisted education for inside education, did the managers teach their people?**

| | All MRP Companies | Class A Companies |
|---|---|---|
| Yes | 23% | 34% |
| Sometimes | 29 | 33 |
| No | 14 | 5 |
| Did not use video | 34 | 29 |

1123 responses; 100% of MRP/MRP II companies.

**14. If you worked with an MRP consultant, did he have previous Class A experience?**

| | All MRP Companies | Class A Companies |
|---|---|---|
| Yes | 39% | 62% |
| No | 11 | 11 |
| Did not use a consultant | 50 | 27 |

1123 responses; 100% of MRP/MRP II companies.

**15. What would you have done differently in implementing MRP/MRP II?**

| | All MRP Companies | Class A Companies |
|---|---|---|
| More Education | 55% | 35% |
| Better Software | 28 | 23 |
| Top Management Commitment | 48 | 20 |
| Other, Not Listed | 21 | 18 |
| Would Do Nothing Differently | 11 | 39 |

**16. What other company projects are you considering or pursuing?**

| | Not Considering All | Not Considering A's | Considering All | Considering A's | Pursuing All | Pursuing A's |
|---|---|---|---|---|---|---|
| Management By Objectives | 40% | 40% | 14% | 12% | 46% | 48% |
| Participative Management | 43 | 33 | 20 | 12 | 37 | 55 |
| Quality Circles | 33 | 26 | 23 | 19 | 44 | 55 |
| Major Quality Improvement Program | 24 | 20 | 19 | 15 | 57 | 65 |
| Kanban | 80 | 70 | 12 | 15 | 8 | 15 |
| Just-In-Time/Zero Inventories | 40 | 29 | 36 | 21 | 24 | 50 |
| CAD/CAM | 26 | 14 | 25 | 21 | 49 | 65 |
| Other | 28 | 17 | 23 | 18 | 49 | 65 |

1327 responses; 73% of all companies.

**17. If you are considering or pursuing any of these projects, how do you feel they compare in benefits to MRP II?**

| | Significantly Less All | Significantly Less A's | Somewhat Less All | Somewhat Less A's | About the Same All | About the Same A's | Somewhat More All | Somewhat More A's | Significantly More All | Significantly More A's |
|---|---|---|---|---|---|---|---|---|---|---|
| Management By Objectives | 31% | 43% | 27% | 24% | 28% | 25% | 6% | 6% | 5% | 2% |
| Participative Management | 26 | 22 | 28 | 31 | 26 | 31 | 13 | 9 | 7 | 7 |
| Quality Circles | 26 | 30 | 30 | 39 | 28 | 22 | 12 | 3 | 4 | 6 |
| Major Quality Improvement Program | 13 | 15 | 20 | 24 | 35 | 35 | 21 | 14 | 11 | 12 |
| Kanban | 52 | 53 | 23 | 22 | 16 | 17 | 5 | 5 | 4 | 3 |
| Just-In-Time/Zero Inventories | 20 | 22 | 22 | 22 | 32 | 32 | 16 | 10 | 10 | 14 |
| CAD/CAM | 20 | 19 | 25 | 24 | 32 | 36 | 17 | 13 | 6 | 8 |
| Other | 55 | 48 | 13 | 22 | 14 | 4 | 7 | 11 | 11 | 15 |

1044 responses; 57% of all companies.

**18. What is the approximate dollar volume (in millions) of your plant or division?**

| | All MRP Companies | Class A Companies |
|---|---|---|
| Under $10M | 10% | 4% |
| 10-24M | 20 | 12 |
| 25-49M | 22 | 31 |
| 50-99M | 18 | 19 |
| Over 100M | 30 | 34 |

1753 responses; 96% of all companies.

**19. Approximately how many employees work at your plant or division?**

| | All MRP Companies | Class A Companies |
|---|---|---|
| Under 100 | 10% | 4% |
| 100-249 | 22 | 18 |
| 250-499 | 24 | 32 |
| 500-999 | 19 | 16 |
| Over 1,000 | 25 | 30 |

1804 responses; 99% of all companies.

Reprinted from APICS 1987 *Conference Proceedings*.

F3   TEN WAYS MRP CAN DEFEAT YOU
Gus Berger, CPIM
The Gus Berger Group

INTRODUCTION

Much is heard today about MRP system failures. The current trend leans toward blaming the people and blaming the company for the inability to successfully implement MRP. The purpose of this presentation is to present a new insight into the problem of MRP II system failures. By proving that MRP II is not perfect, the author proposes to help the MRP II system implementors and users in overcoming the obstacles encountered implementing a system against a "stacked deck" of built-in MRP II logic application problems. With a knowledge and understanding of some of the MRP II logic application deficiencies, the implementor and user are in a better position to avoid both the symptoms and problems encountered as a result of latent MRP II application logic defects.

While finding fault with MRP II logic applications, the author still believes that for a majority of American companies, MRP II still presents one of the best manufacturing planning tools available. It should also be noted, that for those companies considering Just-In-Time (JIT) manufacturing concepts, the MRP II system will still be required as the database for backlog management, as the order-launching vehicle for both purchase orders and release of work to the factory, and as the total integrated database supporting all peripheral systems including Engineering and Finance.

Items identified in the following discussion as weaknesses in MRP II logic applications will not be encountered in every MRP II software system. However, they are the more common problems that the author has encountered in older and in-house generated MRP II systems.

TEN WAYS

1.  The Fallacy of Static Leadtimes
    Most MRP II software systems treat leadtime as a static, fixed element. Once leadtime has been established, it becomes a system constant, retaining its value regardless of other mitigating factors that we will study during the remainder of this presentation. When studying the theories of Just-In-Time manufacturing (JIT) or Optimized Production Technology (OPT), one soon realizes that leadtime is indeed a dynamic variable, subject to multiple mitigating factors. The "fixed factor" approach to leadtime used in most MRP systems proves to be one of the major reasons for shop floor schedule confusion and capacity planning difficulties.

2.  The Mis-Definition of Leadtime
    Defining the elements of leadtime has proven to be one of the major difficulties within MRP II system software. Some MRP II systems instruct the users simply to "load leadtime". Others define leadtime as the series of elements shown in Figure 1. As many companies have discovered, the diligent loading of all leadtime elements shown in Figure 1. usually results in product leadtime so excessive that the company becomes non-competitive in its marketplace!

    The key basic elements of manufacturing leadtime are "set-up time" and "run time". All other elements are what might be defined as "work-out elements." (The objective is to work these elements out to zero or a very minimal amount of time). In some cases there may

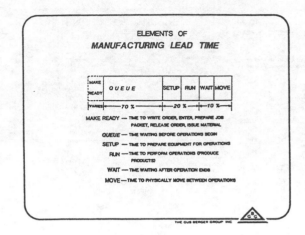

Figure 1.

be a valid need for "move time" due to physical separation of resources. The most glaring fallacy in loading leadtime to the MRP II system database occurs with those systems that recommend the loading of "queue time". The only thing guaranteed as a result of loading queue time is that the queue will exist! "Queue time" is a reality of Murphy at work on the shop floor. The planning of queue time, however, "because it has always existed", will only assure the prolonging of that existence.

For those who've experienced leadtime increase, instead of leadtime reduction after implementing MRP, a study of leadtime elements loaded will usually discover that such things as the automatic loading of "queue time" or the automatic loading of "move time" have been added to every element of fabrication and assembly leadtime, thus creating a leadtime build-up far in excess of the actual time required to produce the product.

3.  Leadtime Vs. Fabrication/Production Quantity
    As determined earlier, leadtime is made up of certain fixed elements which are stored as a total static value. Unfortunately, the production quantity is seldom addressed in the leadtime equation or in the use of the leadtime factor. Most MRP software system logic simply reads the static leadtime value, using it to offset the start of fabrication or assembly from its required completion date, totally disregarding the production quantity.

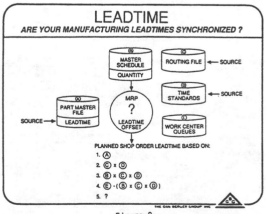

Figure 2.

**128**

© **American Production & Inventory Control Society**

Although we are aware that there can be a dramatic difference in the time required to run one piece vs. one hundred pieces vs. one thousand pieces, to most MRP systems, the static leadtime, whether it was calculated for one or one hundred or one thousand pieces, is always applied, regardless of the actual production quantity. To the uninformed, this becomes an enormous scheduling trap in which large quantities are often put into work with totally insufficient production leadtime or small lots are put into work with excessive leadtimes.

In some cases, companies have realized this danger and calculated lead time for specific lot sizes. All too often, however, the master scheduler and even the production scheduler are not made aware of the lot size rules applied to the leadtime calculation, and therefore schedule work in increments that differ from the lot size used to calculate the static leadtime.

4. The Bill of Material - A Valid Manufacturing Driver?
MRP uses the Bill of Material as the driver for fabrication and manufacturing work orders, yet for many companies the Bill of Material in no way represents the way the product is fabricated and assembled (See Figure 3).

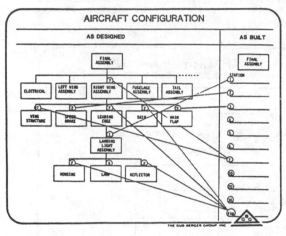

Figure 3.

While a bottom up product structure is representative of the way some companies produce their products, those that produce products on an assembly line usually are far from a bottom up product structure assembly process. As is seen in the case of the aircraft assembly line, items that are called for first in an engineering product structure, may be required last in a production line assembly process, such as aircraft or other major commodity manufacturing.

The author believes that the majority of the software industry is extremely derelict in its responsibilities in terms of providing a Bill of Material explosion process that will allow the production line manufacturer to utilize MRP processing from the bottom up engineering Bill of Material structure, while exploding the product structure to produce pick lists representative of the reality of the way the product is fabricated and assembled without requiring a second "manufacturing" Bill of Material. This is particularly significant in that most companies have substantial difficulty maintaining configuration management with one Bill of Material structure, and virtually all using dual Bills of Material fail to successively maintain synchronized configuration management!

5. MRP - A Tool to Support Bill of Material Revision Control?
Many MRP II systems prove deficient in the ability to maintain change or configuration management. These MRP II systems do not include use of a part revision letter/number as an active addendum to the part number identifier in:

   A. Reading a Bill of Material for MRP explosion purposes

   B. Creating pick lists based on MRP explosions

   C. Reporting receipts and issues to stock.

Most manufacturing companies still encounter difficulty with the "fit/form function criteria" for determining part revision level change vs. actual part number change. These problems are compounded by MRP systems that do not recognize revision level as a source of physical differentiation within a given part number.

6. Leadtime Vs. Routing
MRP II is described as a system to schedule vendors and a system to schedule the shop. Yet, as we will discover, many MRP II software system applications have serious problems with respect to scheduling the shop floor.

As displayed in Figure 4 it becomes apparent that the shop floor scheduling capability is dependent on the Bill of Material structuring. Numerous routing steps may be concealed within a single Bill of Material level. In the example shown, numerous routing operations occur within the twelve week leadtime period for the fabrication level of the Bill of Material structure.

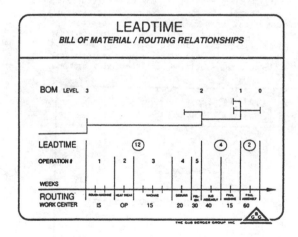

Figure 4.

In fact, it can be observed that within that single Bill of Material level over a period of twelve weeks, the job passes through the same work center twice for a cumulative period of seven weeks out of the total twelve week leadtime. The total net effect is one of being unable to properly schedule the intermediate Work Centers due to the fact that many MRP II software system applications only generate a start date and a required complete date for the Bill of Material level as opposed to stop and start dates for each of the individual routed operations occurring within the Bill of Material level. This characteristic makes capacity planning extremely difficult and often results in overloaded work centers as a result of unexpected conflicting operation start dates that do not appear as a part of the normal MRP II software system scheduling output.

7. The Fallacy of Infinite Capacity Planning
In many MRP II software systems the MRP computation logic assumes that capacity is available to produce whatever has been master scheduled. Few MRP II software systems have an integrated Capacity Requirements Planning (CRP) module that can recognize a shop overload and, in an integrated manner, reschedule the MRP system such that the overload is eliminated and that material will still be available at the correct time and places to support the Capacity Planning driven schedule readjustment.

8. The Real Story of Rough-Cut Capacity Planning
We have been taught that the solution to overloaded work centers lies in rough-cut capacity planning during the Master Scheduling process. Anyone who has ever scheduled in a multi-product, routing intensive job shop will tell you that rough-cut capacity planning lies somewhere between the difficult and the impossible. Basically, the master scheduler is expected to look at the prior MRP and prior capacity load created by the existing Master Schedule and then be able to predict the impact on bottleneck work centers caused by changes made during the current Master Schedule cycle. In essence, the master schedulers are theoretically expected to perform MRP and CRP explosions in their heads, a task that is more than challenging for most computer systems.

As a result, master schedulers have been trying for years to devise methods to improve their rough-cut capacity analysis technique. One of the most common approaches is the use of an equivalent unit algorithm. This algorithm relates all similar products to the most common product produced in the shop (See Figure 5). A base line is created for the common (standard) unit that states its approximate demand in man-hours required against critical bottle-neck work centers (See Figure 6). Other products are compared in terms of a percentage of the standard "equivalent unit" and then summarized as an approximate amount of additional load applied to the specified bottleneck work centers.

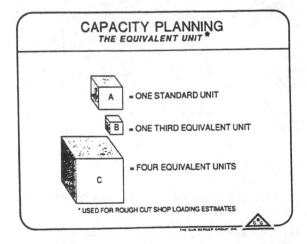

Figure 5.

Unfortunately, this already difficult task of projecting man hours in percentages of a standard unit, is made even more difficult when one attempts to time-phase the addition of the load to the individual bottleneck work centers. The task becomes virtually insurmountable and eventually many master schedulers

abandon the attempt to execute time-phased bottleneck loading analysis. For many MRP systems the only technique available to perform rough-cut capacity planning is to actually run MRP with the new master schedule and then run a Capacity Requirements Planning (CRP) output to determine the impact of the Master Schedule changes. Usually, this solution becomes impractical because of the amount of computer time required to run the initial analysis, let alone to run additional simulations as the master scheduler attempts to capture and overpower "floating bottlenecks" that develop as master schedule changes are simulated.

9. Capacity Planning vs. MRP Logic
One of the greatest failings in much MRP software logic is the lack of integration between Material Requirements Planning and Capacity Requirements Planning during the MRP logic calculation process. As we observed, in the analysis of rough-cut capacity planning, it is extremely difficult to balance capacity through the use of the Master Schedule and rough-cut capacity simulations. Multiple schedule manipulations usually result in non-bottlenecks becoming bottlenecks and the appearance of "floating bottlenecks", that is, bottlenecks that appear and disappear, depending upon the Master Schedule contents.

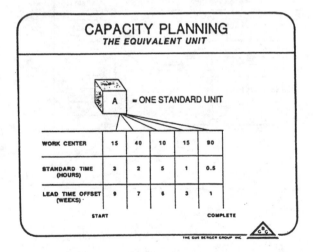

Figure 6.

The only valid solution to this problem is for MRP to run its Capacity Requirements Planning calculation simultaneously with the Material Requirements Planning calculation. The resultant output would be a material requirements plan capable of being supported by available shop capacity. Unfortunately, because most software packages lack MRP/CRP integration, very precisely calculated material plans often disintegrate into confusion when the required capacity is not available to perform some intermediate fabrication or assembly operation on the manufactured product.

10. MRP Logic - A User Confuser
Unfortunately, MRP calculation logic differs from system to system. Many invalid assumptions are often made about how the MRP system will react in response to a schedule acceleration, schedule deceleration or the cancellation of an order that already has work-in-process. The exact application of accelerate, decelerate and cancel messages is not always predictable, particularly with respect to the time

intervals between the occurrences of changing events
that drive these messages and other unrelated
planned/released jobs.

## MRP SCHEDULING LOGIC

| | TIME PERIODS | | | | | | | |
|---|---|---|---|---|---|---|---|---|
| | 1 | 2 | 3 | 4 | 5 | 6 | 7 | 8 |
| REQUIREMENTS | 10 | 20 | | | 30 | 20 | | |
| EXISTING OPEN ORDERS | 10 | | | 40 | | | 10 | 100 |
| MRP RECOMMENDATION  QUANTITY | | 20 | | 40 | | | 10 | 100 |
| ACTION | | △ ORDER | | ▷ DEFER | | ◁ EXPEDITE | | △ CANCEL |

MRP SCHEDULES ORDERS TO MEET REQUIREMENTS
- o MAINTAIN VALID DUE DATES/PRIORITIES
- o SATISFY CHANGING REQUIREMENTS
- o REDUCE SHORTAGES
- o MINIMIZE EXCESS INVENTORY

THE GUS BERGER GROUP, INC.

Figure 7.

It is in the best interest of an MRP system user to
test system behavior with varying combinations of
accelerate, decelerate and cancel messages in an
environment of multiple existing demands. By
understanding the system logic characteristics, the
material/production planner can avoid unnecessary
logic generated crises in the shop and in the purchase
part supply line.

SUMMARY

We have reviewed ten ways to get in trouble while using
MRP system software. I must emphasize again that all MRP
II software systems do not have all of these problems and
some systems successfully overcome many of these problems.
It is safe to estimate, however, that the average MRP II
system user will discover several of the problems
discussed in their MRP software system applications.

Although the items we have discussed may be depressing,
MRP II is still one of the best acts in town. Educated
users, with an understanding of potential MRP logic
application pitfalls, can generate substantial operating
improvement in most companies with the successful
implementation of MRP II software.

BIOGRAPHY

Mr. Berger is an internationally recognized educator,
consultant and President of the Gus Berger Group, Inc., an
organization dedicated to consulting and education in the
commercial and government contracting business communities
internationally. He served as Conference Chairman for the
1980 APICS International Conference and is a Chapter
editor for the forthcoming McGraw-Hill Production and
Inventory Control Handbook, James H. Green, editor.

Prior experience includes executive positions in
Consulting, Material, Purchasing and Software
development/Installation. Mr. Berger has been
instrumental in "turning around" distressed companies,
installing MRP/MRPII systems and developing/implementing
strategic commercial and government contractor business
and information systems planning. Mr. Berger presents
public and in-house lectures, seminars, workshops, and
educational and certification training programs throughout
the world. His publications are found in the annual
International Conference Proceedings of APICS, CAPICS and
in national trade journals. Experience with European and
Japanese manufacturing provides him with a broad
perspective on business issues. He holds a B.A. and an
M.B.A. from the California State University at Fullerton,
where he has taught in the School of Business.

Reprinted from *Production and Inventory Management*, Vol. 25, No. 3, 1984.

# WHY MRP SYSTEMS FAIL: TRAPS TO AVOID

James A. G. Krupp, CPIM*
Sealectro Corp.    Trumbull, CT

## INTRODUCTION

In the last twenty years, American business has poured billions of dollars into material requirements planning (MRP) systems in the form of educational, software, and implementation/sustaining manpower costs. Yet, few companies have systems operating at their full potential. Oliver Wight has hypothesized that the number of Class A MRP users is as few as twenty-five companies. The materials management literature has shown how failures occur. This generally happens during implementation due to the lack of top management support, inaccurate bills of material, lack of education for all users, poor base data, etc. Certainly, many MRP installation failures can be traced to these syndromes. But even companies with excellent implementation plans have had disappointing results with no logical explanations to be found in the classic reasons. How does one explain an installation failure in *these* environments?

Many MRP failures go beyond the textbook symptoms. They involve misunderstandings of the effective operation of MRP systems and/or unrealistic expectations. In this article, *MRP* is narrowly defined as the classic material requirements planning system. Some observations offered here are controversial and run contrary to some of the "accepted truths" about MRP. I have relabelled these "truths" as "traps".

## TRAP #1: MRP IS AN "EITHER-OR" PROPOSITION

The early literature of MRP led many people to believe that MRP was not only the ultimate technological development in manufacturing planning and the optimum system in any environment, but was in and of itself a "stand-alone" system. Two principal factors have perpetuated this myth outside the profession.

1) The changing meanings and evolution of acronyms within the profession may be clear to practitioners, but have confused many others. The subtle attempt to change the inference of MRP from material requirements planning to manufacturing resources planning, and the subsequent development of the acronym MRP-II to distinguish between the two technologies, has escaped the attention and/or understanding of more than a few people outside the profession.
2) The plethora of articles, both within the profession and in the popular press, comparing MRP to such systems as KANBAN, PYMAC, OPT, detailed scheduling, operation sequencing, etc., has led many people (including practitioners) to view the choice of MRP as an "either-or" proposition.

Professionals and practitioners should educate those unfamiliar with the field in the evolving technology which comprises modern materials management systems. The material requirements planning aspect of MRP should be seen as little more than a material planning and rescheduling system. In most environments it takes both material and capacity to make product. In some environments, schedules need to be based on capacity availability and/or utilization, with material being a secondary consideration. In others, the ability to fulfill schedules depends both on material and capacity, with the relative importance of each changing from work center to work center and/or between different stages of the manufacturing process. In still other environments, the sole concern may be availability of materials or process yield, with capacity either highly variable or of little importance.

(ACKNOWLEDGMENT: The author wishes to acknowledge the contribution and insights provided by the Editorial Board reviewers of this article, people whose contributions were invaluable to its effective presentation. A number of the observations in this article resulted from direct input from these anonymous individuals. This article, therefore, is dedicated to these reviewers who contribute so much behind-the-scenes effort to the technology of our field.)

There are few cases in which differing techniques are mutually exclusive. MRP must be viewed as only one tool in a portfolio of techniques which comprise the total scope of manufacturing resources planning. Using this approach overcomes the "either-or" syndrome, and allows development of an overall system which combines complementary tools. The timeliness and level of detail required to develop and maintain valid, realistic schedules are a function of each environment to be managed, and dictate the optimum combination of techniques which form an overall planning package. The success of a particular system must be directly proportional to its appropriateness, i.e., a system will operate best in its own natural environment. To use MRP as a "stand-alone" system may not result in a cataclysm. But neither will the overall system yield the optimum results and support the objectives of system development which could have been realized with a combination of techniques. Thus, the results obtained must be inherently suboptimal.

This phenomenon is not limited to the selection of a system for a company as a whole; it is also important to keep in mind for corporations with diverse operations. Just as a corporation maintains a portfolio of marketing strategies, with each product type assigned a strategy appropriate to its marketplace, so should a portfolio of planning systems be maintained, with each unique operating environment evaluated to determine the most appropriate planning/control system.

## TRAP #2: MRP IS A CLOSED-LOOP SYSTEM

The classic literature of MRP tends to portray it and its related systems (MPS, CRP, SFC, etc.) as a closed-loop technology, with feedback systems integrating all modules in the flow. The fact is, however, that all *automatic* aspects of the system are unidirectional, with a "top-down" emphasis in the decision-making process. The system begins with the master production schedule, which is exploded and netted against level 1, which is in turn exploded and netted against level 2, etc. Thus, the downward progress of the process is automatic, and yields a series of directives and recommendations within a short time, all derived by a specific, well-defined set of standard operating logics.

The feedback mechanisms, on the other hand, do not have the advantage of being incorporated into the system logic. While the generation of exception messages is incorporated in system logic, the feedback mechanisms require manual intervention, analysis, and interpretation, a process which can be so time-consuming in a complex environment as to render the results untimely and/or valueless. If one feedback cycle cannot be completed before the next plan regeneration, it can seem futile to question the output of the first plan.

The feedback techniques themselves have a second drawback. Such systems are, for the most part, informal and ill-defined, with few standard operating procedures to support them. The profession has not really tried to standardize and publicize feedback systems and procedures. When such systems are effective, it is often a direct function of the capabilities and motives of those who conceive and implement them.

The third, and often most deadly, flaw in such feedback systems is the lack of an absolute mandate in the system to recognize identified constraints. If management does not require consideration of valid and relevant user concerns the system loses its credibility with users. All those in the cycle like to feel they have some control over their destiny. When their input is ignored or improperly evaluated, they may become indifferent or negative.

What is the solution? There are no easy answers, but a number of potential alternatives present themselves.

1) Review the system design and, if appropriate, "desensitize" it to avoid an excess of exception messages generated by minor schedule changes. Use damping factors to reduce the number of action items to a manageable level.
2) Review the general practices management of the production plan and master production schedule to ensure they properly represent the environment to be controlled.
3) Develop (and publicize) standard procedures and guidelines for feedback systems. Incorporate mandates to include all feedback before the next system cycle or document why such feedback was modified or disallowed.

4) Develop MRP systems which *must* recognize constraint areas in the automatic planning cycles and replan accordingly; users can load their feedback (subject to review and approval) as part of the master data for the system.

## TRAP #3: THERE IS NO SUCH THING AS A UNIQUE COMPANY

This is actually a corollary of Trap #1. This statement is often misinterpreted to mean that a universal system can be applied in any environment.

One cannot simply take a packaged MRP system, drop it into place, and expect an optimum operating system. Yet, this is the way many people mistakenly view the use of MRP. Manufacturing technology may not be unique to a specific firm (and, in some isolated cases, even this assumption can be successfully challenged), but each firm has special considerations which will make the structure of an optimum MRP system unique. The author does *not* advocate designing every MRP system from the ground up, for many outstanding software packages are available. But each package will require some modification to adapt it to the environment. Some peculiarities which can make an MRP system unique are:

1) audit trails required by U.S. government regulations and/or contractual requirements,
2) specific serial number control on identical items,
3) "available-to-promise" checks below the ordered item level (as with generic end-product numbering systems),
4) multifaceted material requirements (e.g., mixture of virgin and remelt materials in castings and plastic molded parts),
5) "family-of-parts" logic,
6) segregation of "gross requirements" into dependent demand, firm independent demand (customer orders), and forecasted independent demand on all print-outs and displays,
7) "phantom" bills of material, and
8) incorporation of safety stock into system logic.

For any system to establish and maintain its credibility, it must reflect the practices and considerations unique to its operating environment. A basic precept of MRP systems is the formal system will not work unless it can incorporate and eliminate the need for the informal systems. No standard packaged system can fulfill all the requirements of a specific firm. Some customization is mandatory to make best use of it.

At this point, one must also recognize that overcustomizing can be as serious a flaw as no customizing. Some MRP systems add a whole new dimension to the word *overkill*. This is a particular danger in multiplant environments. In their fervor to be "all things to all people," designers of such systems invariably impair total system effectiveness in one (or both) of two ways:

1) the system becomes so complex and massive that EDP is slowed, and/or
2) so much superfluous information is generated that most users find reports unreadable.

In addition, Murphy's Law remains a hidden danger—the more that can go wrong with a system, will. The key to an effective MRP system is to make it appropriate to the operating circumstances. Do not allow excessive sophistication which would impair the systems operating efficiency and usability.

## TRAP #4: MRP IS A STANDARDIZED TECHNOLOGY

Many practitioners have come to treat MRP as an accounting system, with strict and inflexible rules governing universal concepts of application and practice. These rules serve well as guidelines, but should never deter creativity in applying MRP systems to specific technologies.

In its infancy, MRP desperately needed standardized approaches to guide the vast number of novices in this technology. We owe an immeasurable debt of gratitude to professionals such as Joseph Orlicky and Oliver Wight for developing such guidelines and forming the foundations for the recognition and advancement of MRP and the evolution of manufacturing resources planning. Now, however, MRP is reaching maturity, with many experienced (and often bloody) users. Yet, despite the "founding fathers'" intentions, unusual and creative approaches are often stifled because those original guidelines are viewed as dogma. Getting the best results from an MRP installation often means recognizing MRP is a changing technology. Its tools are constantly being refined and/or replaced. Leaders in the field, including these "founding fathers", are constantly developing and publicizing new approaches. Practitioners must monitor these developments closely to fully appreciate the current state of the art. Creativity in both designing and enhancing MRP systems is crucial to ensuring the best fit between system and environment. Optimal systems are consistent with a standard *framework* and are enhanced by environment-specific technology.

## CONCLUSION

Many readers may feel indifference or disillusionment toward their MRP systems. If so, they may be the victim of an MRP failure. An installation does not have to collapse entirely to be considered a failure. Any system which does not yield desired results (provided that the original expectations were realistic) can be seen as a failure. Revamping the system can often be as time-consuming and irritating as the original installation. (An anonymous saying quips, "You never know what you can do until you have to try and undo what you did.") Scrapping your MRP system is never a viable alternative, however. If the classic symptoms given for MRP failures do not apply in your case, consider the points raised in this article and rethink your approach to and/or expectations of the system.

If you have yet to install an MRP system, but wish to do so, be sure you cover all the bases recommended by consultants, educators, and practitioners, including the considerations set forth here. Then, choose a resident skeptic/pessimist (every company has at least *one*) and let him or her describe all the reasons the system won't work. Finally, consider and, where appropriate, compensate for these problems.

In summary, in the technology of MRP (as in the case of *any* technology), heed the words of Dr. W. Edwards Deming, the "father" of quality circles:

Long-term commitment to new learning and new philosophy is required of any management that seeks to accomplish anything of note. . . . The timid and the faint-hearted, and people that expect quick results without effort, are doomed to disappointment.

---

**About the Author—**

*JAMES A. G. KRUPP, CPIM\** is Director of Advanced Planning & Systems for Sealectro Corp., Trumbull, CT. His background includes various assignments in materials management, systems development, engineering, and quality control for such firms as Carlyle Johnson Machine, Picker International, Burndy Corp., Stanley Tools, and Sargent & Co.

Jim's articles have appeared in *Inventories & Production Magazine, Journal of Purchasing & Materials Management, Management Accounting,* and *Production & Inventory Management.* He is the co-winner of the 1978 APICS Production & Inventory Management Journal Award.

Jim holds a BSME and a MBA from the University of New Haven, and also attended the U.S. Naval Academy at Annapolis. He is a member of APICS and NAA, and is certified at the Fellow level by APICS. A member of several APICS committees, he is a frequent speaker at local APICS and NAA society meetings.

Reprinted from APICS 1983 *Conference Proceedings*.

MRP AND KANBAN—AMERICAN STYLE
J. Nicholas Edwards, CPIM*
*Rath & Strong, Inc.*

## I. INTRODUCTION

Much attention has been generated toward the relative merits of MRP versus KANBAN. MRP, a product of the '60s and refined in the '70s, had its roots as a material planning system, first as an order launcher, and then refined as a priority planning system. KANBAN, on the other hand, had its roots in the '70s dealing with the need to operate with the minimum of inventories and space. The real point then is not to determine which system is better, but to merge the best of both in meeting the challenge of world competitive manufacturing.

To better understand how this blending is done, the background of both systems must be reviewed first so that the combined results can be seen in better perspective.

## II. BACKGROUND

### MRP Background

Material Requirements Planning in its current form obtained its start in the late '50s and early '60s when many companies on their own were attempting to find a better way to plan parts than by either the Order Point system or the Project Control method. With the mushrooming computer capabilities, many companies such as Black & Decker, J.I. Case, General Railway Signal, Jones & Lamson, Twin Disk, and others independently installed material planning systems to plan material at all levels of a product by using Bills of Material to create requirements in an "explosion" process. At each level requirements were netted against inventory, both on hand and on order, to plan new orders, either manufactured or purchased. This was fundamentally an order launching process. In time, this was refined to include priority planning capabilities so that shops would work on the most important jobs first based on a date priority scheme.

In the late '60s and early '70s, MRP planning systems took two paths. The first was an MRP replan of all requirements into periodic quantities (File Driven) while the second was an MRP replan of requirements for only those parts whose availability was changed (Transaction Driven). This second approach required knowing what caused these requirements, e.g., the planned requirements must be linked to the source that caused them.

Since requirement quantities in the first case were not isolated to what caused them, the whole process of requirements replanning was repeated from scratch. This was commonly called "Regenerative MRP." The second approach used was where two types of individual detail requirement records were created: one, the independent requirement records caused by customer orders, and second, the dependent requirements from the planning process. These dependent requirement records were "pegged" to the higher level assembly orders that created them. This gave significant improvement in planning visibility. Because of these "pegged" dependent requirements, there was no need to replan from scratch each time, and therefore, "Pegged Net-Change MRP" was developed. Examples of both forms of MRP[1] are shown in Figures 1 and 2, where the key point is that "pegged" or "bucketless" requirements yield a visibility that "bucketed" requirements did not.

[1]Reference: MRP Update, Everdell & Edwards 1979 APICS National Conference, St Louis.

M.R.P. Output
"Bucketed" Requirements

Gross To Net Requirements Planning_____INTEGRATED CIRCUIT

OH = 30    SS = 10    LT = 4 weeks    CLT = 9 weeks    OQ = 4 periods

| | PAST DUE | 1 | 2 | 3 | 4 | 5 | 6 | 7 | 8 |
|---|---|---|---|---|---|---|---|---|---|
| DEPENDENT REQUIREMENTS | | | | 60 | | | | 50 | |
| INDEPENDENT REQUIREMNTS | | 10 | 10 | 10 | 10 | 10 | 10 | 10 | 10 |
| GROSS REQUIREMENTS | | 10 | 10 | 70 | 10 | 10 | 10 | 60 | 10 |
| ORDER RECEIPT | | | 100 | | | | 90 | | |
| PROJECTED AVAILABLE | 20 | 10 | 100 | 30 | 20 | 10 | 90 | 30 | 20 |
| ORDER RELEASE | | 90 | | | | 100 | | | |

* SCHEDULED RECEIPT    ** PLANNED ORDER    Figure 1

MRP OUTPUT
"Pegged" Requirements

8-7-83    Planning Sheet Display    13.20:09

Part #    Description

404574    IC Digital 750MHZ D Type

| OH | SS | LT | CLT | Order Policy | OQ |
|---|---|---|---|---|---|
| 30 | 10 | 4 wks | 9 wks | Periods Sup. | 4 wks |

| Order # | Parent Part # | Desc | D/S | Qty | Date | Proj Avail |
|---|---|---|---|---|---|---|
| 41591 | C/O 124 | | D | 10 | 603 | 20 |
| 41592 | C/O 124 | | D | 10 | 603 | 10 |
| 41593 | C/O 124 | | D | 10 | 610 | 0 |
| M0143 | | Rel Ord | S | 100 | 613 | 100 |
| 67585 | 396192 | PC Mem | D | 35 | 613 | 65 |
| 63436 | 45769 | PC Logic B | D | 20 | 614 | 45 |
| 67888 | 396192 | PC Mem | D | 15 | 618 | 30 |
| 41596 | C/O 124 | | D | 10 | 618 | 20 |
| 41597 | C/O 124 | | D | 10 | 623 | 10 |
| 41603 | C/O 596 | | D | 10 | 628 | 0 |
| P09823 | | Planned Ord | S | 90 | 634 | 90 |

etc.    Figure 2

As a result, most all MRP systems of today are "pegged" in one form or another. Appendix A is a write-up on two common pegging examples, a bill of material peg, and a combination bill of material-order master peg.

The next advance of MRP included the incorporation of Master Scheduling to drive MRP. This resulted in MRP systems that were expanded to include capacity or resource planning. As part of this enhanced process, MRP was renamed MRP II (Manufacturing Resource Planning). MRP II was used as the means to develop total control for manufacturing from initial planning to the latest priority in Shop Floor Control.

MRP systems of the '80s have now been refined to support many characteristics. These include multi-plant environments, single- and multi-level pegging, "as-planned" and "as-built" configuration control, configuration control on a project-by-project basis, repetitive manufacturing environments where material is controlled by schedules instead of job lots. However, the original thrust of MRP has continued to remain, that being the planning of material by part for how much and when needed.

### KANBAN Background

KANBAN received its beginning in the '70s based on work done by the Toyota Motor Company in their effort to lower inventory to an irreducible minimum. In a broader sense, this was an accumulation of many years of effort to eliminate all forms of waste that would not add value to the product. Mr. Cho of Toyota commented on the Elimination of Waste, "...anything other than the <u>minimum</u>

amount of equipment, materials, parts, and workers (working time) which are <u>absolutely essential</u> to production..." sums it very <u>well</u>. As part of this program to eliminate waste, quality programs to reduce defects were instituted to insure that parts were made right the first time. This is one of the essential points to get away from "Just-in-Case" inventory to a "Just-in-Time" philosophy. Also, inventory itself was considered a waste of money and space as effort had to be expended to first store the material, then eventually to retrieve it. Therefore, the need to reduce large setups which created the need for large lots was also a high priority.

In Toyota's drive to reduce inventory, other aspects came along such as the need to schedule assembly lines to avoid surging of components. This meant that instead of making trucks at the beginning of the month and sedans at the end, there was a mixed model assembly line of both vehicles so that the manufacturer of truck axles would be continuously busy as opposed to working feverishly at the beginning of the month and being without work at the end of the month. The eventual KANBAN cards are but the accumulation of many efforts to both simplify and streamline operations.

This review could continue, however, there is numerous good reference material available on KANBAN and Just-In-Time. The ones we have found most helpful are listed in Appendix B with our opinions of their impact. However, the real basic benefits from KANBAN cannot be overlooked: to improve quality and productivity, and reduce inventory, all important characteristics of executing MRP.

III.    MRP AND JUST-IN-TIME--INTEGRATED

MRP began as a planning system for material, KANBAN began as an execution system of quality improvement, inventory reduction, and productivity. Both systems, in their final form, stress the importance of good production planning with synchronization and short lead times being the key to KANBAN. The advantage then of combining both KANBAN and MRP result in a superior system that yields greater flexibility. With this integration of KANBAN into MRP, it is important to cover the significant aspects of KANBAN first so that its effect on MRP is understood.

A.    KANBAN/Just-in-Time

KANBAN, in its literal definition means "card"; however in its relationship to Toyota, it became a culture or an entire style of manufacturing control. The Just-In-Time aspects of KANBAN can have a significant impact for a more effective MRP, for to quote Ed Hay in his article on Japanese Productivity Methods, he refers to it as, "The Winning Combination of Neglected American Ideas." Specifically, we look at these as the "Seven Zeros" of Just-In-Time for a more effective MRP.

1.    Zero Defects

Where is the attitude of making a product right the first time? Let's analyze what a product in intended to do! Dr. Juran calls this "Fitness for Use." This implies designing the process to be capable of meeting the specifications as needed, not to unnecessarily stringent tolerances. This includes establishing a vendor relationship on a cooperative basis as opposed to an adversary basis. Hopefully this is the same basis engineering, quality, and manufacturing operate. With a design and manufacturing process capable of delivering product that measures defects in Parts Per Million, not AQL's (AQL's generally measure defects in percents!), operators can verify quality, eliminating unnecessary inspection. Therefore, no extra lead time for rework or extra material for scrap allowance need be planned.

2.    Zero Set-up

For many years Production Control personnel have accepted set-up as a given. Not only is this costly, it often encourages wasted motion, time, and handling. Also, not nearly enough methods engineering

effort has been spent on reducing setups as has been spent on reducing cycle times.

3.    Zero Lot Size (Lot Excess)

With a markedly reduced setup, it is possible to make only what is required, with none planned for inventory or safety stock. In an MRP system the "discrete" planning logic could be used, or for that matter, the part could be "phantomed" into the higher level. The eventual goal is the "lot of one" throughout.

4.    Zero Handling

By making what is required, there exists no double handling of extra inventory by first delivering it to stores, then retrieving it from stores. Material would be delivered to point of use. Of course, the ideal would be to feed material from operator to operator, and thereby eliminate all interim material handling.

The same holds true for purchased components. The normal sequence would be for purchased components to proceed along the following lines of:

        Vendor Picking
        Vendor Shipping
        Receiving
        Receiving Inspection
        Deliver to Stores
        Pick from Stores
        Deliver to Line

Why not have the vendor deliver to the point of use?

5.    Zero Surging

The zero surging comment applies to both planning and execution. Planning with no surging would mean having a stable Production Plan. Executing with no surging would occur by not letting material pile up at work stations, and by not letting one machine operate faster than the next one. The key then is:

        TOTAL SYNCHRONIZATION

for all aspects of the manufacturing environment from initial planning, material control, level of staffing to delivery.

6.    Zero Breakdowns

So often in attempting to reduce inventory, the old "Just-in-Case" Inventory theory is brought up to protect against the "inevitables" such as equipment or tool breakdowns. Not nearly enough attention is paid to having operators do routine preventative maintenance. Also, keep an extra set of wear tools at the machine so no time is lost "getting tooling" when a tool needs changing. This applies to the tools used for performing change-overs, why not leave them at the machine?

7.    Zero Lead Time

With zero set-up, lot, and surging, and the need for "Just-in-Case" inventory eliminated, then lead times can be reduced to run time by handing a piece from operator to operator. This means that there will be:

    .    No Within Lot Wait (Batching)

    .    No Between Lot Wait (Queues)

This does mean that MRP lead times, usually expressed in days, will have to be restructured, as lead times can be reduced to hours or minutes.

In summary, the seven zeros of just-in-time serve as a guide of how effective we are in making the right item for the right quantity at the right time.

## B. MRP

With the dramatic reductions in lead times and lot sizes that a Just-in-Time environment creates, the operation of MRP is significantly altered as a planning tool. MRP, as a method for planning parts, had its origins in the '30s where cumulative planning systems were used. The current version of MRP beginning in the 50's and 60's, used planned orders, and firm planned orders. This enabled planning to more closely simulate the actual factory environment. With Just-in-Time, MRP needs to be altered again with some revised logic and revised operating parameters. This also expands to even planning with the vendor, for their loads will be more accurate as the total internal manufacturing lead times are in hours and days, as opposed to weeks and months.

### 1. MRP Logic

With the extremely short lead times of JIT, planning logic must be revised for both lead time offsetting and material handling. Also, if there is a heavy amount of options on the end product, they too must be planned to meet the JIT environment.

#### a. Lead Time Offset

Lead time offset, in the attached example, is the time to build a given level of a product. When lead times become small, (daily or hourly) their cumulative effect through many levels could distort the total lead time due to the rounding effect that might occur in an MRP explosion that may round to days or weeks. Therefore, to avoid this distortion, lead time offset should be replaced with a lead time setback approach where MRP explodes, without lead time offset. Upon completion of the explosion, each part is then setback (or started) "X" days prior to completion (or ship date). This does create a small problem if one part is used at many levels, (only one setback per component); however, this potential problem is small in comparison to the improved visibility for every person in the process where they know how they fit in the total timing picture. Also this eliminates the need for lead time adjustment factors (See Figure 3).

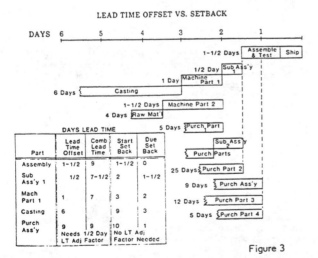

LEAD TIME OFFSET VS. SETBACK

| Part | Lead Time Offset | Comb Lead Time | Start Sct Back | Due Set Back |
|---|---|---|---|---|
| Assembly | 1-1/2 | 9 | 1-1/2 | 0 |
| Sub Ass'y 1 | 1/2 | 7-1/2 | 2 | 1-1/2 |
| Mach Part 1 | 1 | 7 | 3 | 2 |
| Casting | 6 | 9 | 9 | 3 |
| Purch Ass'y | 9 | 9 | 10 | 1 |
| | Needs 1/2 Day LT Adj Factor | | No LT Adj Factor Needed | |

Figure 3

#### b. Material Flow

With material flowing in hourly (or daily quantities), the planning of a one-week lot would not correspond to the delivery of material, as weekly delivery is impractical. Therefore, while the MRP system may plan for up to a weekly schedule and the corresponding requirement may be a week's worth of material, in actual practice the material may be fed to the line in a daily or more frequent basis. To overcome this, the pegged dependent requirement record should recognize both a "release interval" as a quantity and a "released quantity" for delivery in addition to the normal "required" and "issued" quantities that already exist. For example, if a weekly requirement is 100, and the release interval is set at 20, then the delivery release for the first day would be 20. When material is delivered to the line, it would show an issued quantity of 20. On the next day, the release quantity would accumulate to 40, and when delivery occurred (such as on a KANBAN card), the issued quantity would go to 40, etc.

In addition, it often is worthwhile on the released parent assembly schedule to show the expected daily rate along with the lot size or schedule quantity planned. This is especially true for longer running items--over 1 day.

#### c. Option Planning and Control

With the significantly reduced lead times, hopefully options can be planned and scheduled along with the basic product. If full option lead time is not available, then a method for stocking option components must exist. Here the use of flexibility stock is recommended, where the amount of safety stock is proportional to the uniqueness of the part. This implies that a part that is 100% needed for options would not be stocked. The specifics of this approach are covered in a prior APICS conference, "MRP in a Mass Production Environment."[2]

### 2. MRP Parameters

The other aspect of integrating Just-in-Time into MRP include dealing with the operating parameters themselves. These include expanded use of Phantom logic, Deliver-To Locations, Order Policies, Order Quantities, Safety Stocks, and Lead Times.

#### a. Phantoms and Deliver To Locations

The use of phantom logic has the beneficial effect of eliminating levels of manufacturing control. The hope would be to have but a single level from purchased part to finished product. However, that may not be practical, so a two- to three-level manufacturing bill of assemble, subassembly (optional), and fabrication, would be a significant gain in level reduction for complex operations. The resulting collapsing of levels means bills of material become very broad. In order to subdivide these broad levels, logical groupings by "deliver to" locations should be used more. These "deliver-to" groupings then become significant MRP parameters.

#### b. Order Policies and Order Quantities

The first instinct when converting over to a Just-in-Time environment is to change order policies to a "lot-for-lot" or "discrete" policy. Unfortunately, this has the effect of increasing the number of pegged records in an MRP run, thereby adversely affecting computer run times. The important thing here is to determine what the logical schedule quantities are, independent of the JIT considerations, with up to weekly schedules being a good size and resultant order policy for periods of supply. Then, using the "Release Quantity" logic covered before, material issues (or KANBAN cards, if used) can be independent of the schedule quantity. The use of this "Release Quantity" logic must be traded off against the need for configuration control on a unit-by-unit basis.

---

[2]Reference: MRP in a Mass Production Environment, J. N. Edwards, 1979 APICS National Conference, Cleveland.

### c. Safety Stocks and Lead Times

Safety stocks have played a large role in MRP systems as part of the "Just-in-Case" philosophy. With good quality control and shortened lead times, the need for safety stocks is reduced. If, for some reason, safety stocks are required, then they should be set at the lowest level possible, either at the vendor plant for parts, or at the raw material level in the manufacturing location. Safety stocks or banks at intermediate levels could, and should, be sharply reduced or eliminated.

## IV. SUMMARY

In an MRP/Just-In-Time environment, MRP reverts back to being primarily a planning tool for determining material and overall capacity required. Order releasing, scheduling, and material control become part of the Just-In-Time systems. Therefore, with the merging of Just-in-Time practices into MRP, significant gains in on-time performance and inventory reduction can happen. However, for this to happen, a "100% Operating Philosophy" must be established. This means the dedication to:

100% Elimination of Waste
100% Commitment to Improvement by All
100% Visibility
100% Synchronization
100% Education

This is indeed a challenge and based on what has occurred in the past few years, we are witnessing the start of the Second Industrial Revolution.


APPENDIX A

PEGGING IN MRP

### A. SUMMARY

The term "pegging" in MRP is defined in the APICS dictionary as: "In MRP, pegging displays for a given item the details of the sources of its gross requirements and/or allocations. Pegging can be thought of as 'live' where-used information." In actual practice, there appears to be two common types of "pegs," the first, a "bill of material" peg, and the second, a combination "BOM, As-Planned" peg. A description of each follows.

### B. BILL OF MATERIAL PEGGING

A Bill of Material Peg is, as its name implies, the avenue that links the higher level assembly orders (supplies) to the detail dependent component requirements (demands).

The basic concept behind this pegged MRP approach is to use computer records to describe each requirement and its parent replenishment order. These requirement and replenishment records are linked to their respective part number records in the part master file. An example of the approach is as follows:

```
   Bill of Material              File Design Linkage

                          P/S   P/M        Req/Rep
          X                       X ——— Repl X Ord #1
  ┌───┴───┐               X:B┐
  B    etc                     B ——— Req B Ord #1

Where:  X    = Subassembly
        B    = One of the components of X
        P/S  = Product Structure File (describing
               the Bill of Material)
        Req/Rep  = Requirement & Replenishment Order
Detail
               records in a file linked to their
               parts and identified by the common
               order number.
        Ord  = Assembly Order on X calling out
               Requirements on B
```

By having this requirement-replenishment "pegged" identity, it is possible to process an MRP run by a "net-change" explosion where this explosion replans only those parts whose availability was affected (as opposed to a complete regeneration where all parts are replanned). Because of this requirement-replenishment detail, it is not necessary to "throw away" all the requirements and take the time to regenerate all requirements from scratch as an audit trail now exists to keep track of the individual requirements. However, if this detail is _not_ maintained, the longer regeneration approach must be used, as there is no way to audit the accuracy of the requirements. Any engineering changes must be stored on the product structure file with an effectivity scheme available to link the correct dependent requirements to the proper higher level replenishment order. If this does not occur, then some stray requirements may remain in the system, as there is no positive way to purge them if a particular requirement is not satisfied with a withdrawal.

### C. BILL OF MATERIAL--ORDER MASTER PEG

The Bill of Material - Order Master Peg operates in a slightly different fashion where the original linkage is established through the bill of material as in the first example. However, an added step is included to link the dependent requirements (demands) back to their parent replenishment orders by means of a separate order master linkage. This revised linkage modification follows:

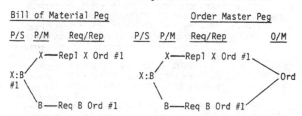

| Bill of Material Peg | | | | Order Master Peg | | | |

| P/S | P/M | Req/Rep | | P/S | P/M | Req/Rep | O/M |

Where:  O/M = Order Master linkage file

The processing sequence then is that the original planning is done through the Product Structure file and all revised planning is done through the Order Master file as if the Product structure file did not even exist! The reasons is that the Order Master file directly links all of the information about a given order. For example, an assembly replenishment order places dependent requirements on components. The order master file links this replenishment to all of its requirements. Likewise, a customer order or a spares order is linked to the requirements for each of the end items or spare parts. By the use of this order master linkage, all records for a given order are linked together, be it an assembly order, customer order, or a purchase order with many split deliveries or different purchased parts.

The use of the order master linkage allows for single and multilevel pegging, "as-built" configuration control, and one easy alternative of handling "use-up" changes for engineering change planning and control. Also, with the addition of configuration control in the product structure data base either by serial or date effectivity, plus special engineering, manufacturing, and phantom configuration coding, it is now practical to have an Engineering B/M, a Manufacturing Planning B/M, and an "As-Built" B/M. The "As-built" Bill of Material, achieved through the use of the order master linkage could include deviations not covered by engineering change control such as rework, MRB, etc.

The net result is that MRP planning follows two explosion approaches. When an item is being planned for the first time, a "product structure" explosion is used. When an item is being replanned, the direct "order-master" explosion is used, as all of the planned effectivity considerations were covered in the initial planning. If an engineering change occurs to something already planned, the "order master" relationship can be altered for the change, or could be entirely replanned to the new structure by cancelling the old.

Detailed examples of single and multilevel pegging using the order master concept are shown in Figures A-1 to A-4.

D. ADVANTAGES OF ORDER MASTER LINKAGE

Since the order master linkage concept as part of the net change MRP has been in use for the past few years, it is now possible to highlight some of its advantages:

1. "As-Built" Configuration. With the "as built" configuration a result of the order master structure--as opposed to the engineering and manufacturing planning configuration in the product structure file--many changes that are not covered in the engineering change control procedure get picked up by tracking withdrawals from the stockroom.

2. Improved Requirement Accuracy. With the use of the order master linkage, giving direct linkage between replenishments and requirements, errors in operating use such as missed issues or incomplete Bills of Material can be highlighted.

3. Shop Floor Control. The order master linkage can serve to generate a process Bill of Material to have material issues to a shop in a staggered sequence without complicating the product structure sequence.

4. Cost Control. With all material issued by order number, it is possible to track all material issued to a job, both planned material and unplanned material. Project cost is thereby easy to maintain with material cost calculated from the order master file and labor cost calculated from a job progress file.

5. Computer Run Time. The order master linkage reduces the amount of record accessing in a pegged net change environment, thereby speeding up computer run time.

6. Easier Computer Access. All that is needed to access the computer is the unique order number. The order master linkage ties all elements of the order together.

7. Simpler Processing Logic. Complex logic is required to handle special configuration control in the product structure explosion because of the different conditions. When an order master is set up, the explosion and resultant computer I/O is considerably simplified using the order master chain.

These are but a few of the advantages of using the Order Master logic. However, it is important to note that any "pegging" approach does add to computer run time. This is especially true if many requirements are linked to high usage, inexpensive parts such as electric components or hardware. Therefore, the total amount of pegging must always be evaluated to keep MRP run times in reasonable control.

Bill Of Material

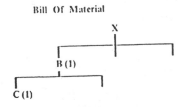

Figure A-1

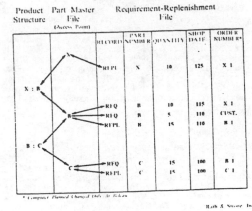

Figure A-2

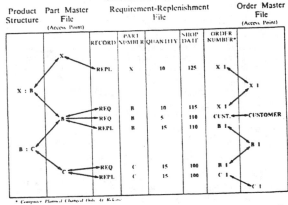

Figure A-3

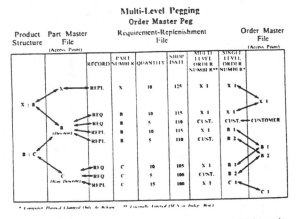

Figure A-4

APPENDIX B

KANBAN OR JUST-IN-TIME Reference Material

A. Background Material

1. Driving the Productivity Machine: Production Planning and Control, Robert W. Hall, APICS. An excellent overview publication of what happened in Japan and at Toyota over the years.

2. Japanese Manufacturing Techniques, Richard J. Schonberger, Free Press. A well organized book that accumulates good background on Japanese manufacturing. We feel it is a "must" to help in basic understanding before embarking on a Just-In-Time program.

3. Study of Toyota Production System, Shigeo Shingo, Japan Management Association. A detailed treatise on the implementation of KANBAN at Toyota. It requires plenty of time as it is difficult to read in its English translation.

B. JIT Implementation Assists

1. Kawasaki USA--A Case Study, Robert W. Hall, APICS. An implementation history on Kawasaki in Lincoln, Nebraska.

2. Japanese Approach to Productivity/Japanese Productivity Methods, Kenneth A. Wantuck & Edward J. Hay, Inventories & Production Magazine, January-June 1983. A series of three articles highlighting the fourteen aspects on dealing with both the elimination of waste and the respect for people.

3. Stockless Production, Robert A. Hall, APICS. A detailed book showing specific examples of what was done on Set-up Reduction, U-lines, etc. An excellent source of ideas for a JIT program.

4. Japanese Approach to Productivity, Kenneth Wantuck and Leonard Ricard, AIAG. A series of four, one-hour video tapes based on a presentation at Ford World Headquarters on Just-in-Time Production.

C. Continuing Programs

1. Repetitive Manufacturing Group, APICS; Founder, Edmund Reznicek, formerly Daisy Manufacturing; Founding Chairman, Rolland L. McCulloch, Briggs & Stratton (1977 to 1982), Current Chairman, Lee Sage, Excello Corp. (1982 to present). An active APICS special interest group that has sponsored twice-yearly seminars on different aspects of Repetitive Manufacturing including Just-In-Time.

2. Automotive Industry Action Group (AIAG). L. A. Higgason, Managing Director, 6560 Cass Avenue, Suite 42S, Detroit, MI 48202, (313) 871-3701. An industry-wide education and problem solving group dealing with supplier/customer productivity such as: Electronic Communication, Bar Coding, Just-in-Time techniques, etc.

# Kanban versus MRP II— which is best for you?

Walt Goddard, a leading spokesman in the field of inventory management, visited Japan for a first-hand look at how the Kanban System works. His findings shatter a few myths and point out how we can gain the best of both worlds.

by Walter E. Goddard, president
Oliver Wight Educational Associates, Inc.

There's more than distance separating Japan and America. In the field of production planning and inventory management, the two countries are going in different directions. To the east, it's Kanban; to the west, it's Manufacturing Resource Planning (MRP II).

The goals of each are identical—to aid manufacturing companies in improving customer service, inventory turnover, and productivity. Spectacular results can be cited by companies employing each. However, the tools used by Kanban are dramatically different from the tools used by MRP II.

After visiting Japan to compare the pros and cons of Kanban with those of MRP II, I came to two conclusions:

● Kanban can succeed only where the user produces highly repetitive products. MRP II, however, works equally well for highly engineered one-of-a-kind environments, make-to-stock products, and finished-to-order products.

● MRP II has better tools than Kanban, but these tools are more costly. It is very important for a company to properly evaluate not only the costs, but what the paybacks will be. Unless the general manager and his staff can visualize a sizable return, they will not invest enough of their time and energy to ensure that the company will become a successful user.

## Lessons to learn from Kanban

There are at least three lessons to be learned through understanding the Kanban System.

Lesson number one is apparent to every observer of the Japanese success story. It's called teamwork. The Japanese companies operate with a tremendous amount of team effort. They pull together. They realize that as a team they will be stronger.

The second lesson is that education is the common denominator. This is as true for the successful Toyota Kanban System as it is for all successful MRP II systems. It is better to have a technically imperfect system that the users understand and want to make work, than a technically correct one without user understanding.

The third lesson is that we should not copy their tools. Rather we should continue in the direction of utilizing MRP II to its fullest potential.

The success that Toyota has achieved is not the result of their tools, nor is it how they use them, although they use them very well. *The key is what they do before using their system that permits it to work so well.*

Without a clear distinction between these Kanban tools versus the attitude and philosophy of

# How Toyota's Kanban philosophy differs from a typical U.S. company

| Factors | Toyota's Kanban | American philosophy |
|---|---|---|
| Inventory | A liability. Every effort must be extended to do away with it. | An asset. It protects against forecast errors, machine problems, late vendor deliveries. More inventory is "safer." |
| Lot sizes | Immediate needs only. A minimum replenishment quantity is desired for both manufactured and purchased parts. | Formulas. We're always revising the optimum lot size with some formula based on the trade-off between the cost of inventories and the cost of set up. |
| Set ups | Make them insignificant. This requires either extremely rapid changeover to minimize the impact on production, or the availability of extra machines already set up. Fast changeover permits small lot sizes to be practical, and allows a wide variety of parts to be made frequently. | Low priority. Maximum output is the usual goal. Rarely does similar thought and effort go into achieving quick changeover. |
| Queues | Eliminate them. When problems occur, identify the causes and correct them. The correction process is aided when queues are small. If the queues are small, it surfaces the need to identify and fix the cause. | Necessary investment. Queues permit succeeding operations to continue in the event of a problem with the feeding operation. Also, by providing a selection of jobs, the factory management has a greater opportunity to match up varying operator skills and machine capabilities, combine set ups and thus contribute to the efficiency of the operation. |
| Vendors | Co-workers. They're part of the team. Multiple deliveries for all active items are expected daily. The vendor takes care of the needs of the customer, and the customer treats the vendor as an extension of his factory. | Adversaries. Multiple sources are the rule, and it's typical to play them off against each other. |
| Quality | Zero defects. If quality is not 100%, production is in jeopardy. | Tolerate some scrap. We usually track what the actual scrap has been and develop formulas for predicting it. |
| Equipment maintenance | Constant and effective. Machine breakdowns must be minimal. | As required. But not critical because we have queues available. |
| Lead times | Keep them short. This simplifies the job of marketing, purchasing, and manufacturing as it reduces the need for expediting. | The longer the better. Most foremen and purchasing agents want more lead time, not less. |
| Workers | Management by consensus. Changes are not made until consensus is reached, whether or not a bit of arm twisting is involved. The vital ingredient of "ownership" is achieved. | Management by edict. New systems are installed in spite of the workers, not thanks to the workers. Then we concentrate on measurements to determine whether or not they're doing it. |

## Eight manufacturing functions: how they're controlled by Kanban and MRP II

| Functions | Categories | Kanban System | MRP II |
|---|---|---|---|
| Rates of output | Families of products | Leveling | Production Plan |
| Products to be built | Finished goods for make-to-stock, customer orders for make-to-order | Master Production Schedule | Master Production Schedule |
| Materials Required | Components—both manufactured and purchased | Kanban Cards | Material Requirements Planning (MRP) |
| Capacity Required | Output for key work centers and vendors | Visual | Capacity Requirements Planning (CRP) |
| Executing Capacity Plans | Producing enough output to satisfy plans | Visual | Input/Output Controls (I/O) |
| Executing Material Plans—Manufactured Items | Working on right priorities in factory | Kanban Cards | Dispatching Reports |
| Executing Material Plans—Purchased Items | Bringing in right items from vendors | Kanban Cards and unofficial orders | Purchasing Reports |
| Feedback information | What cannot be executed due to problems | Andon | Anticipated Delay Reports |

The same functions are performed by every manufacturing company; however, the tools used by Kanban differ greatly from the MRP II tools. Under Kanban, the tools are manual—Kanban Cards, Andon lights, visual checks, and oral orders. Under MRP II, the most important tool is the computer.

the Kanban users, we could easily import the wrong message from Japan.

### Outstanding results at Toyota

The successes achieved by several Japanese companies as measured by increased productivity and increased inventory turns border on the unbelievable. One's first reaction is, "Can they really be that good?"

My visit last year to the Takahama Plant of Toyota was with some of this same skepticism. At this facility, Toyota produces their line of forklift trucks. The plant is modern, completed in 1970, and large, over 24 acres under roof. It's a high volume operation, and it uses the Kanban System.

How's it working? In terms of customer service, very well indeed. "Our on-time delivery performance to the promised date of new trucks is 100%," I was told. "Our delivery performance for shipping service parts the same day as the orders arrive is 97%." It's difficult to top that.

How about lead times? What's their cumulative material lead time, top to bottom, including final assembly, sub-assembly, fabrication, and pur-

chasing? American forklift truck manufacturers would reply in the range of 6 to 9 months. Toyota's response was, "1 month!"

How have they accomplished these results? To answer this you have to understand their attitude towards inventory.

### Toyota's philosophy

Inventory, in Toyota's view, is "a waste." It's a waste of both space and money. As a result, they have an obsession to eliminate all unnecessary inventory. It's attacked with the same degree of vengeance as their campaign to improve quality by eliminating the causes of defects.

In their desire to achieve the elimination of inventory, they have put together a system that attempts to have every part, be it manufactured or purchased, available "just in time." It's a worthy goal. The right part at the right time in the right quantity at the right place is, indeed, what every production planning and inventory management system is striving for.

Toyota supports these words with deeds. They devote great energies to nine fundamentals as each of them contributes greatly to their goals. Our "typical" approach versus theirs is summarized in the table on page 41.

These nine—inventory, lot sizes, set-ups, queues, vendors, quality, equipment maintenance, lead times, and workers—are the foundations for any manufacturing planning and control system. That is, the system does not dictate these to the users, just the opposite. The users must specify them. It is up to the users to provide this information and maintain it for both the Kanban System and MRP II.

The attitude that Toyota's management and workers bring to each of these issues is not inherent to their "culture." In fact, a sizable number of American firms have both the same philosophy and similar results.

Contrasting one Japanese company's philosophy against a "typical American company" philosophy may be somewhat unfair. It may not represent your company's approach. However, it's enlightening as it certainly summarizes Toyota's approach.

The important point is that achieving improvements in these fundamentals would help any system to work better.

### The mechanics: Kanban vs. MRP II

Every manufacturing company has certain functions that it must perform. Eight of these functions are summarized in the table, left, which also lists the tools that both the Kanban System and MRP II use to aid these functions.

In reviewing the table, it is important to note that the Kanban Cards—actual paper cards—simply represent one key element within the Kanban System. In a similar manner, MRP (Ma-

---

*"Toyota says eliminate buffer stocks on the factory floor. When problems occur, they identify the causes and correct them. The correction process surfaces the need to fix the cause rather than hiding the need."*

---

terial Requirements Planning) is simply one key element within MRP II. Neither MRP nor Kanban Cards is a stand-alone system. In both cases, if they were installed by themselves, they would produce few, if any benefits.

Let's review these eight functions that make up the two operating systems and the tools used in both systems:

**Establishing rates of output.** With Toyota's emphasis on "life-time employment," great care and effort goes into determining the rates of output for their facilities. It is top managment's responsibility to determine these rates. The objective is to

---

*"It's not the Kanban System that we should import, but the 'Kando' of Toyota's Kanban that we need more of."*

---

"level," to stabilize the labor force. Only with great reluctance would Toyota expand or contract their labor force.

In the U.S., without debating whether American manufacturing executives put the same amount of emphasis on avoiding layoffs, the process of "production planning" is exactly the same. The objectives are identical. In companies with MRP II, the top management of the company is establishing rates of output which becomes their policy for the other resource planning functions to carry out.

**Determining what products need to be built.** The master schedule specifies what products are to be built out through the planning horizon. At Toyota, the master schedule extends three months. The first month is considered firm, and all changes are resisted. The next two months are considered tentative, and very likely will require modifications.

The approach is the same to maintain a good master production schedule in an MRP II system. The planning horizons vary greatly from company to company, as well as the guidelines for managing changes. Yet, a major difference occurs in how the products are lot sized and sequenced within the Kanban master schedule.

**Determining what materials are required.** There are two types of Kanban Cards—a requisition card (authorizing withdrawal of material from the feeding operation) and a production card (authorizing the feeding operation to produce more of what is being withdrawn). It is a non-computer based system.

With Material Requirements Planning, computer-generated reports advise the material planners what they should order. This process reproduction schedule.

There's one other key objective—to do so by having a minimum amount of inventory on the floor. Every operation in the factory is to "gear-up" to accomplish both missions. They're aided in this task by having multi-skilled operators, and sometimes extra machinery. The combination provides great flexibility in responding to the capacity needs.

In the U.S., with Capacity Requirements Planning, the computer produces reports displaying the time phased loads per key work center. These reports reflect not only open shop orders that haven't passed through the work center in question, but additionally include all of the planned orders (as calculated by MRP) to gain sufficient planning visibility.

This information is typically reviewed by both the planning department and by the appropriate factory managers. They determine the ability to respond to any predicted upturns or downturns in the capacity required.

**Executing the capacity plans.** At Toyota, if not enough parts are being produced, the final assembly line will shut down shortly. On the other hand, if work is accumulating behind a particular work center, this queue means that inventory is not at a minimum and steps must be taken to correct it. Thus, the burden is with the factory personnel to plan and to react if adjustments are required to alter the output.

Within MRP II, input/output reports are produced. The objective of these reports is to provide a formal monitoring system. The flow of hours into the key work centers should match the prediction that came from CRP. The flow of

---

*"The trend in Japan is to reduce the number of suppliers. They feel a single-source supplier has a greater incentive to reduce price, improve quality, and ship on time."*

---

hours out of the work center should reflect the capabilities that the factory agreed to in order to satisfy the capacity plans. If a significant deviation occurs in either, it would signal a problem and cause corrective action to be initiated.

**Determining what manufactured items** should

quires a structured bill of material, inventory records (what's on hand in the stockroom plus what's on order), and is driven by a master production schedule. In essence, the analysis compares what's available for inventory to what's needed to advise the planners what's missing, in other words, the need to get more.

With an MRP II system, typically the planner issues a shop order along with a pick list to the stockroom. The pick list authorizes the stockroom to issue the proper material to make the needed item. The shop order is the authorization for the operators to perform the required functions to make the needed item.

With the Kanban system, there is no bill of material explosion on the computer; yet once a component is depleted on the final assembly line, that triggers the replenishment cycle, top to bottom, in a similar manner as would be done with MRP II on the computer.

The two Cards of Kanban perform the same functions as the pick lists and the shop order. But they do it manually.

**Determining what capacity is required.** With Kanban, it's a non-computer approach. Through knowledge of the daily output volume, the factory foreman and operators determine what they have to do in terms of capacity to support the master be worked on. The Kanban Cards provide this information. The production cards become authorization for the operators to make more. Basically, it's a first come/first serve system—whatever production card arrives first identifies the job that should be worked on next.

Companies using MRP II usually issue a daily dispatch report for each work center. It lists all of the jobs that are physically there in a priority sequence.

**Determining what purchased parts** are required. The actual authorization for a vendor to ship more material is a Kanban Card. The absence of a card means that the vendor is not permitted to deliver material. The objective of their relationship with the vendor is to have a process similar to the relationship within the factory. That is, small lot sizes, frequent replenishments.

Under Kanban, the vendors do get advance notification to permit prior planning to occur. From the master schedule, the customer sends to each of his suppliers a rolling, ninety days projection. The notices to the vendors are treated as "unofficial orders." They are used to aid the vendor in material and capacity planning, but do not constitute a firm commitment on the customer's part.

With an MRP II system, computer reports advise purchasing people what items should be bought. The reports also suggest what existing purchase orders should be rescheduled to either arrive earlier or later, based on the changing needs of the company. The planned orders permit purchasing to provide visibility to vendors beyond the lead times.

**Feedback information.** In both countries, the notification that execution problems have occurred are manually generated. How this information is communicated, though, differs.

Toyota employs an Andon System, which translates into "light" or "lamp." The Andon is hung over the final assembly line. It is large enough to be seen throughout most of the factory. If an operator is having trouble keeping up with the required production, he signals this potential problem by lighting up his work station in yellow.

If the problem cannot be corrected, this is communicated by lighting up the work station in red. This is a warning that the final assembly line will soon shut down. Obviously, this will generate

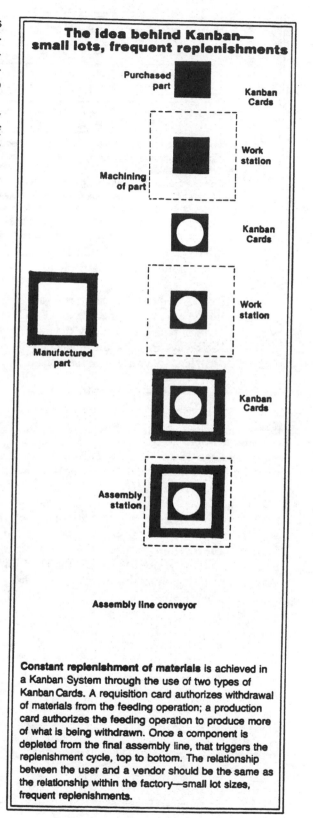

**The idea behind Kanban—small lots, frequent replenishments**

Purchased part

Kanban Cards

Machining of part

Work station

Kanban Cards

Manufactured part

Work station

Kanban Cards

Assembly station

Assembly line conveyor

Constant replenishment of materials is achieved in a Kanban System through the use of two types of Kanban Cards. A requisition card authorizes withdrawal of materials from the feeding operation; a production card authorizes the feeding operation to produce more of what is being withdrawn. Once a component is depleted from the final assembly line, that triggers the replenishment cycle, top to bottom. The relationship between the user and a vendor should be the same as the relationship within the factory—small lot sizes, frequent replenishments.

## A Kanban master production schedule—the future resembles the past

| | Week 1 | | | | | Week 2 | | | | |
|---|---|---|---|---|---|---|---|---|---|---|
| Toyota (Kanban) | A B / A C | A B / A C | A B / A C | A B / A C | A B / A C | A B / A C | A B / A C | A B / A C | A B / A C | A B / A C |
| U.S. (MRP II) | A A / A A | A A / A A | A A / A A | A A / A A | A A / A A | B B / B B | B B / B B | B B / C C | C C / C C | C C / C C |

**There's a big difference** between the master schedule for a Kanban System and for a typical American manufacturer. Suppose a company has an output of 100 products per day, and that marketing forecasts that 50% of the sales will be Product A, 25% will be Product B, and 25% Product C. The typical U.S. plant might make Product A for five straight days, change over to Product B for two and a half days, then produce Product C for the balance of the week. However, under a Kanban System, a Japanese plant will make Product A, followed by B, followed by A, followed by C. Their goal is to schedule every product, every day, and in a sequence which intermixes all products.

sufficient activity to either keep that from occurring and/or to minimize the length of the shutdown.

With MRP II, "anticipated delay reports" are generated by the appropriate people in the factory as well as in purchasing to notify the material planners that delays in achieving schedules will occur. This will lead to a reassessment of the plan.

### Limitations of the Kanban System

If a knowledgeable person were to assess the Kanban System by only looking at the tools, his conclusion would be that we have stepped backwards into the 1960s. The big debate then was, what items should be maintained on a reorder point basis versus MRP II.

Kanban Cards operate in much the same manner as a two-bin system, which is a reorder point approach. The two-bin approach has been around for eons. The inventory is separated into two bins or locations. One is used to satisfy the need for that part and as soon as that bin is empty, that's the trigger to replenish this part number. Until it is replenished, the second bin is used to supply the part.

With both the two-bin system and the Kanban System, what has been used is being replenished. The presumption is that if you have used up your inventory you will need more.

The flaws of the reorder point, and the advantages of MRP II, are so well known today that it would be difficult to find an advocate of the reorder point approach. Then how can the Kanban Cards work?

The answer lies not in the cards. Rather, Toyota has done five things to overcome the reorder point flaws:

**A uniquely structured master production** schedule. The master schedule is put together to ensure that the future resembles the past. Great care is made to plan the same products, not only every month, but within each week, and, in turn, every day. This is possible only where a company is making a highly repetitive product. Without this environment, the Kanban Cards would be replenishing the wrong items—the items used would not be the items needed.

The goal is to schedule every product, every day, and in a sequence that intermixes all products. If such a plan can be executed, then every day all components are being consumed and all are being replenished. Moreover, all that are being replenished will be needed. It's this se-

> *"The successful users of MRP II may not have harmony among all of the players, but certainly they have achieved consensus. What MRP II offers is a way to gain a 'game plan.' Once the group is pulling together, the individual capabilities are magnified."*

quence that puts the Kanban replenishment system in step with the master schedule.

The typical American manufacturing company schedules products differently. It seeks economics and efficiencies through economical lot sizes, and would batch build these products.

With this approach, the Kanban replenishment system would be out of step with the master schedule. The items being consumed would be

*"Technology can be bought; teamwork has to be nurtered. Installing a system on the computer or manually is straight forward. Using it properly is a far greater challenge. Too frequently we install systems for the users, not by the users. It's the kiss of death."*

replenished prematurely. This is one of the problems with reorder points.

**Extremely small lot sizes.** Their ultimate goal is to "use one, make one." The combination of making products repetitively, as well as in very small quantities, causes a continuous demand on all of the components parts.

If the lot sizes are larger, say a month's supply, the demand for the components will be "lumpy." The demand at the lower levels will occur twelve times a year, a month apart. Inventory will be increased due to the larger lot size, and due to making it prior to when it's next needed.

**Very short lead times.** A reorder point system does not identify the need to reschedule. All manufacturing companies are confronted with a steady stream of changes. Forecasts are wrong, bills of material are revised, parts are scrapped, vendors are late, tooling breaks, and so on. However, if the lead times are extremely short, rescheduling isn't critical.

With long lead times, if the schedules are not changed to reflect the up-to-date needs, then expediting will replace scheduling. The factory and purchasing will be running to hot lists to answer the question—"what do you really need?"

**Top down replenishment.** The master schedule and the Kanban Cards are not hooked together as a computer is linked with MRP. Nevertheless, if something is not used in final assembly, no replenishment action will take place underneath it. In essence, Kanban ties everything together via the consumption at the master schedule level.

A conventional order point system does not have these ties. It assumes each item is a stand-alone item, to be replenished independently.

**Informal capacity planning.** The burden is on both the factory as well as vendors to gear up to handle any increased or decreased volume in the master schedule. Because the master schedule generates the need for a steady, repetitive flow of parts, capacity planning at all work centers is fairly straightforward.

Without this feature, the surprises caused by manufacturing a wide variety of parts in a nonre-petitive manner would make this job extremely difficult without a computer.

These constitute the constraints for the Kanban System to work well. Remove any one and the Kanban System comes tumbling down. Therefore, unless a company makes highly repetitive products and unless they can accomplish all five points, they should not use the Kanban System.

### "Just-in-time" deliveries

All of the Kanban tools and all of the Kanban users' efforts are dedicated to the "just-in-time" and minimum inventory objectives. The goals are highly commendable; attaining them would be extremely desirable.

Just picture such a factory where the components required for final assembly arrive just in time and all of the purchased materials show up just in time to support the manufacturing operations. If, in fact, all of this could be achieved, the impact in terms of improved inventory turns and fast response to the marketplace would be spectacular. Additionally, a company would eliminate shortages and thereby gain a tremendous impact on improved productivity.

With MRP II the objectives are the same. Instead of the phrase "just-in-time" our term is "drop dead dates." It means no fat, no lies; it means every schedule lined up to the needs of the company. It means complete honesty to the foreman and to the buyers, valid dates on the factory and purchase orders. It means that if the schedules are executed, the items will come in just when needed. The foreman and the operator know that in the event that a schedule is not met, a shortage will develop.

If a company used the tools of MRP II with the same starting point as Toyota (queues, lot sizes, safety stock, lead times, vendors, and a similar execution of the schedules), the results would be as good. But the opposite would not be so. If the Kanban system was used in a company that did not resemble Toyota's environment, the results would not nearly be as good as with an MRP II system, as explained in the copy box on pp. 48.

## The major advantages of Kanban and MRP II

### Kanban System

**The tools are less expensive.** A number of functions, such as material planning, capacity planning, and dispatching, are done manually. With MRP II, these functions require a computer to keep the vast amount of data up to date. With Kanban, fewer people are required to perform these same functions.

The Kanban System depends heavily on the foreman and operators—the line people. Their job is not to have somebody else tell them whether or not they're performing well, but to make that determination themselves and take whatever corrective action is required. The typical company using MRP II has a number of planners reading output reports, responding to action messages, maintaining data, and the like.

However, if the Kanban tools were employed in an environment different from the conditions that Toyota surrounds itself with, it would simply be an "order launching and expedite" system. The reorder point approach is a very expensive system to operate. It generates excessive inventories of mismatched parts, while at the same time requiring massive expediting to react to shortages. Inexpensive tools that can't get the job done are not a bargain.

### MRP II

**It can plan ahead.** All of the functions that make up MRP II are "forward looking." For example, MRP advises replenishing material only if it is predicted that more is needed.

A Kanban System is "backward looking." It replenishes material when depleted. This is a significant difference. Only when you can make the future resemble the past will they both respond in a similar manner. With a repetitive product, this can be achieved. However, for non-repetitive products, MRP II's approach is far better.

**It can plan other activities.** Activities such as design engineering and drafting are critical "upstream functions" that can be planned by MRP II. Predicting what capacity is required and maintaining up-to-date priorities are important for these highly skilled resources. Companies are also using MRP II to predict the need for tooling and maintenance items.

**It can coordinate distribution centers.** Within an MRP II system, Distribution Resource Planning is the approach that not only plans the resource needs at these remote locations, but, in turn, coordinates their replenishment with the manufacturing facilities. DRP operates in a similar manner to MRP II—it can project the need for material, space, and people at the warehouse, as well as the size of the replenishment shipments in terms of weight, pallets, and cube.

**It can aid financial planning.** A distinguishing feature of MRP II is that the financial planning system is an extension of the operating system. One set of books for the company is the result. For many companies, this is not the case. Rather, their financial people have developed their own set of books. They have learned the hard way that the data coming out of the factory are not reliable. Much second guessing and reserves are required to protect against potential end-of-the-year financial shrinkage.

**It can handle "what if" questions.** Although it costs more to put data in a computer than to handle it manually, a company can do more with the data. For example, one of the most valuable uses of any system is to predict the consequences of alternate plans. The computer doesn't pick the best plan, but it provides information so that management can review the impact of the choices prior to selecting the one that makes the most sense. MRP II can show the consequences in terms of materials, capacity, and money. This would be an asset for any manager.

## Where do we go from here

The list of American companies utilizing MRP II and achieving spectacular results is far longer than the Kanban users. Because of the excellent track record achieved by MRP II, a number of Japanese firms have decided that this is the proper approach. Makita Electric Works, Ltd., and Stanley Electric have material requirements planning systems that work well. Additionally, they have put as much time and effort into the fundamentals as Toyota has for Kanban.

The Japanese have studied our approaches and experiences. They've learned from us. We, in turn, should study approaches such as Toyota's Kanban System and profit from this analysis.

But it's not the Kanban System that we should import. Rather it's the "Kando" of Toyota's Kanban that we need more of. Certainly, it's not simply installing a new MRP II system that will make us better; it's how we use it. But MRP II represents the right direction for manufacturing companies to manage themselves in a more productive manner.

Without a formal scheduling system that works, most American companies will not get all of the players to play team ball. MRP II provides the "glue" that can bond a team together.

A manufacturing planning and control system is made up of two ingredients—tools and people. The ideal combination would be to have the best possible tools and people using them properly. But in the final analysis, team work is the key. It's Toyota's trump card. It is the same trump card for the successful users of MRP II.

Reprinted from APICS 1982 *Conference Proceedings*.

## STOCKLESS PRODUCTION FOR THE UNITED STATES

Robert W. Hall, CPIM*
Indiana University

Most people by now have developed a certain amount of grudging admiration for the accomplishments of Japanese manufacturers. Most do not yet have a clear idea what their response will be. In part, that is because they have not yet become familiar with more than one or two techniques which Japanese manufacturers are reported to use, but even those companies with extensive knowledge of Japanese methods are having difficulty formulating a competitive program. Americans are not likely to compete well by imitation, so while some changes in manufacturing practice will be based on the Japanese experience, other changes will have to be based on American initiative.

The system we will call "stockless production" in this paper is a total manufacturing system, not just a materials management system. The names KANBAN, just-in-time or stock-less production do not suggest that, but the system encompasses everything: Product design, process design, equipment selection, materials management, quality assurance, job design, employee morale, productivity improvement -- even the marketing strategy. The full scope of the system is seldom appreciated even in Japan.

The ultimate goal of stockless production is synchro-nized, streamlined, one-piece production. Within the capa-bilities of the plant, it should be able to make one unit of any product at any time it is wanted. That is the goal of the ideal automated industry, and the objective of stockless production is over the long run to develop not just an automated plant, but an automated industry, conver-ting raw material in the hands of suppliers to the finished product in the hands of the customer with near-zero lead time and zero idle inventory.

Such an attainment is not literally possible today, but that is not the point. It is the concept itself which is important, a view of manufacturing as a physical process, minimally cluttered by the traps of conventional business thinking, which enables us to more clearly see how we must manage the technology we have created.

The proper appreciation of the goal of stockless pro-duction is most important because that allows us to see what is unnecessary in our current practices. Thus unfettered from existing work practices, planning systems and cost systems, we are free to develop new approaches.

This way of viewing manufacturing contrasts with the view often prevailing today in which the manufacturing pro-cess is held to be matter subservient to the business plan of the company. One group designs the product, another designs the plant, still another decides how and when the customer should be served, and then we attempt to devise production systems to "optimize" the current methods of production.

The stockless production way is to develop the product and the production process in a unified way, then develop the business plan so as to physically change the production and distribution processes to bring them closer to the ideal way of doing it. The difference in thinking is subtle, but crucial, the difference between managing production as if it were a humdrum, stagnant activity, and managing it as if it were a production laboratory. Above all, stockless production means creating an atmosphere of constant progress toward a purposeful goal. The resulting transformation in management attitudes works all the magic there is.

Most of this discussion will be on how to implement stockless production in Japan and in the United States. No detail about the practices of stockless production will be discussed, but the basic methods used in Japan are well known:

1. Reduce inventory levels to a minimum, and persist in overcoming the basic problems in the production process which prevent operating at the lowest possible level of inventory.

2. Reduce set up times to a minimum so that any work center can, if at all possible, produce anything it is capable of producing at any time.

3. Reduce and standardize lot sizes. The ultimate goal is a lot size of one unit.

4. Use a pull system of material control. (The Toyota system is best known for using cards to do this, but the assembly "broadcast systems" of the other auto companies do the same thing in a more limited way.)

5. Level the final assembly schedule to make an iden-tical amount of every product every day. (If lead times and inventories can be reduced to extremely low levels, this is less important.)

These methods presume that repetitive manufacturing is possible. Repetitive manufacturing is production actually or potentially controlled by rate. If manufacturing is not done repetitively, the first objective is to make physical changes to streamline material flows to convert as much job shop production as possible to repetitive manufacturing. The proper question to ask is why production <u>cannot</u> be done repetitively, accepting job shop production only when it cannot be avoided. Repetitive manufacturing is obviously more efficient whenever it can be employed.

However, the basic methods of stockless production also apply to job shops except for standard lot sizes and iden-tical schedules every day. The ideas of stockless production are clearer when directed to development of repetitive manufacturing, and they were applied to repeti-tive manufacturing (in the auto industry) earlier and more intensively than to job shop production.

IMPLEMENTING STOCKLESS PRODUCTION

1. <u>Basic and Correct Understanding at all Organiza-tional Levels</u>: This step, as all the others, is necessary in both the United States and Japan. Top managements every-where have declared that the company is going to "do just-in-time" without understanding the scope of that declaration or the commitment required. The method is not natural to Japan or to anywhere else in the industrial world because it requires an intensity of performance not previously practiced and a rejection of past methods of operation. Therefore, its implementation is always accomplished by dissention and confusion. Entering the program without recognizing what it is can only lead to disastrous failure, and it has done exactly that for several companies.

This understanding is required at all levels:

Top management.
Operating management -- the implementation teams.
Workers (and unions where those exist.)

From the successful companies comes the advice not to plan implementation in too much detail. It is impossible to foresee in detail the problems which will occur. In each plant, implementation is a process of self-discovery through experience -- learning by doing.

Most important is to understand that all aspects of production must be changed. Stockless production is not just a program to reduce inventory, for example. Nor is it just a program to modify equipment, or to develop more participative management on the shop floor. The manage-ments with a narrow view of what is needed may think that a very small accomplishment is a great achievement and stop before they really begin.

All successful companies (some after an initial failure) have said that the personal and emotional commitment to undertake the program was the most difficult step. It takes courage to be a vice-president of revolution, especially the positive kind.

All this requires emotional preparation. In all, it appears that an American plant cannot possibly get ready for a stockless production program without six months or more of study and preparing of the workforce for the con-version. It is a tough, confusing process, and morale must be high going into the start of it.

2. <u>It Is an Action Program</u>: All the successful companies have organized in a similar way. A visible, dominant top executive has led the charge, a project

champion powerful and forceful enough to neutralize organizational resistance as it occurs. The uproar is strong enough that the Board of Directors should have a fundamental understanding of what is about to happen and support it.

The implementation happens plant by plant with strong shop floor leaders personally directing the changes. The usual plant implementation team consists of 5-15 people. The most crucial positions are: production control specialist, manufacturing engineer and the foremen of the project area. Many changes are needed in each area of the plant, so the foremen must become project leaders coordinating the changes. Production must continue all through the changeover periods of chaos in both equipment and control systems.

A typical pattern is for the team to have daily meetings to review the status of every little project and set goals for accomplishment each day. As the program moves from a single pilot project to projects all over the plant, the various team members are involved in review meetings almost constantly, many of them stand-up meetings in the shop.

The method is to make problems visible so that everyone can see what is necessary. In fact, the major techniques associated with KANBAN are dedicated to allowing everyone to see where the trouble points in production are, and to allowing everyone to assist in promoting a smooth flow of material through the production process. The idea is to make problems visible, not to hide them. Incidentally, a "problem" is any condition that inhibits a straight-line flow of production according to the precept of stockless production. Without the concept firmly in mind, the problems remain unseen.

The project champion and the implementation teams march the plant through the conversion process by a program of management by objectives. By giving people clear direction about what is to be emphasized in the program monthly, weekly and daily, the Quality Circles or other work participation groups can make their contributions. However, the impetus does not come from the worker groups. It is a directed program.

Most important is the quality and intensity of shop floor leadership. The people selected to direct the program on the shop floor must be both experienced with the plant and its people and capable of leadership at all levels of the plant.

3. Approximate Sequence of Implementation Activity: This is more a conceptual sequence than a chronological one. Once floor activity begins, a great many things may be happening at once, and this is determined by the particular problems uncovered in a given plant.

a. Training: Some formal training may occur both before and after floor activity begins. Top executives typically get several days training, and the implementation team should get both classroom and, if possible, some hands-on training (in a plant already on the system). Floor workers typically get 1-4 days of training. However, much of the education is done by doing it, and one of the qualifications of project leaders is their ability to explain and train people at the spot where they work as needed. Most companies prepared manuals for people at different organizational levels. The major effort has gone into manuals and other training devices for floor workers. They require the simplest, clearest explanations, and their manuals should be prepared in terms of the products and processes with which they work every day.

b. Housekeeping: The need for excellent housekeeping is common sense. The smooth material flows and fast set ups cannot be done unless everything is exactly where it is supposed to be. A production process cannot be automated without precision placement of everything, and that does not happen by itself. Though simplistic, the process goes like this:

(1) Find a proper, correct location for everything necessary for production: material, tools, supplies and accessories. In most plants this requires some nitty-gritty thinking and planning by every member of the workforce.

(2) Remove everything not needed from the production floor. This is not as easy as it sounds. To do it means more detailed decisions about tools, obsolete material, quality holds, etc. Taken far enough it begins to attack the fundamental procedures of the plant, and that is exactly the point. Cleaning up the plant means cleaning up the process.

(3) Institute strict rules on put away and clean up. All tools, dies and materials must be clean and ready for use in their proper place the next time they are required -- a little bit like organizing a fire station.

(4) Remove excess inventory from the floor and from stockrooms. This is done before any formal change in material handling procedures or equipment. It usually means examination of the reasons for holding safety stocks. The purpose is to attack the reasons for the safety stock. (Many companies feel that stockless production is only an inventory reduction program, so they feel elated by the financial results of this move and slow the program at this point -- before it has really begun.)

c. Streamline the Flow of Material: This means "rearranging the furniture" so as to make process flows where job shop flows existed earlier. It may only be possible to do this partway until further development takes place, but straightening the physical flows does much to establish fixed routings of materials where these do not already exist.

At this time the project team should begin to establish stockpoints on the floor, an inbound stockpoint and an outbound stockpoint for each work center. The concept is that one part number should only originate from one place in the plant.

Just to get this far may require considerable rework of routings and selection of operations and equipment. It results in so much increased visibility of the actual problems in production that the good ideas begin to present themselves. Well done, it is an important psychological and mental contribution to the seriousness of the program. The workers know that everyone is going to accomplish something, not just tinker with the symbols of the system. It makes everyone want to do a better job.

Several activities usually start in conjunction with this:

(1) Decrease set up times. For many types of equipment, this is not difficult. It requires only the same kind of care and analysis usually reserved for improving the running rates of equipment. The equipment used should be simple enough to modify, and that itself may provoke some wrenching decisions about mothballing some expensive, complex equipment in favor of simpler, more flexible pieces. The development of the set up process itself really means standardizing the setups so that one person can do them by rote in an easy fashion.

(2) Improve process control. The essential activity is to attack the causes of scrap. This is a neverending activity because one of the main reasons for irregular material flows is defects. The objective is to get rid of the rework.

The best way to do this is to have each machine automatically shut itself off if a defective is produced. Then proceed to correct the cause of the problem. To do this usually requires some original work on the process capabilities of several pieces of equipment.

(3) Preventive Maintenance. A PM program is a must with stockless production. If the plant is to operate with a minimum of inventory, equipment downtime needs to be reduced. It is not unusual to allow one or two hours between shifts for proper maintenance of equipment to take place. Besides if machines are closely linked together, it is desirable to pull the maintenance on them in groups

since downtime on one will stop them all. Also common is the placement of a counter and warning light on each machine which is reset with each tool change. The machine itself gives warning that maintenance is needed. Detailed operating histories are commonly kept in a log on each piece of equipment.

(4) Cross-Train Workers: If a smooth flow of production is to take place, the plant must also not have a bottleneck if a particular. worker is absent. This means giving incentive to workers to learn the operation of many pieces of equipment and to keep current with their operation. American plants with tight job descriptions and rigid job assignments will have a difficult time adjusting to this, and it is sometimes thought that a smooth flow of production can take place without it, but all plants seriously entering stockless production have found multi-functional workers to be a necessity.

d. Reorganize Design Engineering to Improve Product Produceability and Reduce Engineering Changes: It is obviously very important that engineers design the product so that it can be built in the plant that is emerging from this process. Therefore, design engineers must be fully indoctrinated in stockless production, and manufacturing engineers need to be introduced into design teams if this practice is not already being followed.

The start up of a new product is also very important. A typical practice is for Design Engineering in stockless production accompany the new product to the floor and work through the changes necessary to make it work properly at the time of start up. It is done informally and quickly during start up itself. Then only the most necessary changes are required to enter the process after the product is in production.

Another common practice is for Production Control to develop the final bill of material -- the way it really is. That minimizes the little changes that hit the system. The pride of ownership of many engineering departments in keeping responsibility for design is dampened by the practice, but it also frees engineers from a great deal of trivia which they often do not perform with enthusiasm and allows them to concentrate on more substantive design problems.

e. Improve Supplier Quality: Of course the supplier pipelines can be trimmed by having them ship in smaller quantities more frequently. Where this can be done without difficulty it should be done, but this is not the initial objective with suppliers. Initially, the quality of parts or materials should be improved.

Usually this means reducing the number of suppliers, giving the business to those who are capable of providing good quality. If they can provide good quality so as to eliminate the need for inspection, that is more important than cutting the inventory pipeline in the beginning. One of the principles of several companies entering stockless production is not to press for performance from suppliers that the buyer cannot do himself.

f. Level the Final Assembly Schedule: If a pull system of material control is to be established, the final assembly line must be first developed for it. The temptation exists to issue cards elsewhere, and it is often possible to do that, but eventually every operation must take its cues from final assembly.

Leveling the schedule means running a repetitive sequence of models in final assembly so as to provide an even distribution of daily demand for all types of material which should arrive at the line. That means assembling a sequence of mixed models, something like what is commonly done in automotive assembly.

The line must first be physically organized to run a mixed model sequence, and that may take some time. The organization of the line to do this makes it look a little like a storeroom. Every part and every tool should be exactly in its place. Assembly should become a precision operation.

Leveling the schedule means leveling the flow of material to final assembly, not leveling the workload necessarily, though it is necessary to balance the line also.

Also important is to adjust the rate of the final assembly process to the demand of the market. That is difficult because as line rate changes it becomes necessary to rebalance the manning. At this point the need for multi-purpose workers and quick change assembly stations becomes obvious. The alternative is to allow goods to accumulate in finished goods, and it also forces all the feeding operations to work on more a stop-and-go basis than is desirable.

The schedule which is leveled is the planned schedule for final assembly, not the actual final assembly schedule. The actual schedule should be exactly what was planned, but in the plants which build product to order, this may be exceedingly difficult. The schedule attempts to provide the basis of a level schedule, but the purpose of the pull system is to keep material flows synchronized to the actual demand for material in final assembly.

The typical pilot project is one assembly line and several work centers which feed it. Because of that, it is not necessary to level the schedule of a complete product line at once, only the schedule for one final assembly line at a time.

g. Link Material Flows to Final Assembly. The simplest and most common way to do this is by the Toyota card system, and the card system has a distinct advantage over some others. To use it, WIP inventory for particular part numbers must be located at specific points on the plant floor. In fact, the reason the cards are issued initially is to foster a heightened awareness of the need for housekeeping. Once the workforce has the floor arranged and has mastered the mechanics of using cards, then the card system can be used to start a controlled reduction of inventory and attack on the second round of problems which are the root cause of the need for inventory.

In the beginning the card system may be used to withdraw material from the stockroom, but as soon as possible, material should be eliminated from the stockroom and installed on the floor. This is itself a considerable project and is the initial objective of the card system if inventory is not all on the floor when it is begun.

If shipment quantities from suppliers cannot be cut, there may be no way to avoid continuing the raw material storeroom for a while, but the objective is to reduce the need for the storeroom to a point where the receiving area itself is the only raw material storeroom needed. In effect the receiving area becomes a staging area for production, and this cannot be done so long as there are major problems with supplier quality, which is the major reason that the strongest initial action with suppliers is defect reduction.

However, the card system is not the only way to link fabrication with assembly. It is possible to synchronize fabrication schedule sequences with final assembly unit sequences. This is really a tighter method of control than the card system because it is based on a lot size of one.

The sequence of units in fabrication can be set as soon as the sequence of units can be set in final assembly. In the auto business this sequence can most often be firmed as soon as the body has been painted without blemish requiring touch up. Therefore, the production can be sequenced within the lead time established between paint and the point at which a given component must merge into final assembly. The objective is to compress the lead times of fabrication short enough that the maximum number of components can be controlled in this way.

This kind of fabrication in sequence has long been practiced within automotive assembly plants, but only with the advent of stockless production has it been considered feasible to fabricate at one plant and transport to assembly in the sequence required, but this is the ultimate goal, and in fact is beginning to be practiced in a limited way.

h. Maximize Conversion to Full Automation; The level schedules with a pull system of control and short set up times is only an approximation of the full automation desired. The stockless production method of evolving to automation leads many Japanese plants to develop U-lines, or group technology cells. This can be established as soon as inventory has been reduced to zero between operations so that they can be physically located next to each other and all set up at once. In fact, to make this work really well, the set up times should be reduced to a time less than the cycle time of the parts being fabricated. Then the operators can make a circuit of the equipment for set up just as if it were a production cycle with a part to fabricate.

One of the major attributes of stockless production is that it offers guidance in the selection and development of automated equipment. It deters the purchase of equipment which runs at a higher speed than is required or which lacks the flexibility required. It also stimulates a search for the simplest way to accomplish a particular operation and discourages the development of equipment which is unnecessarily complex (and expensive). Since it promotes simple, flexible automation along with careful attention to detail, stockless production develops automation more effectively than a straight engineering approach. The debugging takes place as the automation develops -- not after a complex installation of equipment is already in place.

i. Extend the System to Applicable Suppliers: As previously mentioned, the most important initial objective with suppliers is to improve their quality. Beyond that, the most important assistance given to suppliers is the leveling and stabilizing of the schedule given to them. If suppliers know that they are expected to meet a level delivery schedule with quality material, they have fewer reasons for non-performance.

However, the most important aspect of the relationship with suppliers remains quality. The purpose of decreasing the inventory pipeline between the last operation of the supplier and the first operation where material is used is to provide easy traceability of the cause of defects. Immediate feedback and specific information relating to the supplier's production process is the quickest way to solve the mysteries of defects.

The primary way to reduce the amount of inventory in transit between supplier and customer is to ship smaller quantities more frequently. This is done much more easily in Japan than in the United States. In Japan trucks are mostly side loaded, and they ply a regular circuit between plants, unloading a skid or two and loading a skid or two at each stop. They carry a mixed cargo much of the time, and because of this system, there is little economic incentive to ship in large quantities just to fill a truck.

The same idea is applicable in the United States, but not in the same degree. Companies can cut the pipeline inventory by using consolidation warehouses and organizing trucks to make a circuit of suppliers when bringing in material. Companies are making substantial reductions in purchased part inventories by giving thought to this.

The intention of the program with suppliers is not to push the inventory off on them, though this is a common initial reaction to stockless production, and often an initial fear of the suppliers. In any case, the inventory costs the same in confusion no matter where it is physically held, and the objective is to eliminate it wherever it may be found.

However, companies cannot give much instruction to suppliers on stockless production until they have experience in using it themselves. It is important not to antagonize or frighten suppliers in the beginning of the program when they do not yet understand what it is.

THE AMERICAN RESPONSE

Stockless production has both succeeded and failed in Japan. Americans will doubtless record a number of failures before they get it going. Over the past year I have had the opportunity to observe the early efforts of a dozen American companies venturing into stockless production, and the following observations are distilled from the comments of the managers involved, in addition to personal thoughts.

The major cause of failure in the United States will probably be the same as it was in Japan: Wanting to do the program superficially, putting in a few quick die changes and some Kanban cards, but without doing the hard work of preparing the people and cleaning up the plant. We overlook the basic and the obvious in the rush to install some of the visible trappings of the system and enjoy a few of the short-term benefits.

Almost all American managers who have studied stockless production or thought through how they would implement it have pointed out three practices common to U.S. industry which cannot prevail if stockless production is to be successful:

1. The methods of performance measurement for production managers must eliminate the short-term concern for labor efficiency. This occurs both in direct measures of performance and indirectly because of the way standard costs are developed. The undesirable effect is that people are extremely reluctant to stop production for a set up, and they are encouraged to produce at the maximum possible running rates because this results in the lowest unit costs by the common methods of measurement. Performance measures must change to emphasize the number and magnitude of production improvements made.

2. People must not fear either losing or changing their job. Most of the Japanese companies have been able to greatly increase sales and absorb the workforce into positions created by expansion as productivity doubled or tripled. However, companies in mature industries must find a way to remove large numbers of both staff people and direct labor from the company without losing morale. That is not a problem that managers want to discuss. They will acknowledge its existence, but a program of outplacement for those who are to be displaced is not a subject within the realm of currently accepted thought.

3. Management must become more integrated. Managers must learn to think of manufacturing from a broader perspective than their own narrow technical specialty. This is a well-recognized problem and one with which most managements interested in stockless production have begun to deal with openly.

The major effort for American industry is for a large enough group of managers to come to a correct understanding of stockless production so as to provide leadership in tackling the tough problems of implementation. Once that is done, Americans will likely go about it with innovative vigor. Here are some of the thoughts on how Americans will approach it:

1. Training programs are likely to be far more useful for Americans than Japanese or others. One suggestion by a General Motors manager is to build a small scale model of the plant and its equipment and use it in planning what to do and in walking everyone through the implementation. It is a technique which has been used in construction, but seldom in manufacturing.

American industry has usually been very good in training people when it was obvious that mass training in a hurry was really needed. There is also a great deal of experience from the armed forces on training large numbers of people very quickly on subjects that require physical changes and skills.

2. Americans are likely to work better as temporary teams than as "permanent" groups of people in Quality Circles. The American style is to form a task force or committee to tackle specific problems as they arise without necessarily making them into a semi-permanent social group.

American companies are likely to develop several innovative approaches to suggestion systems. One of them is called by Hewlett-Packard a Corrective Action Request. The individual employee fills out a request to which a supervisor must respond within 48 hours. Both the suggestion and the response are kept on a board so that everyone can see the nature of it and the progress being made. If the problem is difficult enough, a team of staff specialists and floor personnel can be assembled to solve it. The method is a straightforward way of tackling problems.

3. American companies usually have strong engineering power. Because of that, they may leapfrog to full automation very quickly once a good methodology for doing so is worked out. The major weakness in most of the trial projects now in operation is the lack of a mechanism for attacking and solving the basic problems. We tend to think of problems as exceptions rather than as matters to be given attention as they are uncovered, but once this more active mode of thinking about the problems of automating has gained acceptance, American staffs will likely formulate some powerful methods for analyzing the causes of problems. It is a matter of popularizing some of the problem-solving methods we already know and bringing them into full-time use by more people.

4. American companies have a great deal of systems capability. Therefore, we are likely to leap more readily into methods for sequencing fabrication operations directly with final assembly without going through a long process of working up to this point through a card system. The danger is that Americans will try to manage more complexity than is necessary, but once many people understand that the objective of the system is to provide a method of communicating a linkage between final assembly and fabrication and preserving a very short lead time, we should develop some excellent ways of doing this.

Robert W. Hall

Professor Hall teaches Operations Management at Indiana University. Prior to joining the faculty he worked for Eli Lilly & Co. and Union Carbide Corp.

Long active in the American Production & Inventory Control Society, he has served as president of the Central Indiana Chapter and as Vice President of Education for Region 13. He has made numerous presentations at local and national conferences. Recently he has been active with APICS Repetitive Manufacturing Group as a writer of their proceedings and materials, and he is engaged in comparative studies of Japanese and American manufacturing management. He is the author of the APICS publication Driving the Productivity Machine and the case study Kawasaki U.S.A.

Reprinted from APICS 1987 *Conference Proceedings*.

## HOW TO DESIGN MRP SYSTEMS FOR JOB SHOPS

James W. Branam, CPIM
Rockwell-Goss

### INTRODUCTION

This paper is based on the notion that most MRP (Material Requirements Planning or Manufacturing Resource Planning) Systems are designed for either Make to Stock or Assemble to Order environments. The true job shop or Engineered to Order shop is a different business environment. The product of the Engineered to Order shop is not the manufactured goods but is engineering and manufacturing expertise and capacity. Therefore, even though many people have forced them into job shops, present MRP packages do not fit the needs of job shops.

Based on extensive review of many of the major MRP packages available today the author presents a list (generic) of the MRP shortcomings in relation to job shops and a list (generic) of the types of modifications required to make MRP Systems perform properly in a true job shop environment. Specific software packages will not be mentioned either by name or by description.

### BACKGROUND

There are two basic types of companies: Make to Stock and Make to Order. The Make to Order companies further breakdown into two types: Assemble to Order and Engineer to Order. The Engineer to Order company is the true job shop. The major task of manufacturing management is to balance schedule (load) and capacity. Both the Make to Stock and Assemble to Order companies rely on adjusting the schedule (load) to conform to available capacity. On the other hand, the Engineer to Order companies must adjust capacity to balance to the schedule (load). This is obviously a much more difficult task. It is necessary because the Engineer to Order company is usually held to a delivery date based on a contract. This contract may, in many cases, have a penalty clause for failure to meet the contractual due date. This major difference between Engineer to Order (job shop) companies and Make to Stock or Assemble to Order companies must be considered when evaluating an MRP system.

### MANUFACTURING SYSTEMS REQUIREMENTS

Statistics have shown that the majority of time that a part spends in the factory (batch manufacturing) is spent in move and queue. The amount of time that a part actually spends on a machine is not all value added. The majority of that time is spent in non value added activities such as set up, tool change, and in process inspection. The portion of a part's thruput time in a factory that is spent in true value added activity is very small indeed. This percentage has been shown to be less than two percent.

The reason that the true value added percentage is so low is that the majority of manufacturing engineering, corporate and university research efforts have been spent trying to reduce the time involved in this value added portion. The basic functional scheduling, set up, tool change and in-process inspection efforts were left to production schedulers, foremen, material handlers, expeditors and set up men. These people had little, if any, formal training and even less professional help. They were thrown into the vast sea of the manufacturing plant and, in essence, told to sink or learn how to swim. Human nature prevailed and most of their efforts were survival oriented rather than being spent trying to solve the basic problem.

The advent of computers, MRP and exotic scheduling systems did little to alleviate this situation. The most basic and most difficult management task in a manufacturing environment is to balance schedule (or priority) and capacity on a continuous ongoing time phased basis. This basic task must be performed at two levels.

First, schedule and capacity must be balanced at the planning level. The schedule portion is typically performed starting with the Business Plan proceeding on through the Production Plan to the Master Production Schedule and on to the Material Requirements Plan. The capacity side of the equation also starts at the Business Plan level and proceeds on to Resource Requirements Plan, Rough Cut Capacity Plan and Capactiy Requirements Plan. It appears that many companies spend a great deal of effort planning the schedule side of this equation but relatively little on planning the capacity side.

The second level of the schedule vs. capacity equation is at the execution level. At this level the schedule execution side of the equation is mainly concerned with priority control on the shop floor. This takes many different forms but typically involves a final assembly schedule, stock picking schedule, order priorities and operation sequence (or priority). The capacity side of the equation at the execution level takes the form of capacity control via labor control, inventory control, factory order control, machine (or work center) control, tool control, and preventive maintenance. The execution level is similar to the planning level in that one side of the equation seems to receive greater emphasis than the other. The difference is that it is the opposite side! The emphasis at the execution level is on the capacity side rather than the schedule side.

The net result of the heavy emphasis on planning the schedule and execution on the capacity side of the equation is that schedule execution usually leaves something to be desired. This weakness in schedule execution has been one of the biggest disappointments of MRP and other schedule planning computer systems. These systems are long on planning and short on execution.

### BASIC MRP CONCEPTS

The first basic MRP concept of Independent vs. Dependent Demand was well understood by job shop companies. They knew that they could not order component parts until they knew about the end item that they were building. Most MRP to old system comparisons were based on the old system being a reorder point system. However, the job shop people understood the concept of Independent vs. Dependent Demand and ordered components using a "block ordering" approach. This approach typically was to perform a manual bill of material explosion (and then later with computers) and order all components to be due on the same date. This date was based on an arbitrary or historical offset from the ship date.

The second basic MRP concept of component Time Phasing was only partially practiced by the job shops. They time phased the jobs but not the components within the jobs. This lack was more due to a lack of data processing capability than a lack of understanding of the concept. MRP was touted as a system that would bring the components in on an as required basis rather than having them set in inventory for long periods of time. This idea sounds a lot like the Just-In-Time idea of today. However, the MRP approach never realized its full potential because move, queue and safety times were inflated to provide "cushion" in the lead times. This again highlights the weakness in the schedule execution phase of present MRP Systems. The cushion provided by the inflated lead times was deemed necessary because of the weakness in the schedule execution phase. This weakness is more predominant or evident in job shops than in Make to Stock companies because of the less routine or regimented flow of work through the plant.

One further note on MRP concepts. The original term MRP stood for Material Requirements Planning. Since then it has been expanded to mean Manufacturing Resource Planning. This term also seems to mean the same as the term Closed Loop Manufacturing control Systems. The original

Material Requirements Planning concept was a good one. However, it did not give the expected results because of a lack of discipline or regimentaton in other areas (that supplied data to MRP or were to execute the plans developed from MRP). Therefore to properly discuss MRP; the bigger picture must also be discussed.

## WHAT IS THE PRODUCT?

The product of a Make To Stock company is a standard item produced through repetitive production. The assemble to order product is a standard item with options produced via repetitive and batch production (with some quantity and mix variables). The Engineer to Order company produces custom items via job shop production. The product of an Engineer to Order company is its engineering expertise (within a given field) and production capabilites to convert the engineering expertise into the prouct that the customer ordered. Therefore the Engineer to Order company is selling engineering services and manufacturing capacity. Based on this product definition the closed loop manufacturing system must be viewed in a different light. The following sections will discuss the closed loop manufacturing control system with a view towards the differences involved in an Engineer to Order company.

## PRODUCTION PLAN

The matching of forecasted business to production capacity takes place in the Production Plan at a product line level. The Make to Stock company can, in many cases, match an end item forecast to plant capacity. The addition of the option mix makes this matching more difficult in the Assemble to Order company. However, the Engineer to Order company must match the manufacturing content of the forecast to plant capacity. This is the point were the problems first start to arise. The problem is determining the manufacturing content of the forecast. It is difficult to determine the manufacturing content of an item that has not yet been designed. Therefore it may be necessary to have some sort of rough . estimating capability that will easily and quickly estimate the manufacturing content of forecasted business.

Additional problems occur for the Engineer to Order companies on the capacity side of the equation. The mix and product remain fairly constant in a Make to Stock company making it fairly easy to identify and track critical work centers. The variation in option mix for Assemble to Order companies starts to add complexity to the determination of critical work centers. Engineer to Order companies have wider variance in critical work centers since both mix and product vary.

## MASTER PRODUCTION SCHEDULE

Prebuilding to a forecast is rarely used in Engineer to Order companies. Therefore the Customer Order is the next item that would be considered. However, the Customer Order is not definitive enough to use as a Master Production Schedule to drive Material Requirements Planning. The Customer Order in the Engineer to Order company typically consists of specifications or verbal descriptions of what is being ordered. Some type of decision support or artificial intelligence system is needed to configure an order based on a menu or question and answer session. Otherwise the manufacturing fuunction must wait until the engineering is complete to be able to load a Master Production Schedule that is capable of driving a Material Requirements Plan. Even when this has been completed it is not always structured in a manufacturing bill of material. In many cases the engineering will be just a group of parts lists. These parts lists may have to be structured at least to the Customer Order to load them into the Master Production Schedule. Additionally these engineering lists may or may not have the manufacturing content (hours) estimated at this point.

The next Master Production Schedule item is the Available to Promise. The Available to Promise numbers should be in terms of capacity for Engineer to Order companies. However, since capacity requirements for each order are not known until the engineering design is complete it is unlikely that this information will be available on a timely enough basis.

The Available to Forecast portion of the Master Schedule is not used in Engineer to Order companies since forecast is not used. If it was used it would have to be in terms of capacity.

## ROUGH CUT CAPACITY PLANNING

As stated earlier capacity requirements are not usually know at this point in time in the Engineer to Order company. Therefore many Engineer to Order companies do not use Rough Cut Capacity Planning. Those that do use a form of Rough Cut Capacity Planning will use some sort of historical data or, lacking that, rules of thumb.

The lack of definitive load data at this level in Engineer to Order companies is a major problem for manufacturing management. The need for an Estimating System that estimates load by work center (or category of work center) as well as costs and lead times. This Estimating System would have to functon at various levels. Make to Stock and Assemble to Order companies have Standard Cost Systems that provide this data at all levels. These levels range from the Production Plan Level all the way down to the detail operation number on the shop floor. It should be noted that even though many Engineer to Order companies use Standard Cost Systems the standard costs are not developed early enough to be useful in the planning stages. Therefore the need is for an Estimating System that would be useful not only to evaluate pricing but to also supply data at all levels from the production plan to the shop floor.

The capacity side of the equation in the Engineer to Order company also has its problems. Critical work centers are difficult to identify because they vary due to mix changes and mix may change with each order. Additionally, true capacity is not fully known. The nature of a job shop is such that there are several alternate methods to perform each operation. Most job shop people pride themselves in being able to see and use these alternatives. Also, since capacity must be more flexible in a job shop, management usually causes additional alternatives to be developed. They would include such approaches as overtime, layoffs, rearrangement of shop personnel, subcontracting and product redeployment between plants.

These variables illustrate the point that the critical balance between schedule (load) and capacity is more difficult to obtain in Engineer to Order Companies. In addition to the previously mentioned aids to dealing with this problem, an on line what if system is needed at this level. The what if capabilities would not only have to perform what ifs on schedule changes but also on capacity changes and/or alternatives.

## MATERIAL REQUIREMENTS PLANNING

Since each job has custom engineering, bills of material tend to vary greatly, even if some common components are used. The heavy engineering work load and constant push to finish each order tends to result in parts list type bills of material. Manufacturing usually does not have the lead time to restructure the bills of material. Therefore some sort of generic subassembly or operationalized generic assembly routing is developed. Since most MRP packages will not handle generic subassemblies a "work around" solution is developed. The parts list type of bills of materials are often not structured all the way to the top. They may have just quantity references related to other specifications on the customer order.

As mentioned earlier the Master Production Schedule must reflect the Customer Order but since the Customer Order is not directly explodable some interface must be used. The parts list bills of material must be structured to the customer order.

Additionally a method to schedule individual elements of the Customer Order is required if it is a long job.

Predetermined lead times or lead time build ups on the computer may not be possible since many Engineer to Order companies do not have assembly routings. Therefore in many cases assembly lead times must take the form of lead time offsets in the product structure file. However, lead time offsets have the built in problem of not being dynamic based on quantity variables. Component fabrication routings are often prepared using estimates or predetermined time standards. Therefore they may also leave something to be desired as far as accuracy is concerned. Move and queue times vary widely due to the functional processing approach used in these shops. Most MRP packages do not have a dynamic lead time calculation. This is very important in the Engineer to Order shop. This is due to large quantity variations as well as mix and product variations.

Since MRP plans to infinite capacity the following queston then develops: Does it make sense to plan (schedule) to infinite capacity, if, capacity is the product that is being sold? The experts say that you cannot plan to finite capacity using MRP. If this is true then how can the Rough Cut Capacity Plan be valid? The use of finite scheduling in a functional processing environment can be very difficult but it can help (but not solve the problem).

Most MRP packages have only fixed lot size techniques. Only a few have dynamic lot sizing techniques such as least total cost. Most of the fixed lot sizing techniques assume level production (and demand). However, the Engineer to Order company tends to have very lumpy demand. Lot sizing also clouds the traceability of the Customer Order status (components).

The strict make or buy only part classification in most MRP packages is too restrictive for Engineer to Order shops. Most of these shops tend to do a lot of subcontracting to handle peak load periods. Another part classification called "subcontract" is needed. Also, plants that are part of a company that has other plants another part classification called interplant is needed.

The large move and queue times involved in the traditional functional processing and the poor schedule execution of most MRP and/or computerized scheduling systems have forced Engineer to Order shops to move to Group Technology. Group Technology coding and classification of parts has allowed families of similar parts to be developed. These families can then be processed in the same manner. This has allowed the development of group technology work cells and then Flexible Manufacturing System (FMS) cells to convert job shops to a flow processing concept. However, few MRP packages have the ability to handle group technology codes and retrieval. None seem to have the ability to plan and schedule on the basis of groups or families. Group ordering formulas have been defined and published. However, they have not been incorporated into MRP packages so they could be used to combine requirements or orders on a common schedule.

CAPACITY REQUIREMENTS PLAN

Does it balance yes or no? The balance is based on finite capacity vs. a schedule loaded without concern for capacity. If capacity data is good enough to use for balancing then why is it not good enough to use for finite scheduling. Conversely if it is not good enough to use for finite scheduling, then is it good enough to use for balancing? The answers to these questions leave much doubt as to this approach. Also "What If" capability rarely if ever exists. If it does it usually is in reference to adjusting the Master Production Schedule. The Engineer to Order shop is selling capacity and therefore needs to adjust capacity and it probably has the capability to do so. The typical solution to an out of balance Capacity Requirements Plan is to supply manual feedback to the Master Production Schedule. There are two problems with this manual feedback. First, it does not always happen. Second, when it does happen it is either too late to make a change or it is ignored (or overruled).

Another problem area of the Capacity Requirements Plan is that no action is required. It is a reference document only-orders can flow through without ever being reviewed. The same condition applies to work centers. Also no alternatives such as overtime, queue compression, lot splitting, etc., are offered.

SHOP FLOOR CONTROL

The schedule execution is not as well time phased as Just-In-Time but it could be a lot closer than it is. MRP was going in the right direction but somehow seemed to stop short. MRP is based on scheduling to infinite capacity and therefore not realistic. Schedule execution is left to foremen and expeditors to make it happen. The use of Input-Output Control is a feeble attempt at manually controlled finite scheduling. There are no tools in the system to help in actual schedule execution. Dispatch reports are unrealistic and do not link parts together by customer or by assembly requirements (other than by due dates distorted by questionable lead times and lot sizes). Overall there is too much fat and slack in the system. Lead times, queues, move times, safety times etc. All of this fat and slack has been added to compensate for the lack of a good schedule execution system.

The capacity control portion of shop floor control is used mostly as a monitoring system to track and report on the level and use of capacity items such as: labor, inventory, factory orders, machines, tools and maintenance. It does little to actually control the use of these items other than provide reports that are used to criticize the people on the firing line. It then becomes more of an accounting system rather than a schedule vs. capacity balanced execution system.

One final note about Shop Floor Control is that it, like Material Requirements Planning, has no provision for Group Technology. To move away from the old slow functional processing to the flow processing approach it will be necessary to have scheduling capability and capacity viewing by part group.

PURCHASING

Purchased part lead times are even more unrealistic than those for make items. They are not maintained due to a lack of mass maintenance capability (by commodity code) in most packages. Even when they are maintained there is even less leverage to get good information than for manufactured parts.

The large variety of parts and low volume per part create problems in the Purchasing area. Most software packages suffer from a lack of-or have poor contract buying capability. Better contract buying ability is needed. This contract buying ability should allow for the purchase of several items from one vendor. It should also be able to handle both contract and requirements details. These should include capacity buying techniques as well as quantity considerations. Additionally release and receipt status must be constantly updated and tracked against contract terms. To make the size of the contracts worthwhile to vendors and to prevent inventory problems it is necessary that Group Technology techniques again be used to group items into families of parts that can be combined into one contract and ordered from one vendor. The Group Technology techniques can also be used in subcontracting work from overloaded groups. Last, the groups can be used to evaluate prices, determine standards, and prepare estimates.

RECEIVING

The Receiving Department needs the system to automatically flag backorders upon receipt. It is amazing that MRP systems either continue to assume that there will not be any backorders or that expeditors will continue to handle them. Once these backorders are received the system must allow for a combined receipt and issue to issue them from the Receiving Department.

## STOCKROOM AND ASSEMBLY

The Stockroom needs the ability to easily update at least two locations per part. The location update transactions will be considerably higher in volume in an Engineer to Order company due to the higher turnover and mix of parts.

One of the biggest needs in this area is the ability to combine parts from various engineering parts lists via a generic subassembly code into a single picking document and retain the parts list identity. The lack of a manufacturing structure bill of material forces this need. Without these structured bills of materials the Engineer to Order companies often resort to generic subassembly codes to issue parts. The lack of assembly routings and manufactured structures then forces the assembly area to rely heavily on the experience of the assemby workers to properly assemble the subassemblies and the end items.

## SUMMARY

The nature of the Engineer to Order business is such that the product being sold and produced is really engineering expertise and manufacturing capacity. Since many Engineer to Order contracts have delivery penalty clauses the task of balancing load and capacity becomes more difficult. Load cannot be easily leveled by rescheduling the Master Production Schedule. It becomes necessary to adjust capacity to maintain the critical balance between load (schedule) and capacity. Engineer to Order companies have developed many techniques to adjust capacity quickly. However, most MRP packages do not have the required mechanics to allow the system to handle this approach.

The nature of the Engineer to Order Job Shop is that there is a low volume of a high number of part numbers and a constantly shifting mix and item design. The only current techniques which allow this type of company to practice some of the flow processing techniques is the concept called Group Technology. Group Technology groups this wide variety of part numbers into generic families of parts that require similar processing capabilities. To be effective, in the Engineer to Order Job Shops, MRP systems must be able to handle a view of the situation based on the Group Technology concept.

One additional point is that the lack of lead time usually dictates that there is no time to develop a unique manufacturing structure for each Customer Order. Therefore some sort of generic subassembly coding is developed. The system must be able to handle this generic structure in many areas.

Finally, it is important that the Engineer to Order Job Shop have a good Estimating System. This system may or may not replace the standard cost system. This Estimating System must function at all levels from Pricing to Production Plans to Shop Floor Control to Cost Accounting. It must be able to respond quickly to requests for information not only about costs but also about lead times, shop loads and work center capacity requirements.

## AUTHOR'S BIOGRAPHY

Jim Branam has a Bachelor of Industrial Engineering Degree from General Motors Institute and an MBA from the University of Iowa. He has over 25 years of manufacturing experience in four different companies. His product experience includes automobiles, aircraft engines, air conditioners, farm equipment, and large capital goods machinery. He has held management positions in Industrial Engineering, Materials Management and Information Systems. He is a member of both APICS and SME. He has presented papers at the International Level for both of these organizations. He is a past president of the Cedar Valley Chapter of APICS.

Reprinted from APICS Repetitive Manufacturing Group Seminar Proceedings, 1981.

## CLASSICAL MRP IN A REPETITIVE ENVIRONMENT

By Howard J. Bromberg, CPIM
Westinghouse Air Brake Division
American Standard Inc.
and
James A. Mann, CPIM
Champion Spark Plug Company

In the early 60's the initial MRP implementations occurred in batch job shop environments. This led to the standard MRP approach being developed, oriented towards a job shop environment. Most of the early software systems, both in-house developed and computer/software developed, utilized these standard concepts. As the MRP crusade gathered steam and many companies that did not operate in a job shop batch environment began to implement MRP, serious problems occurred. In some cases companies modified their manufacturing process so that they could operate in a standard MRP mode. In other cases significant modifications to the standard approach have been developed. The major problem most repetitive manufacturers have in implementing an MRP System is that their product is in continuous high volume production and material is not issued to the shop in separate batches. Assembly line type environments have material flowing in a more or less constant rate. Production volume is so high that it is not possible to maintain order integrity and issue all the components of a sub-assembly at one time. Also, companies in this environment cannot economically handle the type of shop paper work that would be used in a batch environment.

Recently a study group has been formed made up of representatives of companies having a repetitive manufacturing environment. This study group has developed the typical characteristics of a repetitive manufacturing environment and this is discussed below.

The Repetitive Manufacturing Group was formed and first met two years ago at the Briggs and Stratton facility in Milwaukee, Wisconsin under the auspices of the Milwaukee APICS Chapter. The group met again in Toledo, Ohio at Champion Spark Plug; a third time at Bendix in Southfield, Michigan and co-sponsored with the Detroit and Pittsburgh APICS Chapters a seminar on Japan P&IC Systems and Productivity.

The result of these meetings is that a group of APICS members have developed an interest in what they have come to call Repetitive Manufacturing.

### DEFINITION OF REPETITIVE MANUFACTURING

Repetitive Manufacturing is the fabrication, machining, assembly and testing of standard units produced in volume, or of products assembled to order in volume from standard options. It is distinct from the process industries in that it primarily deals with the handling of discrete units, less with fluids, powders and processes involving chemical change. However, the end items of many process industries are discrete units (cans of paint, for example). It differs from job shops in volume of units produced.

The unique characteristics of repetitive manufacturing processes are as follows:

1. Capacity is dedicated and tooling is likely to be specialized for building a specific product, or a small number of products.

2. Routings are often fixed with the units flowing through the operating stations which are arranged in the sequence in which operations take place. Balancing of production rates at each work center or station becomes much more important than in job shops and is often designed into the equipment used.

3. Processing time is generally short. Queues of parts are short. Work-in-process inventory should be small relative to job shops because physical space is inadequate to allow it to accumulate between work centers.

Note that very little is implied about management methods or about production and inventory control. Repetitive manufacturing situations can be distinguished from job shops primarily on the basis of equipment type and arrangement and on the volume of units produced. Production may be accomplished on long lines of work stations in sequence, or at a single work station operating at high speed (forging box wrenches, for instance). Also, the definition applies to a type of production, not to a type of company. Many companies and plants contain a mix of job shop and repetitive production.

### UNIQUE OPERATING PRACTICES AND CHARACTERISTICS

At the first two meetings of the Repetitive Manufacturing Group, considerable time was spent reviewing the common approaches of the various companies to the scheduling and control of volume production of discrete units. This resulted in further unique characteristics of P&IC practice as it exists today.

1. Use of daily run schedules, not work orders for control of production. Master Schedules culminate in serialized control of production which covers specific lengths of time.

2. Production control must be accomplished without excessive paperwork. This leads to the control of production by production counts at key points in the flow and relief of inventory by exploding the Bill of Material against these counts. There is a minimum of inventory relief by parts being issued using transactions.

3. Overall status reporting is often accomplished by using cumulative totals of requirements, receipts and completions on a month-to-date basis or a year-to-date basis.

4. Cumulative figures are often used as the basic check figures for communicating material flow status between remote locations - feeder plants or vendor plants.

5. Master scheduling is often done on a cumulative basis for a year at a time. That is, total end item requirements are developed as cumulative totals and component requirements are exploded from that, not developed as individual job lot quantities.

6. Master scheduling in the near term planning horizon usually must key on a finished goods inventory system or the needs of a distribution system. Planning of parts and intermediate sub-assemblies usually must key on increasing/decreasing banks of parts feeding next higher assemblies.

7. Long lead time scheduling almost always keys on a forecast, not actual orders. Even those companies which on contract produce materials which go to customers for next higher assemblies must plan to a forecast supplied to them by their customers. The master schedule must often be coordinated with a national sales forecast and distribution plan.

8. Multi-plant production planning and master scheduling is frequently used for "captive" feeder plants. There is often a need to coordinate a change in a very long flow of material extending to many feeder plants and vendors in response to a change in sales requirements.

9. Capacity planning is an intrinsic part of master scheduling in a way different from job shops. It is more difficult to balance capacities in different parts of a total system because many lines or pieces of equipment are either up or they are down. "Work Centers" can less easily be operated at "50% of capacity", and the system must be balanced. That leads to the need for controlling increases/decreases in banks of material, and for planning these.

10. Many companies use a "flat" planning Bill of Material compared with job shops, four or five levels in most Bills, though there are exceptions with some companies having 10 - 12 levels in at least some Bills.

11. Engineering change control must often be accomplished "on the fly" by recording the change at some point in an ongoing production run, not by making them effective on a specific order.

This paper will discuss how two major manufacturers with a repetitive manufacturing environment have modified the standard MRP approach to work in a repetitive shop floor environment.

### WESTINGHOUSE AIR BRAKE DIVISION APPROACH

The Westinghouse Air Brake Division has both low volume job shop batch and high volume repetitive manufacturing shop environments. An in-house MRP System has been developed and implemented to work in both environments. Considerable special programming and logic was necessary to allow the MRP System to operate within their repetitive shop floor framework. Shown below is a chart of the major modules which make up an MRP System.

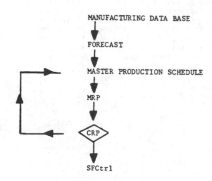

We will discuss the approach used in each of these major systems in a repetitive environment and how they deviate from the standard approach.

## Data Base Module

The major elements making up the data base are the Bills of Material, Routing File, and Item Master Data. The Bills of Material System for repetitive manufacturing requires the extensive use of phantoms since in an assembly line production we typically build through several sub-assembly levels in the Bills of Material. These sub-assembly levels are coded as phantoms so that when orders are released we drop down to the component level for creating allocations. The Routing File of the data base is more or less a standard approach with no modification required for a repetitive environment. The Item Master data contains all of the standard information plus the concept of a floor stock storeroom. This concept involves issuing material from a locked storeroom to the assembly area. While in the assembly area, from an MRP standpoint, it is in a floor stock storeroom. When the end product is shipped from the assembly area, the shipping transaction causes a back explosion to relieve the floor stock storeroom of the components that would have been consumed in producing the quantity of the end items shipped.

## Forecasting

For those end items produced in the repetitive manufacturing environment, the standard statistical forecasting technique is used. However, since production of these items is at an extremely high level, this statistical forecast is used primarily as a guide. A considerable amount of manual review of field intelligence, economical forecasting, etc., is used to modify the statistical forecast.

## Master Scheduling

The Master Scheduling approach from a logic framework standpoint is no different from that used in a job shop batch environment. However, the quantities in the Master Schedule are in weekly time buckets since the same items are in production continually. Also, the Master Schedule is at a consistent level running rate since the assembly lines must be manned accordingly. Any change in the schedule can require a considerable redistribution of personnel and of incoming purchased material.

## MRP Logic

The standard MRP logic is used; however, significant additional features were added to it to support the repetitive environment. When a repetitive item is released, allocations are created against the floor stock account. As stated earlier, the floor stock is made up of material that has been issued to the assembly area but as yet has not been consumed. If the quantity allocated is less than the quantity in the floor stock storeroom, a picking list is generated for the locked storeroom. This serves as authorization to deliver material to the assembly area. When material is delivered to the assembly area it is merely a transfer from the locked storeroom to the floor stock storeroom. It is a transfer of inventory and does not affect allocations. As stated earlier, when end items are shipped, a back explosion takes place which relieves the allocations against the floor stock storeroom and the quantity on hand in the floor stock storeroom.

## Capacity Requirements Planning

The standard approach to Capacity Planning is used. However, it is not as critical as that of a job shop environment because typically once the running rate is established, the manning required is known. It is somewhat complicated from the standard approach since there is extensive use of phantoms coded into the Bill of Material. When the order for the end item is released from an MRP standpoint, the requirement for the phantom order disappears. This can give a false reading as to the amount of capacity required. This problem has been solved by using phantom orders tied to the master order. These phantom orders are relieved as deliveries are made against the master order.

## Shop Floor Control

The approach to Shop Floor Control in a repetitive environment is completely different from a batch environment. Generally, single purpose equipment is used to run the same part day after day. There is no real need for a dispatching function. However, it is extremely important to monitor production rates so that the assembly line is kept stocked with parts. No shop paper is used and production cannot be identified against a unique shop order. As material is completed it is delivered and automatically relieves the oldest shop order in existence. One of the major problems is controlling accurately the amount of material in the floor stock storerooms. A cycle counting system is being developed to solve this problem. An additional feature of the system is that anytime the quantity available in floor stock is less than the allocations against it, a higher priority is created for the items which are purchased or produced in batch areas in order to complete them and get them delivered to the assembly line areas.

The above highlights the significant modifications to the MRP approach that were developed by one manufacturer. The following discusses the approach used at another manufacturer, Champion Spark Plug Company.

### CHAMPION SPARK PLUG COMPANY

The Champion Spark Plug Company is a diversified producer and acknowledged world leader, not only in the manufacture of spark plugs, but also coating application equipment and cardiopulonary and respiratory therapy equipment. Other major products include wiper blades and cold drawn steel bars. Corporate annual sales are in excess of $800 million.

Champion is the world's largest manufacturer of spark plugs with plants in five U.S. cities, Canada, Belgium, England, South Africa, Australia, New Zealand, Mexico and Venezuela.

More automobile manufacturers the world over install Champion spark plugs as original equipment than do the next two brands combined. However, there are some sizable automakers, such as General Motors, who do not install Champion as original equipment. Customers in many instances must be converted from competitive brands. This conversion requires availability of a proven high performance product.

Availability of the product to the customer is the primary objective of Champion's "SPARC" System.

This presentation will address only the domestic operations, and how Champion's System for Priority And Requirements Control "SPARC" is used to support customer service objectives.

Prior to the development of SPARC, Champion's manufacturing orientation had been to provide a quality product at the lowest possible cost. The major goal of SPARC was improved customer service. This was accomplished by integrating marketing and manufacturing planning and control into a single system with common objectives. The system functions are organized very nearly the same as the job shop manufacturing planning and control system framework.

The key factor in integrating marketing and manufacturing planning is the production plan. Top management from both organizations participate in the development of the production plan. The production plan is tightly coupled with the master production schedules to achieve detailed operational plans that meet top management objectives. Master schedule validity is established through "rough cut" capacity checks and the valid master schedules drive classical MRP. Material control is typical of many flow shops in that material movement is used to relieve inventory from the previous level. In short, Champion's system demonstrates that the pattern of material flow is the major determining factor in the design of a manufacturing planning and control system framework, not the manufacturing process.

## Forecasting

Forecasting at Champion is done by the Market Research organization within the Sales function. There are two basic forecasts prepared by Marketing; a long range projection (10 years by year) and an intermediate range forecast (12 months by month). The long range forecast is prepared once a year and projects total unit sales by major market area, market segment like automotive, RV, Agriculture, etc.

Econometric models and market intelligence (judgment) are used to prepare this forecast which is the basis for a manual computation of long range capacity requirements.

The intermediate range forecast is made by SKU for total unit sales and is updated monthly. This forecast is the sales input to the planning process. It is one of the major inputs of the production plan and the master schedule. The initial statistical forecast is generated using a combination of adaptive smoothing and regressive techniques and utilizes a base series and the ABD principle to estimate seasonality. Extrinsic information is also used to modify the statistical projection for such things as promotions, price changes, etc.

The intermediate range forecast is also further forecasted or broken down into geographic areas supplied by each plant and distribution point. These breakdowns are actually a forecast of the geographic mix of demands or sales. The monthly plant totals are then broken down into weeks using the number of Monday's as the number of weeks per month and the weekly forecasts become the input to the master schedule at the plant level. This breakdown technique insures that the production plan and the master schedule are both working to satisfy the same total sales figures. It should also be noted here that only sales has the authority to change the forecast, all other users of the forecast must develop plans to meet the forecast, not vice versa.

## Master Production Scheduling

The Master Scheduling at Champion is done by plant and is based on the demands in the geographic area served by each plant. The master schedule is in units by plug type and its horizon consists of 30 weekly buckets. Master schedule requirements are generated from the monthly forecast by pack configuration "SKU" and the current customer order backlog (if there is one). The monthly forecast is broken down into weeks using the number of Mondays per month and then the forecast and the backlog are netted against current inventory to obtain SKU requirements. The net SKU requirements are then summarized by plug type and scheduled by computerized, "almost traditional" MRP logic for Scheduler review.

Time fences play an important role in the master scheduling process. The Master Scheduler controls all changes in the first thirteen weeks of the schedule. Standard MRP logic is used to monitor the validity of the first thirteen weeks of the master schedule using current inventory balances and customer requirements (backlog and forecast), but all changes are made by the Master Scheduler.

Computerized MRP logic plans all master schedule orders beyond the first thirteen weeks.

## Material Planning & Control

Traditional MRP logic is used to plan all material needs below the plug level. The master schedule drives this process through the remaining levels of the Bills of Material. Replanning is done weekly, following the update of the master schedule. The material requirements plan is prepared in weekly time buckets and matches the thirty week planning horizon of the master schedule.

The master schedule governs the flow of all manufactured parts through the plant and the overall run size. Each intermediate level component is planned by standard MRP logic using lot-for-lot or discrete lot-sizing policies and scrap allowances. The planning orders generated by MRP at each level are treated as schedule targets. Plant schedulers work these targets into detailed schedules in each department. Schedules, not orders, control the production and flow of materials through the plant.

The key word in the planning and control functions is "flow". The intermediate levels in the product structure never enter a storeroom, they flow through the plant as work-in-process. Only raw materials, packaging supplies, and finished products are stored, and then not for very long.

## Capacity Planning & Control

The rough cut capacity check of the master schedule is the primary capacity planning tool in use at Champion. This shows load versus capacity for thirteen critical work centers and it is monitored weekly. Bottlenecks that cannot be resolved by reassignment of manpower or overtime are resolved by master schedule changes. Changes in the capacity level in the first five weeks are rare and only isolated overtime is used. Beyond five weeks the capacity is reasonably flexible.

## Shop Floor Control

The Bills of Material structure supports the shop floor control process. As parts move from one department to another, they advance a level in the Bills of Material, by design. Inventory in the sending department is relieved as materials cross a control point and the Receiving Department inventory is increased by the same transaction. The sending department inventory is "backflushed" using the single level Bill of Material to relieve both floor stock and work-in-process from preceding departments. Accuracy is maintained by cycle counting the work-in-process and floor stock periodically.

The definition of accuracy in the data base is not as rigid as it might be in some environments. Virtually all material is weigh counted which implies a certain degree of inherent error. The other major source of planning inaccuracy comes from scrap. Scrap is the most difficult material factor to control and to monitor. Its historical measurement determines the overall accuracy of the Bills of Material explosions used in planning, given that the Bill has proper component identification. Data base accuracy is still as important at Champion as it is in any other manufacturing firm, but the degree of absolute accuracy which is economically attainable varies.

## SUMMARY

The preceding illustrates how two companies operating in a repetitive environment were able to modify the standard MRP approach to work successfully in their environments. These two systems developed independently have much in common. It is interesting to note the similarities of the two systems. It seems that under the direction of the Repetitive Manufacturing Group, a "standard" MRP approach for repetitive manufacturing will soon evolve.

Reprinted from *Production and Inventory Management*, Vol. 24, No. 3, 1983.

# MRP FOR REPETITIVE MANUFACTURING SHOPS:©
# A FLEXIBLE KANBAN SYSTEM FOR AMERICA

Arnold O. Putnam, CMC

*Rath & Strong, Inc.     Lexington, MA*

## INTRODUCTION

Most of the methodology for manufacturing systems has been devoted to job shops. Frequently, the assumption has been made that, because job shops are the most complicated, their methodology should fit Repetitive Manufacturing as well. A review of some of the basic differences may be helpful in understanding the approach to Repetitive Manufacturing that comes later in the article.

| *A Job Shop:* | *Repetitive Manufacturing:* |
|---|---|
| Has discrete lots. | Operates on a flow of materials and parts. |
| Expands production by larger lots or greater frequency. | Expands production by increase in the rate of flow. |
| Tends to have higher setup costs. | Tends to have lower setup costs or alternatives established. |
| Materials are brought to departments or work centers where each type of operation is performed. | The type of operations are sequenced so that the flow is maintained with short queues and rapid throughput even though different sizes and lengths, etc., have to be accommodated. |
| Uses general purpose equipment. | Uses specialized (dedicated) equipment. |

So an MRP system for Repetitive Manufacturing has to be modified:

—To explode requirements by rates of production within a time period (days–weeks–months).
—To net WIP to assure that valuable resources are not used for deprioritized requirements.
—To pass through requirement need dates to the Shop Floor Control system by time periods and/or cumulative amounts. (Pass-through due dating.)
—To plan and deliver production to either the time requirements and/or cumulative amount needed at that time.
—To report production effectiveness by quantity produced and/or cumulative to date rather than by production lots and operations.
—The link between MRP and Shop Floor described here (see pages 29, 30) are what constitute the "Flexible KANBAN System." In KANBAN, exact quantities of components move every time period (usually a few hours) from the first operation to assembly—arriving just in time. In the system described here the rates of assembly and production may change frequently and also components may be common to several assemblies and thus grouped into different quantities. Yet the desire of the system is the same as KANBAN—keep the parts flowing, arriving just in time—but to meet changing assembly quantities and mixes of models. The conventional tickets and pans of KANBAN can be used or it can be computerized.

This article was prepared with the assistance of Nicholas Edwards, Romeyn Everdell, William Wheeler, and Robert Cronan, all of Rath & Strong, Inc.

Much has been said recently about the use of MRP in Repetitive Manufacturing Shops, but little about how to do it. In many cases, the requirements are exploded but the interface with Production Control is carried out on a manual adjustment basis. *This article describes how it can be logically carried through in a computerized program.*

In order to keep the explanation as brief as possible, it will be assumed that:

—The Company has adequate forecasting.
—The Forecasting and Longer-Range Planning are adequate for Rough-Cut Capacity Planning. The Capacity Requirements Planning may explode directly to resources and dates.

The above programs permit a Master Production Schedule to be developed, revised by Actual Sales Feedback, and maintained to reflect the changes (within Lead-Time Considerations) that Management wants from Production. The relationships of the key subsystems are shown in the Macro-Schematic Flow Diagram (Figure 1).

### Master Production Schedule

This Master Production Schedule should proportion or calculate daily values of units to be assembled in the week, day, or other selected time period designated. It should be revised when signaled from Forecasting or Inventory that the tracking is outside of desirable Control Limits. A

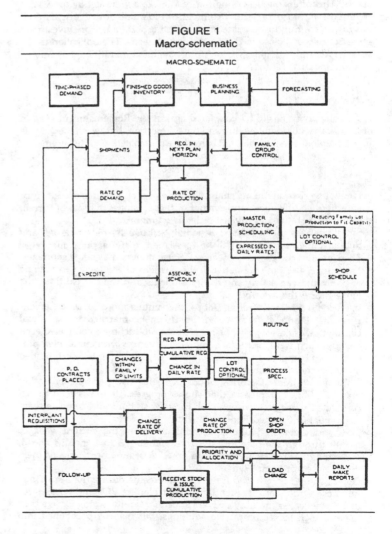

**FIGURE 1**
Macro-schematic

monthly recheck might be worthwhile as well. The Master Schedule feeds the Assembly Schedule and the Shop Schedule (for changes) as well. The Master Schedule may also be impacted by Family Group Control.

### Requirements Planning

Master Production Schedule quantities (expressed in daily or hourly rates) should be exploded weekly. This should be a netting but not a pegged requirement system. These should be stated in rates per hour or per day × working days. A cumulative control value should be maintained as well.

Requirements come directly from the time-phased explosion of the Master Production Schedule to the Time-Phased (dated) Requirements File. These usually match the Master Production Schedule, but the requirements could be ahead of Master Schedule needs where safety quantities have to be built or production increased in anticipation of a jump in demand.

### Shop Floor Control

Planned Replenishments may be scheduled earlier than the required data to allow for safety time, and quantities may be increased to cover unplanned demand, scrap, yields, etc. Thus Replenishment must satisfy requirements but may exceed them in timing or quantity.

### Purchase Releases

Much of the Purchasing for Rate Items is done on an annual or periodic contract basis with estimated release rates and dates against these open orders. This offers the best opportunity to make a volume buy for a price advantage and to get a vendor commitment to a rate of delivery. It is still possible to control the actual receipts (effecting both inventory investment and storage costs) close to the time of actual needs. The obligation to the suppliers is only for released or from scheduled quantities, not for the annual amounts.

### Actual Activity

Actual activity has to be compared against the Replenishment Plan in order to carry out load leveling and time protection, but when the Actuals for the Replenishments Plan fall behind we may expedite to Requirements.

### Comments

- Frequently, Requirements change because of sales volume, product mix, and product difficulties, and evaluating these changes in terms of current production status and revised ordering is important.
- Small changes in the Master Schedule will usually be processed, and Replenishments Planned will be reassigned to the earliest due dates. Then, actuals compared to the new Replenishment may show shortages. The greater the time lag between the position of the increased volume of parts that can satisfy the Replenishments and the current time, the more critical the priority.
- In Repetitive Manufacturing Shops, the cumulation of desired Replenishments (Planned) from a zero point can be matched to the actual cumulation of parts to give plan status. As production is completed each day and each week, the total completed advances with cumulative production to compare against the planned Replenishments or can be tied into customers' requirements.
- In Repetitive Manufacturing Shops, it is this daily completion rather than Lot Size Completion that shows progress. It is easier to match cumulated work done through Job Progress stations and compare them to cumulated Planned Replenishments.
- The requirements should be accumulated from the current week or month through the planning horizon, probably 3 to 6 months ahead, depending upon Procurement lead times. A requirement remains open until revised or completed.
- Orders should be released for the Requirements during the Lead Time. Purchase Orders are frequently co-op or blanket POs and releases for daily, weekly, or monthly deliveries made. Manufacturing Orders may remain open for accumulative additions, but may be partitioned into monthly segments for cost closing. The rates/day and not orders are exploded and accumulated.
- Operations should be such that they are displaced hourly/daily/weekly backwards from assembly. Where more than one operation is done in a week, these may be grouped or shown in detail depending on the degree of control desired. (Zero or minimum queues are expected.)
- The Replenishments values for each part should be accumulated from week (1) backwards from assembly until all replenishments are totaled. A replenishment is shown when ordered and as it progresses until completion.
- Requirements and replenishments should be netted to show: *excess* of replenishments over requirements or *shortages* of replenishments under requirements.
- Where requirements are greater than replenishments, a critical ratio priority scheme could be established that recognizes:
  (1) Number of weeks with an Unsatisfied Requirement.
  (2) Number of weeks the Unsatisfied Requirement increases.
  (3) *The total number of weeks of lead time.* The total number of weeks in the lead time.

Thus, the Critical Ratio can be expressed as:

$$\frac{\text{Weeks of Unsatisfied Requirement} + \text{Weeks Shortage Increased}}{\text{Total Lead Time}}$$

Thus, if it takes 3 weeks at a normal production rate before the plan corrects the overdue, this is worse than an overdue that can be corrected in a single week. If the shortage increases, this indicates a greater problem than if it is stabilized or decreasing.

When the sum of these quantities equals the demand over lead time, we are in continuous trouble. If they reach twice the lead time, the Critical Ratio calculation is 2.0, and the Master Production Schedule needs revision, if such has not already been done.

- Rationing may be required if the shortages in common parts affect planned assembly quantities, otherwise, all of the critical supply may go into a single assembly configuration leaving the other configurations out of stock. Rationing may also be required at packing and filling customer orders so that the first packing configuration or first customer may use up all of the available stock.

## MASTER PRODUCTION SCHEDULING

The primary function of Master Production Scheduling is to load the Plant on a time-phased basis to obtain a doable completion of product that will satisfy the Customer Demand, Inventory, Forecasting objectives of the company's business plan. Without MPS, Requirements can go into MRP in a way that causes too many heaps and valleys of work resulting in bottlenecks and inefficiencies that reduce both total output and profit

The Master Production Schedule in Repetitive Manufacturing may be best expressed in "base units" where group technology is applicable. This provides greater stability. The variations on the base unit such as color fitting, packaging should be scheduled separately at volumes to accommodate flexibility in the final customer demand.

In Repetitive Manufacturing Shops, the requirements should be expressed as Hourly or Daily Rates and the backed-off workloads normally expressed in weekly values where lead times are 4 weeks or longer. Where holidays occur within weeks, it is important that the actual working days be used. Mismatches of days worked per week or per month can produce substantial deviations in output to schedule. (Some companies have variations of 25 to 18 working days in subsequent months.)

In companies where there is less than 4 weeks of production lead time it is better to master schedule by days or consumption periods and to calculate actual production position against Replenishment Schedule on a daily basis (see Figure 2 top).

MPS provides information ahead of decision deadlines. The size/mix of production load affect on the operation can be appraised. Many companies have highly volatile demand which will create a backorder condition, but with good MPS these backorders are scheduled to customer's needs, and acknowledged delivery dates can be given that are consistent

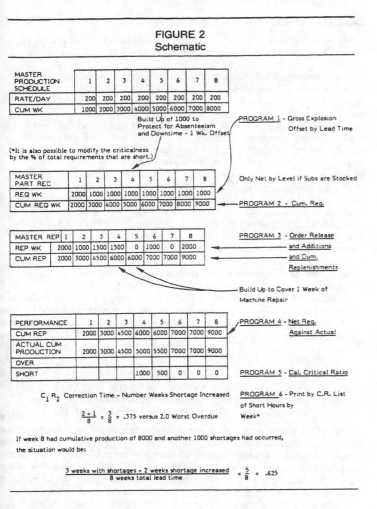

**FIGURE 2**
Schematic

| MASTER PRODUCTION SCHEDULE | 1 | 2 | 3 | 4 | 5 | 6 | 7 | 8 |
|---|---|---|---|---|---|---|---|---|
| RATE/DAY | 200 | 200 | 200 | 200 | 200 | 200 | 200 | 200 |
| CUM WK | 1000 | 2000 | 3000 | 4000 | 5000 | 6000 | 7000 | 8000 |

Build Up of 1000 to Protect for Absenteeism and Downtime - 1 Wk. Offset

PROGRAM 1 - Gross Explosion
Offset by Lead Time

(*It is also possible to modify the criticalness by the % of total requirements that are short.)

| MASTER PART REC | 1 | 2 | 3 | 4 | 5 | 6 | 7 | 8 |
|---|---|---|---|---|---|---|---|---|
| REQ WK | 2000 | 1000 | 1000 | 1000 | 1000 | 1000 | 1000 | 1000 |
| CUM REQ WK | 2000 | 3000 | 4000 | 5000 | 6000 | 7000 | 8000 | 9000 |

Only Net by Level if Subs are Stocked

PROGRAM 2 - Cum. Req.

| MASTER REP | 1 | 2 | 3 | 4 | 5 | 6 | 7 | 8 |
|---|---|---|---|---|---|---|---|---|
| REP WK | 2000 | 1000 | 1500 | 1500 | 0 | 1000 | 0 | 2000 |
| CUM REP | 2000 | 3000 | 4500 | 6000 | 6000 | 7000 | 7000 | 9000 |

PROGRAM 3 - Order Release and Additions and Cum. Replenishments

Build Up to Cover 1 Week of Machine Repair

| PERFORMANCE | 1 | 2 | 3 | 4 | 5 | 6 | 7 | 8 |
|---|---|---|---|---|---|---|---|---|
| CUM REP | 2000 | 3000 | 4500 | 6000 | 6000 | 7000 | 7000 | 9000 |
| ACTUAL CUM PRODUCTION | 2000 | 3000 | 4500 | 5000 | 5500 | 7000 | 7000 | 9000 |
| OVER | | | | | | | | |
| SHORT | | | | 1000 | 500 | 0 | 0 | 0 |

PROGRAM 4 - Net Req. Against Actual

PROGRAM 5 - Cal. Critical Ratio

$C_1R_2$ Correction Time ÷ Number Weeks Shortage Increased

PROGRAM 6 - Print by C.R. List of Short Hours by Week*

$$\frac{2+1}{8} = \frac{3}{8} = .375 \text{ versus } 2.0 \text{ Worst Overdue}$$

If week 8 had cumulative production of 8000 and another 1000 shortages had occurred, the situation would be:

$$\frac{3 \text{ weeks with shortages} + 2 \text{ weeks shortage increased}}{8 \text{ weeks total lead time}} = \frac{5}{8} = .625$$

MPS helps:
- Schedule realistically avoiding peaks and valleys of work.
- Deliver on time, time after time because the program is doable.
- Gain customer confidence because of continued shipment success.
- Increase shop productivity with reduced interruptions and teardowns.
- Avoid last-minute rushes of expediting and splitting lots.
- Improve inventory control by eliminating pile-ups and early arrivals.
- Use equipment/facilities/labor to best effect.
- Examine load/schedule alternatives before commitment.
- Provide maximum flexibility of customer requirements (because it drives the SFC priority system).

In sum, control of the vital planning stages of the operation improves. The advantages from MPS are essential to overall success.

### Scheduling

The listing by date and quantity of product completions, forecasts, and customer orders should be within the Rough-Cut Capacity Limits.

The application to finished goods or to an important status point in the operation—such as packaging options should be available.

Identification of spare parts production, by item or dollar volume or both and allowances for independent demand where necessary.

The Master Production scheduling is a vital input for material requirements planning.

### Product/Resource Data Base

A bill of labor that will adapt to machine time, purchased dollar volume, cash flow, overhead absorption, cost dollars, and sales dollars. This is essential for responding to the rapid change in demand and the projection and appraisal of its impact.

A detailed, or summarized, or by-exception list of required resources for each unit of product.

Time-phasing of resource needs with respect to individual product completion.

### Load Analyses

The load should be applied to product/resource data base and create a projection of greater quantity of resources over a longer period, if desirable.

The capacity should be adjustable down to weekly time periods if desired, smoothing production, increasing productivity.

It is desirable to have an alternative schedule-run capability for improved management decisions.

MPS provides analysis of any manufacturing function for simple and complex products and procedures.

MPS provides a view of alternatives and the answer comes back quickly.

Examples: Figure 3. The final assembly on 7622 looks critical against a normal capacity of 3500 hours, followed by some concern on the cut-off 7620, where the normal capacity is about 2000 hours.

---

**FIGURE 3**

Resource Load Report
Date 03/05/78   Time 15:52:48

| Resource | Date | Hours Load |
|---|---|---|
| Bend | 1 | 1960 |
| Bend | 7618 | 1700 |
| Bend | 7619 | 2050 |
| Bend | 7620 | 1675 |
| Bend | 7621 | 1975 |
| Cutoff | 1 | 2100 |
| Cutoff | 7617 | 1900 |
| Cutoff | 7618 | 2150 |
| Cutoff | 7619 | 1525 |
| Cutoff | 7620 | 2975 ← |
| Final Asy | 1 | 3920 |
| Final Asy | 7620 | 3200 |
| Final Asy | 7621 | 2050 |
| Final Asy | 7622 | 7425 ← |
| Final Asy | 7623 | 4075 |
| Paint | 1 | 2380 |
| Paint | 7619 | 2300 |
| Paint | 7620 | 2600 |
| Paint | 7621 | 2850 |
| Paint | 7622 | 2750 |
| Sub-Assy | 1 | 2100 |
| Sub-Assy | 7619 | 2100 |
| Sub-Assy | 7620 | 2300 |
| Sub-Assy | 7621 | 2300 |

"Production Plan" by family groups is the key to successful repetitive manufacturing. Once you have committed the capacity, you can assign parts priority the way the customer asks you to. The MPS merely serves as a vehicle to launch orders and Shop Floor utilization of resources is done by scheduling at the right time. Also, MPS "can" provide assembly scheduling if throughput (queues = low) is rapid (3–5 days).

## MATERIAL REQUIREMENTS PLANNING

A good MRP system provides:
- Forecasting
- Inventory Control
- Engineering Control (Bill of Material)
- MRP
- Purchasing Control

In some cases these may be separate modules and MRP only accommodates them, but because of the detail quantities, dates, and the Master Part Record, MRP is central to the complete process. The Master Part Record and the Bill of Material combine to maintain much of the basic data in an integrated system.

### Forecasting

—Should separate details of special orders from regular lines, yet integrate them into gross requirements calculation. Where Group Technology applies, the common base should be forecasted separately from the final variables.
—Should analyze order rates and safety stock levels, based on current carrying costs and customer service levels.
—Should review history to select the right forecasting technique for each major line or spare part.
—Forecasts can be based on exponential smoothing, including trend and/or seasonal techniques and modified by Sales or inputted from Sales projections alone.

### Inventory Control

The programs should be able to accomplish all of the following:

—Processes and keeps records of all inventory transactions.
—Handles multiple stocking locations.
—Allows setting individual ordering and control policies for all stocked items.
—Signals and records cycle counting.
—Performs ABC analysis.
—Reports shortages/potential shortages.
—Supports different stock issue techniques.
—Performs inventory/surplus stock valuation, plus inventory investment modeling.
—Prepares transaction history file for full audit trail.

### Engineering Control

—Should provide advance release of partial bills of material without distorting later MRP calculations as well as phantom levels for different structuring and stocking decisions.
—Should provide as-built and effectivity change controls.
—Combines engineering, manufacturing, and planning bills in a common data base so that Engineering material can be to their structure and Manufacturing can build, pick, and assemble to a different listing.

### MRP—Incorporating Family Group Control

In Repetitive Manufacturing there are frequently different sizes, colors, and adaptations of the product making it a Product Family. This is true for shoes, metal fasteners, display hardware, electrical supplies, automotive, jewelry, etc.

The volume of some single items are such that one or more dedicated facilities are used and, in some cases, part of the equipment is left idle when demand is low. The volume of the adaptive items, odd sizes, colors, etc., may require facilities that vary the setup, color, length, etc. These adjustments take time from production and increase the quality and yield losses. For these reasons Family Group Planning has to be introduced at the MPS and/or Production Plan level. Master Production Schedule determines the exact requirements to satisfy the business plan; MRP-Inventory Control may determine that it is economical to produce more ahead of schedule in order to gain efficiency and optimum costs.

### Calculation of Economic Quantities on Run Lengths (ERLs)

*ERL—Economic Run Lengths*—ERLs in Process Batch industries are extremely important in the logistical analysis of the business. They are important in many Repetitive Shops as well.

Many companies have systems that call for major process changes (frequently printing design rolls or chemical blends) and only produce enough amounts of the variations (usually colors, finishes, etc.) to last a short period. They fail to recognize that low stock on a single item of any color can trigger the need to set up the whole design again, but then having made adequate quantities of most items only the low stock ones are produced. The strategy should be to produce a balanced amount of each (related to forecast usage) to bring the stock of each up to equal months of supply, generally known as "Joint Replenishment" logic.

The month of supply should be determined by the Economic Lot or Run Length for the whole group or design volume, depending on the balance of the setup (changeover) costs as well as start-up, trim, clean-out, and quality losses to the costs of carrying the inventory for all the items in the group. Experience shows the most popular groups or designs may run continuously, weekly, or monthly, while the less popular items may warrant production only every 6 to 12 months.

After this calculation, the lot size or run length for each item (color, etc.) can be calculated based on its individual volume and related inventory costs balanced against the cost of the color change and material losses associated with it. The value lower than required to meet the group cycle has to be increased, while other lot sizes or run lengths have to be rounded to match an even cycling, i.e.:

Group Cycle Design A = every 4 weeks

| | |
|---|---|
| Base | 2.5 weeks make 4 weeks supply |
| Switch A | 5.2 weeks make 4 weeks supply |
| Switch B | 7.1 weeks make 8 weeks supply |
| Cover Plate | 15.0 weeks make 16 weeks supply |

If only 2.5 weeks' supply of Base was made, we would have to produce the next batch in 2.5 weeks even though there was ample supply of other items. If we made 4 weeks' supply of Base but only 5.2 of A, when the next run came up in 4 weeks, we would be faced with the dilemma: we have 1.2 weeks of A left but not enough to cover the four weeks' cycle. If we make another 5.2, this will produce 2.4 weeks extra at the end of 8 weeks but still not enough to omit it from the run. If we produce 5.2 weeks' supply of A again at the end of 12 weeks, we have 3.6 weeks of extra or about enough to ship one run. Rounding to 4.0 weeks of A would have avoided carrying extra inventory in the beginning, just as rounding B from 7.1 up to 8.0 weeks gets its production in phase with the 4 week group production cycle.

Group Cycle Design B = every 7 weeks

| | |
|---|---|
| A | 5.6 weeks make 7 weeks supply |
| B | 8.2 weeks make 7 weeks supply |
| C | 12.5 weeks make 14 weeks supply |
| Plate | 29.4 weeks make 28 weeks supply |

In determining the ERL to run for each component, the current inventory should be deducted in each case so that all components are brought into a balanced position.

### Example: Group B

| *Rising Business Recommendation* | *Declining Business Recommendation* |
|---|---|
| Inventory | |
| 10.5 | |
| Switch A 3.5 weeks—make (3.5 + 7) = 14.0 weeks | make 3.5 = 7 weeks of inventory |
| 9 | |
| Switch B 5.0 weeks—make (2 + 7) = 14.0 weeks | make 2.0 = 7 weeks of inventory |
| 15 | |
| Switch C 6.0 weeks—make (1 + 14) = 21.0 weeks | make 1.0 = 7 weeks of inventory |

Plate 10 weeks—do not make—run in next cycle 7 weeks away = 0 weeks.

## Calculations of Economic Run Lengths (ERLs)

Care has to be exercised in calculating Economic Run Lengths. (These ERLs are the counterpart of EOQs, Economic Order Quantities, used in job lot industries.) Considerable misinformation could be generated and actual costs and inventories increased if all the costs and values were used on the final stockkeeping units (SKUs) by each color and these were the only ERL computations made.

The strategy used in the estimating of benefits is the same that should be used in a new operational control system.

If the Group Design cycles every two months, any initial ERL for each SKU that is less than two months is increased to two months usage so that it will not trigger an early call-out of the printing of this design before the two months have elapsed.

Any initial ERL for any SKU between 2.0 and 3.0 months will be rounded down to a two-month usage figure. Any between 3.0 and 5.0 will be rounded to a four-month quantity and cycled every second printing of that design. All larger SKU/ERLs should be rounded to the three, four, or five cycling of the print run of the design.

In sampling for estimation of benefits, the product should be stratified in A, B, C, or Hi, Medium, Low volume categories. It is important that such categorization be maintained in the new system for improved sensitivity of analysis and control.

The Proper ERL for the Commodities and Print Design Groups have to be made using Family Group Control volumes and data.

### Family Group Control

$$ERL_G = \sqrt{\frac{2U_G(S)}{IC}}$$

$ERL_G$ = Group economic run length per setup, per pattern or design regardless of color, size, or whatever differentiates the SKU from the group

$U_G$ = Usage volume for the group or pattern for the time period involved in units (yards)

$S$ = Setup, changeover, and order cost including the loss of materials and slower startup rates of the facility (but not including size or color change) which is accounted for in the next step

$I$ = Total carrying cost, used 25% (different companies use up to 48%)

$C$ = Cost per unit of measure at the point of manufacture

In minimizing quality losses due to color, the scheduler usually works from lights to darks and then cleans out; in changing widths and bottle size, he goes from small to large, crosses over to a new mix and goes down from large to small to minimize changeover time.

Having determined the basic cycling of the Group, the individual SKU can be tested against the cycling of the Group.

### Basic ERLs

$$ERLs\ (SKU) = \sqrt{\frac{2U(S)}{IC}}$$

$ERLs\ (SKU)$ = An initial calculation

$U$ = Volume of SKU

$S$ = Setup, changeover, and material loss for the color or size change alone

$I$ = Total carrying cost, used 25% (different companies use up to 48%)

$C$ = Value per unit of measure at operation being scheduled

The material loss (in printing this would result from getting registration and correct color shading) is an important cost, and this is frequently overlooked in making Run Length Calculations. The loss in yield from the equipment running at lower speeds in order to get everything OK before increasing speeds to production standards was another cost included that is often overlooked.

## Simulation

In a few cases Repetitive Manufacturing Shops have fixed capacity and multiple process steps which make simulation desirable to achieve the optimum Master Production Schedule. The Process Simulator is included in the Appendix and can be used for Critical Work Center control.

## MRP

MRP should include the following features:

—Can be both transaction- and date-driven (bucketless).
—Can process daily change in rate data.
—Should allow control and stabilization of the shop using firm planned rate techniques: master scheduled firm parts; and time fences.
—Offsets lead time and calculates in days.
—Should give exact status of any part at the end of any shift.
—Can account for single and multilevel requirements to higher level replenishment demand rates.
—Can be mechanically driven by master schedule of manual input, with ability to exclude some parts from the planning cycle.
—Performs pass-through dating of open shop and purchase orders, maintains need dates and promise dates.
—Production rates and economic order quantity; minimum/maximum/multiple rounding.

## Purchasing Control

—Should recommend rescheduled due dates based on current requirements status.
—Should monitor status of all open orders.
—Should track purchasing activity from need to release against a purchase order, and receipts from point of use.

## Multilevel Specification

In a Repetitive Manufacturing Shop, the parts unique to the higher level would all be chained (not pegged) and the job progress quantity to the higher-level requirement matched as shown above (see Figure 2).

In appraising plan status, the lower-level availability (of a sub) should be projected on the worst Replenishment Condition (even though all may be listed). The worst projected replenishment should be transferred to the appropriate week of the higher level (a few days, but not more than a week, may be allowed as the sub or final assembly and packaging time itself). Parts available would automatically be reassigned to the higher priority (earlier date) requirement.

Chaining Requirements into common parts would require that these requirements be linked by date due, quantity (rate required over equivalent time period), and higher level number so that they can be accumulated into a total and compared to the replenishment record. Replenishments in excess of Requirements do not create a problem. Shortage of replenishments are a problem, and it may be necessary where rationing is desired for the planner or control person to:

—Maintain date-due filling sequence.
—Maintain date requested sequence.
—Prorate, when parts common to a higher-level are short or overdue.

It is possible for a computer algorithm to prorate if the Planner assigns the same Required Date—any other assignment would fill the first requirement completely and leave all of the shortage in the one with the later date.

Considerable difficulty and reduction in shipping success develops in Repetitive Manufacturing when a part common to several higher assemblies is in insufficient supply but that knowledge appears too late. In the meantime, the part is assembled or packaged into a single end item building its inventory to 1- or 2-month level, while several other assemblies needing the part cannot be completed and go on Customer Backorder.

# SHOP FLOOR CONTROL

## Job Progress and Replenishments

The simplifying feature of this system is to match Job Progress with the number of weeks that the Replenishment is away from completion—so that the quantities in the Replenishment Record can be accumulated and matched to the Requirements.

In a mass production plant for Automotive Fasteners, the maintenance of discrete lots on a daily or weekly basis is at best a headache, at worst, impossible. It is best to release and to accumulate replenishment. For accounting purposes, it is desirable to close out costs on an approximate monthly basis including the proper handling of scrap and rework. This does not have to coincide with month-end exactly, as the work on parts ahead of the divider would appropriately be charged to that sub-order and work after the divider to the following sub-order.

It is important that daily production be identified and that changes that move the replenishments one week (divider) closer to completion are calculated by the increase in total quantity produced for the time period. The difference from a job shop is that the quantity moving is what is produced as a part of a stream and not a predetermined job lot quantity amount (Figure 4).

## Schematic

These production figures feed the Daily Make Report in a non-on-line system. Where the system is on-line the entries are made at terminals.

### FIGURE 4

| Week No. | 0 | 1 | 2 | 3 | 4 | 5 | 6 | 7 | 8 |
|---|---|---|---|---|---|---|---|---|---|
| Job Progress Sta | | 8 | 7 | 6 | 5 | 4 | 3 | 2 | 1 |
| Prior Cum Rep | | 1000 | 2000 | 3000 | 4500 | 4500 | 6000 | 7000 | 8000 |
| Transaction | | 1000 | 1000 | 1500 | 0 | +1000 | +1000 | +1000 | +1000 |
| New Cum Prod Status | | 2000 | 3000 | 4500 | 4500 | 5500 | 7000 | 8000 | 9000 |

The impact of parts being produced over successive weeks to end up with the completed replenishments on schedule and bringing the total cumulative production up to cumulative replenishments is shown in Figure 5.

Consider this explanation as a Flexible KANBAN System for America. Under KANBAN every day (or selected time period) the assembly con-

### FIGURE 5
### Actual production

| DAY OR WEEK | CUM REP | FIN 0 OPER | WORK-IN-PROCESS 1 | 2 | 3 | 4 | 5 | 6 | 7 | 8 |
|---|---|---|---|---|---|---|---|---|---|---|
| | | 8 | 7 | 6 | 5 | 4 | 3 | 2 | 1 |
| 1 | | CUM ACT | | | | | | | | |
| 2 | 2000 | 2000 | 2000 | 1000 | 1500 | #2 500 | 500 | 1500 | 1000 | #1 1000 |
| 3 | 3000 | 3000 | 1500 | 1500 | 500 | 500 | 1500 | 1000 | 1000 | |
| 4 | 4500 | 4500 | 1500 | 500 | 500 | 1500 | 1000 | 1000 | | |
| 5 | 6000 | 5000 | 500 | 500 | 1500 | 1000 | 1000 | | | |
| 6 | 6000 | 5500 | 500 | 1500 | 1000 | 1000 | | | | |
| 7 | 7000 | 7000 | 1500 | 1000 | 1000 | | | | | |
| 8 | 8000 | 8000 | 1000 | 1000 | | | | | | |
| 9 | 9000 | 9000 | 1000 | | | | | | | |

*Advance of production through 8 weeks*—This type of planning shows the developing shortage problem 4 weeks ahead of time. It is easiest when the incremented days or weeks in assembly exactly match daily or weekly segments of production. *It is also easier where the quantities for each period remain constant—it then reflects the Japanese KANBAN System.* With computer control, the quantities planned and scheduled can vary from one time period to another. (The KANBAN system can have pans and tickets if part size variation permits, or it can be maintained by pan number under a computer terminal control.)

#1. If actual production was different from the schedule, it would be shown in "Daily Make (or Production) Report."

#2. Shortage can be predicted 4 weeks ahead of Assembly Due Date.

sumes a fixed quantity. Each day an equal amount advances one day in Production with the final operation being ready for the next day's assembly.

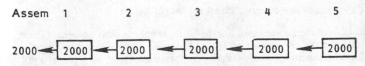

The system described here has two more flexible features:

1. The assembly quantities and configurations may change day by day.
2. The accumulation of the exploded requirements of the common parts may be grouped into different size packages than the 2000 above.

## PURCHASING

Purchasing in Repetitive Manufacturing Shops is substantially different than that in job shops. Contract Purchasing is heavily used rather than being the exception. The items that are used continuously frequently are shipped weekly/daily/hourly against a release. (In automotive houses—big items move daily; in drapery hardware, some items are scheduled in monthly.)

The Purchaser is responsible for costs incurred through the lead time of up to several months, but the rate of delivery can be advanced or slowed down (even stopped) as long as the open releases are finally used. Thus, a change in production rate triggers both a change in production as well as vendors supply rates.

In many industries where common commodities are purchased, the purchaser is responsible only for a slightly higher markup in cost if he does not use the full volume specified in the Blanket Purchase Order.

Cooperation with the vendor can be enhanced by furnishing and updating the information in Figure 6.

### FIGURE 6

| PART NO | | DESC | | P. O. | | | |
|---|---|---|---|---|---|---|---|
| DATE DUE | TOTAL | SHIPPED TO DATE | PLANNED RATE | THIS RELEASE | DATE DUE | % ON TIME | % QA ACC |
| 3/25/81 | 240,800 Anticipated yearly req'ts | 50,000 | 20,000/Mo | 10,000 | 3/30/81 | 95% | 99% |

## PRODUCTION "MAKE REPORTS"

In a job shop, attention is given to operational completion on each job or work order as it moves through the plant.

In repetitive manufacturing shops, "job lots" are nonexistent, except for major product lines and specials. Production Foremen want to know if the target rate for the day or shift has been met. His second concern is whether he is behind or ahead of schedule against a cumulative target figure for the item involved.

A typical daily report is shown in Figure 7.

### FIGURE 7
### Daily production reports

| IDEN | PART | | COLOR | | | |
|---|---|---|---|---|---|---|
| ACTIVITY | REC. | PROD | | CUM PRODUCTION | | BALANCE ON HAND |
| REWORK | SCRAP | | | YIELD | | |
| EFF | SET UP | | RUN | | DOWN | EFF % |
| | STD | ACT | STD | ACT | | |

## Shop Control

The data from the Daily Production Reports is summarized into several Control reports (Figure 8). This report provides Management with the Efficiency against Standard and its cumulative Efficiency Record.

### FIGURE 8

| WC | ITEMS | DAILY PROD | DAILY STD | % OF STD | CUM ACT | CUM STD | % CUM |
|---|---|---|---|---|---|---|---|
| WC SUMMARY | | | | | | | |

The report shown in Figure 9 provides Management with the Scrap and Seconds versus Good Production for a Quality Measure. In some cases, trim losses may also be important—the final figure is the Yield against all input materials.

### FIGURE 9
Performance quality and yield mat

| WC | ITEM | SCRAP | REWORK | GOOD % |
|---|---|---|---|---|
| | | | | |
| WC SUMMARY | | | | |

The report in Figure 10 provides a summary of performance on each piece of Equipment. Setup can be accounted for separate from run time if desirable. Downtime can also be recorded and, if desirable, added to setup to give a total UP-Run Time for the shift or day.

### FIGURE 10
Utilization of equipment labor

| WC | EQUIP | OP | SU STD | SU ACT | SU % | RUN STD | RUN ACT | RUN % | DOWN TIME | % | UP % RUN/DAY |
|---|---|---|---|---|---|---|---|---|---|---|---|
| WC SUMMARY | | | | | | | | | | | |

Labor can also be looked at separately, with Performance separated by Setup and Run Time when desirable (Figure 11). The total Performance and Downtime impact can also be reported by each operator.

These reports can be resequenced alphabetically by operators, by type of material, etc.

### FIGURE 11
Labor by operator

| WC | OPER | SU STD | SU ACT | RUN STD | RUN ACT | TOTAL STD | TOTAL ACT | PERF | DOWN TIME |
|---|---|---|---|---|---|---|---|---|---|
| WC SUMMARY | | | | | | | | | |

## MATERIAL ISSUE TO ASSEMBLY IN REPETITIVE MANUFACTURING

In a repetitive manufacturing environment, material may be delivered in bulk to the manufacturing floor or may be delivered on a daily or weekly rate of manufacture basis.

Where bulk issues are used, the control of this material has been done by many different methods.

### History

Originally, there was little or no control on material, as production workers knew how to fabricate or assemble the product. There was no need, from their point of view, to record what material they used. However, the accountants began to be concerned about the dollar value of work-in-process inventory, and they needed to develop a method to relieve this work-in-process inventory when product was completed. Their approach was to use a costed bill of material of the completed product to determine the material content of the components in dollars. Needless to say, this approach was prone to error, as material substitutions and engineering changes were usually not recorded. With the introduction of production and inventory control personnel, the need to track the amount of material by part number became important in an effort to help reduce shortages that were an inevitable byproduct of the old systems. Therefore, material "pick lists" were developed so that staging of components could be accomplished in order to help search for shortages. This resulted in increased paperwork, but helped attack the shortage problem. With the advent of the computer, these lists could be eliminated by the use of a "back-flush" technique where completed product was "exploded" to relieve the component on-hand balances. In theory, this was a logical approach, as inventory balances could be maintained with a minimum of paperwork. In practice, this "four-wall" inventory approach, as it was often called, was inaccurate due to the inability to easily audit the calculated results.

### Current

With the current emphasis on reduced inventory, the importance of accurate work-in-process tracking is being emphasized. Therefore, the use of the "back-flush" or exploded issue is receiving considerably more attention and is now becoming the second half of a bulk-issue system. The philosophy of the bulk-issue system is to maintain most of the inventory in controlled storerooms. A day or so prior to its use on the assembly lines, this material is bulk issued from the storeroom to the floor. In reality, this is a transfer between two stocking locations, where the stockroom on-hand balance is reduced and the floor on-hand balance is increased. This transfer process may be directed either by a requisition from the floor or by a "group" bulk issue. This "group" bulk issue occurs when the next day's schedule is exploded and consolidated to develop a "group bulk-issue" pick list for the transfer process. With material on the floor, it is now "consumed" by the assembly process. This is recorded by the "exploded issue" process where the completed assembly is "exploded" to relieve the floor on-hand balance of the component. (If the assembly process is short and the material issued on a daily rate, this is usually done as the product transfers to finished stores.) If the assembly process is longer, then the "exploded issue" may occur after completion of the first operation. This exploded issue process will be repeated until the product is transferred into finished goods. The *control* of this bulk-issue approach is achieved by monitoring the amount of actual floor on-hand material in equivalent days. This is achieved by dividing the floor on-hand by the average daily usage. If the floor on-hand is negative, or if the floor on-hand balance is above "X" days (usually 1 to 2 days) or a single container's worth, then it is assumed that the floor on-hand balance needs to be audited, as this balance exceeds its logical control limits.

## SUMMARY

Repetitive manufacturing needs special additions to Standard Material Requirements Planning—Programs that deal in "Rates of Production" and the capability to plan by Family Group (Group Technology) where such exist. These capabilities may produce larger cost savings than the basic MRP system itself.

The features described in this article require computer support though some of the group technology concepts and a simple KANBAN system could accomplish part of the benefits without a computer.

In many Repetitive Manufacturing companies the management process is compounded by rapid changes in forecasts and actual demands particularly in seasonal industries. The ability of the computer system to respond quickly all the way from the Master Production Schedule to the Shop Floor and the vendors is equally important in Repetitive Manufacturing as it is in a complex job shop.

## APPENDIX

### Narrative of Proposed System

The simulation will be used to answer a number of "what if" questions. Most likely a simulation will be initiated by the regular planning cycle reviewing the SKU demand signals, "make up to," special demand, and balance on hand. If the minimum is not covered, a new "make up to" or demand will be recognized. A "make up to" is calculated by subtracting the "on hand" from the ERL for the specific SKU. Thus a balanced ERL position for all SKU is achieved at the end of each group run.

The new demand will be formed into equipment planning units (for a printing press this would include cylinder set, width, and color) through the routing file. Economic run lengths will be reviewed. Priorities will be reviewed. The systems network is shown on Exhibit A-1.

The run loads will be placed on equipment through the facility file and by priority. An option of loading prime or an alternate facility will be available. The first alternative load by operation will be summed and displayed versus capacity. The load can be accepted, held for trial of other alternatives, or recycled. After an acceptable load has been put together for the first facility, the next facility is loaded and so on until the planner, through changes in:

Simulation Variables,
Service Level,
ERLs,
Capacity and Manning, and
Routing

arrives at a satisfactory load for all of the facilities.

The simulator works well for 2 to 5 load centers. As the number increases toward ten and the number of items scheduled increases, it may be advisable to use only the most critical. When work centers are not in the simulator, it is advisable to calculate and maintain a "float of work-in-process inventory" adequate to cover variations from the "simulated-scheduled" work centers.

Loading is the adding of the load to prior load to a capacity at each work center. Scheduling is the sequencing, backdating, or forward dating.

### Simulator Example Narrative

*Main Logic*—Loading starts at the primary or critical operation and is back scheduled into the less critical functions. The schedule is then forward loaded into the other processes based on available capacity. All SKUs with fixed or nonalternative processes are loaded first. Flexible processes are then loaded. Once capacity is exceeded in an operation, the alternatives are tried. If capacity is still exceeded, the load can be pushed forward and

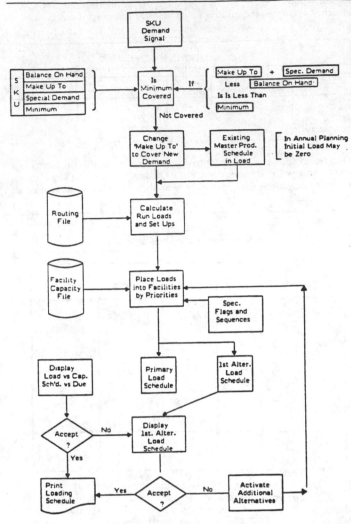

EXHIBIT A-1
Master production schedule simulator

the program can display the schedule date versus the required date. If the date slippage is not acceptable, then a realignment of overall processing guidelines must be undertaken to bring requirements within capacity. Once capacity is satisfied in a process, the system will proceed to the next process. Once the last step is finished, the raw material requirements are backloaded to starting operations. The simulator network for all facilities is shown on Exhibit A-2.

*Primary or Critical Operation*—Items with no alternates are loaded. If capacity is exceeded, a realignment must be done. The restricted items and best method are then loaded. If capacity is exceeded, alternates are used, and then realignment is performed and loading starts again. Once capacity is satisfied, backward and forward scheduling takes place.

*Backward Loading*—Products having no alternatives go first. At this point in simulation, an assumption can be made that backward facility capacity can never be exceeded when loading from the critical if we can have some semifinished goods in process to make up the deficiency. If the yield at various steps requires higher inputs at earlier stages, such are allowed on a percentage basis.

*Forward Loading*—Wide widths go first because in most companies narrow widths can be done on wide machines to level out loads, but wide widths cannot be done on narrow machines. Thus, the wide widths or parts requiring big extruders, etc., always have less flexibility than smaller widths or parts. Demand overcapacity results in realignment. Items requiring Step 1 are loaded. If the load exceeds capacity, the alternate facility is assigned the overload. If the alternate becomes overloaded too, it forces a restart at the primary operation.

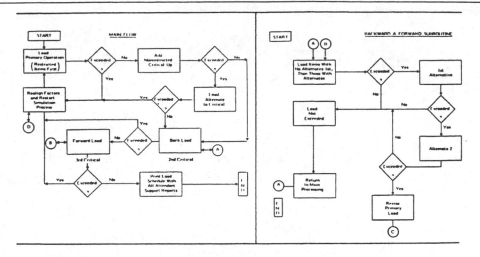

In mixed liquid bottling (paints, etc.), lights go before darks, the line goes from large bottles to small—changes liquid at small and then sizes are increased back to large on the new liquid.

In multipart metal stamping, the master die is loaded with the simplest configuration and punches and cutters added until the maximum is reached. In subsequent runs the most complicated part may be produced first and then the die reduced to the simplest.

In shaft turning on NC lathes, start with the smallest and increase to the longest and largest and then return.

In grinding and mixing, go up or down in color and grit sizes.

*Additional Facilities and Other Operations*—Other operations and alternatives can be added in a manner similar to the first backward and forward operation.

*Input Requirements*—All sizes, colors, restrictions have to be loaded into the data base except for the quantity of each item in order for the simulator to work.

## Summary

Simulation is a series of trial-and-error Master Scheduling steps which allows the Master Scheduler to review the consequences of loading various schedule configurations and assist him in selecting the one which best meets his company's established goals of customer service and cost efficiency. There are special sequences, such as group technology configurations, kept in the data bank that will come to the attention of the Master Scheduler during the interactive simulation process.

## Cost/Benefit Analysis

Cost benefits are from decreasing the number of changeovers, which yields lower material costs, less labor, and greater throughput (increasing capacity), and decreasing the inventory. The calculation is based on ERLs, economic run lengths, and optimizes the cost of acquiring and carrying inventory.

## Interface With Other Subsystems

The subsystem interfaces with the following files:

Demand
Routing
Facility

Bill of Materials
Quality and Examination

The simulator works well for 2 to 5 load centers. As the number increases toward ten and the number of items scheduled increases, it may be advisable to use only the most critical. When work centers are not in the simulator, it is advisable to calculate and maintain a "float of work-in-process inventory" adequate to cover variations from the "simulated-scheduled" work centers.

Loading is the adding of the load to prior load to a capacity at each work center. Scheduling is the sequencing, backdating, or forward dating.

**About the Author—**

*ARNOLD O. PUTNAM, CMC,* is President of Rath & Strong, Inc. His consulting work has included work measurement, wage incentives, statistical engineering, quality control, and inventory and production control. Mr. Putnam's articles appear in *The Handbook of Quality Control* and the *Production and Inventory Control Handbook;* he is co-author of *Unified Operations Management* and author of *Management Information Systems: Planning Developing, Managing.* He is a member of several professional associations, has served as Director of the Boston Chapter of APICS, and is currently a member of the Long Range Planning Committee of APICS. Mr. Putnam holds a B.S. degree from Lehigh University and earned his M.S. degree in business and engineering administration at MIT.

Reprinted from *Production and Inventory Management*, Fourth Quarter, 1981.

# WHY THE PROCESS INDUSTRIES ARE DIFFERENT

Sam G. Taylor
*University of Wyoming*    *Laramie, WY*

Samuel M. Seward
*University of Wyoming*    *Cheyenne, WY*

Steven F. Bolander
*Colorado State University*    *Fort Collins, CO*

Much of the literature of production and inventory management has been devoted to the fabrication and assembly industries. In the past few years APICS has sponsored seminars, workshops, and research projects for the process industries. This has resulted in the development of a planning framework for process industries [3] and the exchange of many ideas. There seems to be a growing consensus within some process industry groups that they are fundamentally different from fabrication and assembly industries. In this article, we will compare the marketing, manufacturing, and financial environments of process industry groups with fabrication and assembly industry groups. These comparisons will then be used to show why many process industry groups require a production and inventory management system with a much different emphasis than the closed loop MRP systems used in fabrication and assembly industries.

## MARKETING ENVIRONMENT

One of the most important factors in developing a business strategy is differentiating a firm's products and services from its competitors'. The amount of product differentiation can be viewed as a continuum from custom products at one end of the spectrum to commodity products at the other end. Examples of commodity products are soda ash, methyl alcohol, cement, beef, lumber and steel. Industry groups and individual companies may have products at several different points along the product differentiation spectrum.

The process industries tend to have less product differentiation than fabrication and assembly industries. Accordingly, the process industries tend to be associated with products at the commodity end of the product differentiation spectrum and products from fabrication and assembly industries are found nearer the custom product end of the spectrum. However, it should be recognized that some fabricated products such as containers and fasteners tend toward the commodity end of the spectrum while some process industry products, such as drugs and specialty chemicals, tend toward custom products. In order to compare the marketing environments of process industries with that of fabrication and assembly industries, we will contrast characteristics of commodity products and markets with custom products and markets.

Table 1 summarizes differences in custom and commodity products and markets. Commodity marketing emphasizes product availability and price while product features are emphasized in marketing custom products. Commodities are often sold from stock while custom products are made to order. Commodity products generally have a limited number of products within a product family (product grades), while custom product families may have an unlimited number of products. Commodity products have few, if any, changes in product specifications while custom products are designed to order. A commodity is generally sold in large volumes to several customers. On the other hand a custom product is committed to a particular customer for a particular use. Commodities frequently have a relatively low value-to-weight ratio which results in transportation costs contributing a higher portion of the cost of goods sold than for custom products.

### TABLE 1
### Comparison of Product and Market Environments

| CUSTOM PRODUCTS | COMMODITY PRODUCTS |
|---|---|
| • Marketing Emphasis on Product Features | • Marketing Emphasis on Product Availability and Price |
| • Many Products | • Few Products |
| • Many Product Design Changes | • Few Product Design Changes |
| • Consumer Demand | • Derived Demand |
| • Low Sales Volume | • High Sales Volume |
| • High Unit Volume | • Low Unit Value |
| • Relatively Low Transportation Costs | • Relatively High Transportation Costs |
| • Discrete Units | • Nondiscrete Units |

Custom products are produced and sold in discrete units. Serial numbers or lot numbers are assigned to each unit. In contrast, commodity products are produced in nondiscrete units and production, sales and inventory records are in pounds, gallons, tons, barrels or similar units of measure.

## MANUFACTURING ENVIRONMENT

Manufacturing facilities can be classified along a spectrum with job shops at one end of the spectrum and flow shops at the other end. A job shop is a manufacturing facility in which materials flow through the shop with routings dependent on each job. A flow shop is a manufacturing facility in which materials flow through the plant with a fixed routing. Most manufacturing facilities fall somewhere in between a pure job shop (random routings where jobs could start and finish in any work center) and a pure flow shop.

Process industries tend more toward the flow shop end of the spectrum than fabrication and assembly industries. In order to compare the manufacturing environment of process industries with fabrication and assembly industries, we will first contrast characteristics of flow shops and job shops and then examine some additional characteristics of process industries.

### Comparison of Job Shops and Flow Shops

Table 2 summarizes differences in job shop and flow shop manufacturing environments. By definition, a flow shop has fixed routings and can use fixed path material handling equipment, such as conveyors and pipes. In contrast, a job shop has variable material routings and must use variable path material handling equipment, such as fork lift trucks and tote bins.

Job shops and flow shops have different plant layouts. The layout of a job shop is by manufacturing process. For example, a job shop may have one work center where all grinding is done and another work center for all welding. If a job required grinding, welding, and then grinding, it would first go to the grinding work station, then to welding, and finally back to grinding. However, the layout of a flow shop is determined by the product. If a product requires grinding, welding, and then grinding, a production line would be designed with two grinding work stations, separated by a welding work station. Accordingly, the production line is laid out according to the processing requirements of the product it is designed to produce.

Job shops and flow shops differ significantly in their capabilities. A job shop has flexible, general purpose equipment which can be used to produce a wide variety of products. In contrast, flow shops have specialized equipment which can be used to produce a group of closely related products.

Flow shops generally have longer lead times for increasing capacity than job shops. In order to efficiently use their relatively high capital investment in facilities, flow shops tend to operate more shifts per day and more days per week than job shops. Thus flow shops have less flexibility to increase capacity by adding shifts or working overtime.

© American Production & Inventory Control Society

## TABLE 2
## Comparison of Manufacturing Environments

| JOB SHOP | FLOW SHOP |
|---|---|
| • Variable Routings | • Fixed Routings |
| • Variable Path Material Handling Equipment | • Fixed Path Material Handling Equipment |
| • Process Layout | • Product Layout |
| • Flexible Equipment | • Specialized Equipment |
| • Low Volume | • High Volume |
| • Shorter Lead Time to Increase Capacity | • Longer Lead Time to Increase Capacity |
| • Capacity Is Difficult to Define | • Capacity Is Well Defined |
| • Labor Intensive | • Capital Intensive |
| • Strikes Shut Down Plant | • Strikes Have Lower Impact |
| • Skilled Craftsmen Who Build the Product | • Highly Specialized, Trained Operators Who Monitor and Control Process Equipment |
| • Significant Work In Process Inventories | • Low Work In Process Inventories |
| • Often Warehouse Work In Process | • No Warehousing of Work In Process |
| • Jobs Not Overlapped Between Work Centers | • Job Overlapping |
| • Equipment Failure Shuts Down a Machine | • Equipment Failure Shuts Down the Plant |
| • Late Receipt of a Purchased Part Delays a Customer Order | • Raw Material Shortage for a Basic Raw Material Shuts Down the Plant |

Since flow shops are production lines designed for a group of closely related products, the line capacity can be determined by examining the bottleneck process. In contrast, a job shop is designed to produce a wide variety of products. In a job shop, the load created by different products in each work center often varies widely. The capacity of each work center can be specified in man hours and machine hours; however, the aggregate capacity of the plant depends on the particular mix of products being manufactured at a point in time. Since the product mix changes frequently in a job shop, the aggregate capacity is difficult to define.

The work force requirements are significantly different for job shops and flow shops. Job shops are generally labor intensive and use skilled craftsmen to build the product. A strike in a job shop will shut down the plant. Some flow shops, such as assembly lines, are also labor intensive and will also be shut down by strikes. However, in many other flow shops, such as oil refineries, the number of operators is low enough so that management personnel can run the plant during a strike.

Job shops and flow shops differ in the relative amount of work in process inventory. Job shops require work in process to buffer variations in work center loads which are caused by variations in product mix. This permits better utilization of work center capacities. In contrast, processes and operations in a flow shop production line are balanced for the limited group of products which can be produced by the line. Thus, work in process is not required to help smooth work loads, although some work in process may be used in a flow shop to buffer sequential operations from short range variations in processing rates. In a flow shop, the amount of work in process inventory is relatively small compared to the throughputs; accordingly, storage facilities for work in process inventories are provided for in the process flow.

Another result of the low work in process inventories in flow shops is the need for reliable equipment. If a particular piece of equipment in a production line breaks down, the entire line must stop production after downstream work in process is consumed or upstream storage capacity is filled. Job shops have more work in process, variable routings, and more flexibility to increase capacity through extra shifts and overtime to speed recovery from an equipment failure. Accordingly, job shops are not as dependent on reliable equipment as flow shops.

The effect of late material is different in job shops and flow shops. In a job shop, the late receipt of a purchased part may delay a customer order and increase inventories of other parts used in the item being made unless these parts are rescheduled. In a flow shop, shortage of a basic raw material can shut down the entire plant.

## Process Industry Manufacturing Environment

Several characteristics of the manufacturing environment of both job shops and flow shops within the process industries are summarized in Table 3. The process industries often obtain their raw materials from mining or agricultural industries. These raw materials have natural variations in quality. For example, crude oils from different oil fields have different sulfur contents and different proportions of naphthas, distillates, and fuel oils. Oil refinery designs, production plans, and operating schedules must account for this variability in crude oil qualities.

Variations in raw material quality often lead to variations in bills of material. For example, variations in the moisture content, acidity, color, viscosity or concentration of active ingredient in raw materials may cause variations in the ingredient proportions required to make finished product quality specifications.

---

### TABLE 3
### Process Industry Manufacturing Environment

---

- Variability in Raw Material Quality
- Variability in Bill of Material
- Product Yields May Vary Widely
- May Have Large Demands for Intermediate Products
- Coproduct Demands Must be Balanced
- Products or Raw Materials May Have a Shelf Life

---

Another factor which causes variations in bills of materials is the price of alternate ingredients. For example, a pet food may have specifications for the minimum amount of proteins, carbohydrates, and fats per pound of pet food; however, the proportions of various ingredients may be varied depending on their current price and availability.

An additional source of variability in a process industry manufacturing environment is product yield. A number of process industries have processes which are difficult to control. Accordingly, when a product is scheduled and run, it may not be produced. For example, in the production of specialty plastic resins or synthetic rubbers, the plant may schedule a target grade. However, in attempting to make this target grade, a highly variable amount of lower quality fallout grades may also be produced.

A characteristic of some process industry manufacturing environments is the large demand for intermediate products. For example, a manufacturer of primary metals may sell some ingots and process other ingots into sheet and plate, bar stock, or wire.

Production of coproducts complicates inventory management for some process industries. In these industries coproducts are produced in proportions determined by chemical and natural characteristics. When producing caustic soda and chlorine by electrolysis of a salt brine, the proportions of caustic soda and chlorine produced are fixed by chemical relationships and cannot be varied by changes in operating conditions or ingredients. Imbalances in demand for coproducts can limit production of one product or create large inventories of the other.

Some process industry groups, such as food and pharmaceuticals, produce products or use raw materials with shelf lives. For example, canneries must process fruits and vegetables while they are fresh, and pharmaceuticals must be used before their expiration date.

## COORDINATING MARKETING AND MANUFACTURING STRATEGIES

A firm's manufacturing facilities need to be consistent with its marketing environment. Figure 1 shows a product-process matrix. Horizontal positions on the matrix represent the degree of product differentiation discussed in the above section on marketing environment. Vertical positions on the matrix represent the material flow spectrum from a job shop to a flow shop discussed in the above comparison of job shops and flow shops. As shown in Figure 1, most industries tend to fall along the principal diagonal of the product-process matrix. Note that some fabrication and assembly industry groups, like containers and steel products, tend toward the commodity and flow shop part of the matrix, while some process industry groups, such as drugs and specialty chemicals, are in the center of the matrix. An industry group's position on the product-process matrix is an important factor in the design of a production and inventory management system.

An individual firm's position on the product-process matrix relative to the position of its competitors can be an important factor in a firm's corporate strategy [1], [2]. A number of firms in the central portion of the matrix are attempting to improve their manufacturing efficiency by moving downward toward the flow shop end of the process spectrum.

## FIGURE 1
### Product - Process Matrix

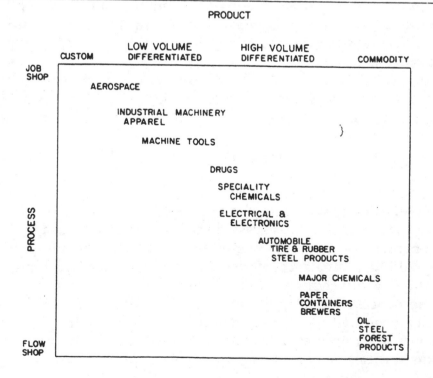

The recent emphasis on group technology illustrates this movement. On the other hand, when a firm moves toward a flow shop, it may lose some of its flexibility to produce many products, or it may need to enforce scheduling sequences which could reduce its ability to respond to rush orders.

## FINANCIAL ENVIRONMENT

An industry group's or a firm's financial structure is closely related to its marketing and manufacturing environment. Table 4 gives financial data for process industry groups and for fabrication and assembly industry groups. The data show significant differences between process industries and fabrication and assembly industries, as well as significant differences among industry groups within the process industries or within fabrication and assembly industries.

In general, process industries are more capital intensive than fabrication and assembly industries. This is demonstrated in Table 4 which shows that the process industries have a ratio of 1.8 dollars of sales for every dollar of gross plant investment, compared to a ratio of 3.1 for fabrication and assembly industries.

Process industries are less labor intensive than fabrication and assembly industries. Table 4 shows that the process industries have $95,000/yr. of sales for each employee while fabrication and assembly industries have $47,000/yr. of sales per employee. Thus two employees are required by the fabrication and assembly industries to generate the same sales revenue as one employee in the process industries.

The inventory data in Table 4 show that inventories turn over faster and that inventories are a lower portion of total assets in the process industries. Nevertheless, inventories represent 20 percent of total assets for the process industries and, if mismanaged, can have a significant impact on a firm's profitability.

## PLANNING SYSTEM CHARACTERISTICS

Having examined the marketing, manufacturing, and financial environments of process industries and fabrication and assembly industries, we will now discuss the impact of these environments on the design of a production and inventory planning system. A firm's production and inventory planning system should be consistent with its position on the product-process matrix. Firms producing commodities in a flow shop environment require a significantly different planning system than firms producing custom products in a job shop environment. Our discussion will divide planning systems into long, intermediate and short range planning systems.

## TABLE 4
### Industry Financial Characteristics

| Industry | Sales/ Gross Plant | Sales/ Employee (1000$) | Inventory Turns | Inventory/ Total Assets (%) |
|---|---|---|---|---|
| **PROCESS** | | | | |
| Chemicals-Major | 1.0 | 83 | 6.3 | 17 |
| Steel-Major | 1.0 | 75 | 8.3 | 14 |
| Paper | 1.1 | 76 | 9.1 | 13 |
| Brewers | 1.2 | 120 | 10.0 | 12 |
| Forest Products | 1.3 | 84 | 8.3 | 14 |
| Oil-Integrated Intl | 1.8 | 315 | 10.0 | 13 |
| Tire & Rubber Goods | 1.8 | 50 | 5.6 | 26 |
| Textile Products | 1.8 | 38 | 5.2 | 29 |
| Chemicals-Specialty | 2.8 | 80 | 6.7 | 22 |
| Drugs-Medical & Hospital Supply | 2.9 | 47 | 4.6 | 28 |
| Soap | 3.1 | 110 | 6.7 | 27 |
| Average | 1.8 | 95 | 7.3 | 20 |
| **FABRICATION & ASSEMBLY** | | | | |
| Containers | 2.1 | 64 | 7.1 | 20 |
| Home Furnishings | 2.3 | 48 | 5.9 | 28 |
| Machine Tools | 2.3 | 48 | 3.5 | 37 |
| Leisure Time Products | 2.5 | 45 | 4.4 | 31 |
| Electronics- Semicond & Comp | 2.9 | 32 | 6.3 | 24 |
| Automobile | 3.0 | 48 | 5.6 | 29 |
| Aerospace | 3.3 | 52 | 5.9 | 27 |
| Industrial Machinery | 3.3 | 49 | 3.3 | 39 |
| Elect. Household Appliances | 3.4 | 51 | 4.4 | 33 |
| Electric Equipment | 3.4 | 47 | 4.6 | 33 |
| Apparel | 5.7 | 34 | 4.6 | 37 |
| Average | 3.1 | 47 | 5.1 | 31 |

SOURCE: *Financial Dynamics*, Standard and Poor's Compustat Services, Inc. 1979.

## LONG RANGE PLANNING

The process industries develop extensive long range resource requirements plans. Because the process industries are more capital intensive than fabrication and assembly industries, capital budgeting decisions have a greater impact on financial performance in the process industries. Accordingly, more attention is given to facilities decisions in the process industries.

Two important long range decisions are plant capacity and plant location. In the process industries, plants are designed for a specified throughput. All equipment is sized for this design capacity. Since the plants generally run seven days a week and three shifts per day, it is impossible to significantly increase capacity with overtime or extra shifts. Thus, increases in manufacturing capacity require the design and construction of new facilities. Since highly specialized, automated equipment is required, lead times of three or more years are often required for significant capacity increases.

Plant location is another important long range planning area. Process industries often transport high volumes of materials which have low values relative to their weight. Thus, transportation costs will represent a higher portion of the cost of goods sold for these industries. In order to minimize transportation costs, firms may use multiple plant locations and break bulk operations through distribution centers. Since products of competing firms have little differentiation, price is a very important factor in marketing these products. A poor plant location can increase transportation costs to the point where a plant cannot compete.

Long range plans for materials, manpower, energy, and waste disposal are also important in the process industries. In order to assure a long range supply of key raw materials, process industries frequently arrange long range supply contracts. Many firms in the process industries require a highly specialized work force. Accordingly, long range manpower plans must be developed to hire and train these workers. Since process industries tend to be energy intensive, long range energy plans are also required. Many process industries have waste products which must be disposed of in a manner consistent with environmental laws. Plans must be developed and permits obtained for emission and disposal of waste substances.

Fabrication and assembly industries which produce custom products in a job shop environment tend to have less emphasis on long range resource planning and more emphasis on product design. In this portion of the product-process matrix, product features are a key factor in corporate strategies. A flexible manufacturing facility which can quickly produce new product designs is important for these firms. Although they must develop plans for equipment, manpower, materials, energy, and waste disposal; fabrication and assembly job shops tend to acquire new resources in less time than process industries. Thus, these firms have less emphasis on long range process planning and more emphasis on product planning.

## INTERMEDIATE RANGE PLANNING

Intermediate range production plans are concerned with developing plans for the utilization of resources. Production plans generally cover time horizons between three and eighteen months. A company may have more than one production plan. For example, during the annual budgeting period, production plans by quarter may be developed. Subsequently, during each quarter, monthly production plans may be developed. Table 5 summarizes areas which are emphasized in process industry production plans.

---

TABLE 5
Areas Emphasized In Process Industry Production Plans

---

- Sourcing Decisions
- Sequencing Products Through Facilities
- Optimizing Product Blends
- Determining Target Safety Stocks
- Coordinating Production and Maintenance Plans
- Temporary Shutdown of Plant or Line to Reduce Inventory
- Exchange or Swapping Agreements
- Determining Material Requirements
- Developing Aggregate Production Plans

---

Sourcing decisions are concerned with assignment of customers to warehouses and assignment of warehouses to plants. Since the process industries tend to have more plants, more warehouses, and spend a higher percent of their sales dollar on transportation; sourcing decisions are generally more important in the process industries than in fabrication and assembly industries. Linear programming is frequently used in the process industries to help develop sourcing plans.

In many process industries, products are made on a regular cycle. The sequence of products is often dictated by product or process technology. For example, products may be sequenced from light to dark, high viscosity to low viscosity, or wide to narrow. Determining the target sequences and cycle lengths is an important production planning problem in the process industries.

Some process industries manufacture blended products, such as gasoline or cattle feed. These industries are concerned with developing a minimum cost blend of ingredients which meets product specifications. Linear programming is frequently used, particularly in the oil industry, to develop minimum cost blends.

Process industries have a tendency to produce products to stock and, as a result, have a large percentage of their inventory investment in finished goods inventory. One function of finished goods inventories is to buffer the plant from variations in product demand. This is accomplished with a safety stock of finished product. The use of statistical techniques to size safety stocks is an important part of process industry production plans.

In a process industry plant, periodic shutdowns are required to perform maintenance. Process industries tend to operate three shifts per day and seven days per week. Thus it is impossible to perform maintenance during an off-shift or on weekends. In addition, process industries have less work in process. Thus when one process unit shuts down, the preceding and succeeding processing units must shut down. Accordingly, when major maintenance is scheduled, the plant or line is not producing. This interruption in production must be accounted for in plant production plans.

When forecasted demand is less than plant capacity, production must be reduced or inventories will build. Two strategies for reducing production are: (1) throttle the plant back to a rate equal to demand, or (2) run the plant at full capacity and periodically shut down to reduce inventories. One major area of cost savings from using periodic shutdowns to control inventory is a reduction in certain energy costs. Since process industry plants tend to be more energy intensive, there is a greater use of the shutdown strategy in process industries than in fabrication and assembly industries.

Process industries tend to produce products at the commodity end of the product differentiation spectrum. When a firm produces an undifferentiated product, it can enter exchange or swapping agreements with competitors in order to reduce transportation costs. Exchange or swapping agreements are a common practice in the petroleum, commodity chemical, and primary metal industries. These agreements are an important factor in developing production plans for these industries.

Some process industries develop material plans for key raw materials directly from their production plans. The production plan sets the rate at which the plant will operate. Some key raw materials are required for every product grade produced. Therefore, after setting the aggregate production rate for the plant, a material plan can be developed for these key raw materials.

Process industry flow shops tend to develop aggregate production plans. It is generally easier to define aggregate capacity for a flow shop than for a job shop. Flow shops have line flow and the capacity of the bottleneck operation limits the capacity of the production line. In addition, flow shops are designed to produce a closely related group of products. Thus, it is easier to aggregate product demands for a flow shop than for a job shop. Accordingly, production plans for job shops tend to have more product and process detail than for flow shops.

Production plans for the labor intensive fabrication and assembly industries require greater coordination with manpower plans than in the process industries. Production plans for fabrication and assembly industries often adjust plant capacity by changes in the work force. This is accomplished by changing the amount of overtime or the number of shifts scheduled.

In reviewing the above differences in the production planning process, it is seen that process industry flow shops must place a greater emphasis on production plans than fabrication and assembly job shops. This is because the marketing and manufacturing environments both allow and require a greater emphasis on intermediate range planning.

## SHORT RANGE PLANNING

Short range plans are concerned with developing operating schedules. These schedules should be consistent with the intermediate range production plans but should have more product, process and time detail. There is often more than one operating schedule. One schedule might cover a period of a month or more, while another schedule might only cover a week but have detailed schedules for each shift within the week.

### Scheduling Methods

The major difference between process industries and fabrication and assembly industries is in the approach to master production scheduling. Fabrication and assembly industries are less capital intensive and more material intensive than the process industries, as shown previously in Table 4. In order to minimize investment in materials, the need date for each order is determined and then the need dates for components (intermediate products) and purchased parts (raw materials) are determined by backward scheduling from the finished product due date. Having determined a schedule of material requirements, the feasibility of the schedule is then checked against equipment and manpower capacities. This approach is a material-oriented master production scheduling method, because materials are scheduled first and then capacities checked. This is the approach used in the closed loop MRP system.

Process industries are concerned with achieving high equipment utilizations. In addition, process industries usually have a good estimate of the capacity of a production line or plant. Thus, process industries tend to first schedule capacity and then materials. This is called a capacity-oriented master production scheduling procedure. A capacity-oriented procedure schedules production runs of various products on each production line such that capacity is utilized at the rate specified in the production plan. Having determined the production schedule, raw material requirements are then determined.

In a scheduling system, both materials and capacity must be planned. The question to be answered is which to do first. To minimize material investment, a material-oriented procedure such as a closed loop MRP system should be used. To efficiently utilize equipment, a capacity-oriented technique should be used. For a job shop producing custom products, a material-oriented scheduling method is appropriate. For a flow shop producing commodity products, a capacity-oriented scheduling method is appropriate. However, as shown by the product-process matrix given in Figure 1, many process industry groups and fabrication and assembly industry groups are not at either of these extremes, but somewhere in between. Nevertheless, firms in these industries must choose either a material-oriented or a capacity-oriented scheduling method.

At the present time, a great deal has been written about material-oriented scheduling methods (closed loop MRP) and many software packages are available. However, there is a general lack of literature and software for capacity-oriented scheduling methods. One of the most promising areas for expanding the body of knowledge in production and inventory control is in the development of capacity-oriented scheduling techniques. Even more exciting and difficult is the possibility of a scheduling system which simultaneously schedules both capacity and materials.

### Scheduling System Characteristics

Table 6 lists characteristics of process industry scheduling systems. The first of these is a greater use of capacity-oriented master production scheduling methods, which has been discussed.

Since the process industries have more plants and warehouses, they place a greater emphasis on distribution requirements planning and interplant transfer planning. In the process industries, the master production schedule tends to be driven more by production plans, short-range demand forecasts, and distribution requirements plans than by customer orders. Because the master production schedule in the process industries is often buffered from customer orders by a finished goods inventory, there tends to be less customer interference in the master production schedule in the process industries.

Lot sizes in some process industry groups may be dictated by facilities design or by manufacturing practices for insuring product quality. For example, a lot size may depend on the capacity of a batch reactor or storage tank. In other cases, such as in canning of meat products, manufacturing practices require a daily washout to maintain product quality.

---

### TABLE 6
### Process Industry Scheduling System Characteristics

---

- Greater Use of Capacity-Oriented Master Production Scheduling Methods
- More Emphasis on Distribution Requirements Planning and Inter-Plant Transfer Planning
- Closer Coupling of Master Production Schedule with Forecasts, Production Plans, and Distribution Requirements Plans
- Less Customer Interference with Master Production Schedule
- Lot Sizes May be Dictated by Facilities Design or by Manufacturing Practices for Insuring Product Quality
- Schedule Is the Authority to Produce
- Sequencing Is Generally Accomplished in the Production Plan or Master Production Schedule
- Schedules Generally Have Smaller Time Intervals

---

These washouts provide logical lot sizes. Nevertheless there are many other situations in the process industries where lot sizes are not constrained. In these plants, lot sizing techniques are an important tool in developing production plans and schedules.

Fewer items, well defined capacity, and fixed routings make scheduling generally easier in the process industries. In many firms the schedule is the authority to produce and manufacturing orders are not issued. Furthermore, since sequencing is generally accomplished in the production plan or the master production schedule, daily dispatch lists are not required. However, since there is no dispatch list, schedules often have time intervals of days, shifts, or hours.

## SUMMARY

The product-process matrix shows why some process industry groups are similar to many fabrication and assembly industry groups and why many process industries are different than most fabrication and assembly industry groups.

Because of differences in the marketing, manufacturing and financial environments, the emphasis on production and inventory management techniques differs between industry groups. The process industries are more capital intensive and place a greater emphasis on long range facilities planning and intermediate range production plans. In addition, in order to achieve high utilizations of expensive equipment, capacity-oriented master scheduling procedures are required.

184

## REFERENCES

1. Hayes, Robert H. and Steven C. Wheelwright. "Link Manufacturing Process and Product Life Cycles," *Harvard Business Review*, January-February, 1979.
2. Hayes, Robert H. and Steven C. Wheelwright. "The Dynamics of Process-Product Life Cycles," *Harvard Business Review*, March-April, 1979.
3. Taylor, S. G., S. M. Seward, S. F. Bolander, and R. C. Heard. "Process Industry Production and Inventory Planning Framework: A Summary," *Production and Inventory Management*, First Quarter, 1981.

## ABOUT THE AUTHORS—

*SAM G. TAYLOR* is a member of the industrial management faculty of the University of Wyoming. He is also a partner in Taylor and Bolander Associates, a consulting firm specializing in seminars and materials management consulting for the process industries. He is a frequent speaker at regional and national conferences and has published articles in *Production and Inventory Management, AIIE Transactions,* and *Chemical Engineering Magazine.*

*SAMUEL M. SEWARD* is an Associate Professor at the University of Wyoming teaching production and operations management courses in the Cheyenne MBA Program. The majority of his consulting and contract research has focused on operational problems in the public sector, including planning for such organizations as fire departments, city and state patrols, and social welfare agencies.

*STEVEN F. BOLANDER* is an Associate Professor at Colorado State University. He is also the Manager for Manufacturing Systems Development and formerly a Program Manager for Rockwell International in charge of designing and implementing a computer-based production and inventory management system. In addition, Dr. Bolander is a partner in the consulting firm of Taylor and Bolander Associates which conducts public and private seminars on inventory management for process industries. He is past president of the Colorado APICS Chapter and now serves on its board of directors.

DISTRIBUTION REQUIREMENTS PLANNING - AND MRP

Quentin Ford, Director, Materials Management
Coopers & Lybrand

Distribution Requirements Planning has been developed as a relatively simple computer planning application. Its function is to intermesh the supply of material within the distribution network, with either manufacturing or vendor sources. Just as MRP has expanded from the relatively simple calculation of material requirements to the larger functions of scheduling, capacity planning and shop floor control, so too DRP can expand to vehicle loading, warehouse planning and dispatching. For any manufacturing company that is involved in distribution, this extension of control is necessary to obtain an enhanced performance of the return on investment in inventory and distribution facilities.

Distribution Requirements Planning is the extension of MRP logic and disciplines to the distribution aspects of the business. For any manufacturing concern involved in distribution, with MRP or contemplating MRP, this extension is vital, for requirements coming in from the distribution network impact the Master Schedule. Without the visibility of distribution requirements, the Master Scheduler works with only a part of the data needed to do an effective job of Master Scheduling. This lack of data prevents the achievement of full MRP benefits.

Distribution Requirements Planning provides a direct link to distribution requirements and the movement of inventory through the distribution network; it provides a better capability to supply the right things at the right time with improved customer service. It has a profound effect upon customer service inventory management and profit--its potential is tremendous.

Exhibit 1

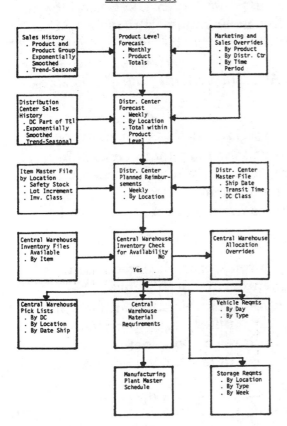

DISTRIBUTION REQUIREMENTS PLANNING LANNING

Generalized Flow Chart

DISTRIBUTION REQUIREMENTS PLANNING - EXPANDING MRP

I. Overview - Distribution Requirements Planning

. Nature of Distribution Networks

The relationship of supply and reimbursement points is very similar to component parent relationships established through a bill of material. In effect, a product structure for each item sold out of a distribution point has passed through a structured network. This structure can be described the same way a product structure is in a bill of material. Expanding the bill of material to include the distribution network thus begins with identifying the distribution point stockkeeping unit at the final level, then identifying the structure of the distribution network behind the stockkeeping unit. This structure becomes an extension of the manufacturing bill. This new expanded product structure then provides a mechanism for cascading requirements back to reimbursing warehouses and eventually to the Master Schedule of the manufacturing or vendor source.

Exhibit 2

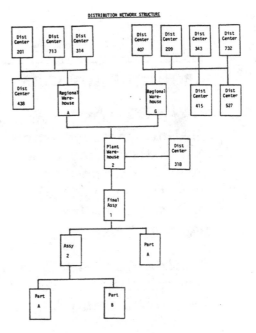

. Dependent-Independent Demand Characteristics in Distribution

The traditional way for defining demand would identify the demand at the final distribution point as independent. But there is often a need to examine this in greater depth. If the demand is greatly impacted by the actions of a relatively few customers or users, then it may not be truly independent. There may be a need to be able to "read" the intentions of these few customers to be able to determine your dependent demand resulting from their actions.

. Source and Distribution Relationships

Just as in a bill of material there is defined a distinct relationship between parents and components, so too must the relationship for each stockkeeping unit be defined. This means that for every level within an item's distribution network, a single source for that level must be defined. However, alternative sources may be handled by making them sublevels or by using the planning bill concept. In this concept, a proportionate split is made to pass demand down to the next lower level.

Also, the same techniques used to maintain the product structure within a bill of material is applicable here also. Such things as engineering change control, with effectivity dating, can be used to alter or modify the distribution network over the time frame of requirements planning.

. Distribution and MRP Relationships

It is clear that all demand below the zero distribution network level is dependent. Therefore, attempting to control the inventory through utilization of order point techniques is inappropriate.

The previous observations about the organization of distribution networks and the nature of demand within them leads to the conclusion that the MRP calculation methodology is applicable in distribution. Use of the MRP methodology should also increase the return on investment performance of inventory in a distribution environment.

Therefore, the beginning point of manufacturing control for a company involved in both distribution and manufacturing is DRP. DRP develops the most accurate set of dependent demand requirements that can be passed onto the manufacturing master schedule.

The responsibilities of DRP as it relates to MRP are:

- Pass requirements accurately
- Update requirements on timely basis
- Allocate as soon as supply falls below defined minimum levels within the distribution network

The responsibilities of MRP:

- Provide high level of on-schedule delivery
- Timely communication of items where schedule change is required

. Support of Improved Asset Management Performance

Most of the assets employed in a distribution function are related to the amount of inventory on hand and to the rate of flow of material. With improvement to inventory performance through the use of DRP techniques, then the projection of requirements of the other assets can be improved. Just as experience has demonstrated that MRP has provided a much better basis on which to determine manufacturing capacity requirements and control over shop floor, these same relationships exist in distribution. They exist with vehicle and storage capacity requirements, and with controls for vehicle dispatching and warehousing operations.

II. Forecast Development

. Forecasting Relationships - Pyramid

One of the key benefits of DRP and MRP is the coordination accomplished by having formal plans that are synchronized within all functions of the business. The downward forecasting process provides a means for developing item forecasts that are integrated with the business of objectives set by management. The forecast pyramid illustrates the relationships of the levels of forecasting from business planning down to individual stockkeeping units.

Exhibit 3

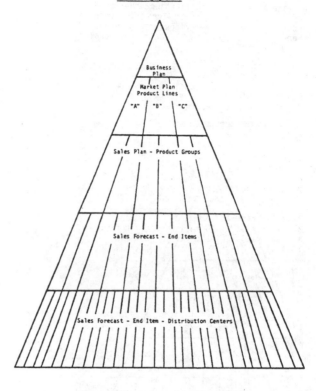

DIAGRAM OF FORECASTING RELATIONSHIPS

Forecasting Pyramids

. Development of Override Capabilities

The need for applying management judgment arises at all levels within the forecasting process. A forecasting system needs to provide accessibility to making overrides to the calculated forecasts. Thus application of these judgment overrides should be done through a number of techniques. As a result, the forecasting systems utilized in DRP provided a number of ways in which overrides could be inserted into the forecasting process.

. Monitoring

Monitoring of forecasts involves the adapting of techniques developed by our fellow quality control professionals.

Forecasts should be left unchanged and then the method of being updated left alone as long as the actual performance is within an acceptable range of the forecast. The limits of this acceptable range are related to actual customer service level and the amount of inventory investment.

Monitoring is done on an individual stockkeeping unit and over a significantly long period of time.

. History

Forecast history should be kept in the same level of detail as the forecast.

End history records should cover the actual performance as well as forecast history.

History records need to cover at least three planning cycles, generally three years, to be statistically significant.

. Ability to Individualize

Individual items often change their behavior patterns independent of the behavior of other items. A forecasting system needs to provide the capability to adjust the forecast of individual items. When this syndrome occurs, the use of overrides that have been properly conceived provides this individualizing capability.

Exhibit 4

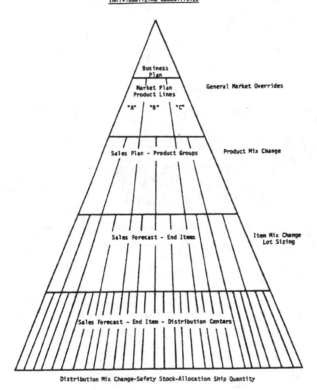

DIAGRAM OF FORECASTING RELATIONSHIPS

Individualizing Capabilities

Business Plan

Market Plan Product Lines          General Market Overrides
"A"   "B"   "C"

Sales Plan - Product Groups       Product Mix Change

Sales Forecast - End Items        Item Mix Change Lot Sizing

Sales Forecast - End Item - Distribution Centers

Distribution Mix Change-Safety Stock-Allocation Ship Quantity

III. Replenishment Planning

. Replenishment Logic

. Replenishment Lot Size Matrix

. Safety Stock Matrix

. Truck Load Planning Overlay

. Shipment Lead Time

. Aggregate Control

. Servicing Special Marketing Efforts

. Pick List Generation

IV. Allocation Control and Customer Service Management

. Allocation Triggering

. Allocation Logic

. Allocation Actions

. Management Control Capability

V. DRP Interface with Production Planning

. Distribution - Production Planning Relationship

. Distribution - Capacity Planning

. Aggregate Input/Output Control

VI. DRP - Interface with Master Schedule

. Allocation Interface

. Master Scheduling Revisions

VII. DRP and MRP Comparison

. Similarities

. Differences

VIII. Distribution Resource Planning (DRP II)

. Future Plans

. Relationships to MRP II

. Resource Planning Bills

IX. Implementation Guidelines

. Education and Training of People

. Installing the System

. Implementation

. Measuring the Results

. Magnitude of Benefits to be Expected

X. DRP in the Future

The present developmental stage of DRP is just scratching the surface of its potential uses in manufacturing/distribution/retailing businesses. For example, DRP can be a basic ingredient in revolutionizing the procurement and inventory practices in the wholesale/retail business. This significant revision of stock replenishment practices will be based upon the ability of each level in the distribution network being able to quickly replenish what has been consumed in the succeeding level. This capability will be provided by using computer technology to link all members of the distribution network together. Also, through the use of basic MRP methodology, within the computer, that can plan and react to changing replenishment demands within these distribution channels will provide this capability.

The fact is there is a lot of idle inventory in today's distribution channels and DRP is the method to reduce it.

Conclusion

Manufacturing companies that sell through a distribution network will find that to achieve a significantly enhanced level of performance requires an integrated system that combines DRP with MRP. This combination of MRP and DRP produces a fully integrated manufacturing/distribution system that provides the capability to increase profits and enhance the performance of return on investment and assets.

About the Author

Quentin Ford is the Director of Materials Management
Consulting for the Chicago Group of offices of
Coopers & Lybrand. He has a comprehensive Materials
Management and Manufacturing background spanning
23 years. Mr. Ford has had continuous experience
with job shop, repetitive and processing manufacturing industries since 1958. Highlights of his
background encompass:

. Development, installation and management of
  five "Class A" MRP systems

. Developed "Class A" MRP-DRP that was published
  as an APICS case study illustrating "State of
  the Art" MRP developments

. Implemented MRP in job shop, repetitive and
  processing manufacturing environments

. Implemented DRP for wholesale/distribution
  operations, in addition to manufacturers

. Developed and conducted educational programs
  in all phases of materials management

. Has been a guest lecturer on Materials
  Management topics at a number of universities;
  has given speeches at many APICS seminars
  and chapter meetings and before AMA, AIIE,
  TIMS/ORSA and other professional societies

Mr. Ford holds a degree in Production Management
from Northwestern University. He has been a member
of APICS for over 20 years and has been Executive
Vice President of both the Chicago and Rochester
Chapters, and Regional Vice President of old
Region V, and is currently a member of the Shop
Floor Control Certification Committee. He is also
a member of the National Council of Physical
Distribution.

Reprinted from APICS 1980 *Conference Proceedings*.

WHICE COMES FIRST, THE BILL OF MATERIAL OR

THE MASTER PRODUCTION SCHEDULE?

Hal Mather, CPIM
Hal Mather, Inc.

Very little has been written about the inter-relationships of
Bills of Materials and the Master Production Schedule. Most discussions treat them as independent variables. However, they are
far from independent; each is directly related to and affected
by the other. Many companies who computerized in the mid 1960's
failed to recognize this when developing their manufacturing
control systems and are now faced with massive changes to their
systems and data. This failing is still being perpetuated by
newcomers to the manufacturing control systems field. It could
have been and still can be avoided with the right approach at
the start.

### INTRODUCTION

Computers have been extensively used in manufacturing companies
since the late 1950's or early 1960's. They were originally
added to handle many financial and clerical chores, simply an
advancement over bookkeeping machinery. The jobs of payroll,
inventory costing, accounts payable and receivable, were all
speeded up compared to the slower tab-card methods.

The next computer uses were for several business functions, for
example inventory record keeping, product costing, pick list
generation and sales statistics, with the middle two requiring
bills of materials in the files. Most companies simply took the
existing bills of materials, usually engineering generated, and
loaded this information into the computer. This worked well for
the needs of costing and pick lists, could also be used for manufacturing assembly instructions, and served the engineers well by
providing them faster retrieval of their information.

The next step was to use the computer for production schedules.
Along came computerized material requirements planning about 1965,
using both bills of materials and inventory balances. These
were already in the files so this job appeared quite straightforward. Most people concentrated on the mathematics of MRP,
the frequency of running, and technical discussions on net change
versus regeneration, hoping for a technical solution to the
problems of high inventory and poor customer service. However,
the success rate of these early MRP systems was very low, regardless of the promises of computer hardware and software people.
But these efforts helped to define what was required to be
successful; the role of the master production schedule became
clear and was seen as the key to success. Emphasis now switched
to how to generate a valid, feasible, master production schedule.
But it was frequently not possible to create this forward looking
plan with existing bills of materials. Products simply were not
forecastable in these entities. In many cases sales statistics
were available but they did not facilitate forecasting, being
based on the existing product definition.

These attempts to generate a valid master production schedule
showed a need to define the product quite differently to the way
it had been defined for manufacturing instructions, costing or
engineering uses. So now the rub, how to link a valid master
production schedule defined in one set of terms to a bill of
material defined in another? And without this how do you run
MRP? It has to be driven by a master production schedule as
proven by the failures of the early systems without it. But now,
how to change the bills of materials to suit the planning and
scheduling activities of MRP with heated resistance from all other
company functions with their systems built around traditional
bills of materials?

### A BETTER APPROACH

The master production schedule should have been defined first.
This is easy to say now, because like the person who swallowed
his contact lenses, we have 20/20 hind-sight. But even with
this hind-sight many companies are still going down the wrong
road. Several who have recently justified implementing computerized systems in manufacturing are following the pattern other
companies followed in the mid '60s. They are loading existing
bills of materials into their computers to generate costs and
pick lists and will face a very difficult conversion when they
finally decide to use MRP.

The first problem is one of definition. When discussing bills
of materials many people conceptualize this as the format of the
document printed out by a computer, not what is stored within
the computer files to generate this information. In the discussion in this article, "bills of materials" refers to the
structures that are maintained within the computer files. The
specific formats of documents that can be generated from these
structures are up to the ingenuity and skill of the programmer
to access, sort and report this information. A good analogy is
a telephone directory printed in alphabetical sequence. It
could just as easily be printed in street number sequence, in

phone number sequence or even in first name sequence. We are
familiar with it alphabetically as that is convenient for retrieval of telephone number information. Yet the information
could be stored using the telephone number or any other convenient data element as the key, with the reporting program simply
displaying the information in the desired format. The primary
objective is to load one bill of material into the computer
which suits all their uses in a manufacturing company. With one
bill of material, the accuracy and integrity necessary to run a
manufacturing business can be obtained.

Many of these uses are shown in Figure 1. Some companies do not
need them all and some companies need even more. The skill is

## BILL OF MATERIAL USES

- DEFINE THE PRODUCT
- MANUFACTURING INSTRUCTIONS
- ENGINEERING CHANGE CONTROL
- SERVICE PARTS SUPPORT
- LIABILITY/WARRANTY PROTECTION
- PLANNING MATERIAL PROCUREMENT
- SCHEDULING THE PLANT
- ORDER ENTRY FACILITY
- PICK LISTS
- SCARCE MATERIAL OR RESOURCE ANALYSIS
- COSTING
- PRICING
- INVENTORY TRANSACTIONS
- MASTER PRODUCTION SCHEDULING EASE

in structuring information within computer files to allow it to
be retrieved to suit all the specific company's needs. Only
when the variety of uses or the specific product design demands
it, should additional structures be added. This way a minimum
amount of redundancy will be carried causing few problems with
maintaining the information accurately.

### PARTICULAR NEEDS FOR THE MASTER PRODUCTION SCHEDULE

Of all the uses for bills of materials, the one causing most
problems is the master production schedule. It is the primary
reason forcing companies to change their traditional bill of
material formats. Figure 2 shows three key characteristics of
master production schedules that have an impact on bill of
material structures.

## MASTER PRODUCTION SCHEDULE NEEDS FROM BILLS OF MATERIALS

- HELP TO PREDICT THE FUTURE WELL
- ABILITY TO OVERPLAN TO PROVIDE CONTINGENCY
- ASSISTANCE IN MEASURING AND MANAGING SALES & PRODUCTION

The first item, the need to predict the future, means the product must be defined in forecastable terms. It is a rare company that has a firm order backlog covering its cumulative lead time of procurement of materials and manufacture of the product through all its stages. Most companies either make-to-stock, where all their planning is based on forecasts, or they have a combination of customer orders short range and forecasts fill out the horizon long range. In this case, if the cumulative lead time of procurement of materials and building the product is 18 weeks but deliveries are quoted to customers in 6, then 12 weeks of activity must occur based on a forecast of sales prior to the order being received. It is simple to see that, in a make-to-order business, especially for products designed to suit a specific customer's needs, finished goods are not the best thing to forecast. But the other extreme of forecasting lower level components as if they were independent, in other words applying order points to dependent components, is probably not a valid alternative either. Some way of using the power of MRP to plan dependent relationships, driven from a master schedule that may be defined quite differently to finished goods, will give much better results in terms of inventory levels, customer service, and co-ordinated planning. So a specific bill of material is needed to link the master production schedule to the raw materials, components, or intermediates that have to be obtained prior to receiving the customer's order.

It's a well known fact that all forecasts are wrong to some degree. This is no different with a master production schedule. A prediction is made of what products customers will buy and these numbers are converted into a master production schedule. This starts many detailed activities moving in the factory and with vendors. It is important to add some contingency in the master production schedule to allow customers to buy what they want, not what we forecast. This will avoid giving either poor customer service with high inventories or jerking the factory around trying to react in the short range to specific customer's orders they did not plan for.

This contingency is often called "over-planning", especially when applied in the master production schedule. Using this approach, minimum total inventories are maintained because shipments are consistently made (you build inventories fastest when shipments drop off), customer service remains high with an ability to react to a range of actual customer orders, and the factory is productive because they see few changes from the marketplace, only those over-planning did not cover.

But what to over-plan? Obviously only those items with large potential forecast error. Items common to a large variety of finished products will see a very stable demand pattern and hence have little need for safety stock. Using traditional bills of materials, if the master production schedule is over-planned it will plan extra safety stock for common items as well as the uniques. This means inventories will be in excess of what is really required to provide the desired customer service level. Hence the bill of material must segregate items unique to each finished product from common items, so over-planning can occur on only those parts where it is needed. Again the need arises to have a different bill of material structure to the traditional format.

The last need is to be able to measure and manage the master production schedule. The objective is to either sell what is being made (Sales may not agree here) or make what is being sold. This requires constant measurement of incoming orders versus the master production schedule so timely adjustments can be made to either react to or control the marketplace. And if the master production schedule is defined in terms different to finished goods then the bills of materials must help to correlate these two sets of numbers. The master production schedule, finished products, and bills of materials must all link together so this measurement and management can occur.

### TYPES OF STRUCTURES

There are many ways of structuring bills of materials within a computer file. Four of the most common will be analysed to see how well they meet the needs of the master production schedule. The ability of these structures to satisfy other uses of bills of materials will be discussed where this is significant.

Modular bills of materials - The classic example for this type of bill of material is the automobile. The number of options available to the general public to create their own personal car causes the number of different cars that could be made, no two alike, to be in the billions. The American car industry in a good year produces about 10 million cars. Back in Detroit each of the car companies has a master scheduler with a very large head; they are all very clever. They predict which 10 million cars out of billions of choices customers will buy and when, and put their prediction in the master schedule!? That's not true. It's obviously impossible to forecast and master schedule specific assembled cars when there are billions of choices and only 10 million cars to make. It is just as ludicrous to consider that stored in a computer are billions of bills of materials defining all the choices just in case somebody buys one.

# MODULAR BILLS OF MATERIAL

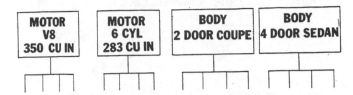

The approach many car divisions use is shown in Figure 3. Bills of materials are created for product modules, in essence the items customers can select as options. For example, bills of materials exist for each engine and body style a customer can select. There are bills of materials for transmission varieties, air conditioning options, radio and tape deck selections, seat options, etc. There are no finished cars in the master production schedule, only options. Simply defining how many of a given engine is to be produced in a given time frame and exploding this through MRP provides all the necessary information to procure the parts and schedule the factory to make engines at the right rate. Any over-planning is applied to the modules, more on the volatile options and less on the stable ones. A wide variety of customer demands in a given time period can now be accepted with no impact on factory schedules. The only adjustment is on the assembly line; which specific automobiles containing which combination of options are produced.

Working at the options level is a much easier forecasting job. Instead of billions of finished products to forecast, only a few thousand options end up in the master production schedule. Sales statistics are kept on the options to assist in forecasting the specific mix that should be placed in the master production schedule.

Order entry becomes similar to ordering a meal in a restaurant. The specific finished product, a mix of options, is selected either by a distributor, a need to replenish the warehouse, or by the customer. Just like a restaurant, an almost infinite variety of finished products can be created from a relatively few alternatives customers can select from. And just like a restaurant, there is no bill of material for the finished product the customer gets except for the short time it takes to produce that particular product, give it to the customer, and bill him. After that the information goes into a historical record. And the bill of material for the finished product is simply a conglomeration of all the individual modular bills of materials that were selected. Because order entry is in the same terms as the master production schedule, it is easy to measure and manage what is being sold versus what is planned to be made. By conceptualizing options are independent items the whole process of master production scheduling, forecasting, measuring and management occurs in the same product definition and is clear to all.

With only option bills of materials stored in a computer, the skill is to mix and match these bills of materials for a specific finished product to create pick lists, manufacturing instructions, costs, prices, etc. This requires a much higher level of expertise within the engineering department to make sure the wide variety of options customers might buy are compatible with an almost infinite selection variety. This may cause additional product costs for the redundancy necessary to handle a wide variety of options. However, this additional cost for standardization frequently results in a reduction in overhead costs, it certainly does reduce inventory, gives better customer service, and in some cases results in better product designs. Modular bills of materials also need higher skills in data processing, to write the programs to select the correct mix of bills of materials, sort them together, and print them in terms useful for all functional groups.

A company that has grown up with traditional bills of materials has a particularly severe problem if they wish to restructure into the modular format. It normally demands a significant effort from the engineering people to evaluate their current data and convert it into formats suitable for master production scheduling. Many companies who have gone through this effort though, say it was worth every penny of it. The difficult job is to get the necessary degree of enthusiasm up front based on the objectives of customer service and inventory reduction, neither of which feature in the engineer's objectives and are not his hot buttons.

Percentage Bills of Materials - These are sometimes called Ratio or Planning bills of materials. They are usually used when the number of options or variants is too high for them to be forecast as individual items. An example of a percentage bill of material

is given in Figure 4. The percentage figure is the ratio of
usage of each variant compared to the usage of the parent item.

## PERCENTAGE BILL OF MATERIAL

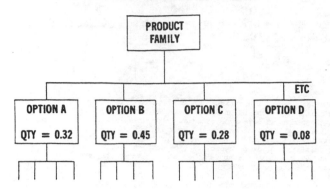

This technique forces redundancy within computer files defining
bills of materials as the percentage linkages are a completely
new set of structures additional to the traditional engineering
bill of material. This redundancy causes accuracy and maintenance problems as engineering changes flow through the system.
And a percentage bill of material frequently requires some restructuring of the traditional format although usually less than
required for the modular approach.

The percentages should be maintained to reflect the latest events
in the marketplace. However, they are frequently maintained
poorly, either because it is a manual system and hence they are
changed spasmodically and erratically if ever, or a computer
system changes them automatically based on historical usage,
causing too many revisions to lower level part schedules. It
also lets the sales and marketing people off the hook. There is
no pressure for them to provide inputs about future changes or
trends within the option mix they may know about.

Over-planning can occur in the master production schedule, in
which case all items in the bill of material get equal amounts of
safety stock, or percentages can be selectively increased above
the historical rates on the volatile options to put extra planning
only where it is needed. It is not as visible to the management
of the business in this latter case but is more effectively
applied.

Percentage bills of materials are not so easy to measure and
manage at the detail level. They are easy to manage at the gross
level, simply by looking at the total amounts of products in a
given product family that are being sold compared to the production plan. They are not easy to manage in terms of specific
variations being sold within the product family. The assumption
is that the percentages in the bill of material relate closely to
the mix actually being sold. Hence the family master schedule
is simply replaced with specific finished products that make up
this family as they are sold. Of course, detailed analysis of
the specific product mix being sold versus the planned mix can
occur, although this is frequently time consuming and often
happens after orders have been promised to customers.

The main advantage of this bill of material is it reduces the
number of items in the master production schedule. As a general
statement, this technique is good for those companies with a
significant order backlog so the percentage bill of material only
comes into play in the far out portion of the master production
schedule. It simply serves to get material procurement activities started today for that time frame. Provided the long lead
time material is common to a product family, then the percentage
bill of material works well. If there is a lot of unique
materials in the family or if the master production schedule
driving the percentage bill of material gets closer to today,
more discrete actions are in process which may or may not match
up with the actual customer's orders being sold.

Super Bills of Materials - This technique is quite similar to the
percentage approach except the percentages are placed on top of
existing bill of material structures. An example is shown in
Figure 5 for a company making truck axles. This technique can
also be used to handle a large catalog of finished items made to
stock. They cannot be handled individually so are frequently
planned in product families. After the master production
schedule for the product family has been set, the super bill of
material simply translates this into specific items to support
this family plan.

## SUPER BILL OF MATERIAL

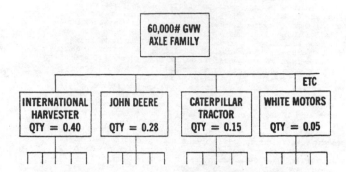

With this technique, the redundancy of information in the computer
files is above the existing or traditional bills of materials,
hence there is no need for restructuring and no additional demands
on the engineering group. As with the percentage bill of
material, the master production schedule can either be over-
planned directly or the percentages of specific items within the
product family can be boosted to always add up to more than 100%.
This bill of material is easier to measure and manage than the
percentage bill of material because it contains the traditional
bill of material definition which is how sales are made. It
does suffer from the same maintenance problems of keeping the
ratios updated as the percentage bill of material, though.

This approach is good where the mix is relatively stable and predictable or where there is a significant customer order backlog.
This means the super bill of material is being driven by the long
range portion of the master production schedule and is simply
planning long lead time material procurement. Provided this is
common to a family, few problems should occur when converting
from a family master production schedule to the specific products
sold.

Add/Delete - This is sometimes called a "Comparative" bill of
material or "Same as, Except", and is shown in Figure 6. This
is a picture of what is actually stored in the computer. It is
not a picture of the maintenance documents used to create
completely new bills of materials. Bills of materials simply
relate new products to a standard product and define which items
to leave off and which to add.

It is a good way of giving information to the plant. These bills
of materials are simple to understand and people quickly see the
differences between one product and another. It is easy to
write new bills of materials so in a company with a lot of
specials and variations it minimizes the engineering activity.

They are very difficult to make accurate. Engineering changes
must not only consider what is in the standard bill of material
but what was planned to be deleted by any special bills of

## ADD/DELETE BILL OF MATERIAL

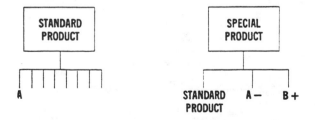

materials. Many companies who use this technique find their
special bills of materials carry negative quantities of things
that aren't present in the standard product because an engineering
change replaced it with another part number and the special bill
of material was not maintained. One company ended up with
negative standard costs for some products this way. The
financial people haven't yet figured out whether to sell or buy
these products to make money!

It is also very hard, if not impossible, to get the positive and
negative quantities to line up and net to zero in the right time
frame. With MRP, the bills of materials are being used to plan

192

items several weeks or months into the future. This means that plans to make standard products and special products have to be carefully co-ordinated in particular time frames so the plus quantity of the standard product and the negative quantity in the special do net out to zero in the right time bucket. If this is not done, MRP sees negative requirements in some time buckets with the corresponding positives in others. This also occurs with errors in the bills of materials as mentioned earlier. Most software packages were not designed with this kind of information in mind. They have no idea how to handle a negative requirement. Some packages even ignore the sign on a requirement quantity and assume it is always positive. This double-plans requirements (instead of the positive and negative quantities netting to zero they now add) and causes significant building of inventories of items that are not required.

The master production schedule has to occur at the finished product level. This is frequently a very difficult place to forecast because of the number of specials that can be sold. This technique does not make the forecasting job easier.

It is also very difficult to over-plan in this environment. If additional quantities of specials are put in the plan, this will get more of the unique components planned adequately but it also over-plans the negative quantity of the standard components meaning we are now short of items to make standard products.

The measurement of the master production schedule all occurs at the finished goods level but because there are so many finished goods it is difficult to compare what is happening in the market-place with the plans to produce. Usually sales information is summarized to a product family and compared at this level to the master production schedule. However, many times the specific items being sold within the family deviate from the finished goods that were forecasted, causing significant disruptions within the factory and with the vendors trying to react to a mix that was not planned.

### CONCLUSION

The subjects of master scheduling, forecasting, and bill of material structuring are inextricably intertwined. These three subjects cannot be discussed independently but must always be discussed as a cohesive group. Too many companies consider them separate and treat them as independent variables. This is not the way to get success within a manufacturing control system because of the strategic importance of the bill of material as the skeleton for all detail planning.

There is too much protectionism within the various organizations that use bills of materials, especially those who can use traditional versions such as the engineering department, sales people, and the accounting and financial groups. They want a bill of material that suits them and the traditional formats do that. We have got to help them see the bill of material for what it is, a linkage of one part to another. These linkages must be created to maximize the return on investment of the business, which will only be done if they support all the uses of bills of materials in a modern manufacturing control system. Hence, they must be structured to suit all the functions, not the select few who want to stay with their traditional approaches. With understanding, co-operation and some ingenuity from all affected people, the best form of structure can be developed to satisfy all the objectives.

### ABOUT THE AUTHOR

Hal Mather is President of Hal Mather, Inc., Atlanta, GA. specializing in management counseling and education in the area of manufacturing control systems, their design and effective use. Recent assignments have taken him to Australia, New Zealand, Holland, France, England, Canada and throughout the U.S.

Hal is a frequent speaker at professional society meetings, conferences, seminars and universities. He is co-author of a booklet, "The Master Production Schedule", and the author of several articles covering manufacturing control subjects.

He has been certified at the Fellow level by APICS, is the founder of the Piedmont Triad Chapter and was its first President.

Reprinted from APICS 1983 *Conference Proceedings*.

WHICH FIRST: MRP OR PRODUCTION ACTIVITY CONTROL?
Neville P. May, FBPICS
*GMD Systems International, Inc.*

Figure 1: The Manufacturing Control System

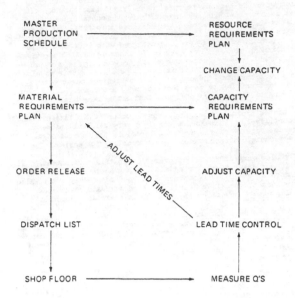

## INTRODUCTION

Many companies starting out on the road to implementing manufacturing control systems ask the question "Which should we do first, Materials Planning (MRP) or Production Activity Control (PAC)?" The underlying reasons for this question being raised are:

- The effort required to do both MRP and PFC at the same time can appear to be beyond the resources available.

- MRP often appears to be an objective obtainable in the longer term (e.g. one to two years).

- PAC could cure at least some of todays problems in the short term (e.g. six to nine months).

The answers to the question have varied over the years, both in the US and overseas. The objective of this paper is to provide an examination of the relevant factors with guidance to assist decision making for companies that are in the process of implementing such systems.

The paper will deal with the following topics:

- The manufacturing system functions.
- Why not both PAC and MRP in parallel?
- The functions and dependencies of MRP.
- The contributions to MRP by PAC.
- The functions and dependencies of PAC.
- The contributions to PAC by MRP.
- Summary of the considerations.
- Conclusion.

## MANUFACTURING SYSTEMS FUNCTIONS

The manufacturing control system is illustrated in Figure 1. The left hand side of the chart is the priority planning and control function, with capacity planning and control on the right. This system can be described as a typical "closed loop".

At this point we can review the diagram and consider:

- If MRP is first, then all functions after order release are lost, other than the manual production control systems of today.

- If PAC is first it will have to exist on the basis of today's material and capacity planning systems.

Which is the lesser evil? At this point the answer is unclear, but it is appropriate to state that:

- MRP (with master scheduling, valid forecasting etc.) is a "new way of doing business." It is essential that it be implemented well, and typically requires changes of attitudes, education, etc.
- Some PAC is being done everyday. Shop floor control is not necessarily a "new way" of doing business other than from the MRP interface aspects.

Therefore it is worth considering that it could be feasible to implement the basics of PAC and refine the system later, after MRP is installed. It would be exceedingly dangerous to try such a two stage approach with an MRP system. If MRP does not go in as a credible system, it can die. PAC "in stages" does not have the same mortality rate due to interim progress. It is easier to explain, for instance, that the PAC system will get better once MRP is effective, and that in the meantime it helps identify and correct some of the current problems. It is difficult to explain that MRP will work better once a forecast and frozen zone is available to make master scheduling credible. Too many middle managers and supervisors will feel animosity toward this lack of upper management commitment to the system.

## WHY NOT BOTH IN PARALLEL?

Why not install both the planning and operational systems at the same time? With this approach we do not have to worry about which should be first. Unfortunately this is normally impracticable except under two sets of circumstances:

- A completely assembly oriented company, probably with single level bills of material, where shop floor activity is minor thus allowing PAC to be implemented without major effort. Examples are flow line assembly, bottling or packaging plants.
- A fabrication shop of simple parts or components where there simpler planning problem e.g. there is a single level bill of material and often only one raw material for most items. Manufacturers of fasteners, and simple machined components from bar stock or castings are typical examples.

Notice the common denominator in these examples. Either the PAC or MRP problems are basically simple. Therefore much less effort is involved in one of the application areas, so it can be implemented in parallel with the "major" system. In most companies, particularly the mixed fabrication and assembly operation, this is not the case. Both MRP and PAC are major undertakings, and if both systems are settling in at the same time it becomes more difficult to identify and resolve the problems because of the intricate inter-dependencies. Too many things being changed at one time will usually degrade the implementation and success of both systems.

FUNCTIONS AND DEPENDENCIES OF MRP

To properly examine the case for MRP first, we should define the functions of MRP as illustrated in Figure 2. Sales forecasts and customer orders are analyzed and managed in the master schedule. Depending on the availability of finished goods to meet this demand (which is a netting, lot sizing and lead time offsetting exercise in itself) the required production schedule is subject to a rough cut capacity or resource planning function. If feasible the plan is then:

- Extended by the bill of material.
- Netted against projected available inventory.
- Lot sized according to the order policies.
- Offset by lead time to calculate start dates.

The planned orders and recommendations for changes in priority are then available to the planners. Actions taken on these outputs are used to establish priorities and control the inventory of components and materials.

Figure 2: MRP Functions

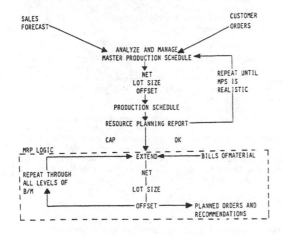

What does MRP need to be effective? These prerequisites have been well defined in many publications:

- Customer orders.
- Sales forecasts.
- Cooperation between marketing and manufacturing to establish a valid master schedule.
- An accurate statement of the availability of materials, including both inventory balances and order quantities and dates.
- Accurate bills of material.
- Valid or reasonable planning lead times
- A dispatching system that allows the priority plan to be promptly actioned by the shop floor.

This list is daunting, and has defeated many potential users. However, of these dependancies, which is the longest lead time item? Identifying the major task or critical path is always helpful in project control.

In my experience the largest lead time item is achieving a valid master schedule. To reach this objective, marketing, manufacturing and most of executive management have to agree to a new way of doing business, provide the forecast data, and allow the

master scheduler to implement the plan for the business. This task must not be underestimated, or undervalued in its importance to an effective MRP system. In the best situations, from the start of the project (i.e. setting up bills of material) it will usually take nearly a year to achieve this master scheduling prerequisite. This time period is normally used to prepare the rest of the system for MRP, by establishing the other aspects in the list.

In most cases considerable effort is then expended to validate the bills, estimate the lead times etc. Unfortunately this is often done without any help from a system; only human resource is employed to prepare the data, which is not able to properly validate or check on the information being collected. We end up with unproven data being used by the shiny new MRP system, and the results are a bitter disappointment. Validation of this data prior to MRP is a point to which we will be returning in the next section.

THE CONTRIBUTIONS OF PAC TO MRP

The MRP prerequisites have been defined in the previous section. We are now in a position to examine those on the list which can be helped by the PAC system.

Accurate Inventory

This phrase has been used over the years, and a figure of 95% accuracy quoted as the basic objective. So you work hard, enclose the stockroom, obtain the 95% accuracy of the stock level and balances, yet MRP is still not working well. How does this happen? The reason is that MRP uses the stock balances as only one part of the projected statement of availability. There are two other figures that must be considered:

- The material "allocations" against manufacturing orders in the release process or work in progress.
- The replenishment orders, which for manufactured items are part the PAC system, in terms of quantity that will be completed and on what date.

Therefore, MRP is extremely dependent on the PAC system for a realistic view of when manufacturing orders are likely to be completed. In fact it is probably fair to say that in many instances order accuracy is more important to MRP than stock room accuracy. I do not know how any respectable level of order accuracy can be achieved without a PAC system to update MRP with this crucial data.

Accurate Lead Times

Inaccurate lead times can kill the success of an MRP system, far more easily than poor lot sizing. Understated lead times cause excessive expediting, but are not the usual problem because everyone who feeds lead time data into the system will be buffering the figures. Overstated lead times cause early release of orders, higher work in process and associated control problems. How can the accuracy of lead times be validated, and monitored as conditions change in the future. The answer is that the usual (or average) process and inter-operation times can only be effectively monitored by a PAC system which provides output reporting of these figures.

Accurate Bills of Material

An effective MRP system requires that the bills of material be accurate, and properly structured according to the way that a product is manufactured. Many companies spend considerable amounts of resource in investigation, validation and modification of bills of material in order to meet this objective. It is much simpler, and less costly, to use feedback from the shop floor and inventory issues against a picking list to achieve the validation task. In fact, the only place that can really check a bill of material is the manufacturing area, and the PAC or operational system is part of this feedback loop.

## A Dispatching System

The Master Schedule and MRP/CRP system is an unsurpassed priority planning mechanism. Material, component, and assembly schedules are continually updated and the new and changed order quantities and due dates reported. What do we do with this output? Go out to the shop floor, find the jobs and chalk the new due dates on the pieces, or change the due date on the shop packet?

Obviously these are not the methods we need, but without an "automated" dispatching system we are unable to:

- Recalculate the open manufacturing order priorities. This needs to be done on the basis of time available to due date compared with time required to complete the job.

- Communicate the latest priority list to the foreman or scheduler in a form that allows him to assign work to different machines, and to organize the support services needed (e.g. tooling, drawings, materials handling etc.).

The dispatching system has to be part of the PAC system, and without this in place the outputs of MRP fall on stony or infertile ground. It should be noted that this worklist communication vehicle should be in place at the start of MRP in order to execute the plan. Later availability is a serious exposure, and can impact the credibility and results of MRP.

## FUNCTIONS AND DEPENDENCIES OF PAC

The Production Activity Control system consists of the functions shown in Figure 3.

Figure 3: PAC Functions

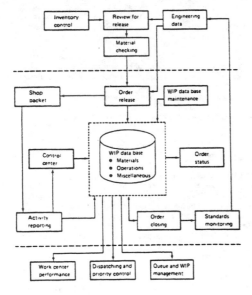

The work in process data base of orders, with associated individual material and operation records, is established when a manufacturing order is released. This data is normally extracted from the basic files in the engineering or production information data base i.e. from item master files, routings, work centers and bills of material. The essential planning information that is made available at order release time is the due date and quantity of the order. The materials planning system controls these from the viewpoints of material availability and schedule (i.e. start and due date.).

The work in process data base is then updated by activity reporting, which includes material transactions and production reporting for the operations to be performed on the order. There are some additional activities that are required to maintain (or alter) the data base to cater for engineering changes, rework

operations etc. Activity reporting in a timely fashion and the maintenance of the data is usually augmented by the creation of a "control center" within the production control department. This center co-ordinates the various system activities, and is aggressive in the pursuit and correction of activity reporting errors.

Once the data base is established, maintained and activity reporting being applied then the basic elements are in place. The problem is that many companies do not apply their resource to these tasks in a committed, urgent or realistic fashion, particularly the data collection or activity reporting task. In such cases the implementation of a successful system can be delayed, just as MRP can be delayed by lack of progress on its own essential prerequisites. However, it is possible to have a staged approach to activity reporting, such as:

- Initially only "operations complete" reporting is undertaken. This means that order progress or status in the system could be somewhat out of date, by a day or so. This is often a minor imposition when, typically, progress information was unavailable except when someone went out and physically checked the job.
- Later (but not too much later) full "start, stop and complete" operation reporting can be implemented. This will tune the system, assist in accurate reporting of labor and machine hours, and allow more timely and thorough error correction.

The key issues of activity reporting are:

- Timeliness is needed to achieve prompt error correction and accuracy, not "up to the second" management information.
- Accuracy requirement is highest for the costing system.

The point of this discussion is that effective activity reporting can be achieved. In the context of this paper this can or should be achieved in a reasonable time frame which is less than some other aspects of the system.

Even in the initial approach above improved and additional control of the shop floor is achievable, with associated benefits of better productivity, reduction of lead times and WIP investment, and some better delivery achievements. This has been proved by the widespread use of standalone (non-MRP) shop floor control system in Europe.

## CONTRIBUTIONS OF MRP TO PAC

The major aspects of MRP that can impact PAC are in the areas of material availability and the schedules provided by priority and capacity planning.

### Material Availability

Release of orders to the shop floor with materials shortages will be regulated by MRP, which detects the shortages in advance. Obviously this is the true solution. On the other hand a thorough availability check at the time of order release, with appropriate adjustments to release quantities and/or due dates, can prevent the productivity impact becoming too severe if the PAC system is not supported by MRP.

### Priority Planning

Without MRP the PAC system is exposed to the dangers of "invalid" due dates and production schedules which are overstated when compared with the capacity available. This is the major problem area, and emphasized by protagonists of the "MRP first" approach who suggest that PAC cannot work under these circumstances. But what is new about this situation? Every shop floor in every plant in the western world (and Soviet bloc?) has suffered or still suffers from these diseases. We want the cure, but are used to living with them. The facilities of a properly used PAC system will assist production management with dealing with them until such time as the full MRP/CRP system is in place. The PAC system will not die without MRP. It will achieve less control and benefits than when a fully integrated or closed loop system surrounds it, but can still contribute significantly to an overall improvement.

## SUMMARY OF THE CONSIDERATIONS

In the examination of PAC and MRP functions and dependancies, and the mutual contributions, we have established the following key points as the basis of success for the two systems:

| PAC | MRP |
|-----|-----|
| Valid priorities (Due Dates) | Sales Orders and Forecast |
| Work in Progress Data Base | Master Schedule |
| Effective Activity Reporting | Accurate Inventory |
| | Accurate Bills of Material |
| | Accurate Lead Times |
| | MRP |
| | Dispatching System |

Some commonly quoted elements are missing from this list, and should now be considered before proceeding further:

### Education Effort

The education effort that has to be undertaken is similar in size (but not content) for both MRP and PAC. Therefore it has been omitted as a "contra" entry on both sides of the "ledger".

### Routing Accuracy

There has been a misunderstanding for many years that operation times have to be accurate before implementing a PAC system. This is simply not true. The impact of incorrect inter-operation times (i.e. queue plus move) has a far more serious impact than inaccuracies of operation setup and run times. Queue times should be established and monitored, but the impact of operation time inconsistencies can be "massaged" out of the system by judicious use of work center efficiency factors. The author has personal experience of successful shop floor control scheduling systems where the operation times were over 100% out. This was because the standards were established as the basis of incentive pay schemes.

However, the more serious aspect of routing accuracy is correct operation sequences. If operation 30 is performed before operation 20, for example, then the manufacturing order status, schedule and dispatch list will suffer. Fortunately this is manageable, particularly if emphasis is placed on the discipline of sequence, and changes of sequence subjected to specific (rather than off the cuff) conditions and approval.

### Capacity Requirements Planning

Both the PAC and MRP systems require that capacity requirements be analyzed to match loads against the available resource. The materials plan is validated by CRP, but must have the current status of open manufacturing orders available in PAC in order to be effective. On the other hand PAC needs a capacity planning function prior to order release, for essentially the same reasons as MRP. Therefore, since both systems require capacity planning, this aspect is considered to have equal impact, and is omitted from both sides of the list.

Returning to the list at the beginning of this section it can be seen that although both PAC and MRP are mutually dependent there are more tasks to be achieved prior to effective MRP than PAC. The first point to consider is that in most situations the implementation path to MRP will take longer. Therefore the possibility of more immediate assistance to

management by the earlier implementation of PAC would be advantageous.

The next consideration is that (as mentioned earlier) the shop floor side of the business could be subject to a two stage implementation and still be effective. MRP is in mortal danger if such an approach were employed in its implementation. The new way of doing business must succeed, or forever be held in disrepute until such time as a costly reimplementation is undertaken.

Notwithstanding these two factors, by far the major issue is the contributions to MRP success that can be achieved by installing the shop floor or operational system first. Validation of bills of material and manufacturing lead times from data that is available from the operational system (rather than guessed) is a key factor. The readiness of a dispatching system to receive MRP's priority plans is also a truly significant contribution. To these three must be added the other crucial issue of inventory accuracy. Remember, MRP is the supreme optimist. It is informed that a manufacturing order for a component has been released and will be completed on the due date with the quantity to satisfy the requirement. MRP will implicitly believe these inputs! Whoever heard of anything or anyone that believed such preliminary facts? Just ask your customers, marketing or assembly foreman if they would believe it? MRP has to have the plan updated, as in Figure 4, by the operational system, because order progress, estimated completion, and quantities good and scrap all require continual feedback. Only in this way can MRP examine the projected availability of material with any credibility. The shop floor system brings the planning system into the world of reality.

Figure 4: Planning and Operational Systems Communications

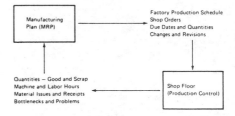

There are two other considerations that are worthy of review at this time, independent of the mutual MRP/PAC dependancies and contributions:

- The usual manufacturing system allows the user to easily recalculate product costs (material, labor, machine, overhead) using the basic data in the item, structure, routing and work center files. The principal uses of this facility are for standard and current costs. However, the feedback on actual costs is derived from the PAC system, to be used in evaluation of performance and profitability. Therefore PAC can provide this key function earlier if installed first.

- The PAC system can give unparalleled insight into the shape of the business, shop floor practices, and provide assistance to engineering and other departments. Again this is an extremely valuable aspect of business information

## CONCLUSION

When all the aspects are added up it should be clear that the implementation of PAC first must be a major consideration. I submit that in most cases it should be first. An effective shop floor control system is the foundation on which successful MRP can be built.

The exceptions to this general rule are:

- If the lead time to implement PAC is larger than that needed for MRP.
- If the PAC need is significantly less than the need or benefits of MRP, such as in the assembly plant environment.

What is the proof of the argument for PAC first, or is this paper just theoretical? The author is fortunate is having had the opportunity, over the last fifteen years, to examine the performance of many users of IBM systems. It was very noticeable in the United Kingdom, from 1970 to 1977, that the companies who obtained the best benefits and use of MRP were those who had used shop floor control first. For two particular systems the successful MRP user list was (very noticeably) comprised of "PAC first" companies. The other proof is those companies which have installed without shop floor control. Even after extended periods of time they still have no formal way of validating lead times, or communicating priorities to the shop floor. At best their MRP systems have achieved some degree of better control, but at a level far below that which is possible, or that which should be achieved as the

justification for the expense and effort of implementation. Talk to MRP users at this conference. Many are in this situation, and will be prepared to talk frankly.

There is also a growing strength of opinion among consultants in favor of PAC first. For many years this was not the case, mainly because most implementation experience and expertise was in the materials area, not shop floor. The 1978 APICS survey revealed that less than half of established MRP users had even implemented the basics of a PAC system. Times have changed dramatically, partly due to the fact that in the USA direct labor productivity has mushroomed from a relatively minor issue to a major concern. More companies are turning to PAC systems, and many are wishing they had installed these before materials planning applications.

Therefore, I encourage you to review the topics in this paper, and amend them according to their significance in your own business operation. Compile a ledger of the debits and credits, and come to your own decision. Please do not just go one way or the other without recognition of the issues and inter-dependencies.

Neville May is a Vice President of GMD Systems International, a manufacturing systems and consultancy firm based in Atlanta, Georgia. GMD specializes in education, software enhancements and implementation services in support of the IBM MAPICS application packages.

Prior to the foundation of GMD, Neville was Manufacturing Industry Marketing Consultant for IBM United Kingdom, General Systems Division and came on assignment to the USA to work on international aspects of manufacturing applications software.

He has been working on the implementation and design of PIC systems for fourteen years, particularly in the area of shop floor control. He is a fellow of both the Institute of Production Control and the British Production and Inventory Control Society, as well as an active member of APICS since he has been in the USA. His activities have included APICS International Conferences, BPICS European Conferences, as well as IBM sponsored conferences in both the USA and Europe. He is also the principal author of a series of IBM courses on Shop Floor Control.

Reprinted from APICS 1979 *Conference Proceedings*.

THE IMPACT OF MRP ON SHOP FLOOR CONTROL

William R. Wassweiler
Management Resource Management, Inc.

The major advantage of a Shop Floor Control System driven by MRP is the inherent capability of MRP to establish priorities and then maintain them. This important characteristic can easily be communicated to the shop floor through a dispatch list indicating the relative priority of all work-in-process by routed operation and work center. This signal feature is the primary reason why MRP driven Shop Floor Control Systems can improve customer service and reduce work-in-process inventory. In addition to priority planning, MRP and its supporting data base provide the necessary framework for other information that further enhances the control of the shop floor.

The following is a review of some of the additional features and functions that MRP provides.

Component Availability Checking

There is no need to stage material to determine part shortages, because a material availability checking program can easily be added to an MRP system. This feature allows a planner to check the availability and status of components prior to the release of a production order to the stockroom for picking. The program indicates either the order is complete - or the part numbers and quantities short are listed. Furthermore, the due date of the shortage is indicated along with previous claims of other production orders that have the same shortages. If appropriate, this feature can be programmed to automatically release orders based on the start date for an order. At order time, the availability of all components will be checked, based on the on-hand plus on-order, minus committed balances for each part. If shortages exist, the order paperwork will not be prepared unless the planner issues a forced release transaction. A by-product of this exercise is an availability report (or mechanized shortage list) to aid the planner in taking necessary actions.

On-Hand Balances and Stock Locations

Knowing the location of material facilitates order release, follow-up, cycle counting and order picking. One on-hand field within MRP that reflects a four wall condition will not effectively support shop floor control. It is necessary to delineate the on-hand position of inventory by displaying material physically in the stockroom, in receiving (either receiving inspection or the receiving department), in floor stock, or material loaned to manufacturing. The later category is best explained by the example of disbursing a whole coil of steel to the press department instead of ten feet to support the order quantity. Stock parts can be loaned to an order when it is convenient to withdraw more than the required quantity and a return is expected of the excess. This feature alerts the planner to the on-hand status of the material, which could influence his release of additional orders calling for the same material.

Multiple locations in the stockroom are necessary because of space limitations and the need to record the storage of overflow material. The stockroom location file provides the input necessary to print picking lists in location sequence, which can substantially reduce the time and effort in kitting material. It is possible to maintain on-hand balances by location in FIFO sequence to insure the timely disbursement of material with limited shelf life.

Net Change

The shop floor by its very nature is dynamic and in a constant state of activity. This environment requires an MRP system that can react to change on a timely basis. Net change has this quality, for it is a change-driven system, which means it can respond to scrap, lead time changes, bill of material changes, inventory adjustments, order cancellations, master schedule changes, material receipts and disbursements as frequently as the user requires. This characteristic keeps the information in the Shop Floor Control System up to date and, therefore, provides more capability than a weekly regeneration system.

Net Change provides the opportunity to automatically change shop priorities daily as a result of MRP exception messages to cancel, expedite or retard material. Care must be taken when using this feature. Automatic rescheduling of expedite messages on the daily dispatch list without planner review for reasonableness, will create unrealistic shop priorities.

Lead Time

To facilitate Shop Floor Control, MRP must support the setting of lead times by a fixed time period, preferably in days, and also by calculating lead times into days by considering transit, queue, set-up and run time. Fixed lead times are helpful in controlling assemblies because of minimum setup, and calculated lead times are appropriate for machined parts with numerous routed operations. This flexibility is necessary to maintain reasonable planning lead times.

Tooling

Insuring the availability of tools to support shop order schedules can be improved by using the planned order start dates of MRP as a need date for tooling. As planned orders in MRP generate requirements for lower level components, they also can indicate a time-phased requirement for tooling. A report can easily be prepared for scheduling the tool room by indicating the tool numbers for a component or assembly in its item master and then listing tool requirements by planned order start date.

The effectiveness of a Shop Floor Control System can be impaired by the abuse or lack of understanding of the standard features of MRP, such as: Lot sizing, safety stock, and length of the time bucket. Lot sizing techniques are necessary and very useful, but care must be taken to apply the proper approach to the appropriate level within the bill of material. Careless application will create a cascading effect which will increase inventory plus indicate false priorities on the shop floor. It is easy for a dynamic lot sizing technique at one level to cause an emergency order at a lower level that may not be critical.

Safety stock is another feature that is essential to good planning and control, but its excessive use will increase inventory that does not turn and cause shop order priorities to be inconsistent with assembly requirements. Safety stocks tend to distort the actual priorities of items and make it necessary to go around the formal system by working to a hot list of assembly shortages.

For effective scheduling, MRP time buckets cannot be longer than one week. A period greater than a week, like a month, will increase lead time through the offsetting process plus create schedules that are not fine or specific enough for a foreman to follow.

MRP is, without a doubt, the key to Shop Floor Control success. This condition will further develop with a little imagination on the part of the user and continued support from data processing.

**Reprinted from APICS 1982 *Conference Proceedings*.**

## THE SYNTHESIS OF MRP, GROUP TECHNOLOGY, AND CAD-CAM

Earl R. Lewis
CTI-CRYOGENICS
A Division of Helix Technology Corporation

Paul G. Conroy, CPIM*
Coopers & Lybrand

### INTRODUCTION

Today, management is faced with a focused challenge - "Improve Productivity." This is not another productivity seminar or lecture on Japan, Inc. It is an attempt to define and explain various techniques used to improve productivity and to describe how they interrelate. Proceeding from one acronym to another in search of improved productivity is not a wise strategy. A better approach is to first understand what is important to your business "up front", and then proceed with an orderly focused plan. The technologies that will be discussed are Group Technology (GT), Computer-Aided Design (CAD), Computer-Aided Manufacturing (CAM) and Flexible Manufacturing Systems (FMS). I will pay particular attention to GT, as I believe this is the glue that holds these technologies together.

Fredrick Taylor offered one of the first strategies for productivity called "Scientific Management." His strategy was to divide work into small specialized repetitive tasks, organize so that these similar tasks are performed by the same people, then measure and improve the performance on each task. During Taylor's time, production lines were springing up and the industrial revolution was in bloom. Shops were organized by function - not by product. A result was the ability to quickly train low-skilled workers, however, there were some serious disadvantages. These included complex scheduling, high inventories and long process times. Today we have a better educated work force, quality of work is important and has been proven to be a factor in productivity. The question is does this classical organization for production fit today's needs?

We believe there is a solution for many companies that will improve productivity, reduce process times and inventory requirements. We also believe this solution is a necessary step in the progression from manual labor and manual management of the production process to the automation in our future.

### GROUP TECHNOLOGY

Over the next several years, the majority of industrial manufacturing forms are expected to introduce GT, a little-known but potent methodology that provides an alternative approach to manufacturing.[1] Group Technology streamlines batch production, the mode in which 60 - 70% of all manufacturing in the United States is currently performed, by restructuring the work flow within a factory.

Group Technology is based on the premise that "similar problems have similar solutions." It is similar to more familiar methodologies such as "Quality Circles" in that it enhances workers' involvement with the total requirements of production. This, in fact, has been described as its principal benefit. But although "job enrichment" is indeed one of GT's benefits, it may be more relevant to think in terms of "company enrichment."

Although Group Technology has been documented since the early 1930s, and has been successfully applied from Russia to Scandinavia, from Europe to Japan, to date it has had few publicized applications in the U.S. This may be due to the current emphasis on using computer software to solve production scheduling problems -- or because management has not yet been fully apprised of its potential.

---

[1] Two recent surveys defined the following projections.

"By 1988 more than 50% of industry will use GT" University of Michigan. The International Institute for Production Engineering Research (IIRP) says that "By 1990, 70% of industry will use Group Technology in manufacture."

Batch manufacturing has long been plagued by certain inherent inefficiencies that affect not only product cycle times, but overall output as well. Many of these inefficiencies result from the standard structure of batch manufacturing, in which a number of specialized departments participate in production. Typically, these departments are functionally oriented (i.e. turning, welding, milling, assembly, etc.), and work is routed through them as shown in the example below.

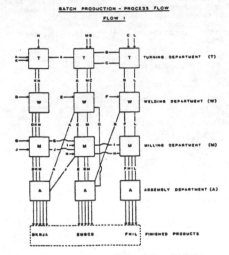

In Flow I, work-in-process is queued up behind each department, waiting to be worked on according to its priority. Determining this priority is an extremely complex task in a functionally-oriented flow. As Jeff Miller writes, "literally hundreds of different ways exist for assigning priorities to the work, among them the following:

1. Most important customer
2. Highest sales volume
3. Least cost (economic lot size)
4. Earliest due date
5. Satisfy the most customers."

These factors are primarily external to manufacturing, but there are also many internal considerations that can affect priorities. For example: critical machines down; absenteeism; material shortages; scrap; rework; test failure; and so on. "The sum total of thousands of priority work decisions that may be made each day in a large factory determines that factory's output," concludes Mr. Miller.

There is a direct correlation between a product's cycle time (the time required to build it within the factory) and the number of priority decisions required during its production. This relationship is significant in batch production in a functionally-oriented flow, because the process, by its nature, is subject to frequent change. Management plans production to satisfy the requirements of a master schedule, and attempts to build a modified economic lot-sized batch. However, the factors described above will frequently disrupt production as planned, and scheduled quantities must often be increased to some more economic lot size. Forecast inaccuracy, too, can generate many changes, especially since "Forecast accuracy is a function of time. The further out in the future the forecast is made, the less accurate it is likely to be."[2] Forecast accuracy is thus a key determinate in the number of changes that must be made to production schedules.

Schedule changes are translated into new priorities on the factory floor as actual orders arrive. But although the original master schedule takes into account each department's capacity, it is virtually impossible to restructure a new master schedule as daily priorities change. Job A may now, because of a higher priority, push out Jobs B, C, and D, causing them to be late, as a higher-priority job can absorb a department's total capacity, precluding production of all other jobs. The jobs that are pushed out then cause random capacity problems or "bottlenecks" -- in one department one week, in another the next.

---

[2] G.W. Plossl and O.W. Wight, *Production and Inventory Control*

This problem is compounded if product cycle times are long to begin with. The longer the cycle time, the more changes in priorities. The more changes, the longer the lead time, and the more likely that the manufacturing process can become "out-of-control."

It is important to stop here and address one well-documented fact: that typically over 95% of a product's cycle time, from its release to the factory floor to shipment out the door, is wait time or queue time -- the time that it sits waiting to move on to the next operation required in its production. Group Technology offers a viable solution to this "chicken and egg" problem.

Group Technology approaches production by means of a simple, but quite different, structure. In a GT factory, manufacturing is performed by combining similar work. First, similar products and parts are identified and analyzed. In a complex factory, a classification coding system is usually employed to accomplish this. Next, the machines and/or skills needed to manufacture them are defined. Workers are cross-trained so that they are capable of performing all operations required to produce a product; in effect, they become generalists making similar products instead of specialists with one specific skill, and work therefore becomes easier to understand.

Machines and skills are then grouped together in "cells" on the production floor. Each cell has the capability to manufacture an entire range of similar products or parts, operating, in essence, like a factory within a factory. (See Flow II, following.) The significance of this difference is difficult to convey, but it is indeed significant. Consider the following effects of the GT approach.

BATCH PRODUCTION - GROUP FLOW

FLOW II

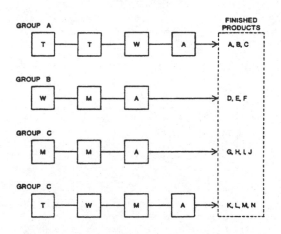

Because products in a GT system can be manufactured from start to finish in one area instead of being routed from department to department all around the factory, product cycle times are reduced. Group Technology thus effectively attacks the link between cycle times and priority decisions. Since cycle times are shorter, fewer priority decisions need to be made. For the same reason, GT cells gain the critical flexibility needed to respond quickly to changes mandated by market conditions or by management.

Since GT cells are dedicated to similar work, workers do not need to prepare as many special setups, and setup costs go down. This reduces lot sizes, and, consequently, work-in-process, or inventory. Because lot sizes are reduced and cycle times are shorter, scheduling of a GT cell is a straightforward process, and it is easier to make changes. The capacity to manufacture the products assigned to a cell is simply the total manhours available, as similar products require similar capacity. Machines and tools can easily be allocated to meet the management-defined output.

In fact, GT foremen and workers can and should accomplish the daily scheduling of their cells. They are better able to use their time effectively when they understand

the final product requirements, are given a defined output to produce, and have the possibility of performing any one of many operations on the product. In addition, since one worker can do another's job, workers are more fully utilized, and the problems usually created by key persons' absenteeism are reduced considerably.

Summary

Group Technology reduces total cycle time, and hence inventory, for several reasons:

°   Management commits only similar work to be produced in certain cells. This allows for tooling that needs to be varied only slightly, thus reducing both setup times and lot sizes.

°   With smaller lot sizes, production changes are easier to schedule.

°   Wait time between operations is reduced, as capacity is easily planned, and only parts that are required are available to be worked on.

°   Workers are more flexible, and management is hence less vulnerable to worker absence.

°   Demand as seen by production foremen is not random, but can be easily planned to match the output required.

For a comparison of GT vs functional organization see Chart "A".

CHART "A"

Group Technology Cells vs Functional Organization

|  | Functional Organization | GT Cells |
|---|---|---|
| In Process Time | long | short |
| Shop Scheduling | complex | simple |
| Master Schedule Change Horizon | long | short |
| Work in Process Inventory Investment | high | low |
| Worker Satisifaction | low | high |
| Training Cost | low | high |
| Equipment Utilization | high | low |

TOWARD THE AUTOMATED FACTORY

While we have heard the acronyms CAD and CAM used over and over it is important to realize what they mean in the simplest of terms, then to describe what can be accomplished with these technologies. The automation of design recognizes the basic similarities of definition. Libraries exist containing designs of common or similar parts (shapes, forms, etc.). CAD seeks to bring these similar designs into the designer's hands in a manageable, controlled way in order to eliminate the repetitive nature of the designer's task. CAM which seeks to automate the factory operations consist of a similar library of tape, N.C. tapes or D.N.C. programs stored in a computer memory. These are called out to perform various machining operations. Put into the simplest of terms - we need a library code system to retrieve this CAD/CAM information. This code system will be discussed later. Group Technology requires a similar library to identify similarities. These classification schemes are therefore the focal point required to integrate these three productivity improving techniques. How do we accomplish all this - integrate CAD, CAM, GT and justify automation. First we need to link these technologies together to identify similar parts in order to organize the factory floor, to find similar designs and similar programs. Coding systems are designed to help recognize these similarities, to identify them in order to act in a manner that allows us to use the past work to reduce costs in the future. These systems are available commercially - some are even free.

We are constantly struggling with actual applications of Advanced Automation Techniques, e.g. robotics, flexible Machining Systems etc. For many companies it is extremely difficult to justify the applications. Part of the problem is in our approach. The automation of a single activity in a functionally oriented shop is by definition unique to a function - (drilling, milling, welding, etc.). The true promise lies in the automation of manufacturing of a product - not the automation of a function. In a functional organized shop, families of like products are difficult to isolate and hence to automate. Group Technology forces these similar products into work cells where the operations become repetitive. For the most effective application of automation work must be organized by product. This organization of work by product is also the goal of GT. Therefore, the move to GT is also a necessary move toward automation.

## TOWARD CONTROLLING THE AUTOMATED FACTORY

### GT and MRP

The MRP technique calculates production requirements without regard for the availability of capacity to produce. This is referred to as "infinite loading", that is, capacity is considered to be infinite. A perfect match of production requirements with production capacity never occurs, therefore, a number of techniques have been developed to resolve this difficulty.

The first approach is based upon the premise that capacity can be changed to accommodate the production requirements. Thus, we have rough cut capacity planning used to test the feasibility of a master schedule and shop loading that calculates the man and machine requirements for MRP planned orders and in process orders on a day-to-day basis. We can never change capacity to perfectly match production requirements. To do so would require enough capacity to handle the highest peak requirements with the resulting very low average utilization. Therefore, we set capacities that "on the average" will meet the production requirements.

To complete the resolution of production requirements with capacity we have two approaches to choose from. The first is to allow sufficient lead-time for the manufacture of the parts for the detail scheduler to match requirements to capacity by producing most parts ahead of the MRP need date. The second approach is called "finite scheduling." The production requirements are scheduled to the capacity planned and the scheduled completion date is communicated to the planning system where higher level production that is dependent upon the part is rescheduled as required. The finite scheduling approach is almost never used. Even though it has significant advantages in reduced inventory requirements and shorter manufacturing lead-times, its use is precluded by the complexity of the scheduling and rescheduling procedure in the typical functional shop. In the Group Technology shop with a small number of cells to be scheduled, finite scheduling becomes a real possibility.

As we have seen, in the future, Group Technology cells will be replaced by automoted process. As this occurs we will be released from additional constraints. Working a machine twenty-four hours to cover requirements one day, and six hours the next day, is much more of a possibility in the automated factory. Workers in the automated factory are there to start the machines, stop the machines, correct problems and maintain the machines. Their numbers vary only with the general activity level of the plant and not with the activity of any particular automated process. The penalty for short-term radical load changes disappears with automated work centers. Therefore, our ability to finite schedule the automated factory is even greater than our ability to finite schedule the group technology factory.

In this new environment the MRP system that is not fully integrated with a finite scheduling system, will be as obsolete as a reorder point system would be today, if used to plan requirements for dependent demand items. We are entering a new era in manufacturing where there is renewed interest in the process as distinct from the operations. The movement to Group Technology and then to automated processes will move swiftly and together. We must be prepared to evolve our control systems to adapt to these changes.

## CONCLUSION

Some of the major points discussed are summarized below.

1. CAD/CAM involves the same grouping of manufactured parts as GT. Similar classification techniques are used.

2. GT simplifies the scheduling task and therefore reduces lead time and inventory requirements.

3. MRP will have a shorter planning horizon allowing faster response to market changes.

4. Future MRP development will be required to integrate MRP with finite scheduling.

5. Manufacturing is moving towards automation. The organization of work required for application is the GT organization.

Productivity improvements are being focused on with much greater emphasis than in the past. This focus has defined many new technologies all with the promise of greater productivity. In order to reap the potential of these new technologies it is necessary to define a global plan that encompasses each of these technologies. Group Technology offers the glue or bond that should be utilized as the basis of the long-range productivity improvement plan, as it is the foundation for the automated factory of the future.

- - - - -

Earl R. Lewis is Vice President of Manufacturing for CIT-CRYOGENICS, a Division of Helix Corporation, located in Waltham, MA. Previously he was associated with Westinghouse Electric Company in a number of Materials Management positions, and with Alfa-Laval (a Swedish company) who owns manufacturing facilities worldwide. He spent two years in Europe working on numerous manufacturing assignments, including studies of Group Technology. He has implemented the Group Technology concept as a Line Manager in two factories - as Corporate Director of Manufacturing for Alfa-Laval (U.S.) and in his current position with CTI-CRYOGENICS.

Paul G. Conroy is a Management Consultant with Coopers & Lybrand in Boston, MA. He has specialized in manufacturing industry consulting for the past fifteen years. With this article he continues his interest in the relationship between work organization and production control that began with his 1975 article in PRODUCTION & INVENTORY MANAGEMENT - 4th Quarter, "Work Flow and Production Control."

Paul is a member of the North Shore Chapter, a past president and founding member of the New York City Chapter and he is certified by APICS at the Fellow level.

MODULAR PLANNING BILLS: THEY EXPLODE TO THE
BOTTOM LINE
James R. Schwendinger, CPIM
*SOM Associates, Inc.*

Planning bills of material remain one of the under
utilized techniques within materials management. Yet, the
potential benefits for companies who have a combination of
make-to-stock and assemble-to-order are substantial. Many
companies start out highly motivated with the knowledge
that the use of planning bills normally results in a
drastic reduction of the number of end configurations to
forecast and master schedule. This enthusiasm turns to
frustration when the practioner discovers that no one in
his company is willing to give up their end item bills or
is confortable with a two-level master scheduling process.
The objective of this paper is to clarify and simply the
use of modular planning bills of material to facilitate
master production scheduling.

THE CASE FOR ASSEMBLE-TO-NEED

Many manufacturing firms have found that the nature of
their business has changed over the years presenting a
whole series of new problems. The type of company referred
to here is the company that develops a relatively simple,
new product that is well received in the marketplace. In
the early days the product is only offered in one configuration. The company develops a strong customer service
orientation and adopts a make-to-stock, ship off the shelf
orientation. The company thrives with its new product and
grows. Before long either the customers or the product
engineers, or both, have identified and requested new
variations of the initial basic product. At the time, the
change seems minor, it doesn't significantly impact product
cost, and after all, it is a better product utilizing the
same technology the company has previously developed. The
new product variations are also treated as make-to-stock.

The process of creating product hybrids from the
initial product continues over the years with the same
basic product. Ultimately the company's view of the once
simple, basic product expands to a view of a product line
having the following options available:

    - Size:              6 available
    - Style:             3 available
    - Material:          2 available
    - Pressure Rating:   4 available

We all recall from some of the early classical bill of
material structuring articles that with this number of
options, and assuming none to be mutually exclusive, that
the total number of possible configurations were:

        6 x 3 x 2 x 4  =  144 possible configurations!

Like many companies, only a small percentage of the
possible options had actually been designed and sold. An
analysis of the sales history indicated that only 38 unique
part numbers had actually been sold.

The engineers had created 38 specific end item bills
of material. The company found that it no longer referred
to the basic product, but instead, now talked about the
product line. The company management now found that the
once easy to manage product was now a frequent topic of
discussion as a problem product line. Inventory levels had
increased significantly and customer service was now a
problem. Master scheduling was difficult to manage. There
really was no one factor leading to this change, but rather
a group of factors interacting with each other. The
typical causes are worth noting:

A.  Increase in competition
B.  Tendency to respond to customer requests for product
    variations
C.  Product configurations growing faster than share of
    market
D.  Significant increase in forecasting error for end
    items
E.  Continued emphasis as a make-to-stock product line
F.  Genuine improvements made by the engineers without

phase out of old designs
G.  Inability of planning systems to respond to changes
    in mix

If the above scenario sounds similar to your company
you are a candidate for using planning bills of material.
This particularly is the case if the company is able to
adopt an assemble-to-need orientation. Some products will
continue to be stocked in a finished, on-the-shelf condition with the significant portion stocked at the module
level with a short final assembly.

DEFINITIONS

One of the principle causes of confusion with regard
to planning bills is that there is a lack of standardization from company to company in the ways planning bills
are used and their terminology. Let's define some of the
terms:

Planning Bill     - An artificial grouping of items, in bill
                    of material format which is used to
                    facilitate master scheduling and/or
                    material planning. This definition is
                    highly generic to cover a broad spectrum
                    of interpretations and uses.

Figure #1 represents a typical Planning Bill in that
the bill relates a forecast for the product family XYZ to
specific end configurations within the family.

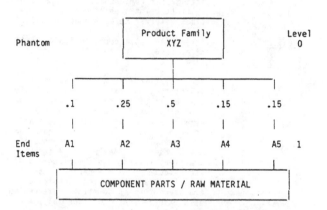

FIGURE #1

MODULARIZED BILL - A type of planning bill which is
                   arranged in product modules or options.
                   Often utilized where the products have
                   many options. Products are modularized
                   to facilitate master scheduling and to
                   ease the forecast task.

COMMON PARTS      - Type of planning bill which groups all
                    common components for a product or
                    family of products into one bill of
                    material. The segregation of common and
                    unique parts make it possible to mini-
                    mize inventory investment in common
                    parts and allow for different decisions
                    to be made for the unique parts nec-
                    essary to provide an acceptable level of
                    customer service.

SUPER BILL        - A type of planning bill, located at the
                    top level in the structure which ties
                    together various modular bills to define
                    an entire product or product family.

                    Quantity per relationship of super bill
                    to modules represents the forecasted
                    percentage popularity of each module.

                    Master scheduled quantities of the super
                    bill explode to create requirements for
                    the modules which are also master
                    scheduled. Figure # 2 is an example of
                    a super bill.

FIGURE #2

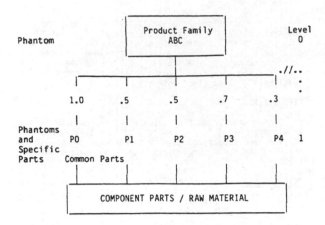

**PHANTOM**     - A non real item that appears within a planning bill. A phantom item receives special coding in the bill of material logic. A phantom item is not stocked, has no stock balance, zero lead time, and is planned for on a lot-for-lot basis. The planning logic drives the requirments straight through the phantom item to its components. A planning bill which contains a phantom item is sometimes referred to as a phantom bill.

**TRANSIENT**     - A real item that appears within a bill of material. The transient item is similar to the phantom item except that it is possible to have a stock balance for a transient item. The existance of inventory is unplanned and is normally the result of a production line change-over or salvage. The logic of MRP permits the netting of any occasional inventory against the gross requirements before exploding to the components of the transient. The lead time for the transient is zero and the planned orders are calculated on a lot-for-lot basis. A bill of material which contains a transient item is sometimes referred to as a transient bill of material.

WHY DO COMPANIES USE PLANNING BILLS?

Companies generally utilize planning bills for the following reasons:

° Ease the forecast problem

° Coordinate the product options

° Reduce the MPS volume

° Provide relief for order promising

° Improve flexibility

° Improve inventory management

° Address customer service problems

MODULARIZING BILLS OF MATERIAL

Modularizing the bills of material is a process of taking the end item bills and restructuring these bills to group the parts into logical modules. The objectives of modularizing the bills of material are as follows:

° To "disentangle" the product options

° To separate the common parts from those which are unique to specific end configurations

Each of these objectives has a different purpose:

° Disentangling is to facilitate forecasting

° Separating the common from unique is to minimize inventory of common parts and facilitate the use of safety stock for the unique parts.

THE TWO-LEVEL MASTER SCHEDULE

Many companies who are attracted to the benefits of utilizing planning bills have encountered difficulties in managing the planning process. This is particularly true for the mature company who has previously educated its employees and its customers with an end item, make-to-stock orientation. Within these companies there is strong resistance to changing from an end item approach. Frequently, these companies find that their forecast, when aggregated to the product family, are reasonably accurate. However, the individual end item forecasts within the product family experience substantial error on a part by part basis. This, in conjunction with the make-to-stock approach, results in excessive finished goods, and a lack of the components available to satisfy the requirements when needed due to the forecast error. The solution is to utilize planning bills and to modularize to permit forecasting and master scheduling at the options level.

In this way, the company can identify some popular items which should be stocked in anticipation of the arrival of demand from customers or distribution. These popular end items can be controlled with a time phased order point to maintain the appropriate end item stock. The time phased order point will generate replenishment orders for end items which must be used to consume the production forecast for the option modules. The success of this approach depends on:

- Capability to respond with quick final assembly upon receipt of the demand

- Location of the options within the bill structure

The technique for balancing the Production Plan and the production forecast for the option modules is a key element for maintaining planning integrity. Referring to Figure #2, the planning bill consists of a phantom part as the parent representing the product family ABC with a combination of phantoms and specific unique parts or subassemblies (PO, P1, P2, etc.) as the children. The relationship between the phantom parent and the components is expressed as a percentage reflecting each items' relative family popularity. In this manner, the popularity percentage is in reality a forecast. The popularity percentages should be revised as needed based on the projected change in mix within the product family. The Production Plan established for the product family ABC generates requirements for the options PO, P1, etc. as described in Figure #3.

FIGURE #3

| PRODUCTION PLAN | | 1 | 2 | 3 | 4 | Total |
|---|---|---|---|---|---|---|
| | | Weeks | | | | |
| XYZ PRODUCT FAMILY | | 40 | 40 | 40 | 40 | 160 |
| PLANNING BILL | Q/P | | | | | |
| PO | 1.0 | 40 | 40 | 40 | 40 | 160 |
| P1 | .5 | 20 | 20 | 20 | 20 | 80 |
| P2 | .5 | 20 | 20 | 20 | 20 | 80 |
| P3 | .7 | 28 | 28 | 28 | 28 | 112 |
| P4 | .3 | 12 | 12 | 12 | 12 | 48 |

The Production Plan for ABC is planned at a rate of 40 per week. The Production Plan for the phantom parent, ABC, will appear as follows in Figure #4.

FIGURE #4

| PRODUCT FAMILY ABC | Weeks | | | | | | | |
|---|---|---|---|---|---|---|---|---|
| | 1 | 2 | 3 | 4 | 5 | 6 | 7 | 8 |
| Production Plan | 40 | 40 | 40 | 40 | 40 | 40 | 40 | 40 |
| Demand | 18 | 6 | 12 | | | | | |
| Production Plan Coverage | 40 | 0 | 40 | 0 | 40 | 0 | -40 | -80 |
| Master Schedule | 80 | | 80 | | 80 | | | |
| Available to Promise | 56 | | 68 | | 80 | | | |

SCHD

DEMAND PEGGING

| DATE | CUST # | QTY |
|---|---|---|
| Wk #1 | 1-P1/P3 | 10 |
| Wk #1 | 2-P1/P3 | 8 |
| Wk #2 | 3-P2/P4 | 6 |
| Wk #3 | 4-P2/P3 | 7 |
| Wk ## | 5-P1/P4 | 5 |

Where:

P.P. Coverage = MPS - Production Plan

Available-To-Promise = MPS - Demand till next MPS

FIGURE #5

ITEM PO
100% of ABC FAMILY
PO is COMMON PHANTOM

| | Weeks | | | | | | | |
|---|---|---|---|---|---|---|---|---|
| | 1 | 2 | 3 | 4 | 5 | 6 | 7 | 8 |
| Service Forecast | | | | | | | | |
| Production Forecast | 56 | | 68 | | 80 | | | |
| Demand | 18 | 6 | 12 | | | | | |
| Proj. Available | 0 | 0 | 0 | 0 | 0 | 0 | 0 | 0 |
| Avail.-To-Promise | 56 | | 68 | | 80 | | | |
| MPS | 80 | | 80 | | 80 | | | |

DEMAND PEGGING

| DATE | CUST # | QTY |
|---|---|---|
| Wk #1 | 1-P1/P3 | 10 |
| Wk #1 | 2-P1/P3 | 8 |
| Wk #2 | 3-P2/P4 | 6 |
| Wk #3 | 4-P2/P3 | 7 |
| Wk ## | 5-P1/P4 | 5 |

The production forecast for the common parts phantom item, PO, is derived by exploding the ATP from the parent phantom item ABC. Since every customer demand scheduled will require one common parts, PO, item the ATP from ABC is directly transferable as the production forecast for PO. The ATP of the common parts is the same as the parent item, ABC.

FIGURE #6

ITEM P1
50% of ABC FAMILY
P1 is NOT STOCKED
No Service Requirements

| | Weeks | | | | | | | |
|---|---|---|---|---|---|---|---|---|
| | 1 | 2 | 3 | 4 | 5 | 6 | 7 | 8 |
| Service Forecast | | | | | | | | |
| Production Forecast | 28 | | 34 | | 40 | | | |
| Demand | 18 | | 5 | | | | | |
| Proj. Available | 4 | 4 | 5 | 5 | 5 | | | |
| Avail.-To-Promise | 32 | | 35 | | 40 | | | |
| MPS | 50 | | 40 | | 40 | | | |

DEMAND PEGGING

| DATE | CUST # | QTY |
|---|---|---|
| Wk #1 | 1-P1/P3 | 10 |
| Wk #1 | 2-P1/P3 | 8 |
| Wk #3 | 5-P1/P4 | 5 |

In Figure #6, item P1 is a non-stocked phantom with a 50% popularity. The ATP for ABC is exploded to P1 factored by the 50% quantity per. In the case of a phantom item, a positive projected available balance indicates overplanning on the part of the master scheduler. Likewise, the ATP will be larger than the 50% mix thus providing some additional availability should the 50% popularity percent be in error during this time. It should be pointed out though that the overplanning was only done via a positive act by the master scheduler.

FIGURE #7

ITEM P3
70% of ABC FAMILY
P3 is a STOCKED ITEM
Has Service Demand
OH = 70  SS = 5
OQ = 60

| | Weeks | | | | | | | |
|---|---|---|---|---|---|---|---|---|
| | 1 | 2 | 3 | 4 | 5 | 6 | 7 | 8 |
| Service Forecast | 2 | | | | 3 | | | |
| Production Forecast | 40 | | 47 | | 56 | | | |
| Demand | 19 | | 7 | | | | | |
| Proj. Available | 9 | 9 | 15 | 15 | 16 | 16 | 16 | 16 |
| Avail.-To-Promise | 51 | | 53 | | 60 | | | |
| MPS | | | 60 | | 60 | | | |

DEMAND PEGGING

| DATE | CUST # | QTY |
|---|---|---|
| Wk #1 | S-P3 | 1 |
| Wk #1 | 1-P1/P3 | 10 |
| Wk #1 | 2-P1/P3 | 8 |
| Wk #3 | 4-P2/P3 | 7 |

In Figure #7, item P3 is a stocked item with a current on-hand balance as well as service forecast. There is also a service order (S-P3) in week #1 to be serviced. Since P3 is a real part, the netting against its stock on hand must be done to derive the projected available balance. Note that P3 has a safety stock on the option to cover the uncertainty of the usage percent of P3 being in excess of 70%.

In this example, we are actually master scheduling at both the Production Plan level as well as the level 1 options and common parts modules. As additional demands arrive, the Production Plan for the family, ABC, is consumed utilizing one of the following forecast consumption rules:

° Current period consumption
° Cumulative consumption (Current, Past, Forward)

The entry of the demand will reduce the available-to-promise for the family ABC. This will likewise result in a change in the production forecast for the unique options and common parts module at level one of the planning bill. The key for maintaining balance of the plan at level 1 is to reexpress the actual demands for end items at the options level. In this manner the master scheduler can determine if he needs to respond due to an unexpected change in mix. If the customer service personnel are utilizing the ATP of the common and unique options at the time of order promising, the commitment date will have integrity. If the actual demands vary by more than the projected availability generated by overplanning or safety stock the master scheduler will know immediately of the problem for the specific option thus improving the chances of being able to respond.

SUMMARY

Planning bills offer a tool to improve inventory management and customer service for assemble-to-need companies. The techniques of managing the two-level master schedule require a change in thinking in contrast to traditional end item master scheduling approaches. The hurdles to overcome include both the re-education of people and creation of the system mechanics to create and maintain the planning. While planning bills offer benefits to many it is not a technique that is well suited to all situations. A careful analysis must be done to fully understand the true need as well as the essential elements. For those willing to do the homework to determine if the requirements match the capabilities, planning bills are a powerful management tool.

ABOUT THE AUTHOR

Mr. Schwendinger is Vice President of SOM Assocites, an international consulting firm specializing in materials management and located in Houston, Texas. He has a number of years of industrial experience concentrating heavily in manufacturing control systems and materials management. Previously, he was the Materials Manager for CAMCO, an oil tool manufacturer in Houston. He held serveral positions within the Management Systems and Manufacturing Operations organizations at TRW Mission. He began his career at U.S. Steel developing production and inventory control systems in Gary, Indiana.

Mr. Schwendinger is a graduate of the University of Wisconsin with a MBA with a concentration in production and operations management. His undergraduate was a Bachelor of Science degree in Economics from Carroll College in Wisconsin.

Mr. Schwendinger has been active in APICS for several years both as a speaker and in chapter management. He is a certified practitioner. He was a speaker at the 1978 International APICS Conference and is a frequent speaker at chapter meetings. He is a past president of the Houston APICS Chapter. He currently is serving as the Region VI (Southwest) Vice President and member of the Society Board of Directors.

Reprinted from *Production and Inventory Management*, Vol. 20, No. 4, 1979.

# OPTIMIZING INTERMITTENT PRODUCTION SYSTEMS THROUGH GROUP TECHNOLOGY AND AN MRP SYSTEM

Nallan C. Suresh

*Brakes India Ltd.     Madras, India*

The complexities of the functional layout based job shop environment have been confronted in recent years through two differing approaches. One approach has been through computer systems like the MRP and its priority planning extension to shop floor control; and the other has been through the replacement of the functional layout by a group layout and the implementation of Group Technology.

The first of these approaches, the implementation of an MRP system and its extension to shop floor control, has been more popular and widely implemented. However, establishing a successful MRP system in a majority of cases has not been easy. A great many of these systems are still "order launching systems, coupled with computer aided dispatching" and there have been a number of failures (1,2). This only highlights the inherent complexities of the batch production situation based on the functional layout, which involves the complex routings of components across the shop floor, complex interactions between jobs, etc.

An alternate approach has been the implementation of Group Technology (GT). GT involves among other changes, the adoption of the group layout—which is based on component families instead of machine families, as in functional layouts. This could be viewed as a somewhat radical change, considering the fact that the general approach to batch production operations through the use of the functional or process layout, has remained practically unchanged since the days of the Industrial Revolution (3). While GT had been propagated initially as more or less a panacea for the small batch/large variety situation, very few companies have actually implemented GT. But where implemented (e.g., Serck Audco, Ferranti of UK), the performance of GT has been indisputably successful. In the industrial nations, given such factors as increasing customer imposed product variety, smaller runs, and competitive pressures shortening lead times in recent years (4,5), GT was viewed as a new way to counter the diseconomies of larger variety/lower volume operations. But it has always been realized that GT as a technique is more appropriate for a low-technology context, as found in the less developed countries (LDCs) and has several limitations (6), which reduce its area of applicability. It had been pointed out for instance that (7), "the application of GT will grow in the smaller companies of the leading industrial nations or in those nations which have labor-intensive manufacturing industries."

The following sections which describe the operation of an MRP system in a Group Technology framework, are based on the personal experiences of the writer while implementing an MRP system in an automobile ancillary industry in India. The company caters to OEMs of automobiles, tractors, commercial vehicles, etc., in this country and to the spares and export markets. The manufacturing operations are based on what could be called a group layout. While there has been no explicit or systematic approach towards adopting a group layout, given the easily distinguishable component families, such a layout has evolved automatically. Superimposed on this, however, is a set of practices which would be more applicable in a functional layout. For instance, the manual Kardex-based planning system assumed like most manual systems, standard lead times for most components as one month (ordering is on monthly cycles). But the actual lead times, given the group layout, were much shorter. These and several other inconsistencies, by no means uncommon in the Indian engineering industry, can be resolved through a computer based MRP modified to operate in a GT context. The theoretical basis for such a system is outlined below.

## THE THREE ASPECTS OF GT IMPLEMENTATION

The implementation of GT involves primarily, 1) the changeover from process to a group layout, 2) establishing a Production Planning and Inventory Control system which would be compatible and optimal for operations based on a group layout (and which, as we shall show, is achieved through MRP), and 3) a scheduling and machine loading approach based on the GT concepts of tooling and material families, in addition to other factors such as machine and labor utilization levels.

The changeover from conventional process layout to a group layout and other changes, enable the extension of mass production economies to the batch production situation, which forms the ultimate objective with GT. In group layouts the arrangement of machines is based on component families instead of machine families as in functional layouts. For a given family of components, most or all operations are carried out within a particular group of machines, unlike functional layouts where a component has to travel to various departments for various operations. This not only leads to a simplified work flow and reductions in material handling, but also greatly reduced throughput times, which are more predictable than in process layouts; better delivery performance; reduced WIP; finished goods inventories; and easier control over shop floor operations.

The other benefits realized through GT include the considerable reductions in setting times, through machine loading based on tooling families and minimization of raw material wastages by application of the material family concept. Reduced manpower and documentation for Costing and Production Control is usually another advantage with group layouts.

To establish the group layout, the component families need to be identified. Various techniques are used, like Production Flow Analysis or the PFA (8), or one of the several component classification and coding systems such as Brisch, Opitz, SAGT (9) and also rule-of-thumb methods when the "component families are self-obvious" (10). Reference 11 describes a PFA of large quantities of uncoded components by computer sampling methods utilizing the BOM Processor and Routings master file. A systematic approach to GT along these lines also results in Design Rationalization and Variety Reduction.

Thus in a small batch/large variety situation, where the conditions are appropriate for GT, the optimal Production system consists of the following: a group layout; a "short cycle-flow control" approach for direct materials planning and ordering; and a scheduling approach based on tooling, material families in addition to other relevant factors. Burbidge (12) uses the OR technique of AIDA (Analysis of Interconnected Decision Areas) to substantiate the optimality of the above combination.

The following sections will be directed at the second of the above mentioned aspects, ie., the short cycle-flow control approach required in a GT situation and how this requirement is met by an MRP system.

### Short Cycle-Flow Control and Time Phased Requirements Planning

To establish the applicability of an MRP system in a GT context, a reconciliation of differing terminologies is in order.

The flow control approach refers to (13), "an ordering system based on the 'explosion' of a series of short term programmes . . . which is essential for the successful application of Group Technology." It is seen to approximate the Time Phased Requirements Planning approach, which involves the explosion of the Master Production Schedule using the Bills of Material. For GT, the flow control has been recommended in place of stock control, for various reasons. Stock Control refers to techniques like the Reorder Point. Basically, the need for flow control instead of stock control in group layouts is equivalent to the necessity for Requirements Planning instead of Reorder Point, for dependent demand items. This need also arises in group layouts due to the differing nature of operations.

The short cycle flow control, alternately referred to as the single cycle Period Batch Control, is defined as (14), "an ordering system of the flow control, single phase, single cycle type which is used mainly to control the ordering of materials and parts for assembled products to standard design in continuous or intermittent productions."

The key words in this definition are **flow control, short cycle,** and **single phase-single cycle.**

### Short Cycle—Flow Control

The necessity for short cycle ordering is due to the fact that in group layouts the throughput times are greatly reduced and are far more predictable than in functional layouts.

In functional layout the manufacturing lead times, which are long and uncertain, consist mostly of queuing times which could account for as much as 90% of the total cycle time. The lead times vary greatly depending on the priorities assigned to a given order. Thus, the planned lead times assumed in process layout-based MRP systems rarely coincide with the actual lead times. The lead times, which are fixed on a rough basis in functional layouts, are far more accurate and reduced in group layouts. This is due to the operation overlaps which can be effected within the GT cells. Material transfers between machines within the group may be in subbatches (or in the case of rush orders in single components). The throughput time is ≤ total operation times, whereas in process layouts this includes the sum of all operation times; the large queuing times; handling; and stage-by-stage inspection times. Delivery performance improves greatly, since machining and assembly can be carried out just prior to the date of need. And in-line with short cycle operations, short cycle ordering results in reduced WIP and finished goods inventories.

Reducing the cycle time (which is consistent with the objective in MRP systems to reduce the bucket size) results in greater precision in timing the orders and greater flexibility since firm orders need to be given only for the immediate period. However, in a GT context there are constraints with respect to minimizing the cycle time: 1) it should not be less than the longest throughput time; which is, of course, reduced in group layouts and 2) the proportion of setting times should not increase unduly. These constraints arise because of the single cycle ordering.

### Single Cycle—Single Phase Ordering

The inapplicability of classical EOQ/EBQ models for discrete demand situations has led to the development of several lot sizing models, which could be incorporated within an MRP system (15). But in a Group Technology context, it can be shown that the use of the EBQ or any other multi-cycle approach involving independent component lot sizing precludes or defeats the very purpose of GT application. Multi-cycle ordering requires the manufacture of components in quantities in excess of the immediate requirements. The residual inventories are in unbalanced sets for final assembly schedules and are vulnerable to engineering changes. Even in functional layouts, the independent component batching in an MRP system introduces this problem. While excelling with respect to timing of material orders and maintenance of relative priorities, the MRP with multi-cycle ordering introduces the problem of unbalanced sets and control over load inputs and planned sequencing (crucial for GT) become difficult (16). The utility of a single cycle approach—which has been confirmed in practical applications of GT—can be explained as follows.

For one thing, the diseconomies of a batch size other than the EBQ are only marginal over a wide range of batch quantities. Consider the EBQ model for instance. The cost functions, the set-up costs, inventory carrying costs and the total costs per unit with respect to batch quantity are as shown in Figure 1a. The total cost is seen to have a fairly well

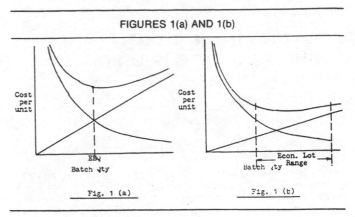

FIGURES 1(a) AND 1(b)

Fig. 1 (a)    Fig. 1 (b)

defined minimum point corresponding to the EBQ. But it has been shown that this function is very often flat in the vicinity of the optimal point and is relatively insensitive to batch size over a wide region (17). It has been proposed for instance that the use of an economic lot range, instead of a rigidly fixed batch quantity offers freedom and flexibility for the scheduler (18). This is seen in Figure 1b. Reference 19 illustrates a case where halving the batch quantity only results in a 0.1% increase in total costs. The implication of all this would be that considering the overall benefits of GT, "The gains when one changes from a multi-cycle to a single cycle system are far greater than any possible gains from varying the batch quantity" (20, 21, 22, 23).

In the above model, as in the several discrete demand lot sizing models, set up costs are assumed to be fixed costs, which is not valid in a GT context where the setting times are reduced sizably and in varying degrees, by planned loading sequences. It is well known in practice that the set up time for a given job can be greatly reduced if the job is similar, "toolingwise," to the previous job. Scheduling rules also exist, for example, which are analogous to the traveling salesman problem, to minimize the set up costs (24). In practical applications of GT, it has been found that the setting time reductions through sequencing based on tooling families have been substantial. The tooling families associated with the critical machines in each group are the vital ones.

Furthermore, it has been pointed out that the notion of the "batch" is somewhat restrictive in practice. This is especially true in a GT situation where material transfers are in subbatches between machines within the group (to effect operation overlaps and reduce the throughput time) and set-ups are "commonized" wherever possible for several batches, etc. In such a case, instead of the batch, "order quantity," "run quantity," "transfer quantity," etc. (12) would be more meaningful.

It follows that in a GT context, lot sizing on an item by item basis is an exercise in sub-optimizations which does not result in a total optimal system. And the achievement of GT has been to extend mass production economies to the batch production situation, enabling short and single cycle operations to be carried out economically.

### Shop Floor Control

The priority extension of the MRP system, in a job shop environment enables shop floor control, through the dynamic updating of priorities, subsequent to issue of production orders. An important aspect to be noted here is that priority is assumed to be equivalent or directly related to due-date. The relevance of this assumption and its requirement for a dispatching rule directly related to due dates has been questioned by New (16) in the case of functional layouts. In a GT context in place of the order due dates and the priorities derived from them, it is the planned loading sequence based on tooling families that is important. Furthermore, the whole approach to Production Control is different and simpler in group layouts. After the generation of Net Requirements schedules for all components (by an MRP system with single cycle ordering) these have to be classified on the basis of the groups within which they are machined. For the purposes of planning the loading sequences, sequence-codes could be developed. Alternatively, the list of components to be manufactured is issued to the groups and loading and control are left to the group personnel themselves. Firm orders need be given only for the immediate period and given the short cycle operations, the due date corresponds to the period-due. The calculation of capacity requirements and the reworking of the Master Schedule are much easier, given the absence of independent component lot sizing.

## GT-BASED MRP SYSTEM

Thus the operation of the MRP in a Group Technology framework (Figure 2) is affected by the following factors:

1. Manufacturing lead times are much shorter and more predictable than in functional layouts, where they are long and uncertain. Priority planning subsequent to production orders issue is obviated in group layouts.

2. The requirement for single cycle Period Batch Control form of ordering for all but a few items.

3. More ordered and streamlined work flow than in process layouts resulting in easier control, with less documentation and expediting requirements.

4. Reduced shop floor, other WIP and finished goods inventories and simplified materials movement and control; easier monitoring of scrappages, etc., contributing to greater accuracy of inventory records, which remains a problem in functional layout-based MRP systems.

The basic requirements of MRP like the proper structuring of the BOM, realism of the Master Schedule, and accuracy of records are unaffected.

The above factors make the experiences in Serck Audco, as related by Edwards (25) interesting reading. A more detailed account of the Audco experience is offered by Ranson (26) in his book on GT. The implementation of GT and the requirements imposed by GT on the material ordering system are described in detail. With the adoption of GT, organizational restructuring to form an integrated, materials management section independent of Sales and Works departments became necessary. (An integrated Materials Management form of organization has been found to contribute to the success of an MRP system even in a conventional intermittent production system: Ref. 27). The materials planning and ordering was based on a Time Phased Requirements Planning approach, using data processing methods. Through this overall approach to GT, the following results were achieved: sales increased by 67%; inventories reduced by 46%; manufacturing lead times reduced on an average from 12 to 5 weeks; dispatches per employee increased from £ 2218 to £ 4068; and average annual earnings increased from £ 714 to £ 1163.

## REFERENCES

1. Wight, Oliver. "How to Control Job-Lot Flow," *Modern Materials Handling*, September 1974.
2. Hall, Robert W. and Vollman, Thomas E. "Planning Your Material Requirements," *Harvard Business Review*, September/October 1978.
3. Burbidge, J. L. *Introduction to 1st International Conference on Group Technology*, ILO, Turin, Italy, 1969.
4. Starr, M. K. "Modular Production—A New Concept," *Harvard Business Review*, Vol. 43:6, November/December 1965.
5. Skinner, Wickham. "Production Under Pressure," *Harvard Business Review*, Vol. 44:6, November/December 1966.
6. Leonard, Raymond, and Rathmill, Keith. "Group Technology Myths," *Management Today*, January 1977.
7. Grayson, T. J. "Group Technology—A Brief International Appraisal," *Advances in Manufacturing Systems-Research & Development*, Ed. Prof. J. Peklenik, pp. 60, Pergamon Press, 1971.
8. Burbidge, J. L. "Production Flow Analysis," *Institution of Production Engineers Journal*, Vol. 42:12, 1963.
9. Abou-Zeid, Mohammed R. "Group Technology," *Industrial Engineering (AIIE)*, Vol. 7:5, May 1975.
10. Durie, F. R. E. "A Survey of Group Technology and its Potential for User Application in the UK," *Production Engineer*, March 1970.
11. Schofield, R. E., and Masey, N. C. "The Production Flow Analysis of Large Quantities of Uncoded Components by Computer Sampling Methods," *Development of Production Systems and the Need for Further Research—Proceedings of 2nd International Conference held at Copenhagen, Denmark* (London: Taylor & Francis), (U.S. distributor: Halsted Press), August 1973.
12. Burbidge, J. L. *The Introduction of Group Technology*. Heinemann, London, 1975.
13. Burbidge, J. L. "The Case for Flow Control," *Managing Materials in Industry*, Ed. Peter Baily and David Farmer. London: Gower Press, 1972.
14. Chapter on Period Batch Control, Reference, 12.
15. Orlicky, Joseph. *Material Requirements Planning*. N.Y.: McGraw Hill Books, 1975.
16. New, Colin. "MRP & GT—A New Strategy for Component Production," *Production & Inventory Management Journal*, 3rd Quarter, 1977.
17. Eilon, Samuel. "A Note on the Optimal Lot Range," *Management Science*, Vol. 7:1, 1961.
18. Solomon, Morris J. "Economic Lot Range," *Management Science*, Vol. 5, 1959.
19. Tate, T. B. "In Defense of the Economic Batch Quantity," *Operational Research Quarterly*, Vol. 15:4, 1964.
20. Burbidge, J. L. "Dragons in Pursuit of the EBQ," *Operational Research Quarterly*, Vol. 15:4, 1964.
21. Eilon, Samuel. "Dragons in Pursuit of the EBQ," *Operational Research Quarterly*, Vol. 15:4, 1964.
22. Duckworth, W. E. "Dragons in Pursuit of the EBQ," *Operational Research Quarterly*, Vol. 15:4, 1964.
23. Burbidge, J. L. "The Case Against the Economic Batch Quantity," *The Manager*, January 1964.

## FIGURE 2
## A GT Based MRP System

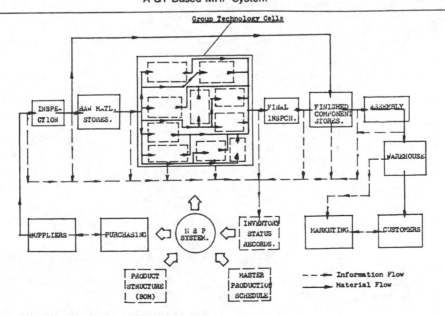

Group Technology Cells

- - - - ▸ Information Flow
──────▸ Material Flow

24. Johnson, Lynwood A., and Montgomery, Douglas C. *Operations Research in Production Planning, Scheduling and Inventory Control.* John Wiley & Sons, 1974 (Chap 5-2.6: Scheduling to Minimize Set-up Costs.)
25. Edwards, G. A. B. *Readings in Group Technology*, pp. 108, Chap. 8: "Some Practical Applications," United Kingdom: The Machinery Publishing Co. Ltd., 1971.
26. Ranson G. M. *Group Technology.* McGraw Hill Book Co. (UK), 1972.
27. See pp. 112, Reference 2.

---

**About the Author—**

*NALLAN CHAKRAVARTHY SURESH* is currently a Systems Analyst with Brakes India Ltd, Madras, India. He holds a Bachelor of Technology degree from the Indian Institute of Technology, Madras and an MBA from McMaster University, Hamilton, Ontario, Canada. Suresh is a member of the Madras Management Association, and a student member of the Indian Institution of Industrial Engineering (IIIE).

Reprinted from *Production and Inventory Management*, Vol. 25, No. 2, 1984.

# THE VENDOR-CUSTOMER RELATIONSHIP TODAY*

Dean Bartholomew

*Newell Window Furnishings*      *Freeport, IL*

## PREFACE

A great deal has been written within recent years with respect to the problems of American business, especially when compared to Japanese advances during the same period of time.

From a production and inventory control standpoint, two basic topics are invariably discussed: inventory and manufacturing throughput times.

Like so many other things, minimization of inventory in Japan was not so much a goal as a necessity. An economy devastated by a world war mandated strong controls over scarce resources, among them inventory. Not without significance was the lack of physical space in Japan, which necessitated supplier plants in close proximity to one another and the minimization of inventory for all concerned.

Necessity was the mother of invention. Vendor-customer relationships became close and intertwined to the point that customers began scheduling vendors just as they would another department.

The Kanban system of production and inventory control has generated much debate in this country as to the probability of its success within major American industries.

The success of Kanban is heavily dependent on a close vendor-customer relationship, to the point that single-sourcing in Japan is more often the rule than exception. Their business climate demanded it and the response was made.

The end of World War II created a substantially different business climate for American industry. Industry had geared up to support the war effort and, indeed, had awed the world with its ability to produce material and reduce lead times to get the material where it was needed faster. Kaiser, and his ability to produce—via his PERT methods—Liberty ships with lead times previously thought impossible, created a new school of thought. The war ended with capacity in U.S. industry at unheard-of levels.

Just as important, American industry had not suffered the devastation experienced by other economic powers such as England, France, Germany, Japan, the Soviet Union, Italy, etc. We had capacity to burn and, with our competitors devastated, set about supplying the world. The result was an economic boom for this country unparalleled in its history.

As profits rose, so did demands for wages, benefits, and work rule modifications. Union activity in the late 40s and early 50s rose with labor determined to share in the prosperity.

Truman's nationalization of the railroads was the most memorable of many confrontations. Most corporations were loath to endure substantial labor strife. Profit margins were high and the business climate was conducive to accommodation. It was during this period that many of the major work rule changes came about (e.g., restrictive job classifications, voluntary overtime, etc.). The profit situation allowed many companies to engage in what we recognize today were, and are, extravagant activities.

Oliver Wight told a story about being confronted by an executive who, in belittling the need for MRP, commented that his firm seemed to be making a pretty fair profit despite its absence. Mr. Wight's comment was "Yes, but I know your competitor." It was another way of saying that firms, and people, either go back or go ahead, but seldom stay the same. Many of the industrial giants of U.S. industry were content to pursue "business as usual" with wartime policies while at the back door foreign competition, which had been forced to innovate, began to knock. It is interesting to note that automotive involvement in the American Production and Inventory Control Society is a relatively recent phenomenon.

* This report is the result of a study funded by a research grant from the APICS Educational and Research Foundation.

So today the needs have changed. Necessity has again become the mother of invention; and American business has not stood still during the last twenty years.

During that time, APICS has developed into a viable organization. MRP is an American development.

To be sure, old dictums and philosophical points of view will need to be re-examined. One of them is the thrust of this discourse. Almost from the inception of MRP, the contention was that one should be able to give his MRP generation to his vendor and, in effect, schedule the vendor's shop. This is what the Japanese have done, and it is important to note that they did it with American tools. We will examine why that close relationship does not exist today and what the possibilities are that a change may come about in the future.

## THE VENDOR-CUSTOMER RELATIONSHIP TODAY

For most of the history of this country, American firms generally operated with single-sourcing policy. Logistics played a major factor in that policy decision. Vendors needed to be close at hand due to the nature and time of freight movement prior to the advent of the internal combustion engine. Thus, the vendor closest to the manufacturing facility, all other things being equal, likely would have been the vendor of record.

The turn of the century brought new and improved modes of transportation and substantially altered the equation. Speed of delivery and freight charges were no longer the prohibitive factors they once were. Now the key factors were pricing, delivery performance, and quality.

Because the logistics considerations had been substantially reduced, where there had once been one or two vendors (by virtue of their location), there might now be four or five, etc. It was readily perceived that this could provide the customer with a larger amount of leverage. This led to a new P&IC philosophy, still in vogue today, known as *Dual Sourcing.*

The central tenet of dual sourcing is to always have more than one vendor for the same item and to split purchase orders periodically between the two.

This, theoretically, provides the customer with a substantial amount of leverage over the vendor in terms of cost, delivery performance, and quality. During my professional years, a purchasing agent who did not pursue such a policy was regarded as, at best, inefficient or, at worst, criminal.

The fact is that this is probably the primary reason MRP integration between vendor and customer has yet to substantially occur in this country. Even more important, it has been the inherent factor in limiting stronger vendor-customer relationships.

Dual sourcing has advantages, most notably the ones previously described. The introduction of new inventory control techniques, among them MRP, has opened new vistas for controlling production and inventory. Their effective use will demand stronger vendor-customer interface. Dual sourcing does not lend itself to MRP interface. To achieve a successful relationship using MRP, the presumption is that the vendor will be given substantial insight into future customer requirements, which would allow him to minimize inventory and capital equipment requirements, level production, and convert that allowance into cost savings and improved delivery performance for the customer.

Dual sourcing assumes that material will be supplied by more than one vendor and orders will flow to one vendor or another in proportion to their price, quality, and delivery performance. Thus, commitments for future purchases will be limited and, by implication, so will the vendor's ability to reduce inventory and capital equipment requirements and convert that savings into reduced cost and increased vendor delivery performance.

Jack Hoyt (President, Durable Wire) in a recent article, made the following prophetic statement:

A quiet revolution in American business is enabling companies to slash inventories to a minimum and free millions of dollars in captive capital.

Using the computer as its primary tool and applying stringent scientific and management controls, the revolution also is forging new partnerships between suppliers and customers. New avenues of trust and cooperation are opening up, allowing progressive businesses to convert lumps of inventory stock piles into smooth flowing streams of material.

. . . . It seems inevitable that the next step will be for companies and their customers to participate together to control inventories.

What will be needed to make this combined operation successful is communication—the same free flow of information between two companies that exists between the departments of an individual company.

In essence, the supplier will need to be privy to his customer's history of operations and his projections. New avenues of trust and cooperation, which are beginning to open up, must be maintained. The entire system is based upon this partnership.

Everything is there for us to use and the benefits are ours to reap. If American industry does not choose to recognize materials control as a science to be used to its fullest as an instrument of management, there's a real danger that the footsteps we now hear behind us will soon be very far ahead.

In the following section we will examine the present-day situations of selected companies and their thoughts on the possibilities of increased vendor-customer relationships.

## STUDY GROUP ANALYSIS

In selecting a combination group of vendors and customers, the emphasis was to select companies with a demonstrated interest in "Just-in-Time" techniques. The vendor-customer relationship in Japan has been a key to their consistent productivity enhancements and consequent competitive edge. The philosophic difference from their American counterparts is easily demonstrated by comparing the number of Nissan Motor's suppliers (460) to Ford's (2,500). The basic difference is an increased willingness on the part of Japanese industry to engage in single-sourcing. 98% of Nissan's horns are produced by one vendor. This has allowed that vendor to engage in long-term research and development and capital equipment acquisition with the realization of productivity gains and cost savings for the customer. This type of relationship is not a Japanese invention. Single-sourcing was extensively practiced in the U.S. prior to the turn of the century, as discussed previously.

The fact that Japanese auto companies have been so successful in employing these techniques has led their American counterparts to be among the first to consider instituting them. Indeed, all of the major U.S. automotive firms profess to have an ongoing JIT program at this time. For that reason, study companies were selected from the auto industry and its suppliers. In using auto industry firms and their suppliers, other factors come into play as opposed to the rest of U.S. industry. A major question today, with respect to JIT in the U.S., is whether it will serve as an adjunct to MRP or become a total replacement of it. It is getting difficult to find a firm over $15 million in sales that does not either have MRP, is actively trying to install it, or has made the attempt and failed. The notable exception to this rule has been the auto industry.

Although time-phasing through a bill of material on a gross requirement basis is generally accomplished, netting of inventory during the throughput process is limited, leading to a substantial expedite mode. There appears to be a feeling in the industry that full MRP cannot be accomplished because of the large amount of SKU's and limited throughput time. One mid-level auto executive commented "MRP doesn't mean squat to us." Another executive with a major automotive supplier, who had been to New England to take Oliver Wight's executive courses, chastised him—and APICS—for preaching the gospel of MRP: "We're different." Poor Mr. Wight. How many times he had heard people say that. Shop floor control has been a problem with many firms approximating the auto industry, in terms of SKU's and throughput time, and has been successfully addressed through MRP.

The 1981 proceedings of a seminar sponsored by the Automotive Industry Action Group (then a committee of the Detroit Chapter of APICS) contained the following exerpt describing interplant shipments by U.S. auto firms:

Under scope, the shipping plan development is as volatile as the assembly plant's immediate needs. In some cases, the informal system—the phone call—becomes the best shipping plan. That is, when the assembly plant calls and says that they need 200 engines with air conditioning and manual shift by noon the next day or the assembly line will be shut down, the manufacturing plant's shipping plan immediately begins to develop.

The key word, of course, is "informal" (expedite, expedite, expedite). It has been said, by DeLorean among others, that one of the limitations facing U.S. auto industry is its degree of insulation. Mid and upper level management personnel have almost exclusively spent their careers at that particular firm with very little hiring done on the outside. GM even had, until recently, its own university.

On the supplier side, several firms utilize successful MRP systems.

Between the auto firms and their suppliers, nearly unanimous agreement exists that JIT could not operate on a stand-alone basis. Most felt a time-

phased system would also be required, for predominately logistics reasons. U.S. automotive suppliers are frequently not as geographically convenient as their counterparts in Japan and, thus, daily deliveries may be unavailable. A supplier in San Jose, California would probably be unable to deliver with the frequency of a vendor in Livonia, Michigan. Time, then, becomes a factor; hence the requirement to time-phase. It seems likely that companies considering adopting JIT techniques must assume their integration with some form of time-phase system. The question of whether suppliers will move closer to their customers will be addressed further on.

The auto firms studied, again, all stated that they were involved in implementing JIT techniques in varying degrees. Their level of activity frequently paralleled their willingness to discuss their program in detail. Those that had a substantial program tended to be very forthright in discussing it. Details on interviews and program review for two firms (General Motors and Deere & Co.) of the five studied (AMC, Ford, General Motors, Chrysler, and Deere & Co.) follow. General Motors is displayed because of its leadership in the industry.

Deere & Co. is displayed because it had far and away the most active program in terms of defined goals, assigned accountability, and demonstrated level of accomplishment.

### General Motors

In terms of the vendor-customer relationship, it should be remembered that GM has been a group of substantially autonomous divisions (Chevrolet, Pontiac, etc.). In terms of procurement these divisions have, up to this time, been allowed to operate fairly independently. An effort is now going on to institute a more cohesive structure. In terms of P&IC systems, they are somewhat home-grown within each division and integration is a major obstacle they are attempting to hurdle.

Primary emphasis for their JIT program is provided through the corporate materials management department, headed by Robert Stone. His thoughts as to what GM foresees in the future are illustrated in his comments to the Automotive News World Congress in 1982:

For the Just-in-Time system to work well, an integrated supplier approach is necessary. This means several things:

1. Selection of suppliers early in the design stage with full supplier participation in the design process to insure that the designs incorporate the best technology, are economically produceable, and require minimum investment.
2. "Family of parts" sourcing to concentrate and take advantage of expertise.
3. Supplier process controls and quality certification must be in place in order to achieve the improvement in quality that is essential.
4. Long-term relationships to encourage mutual cooperation and capital investment with cost analysis-based price negotiations and last—a reduction or elimination of routine paperwork such as shippers, receiving slips, and invoices.

Over a number of years this approach will naturally result in a smaller supplier network. This means tremendous opportunity for growth for those suppliers who can improve their quality control costs and provide Just-in-Time delivery. We believe that those suppliers who adopt a total process approach, including the Just-In-Time system for their own operations are the ones who will succeed.

The following comment should also be noted:

An added benefit of Just-in-Time systems is a reduction of computer and people required to support the production process. In the Japanese automotive world there are no inventory records for parts and no expeditors to follow shipments. Our Japanese competitors get by with a small fraction of the head count we use for production and material control and logistics functions.

Interviews with mid-level materials management personnel elicited the following:

1. GM has made substantial gains in inventory reductions (overall inventory turns have increased from 4.5 to 6). However, inventory reduction is really the icing on the cake and their main goal is improved productivity.
2. There will not necessarily be a major shift in inventory to GM's suppliers. GM desires, more than anything else, increased flexibility from their suppliers. It is expected that the number of suppliers will be reduced. GM wants to go to "family of parts" sourcing where similar parts would go to the same vendor.
3. In response to a question as to whether GM would do more outsourcing and sub-contracting, the question was avoided and it was stated that they have no contractual agreement not to outsource

but that the union has the opportunity to provide concessions to keep the business.

4. GM's inventory in assembly is presently averaging 10–11 days.
5. Just-in-Time would not be more difficult to implement in a heavily unionized Michigan environment, but easier because of all the staff support available. They are presently using a test Kanban system with one outside vendor and one internal manufacturing department and both were successes to date.
6. With respect to corporate attitudes, two years ago 95% of the corporation didn't believe JIT existed in the real world. Today, 80% now believe it can work.
7. On the subject of warehousing, the Toyota concept that the size of warehousing for manufacturing purposes should be zero was brought up. When asked if GM was pursuing that policy, it was felt they were sending mixed signals. They had recently built three assembly plants with substantially large stores capacity that were clones of the Oklahoma City plant which was designed in the late 60's. They are now trying to bring in fabrication operations to use the stores areas for other purposes. Future plants are being designed without storage space.
8. With respect to top management commitment, it was felt that they had blessed it but were not heavily involved and didn't necessarily understand it. Mid-level management involvement and support is extremely heavy.
9. As to supplier involvement, a large quantity are interested in Just-in-Time but have a lot of concern about inventory being shifted to them.
10. Disagreement was displayed with the contention that vendors need substantial insight into their customer's future to make Just-in-Time work effectively. It was felt that GM intended to continue their policy of no firm vendor commitments beyond 13 weeks.
11. GM's manufacturing systems are home-grown division packages that do not interface.
12. Purchasing activities are presently decentralized, which was felt to be a disadvantage in terms of JIT.
13. With respect to daily line mixing to provide stability to the vendor, GM produces each model on a daily basis, with the exception of color, because of the expense and quality problems associated with a paint line change. Vehicles with a high labor content are more interspersed (i.e., they are not produced on Monday and Friday due to a higher rate of absenteeism).

GM apparently has several active JIT test sites (Buick is the one most frequently mentioned) making it one of the few companies that has taken their program off the drawing board to any great degree.

## Deere & Company

Deere & Company's JIT program represented a dramatic departure from others in several notable areas, including long-range planning, top management commitment, and program institution beyond the design stage.

Emphasis was initially placed on phased program development. A formal program was then submitted to the corporate board of directors along with relevant cost considerations. The program was subsequently approved by the board of directors and executive staff and approximately $2 million allocated for development and implementation. At no other firm reviewed was such a review structure and formalized top management commitment visible. It should be noted that Deere also displayed the most concrete implementation activity as opposed to other review sites. For example, part of the allocated expenditures are to convert their Horicon, Wisconsin facility (which produces their lawn and garden implements) to a full Just-in-Time program. At other firms with internal test sites, testing was limited to selected departments rather than a plant-wide approach. Also, very few firms had internal test sites where they were attempting to employ JIT techniques. Most were concentrating on the external supplier side with an eye toward raw material inventory reductions. Lip service was usually paid to attacking the shop floor "down the road" but a formal plan was seldom in evidence.

Interviews with executive level materials management personnel elicited the following comments and perceptions on the future of vendor-customer relationships and Just-in-Time at Deere: Richard Wharton, Corporate Director/Materials Management:

Deere is presently turning inventory six times annually which is a somewhat lower figure than the previous year due to sales projection shortfalls. Deere's goal is to increase turns to twelve.

With respect to JIT, its implementation does not mandate a shift in inventory from customer to supplier. The objective is to achieve least total cost. JIT does not also imply a trend toward increased outsourcing. It will definitely result in a reduction of the total number of suppliers (as an example, Deere has reduced the number of coil steel vendors from six to three). More coordinated purchasing *negotiation* will increase as a result.

Deere is making a concerted effort to reduce their inspection force through improved quality control at the source.

Geography may be a factor in successfully implementing a JIT program (i.e., it may be easier to install in Mississippi than Michigan).

Using Kanban cards to trigger a vendor shipment would be an archaic approach as opposed to some form of electronic trigger.

Some form of centralized stores must remain in selected factories, in Deere's case, because of seasonality and volume considerations.

Deliberate restriction of warehouse space is not necessarily an ideal approach, but enlightened facilities design should take into account inventory turn projections.

With respect to project team operation and top management involvement relative to JIT, a full-time project team is in place and heavily involved in implementation. Top management involvement is extensive and knowledgeable.

As to whether vendors should be allowed increased visibility into their customer's future requirements, Deere is presently providing twelve-month rolling schedules to selected suppliers.

Deere is working toward a closer relationship with their vendors, but *dual-sourcing* will remain for a period of time. The vendor-customer relationship in the U.S. is still more adversarial than it is in Japan. In Deere's case, they are single-sourced in too many areas.

### Ron Sonnenburg, Manager/Production Control:

Just-in-Time's future relationship at Deere will be as an adjunct to MRP rather than a replacement to it.

Deere will concentrate on interdepartmental implementation first and then work on supplier installation. There will eventually be a substantial reduction in the number of Deere suppliers.

Deere will not engage in a deliberate reduction of space to force down inventory levels.

MRP and JIT must work in tandem at Deere because there are some jobs that must be run in a batch mode, thus negating the desirability of JIT.

Electronic order releasing, both internally and externally, is a major goal.

Deere is working toward container configurations that will make it easier to perform inventory checks.

There will probably be a trend toward suppliers locating physically closer to their customer. Many vendors, however, will trend toward setting up warehouses rather than production facilities and, in that situation, it's questionable how much cost improvement would result.

For many vendors outside the Quad-City area (that individually don't have sufficient *daily* trailer volume) Deere has established daily or weekly in-bound freight consolidation. In some cases, Deere sends out their own trucks to multiple vendors on a daily basis to make pickups, or uses them to pick up freight from consolidation points.

There are four desired alternatives:

1. Daily delivery from an adjacent vendor.
2. Customer sends out consolidation trucks on a daily basis.
3. Supplier consigns inventory on the customer's premises. Customer only pays for inventory as it's withdrawn.
4. Merchandise is bought in quantity, stored *off-site* at *rented* warehouses and then brought in as needed.

Just-in-Time may imply a partial shove-back of inventory to the suppliers, particularly in the early stages of JIT involvement.

Deere's master scheduling is presently decentralized, but they are gearing toward a more coordinated approach in the distant future where indicated by capacity constraints and interfactory supply relationships.

With respect to increased outsourcing as a result of JIT, such a situation presently exists in Japan. However, the existing adversary aspects of vendor-customer relationships in the U.S. will probably continue for some time, limiting extensive outsourcing. This might change over a lengthy period of time.

Deere is monitoring developments in bar-coding. They are currently doing extensive processing via magnetics. Long term, they believe bar-coding will assist in linking-up with suppliers, getting the paper off the shop floor, and reducing operator input.

### Terry Carlson, Corporate Purchasing Manager:

There has generally been no supplier resistance toward Just-in-Time at Deere, but certainly a lot of questions. It will initially cause suppliers to carry more inventory for Deere. There will be a trend toward moving inventory closer to the customer, but not necessarily production.

Deere is presently designing a purchasing system that will accommodate direct data hookups to their suppliers. This would allow an expansion of providing extended forecast information to their suppliers.

There will ultimately be a trend toward single-sourcing, but the dual-source philosophy is deeply ingrained in American business ethic. Thirty percent of Deere's purchased items are presently single sourced.

Deere is looking toward more statistical process control but haven't yet asked their suppliers to commit to it. They intend to institute a *certification* process relative to the JIT program. For a supplier to be involved in the program, he would have to be certified by Deere. Criteria for certification would include quality, timeliness of delivery and, possibly, logistic convenience.

In the U.S., vendor negotiation may become more centralized eventually, but will remain substantially decentralized for the near term. Corporate at Deere presently acts as a catalyst and support organization, but sourcing and price negotiation are the responsibility of operating units using the lead factory concept.

Deere plans to involve their suppliers more in the design stages than they do today. "Quality Conferences" have already been instituted with select suppliers.

Greater emphasis will also be placed on bar-coding for manufacturing purposes which will result in substantial involvement on the part of Deere's suppliers.

Deere has examined direct department receipts of raw material as opposed to receiving it through a centralized stores area and then forwarding it to the department and does not intend to pursue at this time.

Frank Becker, Manager/Operations Research:

Deere has substantial executive involvement in the JIT program through their Productivity Quality Group which is made up of corporate directors and vice-presidents from all areas (except Marketing) and has direct oversight.

Five plants are presently involved in JIT testing (Lawn and Garden, Engine, Component, Harvester, and Plow and Planter Works).

Project effort is spaced over a fifteen-year period. With respect to organization, structural and jurisdictional changes are anticipated.

An education program has been developed as part of the implementation. The program consists of three modules and is slide/tape oriented. The first module illustrates the problems Deere faces in the marketplace today. The second module shows the new directions Deere is charting to meet these problems. The third is an appeal for help and a request for patience while changes are going on.

Other existing JIT projects include:

1. Overhead impact study
2. Aggregate lead times study
   a. Should there be leadtime *goals*
3. Multiple front-end tracking
4. Data *reduction* analysis
5. Machine readable study (bar coding)

Reading these comments, one gets the impression of a well-planned program on its way to becoming reality. The level of commitment displayed at the executive level serves to reinforce the program and advance it to the degree shown.

## Suppliers

To insure candor and eliminate the possibility of customer intimidation, suppliers were assured their corporate names would not be published in connection with the study. Four suppliers were reviewed on-site. A further six were reviewed through correspondence. All serve the automotive and agricultural industry. All are located in the Detroit area.

As might be anticipated, there was supplier concurrence in many areas with respect to JIT and the future of vendor-customer relationships. Areas of disagreement were also in evidence.

Two supplier interviews will first be presented and then the results of a questionnaire will be reviewed:

Supplier I:

Suppliers will be forced to carry more inventory for their customer unless they also go to some form of Just-in-Time.

Increased outsourcing by the automotive industries is likely to occur. Increased single-sourcing is mandated by JIT. The supplier pros to this are:

1. Early design development
2. Closer relationship to customer
3. Expanded visibility into customer's planning horizon

With respect to the last item, two major auto firms, with active JIT programs, have been less than forthcoming.

Customers with JIT programs must gear toward "gateway" production. JIT's effectiveness will be limited without it.

To support this kind of program, electronic purchasing linkage will be essential between the vendor and customer.

Our firm will build no more plants with large centralized stores areas. We are presently providing direct receipts to manufacturing departments of one major agricultural implement company.

Our customers are presently pressing us for:

1. Zero defects
2. Just-in-Time delivery
3. Statistical Process Control
4. Zero cost increases

We are pressing them for:

1. Greater visibility into their planning horizons
2. Increased demand stability
   a. Our customers have not improved in mixing line production to insure consistent demand such as the Japanese auto firms have.

Our customers are involving us more in design stage planning.

The "little job shop guy" will not be around in the future.

We must go to Just-in-Time to compete. However, JIT will have to co-exist with MRP especially with respect to the shop floor.

Just-in-Time must have total employee involvement to implement. It will be tougher to install in Michigan. The UAW is presently a problem.

We are presently pursuing QC at the source with our vendors and are attempting to reduce our inspection activity on the shop floor.

Limiting stores areas to force inventory down is a logical concept.

Our top management is heavily involved in our JIT program and are making presentations to our employees as well as conducting discussions.

Reducing the supplier base is essential for us also. As an example, we have reduced our casting suppliers from 112 to 50.

Purchasing activity should be *centralized.*

Nothing is sacred with respect to out-sourcing for our firm. We are seeing increased out-sourcing activity from one auto company.

We are one of five or six auto suppliers with JIT programs. Most have yet to become active internally.

JIT will be different in the U.S. Suppliers will *not* move their plant facilities closer to the customer.

Engineering standards on the part of the customer must stress conformity. If one varies, all must.

Forecast accuracy on the part of our customers would have to be characterized as poor.

We are presently consigning inventory to selected customers.

Supplier II:

Most of the auto firms are presently trying to use JIT to reduce inventory rather than change processes internally. One is making significant strides internally.

Telecommunication interface between vendor and customer will be required to support JIT.

Present visibility into our customer's planning horizon is minimal.

Buying procedures from our customers still tend to be fragmented.

We don't anticipate that the auto firms will increase their outsourcing activity in the foreseeable future.

Our response to being asked to move plant facilities closer to support daily shipment to customers is, "fat chance."

We believe the auto companies will stay with a centralized receiving function.

We have yet to see increased demand stability from our customers, which is a prerequisite of JIT.

Unions, per se, are not an inhibiting factor to JIT implementation.

Just-in-Time will not replace MRP, but co-exist with it.

As to whether or not we would consign inventory, our response is also, "fat chance."

With respect to deliberately cutting storage space to cut down inventory, many of us agree with it, but our top management is still sitting on the fence.

Purchasing negotiation should be centralized.

We plan on reducing our inspection force, but expect great resistance. We are pressing our vendors for increased Q.C. at the source.

Two of the major auto companies are using standardized containers that assist in performing inventory counts.

Suppliers are presently skeptical that the auto companies will fulfill their commitments in terms of Just-in-Time.

### Questionnaire/Survey Results

| Question | Response | |
|---|---|---|
| | *Yes* | *No* |
| 1. Does "Just-in-Time" imply a shift in inventory from customer to supplier? | 100% | 0% |

*Comments:*
a) "If you mean inventory in the short term, yes. Over a longer term (4–6 years) the entire supplier chain will operate with less inventory than currently."
b) "The concept of JIT does not imply a shift of inventory responsibility from customer to supplier. However, in practice, domestic manufacturers have been far more concerned with achieving their own individual cost reductions than increasing the productivity and cost effectiveness of the domestic industry as a whole. They tend to simply push inventory back through the pipeline."

| Question | Response | |
|---|---|---|
| | Yes | No |
| 2. Do you foresee a trend toward increased out-sourcing? | 83% | 17% |

*Comments:*
a) "New products like specialty steel and plastics and electronic components which require large initial capital investment will probably be outsourced. Products for which customer facilities already exist may well tend to be in-sourced unless the supplier can guarantee price advantages over the long term."

| Question | Response | |
|---|---|---|
| | Yes | No |
| 3. Will "Just-in-Time" result in more single-sourcing? | 86% | 14% |

*Comments:*
a) "Not so much single sourcing as fewer sources for the same items or commodities. The OEM's will continue to exercise pricing leverage by having more than one supplier."
b) "High value, quality intensive products will be prone to single sourcing. Low value commodity-type products will continue to be dual sourced to maintain price leverage on the suppliers."

| Question | Response | |
|---|---|---|
| | Yes | No |
| 4. Do you anticipate a trend toward suppliers moving their plant facilities logistically closer to their customers? | 57% | 43% |

*Comments:*
a) "Yes, or suppliers providing warehouses closer to the customers."
b) "The really aggressive supplier who wishes to "lock-up" a specific customer will at least open nearby warehousing facilities in return for long term purchase commitments. As the relationship grows, the supplier will see the benefit of converting such warehousing into highly focused, small manufacturing facilities. In general, however, relocation will not be a prerequisite of JIT participation."

| Question | Response | |
|---|---|---|
| | Yes | No |
| 5. Do you see a trend away from a centralized stores function? | 86% | 14% |

*Comments:*
a) "Eventually, yes. Requires a whole new approach toward quality assurance and manufacturing processes."

| Question | Response | |
|---|---|---|
| | Yes | No |
| 6. Do you believe direct receipts into manufacturing will eventually replace the traditional receiving function? | 29% | 71% |

*Comments:*
a) "Not in the USA, except in a very few cases where products are very simple."
b) "At the customer level, yes. The supplier, however, will have to exert much more influence over the process of *his* suppliers before direct receipts into manufacturing are feasible. A major issue for many first-tier suppliers will be that the second-tier supplier may be larger and less automotive oriented than his customer. So, the first-tier supplier may never be able to influence the process sufficiently to allow direct receipts."

*Question*
7. What are your customers asking from you today?

*Comments:*
a) "Daily, rather than weekly, shipments."
b) "Price, quality, delivery. Some *talk* JIT."
c) "Greater process capability, more schedule flexibility, lower price.

*Question*
8. What would you like to see from them in return?
a) "Minimal schedule changes, improved planning dialogues, and understanding the supplier's processes, lead time, and financial commitments."
b) "Higher market share."
c) "Improved forecast visibility."
d) "Greater commitment to the principles of JIT at the middle management level, not just at the top and on the banquet circuit where it sounds good."

| Question | Response | |
|---|---|---|
| | Yes | No |
| 9. Are you participating in design stage planning with any customer? | 100% | 0% |
| 10. Do you feel "Just-in-Time" is a viable philosophy in U.S. industry.? | 100% | 0% |
| 11. Are you presently using an MRP system? | 86% | 14% |

## CONCLUSIONS

With reference to the future of vendor-customer relationships, it would appear from both sides (supplier and customer) in the auto industry that there is substantial concurrence that Just-in-Time is a viable manufacturing philosophy. As a result, vendor-customer relationships will likely evolve into something substantially different from what we see today.

It seems clear that JIT will not replace MRP but serve as an adjunct to it. As evidenced by supplier comments, vendor plant moves closer to the customer's site will occur over a lengthy period of time, if at all. This translates into the likelihood that at least a portion of a customer's supplier base would be unable to make daily, or "Just-in-Time" deliveries. Thus, time-phasing becomes a requirement and reinforces the need for MRP to co-exist with Just-in-Time.

To support a Just-in-Time situation, the trend toward single-sourcing is equally clear. Just-in-Time deliveries require an extremely close relationship between vendor and customer in terms of interface. Dual sourcing would severely inhibit the ability to communicate on a close basis.

Supplier bases will be reduced. Those suppliers that remain will probably be the ones that can do at least a portion of the following:

1. Interface electronically with their customer (purchase transactions, bar coding, etc.)
2. Make Just-in-Time deliveries
3. Perform quality control at the source
4. Move their facilities logistically closer to their customer

For the supplier to provide these benefits to the customer, and remain profitable, they must insist on the following:

1. Long-term commitment
2. Substantial insight into the customer's planning horizon
3. Demand stability in terms of mixing production (i.e., producing a model daily instead of every other week)

For these changes to occur, the adversary relationship that exists today between vendors and customers must change to one of partnership.

Finally, to effect changes of these proportions will require more than a segmented commitment. A customer cannot demand philosophic change from his vendor without embracing it himself for the program to have a reasonable chance for success.

Despite these changes, U.S. vendor-customer relationships will never mirror Japanese, just as our societies do not mirror each other. For these changes to be successful, as the Deere program exemplifies, the key is to analyze, test, and modify as needs dictate; and, above all, get executive commitment. As the saying goes: "Without a foundation, the house will fall."

Reprinted from *Production and Inventory Management*, Vol. 20, No. 2, 1979.

# THE CONTRIBUTIONS OF MATERIAL REQUIREMENTS PLANNING (MRP) TO BUDGETING AND COST CONTROL

Robert J. Campbell
*Miami University      Miami, FL*

Thomas M. Porcano
*Miami University      Miami, FL*

The cost accountant today should seriously consider the opportunities for improved budgeting and cost control offered by new production and materials management systems. These systems, made possible by high speed electronic data processing equipment, emphasize large volume of data and rapid updating of information. There is commonality of data as computer data files are available to all users, the accounting department as well as the production scheduling and materials management personnel. The challenge to the cost accountant is to integrate the data generated by production and materials management systems into the budgeting and cost control functions actively supported by the firm's accounting department.

## The Materials Requirements Planning System

A relatively new and important production and materials acquisition system is materials requirements planning (MRP). This computer-based system is concerned with maximum efficiency in the timing of ordering raw materials from vendors to be used in the production process and ordering the machining and/or assembly of component parts needed in the assembly of the final manufactured product. The objective of MRP is to minimize on-hand physical stocks of raw materials and component parts while providing assurance of the availability of needed stocks for planned production runs with a high degree of confidence. The results obtained should include:

1. minimal dollars tied up in on-hand inventory;
2. fewer production run disruptions due to stock-outs of required material(s);
3. reduction of added costs associated with rush or expedited orders both from vendors and within the firm's own shop;
4. reduction in handling costs of orders as a result of advance planning on order release;
5. reduction in storage costs associated with inventories.

MRP is an inventory control system which is suited for manufacturing firms whose products are machined and assembled in stages. Assuming that production scheduling is carried out to time periods in excess of lead times on manufacturing of component parts and that demand is based on reasonably reliable forecasts, MRP can make a significant contribution to planning for materials and component parts order release timing.

Ideally, we would like to have added to stock those raw materials and/or components just prior to the point of time (day or week) when they are required for use in actual production runs. The MRP system is based on the concept that final product assembly is tied to *independent* customer demand while raw materials and components requirements represent a *dependent* demand since the proportion or amounts of these items going into final products are known. Once we know the time schedule for final product assembly, the computer MRP program can "explode" this production schedule back in time to develop dependent demand schedules for materials and components.

The requirements for "exploding" the production schedule into meaningful information on material and component acquisition are as follows:

1. a reliable and up-to-date production schedule detailed by product or product grouping;
2. knowledge of reliable lead times for acquisition of raw materials from vendors and fabrication of component parts plus assembly in the factory;
3. bills of materials with up-to-date engineering specifications.

The MRP system produces time-phased records for each component part or raw material by specifying for a series of time periods (weekly over the next year, for example) various items such as (1) stock requirements by week, (2) scheduled receipts or completion of component parts, (3) planned on-hand inventory and (4) planned order releases for specific time periods.

The output of MRP systems is a forecast of the physical status of specific products which are planned to be in varying stages of completion plus the forecasted level of raw materials at various points in time. Thus, aggregating the individual product forecasts provides us with the opportunity to forecast standard cost of goods sold, work-in-process, and raw materials inventory directly from production schedules where a standard cost system is in use.

## Budgeting in an MRP Environment

Utilizing the MRP system as a budget generating device would not only provide more accurate predictive capability than current approaches based on trend analysis or percentages of sales, but would also provide the discipline necessary to insure that continuous review would depend more on computer system promoting than human prompting. An inventory addition (including in-process and finished goods) and cost of goods sold budget could be generated periodically by the MRP system. This budget would be based on the *forecasted* production schedule with specified completion dates plus standard costs and would provide management with a reliable preview of the investment in inventories and cost of sales at numerous points in the future.

## The "MRP Budget"

The MRP budgeting process would begin just as most of the current "planned" budget processes. This would entail the following:

a) **Sales forecast:** A forecast of sales by product in units and dollars would be prepared. In large organizations, this forecast could be further divided by territories; in organizations having only a few major buyers, the breakdown could be by customer, product, etc. In any case, the sales forecast should be broken down in such a way that it insures ease of entry to the MRP system. For example, if there are numerous plants throughout the country, the expected sales should be matched as nearly as possible with the appropriate plant.

b) **Production forecasting:** To simplify our discussion, we will assume that the sales forecast is within the strategic and financial objectives established by top management. An additional assumption is that the capability exists to simultaneously perform "MRP budget" processing and "MRP actual" processing. This is a critical assumption for firms that already have an established MRP system because preparation of the "MRP budget" may require computer work and computation which cannot be permitted to contaminate the data used for the ongoing MRP system in its capacity as a production and materials acquisition support system.

Once the sales forecast has been thoroughly evaluated and refined, the production manager will review the forecast to determine if it is within the physical capability of manpower, plant, and equipment. It is during this review process that the expended capability of an MRP system will begin to illustrate its use as a planning device.

If the sales demand is fairly steady during the forecast period, then the initial computer calculations for MRP would serve to highlight excessive or deficient capacity. The production manager may provide to the computer such constraints as capacity limits at each work load centre and tentative production schedules by week over a selected future time period such as one year. The production schedules will have to include forecasts for individual products or product groups. These forecasts will be based on estimated sales and desired delivery dates if

Reprinted, with permission, from the January-February 1979 issue of *Cost and Management.*"

known. The MRP program will print out a schedule of peak demands on key work centres indicating whether or not the proposed production schedules violate capacity constraints.

The computer-based MRP computations are based on minimal lead times. Therefore, the production manager may stretch out production schedules to work within capacity constraints, assuming that later completion and delivery dates would be acceptable to the marketing department. An alternative would be to adjust capacity.

If sales are lumpy, which is more likely, then it is highly probable that work centre capacity would be exceeded by demand at some points during some time periods while excess capacity would be available at these same points at other times. In this situation, the initial "MRP budget" results would provide data to assist the production manager in analyzing work centre loads and capacity requirements planning. The production manager could then make adjustments to work centre loads to insure the best use of capacity while remaining within the sales forecast requirements. Once this has been done, probably through several more calculations of the master production schedule program, the MRP budget may still indicate under- or over-capacity demands. If we continue to assume the validity of the sales forecast, then the appropriate recommendation, i.e., decrease or increase capacity, modification, etc., should be forwarded as an attachment to the MRP budget for financial and top management review.

c) **Financial and top management review:** This is perhaps where the MRP system, as a budgeting device, will prove to be most useful. The potential of the MRP system for improving the production forecast has been briefly discussed above. However, while the production department is concerned with costs, it would still, for the most part, be using the MRP system as a predictor of unit requirements. If we assume that as part of the "revised bill of material" we add all assignable costs such as dollar value of material, labor variable and any other costs that can be associated with the production of specific units, we would have something that might be better called a "bill of costs."

The vastly improved data base of the MRP system which permits easy tracking of the inputs to a specific end item would also permit easy tracking of all related costs. Therefore, when the MRP budget results are presented for review along with sales dollar forecasts, top management would have documentation which greatly increases the visibility of financial success or problem areas. For example, as mentioned earlier, excessive or deficient demand may occur at certain work centres or throughout the entire plan. In a deficient demand situation, top management could use the cost data as indicators of which area(s) the R&D and the marketing departments should research for new product development to make better use of the deficient capacity. In excessive demand situations, they could use these same cost data to determine whether recommended expansion actions would prove profitable.

Other applications of the MRP system would lie in product continuation decisions. For example, under the old economic order system some products may have become progressively more expensive due to maintenance of costly inventories. With the reduced inventory costs resulting from the MRP system, some products that would have been dropped based on the older cost programs will be continued. This could be very critical in situations where the unprofitable product was a major contributor to a firm's reputation and assisted in bringing in other orders. On the other hand, by using a "bill of cost," especially one revised with the most likely values for the budget period, the "MRP budget" will also assist in identifying those items which have greatly decreased in profitability. Thus, current products can be analyzed for price increases, modifications or outright deletion.

We have attempted to depict one possible flow sequence of the "MRP budgeting process" in Figure 1. This exhibit is an extreme simplification of what might occur. For example, the MRP budget might be analyzed by the R&D or personnel department to determine areas in the "bill of costs" where reductions should or might be made. There would be numerous feedback lines of communication throughout the flow process presented. However, the exhibit was intentionally kept simple for illustrative purposes.

In summary, time-phased data allow management to better cope with the future. Time-phasing provides information which aids management in planning for: (1) material acquisition and disposition; (2) cash flow and cash needs; (3) long-term acquisitions (e.g., equipment); and (4) overall resource allocation.

## Analysis and Control

Reports for analysis and control (performance reports, variance reports, etc.) usually contain data dealing with actual performance and standard (expected) performance. They may also contain data that can be projected and used to determine expected future performance. Reports should identify responsibility areas, analyze differences in costs, indicate the behavior of costs, and measure operating efficiency. The integration of the cost accounting with the MRP system can be very beneficial here. Figure 2 specifically shows where the integration should occur. MRP can be useful in providing more relevant and detailed information and would allow the cost accounting system to produce reports that contain most of the above features.

Reports currently generated by cost accounting systems do an adequate job of relating to and identifying areas of responsibility. MRP would not improve this aspect. However, there is room for improvement in analyzing costs, measuring operating efficiency, and tracing the behavior of costs.

MRP can be useful in variance analysis. By providing more accurate and detailed information, the information system can help to identify the causes of variances. Such variances can be traced through the whole system, pinpointing where they took place. The reasons why the variances took place can be obtained more readily because of the detailed records contained in the MRP system. For example, the MRP records contain expected arrival dates of material and work dates for products. Backlogs may be due to late arrivals of material or poor performance by a particular department. Using the "pegging" function, the cause of the variance can be traced through the system and pinpointed to the specific department where the problem first occurred.

The detailed information allows management more effectively to measure efficiency and cost behavior. The example above shows how efficiency measures can be made more effective by locating the specific causes of variances. The MRP data base also contains detailed data concerning costs of labor and material. These data can be used to generate various budgets and standards which sould be more accurate and precise than those developed without the MRP data (a benefit of which is that better standards and budgets should produce additional motivation for work effort).[1] Such costs, broken down into different time periods and classifications, can be generated as output of the system and would be very useful in controlling performance of the operations. From this output, management could determine specific behaviors of cost (e.g., consistently in-control or out-of-control, trends, etc.). Some of the reports that could be generated by the system are:

(1) Open order reports—contain information about all open orders; dates, quantities, etc. which can be useful in expediting.

(2) Obsolete and surplus reports—contain information about inactive and excess material; quantities, time period, etc. which can be useful in developing material acquisition strategies.

(3) Shortage reports—contain information about low inventory levels, stockouts, and backlogs. This can be generated for actual materials and projected for future periods.

(4) Performance reports—contain information about actual company performance, expected performance, variances, and information about future needs and performance. These reports can be furnished to all departments, foremen, and higher management; the higher up on the organizational chart, the more condensed the report will be. Some specific examples are reports to the production department concerning the current rate of operations, expected rate of operations, individual parts locations, expected arrival dates, etc. Reports that will be used for inventory control and production scheduling will be sent to the production department. Reports concerning inventory costs and levels (actual and predicted) may be useful in determining pricing strategies, product mix, etc.[2]

---

[1] Since the MRP system has inventory status data which are current and kept up-to-date, standards and budgets can be revised more often as needed, enabling them to reflect the current state of affairs.

[2] For some additional reports, see G. Crossno, "Programmed Requirements Planning," *Management Accounting*. March 1974, pp. 23–27.

## FIGURE 1
## MRP Budgeting process

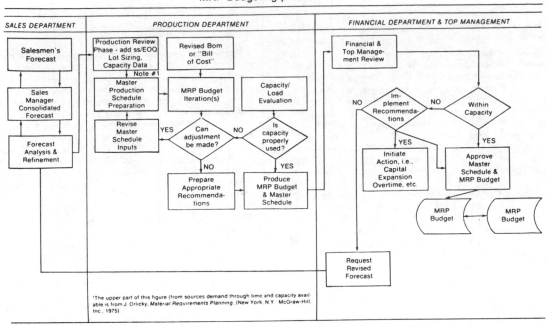

¹The upper part of this figure (from sources demand through time and capacity available is from J. Orlicky, *Material Requirements Planning*, (New York, N.Y.: McGraw-Hill, Inc., 1975)

## FIGURE 2
## Integrating the MRP system and the cost accounting system¹

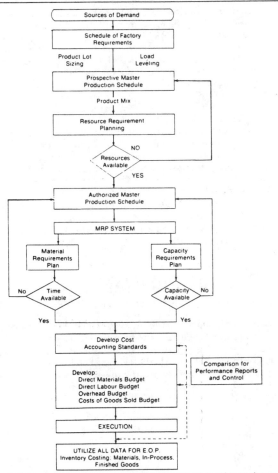

¹The upper part of this figure (from sources demand through time and capacity available) is from J. Orlicky, *Material Requirements Planning*, (New York, N.Y.: McGraw-Hill, Inc., 1975).

The integration of the MRP system with the cost accounting system will enable the firm to produce information (reports) that will allow management to control operations closely and plan for the future. Without the MRP system, the cost accounting system will likely produce information that is not as useful as the information produced when the two systems are integrated.

**About the Authors—**

*PROFESSORS CAMPBELL and PORCANO* are Assistant Professors of Accountancy at Miami University, Oxford, Ohio. They both hold DBA degrees from Indiana University, and both are members of NAA. Professor Campbell is a member of AIDS while Professor Porcano is also a member of AAA and has had articles published in *Taxation for Accountants* and *The CPA Journal*.

Reprinted from *Production and Inventory Management*, Fourth Quarter, 1984.

# VENDOR CAPACITY PLANNING: AN APPROACH TO VENDOR SCHEDULING

Phillip L. Carter
*Michigan State University*     *East Lansing, Michigan*

Chrwan-jyh Ho
*Oklahoma State University*     *Stillwater, Oklahoma*

## INTRODUCTION

The interaction between purchasing and production/inventory control (PIC) has been a weak link in closed-loop material requirements planning (MRP) systems [1]. Although the significance of bridging the gap between purchasing and PIC has been well recognized [1], [2], [8], vendor scheduling using MRP output has apparently been successfully implemented in only a few companies [5], [11], [13]. One reason for this is the difficulty in matching short-term customer requirements (as calculated by MRP) with short-term vendor capacity. This paper presents a planning mechanism which can be used to achieve a better match between customer requirements and vendor capacity and thereby facilitate the implementation of MRP in purchasing.

## VENDOR CAPACITY PLANNING

The major reasons for purchasing parts instead of manufacturing them in house include cost, the vendor's unique technology, and a shortage of in-plant capacity [6]. From a PIC perspective, purchasing can be viewed as a means to supplement in-plant capacity, either short term or long term.

Purchase agreements are one way to reserve a vendor's capacity over a period of time [4], [7]. Based on a projected annual requirement, the buyer can negotiate a contract with the vendor specifying price, terms of delivery, and so on. Theoretically, the vendor should reserve his capacity to meet the annual requirements according to an agreed-upon order release pattern. Practically, a purchase agreement can only guarantee that the total supply within the contract period will satisfy the total estimated demand within the same period. An MRP system, however, requires that the demand in each week be satisfied. There is no way that a purchase agreement can accomplish this requirement without additional terms in the contract. Vendor capacity planning (VCP) is proposed as one way to achieve the objective of matching supply and demand period by period.

Figure 1 illustrates the role of VCP in a production planning system. VCP requires inputs from the purchase order schedule (POS) and vendor capacity report (VCR). The VCR is a time-phased production schedule for each part or part family provided by the vendor. The POS is a time-phased schedule of requirements for each part or part family derived from the MRP output.

Following a review of the MRP output by the buyers or purchase part planner, a POS is sent to each vendor. The vendors use the POS and their own master production schedule (MPS) to prepare the VCR. The VCR, in turn, is sent to the buyers. The VCR received from the various vendors are then aggregated by the buyers into a VCR summary which serves as input for VCP. The details of the POS, the VCR, and VCP as well as their relationships are discussed below.

**FIGURE 1**
Production planning incorporating vendor capacity planning

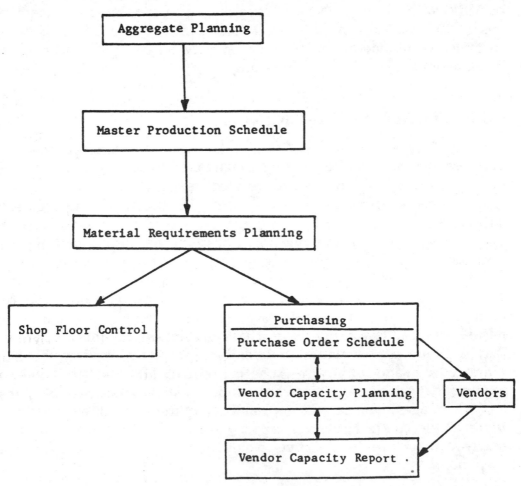

## Purchase Order Schedule

The POS can be derived from the MRP output and shows the time-phased requirements by vendor. If the total quantity required is split among several qualified vendors (Figure 2), the POS for each vendor can

---

FIGURE 2
Distribution of percentage split

| Part Family Number | Vendor X | Vendor Y | Vendor Z |
|---|---|---|---|
| A | 60% | – | 40% |
| B | 70% | 30% | – |
| C | 40% | 30% | 30% |
| D | 50% | 50% | – |
| E | – | 60% | 40% |
| F | 100% | – | – |

---

be obtained by multiplying this predetermined percentage split by the MRP output (Figure 3). The aggregation of individual parts into part families may better serve the objectives of VCP, depending upon the relative significance of an individual part. A vendor may be reluctant to provide a capacity report for a C item, such as an air valve. If the part family, instead of the individual part, is used in VCP, the buyer should combine the requirements of each individual part in this part family in order to obtain the aggregate demand. The schedules in Figure 3 labeled Vendor X and Vendor Y are the POS's that these vendors would use to prepare their VCR for part family A. The bottom schedule in Figure 3 shows an aggregate POS which summarizes purchase requirements by part family over a period of time. This aggregate POS serves as an input of the VCP system.

## VENDOR CAPACITY REPORT

The VCR is a time-phased statement of available production capacity for each purchased part family or part number over a time horizon. A

# FIGURE 3
## Purchase order schedule

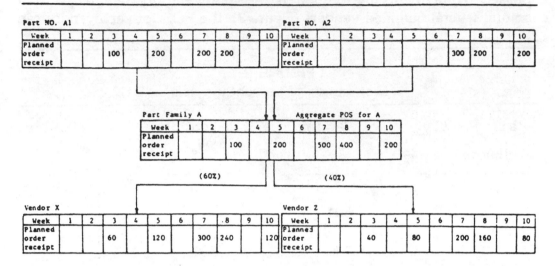

Aggregate Purchase Order Schedule

| Part Family | 1 | 2 | 3 | 4 | 5 | 6 | 7 | 8 | 9 | 10 |
|---|---|---|---|---|---|---|---|---|---|---|
| A |  |  | 100 |  | 200 |  | 500 | 400 |  | 200 |
| B |  | 200 | 200 |  | 300 |  |  |  | 500 |  |
| C |  |  |  | 300 |  | 400 |  |  |  | 800 |
| D |  |  |  | 500 |  | 600 |  |  |  |  |
| E |  |  |  |  | 400 |  | 400 |  | 700 |  |
| F |  |  |  |  |  | 800 |  | 600 |  | 600 |

vendor should consider the VCR as a marketing tool, not just a disclosure of his capacity information to his customers. An appropriate implementation of VCP would help vendors establish a long-term relationship with the buyer. As for the buyers, the production strategy of the vendors can be detected through a careful examination of the VCR. For instance, the requirements for vendor X in periods of 3, 5, and 7 of part family A are 60, 120, and 300, respectively (refer to Figure 3). However, vendor X tries to smooth out his production rate by quoting 60, 60, 60, and 100 for periods 3 through 6 (see the top schedule in Figure 4). Vendor Z adopts a different production strategy and reports more available capacity

# FIGURE 4
## Vendor capacity report

Vendor X

| Part Family | 1 | 2 | 3 | 4 | 5 | 6 | 7 | 8 | 9 | 10 |
|---|---|---|---|---|---|---|---|---|---|---|
| A | | | 60 | 60 | 60 | 100 | 100 | 100 | 100 | 100 |
| B | | 150 | 150 | | 210 | | | | 350 | |
| C | | | | 120 | | 150 | | | | 300 |
| D | | | | 250 | | 300 | | | | |
| E | | | | | | | | | | |
| F | | | | | | 800 | | 600 | | 800 |

Vendor Y

| Part Family | 1 | 2 | 3 | 4 | 5 | 6 | 7 | 8 | 9 | 10 |
|---|---|---|---|---|---|---|---|---|---|---|
| A | | | | | | | | | | |
| B | | 80 | 80 | | 100 | | | | 150 | |
| C | | | | 100 | | 150 | | | | 250 |
| D | | | | 300 | | 300 | | | | |
| E | | | | | 160 | | 160 | | 300 | |
| F | | | | | | | | | | |

Vendor Z

| Part Family | 1 | 2 | 3 | 4 | 5 | 6 | 7 | 8 | 9 | 10 |
|---|---|---|---|---|---|---|---|---|---|---|
| A | | | 50 | | 100 | | 200 | 160 | | 80 |
| B | | | | | | | | | | |
| C | | | | 100 | | 120 | | | | 250 |
| D | | | | | | | | | | |
| E | | | | | 250 | | 250 | | 300 | |
| F | | | | | | | | | | |

than the POS requires. Vendor Z may induce more business to supplement the expected low demand at these periods. Thus, the buyer should take advantage of the extra information conveyed in the VCR for planning the placement of future requirements of purchased items.

Actually, the VCR can be viewed as the difference between the vendor's aggregate production plan and the vendor's MPS. From the MPS, the vendor knows the committed capacity and the open capacity in his shop. Through an appropriate adjustment in order to incorporate the production plan, a VCR can be prepared. The following features, which are quite comparable to the master production schedule, are discussed to illustrate this basic characteristic of VCR.

### Expression of Vendor's Capacity

Capacity is usually expressed in terms of production resources, such as machine hours or labor hours, available over a period of time. In the VCR, capacity is expressed as the amount of each part number that can be supplied per week. If this level of detail is too difficult for vendors to deal with, the available capacity for a part family can be reported instead. However, the degree of detail in the VCR depends upon the importance of the item. The capacity report for an A item, such as a generator, could be by part number, while for a C item, such as an air valve, the capacity report could be by part family. In order to obtain a capacity report for a part or part family, the vendors can determine the unit production time on the critical facility for each item. By comparing the available (i.e., uncommitted) production resource and the MPS time period by time period, the VCR can then be prepared. The VCR should be expressed in terms of delivery dates in order to be consistent with the MPS and POS.

### Time Fences in the VCR

A vendor should establish time fences in the VCR similar to the establishment of a time fence in a master production schedule. Typically, capacity would be fixed from current time out to the first time fence. Between the first time fence and the second time fence, capacity could be changed by short-run adjustments such as overtime, second shift, or subcontracting. Beyond the second time fence capacity could be changed by plant expansion, new plant, new equipment, etc.

### Updating the VCR

The VCR should be updated on a weekly basis after the vendor has received the latest POS and updated the MPS. The planning horizon should correspond to that in the MPS.

## Vendor Capacity Planning

Two levels of VCP will be illustrated. The aggregate level of VCP is used for overall planning of purchasing requirements. The cumulation of all the vendors' capacity reports by part number or part family (as shown in Figure 4) is called the VCR summary. Figure 5 gives an example of the VCR summary. By comparing this VCR summary with the aggregate POS, the deviation between required and actual capacity can be identified throughout the planning horizon, as shown in Figure 6.

FIGURE 5
Vendor capacity report summary

| Part Family | 1 | 2 | 3 | 4 | 5 | 6 | 7 | 8 | 9 | 10 |
|---|---|---|---|---|---|---|---|---|---|---|
| A | | | 110 | 60 | 160 | 100 | 300 | 260 | 100 | 180 |
| B | | 230 | 230 | | 310 | | | | 500 | |
| C | | | | 320 | | 420 | | | | 800 |
| D | | | | 550 | | 600 | | | | |
| E | | | | | 410 | | 410 | | 600 | |
| F | | | | | | 800 | | 600 | | 600 |

FIGURE 6
Aggregate level of vendor capacity planning

Part Family
A

| week | 1 | 2 | 3 | 4 | 5 | 6 | 7 | 8 | 9 | 10 |
|---|---|---|---|---|---|---|---|---|---|---|
| VCR | | | 110 | 60 | 160 | 100 | 300 | 260 | 100 | 180 |
| POS | | | 100 | | 200 | | 500 | 400 | | 200 |
| Cumulative Deviation | | | +10 | +70 | +30 | +130 | -70 | -70 | +30 | +10 |

When a negative deviation occurs (i.e., insufficient capacity), the detailed level of VCP can be used to help identify corrective actions.

The purpose of the detailed level of VCP is to identify the capability of an individual vendor to conform with the POS issued by the buyer. An example is given in Figure 7, which shows a positive deviation of part family A for vendor Z. Figure 6 shows that a negative cumulative deviation occurs in period 7 at the aggregate level of VCP. Combined with the detailed level of VCP of vendor X, the other supplier of part family A, the buyer can determine how to allocate the requirements during shortage periods. In this example, vendor X estimates that he cannot meet the buyer's purchasing requirement after period 7, while vendor Z has slack capacity for not only part family A but also part families C and E. It is obvious that this problem can be resolved by re-allocating requirements from vendor X to vendor Z without forcing vendor X to change his production plan.

## EXPECTED ADVANTAGES OF THE VCP

Several advantages, derived from sharing information in the POS and the VCR with the vendors and buyers, can be expected from implementing VCP.

### Forward Visibility

VCP projects purchasing requirements into an intermediate future through the use of the VCR and MRP's revised POS. With this forward visibility, PIC and purchasing people can work together to make the adjustment necessary to narrow the gap between the vendors' available capacity and the planned purchase order schedule. If insufficient vendor capacity develops over a period of time, the planned purchase requirements can be adjusted accordingly through other alternatives, such as in-plant manufacturing.

### Effective Communication

Current purchasing practice has been criticized for a lack of responsiveness to unexpected changes [3]. It is suggested that a buyer-planner be used to take control of the direct communication between PIC and vendors about the due dates and requirements of the needed items [12]. The communication can be further enhanced with the use of VCP. The buyer can contribute considerably to the overall planning system through the impact of VCP on the MRP system.

### Mutual Benefits

Through the VCR, vendors can inform purchasing about any potential or actual supply disruptions, allowing the buyer to react to these

226

unexpected events promptly. The vendor also knows the future purchase requirement and can determine his own strategies for capacity adjustment. The vendors can initiate their production planning to best utilize their capacity. The POS also provides a basis for estimating annual requirements, which gives vendors a better estimate of how much long-term capacity is needed to meet the estimated annual requirement of the customer.

**FIGURE 7**
The detailed level of the vendor capacity planning

Part Family A         Vendor Z

| week | 1 | 2 | 3 | 4 | 5 | 6 | 7 | 8 | 9 | 10 |
|---|---|---|---|---|---|---|---|---|---|---|
| VCR | | | 50 | | 100 | | 200 | 160 | | 80 |
| POS | | | 40 | | 80 | | 200 | 160 | | 80 |
| Cumulative Deviation | | | +10 | | +30 | | +30 | +30 | | +30 |

Part Family C         Vendor Z

| week | 1 | 2 | 3 | 4 | 5 | 6 | 7 | 8 | 9 | 10 |
|---|---|---|---|---|---|---|---|---|---|---|
| VCR | | | | 100 | | 120 | | | | 250 |
| POS | | | | 90 | | 120 | | | | 240 |
| Cumulative Deviation | | | | +10 | | +10 | | | | +20 |

Part Family E         Vendor Z

| week | 1 | 2 | 3 | 4 | 5 | 6 | 7 | 8 | 9 | 10 |
|---|---|---|---|---|---|---|---|---|---|---|
| VCR | | | | | 250 | | 250 | | 300 | |
| POS | | | | | 160 | | 160 | | 280 | |
| Cumulative Deviation | | | | | +90 | | +180 | | +200 | |

Part Family A         Vendor X

| week | 1 | 2 | 3 | 4 | 5 | 6 | 7 | 8 | 9 | 10 |
|---|---|---|---|---|---|---|---|---|---|---|
| VCR | | | 60 | 60 | 60 | 100 | 100 | 100 | 100 | 100 |
| POS | | | 60 | | 120 | | 300 | 240 | | 120 |
| Cumulative Deviation | | | 0 | +60 | 0 | +100 | -100 | -240 | -140 | -160 |

## PREREQUISITES AND LIMITATIONS OF THE VCP

As with an MRP system, there are several important prerequisites of a VCP system.

### VCR Availability

The most important prerequisite may be the availability of the VCR. Some vendors may not be willing to reveal their capacity information in detail, given the effort required to obtain these data. Just as vendor education is necessary to extend the MRP system into the vendor's shop [10], vendors can be educated about the advantages of preparing an adequate VCR for the buyer. The extra effort to prepare the VCR will be compensated by the expected advantages of VCP for the vendors.

### POS Conformation

Large vendors may not want to conform with the buyer's POS. They may only be willing to provide a predetermined available capacity for each customer based on their own production schedule and marketing strategy. Faced with this situation, the buyer would need to modify the POS to meet the suppliers' VCR. In the extreme case, the buyer needs to inform PIC to adjust the master production schedule to cope with an anticipated shortage.

### POS Stability

The objective of MRP's rescheduling capability is to keep priorities up to date and valid [9]. However, this may change the actual need date or quantity within the firm portion of the POS. In turn, open purchase orders tend to change from time to time. This nervousness will cause problems with the buyer's POS and, eventually, will obscure the future VCR such that VCP will be invalid for planning purposes. Therefore, trade-offs exist between constantly rescheduling purchase requirements and planning vendor capacity. A mutual agreement about the treatment of purchase order changes must be developed in order to ensure a better performance of VCP.

### SUMMARY

As MRP systems become the dominant production scheduling technique, an effective two-way communication between PIC and related functions becomes essential. This article stresses the significance of the purchasing function in an MRP system and describes how purchasing can play a more effective role in vendor scheduling using VCP. Because effort and persuasion are required to obtain a valid and realistic VCR, the purchasing manager is the best person to be responsible for implementing VCP. On the other hand, to make VCP work best, PIC should be responsible for providing stable purchase requirements within the firm portion of POS. The VCP concept cannot be achieved without cost, but the additional effort and cost can be justified by the advantages of implementation.

## REFERENCES

1. Aiello, J. L., "Successful Interaction Between Purchasing and Production and Inventory Control," *APICS Annual Conference Proceedings 1979*, pp. 234–236.
2. Benson, R. J., "Can Purchasing Supply Tomorrow's Factory?" *APICS Annual Conference Proceedings 1981*, pp. 355–359.
3. Brunelle, P. E., "Controlling the Outside Factory by Purchasing Manager," *APICS Annual Conference Proceedings 1977*, pp. 148–155.
4. Burlingame, L. J. and Warren, R. A., "Extended Capacity Planning," *APICS Annual Conference Proceedings 1974*, pp. 83–91.
5. Carter, P. L. and Monzka, R. M., "Steelcase, Inc.: MRP in Purchasing," in E. W. David, ed., *Case Studies in Materials Requirements Planning*, APICS, Inc., Washington, DC, 1978, pp. 105–129.
6. Leenders, M. R., Fearon, H. E., and England, W. B., *Purchasing and Material Management*, Richard D. Irwin, Inc., Homewood, IL, 1980.
7. Morency, R. R., "A Systems Approach to Vendor Scheduling under Contract Purchasing," *APICS Annual Conference Proceedings 1977*, pp. 458–466.
8. Olsen, R. E., "Bridging the Purchasing-Production Control Credibility Gap," *APICS Annual Conference Proceedings 1977*, pp. 450–457.
9. Orlicky, J. A., *Material Requirements Planning*, McGraw-Hill, Inc., NY, 1975.
10. Papesch, R. M., "Extending Your MRP System into Your Vendor's Shop," *Production and Inventory Management*, Vol. 19, No. 2, 1978, pp. 47–52.
11. Pellegrini, D., "Vendor Scheduling: It Really Works," *APICS Annual Conference Proceedings 1982*, pp. 358–363.
12. Plossl, G., *Manufacturing Control: The Last Frontier for Profits*, Reston Publishing Co., Inc., Reston, Virginia, 1973.
13. Smolens, R. W., "MRP II Systems: Does The Purchasing Function Change?" *APICS Annual Conference Proceedings 1982*, pp. 355–357.

## About the Authors—

*PHILLIP L. CARTER, CPIM,** is professor of management and Chairman of the Department of Management in the Graduate School of Business at Michigan State University. Dr. Carter is a past cochairman of the APICS Academic Practitioner Liaison Committee.

*CHRWAN-JYH HO, CPIM,* is assistant professor of production management at Oklahoma State University. He holds an MBA from the University of Georgia and expects a PhD from Michigan State University. He is a member of APICS, AIDS, and TIMS.

Reprinted from APICS 1987 *Conference Proceedings*.

## HOW TO AUDIT YOUR MRP SYSTEM FOR CONSISTENT RESULTS
Craig R. Erhorn, CPIM
Coopers & Lybrand

The objective of this presentation is to provide attendees with a practical method of continuously assessing the accuracy of the data which their material requirements planning system must use. It reaches beyond the scope of the "ABCD" checklist with a detailed look at what is really required for consistently valid MRP output and successful operation. The focus is on the need for quality in all phases of system operation.

The presentation offers an alternative to a periodic audit, and discusses the advantages of a continuous program. It includes a discussion of what information will be required, what personnel requirements are appropriate, and a suggested methodology for establishing a program.

### BACKGROUND

This discussion is intended for those who are implementing (or re-implementing) MRP and are genuinely committed to using the tool to full advantage. MRP has the potential to let us MANAGE our operations instead of REACTING to a stream of crises; to anticipate trouble and avoid it by planning carefully and managing to the plan. This will not happen without excellence in the way we operate the system. Even relatively short lapses in data accuracy and operational disciplines could affect our planning at a critical time, with potential long-term consequences. Continuous monitoring and consistently accurate data are essential if we expect to get a worthwhile payback on the considerable amounts of time and money spent installing the system.

### PERIODIC VERSUS CONTINUOUS AUDITS

A continuous assessment of system performance and data accuracy is similar to the concept of the cycle count program for physical inventory. Data is sampled daily, errors are recorded, investigation is carried out, and the CAUSES of error are tabulated. Corrective action is taken to eliminate the situations which are causing the errors. Eventually, the continuous refinement of procedures to eliminate causes of error results in a consistent level of excellent performance. Consequently, accuracy is usually better than with a periodic assessment, and the difference may be significant enough to make the difference between acceptable and unacceptable levels of performance.

Periodic audits tend to be limited in scope, and are somewhat akin to the annual physical inventory. They may present an accurate picture of performance if they are well organized and carefully executed, but are handicapped by the fact that they are limited to a specific time period which is well known to everyone involved. Typically, there is enough advance notice to allow for some housecleaning and other preparation, which skews the results toward a more favorable outcome. Periodic audits usually involve people who have been assigned to the audit team temporarily, have little experience in an auditing capacity, and are checking a functional area they may not be familiar with. Typically, their job performance evaluation will not include the audit activities, hence they have little incentive to really "dig in" and find the problems. Time constraints also contribute to cursory investigations, which may totally bypass significant data.

To summarize, the primary benefits of a continuous audit are the steady improvement resulting from researching and correcting the causes of errors, higher and more consistent levels of accuracy, and consistently high levels of performance.

### GETTING STARTED

The best time to set up a program of this type is during the MRP implementation effort. Management is very much aware of what they are spending in terms of money and human resources to implement the system, and they should be receptive to efforts to ensure that there is a significant return on the investment. An MRP implementation is also a time when major changes are introduced in the way the business is run, and the audit can be seen as just one of many requirements of the new system. Do not request authorization to set up an audit, instead design a program for your situation and present it to your management Steering Committee as a required activity. Discussion should center on what resources will be allocated to the effort and not on whether there should be a program.

### METHODOLOGY

Early in the design process, education must be considered. Anyone who directly or indirectly has input to the MRP system must understand that they have a role in keeping it accurate. Many errors can be prevented by educating operating personnel to anticipate the consequences of specific actions in advance. Since MRP education is normally a part of the implementation effort, efforts should be made to include material that reinforces the need for accuracy and emphasizes following good operating procedures.

One situation that is frequently overlooked is what to do for the new employee. When personnel change, some provision must be made to educate and train new employees. Over time, the level of performance in a department can deteriorate as experienced employees leave, unless a deliberate effort is made to educate and train the new person. Informal orientation and "on the job" training will not be sufficient. Include provisions in the education planning for an on-going program which will maintain standards of competence in the future, and formally state what the standards are.

The next step is to define measurements. Considerations include sources of data and any specific data collection or reporting requirements that must be included in the system to facilitate measurement. The actual process of conducting each measurement should be outlined in a procedure which defines the data source and frequency of measurement. For each measurement, clearly define the target level of performance and any tolerances which will be allowed.

Once the scope of the audit program is defined, it should be apparent what level of human resources will be required to support it. Personnel requirements can be estimated from the number of items to be checked daily, weekly, monthly, etc. It would be wise to keep resource requirements in mind when designing the measurements, to minimize the budget impact and help ensure approval of sufficient staff to operate an effective program. Be prepared to demonstrate to management that you have designed a program which uses a minimum of human resources, and at the same time, will not jeopardize the success of the system.

Selection of the people who will perform the audit follows approval of the program. There are many ways of staffing the effort, depending on the size of the company and the scope of the program. As a general rule, good results will be obtained by dedicating full-time staff to the data accuracy activities. Performance measurements can often be performed by the computer, through the use of reports. If this is not possible, manual methods may be necessary to measure how well the system is being used. Excellent results have been observed in situations where the full-time staff are organized in a "data control" department which verifies transaction entries, administers the inventory accuracy program, conducts accuracy audits of master files, tracks performance measurements, and oversees adherence to procedural disciplines. The overriding concern must be to assign competent, experienced people.

Whether or not a data control department is established, there must be one person assigned the responsibility for the audit program and its successful administration. Individuals assigned to the audit should be selected based on demonstrated qualities such as functional experience, analytical ability, people skills, objectivity, and commitment to success of the program. The manager responsible for the audit function should establish procedures for measuring accuracy and performance data, standard analytical methods, and reporting standards. Training should be provided to each person involved in the audit to ensure that the procedures are understood.

Once the audit program is underway and results are being recorded, a periodic management review meeting should be established. The purpose of the meeting is to review progress in meeting objectives and to involve management in achieving the desired results. If employees observe active management interest, they will support the audit program. Attendees should include top management at the facility, audit personnel, and every functional manager whose department is covered by the audit. Audit personnel should present a report of the most recent measurements versus goal, with historical data to indicate whether progress is being made. Recommendations to correct the causes of error should also be discussed at this point, with management assigning responsibility for corrective action.

PROCEDURAL DISCIPLINES

One of the most important considerations in organizing for MRP excellence is to build in routine checks and procedures which will help achieve and maintain accuracy. It is best to identify as many as possible in the planning stages of the implementation, so that each activity can be included in the project plan. In this way, responsibility and timing are clearly spelled out, and progress in implementation is subject to regular management review. Examples of the kinds of routine checks and operational procedures which should be established are given below:

- Verification of all transactions to their source document. This is one of the most frequently overlooked areas in companies implementing a computerized system for the first time. It is also where a significant amount of errors occur. Checking that the transaction was entered correctly is accomplished by comparing the system transaction log to the transaction form which was used to communicate that a transaction took place. This activity must be performed daily to identify problems as they are entered, and initialed by the person who entered the transaction. This information aids in error investigation and helps identify individuals who need to improve the accuracy of their data entry.

- In on-line systems, require that all transactions be input as they occur. Many companies require their system to perform on-line transaction processing, yet transaction documents are really entered in batches. Companies have been observed spending significant amounts of time researching apparent transaction errors, only to find that the problem was due to delayed transactions. If your company truly needs the capability of on-line, real-time transaction processing, enforce the discipline necessary to make it reliable.

- In batch processing systems, provide for immediate correction and reprocessing of rejected transactions. Rejected transactions allowed to age beyond the next batch processing run will create additional rejects and cause accuracy of the affected files to deteriorate. Decisions based on this data will be incorrect.

- Review system variables or control settings regularly. Most systems today have optional features and critical parameters controlled by user accessible software "switches". Many of these can affect MRP output in undesirable ways if set incorrectly. In one popular MRP package, variable settings could cause MRP to use requirements from a previous run or to stop exploding requirements through phantom BOM's.

- Create reports to trap obvious errors in static data. Report items coded incorrectly in the item master file, such as: phantoms coded as master scheduled, items with no lead time, items with extremely long (and unlikely) lead times, items coded manufactured with no bill of material, phantoms with positive QOH, items with no planner code, items with no order policy code, items with order modifiers (EOQ, minimum, multiple, shrink factor, etc.) not permitted by policy, etc. Errors in static data can have major impact on MRP output, due to their use in the calculation of net requirements.

- Create reports to identify possible errors for further investigation. Examples of this type of report include: items in receiving more than "x" days, orders past due more than "x" days, items with shortages and a positive balance on-hand, closed orders with a balance due greater than 0, and closed manufacturing orders with outstanding component shortages. Each of these situations may be providing MRP with erroneous data, and could cause the system to recommend incorrect action.

- Require individuals who work with the MRP output to "sanity check" all planning data when responding to an action message. This makes planners responsible for their decisions, not "the computer". Planners should scan static data which affects decision making, such as unit of measure, order policy, lot sizing, safety stock, order modifiers, and lead time. Verification of past due open orders and unusual inventory balances (negative?) are also advisable. Reschedule or order action messages which signal a significant change in schedule should be traced back to the demand source and verified. In many actual situations, "pegging" back to the source of a demand has revealed a major error in the master production schedule, rendering the MRP output useless.

- Bill of material effectivities must be reviewed for validity on a routine basis. Here is another frequently ignored area. Setting a phase-in/phase-out or use-up effectivity date and then forgetting about it virtually guarantees that it will not happen as planned. Unplanned issues, cycle count adjustments, scrap, or changes in demand occur constantly and alter the timing of the change. Unless effectivities are managed in step with the changing requirements, MRP will continue to plan the original (and now incorrect) effectivity.

- Establish a master production schedule policy which will prevent "impossible" schedules. Far too many companies with good data accuracy fail to get real benefits from MRP because the master schedule is poorly controlled. A good MPS policy needs to consider capacity and material availability in determining rules governing changes to schedule. Time fences should be established based on these factors and the cumulative product lead time. Accuracy of forecast data and other inputs to the MPS should be verified before each MRP run. Lot sizing and safety stocks at this level should also be reviewed, since they directly affect lower level items, and can cause unnecessary rescheduling.

- Establish a policy which designates who is authorized to maintain system data. Ability to change data elements must be restricted if accuracy is to be maintained. One person should control all security authorizations and should periodically review access to the system as people change functions within the company.

- Establish counting disciplines throughout the operation. A frequent cause of poor data accuracy is the acceptance of written counts at points where transactions occur. Any material movement requiring a transaction should also require that the quantity be physically counted. Accepting a vendor's count on a receiving document, or a previous department's move ticket without physically verifying the quantity is certain to introduce errors. The stockroom should never issue or receive any material without physically counting it. An excellent idea for the stockroom is to set up a count quality program which would sample the count accuracy of material being issued and received.

## DATA ACCURACY

The basis for an effective system is the data it uses to perform its intended function. Although there are many other requirements for valid MRP output, the most basic requirement is that ALL the data input to the system be as accurate as possible. If the accuracy of the data in the system is not being continuously tested, then the validity of the MRP output will not be apparent until it is too late!

### Static Data

Static data includes information stored in the Item Master, Bill of Material, Routing, and Work Center files. Although this data is not constantly being updated and changed, enough maintenance does occur to require continuous accuracy testing. Since these files can be large, the selection of items for checking is usually done on a sample basis. Samples may be determined statistically, by ABC classification, or by other means.

### Item Master File

The Item Master file is the primary part record and contains elements which affect MRP significantly. The following fields should be verified by the people who are designated to control them:

- Unit of Measure
- Inventory Classification (for reporting purposes)
- Item Type (phantom, make, buy)
- Order Policy (lot sizing method)
- Master Schedule Code (MPS item?)
- Lead Time
- Planner Code
- Safety Code
- Lot Size (EOQ)
- Shrinkage Factor
- Order Quantity Modifiers (minimum, multiple, maximum)

If any of the elements in a particular Item Master are found to be incorrect, that entire record is counted as an error, regardless of how many elements were wrong. Accuracy measurement for the file is the number of Item Masters with no error, divided by the total number audited.

### Bill of Material

The Bill of Material file should be checked using single-level bills of material, as this corresponds to the way Engineering documentation is typically produced; one assembly at a time. Each assembly is compared to the documentation to verify that all components are included and that quantity-per and unit of measure are correct. If any component on a particular BOM is incorrect, or there are additional components not on the Engineering documentation, or a component is missing, that bill is counted as an error. The accuracy measurement is the number of single-level bills with no error, divided by the total number checked.

### Routings

Routings should be compared to the manufacturing process documentation developed by the industrial engineers. Each routing for a manufactured item must agree with the documentation on the number of operations, the sequence of operations, and the set-up and run times. If any of these items are incorrect, the routing is counted as an error. Routing accuracy equals the number of correct routings divided by the total number checked.

### Work Centers

Another static file which indirectly affects the quality of MRP output through its role in capacity planning and production scheduling is the Work Center file. Data typically stored in this file include machine hours available, labor hours available, crew size, and queue times. Since there is seldom any written documentation for the data in this file, it should be checked by a qualified person. Accuracy measurement would be the same as for the Bill of Material and Routings.

### Volatile Data

Volatile data includes items in files which are constantly being changed. Files in this classification contain such things as inventory balances, inventory locations, manufacturing orders, and purchase orders. An important consideration in checking volatile data is cut-off control. Provision must be made to check these items during a period when no transactions are being made, and when all previous activity has been entered into the system. Good practice requires that someone verify that the transaction cut-off has been established before proceeding with accuracy checks.

### Inventory Balances

Assessing the accuracy of the inventory balances should be accomplished by cycle counting. The cycle counting concept of continuously auditing the inventory records using trained personnel, recording the causes of error, and eliminating the causes is well documented in the literature. It is also the basic concept of the program being proposed here for ALL data used by MRP. Accuracy is recorded as the number of correct inventory balances (within specified tolerances), divided by the number of items counted.

### Inventory Locations

Many systems provide the capability to record where inventory is stored through a locator system. If this data becomes inaccurate, it can cause inventory to be lost or misplaced, resulting in unanticipated inventory adjustments. The effect is the same as inaccurate inventory balances, with significant impact on MRP. Audit of the inventory locations can be included in the cycle count program, or can be performed as a separate activity. In either case, it requires checking that items recorded on the system in a specific location are actually there. Inventory location accuracy is the number of correct locations, divided by the number of locations checked.

### Work in Process

Work in process inventory is an area that is often substantially incorrect and just as often ignored in inventory accuracy programs. Unfortunately, it has just as much impact on MRP results as an incorrect stockroom balance. As far at the MRP calculation is concerned, work in process quantities are "on-hand" and become available for use on the manufacturing order due date. Unreported scrap, over-production, or material shortages are common occurrences which will cause the actual receipt of finished work to be different from what the system expected. Provision must be made to cycle count work in process at a level which allows comparison of the quantity actually being manufactured to the quantity shown on the open manufacturing orders. Common cycle count accuracy measurements and tolerances are applicable. Estimation of the work remaining versus due date should be performed to give an indication of the validity of the due date.

### Purchase Orders

Purchase order information is treated the same as work in process by MRP, and the same accuracy requirements apply. Selection of purchase orders for "cycle counting" should be handled in the same manner as manufacturing orders. The actual "counting" is accomplished by contacting the vendor and verifying quantity in process and due date.

## PERFORMANCE MEASUREMENTS

In addition to keeping data accurate, performance measurements provide an indication of how well the system is being used, and point to areas which need corrective action. Data in the system can be sufficiently accurate, but provides little benefit if the system capabilities are not being used or are used incorrectly.

Performance measurements should be an integral part of any program to audit MRP. They help to ensure that the potential benefits of the tool are realized, and they are also useful as reasonability checks on the accuracy measurements. If reported data accuracy is in an acceptable range, but a related performance measurement is not (even though correct disciplines are in place), the accuracy measurement is suspect. Management should set targets or objectives for each measurement, and review progress on a monthly basis. Performance in meeting the target levels should be used as incentives for excellence by associating attainment of target levels to the employee's performance review.

### Suggested Performance Measurements

Master Production Schedule Change Analysis - an indicator of overall system nervousness which will show how volatile the master schedule is inside the time fence. This analysis should be performed on a weekly basis, and will show the number of MPS items changed inside a predetermined time fence, and the magnitude of the changes. An appropriate level of system nervousness should be determined in advance, with the establishment of allowable percentage changes at various points inside the time fence.

Shipping Performance Analysis - indicates if product is flowing as scheduled or if the "month-end crunch" mentality still exists. The actual measurement is the percentage of line items shipped on time and complete, based on the date shipment was promised to the customer. This analysis can be used in reviewing a master scheduler's ability to schedule effectively, and as an indicator of system effectiveness in improving customer service. Information on the total number of units and dollars shipped reflects performance to the Production Plan.

Lead Time Violation Analysis - tallies how many items (purchased and manufactured) were ordered with less than the normal planning lead time, and what percentage of the lead time was violated. The number of items in violation may also be expressed as a percentage of the total number of orders placed, to add perspective to the measurement. High levels of lead time violation usually indicate an unstable master schedule or poor planning disciplines.

Miscellaneous Issues From Stores - is an additional test of bill of material accuracy. An excessive number of miscellaneous requisitions for component items normally issued on manufacturing orders may be due to inaccuracy in the quantity per assembly on the BOM. If there is commonality of component parts across the product line, items may be on some bills and missing from others. Care must be exercised to investigate all possibilities. Manufacturing supervision should be encouraged to report apparent bill of material errors.

Assembly Shortage Analysis - is a weekly count of how many assemblies are being delayed due to component shortages, and how long they have been waiting. This measurement is often one of the best indicators of the overall performance of material planners, provided that data accuracy in the system is at acceptable levels.

Manufacturing Schedule Performance - compares the number of items completed by the schedule due date to the total number of items due, on a weekly basis. This analysis can give a reliable measurement of shop performance in support of the schedule, as long as items delayed due to material shortages are factored out of the calculation.

MRP Exception Message Analysis - reveals the percentage of items with MRP action messages, by planner, on a weekly basis. When exception levels are tracked over a period of time, this measurement can be used to rate planner performance and to assess nervousness. Planner workloads can also be adjusted for maximum efficiency based on this analysis.

Excess and Obsolete Inventory Analysis - classifies inventory on-hand in excess of requirements, and assigns a dollar value to each category. Obsolete material is usually identified by the fact that it has no where-used, or that it is a component of an assembly that is designated obsolete. Excess material is material available beyond all known requirements, for a product that is still active in production. Excess is a measurement of planning performance, while the level of obsolete material indicates how well Engineering changes are being implemented.

Inventory Input/Output Analysis - reports actual performance against the inventory plan. This is a good measurement of overall inventory management, and requires development of an inventory plan which takes into consideration starting inventory, planned receipts, and planned production to project an inventory value at the end of the planning period. Actual data is compared to the planned values monthly, and will point to areas needing corrective action if the company is to meet the planned inventory levels.

Vendor Performance Analysis - evaluates vendor performance in terms of on-time delivery and rejected orders. This measurement may also be used to assess the effectiveness of Purchasing in managing procurement. On-time delivery is measured as the percentage of line items on purchase orders delivered on or before the due date. Rejected orders are reported as the percentage of line items on purchase orders which were either fully or partially rejected, within a specified reporting period designated by management.

SUMMARY

Continuous monitoring and consistently accurate data are essential to achieving excellent results from MRP. Periodic audits can be useful, but are handicapped by time constraints and the tendency of people to prepare for them. A methodology has been presented here which will assist practitioners in establishing an MRP audit program. It begins with establishment of an awareness of the need for accuracy throughout the company, provides education in the required disciplines, defines measurements, and requires dedicated human resources. The methodology also requires that one person be held responsible for the overall program, and that management regularly review the results of the audit. Examples of procedural disciplines, data accuracy measurements, and performance measurements have been discussed to illustrate what should be included in an audit program.

ABOUT THE AUTHOR

Craig Erhorn is currently a manufacturing systems consultant for Coopers & Lybrand in New York City. He has held a number of materials management and manufacturing systems positions since 1974, in industries ranging from metal-cutting to electronics. Responsibility for a number of MRP-II implementations are included in this experience.
Active in APICS, Craig has presented papers at the 1981, 1983, and 1985 APICS conferences, and has served as President of the Mid-Hudson chapter and Vice-President of the Mid-Carolina chapter. His work has also been published by Auerbach Publishers, in the P+IM Journal, and in the Production and Inventory Control Handbook.

Reprinted from APICS 1985 *Conference Proceedings*.

## PDQ: PURCHASING TO SUPPORT MANUFACTURING, OR "WHERE'S THE REQ?"

John P. Flavin, CPIM
Thomas H. Fuller, Jr., CPIM
Burroughs Corporation

### INTRODUCTION

The purchasing activity offers a fertile field for direct and indirect returns from a well-run manufacturing control system. Contemporary authors and practitioners document reductions of five per cent and more of the actual purchased component of cost of goods sold. Since this is for most manufacturers the largest component of cost of good sold, it certainly deserves to be investigated. Stated negatively, a poor manufacturing control system (or a system out of control) can mean that you're paying five per cent more than you need to for purchased components.

The purpose of our talk is to flesh out this five per cent with specific examples of the effective use of modern purchasing systems. PDQ stands for price, delivery, and quality - all of which must be carefully managed if purchasing is genuinely to support excellence in manufacturing.

### IS PURCHASING SEPARATE FROM MANUFACTURING?

Half a dozen years ago Joe Aiello gathered together the mission statements of the two groups and put them side by side (1):

"It is our responsibility to see that the finished product is made to the right quality and quantity and at the right time to satisfy the needs of our company at a cost which will allow our company to earn a reasonable profit."

Production and Inventory Control

"It is our responsibility to purchase materials to the right quality and quantity and at the right time to satisfy the needs of our company at a cost which will allow our company to earn a reasonable profit."

Purchasing

On the face of it, these two departments of the company do not appear to be in opposite businesses. Ideally, they are in the same business supporting the same objectives with many of the same methods. Cooperating, these two groups have great potential to contribute to the smooth flow of material through the plant, reduced leadtimes, and productivity that contribute to the profitability, and competitiveness of the company. Again, to restate this point negatively, if these two functions are allowed to engage in finger pointing and assignment of blame, they have the potential to drain away a company's opportunity to excel, or even survive in today's demanding markets.

### THE BUYER'S DAY

Increasingly we are coming to respect the elements of professionalism demanded in today's world of purchasing. The market the purchaser, or buyer, surveys is no longer limited to a handful of nearby vendors. Not only must he seek the right part at the right quality at the right time, but now he wants that part with the right packaging, from a nation with the right infrastructure and the right exchange rate, deliverable in the right time at the right transportation cost, with the right customs documents, and on, and on.

Into this complex world we inject today's buyer. His day is often ten hours long with non-stop action - expediting, missed phone calls, busy signals, canceling, re-ordering, checking up on price quotes, cold coffee, panic, and exasperation. Lest I give you the wrong impression, let me point out that many days are not this smooth. There were many days as a buyer that I probably got only one productive hour out of a day, and a good two-hour lunch with a willing vendor. The rest of the day was full of catching up to where I should have been before starting to catch up to where I was.

How does the buyer lose control over his time? More importantly, how can he buy it back?

Consider how the day develops. From the time he hangs his coat on the nail, he is expediting production parts, newly introduced parts, substituted parts, tooling, maintenance items, and general supplies. In front of this continuous background tapestry is each day's parade of negotiations, salesmen, value analyses, price increase announcements, and new order placements. In such an environment, many very worthwhile things (value analysis, sourcing, negotiation, supplier training and development) are more easily put off than the emergencies du jour.

From this haggard buyer's perspective:

- The time to develop forward-looking plans and to control his environment no longer belongs to him.

- He can never stop expediting for a moment, or the plant will shut down, and he will get yelled at.

- He is largely at the mercy of his vendor's capacity, his sub-contractor's billing, and the finance department's costing.

- Negotiations only happen in Geneva.

- Value analysis must refer to choosing between Captain Cornflake and Nut Nugget at the supermarket on Saturday.

What causes the many little emergencies, and the ensuing panic of expediting? The trigger events run the gamut of poor planning and poor control - untimely engineering changes, missed communications, erratic market demands from the plant's own customers, vendor shortfalls, inaccurate inventory records, failure to include purchasing constraints in the master production scheduling process, paperwork errors, and so on. Many of these could be summarized as a failure to, in Plossl's words, "handle the routine elements of the job routinely."

Figure 1 shows a table depicting the buyer's day at the Tennant Company (2). The column on the left depicts his division of an eight-hour day (if he had one!) prior to the installation of a sound manufacturing control system. The table on the left shows the same buyer's typical day after a closed loop MRP II system had been installed and understood.

---

### FIGURE 1

### TYPICAL BUYER'S DAY

==============================================================

#### BEFORE MRP IMPLEMENTATION

| ACTIVITY | HOURS |
|---|---|
| Expediting | 4.0 |
| De-expediting | 0.2 |
| Order processing, calls, meetings | 1.5 |
| Sales interviews | 1.0 |
| Cost reduction, value analysis | 0.8 |
| Negotiations | 0.5 |

==============================================================

#### AFTER MRP IMPLEMENTATION

| ACTIVITY | HOURS |
|---|---|
| Expediting | 1.0 |
| De-expediting | 1.0 |
| Order processing, calls, meetings | 1.5 |
| Sales interviews | 1.5 |
| Cost reduction, value analysis | 1.5 |
| Negotiations | 1.5 |

==============================================================

We observe that the lion's share of the day is taken up with expediting. Virtually no time is spent in de-expediting. This nearly guarantees the accumulation of a large backlog of orders at the vendor's plant. Since the orders are not called for by the buyer, the vendor assumes that there is very little relation between the due dates that appear on the orders and the date of actual need. As in our own plant, this phony backlog (to use Wight's phrase) torpedos the formal system in the vendor's eyes as surely as a phony backlog in the plant would sink the formal shop floor control system.

We further note that less than a third of the buyer's day is spent in the activities that could have a great impact on the cost of goods sold - cost reduction/value analysis, negotiations, and sales interviews. After the closed-loop MRP system was operational, we see that expediting and de-expediting occupy about the same amount of time and that these two add up to only two hours of the day. If we are to keep the priorities valid, it is natural that as many orders would be de-expedited as expedited. Also we see that the three high impact areas named above have increased to four and a half hours of the day.

As the purchasing function makes use of the output of sound production control systems, and increased stability in the scheduling process, they gain the discipline and tools to stabilize the tasks of purchasing. We can never eliminate all of the changes that challenge us daily, but we can handle routine orders routinely. As marketing buffets the schedule with under-forecasting this month and over-forecasting next month, we can build the flexibility into our systems to respond to these challenges with insight and cost-sensitive analysis. Before examining these purchasing support systems, let us take a few moments to analyze the evolution of both manufacturing and purchasing systems.

## REVISITING PLAN/CONTROL, PRIORITY/CAPACITY

Just over a decade ago, Ollie Wight focussed much of the emerging technology of manufacturing control systems by dividing the vast arena of production and inventory control into a two by two diagram. He stated that we really practiced only two things - we planned and we controlled. We formulated plans for end-items (called Master Production Schedules, or MPS), plans for material, plans for the work centers, etc. We also controlled. We control the flow of material, manpower, money, etc. He further simplified this model by suggesting that we apply these two managerial practices to just two things - priority and capacity.

This model of the tasks of production and inventory control is simple, but still valuable in analyzing our tasks. We plan priorities by creating a material require-ments plan that arranges parts by the proximity of their need. Its mechanical logic maintains the relative priori-ties of the thousands of possible part orders in lockstep priority sequence. We plan capacity with such tools as the Rough-cut Capacity Plan (RCP) applied to the MPS, and the Capacity Requirements Plan (CRP), if needed, to the MRP.

Having made the plans, we now control the execution of the priorities by distributing the dispatch list to the legions on the shop floor. Having instilled the necessary discipline and reporting, and adding an element of judg-ment and wisdom occasionally, we are confident that the right items will appear as they are needed. In a similar manner, the Input-Output technique gives us a method of monitoring the loads throughout the plant. We can then take corrective action to cause these to correspond to our previously-made plans. If more capacity is required, we may schedule overtime, subcontract work, or add additional facilities to meet the requirement.

In recent years, manufacturing professionals have discov-ered that these processes can be simplified in the envi-ronment where the same types of parts are regularly following the same flow through the shop floor. This has been called "repetitive" manufacturing, although some parts of traditional job shops can be conformed to this pattern. In such an environment, the planning and control of both priority and capacity is simplified with the "pull" method of control. Whether implemented by kanban cards, lights, empty containers, or keen eyesight, this method causes parts to move through the processes in a nearly unbroken flow that is largely self-regulating. This can simplify or even eliminate some of the planning techniques named above in some cases.

Against this historic backdrop, let me comment on a few trends observed in the world of purchasing during the past few years. The challenge is to communicate the priorities of the many orders active at a given time with a vendor. The MRP has proven a valuable tool in keeping these priorities in line with actual need for both planned and actual orders with the supplier. This is obviously priority planning. Also, it is considered important to good vendor relations to let them know the immediate requirements, and to formally communicate changes in relative priority. This is typically done with open purchase order reports, arranged for each supplier. This is clearly analogous to the dispatch list. If sufficient trust and discipline have been developed, we can feel confident that the vendor is working to our actual priori-ties - at least to the best of his ability. This is priority control.

Notice that I said "to the best of his ability". We also hear increasingly that the manufacturer owes it to him-self and his supplier to take that supplier's capacity into account when formulating plans. In some cases, this is even a part of the MPS generation. This implies that some suppliers may be considered "critical work centers" to the buying plant. The gray iron foundry that supplies blocks and heads to an engine plant is an obvious example. This is certainly planning capacity in conjunction with the vendor. If a vendor gets bogged down, we may open up a second source, or work with him to help him meet the increased need. This is a type of capacity control in the world of purchasing.

In fact, many purchasing professionals are now developing longer schedule horizons with favored vendors to give them more visibility for their own plans. In fact, several firms (Black and Decker was an early one) are actually committing to a portion of the near-term schedule to bring a measure of stability to the vendor's schedule. In fact, this ideally corresponds to the vendor's assembly leadtime. This further improves the capacity controls available to the purchasing function. This sounds a lot like good MPS management for the buyer's plant also, doesn't it? In fact, it is difficult if not impossible to call this the golden rule of purchasing. "Do unto your supplier's schedule as you would have the master scheduler do unto your schedule." This applies to priority maintenance, capacity checks, and stability.

In a similar vein, the remarks made about simplifying the planning and control of manufacturing through the flow techniques of stockless production apply equally well to purchasing. In fact, it is difficult if not impossible to really succeed in ZI or JIT in your own plant without moving significantly in this direction with your suppliers as well. It is obvious that the issues of cost control and quality are similarly linked between supplier and buyer.

## PURCHASING SUPPORT SYSTEMS

We make the assumption in this talk that the purchasing system is being used in conjunction with some kind of manufacturing control system. A number of the elements of a successful purchasing support system are intertwined with the elements of the manufacturing control system. This includes but is not limited to valid priority manage-ment, consideration of critical supplier constraints in the scheduling process, engineering data control, and sound inventory management.

In addition to these basic production and control features a good purchasing support system should include:

- Quotation processing (RFQs, price, quantity, effectivity)

- Purchase order and requisition processing

- Buyer data (commodity codes, parts, etc.)

- Transportation, receipt, inspection processing

- Vendor relationship management

    - Vendor information maintenance

    - Delivery performance

    - Price performance

    - Quality performance

    - Problem identification and resolution

    - Purchase order management (with or without paper P.O.)

- Value analysis support

- Purchased component cost forecasting and analysis

- Decision support (flexible inquiry, "what if" modeling, summarized and exception reporting)

## MASSEY-FERGUSON, INC., AN EXAMPLE

One of the critical dimensions of improving vendor relationships is a clear working knowledge of how a particular vendor affects our firm, our products, and our prices. This strengthens our ability to focus on the "critical few", while managing the "trivial many" professionally, but routinely. This is important to help the buyer get control of his environment as well.

When I worked in purchasing in the Detroit plant of Massey Ferguson, I was responsible for 900 parts from 110 vendors worth about $12 million a year. This included screw machine parts, hydraulic tubing, and machined castings and forgings. I received requests for price increases nearly every day. The reasons for these increases were typical - labor went up, raw materials increased, etc. Before the advent of the manufacturing control system, I would have to pull the file of the particular vendor (and my industrial strength calculator) and calculate the impact of the new prices, part by laborious part. I gathered information on the date of the last increase, percentage of increase, split sourcing availability, timing of labor contracts (for the vendor), overall purchases from this vendor, and the impact on our manufactured products. This was the basic information necessary to enter into the process of negotiating our response to their request for the increase.

Even if I found the time to do all of this research in our department, a number of elements of the whole picture were missing - elements that should significantly influence the decision. Upcoming engineering changes might change the demand for the parts (up or down). Vendor performance (quality, for example) was relatively unknown. Long term plans for the end-items that required the parts were not available. The absence of this information made the process of preparing for vendor negotiation difficult and patchy. The hectic pace of the buyer's day caused much price (and delivery, and quality) negotiation to be handled reactively or by unthinking default from a weak position.

To correct this, Massey implemented a sound manufacturing system and then tied in a purchasing support system. The request for a price increase could now be met with much more confidence. Now we could quickly get the whole history of our dealings with a vendor. I knew what parts would be affected and how these parts affected overall costs. The long term effects of engineering changes, or reduced marketing forecasts were apparent. If larger lots or longer term commitments would give us a better price, we were in a position to take advantage of them. We started developing performance ratings on each of the vendors to rank them among their peers in critical areas such as delivery and quality. This left us in a much stronger negotiating position with our vendors. As well, it helped select the vendors that deserved our attention in developing stronger relations. It was invaluable in weeding out the weaker performers.

On occasion, we would run a long term analysis of annual demand on a vendor's parts, cycle of probable increases, and impact on cost of goods sold. This was an important part of establishing standard costs for the next fiscal year.

## ANOTHER EXAMPLE - FROM THE SUPPLIER'S PERSPECTIVE

Henry Horldt owns Leader Machine. He machines castings and forgings for the automotive industry. Two of his products are clutch housings and engine flywheels. One of his principle customers is Ford Motor Company. Being a smaller manufacturer, he is perfectly positioned to give us the vendor's view of these new trends in purchasing. The most notable dimension of the new wave of purchasing is quality. When Ford boasts that "Quality is Job 1," Ford's suppliers like Henry Horldt can verify that Ford is deeply serious. Once a potential supplier has been identified by Ford purchasing, the supplier needs first to be approved by the production control and quality control groups before any order can be placed.

The production control folks will let purchasing know if this supplier has ever let a late part shut down the line. Quality control keeps the same sort of records on the quality of all parts from the supplier in question. As well, the supplier must demonstrate technical competence in his field, and willingness to cooperate with the engineering department. A negative answer in any of these areas can be enough to crowd the supplier off the shrinking island of approved Ford vendors.

The Ford quality program with their vendors seems to be the toughest in the industry. Leader Machine is continually subject to a quality audit. During a quality audit, the Ford QC team spends two full days scrutinizing every facet of the processes of Leader Machine. They verify such items as gauge control - each gauge is certified by its serial number down to the last revision level of the related print and the date of the last certification. After the exhaustive two-day scrutiny, Leader Machine is given a rating from 0 to 100. A rating of 75 is exceptional. In fact, this is enough to qualify a vendor to be nominated to the most exclusive rank among Ford's supplier network - The Q1 elite. Of course more stringent performance is required to actually enter this high caste. Leader Machine, by the way has just been nominated! The premier Q1 suppliers enjoy a streamlined order acceptance procedure and a massive thank you annually in Ford's ad in the Wall Street Journal.

A rank of 65 places the vendor on what insiders call the "intensive care" list. This means that the vendor has 90 days to significantly close the gaps - to clean up his processes - or be removed from the approved list of vendors. None of the vendors that we talked to knew how to get back on that list once removed. Therefore this program is taken with brutal seriousness by the cadre of remaining suppliers.

Up till this section, we had been talking about the benefits of PDQ performance from the viewpoint of the buying manufacturer. These programs are developed by purchasing to further their support of the manufacturing processes in their plant. How about the supplier? How does Horldt feel about the enormous pressure and constant scrutiny by his largest customer? Henry says that this program has been great for his business. While very tough, the program has also been educational and stirring.

Quality has risen to stay abreast of the exacting standards of his customer. Among all of Leader Machine's customers, the firm is known for uncompromising quality. His reputation has grown commensurately. "We are more competitive than ever," he says, "and you have to be to survive is today's marketplace." Obviously, both Ford and Leader Machine have benefited from the time and effort invested in this program.

## BURROUGHS - TEN THOUSAND COMPONENTS THAT ALL DEPEND ON EACH OTHER

That was the description that a quality engineer gave the tour group a decade ago as they visited our Tredyffrin plant. This plant in "Silicon Gulch" near Valley Forge, Pennsylvania, builds our multi-million-dollar-size computers. One of the most critical work centers (and a significant contributor to in-plant leadtime) was incoming inspection. Because the final product contains literally millions of junctions that are enormously interdependent on each other every second, the tolerance for faulty incoming parts is ruthlessly low. Incoming integrated circuits were steamed, frozen, heated, and subjected to the shake and bake tester.

Today, only a fraction of the parts are still so tested. The tolerances are tougher than ever, but our vendor certification program has greatly reduced the need for inbound testing. This had not only freed up the highly skilled staff associated with this program, and eliminated a critical bottleneck in our process, it has also shortened leadtime within the plant, thus contributing to our march toward just-in-time production.

## HOW TO EXPLAIN PDQ TO AN EXECUTIVE - A FINAL CASE STUDY

The average executive has an attention span dictated by the flow of ticker tape from the stock transaction recorder. It is never wise to attempt any highly conceptual explanations with a senior exec, and even a mildly conceptual discussion of purchasing to support manufacturing better gravitate to the bottom line in a persuasive and rapid manner. The case study of Steelcase, Inc. gives a first-rate example.

APICS has published the details of the case (3), so I won't include all of them here. Suffice it to say that the installation of a sound closed-loop material requirements planning system, coupled with a well integrated purchasing system, worked economic wonders for this company. Steelcase's Grand Rapids, Michigan plant includes four and a half million square feet on 250 acres of land (420,000 square meters on a square kilometer of grounds). They are the largest supplier of office furniture in the world with plants here in Toronto, as well as in California, North Carolina, with joint ventures in France, and Japan.
The implementation of MRP in the purchasing area caused several significant changes in the purchasing way of life at Steelcase. This included changes in vendor relations, department organization, reporting, and others. With the reduction in clerical workload, and better planning, much more attention was given to the issues of value analysis and vendor performance. In turn Steelcase strengthened its commitments to honor the schedules given to vendors if raw material had been acquired as a result of the schedule given to the vendor by Steelcase. Leadtimes for some fabrics fell from ten weeks to three weeks.

A cost reduction program, based on value analysis and vendor performance analysis was slated to save $500,000 over two years. In fact, it saved $5,000,000! The percentage of past due orders fell from 35% to 3.2%. After one month of MRP, it fell to 20% just by re-scheduling unneeded orders. Part shortages in the plant fell from 33 per week to 4. Over a two year period of 59% growth in sales, the investment in purchased part inventories rose only 12%.

All this adds up to very impressive results on the bottom line. Successful cost-reduction and improved productivity is music to the ears of any executive. Success of this magnitude is virtually a Viennese waltz to them. This is how to explain PDQ purchasing to an executive - with the right background music.

## WHAT DOES THE FUTURE HOLD FOR PURCHASING?

It is clear that the trend toward integration between supplying and buying plants will continue. By early next year, virtually all of Ford's Body and Assembly Division suppliers will be on line to Ford for direct computerized release processing. By mid-1986, this will be extended to suppliers of Ford's Engine Division. Increasingly vendor capacities and processes will be made a part of the planning cycle of their clients. Within only a few years we will see computer-aided engineering systems that not only formulate the specs of a new product, but also formulate the processes necessary to manufacture the needed parts. Furthermore, this system will load these product and process specs to the suppliers for use in their own computer-controlled work cells. Already, some firms in northern Europe have moved beyond just negotiating price with their vendors. Now they negotiate the vendor's cost. How efficient can the processes be made? If both supplier and buyer get better and better, then

there is more profit to share.

Some vendors and some buying firms will fall along the wayside during the trying times ahead. Others will seize the opportunity to become world-class competitors. The waymarks to excellence are clear: price, delivery, and quality - PDQ. The steps are well documented - top management commitment, excellence at every level, education to strengthen the only appreciating asset (your people), and a driving desire to get better each day.

We challenge and welcome you to join us!

---

NOTES:

(1) Aiello, Joseph L., "Successful Interaction between Purchasing and Production and Inventory Control," 1979 Conference Proceedings, pp. 234 - 236.

(2) Bevis, George, "Closed-Loop MRP at the Tennant Company." Included in Vollmann, Berry, and Whybark, Manufacturing Planning and Control Systems, Dow Jones-Irwin, 1984

(3) Carter, P.L., and Monczka, R.M., "Steelcase, Inc: MRP in Purchasing," Case Studies in Material Requirements Planning, 1978, pp. 105 - 129.

===============================================================
## BIOGRAPHIES

John P. Flavin, CPIM acts as a manufacturing consultant for Burroughs Midwest Region. He formerly taught courses in manufacturing for Burroughs. He served on the AMES (Applied Manufacturing Education Series) Development Committee, and conducts certification seminars.

John received a B.S. in Business Administration from Eastern Michigan University. He worked for two years at Ford Motor Company, and eight years at Massey-Ferguson, Inc. His titles included Shop Floor Planner, Expeditor, Production Buyer, Material Control Supervisor, and Production Control Manager. John brings extensive expertise in purchasing and its relation to manufacturing.

Thomas H. Fuller, Jr., CPIM* is Manager of Educational Quality for Burroughs Corporation. He also served on the AMES Development Committee. He serves on the MRP subcommittee of the Curriculum and Certification Council.

Tom received a B.A. in Math from Amherst College, and an M.S. in Education from Old Dominion University. He has worked in the warehouse and on the production floor of CPC, International, and for the manpower planning department of the Naval Air Rework Facility, Norfolk, Virginia. He has held several marketing and training positions at Burroughs, where he currently manages various training projects. Tom has published articles in Production and Inventory Management and the Auerbach Series on Manufacturing, and often addresses APICS meetings, including the First World Congress of Production and Inventory Control.

## PURCHASING—THE NEW FRONTIER
Michael J. Stickler, CPIM
Xerox Computer Services

In the past, a tremendous amount of effort has been invested trying to improve the productivity of direct labor and the manufacturing process; there have been several companies within the U.S.A. and abroad who have been extremely effective in doing this. While this is necessary and benefits have been forthcoming, in some companies the purchasing effort has been taken for granted. This presentation will address the proper role of the procurement function as it scrambles to support MRPII and the Just-In-Time crusade.

Discussions will center on:

- An Introduction To A "New Philosophy" Of Procurement.
- Vendor Capacity Management - The Other Shop.
- Blanket Versus Regular Purchase Orders.
- The Use Of Stocking Agreements To Shorten Lead Times.
- Vendor Quality Programs To Provide Pre-Inspection.
- Contract Purchasing And The Interface With MRPII.
- Receiving And Dock-To-Stock Problems.

This presentation will provide examples showing cause and effect in each of the noted areas.

### THE "NEW PHILOSOPHY" OF PROCUREMENT

The relationships that once existed with vendors, one of conflict and mistrust, must be revised. To include the vendor as part of the manufacturing process provides a much better material flow into the plant.

In the past, Purchasing's main thrust was to try and get the better of the vendor. This type of environment creates more problems than can be counted!

The procurement goals have centered on purchasing the:

|        |                |
|--------|----------------|
|        | right material |
| at the | right price    |
| at the | right quantity |
| at the | right quality  |
| at the | right time     |

These goals are in conflict, just like the goals of production and inventory control (maximum customer service, minimum investment in inventory and maximum productivity).

It seems that in some companies, the real goal of procurement has been overlooked or forgotten! The real goal is .....  **SUPPORT THE MATERIAL PLAN !!!**

In order to accomplish this goal, the basic functions of procurement should be revisited. They are:

1.  Development of reliable vendors who can deliver on time with minimum lead time and required quality.

2.  Scheduling of vendor deliveries just-in-time and in the quantities required for immediate production.

3.  Help in the development of a vendor value engineering program which will reduce procurement costs.

Granted, these functions are ambiguous to say the least, but they are essential in order to fully move into the MRPII or Just-In-Time environments that manufacturing is striving for.

The implication of these functions is that both the supplier and customer are working in the same direction not at cross-purposes.

These functions would also indicate arrangements that are typically longer term. The vendor is considered a member of the family and is a key member/participant in the manufacturing process.

In some companies, the vendor is involved as a member of the development/design team along with being a consultant on the use of new materials, manufacturing processes, tooling and quality assurance to name a few.

As you can see this "new philosophy" is not really new, implementing it is!

### VENDOR CAPACITY MANAGEMENT - THE OTHER SHOP

The real power of MRPII and Just-In-Time comes from executing the plan. Vendor Capacity Management (VCM) is becoming very important in order to insure the flow of materials into the manufacturing process. VCM can insure that the vendor can really come through!

Once a proper relationship is established with the vendor, his reception to someone else reviewing the cause and effect of the load his buyer is imposing should deminish. (A proper relationship puts the vendor and the buyer onto the same team, both working towards helping each other to greater profits).

The same approach used in-house to do capacity requirements planning can be applied to the vendor environment. The problem is how much of the vendor's total load does the buyer represent. At a minimum, you can at least see what load you impose on his environment. (A caution: Do not go into detail; CRP, if rough cut, provides a good picture). Within a good vendor/buyer relationship, the vendor will respond and the helpful.

In order to develop feedback for the relationship to grow strong, an agreed upon set of performance measurements should be established. These measurements should include the following at a minimum:

Regular Capacity Planning Meetings
Response To Changes
Actual To Scheduled Delivery
Number Of Time Fences And Lead Time Violations

It should be stressed that these performance measurements must be used in a positive manner, as a means to identify problem areas for correction! These performance ratings should be included in an overall vendor rating system.

By not doing VCM, it would be easy to duplicate the following: A company that manufactures machine tools for industry was in a situation where the load in their engineering department forced them to sub-contract some of the engineering design effort. While they were at it, they allowed the vendor to also procure the designed component assemblies. While on the surface this appears to be a good decision, the effect was disastrous. The vendor who did the design effort somehow picked the same vendor to build the component assemblies that the original builder had picked. This resulted in two problems:

- They overloaded the vendor who did the production of the assemblies.

- They created a conflict in priorities (both the vendor and the original contractor trying to set priorities) within the limited capacity.

If you develop good relationships with the vendor and do VCM, this situation can be avoided.

### BLANKET VERSUS REGULAR PURCHASE ORDERS

The use of blanket purchase orders is expanding every day. A blanket purchase is a purchase order for a large quantity with multiple delivery quantities and dates. Normally the quantity on this blanket purchase order is determined based on output from a MRP system and an order policy. The multiple delivery quantities and dates are a result of again looking at the MRP output. The result is the creation of one purchase order, where in the past several individual regular purchase orders were created.

This could represent considerable savings to the supplier as well as the vendor! On the supplier's side, some of the advantages are:

- Improved Material Plan (this input of demand will help the vendor plan material requirements and support in-house efforts to support the buyer).

- Improved Capacity Plan (this input of demand will help the vendor plan capacity requirements to support the in-house efforts to support the buyer).

On the buyer's side, some of the advantages are:

- An improved material flow into the plant.

- A handle on vendor lead time. If the blanket order extends out further than the vendor lead time, minor changes in the vendor lead times will not have an effect.

While upon close inspection, blanket purchase orders appear to have an advantage over regular purchase orders. Some problems, however, still exist:

- As the MRP plan changes, maintenance on the quantities and dates could be extensive.

- The liability that exists with the commitment created by the blanket purchase orders could be prohibitive.

A caution: The MPS and MRP plan should be "good" prior to the implementation of a blanket purchase campaign.

### THE USE OF STOCKING AGREEMENTS TO SHORTEN LEAD TIMES

The idea of having a vendor maintain inventory levels for a buyer is not new. Vendors will provide this service at a cost. The costs, if not policed, could grow into a considerable sum.

Stocking agreements usually fall into two (2) categories. The vendor maintains inventory in the buyer's facility. The second, when the vendor maintains inventory within his finished goods, at specific levels.

The major advantage of these arrangements is lead time; the parts become a secondary concern. An additional advantage is that the vendor does most of the work. In the environment where the vendor maintains inventory in the buyer's facility (normally hardware) on a regular basis, the vendor reviews quantity on-hand and replenishes to an agreed upon level. A company who assembles motors has used this approach for several years and they have never run out of material. The problem is that the buyer has on an average six (6) to eight (8) weeks worth of hardware, and that adds up to a considerable amount of money. With this arrangement, stocking levels must be reviewed on a regular basis.

In the environment where the agreement is to maintain inventory levels within the vendor's facility, some additional thought is necessary.

The material that is stocked in the vendor's finished goods might or might not belong to the buyer. This is dependent upon the agreement established up-front.

An electronics company took this approach for many of its long lead items and they have met with a lot of success. They have only a small number of items which are not set up on this type of stocking program. As a result they can be very responsive to their customers. It is important to note that their customers pay for the responsive action and that an item is not set-up in a stocking program until design is complete and the risk of change if minimal. A majority of the parts are set-up with a sliding stocking arrangement.

Items have a minimum and a maximum level based upon lead times from the suppliers. For example: A simple 'C' part with a lead time of three (3) weeks (under normal conditions) will be stocked at the vendor's location in quantities projected to be needed based upon the last MRP run. The vendor is asked to maintain a minimum of six (6) weeks supply. The level to be stocked is based on ABC classification, the MRP plan and the lead times from the supplier. Granted, costs are considerably higher for both the vendor and the buyer with this type of program, but their customers want responsiveness.

An additional point ..... material is moved from the vendor into the buyer's environment on a weekly basis.

### VENDOR QUALITY PROGRAMS TO ELIMINATE RECEIVING INSPECTION

The move to improve quality is on, in virtually every industry. As the move to zero inventory is made, probably the biggest headaches will come from having rejects or scrap. The system will not work without eliminating or at least minimizing these problems.

Highly stable yields will allow the system to operate more effectively as a pull system.

Quality implies more than conformance to design. It also implies functionality, durability, reliability and also a pleasing appearance. Each and every part or product is a result of the quality of the manufacturing process. If a production process cannot manage well enough to complete a product that meets or exceeds what is expected, it doesn't matter if the design specifications were met.

In dealing with vendors, we must set a level of expectation that we will not tolerate inferior products and that it is their responsibility to make sure that the materials are acceptable. It is important for the vendor to understand that by just tightening inspection and telling people to be more careful will not solve the problem, at best it is only temporary help. The vendor must be aware of the variance of the manufacturing process along with the variance of the part and his efforts towards zero defects should be directed towards the minimization of variances in the process.

The key here is that if the part leaves the vendor at a high level of quality, the process of re-inspection upon receipt at the buyer's is an additional costly step that can be eliminated. In Bob Hall's book Zero Inventories, he devotes all of Chapter Seven (7) to the discussion of quality programs. These programs can be applied in the vendor environment as well as within the buyer's area.

### CONTRACT PURCHASING AND THE INTERFACE WITH MRPII

Contract purchase orders are used to insure a continuous supply or flow of material, with the capability to minimize forward commitments and yet still provide the supplier with an estimate of future requirements, time phased into the planning horizon. Using this technique, contracts issued to a supplier will contain several part numbers, the anticipated usage (quantity and date needed) and the agreed upon unit cost.

The contract purchase order review technique discussed here is also known by the acronym as SMART (Systematic Material Acquisition And Review Technique). The primary function of the SMART contract is to give the material planner (analyst) direct access to the vendor, by-passing the buyer, thus saving time. Once a contract has been negotiated by the buyer, all subsequent deliveries can be scheduled by the planner. The planner uses the MRP output to determine the quantity and the delivery date of the part.

The document provided to the vendor should contain the following at a minimum:

- Date
- Supplier
- Ship-To
- Part Number
- Description
- Purchase Order Number
- Contract Number
- Release Number
- Lead Time
- Print Revision Level
- Net Receipts To Date

```
    * Actual
    * Scheduled
  - Date Of Last Receipt
  - Cumulative Release To Date
  - Current Schedule (From Previous Releases)
    * Date
    * Quantity
  - Changes To Current Schedule
    * Date
    * Quantity
  - New Deliveries - This Release
    * Date
    * Quantity
  - Estimated Future Requirements
    * Month
    * Quantity
  - Comments
  - Originator
```

Figure One (1) shows a typical SMART contract document format.

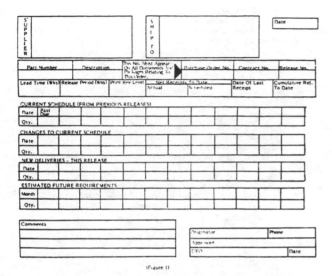

(Figure 1)

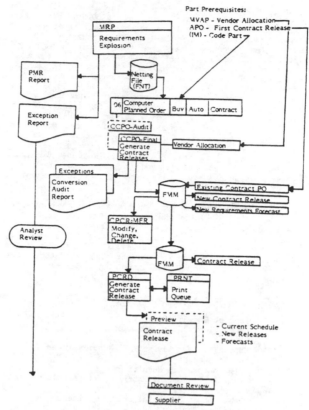

Flow Diagram Of A Contract Purchase Order Release

(Figure 2)

In order to insure that releases are automatically issued against contract purchase order .....

- MRP must recognize that a contract purchase order exists for a given part. The MRP explosion creates computer planned orders for unsatisfied demand. If the part with the unsatisfied demand has been flagged as a SMART contract part, MRP looks for the SMART contract number and the vendor allocation table for the part. Based upon this information, MRP suggests the issuance of a release against the contract to satisfy the demand. This suggested release is previewed before finalizing. The ability to add, change, and delete to the current schedule, new deliveries and estimated future requirements area is necessary as part of finalizing the release.

Upon finalization of the release, the document is printed, reviewed, and forwarded to the supplier. Figure Two (2) is a flow diagram of a contract (SMART) purchase order release.

The power of the SMART contract is that once a vendor is selected and a contract negotiated, the material will **flow** into the manufacturing process. This technique is a winner for both the buyer and the supplier. On the supplier's side the advantages include:

- A Contract
- Information For Planning Capability And Materials
- A Longer Relationship
- A Relationship That Could Grow

On the buyer's side, some of the advantages are:

- A Contract
- The Buyer Is Out Of The Loop (The Planner Takes Over)
- Quicker/Automatic Updating Of Priorities From MRP
- A Longer Relationship
- A Relationship That Could Grow

SMART contracts are a good means of communicating priorities and changes to those priorities. However, like other tools, they are only as good as the people using them and the system supporting them. Imagine the catastrophic effects created by a mis-managed master schedule or poor data accuracy with this dynamic tool!

## RECEIVING AND DOCK-TO-STOCK PROBLEMS

This area has always been a source of problems, from the queue of trucks waiting to unload materials that are not needed for a month, to the trouble shelf where material sits, and let's not forget the three (3) to four (4) month backlog in receiving inspections.

Each of the situations should be addressed in turn.

The first, that queue of trucks waiting to unload materials that are are needed for a month. Many vendors, towards month-end do a scramble and ship orders early in order to make the monthly shipping dollars. Sometimes, they ignore the fact that you do not want the material.

A tool that can help control this situation is an Overshipment/Overschedule Analysis Window. This tool reacts when a receipt is entered. The system is triggered to edit the basic purchase order information against the receiving information versus a set standard. The Overshipment/Overschedule Analysis Window helps to control two (2) areas: early shipments and overshipments. Early shipments are controlled by specifying the maximum number of days early a shipment will be accepted for delivery (e.g. 10 days). Based on this time frame, a second control specifies that constant dollar amount allowed for overshipments that arrive early, say $300.00. With these criteria, a shipment would be accepted only if it were not more than ten (10) days early and the shipment did not exceed the purchase order line item amount by more than $300.00. If either one of these parameters is exceeded, the shipment cannot be received. (This tool can help get a handle on cash flow!) The overscheduled/overshipped items should provide the capability which would allow you to accept items which exceed the ordered quantity by not more than an established percentage - for example 10% and as long as it does not exceed a dollar value limit. This enables the receiving person to receive more goods than ordered within an established tolerance range.

This is a tool that can be put into use overnight. However, you must educate your vendors and start with larger tolerances, eventually working them in the desired direction.

The second area is the trouble shelf, where material sits and sits and sits and sits. Material disposition seems to be a problem on just about everyone's receiving dock. Not knowing if the material received is accepted, scrapped, to be reworked or even to be returned to the vendor, can create havoc for the material expeditors. The flow of material through the receiving department should be kept simple, yet provide for disposition.

At a minimum the system should provide for:

- Receipt Of The Material
- Generation Of A Document (Move Tag/Receiving Report)
- Capability To Assign Lot Numbers (Even Split A Lot If Necessary)
- Enter Inspection Results
- Transfer Discrepant Material Into A Holding Area
- Accept Material Into Inventory
- Create Debit Memos And Shipping Orders
- Track The Costs Of Rework
- Dispose Of Scrap And Return Material To The Vendor
- Interfaces To Accounts Payable And Purchasing
- Define What Material In This Area Is Nettable For MRP

Figure Three (3) shows a typical flow in the Dock-To-Stock area.

The third area becomes even more interesting.....the backlog in receiving inspection. This department is many times overlooked. How many companies do capacity planning for this area or even generate a dispatch list? The same basic tools that are used for other work centers can be applied in the receiving inspection department. The real goal should be to eliminate this bottleneck in the manufacturing process. By moving to source inspection, vendor quality programs, using the Overshipment/Overschedule Analysis Window and a sound material disposition (dock-to-stock) system, this problem should cure itself. However, until it does, capacity planning and a dispatch list can help.

### SUMMARY

Procurement cannot stand alone. The programs discussed require commitment and support. The benefits are many and the results can be impressive. Some of the improvement opportunities include:

- On Time Deliveries/More Frequent
- Reduced Costs
- Higher Quality
- Less Paper Work
- Shortened Vendor Lead Times
- Reduced Inventory
- More Responsive Suppliers

- Less Expediting
- Purchasing Negotiating
- Reduced Material Handling
- Longer Vendor Supplier Relationships
- Visibility And More Stable Plans
- Better Flow Of Materials
- Improved Profits

**Purchasing - The New Frontier, Let's Make It The Old Frontier.**

### REFERENCES

1. Hall, Robert W., "Zero Inventories" Homewood, Illinois, 60430, Dow Jones-Irwin, 1983.
2. Andrew, Charles G., "Putting The Co-Maker Concept Into Practice", Proceedings, APICS 1983 Annual Conference, November, 1983, New Orleans, Louisiana.
3. Landis, Gary A., "Vendor Capacity Planning: A New Frontier For The 80's", Proceedings, APICS 1983 Annual Conference, November 1983, New Orleans, Louisiana.

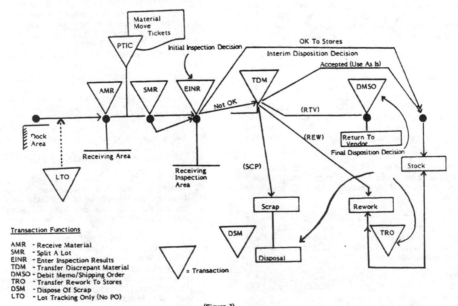

Transaction Functions

AMR - Receive Material
SMR - Split A Lot
EINR - Enter Inspection Results
TDM - Transfer Discrepant Material
DMSO - Debit Memo/Shipping Order
TRO - Transfer Rework To Stores
DSM - Dispose Of Scrap
LTO - Lot Tracking Only (No PO)

(Figure 3)

## ABOUT THE AUTHOR

Michael Stickler is an Education Consultant with Xerox Computer Services. He has over 14 years experience in manufacturing and has held positions as a Plant Manager, Manager of Production Scheduling and Manufacturing Systems Coordinator. He has worked with MRP since 1973. Mike is an active member of APICS. He is on the Board of Directors for Region 13, is on the Board of Directors for the Chicago Chapter, and is Chairman of the highly regarded Eight (8) Week Education Classes. He is also an Instructor for the MRP Certification Review sponsored by the Chicago Chapter. Mike is a frequent Seminar and Dinner Speaker throughout the U.S.A. and Canada. His papers "Capacity Management - Case Study", Performance Measurements For Productive Management have both been published in the 1982 and 1983 APICS National Conference Proceedings respectively. Michael has been recognized as a Certified CPIM since 1980.

## SUB-MRP: THE MINIMUM SYSTEMS STRATEGY
Philip Allor, CFPIM
Deloitte Haskins & Sells

Sub-MRP is a new concept in manufacturing planning and scheduling systems. Whereas the use of conventional transaction based manufacturing systems might be viewed as a maximum systems strategy, the use of Sub-MRP represents a minimum systems strategy. Such a strategy is appropriate for small and medium size manufacturing facilities where there is a need for automated systems to support planning and scheduling activities but there may not be the time, money or people to implement a conventional transaction based system.

### THE PLANNING AND SCHEDULING PROBLEM

A key question that confronts every manufacturing manager every day is determining what should everybody be doing today to make the manufacturing plan happen. This is by no means an easy thing to do. The fact that it is difficult has given rise to all manner of manufacturing systems from MRP II to Kanban.

Everyone seems to be looking to implement bigger and more sophisticated systems to get a better handle on the problem. But more sophisticated systems create other problems. Often, a disproportionate share of management attention has been focused on systems rather than on the real business of manufacturing -- making product and getting it to the customer.

Given an environment in which increasingly sophisticated systems have become the norm, what if one were to adopt a counter approach? There must be simpler means to the same end. Instead of a maximum systems strategy, what if we were to adopt a minimum systems strategy? What if we were to give up a little of functionality of a conventional system in order make big gains in ease of implementation and ease of use? This is the basic concept behind Sub-MRP, a no-frills approach to manufacturing systems.

### THE TRANSACTION BASED SYSTEM

A transaction based system is one which requires a steady stream of transactions to be input and processed in order to be functional. Most accounting systems are, for example, transaction based. There are two main problems inherent to transaction based systems. One relates to implementation. It's a big job. It takes a lot of time, consumes considerable resources and it is not without some risk. The other relates to keeping the system operating of a go forward basis. This is potentially a much bigger job. The reason, and hence the main weakness in conventional transaction based manufacturing planning and scheduling systems, has to do with the simultaneous occurrence of:

- High Data Accuracy Requirements - most manufacturing systems are highly sensitive to data accuracy. As inaccuracies (in inventory records, open orders, bills-of-material, etc.) creep in, system effectiveness erodes considerably.

- High Transaction Volumes - aside from effort required in processing, high transaction volumes bring with them the one thing that manufacturing systems can't tolerate: a high volume of errors. Further, the nature of the environment is such that the errors tend to accumulate over time rather than cancel each other out, making things even worse.

All of the effort we currently see relating to improving record accuracy (i.e., paperless systems, barcoding, cycle counting, etc.) points up the fact that data accuracy is not what it should be and that its causing big problems. We could attack the symptom (i.e., by doing more cycle counting) or we could attack the root cause by eliminating the dependence on transactions through the use of a non-transaction based system such as Sub-MRP.

### HOW SUB-MRP EVOLVED

At the time Sub-MRP was developed it was not apparent there was any pressing need for a non-transaction based manufacturing system. Sub-MRP's origin was essentially a pragmatic response to a extreme situation. It grew out of work some years ago with severely troubled companies. The circumstances were such that there was a pressing need effect improvements but few resources with which to do it and even less time. It was pointless to look at the long-term; if the problems weren't corrected in the short-term, there wouldn't be any long-term.

We began to look closely at the problem. There was a clear need for manufacturing systems but a maximum systems approach (i.e., MRP II), given the constraints within which we needed to work, was out of the question. We then began thinking terms of a purely interim system - something to get us by until we would be in a position to implement a more permanent solution.

We asked ourselves what is it that we really need to do and what is the absolute minimum in terms of systems that we could get by with? In doing this we made an interesting discovery, that much of the complexity, cost and implementation difficulty associated with a conventional manufacturing planning and scheduling appeared to be related to transaction processing. If we could somehow eliminate or significantly reduce transaction processing, we would be able to go with a far simpler and less costly system. We began focusing our efforts in that direction and the result became Sub-MRP.

When we implemented Sub-MRP, it worked far better than we had ever anticipated. So well, in fact, that it became apparent that there was really no point in implementing a maximum system as our final solution. Sub-MRP was our final solution. Since that time, Sub-MRP implementations have been made at a number of different companies with essentially the same results.

### WHAT IS SUB-MRP

Sub-MRP represents a minimum systems strategy for manufacturing resource planning. It uses the "brains" of MRP II but avoids the "grunt work". It consists of a collection of application modules incorporating the following general characteristics:

- It is non-transaction based

- It uses much of the planning and scheduling logic used by MRP II

- Special manual procedures are used to get appropriate data into the system

- Data is presented to system users in simple spread sheet format.

### EXAMPLE SUB-MRP APPLICATION - INVENTORY MANAGEMENT

At this point I would like to walk through a typical application of Sub-MRP, an inventory management system. Modern inventory management systems do a lot of things. But, the key function that we look for an inventory management system to do for us is to tell a material planner:

- What to replenish

- When to replenish

- How much to replenish.

If an inventory management system does a reasonably good job at this, irrespective of everything else, it must be a reasonably good system.

Traditional manual inventory management approaches (i.e., periodic review and two-bin) clearly had advantages in that they were simple and non-transaction based. But, they also left much to be desired in their ability to manage and control inventories. Replacing them with a more modern inventory management approach (i.e., a perpetual inventory system) represented a big step forward in that we could now control inventory a lot more precisely. But, this new capability did not come free. The price was going from a non-transaction based system to a transaction based system. Figure 1 contains a block diagram of a typical perpetual inventory system illustrating the principal data and transaction flows.

### Figure 1.

### Conventional Perpetual Inventory System

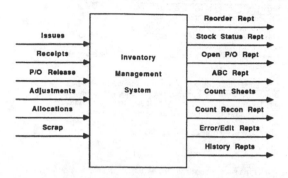

As presented in Figure 1, considerable data (as depicted by arrows) flows into and out of the system. On the input side, this flow of data corresponds to transactions that must be entered and processed. This often requires considerable effort.

On the output side, the flow of data corresponds to reports which must be read and interpreted. Only one of these reports, the Reorder Report, directly addresses the systems principal objective, that of determining what, how much and when to reorder. All the rest of the reports are there to ensure data integrity, in other words, to detect and correct errors in input transactions. This demonstrates the problem of maintaining inventory record accuracy in an environment of high transaction volumes. All sorts of strategies have been put forth to deal with it:

. Annual Physical Inventories

. Location Audits

. Cycle Counting.

Of these, cycle counting seems to be the accepted practice. To maintain high record accuracies, one must do frequent cycle counts -- very frequent cycle counts in the opinion of some authorities in this area. In one extreme case, I know of a high volume repetitive manufacturer where 25% of the part numbers are counted every day. With this volume of counting, one has to question whether the inventory system is truly "perpetual".

In this context, perpetual inventory appears to be a flawed system. In order to maintain high record accuracies required by the system, one has to do frequent counting. But, frequent counting is what perpetual inventory systems were supposed to eliminate.

Consider now the Sub-MRP approach to inventory management. The data flows associated with such a system are illustrated in Figure 2.

The most striking thing about Figure 2 is that there isn't much to it, not much in the way of inputs, not much in the way of outputs. Since there is no perpetual inventory, there are no transactions to process. Instead, periodic inventory counts are taken and directly entered into the system. Purchase order information (new orders released, old orders received complete or cancelled) are accumulated on a log (either manual or automated) and also entered into the system.

The processing logic of the system uses the inventory counts and purchase information to calculate:

. Forecasted Demand

### Figure 2.

### Sub-MRP Based Inventory System

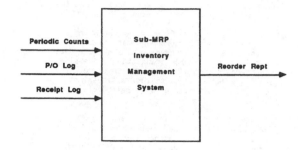

. Forecast Error (demand variation)

. Safety Stock Level

. Order Points

. Order Quantities.

With no transactions and far less potential for error, most of the outputs can be eliminated. The sole output of the system is a Reorder Point Report, containing replenishment recommendations, which would go to a material planner. A representation of this report is presented in Figure 3.

### Figure 3.

### Sub-MRP Reorder Report

| Sub-MRP Reorder Report | | | | | | | |
|---|---|---|---|---|---|---|---|
| Description | Demand | Error | Order Point | On Hnd | Forecast Recvd | On Order | Order Qty |
| Item A | 1200 | 150 | 1500 | 900 | 3000 | 0 | 3000 |
| Item B | 2400 | 300 | 3000 | 2000 | 0 | 0 | 8000 |
| Item C | 6000 | 400 | 9000 | 7000 | 0 | 10000 | 10000 |

This report also same format used for data entry. A user need only become familiar with one data format.

OTHER SUB-MRP APPLICATIONS

The Sub-MRP concept can be applied to areas other than just Inventory Management. Other Sub-MRP applications include:

. Master Production Scheduling - establishing overall production rates for a plant, controlling demand input, managing backlog and finished goods inventory levels. This is an ideal area for the use of Sub-MRP since it tends to be more logic than transaction oriented. A key consideration will be the establishment of appropriate mechanisms for the collection of needed data:

.. Customer Demand

.. Backlog

.. Finished Goods Inventory Level

- Rough-cut Capacity Planning - generating a partial capacity plan (i.e., for key resources) directly from the Master Production Schedule. This is also an ideal candidate for the use of Sub-MRP since there are no transactions and the required data is already resident in the MPS.

- Material Requirements Planning - generating a time-phased plan for component material. This has the potential for needing considerable data a possibly considerable transaction processing when there is a complex product structure. The use of Sub-MRP is thus limited to situations where the product structure is relatively simple.

- Tool Requirements Planning - generating a time-phases plan for perishable tooling used in the manufacture of a component or end item. Conceptually this is very similar to MRP and thus it has similar processing logic. Since a tool bill is usually less complex than a material bill, this tends to be an even better application for Sub-MRP than MRP.

- Shop Floor Control - controlling work in process on the shop floor. Since this application has the potential for generating considerable transaction volume, particular care must be given in developing associated manual procedures so that the system is not overwhelmed.

- Production Reporting - reporting overall attainment of plant operational goals:

  .. Production

  .. Quality

  .. Shipping Performance

  .. Schedule Attainment.

  Key considerations in implementing this application are what needs to be regularly reported to management (i.e., performance with respect to critical success factors) and the availability of data.

This is most probably not a complete list. Sub-MRP is still evolving. Other applications will no doubt be developed in the future.


IMPLEMENTING SUB-MRP

For a single location, it is quite possible to implement a Sub-MRP application in a few weeks using a microcomputer. Before moving ahead with a Sub-MRP implementation, however, it will be necessary to do some groundwork. In particular, you will need to:

- Define the Problem - specifically identify the problem or problems that Sub-MRP is expected to solve. Why are we doing this? What specific things do we expect Sub-MRP to accomplish? If you can't answers this and get a broadbased consensus among your company's management ranks, you probably aren't in a position to implement Sub-MRP or any manufacturing systems for that matter.

- Assess Whether Sub-MRP Will Fit - Sub-MRP has clear limitations. In general it is geared to a small to medium size manufacturing facility with a relatively simple product structure.

- Get an Up-Front Commitment to Make Operational Changes - expect that Sub-MRP will precipitate some changes in the way we run the business. It must. If we still run the business the same way (i.e., by merely automating what currently exists) we will have derived little benefit from Sub-MRP. This is true to some extent for

all manufacturing systems but more so for Sub-MRP. Since the system is simple and easy to install, the focus of the implementation effort tends to be on making needed operational changes.

- Designate a Project Sponsor - you will need some heavy weight management support to get the job done properly. Line up someone in senior management who has a vested interest in a successful implementation and with enough authority to get the operational changes made.

- Establish a Mechanism for Focused Problem Solving - there will be problems to solve some of which will be multidimensional and will impact more than one functional area. To get these resolved and to get a consensus regarding the solution, establish Sub-MRP task force with representatives from the key functional areas impacted.

- Get Some Outside Help - find somebody who has been through it before. Most companies who implement manufacturing systems utilize some outside assistance either from a vendor or an educator or a consultant. It can get you up the learning curve a lot faster.


CONCLUSION

Conventional transaction based manufacturing systems manufacturing systems are both a blessing and a curse. They allow us to operate our manufacturing facilities in ways that would have been impossible before. But, they also create many new difficulties. Mostly this stems from the fact that they are transaction based.

Sub-MRP offers an alternative. It is a non-transaction based minimum systems strategy. It is easier to implement, easier to operate and far less costly. It permits manufacturing managers to focus their attention more on the real business of manufacturing -- making and shipping product to customers.

PHILIP ALLOR, CFPIM

Philip Allor is a Senior Manager with Deloitte Haskins and Sells (DH&S), a major international professional services firm. He is located in Detroit where he specializes in manufacturing systems consulting. He has a broad background in manufacturing and manufacturing systems and has served a wide variety of clients including repetitive manufacturers, job shops and process industry manufacturers.

He is the originator of the Sub-MRP concept and over the past several years has conducted a number of successful Sub-MRP implementations.

He holds a BME degree in Mechanical Engineering and an MBA from the University of Detroit. He is a Certified Data Processor and is certified at the fellow level by APICS. He is a former vice-President of Education for the Detroit APICS Chapter and is an instructor in the chapter's certification workshop program.

Prior to joining DH&S, he worked in various capacities for Control Data Corporation and General Motors.

Reprinted from *Production and Inventory Management*, Vol. 25, No. 2, 1984.

# IMPROVING FACTORY PERFORMANCE WITH SERVICE REQUIREMENTS PLANNING (SRP)

Richard S. Bojanowski

University of Houston     Houston, TX

## INTRODUCTION

The past decade has been viewed as generating high inflation increased government regulation, a decline in worker productivity, and reduced business profits. The seventies also produced a high rate of technological development. Many technically advanced management systems were developed to improve industrial productivity and profitability. Due to reduced sales growth and constricted profits, industry opted for slow assimilation of some management systems which required an investment of time and capital [1, p. 54].

Material Requirements Planning (MRP) is a computerized material management system which has generally achieved very good results. But it required over ten years to develop slightly more than a thousand well-functioning MRP installations by 1980 (2, p. 337]. MRP increases the length of production runs, minimizes inventory, expedites rush orders to reduce related cost, and reduces handling cost caused by advance planning problems. MRP controls raw material, work-in-process, and finished goods inventories.

Service Requirements Planning (SRP) is primarily concerned with reducing the probability of production machinery failure by identifying and prioritizing routine mechanical inspection and machine maintenance sequences. The result of the application of these sequences is improved production machine and assembly line performance.

Secondarily, SRP is concerned with the reduction of Maintenance, Repair, and Operating (MRO) inventories. Time phasing and lateral scanning are two computer techniques which aid in achieving this goal.

Third, the SRP system has the ability to develop repair labor and material actual costs, budgeted costs, and cost variances by machine, production line, department, or total plant dependent upon the sophistication which management desires. They should be mutually supportive management systems.

SRP is a hybrid management system which is derived from MRP system logic. SRP was designed to function independently of MRP, to act as a catalytic base for MRP, or as an adjunct to a MRP system.

## THE SCOPE OF SRP SYSTEM DEVELOPMENT

SRP was developed as a result of research in materials management systems and organizational designs. Part of the research included a survey of twenty-five factories located in eleven states. All but one factory (a chemicals manufacturer) produced either metal products or machine tools. 60% of these factories utilized highly automated production systems. The remainder were sophisticated job shops.

During the factory survey, it became apparent that each factory or parent company had, at least once during 1971–1981, modified its materials management system and/or organization. This was done as a response to high interest rates, slow sales growth, and generally depressed profits. The performance improvements for materials management were expressed in terms of improved turnover of raw, work-in-process, and finished goods inventories. The strategy was good, since about 65% of product cost for metals manufacturers is comprised of metal. The problem was that Maintenance, Repair, and Operating (MRO) inventories were generally not managed as well as production inventories. The reason for this was determined to be a lack of machine service requirements planning as opposed to material requirements planning (MRP) systems which have been available since the early seventies.

Since the ordering cycle for many steel products requires 90 days, it is often difficult for manufacturers to turn over process inventories more than four times per year. Thus, for a factory which has sales of 50 million per year and a gross profit margin of 35%, standard product cost would approximate to 32.5 million. In many factories, 65% of product cost would be attributed to steel cost (raw, w.i.p., and f.g. inventories) of about 21.1 million. With a turnover rate of four times per year, this hypothetical factory would be managing average process inventories of 5.3 million at any given period.

Surveys have shown that MRO inventories average 15% of process inventories [3, p. 91]. In our model factory, MRO inventories were valued at 3.2 million. But by comparison, MRO inventories (predominantly repair parts) turnover less than twice annually compared to process inventories at four times or more. The 3.2 million MRO value turned over 1.9 times per year would provide an average inventory of about 1.7 million. Another problem with MRO inventories, which is substantiated by data from the factory survey, is that the cost of obsolescence of repair parts (roughly 60% of MRO inventory) is at least double the process inventory obsolescence for many factories.

Obviously, the gap between average process and MRO inventories has diminished. It is sometimes less than a 3:1 ratio, depending on raw material value and the number and sophistication of machines used. There is no doubt that MRO inventories require good management. There are three primary reasons why this has not always occurred in the average management environment:

1. Failure to extend a more centralized materials management organizational design to the MRO inventory sphere;
2. Interdisciplinary problems concerning repair parts and labor expense problems between line and staff organizations;
3. Lack of computerized management systems which afford routine machine service requirements planning and data base information.

The scope of SRP system development was not limited to improvement of MRO inventory management. A major concern was to design a machine servicing system which could plan servicing sequences at the correct time interval, thereby reducing the probability of failure for the component, the production machine, or the assembly line. Machine reliability theory states that if a single component fails, then the entire machine fails. If the malfunctioning machine is part of an assembly line, and there are no parallel machines which perform the same function, then the line also fails to function. Thus, if a machine has n = 50 components in series, and each component has an average reliability of 99.6 percent, then total machine reliability is only about 80 percent. Because the probability of failure of each component is $1.000 - 0.996 = 0.004$, then the probability of machine failure due to a single component failure is 0.20 [2, p. 417]. Improved performance of production equipment through SRP emphasis upon reduction of probability of machine failure is estimated at 3 to 10 percent per year. For most factories, gains in production efficiency of this magnitude are even more valuable than the 20 percent MRO inventory reductions which are possible with the system.

Any management system design must be able to function within an appropriate organizational design. Even the best designed system will not function well if organizational design and implementation can't support it. All of the factories which were surveyed had reorganized its materials management organizations at least once during the past decade. Almost all of them had opted for a centralized materials management organizational design. With this design, the materials manager has primary responsibility for process inventory. Subordinate managers for functions such as receiving, warehousing, shipping, purchasing, production control, and electronic data processing report directly to the materials manager. With this organizational design, the materials manager can control material from the production planning phase, through the manufacturing process, and finally through warehousing and distribution.

The highly significant trend toward centralized materials management was no accident. Centralization of organizational design occurs almost invariably when managements are faced with high production costs, high interest rates, inventory carrying costs of 20 to 30 percent, reduced sales, and declining profits. Centralization is a normal management technique which is used when more sophisticated and disciplined controls are required. It is also very common when intensive government regulation prevails over certain segments of business operations. Conversely, decentralized organizations become prevalent in beneficial business environments in which business expansion, new product development, and new markets become primary objectives.

Unfortunately, management of machine servicing and MRO inventories often functions in a state of semi-limbo regardless of the type of organizational design which is used. The reasons for this are quite common:

1. First, the operating manager normally has budget-level responsibility for repair parts and repair labor cost but he has little influence over repair part prices and delivery times or plant machine shop scheduling or costs;
2. Second, the engineering/maintenance manager is generally responsible for MRO storeroom operations but is unaware of production trends and usually resorts to a perpetual inventory system to avoid stockouts;
3. Third, based on the significant performance gains achieved by factories which used a centralized materials management organization, or MRP, or both, there seems to be a real case for placing MRO inventory under centralized control and with a common information system.

The essence of the SRP developmental scope was more pragmatic than contemplative. Four very clear redundant management problems emerged from the factory survey:

1. Machine servicing systems were not responsive to independent production demand;
2. MRO inventories were locked into a perpetual inventory system which was not connected to independent production demand nor a master production schedule;
3. There was a large inability for managers to determine the relationship of machine servicing work performed to production efficiency or product quality level;
4. Managers were unable to determine service and repair costs, repair budget variances, or routine machine servicing plans on a real time (daily) basis because it is impossible without a decisional computer system.

Service Requirements Planning essentially deals with each of these issues.

## A BRIEF REVIEW OF MATERIALS REQUIREMENTS PLANNING (MRP)

In order for the reader to clearly understand the SRP system, it is necessary to review the basic principles and features of MRP which have provided the systems logic foundation for SRP. An MRP/SRP matrix of management functions is required to identify some similarities and differences which are characteristic of the two systems (Table 1).

When an MRP system is properly designed, installed, and utilized, it actually functions on three separate levels. It plans and controls inventories. It plans open-order priorities whether they are purchase orders or production orders. Finally, it provides input to the capacity requirements planning system [4, p. 141].

MRP accomplishes results by using the following logic [4, p. 57]:

1—A master production schedule is used to drive the system. It is the primary system input. The schedule states end (finished) item production requirements in terms of time and quantity. End item production periods are normally stated in weeks, but the master schedule usually has a one year time span. The master production schedule is a procurement and subassembly schedule which insures component availability. Pre-determined lead times are utilized to assure component and end item delivery integrity.

2—Two other MRP system inputs are inventory status records and product structure (bill of material) records. Inventory status is modified by inventory transactions and independent demand (sales orders for finished items). Inventory records contain planning factors such as lead time, buffer stock, spoilage allowance, and lot-sizing criteria. File records provide status data for determination of net requirements. MRP accesses the product structure record to determine the components required for an assembly or parent item.

### TABLE 1
### MRP/SRP System Matrix

| Management Function/Concern | MRP System | SRP System |
|---|---|---|
| Inventory Responsibility | RAW, W.I.P., F.G. large reductions possible | MRO: reductions of 20% plus |
| Productivity Increase | Reduces delays due to stockouts | Increases productivity by 3 to 10% by reducing machine failure probability |
| Product Quality | Little Effect | Direct relationship to machine & tool condition |
| Independent Demand Schedule | Very Significant | 3 to 10% increase on real capacity |
| Production planning | Very Significant | Little Effect |
| Machine Servicing Planning | Develops alternate production plans | Very Significant |
| Contingency Management Index | No | Yes |
| Closed Loop System | Highly desirable | Desirable, but has a contingency system index |
| MRP/SRP System Compatibility | Both systems are mutually supportive. They can operate independently, but installation costs are greatly reduced if installed together or added on. | |
| Coordination with Management Functions | Coordinates material management & operating management | Should be coordinated by materials management. Coordinates engineering/ maintenance and operating management |

3—Once the net requirements for a finished asembly are known, MRP explodes these independent demand schedules backward into time to generate dependent item schedules for materials and components. The explosion process enables the system to compare component availability to the independent demand schedule.

4—Time phasing is the addition of the time dimension to inventory status data. Thus, the three direct system inputs (master production schedule, inventory status record, and product status record) are time phased by system computation ability which produces two outputs: planned purchase and shop order releases.

5—Prior to execution of the purchase and shop order releases, these requirements are passed through a material requirements (purchasing) plan or a capacity requirements (shop order) plan.

6—If either time is unavailable for material procurement, or capacity for shop orders is unavailable, then the master production schedule must be modified through a closed-loop feedback system or modified manually. If time or capacity are available, then purchase or shop orders are executed as planned by the MRP system.

The processing logic and input-output relationships are further explained in Figure 1, which was excerpted in its entirety from Joseph Orlicky's definitive work, *Material Requirements Planning* [4, p. 13].

The basic differences between MRP and SRP systems are immediately apparent in Figure 2. SRP is not concerned with independent item demand nor process inventory. It compares the master production schedule to actual production. Three of the six system outputs are different than MRP outputs.

## DEVELOPMENT OF A SERVICE REQUIREMENTS PLANNING (SRP) SYSTEM

There are five developmental steps that must be accomplished before an SRP system can function properly:

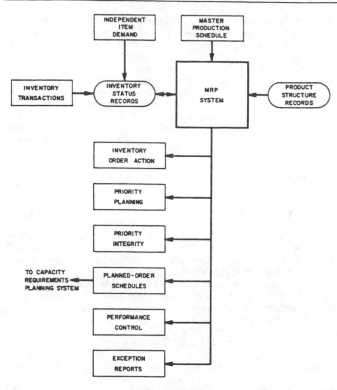

**FIGURE 1**
MRP System: input–output relationships

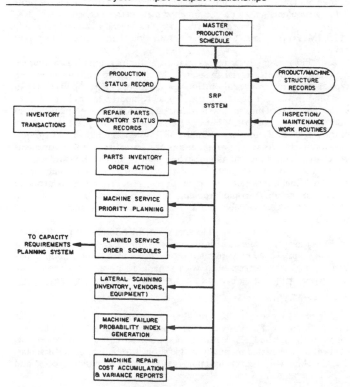

**FIGURE 2**
SRP System: input–output relationships

1. All production and machinery components must be generically identified for computer field display.
2. A lateral scanning loop must be installed so that generically common components may be identified.
3. Inspection and maintenance sequences must be properly designed and timed for production, not calendar intervals.
4. A Machine Failure Probability Index (MFPI) system should be constructed for decisional use in contingency management situations.
5. A cost accumulation and analysis loop must be developed so that actual machine servicing labor and parts costs may be constantly compared to budgeted costs. Total machine servicing costs must be historically accumulated by unit or assembly line.

## GENERIC IDENTIFICATION OF PRODUCTION AND MACHINE COMPONENTS

Each independent demand item (finished or end item) must be identified with a specific computer item code. Many systems use a ten-digit code field in which each field position (combination of position and digits inserted) identifies the end item as a unique assembly which uses certain components, processes, finishes, and packaging.

If SRP is used as an independent system (without MRP), item codes for purchased materials required by either end or component production items are not used. This is because SRP insures machine reliability and not the deliverability of the finished product. The system is concerned only with the utilization of factory machinery and resultant production.

SRP normally utilizes a twenty-digit item code (which is variable) to determine end item, production component, assembly (which is variable) to determine end item, production component, assembly line/machine, or machine component item codes. The twenty-digit code field is used with SRP so that machine components may be identified generically (commonality of machine components is established through engineering specifications rather than by sole use of machine manufacturer's independent drawing numbers.)

Rapid determination of machine part numbers has been a traditional problem for materials, engineering/maintenance, and operating managers. The reason for this was that replacement machine parts had to be ordered by using the machine manufacturer's drawing number. It was very difficult, if not impossible, to determine that identical parts were used in different machines produced by different manufacturers. With generic machine part identification, identical parts are identically coded. Only the assembly line or machine identification prefix is different. Also, the manufacturer's part number is cross-filed, or chained, with the generic part number.

## LATERAL SCANNING

Lateral scanning is the SRP system loop, or sub-routine, which enables a manager to view repair parts as entities or groups without being limited by machine, assembly line, department, or factory (assuming a multi-factory system) boundaries.

This feature is very important to the purchasing manager. For example, he may now determine that the same bearing is used 52 times in 12 different machines which are located in 3 different departments in the same factory. The knowledge that lateral scanning provides has large implications for volume discounts and contract purchases. It enables the purchasing manager to contribute more to managing repair part purchases rather than responding to the panic that normally accompanies the failure of a critical piece of production equipment.

Most factory parts storerooms are centralized to maintain security. Most repair parts are then organized departmentally according to factory departmental organization. This is done to expedite service requests and to reduce queuing. With this type of storeroom organization, and with six factory departments, it is also possible to store the hypothetical bearing in six different locations in varying quantities. Through the use of lateral scanning, a computer system, and data terminals, this problem is eliminated.

Traditionally, most MRO storerooms are operated by the engineering/maintenance department. The reason for this is that the maintenance shop is centrally located in most factories. Also, raw material for shop repair jobs is located in the central storeroom. But the inventory systems used in many MRO storerooms leave something to be desired. Most of them still use Kardex-type records with min./max. levels which were popular in the 1950s. Several factories surveyed utilized statistically based reorder-point systems. None were responsive to fluctuations in independent demand.

With SRP calculation speed, and the lateral scanning feature to reduce purchasing reliance upon engineering and operating jargon, much MRO inventory may be kept on the supplier's shelves rather than the factory storeroom. When all generic and corresponding manufacturer's part identification numbers have been entered in the system, the lateral scanning sub-routine prints out descriptions of all common machine parts, their locations, and total quantities used. The second task for the sub-routine is to print out quotation requests for part prices, terms, and delivery periods. When this information is received and entered in the SRP system, it provides the first usable input to the data base. The volume of quotations required is greatly reduced through the use of lateral scanning. Once the vendor information file is initially established, periodic or multiple quotation requests to vendors are quickly and easily accomplished.

## DESIGN OF MACHINE SERVICING INSPECTION AND MAINTENANCE SEQUENCES

One of the principal differences between SRP and other servicing or maintenance systems (computerized or non-computerized) is that SRP servicing intervals are determined by actual production generated by a particular machine or assembly line and not by calendar periods or operating hours. Thus, the servicing sequences which are found in original equipment manufacturer's publications must be converted from time periods to production units.

The SRP system requires servicing intervals to be expressed in terms of units produced in order to reduce calculation time and data storage capacity. But beyond system design, there are a number of management advantages when servicing intervals are determined by units produced:

1. Production, inventory, and budgets are expressed in terms of units produced and this application to servicing intervals increases line and staff comprehension of service requirements and problems;
2. Needless and repetitious machine servicing work is eliminated by ordering the correct sequence at the predetermined volume of production;
3. Management scheduling of SRP orders is simpler and more effective due to the randomness of production intervals (the need for servicing overtime is reduced);
4. With properly designed inspection sequences, much of this servicing work can be performed while the equipment is operating.

Based on sixteen years of experience with complex metals manufacturing machinery and assembly lines, the author has determined a rough distribution for causative factors of machine failure: 50% of failures were caused by lack of awareness (caused by lack of inspection) of impending machine failure; 20% of failures were caused by lack of machine servicing at proper intervals, 15% of failures were caused by misadjustment, use of sub-standard material, or accidents; 15% of machine failure was due to normal wear.

The SRP inspection sequence is labor intensive and the maintenance sequence is capital intensive. When properly executed, the inspection sequence may prevent the greatest single cause of mechanical failure. It includes machine cleaning, lubrication, adjustment, visual checks, and dynamic tests of equipment. The basis for sequence design is the O.E.M. manual plus input from the factory engineering/maintenance and operating groups. System inputs from the group are an encoded description of the sequence, a brief description of the sequence task, and a measured or estimated time for task completion. Exception codes for problems, incomplete tasks, or indications of imminent failure are established via generic coding.

The inspection sequence must be designed to properly analyze *all* sections of a machine or assembly line. Access covers must be removed. The technician then inspects for proper fluid levels, poor lubrication, broken or damaged lubricant or coolant lines, broken gear teeth, worn chains or belts, etc. Dynamic inspections include checks for excessive mechanical play, excessive noise or vibration, odors caused by overheating, transfer problems, and poor product quality. Appropriate deficiency sub-codes are entered in the system for the machine which has been inspected, and they remain a part of the machine record until the condition has been corrected. For a machine or assembly line, the inspection sequence is repeated on a sequentially programmed basis in order to achieve machine reliability.

Maintenance servicing sequences are easier to define and manage than inspection sequences. They are also extracted from O.E.M. service manuals and modified according to plant engineering and operating practices. Management of these sequences is simplified because mechanical parts are routinely replaced. This is especially true of high wear parts such as tools and dies, especially progressive die sets, which perform such functions as forging, blanking, forming, piercing, notching, assembly, etc. Wear part lives have a very specific relationship to production. SRP ensures that tool and die wear is "tracked" for proper servicing intervals. Using predetermined tool and die replacement intervals, the system explosion of tool and die set parts into components with shop and purchase order lead times assures that repaired or replacement tool and die sets are available at the planned servicing interval. Adherence to the planned servicing interval will reduce the average cost of tool and die repair or replacement and it will optimize production and product quality. In a general way, this rule holds true for all maintenance sequences.

## MACHINE FAILURE PROBABILITY INDEX

Considering only materials management systems such as MRP, there is a generally acknowledged management aversion to closed loop systems. Over 50% of installed MRP systems in 1980 were modified or open-loop systems. The reason for this is that managers are concerned about contingency situations which may lie beyond system parameters. Examples of these situations may be environmental, regulatory, marketing, or profitability problems. Based on contingency management concerns, SRP was designed as a routine closed loop system with a Machine Failure Probability Index (MFPI) for use as a management analytical and decisional support device.

An MFPI is a graphical representation of the performance data which management desires to be measured. In a standard cost environment, typical measurements would include production, quality, spoilage, repair cost, and the cost of operating supplies as compared to engineered standards. This type of information is normally provided through management information systems (MIS), but it is more meaningfully presented as part of the weekly SRP summary. With the SRP system, simplified MFPI graphs can summarize weekly performance inputs from staff and line departments which depict machine and assembly line performance with regard to standard, budgeted and actual levels of performance. In contingency management situations where the labor supply, production requirements, or budget constraints become problems for SRP routine maintenance, an MFPI becomes an invaluable tool for management in determining servicing priorities.

Even though MFPIs are used to alter servicing priorities, the SRP system continues to accumulate records of work performed, and continues to order servicing work based on generated production units. Work priorities may be altered, but the total servicing work schedule is never lost in the system.

## MACHINE REPAIR COST DATA ACCUMULATION, RETRIEVAL, AND ANALYSIS

One of the most redundant problems in manufacturing cost control is the development of accurate data for construction of machinery labor and repair costs and budgets. Without computerized cost accumulation, this data must be extracted manually and is subject to both line and staff bias. The development of servicing budgets is often a negotiation process and occurs without regard to factual information because it simply does not exist in easily retrievable and validated form.

SRP system design, by its data base asemblage, has the power to accumulate machinery repair labor and parts costs during the life of a machine or all machines. If the system is provided with budget information, it will generate budget variances at any point in time and provide them to anyone with authorized data terminal access. This has already been suggested for MRP systems [5, p. 70].

Another complex decisional area for managers is the frequency and cost of machine repairs versus the frequency and cost of overhaul prior to machine replacement. This is known as the repair, overhaul, or replacement (R-OH-R) decision chain. There are a number of economic strategies available, but all of them are based on a long time frame, and all require detailed repair and overhaul costs for the life of the production machine [2, p. 440]. The SRP data base accumulates repair and overhaul costs as a perpetual history for the life of the machine. Decision-tables may be constructed from these values to assure that costs are optimized. Even in contingency situations when capital expenditures are constricted, it is necessary to be able to project the additional machine repair and overhaul costs which are increased by pro forma non-replacement policy. The ability to rapidly analyze and project excessive machine servicing costs by factory managers may even alter rigid non-replacement policies.

## CONCLUSION

There are other computerized maintenance planning systems. However, SRP was designed to fit the newer and more effective integrated materials management organizational designs. The system is not only compatible with MRP, but uses a great deal of MRP logic which has been proven successful. SRP is structured heavily toward the use of participative management through the use of remote data terminals, the lateral scanning feature for purchasing and inventory control managers, the use of a MFPI by almost all staff departments, and the wide dissemination of repair costs, budgets and variances. Most important, the system generates machine servicing plans which are based on planned and actual factory production. This innovation alone enables SRP to be an effective tool for improving factory performance.

## REFERENCES

1. Belt, B.: "Men, Spindles and Material Requirements," *Production and Inventory Management,* First Quarter, 1975.
2. Buffa, E. *Modern Production/Operations Management.* New York, John Wiley and Sons.
3. Taylor, S.: "Production and Inventory Management in the Process Industries. *Production and Inventory Management,* First Quarter, 1979.
4. Orlicky, J. *Material Requirements Planning,* New York, McGraw-Hill, Inc.
5. R. J. Campbell and J. M. Porcano: "The Contribution of MRP to Budgeting and Cost Control," *Production and Inventory Management,* Second Quarter, 1979.

**About the Author—**

*RICHARD S. BOJANOWSKI* has been an Assistant Professor of Industrial Technology at the College of Technology, University of Houston—Central Campus since 1981. He teaches in the areas of production/operations analysis, industrial organization and management, and labor relations. His research interests are centered about production/operations management and occupational safety and health. Prior to this academic position, Mr. Bojanowski spent 21 years in industry. Eight years were spent in staff (industrial engineering) positions, and thirteen years were spent in various operating management positions. He received his B.S. and M.A. degrees from Johns Hopkins University and is currently pursuing his doctorate in Behavioral Sciences from the University of Texas School of Public Health. Mr. Bojanowski is a member of the National Association of Industrial Technology and of the Southwest Division of the Academy of Management.

Reprinted from *Production and Inventory Management*, Third Quarter, 1989.

# WHICH LOT-SIZING TECHNIQUES ARE USED IN MATERIAL REQUIREMENTS PLANNING?

JORGE HADDOCK
*Department of Decision Sciences and Engineering Systems, Rensselaer Polytechnic Institute, Troy, NY 12180*

DONALD E. HUBICKI
*Aluminum Company of America Massena Operations, Massena, NY 13662*

Which lot-sizing techniques are actually being implemented in the day-to-day operation of manufacturing facilities? The methods considered here are: economic order quantity (EOQ), period order quantity (POQ), part period algorithm (PPA) [4, 10], part period balancing (PPB), least unit cost (LUC), least total cost (LTC), Silver-Meal (S-M), Wagner-Whitin (W-W), lot for lot (LFL), fixed order quantity (FOQ), and fixed period quantity (FPQ). References containing detailed information about the methods are ([11, 12] for simple explanations; for survery and comparison papers see [1, 2, 5, 6, 9, 13]). Are companies embracing EOQ models because of their simplicity? Do production planners perform calculations of the S-M heuristic in establishing lot sizes? Are manufacturers using combinations of techniques such as EOQ for constant demand items and W-W for variable demand items?

To investigate this issue, a survey was conducted of the materials requirements planning (MRP) software systems currently implemented in manufacturing facilities. The questionnaire was mailed to marketing directors of 263 companies claiming to offer MRP systems. A surprisingly high survey return rate of nearly 30% was realized, substantiating the claim that lot sizing is an area of current interest in industry. The responses represented 65 different MRP systems with a combined total of more than 25,000 installations worldwide. Table 1 contains a list of those companies / systems represented by these results.

To promote consistency of interpretation, the survey included a one-page summary of the 11 different lot-sizing techniques listed above. For FOQ the user specifies a fixed value to be the lot size, and for FPQ the user specifies a fixed number of planning periods, and the lot size is calculated as the quantity necessary to satisfy requirements for that number of periods. The survey asked three simple questions of the respondents: (1) which lot-sizing techniques are standard with their MRP system, (2) which lot-sizing techniques can be customized for use with their MRP system, and (3) which two lot-sizing techniques do they see most commonly used by client companies?

## RESULTS

Compilation of the survey results produced rather interesting insights and are displayed graphically in Figures 1, 2, and 3.

Most systems which do not offer FOQ and LFL as standard do so as a customized feature. FPQ is offered as standard or custom in 89.3% of the systems. EOQ is offered in over three-fourths of the systems, and POQ in 70.8%.

There was only one MRP system which provided S-M as a standard lot-sizing technique, and one other system which provided W-W as a standard offering.

The 41.5% of "other" lot-sizing techniques included such methods as minimum, maximum, multiples, demand order quantity, and order exact requirement plus safety. One respondent explained that NRN (nice round number) was a standard offering.

The most revealing results of the survey lie in the most common usage of lot-sizing techniques indicated by client companies of MRP vendors. One respondent expressed the opinion that EOQ is already "obsolete," but it appears that EOQ is not being replaced by the more intensive techniques developed by researchers. Rather, the more simplistic demand-driven lot-sizing techniques such as LFL, FOQ, FPQ, and POQ are being utilized most commonly. Only a few of the MRP systems vendors recognized PPA, PPB, LUC, LTC, S-M, or W-W as being the common lot-sizing techniques of choice by client companies.

The average MRP system offered three to four different methods from which the user could choose. The fact that a selection was often provided implies that there is not one universal lot-sizing model. Some system descriptions suggest use of one technique for certain items and another technique for other items (e.g., LFL for non-stocked, custom-built, high-cost items and EOQ for repetitive, lower-cost items).

**TABLE 1: Companies Whose MRP Systems are Represented in the Survey Results**

| Company | System | Company | System |
|---|---|---|---|
| ABLE Technical Products Corp. | ABLE MRP II | Helmsman Systems, Inc. | H-MRP |
| Advanced Computer Management Corp. | ACM Manufacturing Software | Info-Power Software Corp. | I-Manufacturing |
| Aftec, Inc. | PRO-III-MASTER | Interactive Applications, Inc. | MCS |
| Alessi Data Technology | MRP V | Interactive Information Systems, Inc. | IMCS |
| All Type Software, Inc. | MANCOS | Intertec Diversified Systems, Inc. | MAP/3000 |
| Applied Information Development, Inc. | AID-MCS | Intro-Logic, Inc. | Manufacturing III |
| | | Louis A. Wright & Associates, Inc. | AMPS |
| ASK Computer Systems, Inc. | MANMAN/MFS | M & D Systems, Inc. | Myte Myte |
| Axis Computer Systems | AXIOM | MAI Basic Four | MANBASE |
| Bedford Data Systems, Inc. | IBM's MAPICS-II | Management Resource Partners, Ltd. | PACS/38 |
| Cimpac, Inc. | CIMPAC Manufacturing | | |
| Cincom Systems, Inc. | CONTROL: Manufacturing | Manufacturing Decision Support Systems, Inc. | (not available) |
| Compusource Corp. | DYNAMIC | | |
| Computer Cognition | ACUITY | Manufacturing Resource Consultants | MCS II |
| Computer Integrated Modular Systems Inc. | New Dimension Mfg. System | Martek, Inc. | AIMS |
| Computer Solutions, Inc. | Growth Power | Mini/Micro Computer Systems | (not available) |
| Computer Systems Consultants | Inventory/MRP | Minx Software, Inc. | MINX |
| Computer Systems Development, Inc. | IMPCON | Mitrol, Inc. | MFG |
| | | MMS International | SYMAN—Advanced Mfg. |
| Control Data Corp. | ACTIVATOR | MRM, Inc. | PACS |
| Cullinet Software | CMS | MSA Advanced Manufacturing, Inc. | AMAPS |
| Computer Strategies, Inc. | RMS | Probe Software Sciences Ltd. | SIP 3000 |
| C. R. Smolin, Inc. | E-Z-MRP | Prodstar America | Prodstar MRP II |
| Data 3 Systems, Inc. | MRPS38-S | Proman | PROMAN |
| Data Systems for Industry | QED | Relevant Business Systems | INFIMACS |
| Datamation, Inc. | PRO MAN | Response Data Systems | Pilot Mfg. Package |
| David B. Murphy & Associates, Inc. | RT-MRP | Saguaro Data Systems, Inc. | Mfg. Management & Control |
| Driver-Harris Systems, Inc. | SuzyMRP | | |
| Dymaxion Research Ltd. | Dymaxion MRP | Solid State Software, Inc. | MPAC |
| Eastman Micro Systems | SAMM | STSC, Inc. | IMSS |
| Escom, Inc. | MMC | Unisyn, Inc. | Unisyn Integrated Mfg. Sys. |
| Falk Integrated Technologies, Inc. | BPCD | | |
| Formation, Inc. | FORMAN | Unisys Corp. | BAMCS |
| Fourth Shift Corp. | FOURTH SHIFT | Unisys Corp. | UNIS-1100 |
| Friedman & Associates, Inc. | HFA | Unisys Corp. | UNIS-80 |

## CONCLUSIONS AND SUMMARY

Researchers have proposed numerous ways to make lot-sizing decisions, yet manufacturing operations are implementing MRP systems which use simplistic approaches to establishing lot-size quantities. There are several reasons for this paradox.

First is **simplicity** itself. The production controllers who are responsible for managing the activities of a facility need to understand the schedules, from the top-level master schedules to the low-level daily dispatch schedules. They need to understand how and why lot-size quantities are what they are. Simple approaches such as LFL can easily be interpreted.

Another reason is **user acceptance.** Manufacturing personnel are much more likely to accept a computer-generated schedule if the lot-size quantities reflect what their manual calculations would have concluded, rather than to accept lot-size quantities which a relatively complex algorithm calculated as being most economical. Moreover, user acceptance is a measure of the success of an MRP system.

**Speed of computer processing** is another reason which may have motivated the developers of early MRP systems to use simpler techniques, thus improving on run-time performance. With advancements in technology, such concerns no longer exist today; however, the original implementations imbedded these

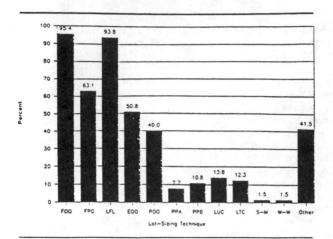

FIGURE 1: Lot-sizing techniques as standard offerings

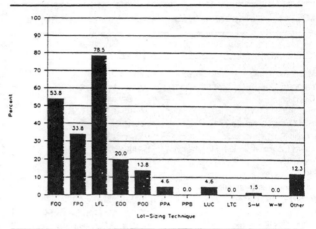

FIGURE 3: Lot-sizing techniques most commonly used

simpler techniques into the thinking processes of many companies.

Finally, manufacturing personnel recognize the **complexity of** the lot-sizing **decisions and**, perhaps, even question the **feasibility of** determining "**optimal**" lot size quantities. These people understand the multiple factors which both influence this decision and are influenced by this decision: setup costs, carrying costs, ordering costs, quantity discounts, material-handling considerations, storage considerations, learning curve factors, capacity constraints, product mix and volume, tool life availability, lead time factors, and many more.

Some researchers have acknowledged the myriad of factors involved with lot-sizing decisions. Collier

[3] pointed out over a decade ago the different levels at which lot-sizing decisions have to be made: end-item and intermediate. Schussel [14] recognized even earlier that there is a distinct difference between an EOQ model for determining lot sizes for ordering from an outside vendor and an economic lot release size for in-house production.

Lot-size quantities have been considered in relation to such things as manufacturing lead times, equipment utilization, and sequencing delays by Karmarkar [7, 8]. Many companies are instituting JIT programs aimed at reducing setup times. If successful, these changes would drive down lot-size quantities which could result in negative impacts on productivity as traditionally measured.

Rather than expecting algorithms to calculate optimal lot sizes, manufacturing personnel have, instead, chosen to embrace simplistic approaches which afford them the ability to understand the schedules generated by their MRP systems. They appear instead to be using their resources to address problems such as reducing setup times, improving tooling durability, and insuring quality production.

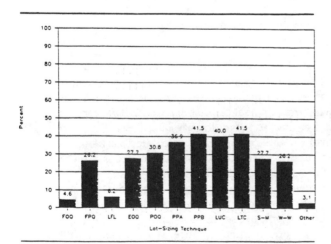

FIGURE 2: Lot-sizing techniques as custom offerings

## REFERENCES

1. Bahl, H. C., Ritzman, L. P., and Gupta, J. N., "Determining Lot Sizes and Resource Requirements: A Review," *Operations Research*, Vol. 35, No. 3 (May–June 1987), pp. 329–345.
2. Bitran, G. R., Magnanti, T. L., and Yanasse, H. H., "Analysis of the Uncapacitated Dynamic Lot Size Problem," Sloan School of Management Working Paper Number 1282-82, Massachusetts Institute of Technology (1982).
3. Collier, D. A., "The Impact of Multi-Level Lot Size Strategies on Capacity," Graduate School of Business Administration

Working Paper Number 223, Duke University (November 1977).

4. DeMattais, J. J., "An Economic Lot-Sizing Technique: I. The Part Period Algorithm," *IBM Systems Journal*, Vol. 7, No. 1 (1968), pp. 30–38.

5. Kaimann, R. A., "A Fallacy of EOQing," *Production and Inventory Management*, First Quarter (1968), pp. 82–87.

6. ———, "Revisiting a Fallacy of EOQing," *Production and Inventory Management*, Fourth Quarter (1968), pp. 12–19.

7. Karmarkar, U. S., "Lot Sizes, Manufacturing Lead Times and Utilization," Graduate School of Management Working Paper Number QM312, University of Rochester (May 1983).

8. ———, "Lot-Sizing and Sequencing Delays," Graduate School of Management Working Paper Number QM8314, Univesity of Rochester (June 1983).

9. Karni, R., "A Study of Lot Sizing Algorithms," *IIE Transactions* (December 1986), pp. 356–366.

10. Mitra, A. A., Cox, J. F., Blackstone, J. H., and Jesse R. R., Jr., "A Re-examination of Lot Sizing Procedures for Requirements Planning Systems: Some Modified Rules," *International Journal of Production Research*, Vol. 21, No. 4 (1983), pp. 471–478.

11. Orlicky, J., *Material Requirements Planning*, McGraw-Hill, Inc., NY (1975).

12. Peterson, R. and Silver, E. A., *Decision Systems for Inventory Management and Production Planning*, John Wiley and Sons, NY (1979).

13. Ritchie, E. and Tsado, A. K., "A Review of Lot Sizing Techniques for Deterministic Time-Varying Demand," *Production and Inventory Management*, Third Quarter (1986), pp. 64–79.

14. Schussel, G., "Job-Shop Lot Release Sizes," *Management Science*, Vol. 14, No. 8 (April 1968), pp. 449–472.

## About the Authors—

*JORGE HADDOCK is an assistant professor of industrial engineering and operations research at Rensselaer Polytechnic Institute. He holds a BS in civil engineering from the University of Puerto Rico, an MS in management engineering from Rensselaer Polytechnic Institute, and a PhD in industrial engineering from Purdue University. Among Professor Haddock's research interests are simulation and optimization of production / manufacturing and inventory control systems. He has several publications in journals such as this one,* IIE Transactions, Computers and Industrial Engineering, Journal of Applied Mathematical Modeling, Simulation, *and* Material Flow, *as well as a software monogram,* Operations Research Methodologies. *Professor Haddock has been a consultant to several companies including Baxter-Travenol Laboratories, Citibank / Citicorp, and Michelin Tires. He is a member of Tau Beta Pi, Institute of Industrial Engineers, The Institute of Management Science, the Society for Computer Simulation, and the National Academy of Engineering of Mexico.*

*DONALD HUBICKI has spent the last five years managing various CIM-related projects in the shop floor and inventory control areas. He is currently employed at the Aluminum Company of America's Massena Operations in Massena, NY. Hubicki holds a bachelor's degree in computer and systems engineering and a master's degree in industrial and management engineering, both from Rensselaer Polytechnic Institute. He is a member of IIE and SME.*

Reprinted from APICS 1988 *Conference Proceedings*.

## LEVER YOUR ROAD WITH ADVANCED MRP

Jeffrey W. Moran, CPIM
MSA Advanced Manufacturing

### INTRODUCTION

The most publicly visible indicator of a company's manufacturing performance is Return on Assets (ROA). Return on Assets is the rate of return on assets used directly or indirectly in company production activity (Revenue - Costs/Assets). Manufacturers who have already implemented MRPII are now attempting to increase ROA on two broad fronts--Just in Time (JIT) and Computer Integrated Manufacturing (CIM). However, relatively minor refinements in the use of MRP in key areas can still yield significant increases in ROA.

The objective of this paper is to encourage renewed effort toward decreasing variable production costs and reducing company assets through the fine-tuning of MRP. The first part of this paper explains the concept of leverage--applying existing tools with a minimal effort to get a maximum payback. Then, we'll look at a number of techniques frequently overlooked by advanced MRP users for leveraging ROA.

This paper is directed to the experienced MRP user who is looking for ways to tighten current practices. This user has already dealt with the issues of data accuracy, communication, and top management support and has in place good procedures for cycle counting, forecasting, and master scheduling. He or she is now considering JIT or CIM as the next logical step on the path toward manufacturing excellence.

### MRP AND JIT

It is clear that MRPII and JIT will coexist in plants in the future as part of a larger concept called Computer Integrated Manufacturing. Emphasis should not be placed on eventually replacing one with the other, but instead on determining which can be applied most cost effectively in a particular time period for a given product or process.

MRP and JIT are basically different types of information systems. JIT is an organic approach that stresses simplicity and visibility of inventory levels, quality, and production status. MRP is a computer-facilitated method that generates a plan through computer modeling. As such, it has advantages inherent in on-line systems--history, quick retrieval of summarized data for decision support, and simulation capability.

Any company JIT or CIM program that does not mention how MRP use will be refined is seriously negligent. We want excellence to extend to all areas, including MRP. As we strive toward attaining the ideals of JIT production, we also by implication want to work to become not just class A MRP users but class AAA!

### INVENTORY TURNS OR ROA?

Inventory Turnover (Cost of Goods Sold/Inventory) measures operations management's ability to convert inventory assets into sales revenues. It is widely touted as the most important performance measurement for evaluating a company's progress toward JIT. However, exclusive attention to improving inventory turnover may do more harm than good. Inventory turns may be improving, yet a company could be headed out of business if it is not pricing its products to return an adequate profit. More seriously, a massive investment in automation may allow inventory turns to suddenly rise while reducing sharply the overall company rate of return on assets.

JIT and CIM are really geared more to boosting ROA than to boosting inventory turns. ROA is a more inclusive performance measurement because it reflects contributions to increasing productivity from groups besides Manufacturing, Material Control, and Production Control. It reflects Engineering's efforts to boost its own productivity and eliminate overhead through CAD. It reflects the Maintenance group's efforts in the areas of preventive maintenance and facilities management. It reflects Sales and Marketing's contributions in streamlining practices and adopting JIT demand management principles.

A focus on increasing ROA forces a company to improve its overall use of existing assets before signing to purchase new automation. From this viewpoint, inventory turnover is too parochial--it doesn't force the issue when it comes to improving methods vs. automation.

### OPERATIONS LEVERAGE

In corporate finance, the term leverage is applied to the use of debt financing (bonds, notes) to get nonowners to help fund company assets. This has the benefit of increasing assets and subsequent revenues without diluting shareholders' ownership in the firm. The treasurer applies leverage, in effect, to ROA to get a higher return for stockholders. Leverage is here defined as the percent of total assets supplied by creditors as opposed to common shareholders. Treasurers are evaluated on their ability to take a firm's given ROA and lever it up to a higher value (Return on Equity) through debt financing. The firm looks more profitable as a result, but additional value or capability hasn't necessarily been added to operations.

Leverage is also applied in manufacturing operations to mean the replacement of existing assets or processes with automation to reduce operating costs and increase ROA. The JIT movement has added its own twist to this by defining leverage as using existing assets better to get a higher rate of return without necessarily increasing the number of assets. In this sense, operations leverage is the additional return made possible by lower operating costs divided by the cost expended to obtain it. The benefit to the firm is that operations leverage adds real value to the firm. Owners don't have to obtain additional plant or equipment but can get a better return from assets they already have through better methods.

How can they get a better return from existing assets? The JIT philosophy calls for manufacturers to "work smarter, not harder." Through improved methods and value-added manufacturing and engineering, companies can gradually lower costs and reduce assets using existing tools. Buying new equipment is only a last resort.

MRP remains a powerful tool for applying operations leverage to obtain additional return from existing assets--even in established user companies who are now considering JIT. The computer's ability to access large data bases and process at high speeds enables human energy and brain power to lever up ROA significantly. MRP can be pictured as a fluid that not only transmits information through a bill of material or a time-phased schedule, but magnifies it to your benefit (or possible detriment).

MRP can provide operations leverage to improve ROA three different ways. First, through bill of material explosion and time-phased backscheduling logic, it can leverage brain power to reduce inventory investment. A little more thoughtful planning in the right places can result in significant benefits overall when blown through the schedule. Second, MRP can leverage effort and energy so it's applied more effectively by helping us focus on improvements that stand to provide the biggest payback. ABC Classification Analysis is one example of this. Third, MRP can leverage time in the sense that doing things right the first time will result in flexibility and lower costs in the future. Overall, MRP will help us work smarter, more efficiently, and more quickly to raise ROA.

### LEVERAGING ROA WITH MRP

MRP has a major impact on ROA by reducing fixed and variable production costs and reducing total company assets.

Types of costs that can be reduced through

improved use of MRP include:

- supplies
- obsolescence/spoilage
- setup/purchase order costs
- direct/indirect labor
- rework
- subcontracting
- material handling
- inspection
- inventory carrying costs
- expediting/deexpediting

Assets that can be reduced include general company plant, equipment, tooling, inventory, and cash.

A large number of techniques exist within MRPII to reduce these costs and assets, ranging from cycle counting and ABC classification to refined lot sizing logic. The following discussion covers several techniques which are often overlooked by MRP users. They are simple to implement, yet they can have a multiplying effect in levering up ROA.

## USE MRP IN NEW PRODUCT INTRODUCTION

An application of MRP that is frequently overlooked is the new product introduction process. New product introduction touches every function in the company and can be very costly if not managed correctly. MRP can provide a powerful control tool if brought into the process early enough--at initial design!

Recommended procedures include:

1. Structure items, bills and routings into the system from initial idea stage through pilot. This allows user to maintain design history and documentation control at all steps.

2. Assign a special range of pre-release revision levels to various design versions (e.g. 00-19 prereleased, 20-99 released)

3. Use master scheduling to bring in prototype material so it's visible!

4. Use Rough-Cut Capacity Planning to evaluate load on new and existing resources.

5. Use costing capabilities to drive down product costs during design stage and to support project budgeting.

6. Use MRP to track the ongoing costs of scrap, rework, new tooling, and vendor negotiations.

7. Manage the cutover process to production through item policy coding and bill of material demand explosion coding.

## MASTER SCHEDULE INSTEAD OF MRP

The rule of thumb most master schedulers follow is the 20 percent/80 percent rule: Master schedule the 20 percent of the items that contribute 80 percent of usage costs. This is necessary due to the large number of items in any company that are candidates for master scheduling.

However, there is a tendency to fix on a set grouping of items and master schedule them indefinitely, regardless of changing priorities. Many schedulers are not spending their time constructively to get the most impact.

The master scheduler should look for new items that can benefit from maximum control even if for brief periods of time. This "magnifying glass" approach supports the JIT principle of continual search for improvement. To identify new items to master schedule, it might help to examine the 20 percent of the items that:

- monopolize 80 percent of material planners' time
- account for 80 percent of expediting costs
- account for 80 percent of late deliveries
- account for 80 percent of customer returns
- have 80 percent of the excess inventory

## STABILIZE THE MASTER SCHEDULE

Changes to the master schedule are transmitted through the bill of material like a shock wave, causing rescheduling, expediting and deexpediting--at a heavy cost! To maintain proper schedule stability, properly defined and enforced time fences still represent the best payback. A time fence is a policy decision as to when the schedule can be changed and how severe the change can be. It is arrived at by consensus between manufacturing, marketing, and finance. It can be violated only upon sign-off by someone in high authority.

It is unrealistic to expect time fences to always be a hard and fast rule. They must be sensitive to material and capacity realities as well as to customer service priorities.

In practice, time fences have been a dismal failure for most manufacturers. This can be attributed to either a lack of consensus between parties involved, lack of knowledge of the costs they will save, lack of understanding of customers or market, or lack of fortitude in enforcing them.

To implement time fences effectively, users should have a good idea of the costs incurred when violating time fence policies. These costs may include any of the following:

- setups/teardowns
- expediting/deexpediting orders
- overtime/extra shifts
- outside vendor costs
- inventory carrying costs
- impairment of quality
- phone calls

These costs should be estimated and made highly VISIBLE so that violating parties have no doubt as to the costs they are incurring by ignoring time fences. Who will be charged for these additional costs--the department responsible or the customer?

Properly enforced time fence policies result in much smoother production and purchasing environments.

## STATISTICALLY CALCULATE SAFETY STOCKS

There is still a lack of attention as to the proper role and amount of safety stock used by many MRP users. Safety stock can be broadly defined as additional inventory investment maintained to protect the company from erratic replenishment (poor vendor or shop floor performance) or erratic demand (forecast error). Ultimately, supply performance problems can be resolved, leaving forecast uncertainty as the only true valid reason for carrying safety stock.

Many MRP users quantify safety stock in terms of weeks of supply and build up massive amounts of inventory at replenishment time that really aren't necessary. The solution is to statistically calculate safety stock levels as a function of customer service level and standard deviation of forecast demand.

Company A, a beverage manufacturer, examined statistical safety stock levels for the first time and discovered that the amount of safety stock needed varied about eight times a year as demands seasonally changed. The amount they traditionally carried turned out to be anywhere from two to six times more safety stock than was statistically justifiable. They were able to immediately order safety stocks cut back by an average of $300,000 per time period, with no detrimental effect on customer service.

## REDUCE SCRAP AND SHRINKAGE

Scrap and shrinkage are safety stock contingency factors below the finished product level. They have an insidious ability to increase inventory as they blow through the bill of material with a snowballing effect. Scrap is a planning percentage that inflates demand quantities in anticipation of loss of material in process. Shrinkage inflates supply quantities as a result of inspection or receiving loss.

Company B, an electronics manufacturer, made an arbitrary decision to load all items and components with a 5 percent scrap and shrinkage factor during MRP implementation. Their first MRP run called for

purchasing to order in excess of $100,000 per week
for individual purchased items. The cumulative
effect of all this over a twelve-level bill blew
their schedule and inventory levels right out of the
water. On the next MRP run they corrected this
situation and eliminated most of these factors.

A small decrease or elimination of scrap and
shrinkage factors can have a tremendous effect in
reducing company inventory and levering up ROA.

## COMPRESS INTEROPERATION LEAD TIMES

Interoperation move and queue times are often
built into standard product lead times as "slush," to
give production control scheduling flexibility.
Unfortunately, the result is usually less
flexibility, more orders, and added inventory
investment. This excess lead time causes loss of
proactive ability, which translates into extra
inventory.

The benefits of reducing or eliminating move and
queue from the schedule are tremendous, the risks
small. These benefits are in direct proportion to
the number of levels in the typical bill of
material. By reducing overall build time, the
company is much less likely to have invested in raw
materials inventory to support manufacture of
subassemblies several levels up the bill structure.

Move and queue can and should be compressed
continuously. Replace inflated guestimates with good
solid planning numbers. Then work to reduce them to
zero. They are non-value added activities.

## CONCLUSION

Companies in search of manufacturing excellence
are advised to look for ways to improve MRP
utilization as they move to JIT and CIM. Relatively
low-cost techniques can yield significant increases
in the ROA measurement.

ROA is the operations performance measurement
most readily available to potential investors and is
a good all-around indicator of company productivity
improvements. While total inventory turnover can be
obtained from published financial reports, it
generally can't be broken out into raw materials,
work in process, or finished goods turnover. Also,
an increase in automation can improve inventory turns
while at the same time decreasing ROA.

Treasurers are judged by their ability to
maximize Return on Equity through the use of debt
financing, tax avoidance, and merger and acquisition
activity. Operations managers are ultimately judged
by how well they produce operating margin--as
indicated by ROA.

Jeff Moran is currently Manager of Software
Instruction for Management Science America, Inc.,
where he is responsible for training instructors and
scheduling and teaching AMAPS workshops. Prior to
this he held materials, production control, and
quality control positions in companies that
manufacture custom molded rubber products, radios,
and electrical transformers. He holds an MBA degree
from the University of Minnesota, and is CPIM
certified by APICS.

Reprinted from APICS 1987 *Conference Proceedings*.

CAPACITY MANAGEMENT AND
ARTIFICIAL INTELLIGENCE:
A NEW APPROACH TO A CHANGING WORLD

Barbara J. Perrier, CPIM
New Enterprise Associates
Mary E. Cross
Palladian Software, Inc.

## INTRODUCTION

The United States is very concerned about the impact of foreign competition on its perceived position as the world leader in manufacturing. The world economy has been shrinking as purchasers of goods and services look for the most innovative products at the best price with the fastest delivery, regardless of the geographical location of the supplier. As a result, the problems faced by all manufacturers have taken on common themes:

- Fickle but demanding customers;
- Antiquated plants and equipment;
- High overhead rates;
- Increasingly restrictive labor rules;
- A requirement to produce the latest technology at ever decreasing costs.

While we may recognize and agree on the problems, we seldom recognize or agree on the solutions. The general reaction is to focus on short-term approaches that deal with meeting competition and shipping the product today. In order to best do this, companies recognize the need to have key resources on hand to meet manufacturing requirements. One of those key resources is capacity. Unfortunately capacity planning becomes increasingly difficult to address as the characteristics shown in Exhibit 1 display.

Companies characterized as having an "easy" level of difficulty are often comfortable with capacity calculations done on the back of an envelope; companies facing a "tough" challenge are probably attempting to use computers for traditional approaches to managing capacity such as capacity requirements planning (CRP) or linear programming; companies which fall into the "tough" group are probably using traditional techniques but with frustratingly inadequate results.

## TRADITIONAL APPROACHES TO CAPACITY MANAGEMENT

Several standard approaches are traditionally used for capacity management. Ranging from very sophisticated advanced mathematical techniques to the use of instinct and judgement, each approach has met with some what limited success. These approaches are displayed in Exhibit 2.

### Capacity Requirements Planning (CRP)

The most common form of CRP is infinite or rough cut capacity planning. This technique focuses simply on how much overall capacity is needed. No assumptions are made and no analysis is done; CRP merely identifies the capacity needed to meet a defined schedule.

The second most common form of CRP is finite capacity planning (often found in closed looped MRP systems). This type of capacity planning does recognize limitations on capacity; however, once a limitation (bottleneck) is reached, the system identifies it and stops its analysis until the problem has been corrected. The system then continues until it finds the next bottleneck. This approach results in a series of suboptimal decisions because judgments are made regarding capacity with very limited insight into the overall production environment.

Other, more advanced, forms of CRP include critical analysis and input/output analysis. Both of these approaches has the ability to identify problems, but no techniques have been developed under CRP for solving them.

### Simulation

Simulation takes a very rigorous approach to looking at capacity problems. It requires that the proposed solution to the problem be identified in advance (even though you may not know exactly what that solution should be). As a result, simulation analyzes a specific situation looking for one and only one answer; it is not goal-driven.

Another major drawback is that simulation requires someone quite skilled in developing appropriate models. This technical expertise must then be coordinated with someone knowledgable about

| Characteristic | EASY | TOUGH | TOUGHER |
|---|---|---|---|
| Competition | Few | Many | Better than you |
| Marketplace | Stable | Demanding | Constantly changing |
| Delivery Time | Long | Short | Off-the-shelf |
| Product Line | Limited | Wide | Rapidly changing |
| Capital Equip & Skilled People | Little required | Quick availability | Long time to procure |
| Space and Money | Little required | Accessible | Required and costly |
| Manufacturing Process | Contin. process; highly repetitive | Functional work center with predictable paths | Functional work centers with varying paths |
| Bottlenecks | Obvious | Hard to predict but equip and operator flexible | Hard to predict; operators and equipment inflexible |

**Capacity Planning Degree of Difficulty Evaluation**

Exhibit 1

application to develop an effective simulation approach.

Because of this focus on one answer to one problem, it is quite difficult to explore a variety of options. For every option you want to explore, a new simulation program must be developed.

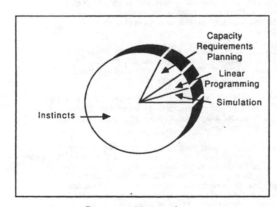

**Current Alternatives**
Exhibit 2

### Linear Programming

Unlike simulation, linear programming is goal driven (i.e., you can identify a specific goal such as minimizing unit cost, subject to a set of predefined constraints). However, a limitation of linear programming is that it depends on linear relationships. Unfortunately the world does not exist in a linear mode. As anyone driving to work knows, a 10% increase in the number of cars trying to cross a single-lane bridge does not generally mean only a 10% increase in the length of time it takes to get across that bridge. Likewise, a 10% increase in demand may not result in simply a 10% increase in work-in-process inventory. This assumption of linear relationships is a major drawback of linear programming.

Another drawback is that linear programming is deterministic and not probabilistic. Using a deterministic model means that the user must identify a specific value for every critical variable or parameter. Once again, the world does not tend to act in this way. If you are looking at a particular product, it is unusual for demand to be set at a fixed 20 units per week. The more common situation is while demand is usually 20 units a week, sometimes it is 15 units and sometimes it is

27 units. Therefore a range of values dictates a more realistic view of the environment. Linear programming cannot handle such variability and so is limited to considering only the average value.

### Instincts

Finally, of course, there's Charlie (or Fred, or Sally, or John). When new problems or opportunities arise, most companies just ask Charlie. After all, Charlie was the one who was here the last time something new was tried, and he's pretty good at predicting the outcome of new situations. So your best bet is to just ask him. However, if Charlie's not around or if Charlie happens to be wrong, this approach of using instincts may not be the best way to do capacity planning for the future. But by plan or by default, most companies use instincts to do capacity planning today.

It is clear that a new approach, one that addresses the drawbacks of these traditional techniques, is required.

## WHAT IS ARTIFICIAL INTELLIGENCE?

Artificial intelligence (AI) is a computer technology concerned with capturing distinctly human capabilities such as thinking about problems, recognizing patterns, and reacting appropriately to unique situations. While AI is used in robotics, speech recognition, and natural language processing, it also refers to the decision-making capabilities known as expert systems. Expert systems use AI technology to provide broader access to the knowledge and reasoning of experts and are simulated on computers designed to handle concepts and symbols as well as numbers. Expert, or knowledge-based, systems have distinctive differences from conventional software.

Data vs. knowledge. Conventional software deals in absolute data values while expert systems can use incomplete or imprecise data.

Quantities vs. qualities. Conventional software manipulates numerical values, 1+ 1 = 2, while expert systems can produce qualitative as well as quantitative results. They can reason by analogy, discard irrelevant background information, and apply past experience.

Passive vs. active. Conventional software responds to user instructions. Expert systems can participate actively, alerting the user to inconsistencies, short-comings, or overlooked opportunities.

The manner in which an expert system analyzes questions involves the use of several different approaches: contingent inheritance schemes, object-oriented programming, production rules, model-based reasoning, and goal-directed control.

A contingent inheritance scheme is a means of extending relevant information from one scenario to derivative scenarios while remaining flexible enough to override specific details. When higher level assumptions are overidden, the exceptions and their justifications are tracked, and that information is immediately available to anyone comparing or reviewing individual analyses.

Object-oriented programming is a technique for defining objects as collections of attributes with results that the system can understand and manipulate. Through descriptions of what specific images represent, the system understands information about these images and how they are to be organized. For example, the system can recognize the concept of a department in symbolic form and can understand arrows as representing product flows.

Production rules. sometimes referred to as if-then rules, typically first describe a situation for which the rule is appropriate and then describe an action to be taken in that situation. In addition, these rules may also be used to check the consistency and appropriateness of the underlying data.

Model-based reasoning is a way to represent highly integrated qualitative and quantitative thinking in an efficient and finite fashion. This approach matches options available in given situations with the ways in which exercising those options affect other portions of the system.

Goal-directed control is a methodology for associating

possible actions with their prerequisites. Goals are packs of information about possible actions which, when associated with rules, can suggest themselves to users at appropriate times. They make it possible to offer the user more responsive, context-sensitive choices.

By making use of a combination of artificial intelligence techniques, new advances in expert systems applications are possible. Because expert systems can incorporate qualitative as well as quantitative wisdom, the knowledge and experience of seasoned users can be integrated into systems which can guide, interpret, simplify, interact with, and construct relevant models for and approaches to real problems.

## CAPACITY MANAGEMENT AND ARTIFICIAL INTELLIGENCE - A NEW APPROACH

The application of expert systems has enabled managers to make use of advanced management science techniques when addressing real operational problems. When applied to the field of capacity management, AI has already been shown to add significant benefits to the strategic and tactical management of manufacturing and complex operations.

The first step to effective capacity management involves consolidating plant operations into meaningful groups. By grouping end items into product families and machines into work centers or manufacturing cells, an environment can be simplified without losing much detail. The system can then analyze these groupings to understand the operational flows throughout the factory. The flow between these operations is represented as the network shown in Exhibit 3. This method of symbolically displaying the flow of products through the factory quickly passes a significant amount of critical data to an AI-based system.

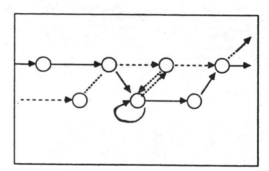

**Factory Representation**
Exhibit 3

The second step is to enter the data characteristics of each operation. These data can be defined in a non-deterministic fashion. Typical application programs permit only one number for critical parameters such as demand, lot size, set-up time, and operation processing time. Unfortunately, as noted previously, the world usually is not deterministic. It probably does not always take 20 minutes to process a particular product family at a specific work center; more likely, it usually takes 20 minutes, but it could take 12 minutes (on a good day) or 37 minutes (on a bad day). Identifying variability or uncertainty in the data creates a much more realistic picture of actual operating conditions. Advanced manufacturing application programs can take this uncertainty and effectively model it by translating it into a distribution function which is then used to evaluate the factory.

Key parameters must be identified in any effective capacity management program. These key parameters include:

- Work-in-Process Inventory
- Lead Time
- Capacity
- Utilization
- Throughput
- Product cost

The relationships between these parameters are diagramed in Exhibit 4.

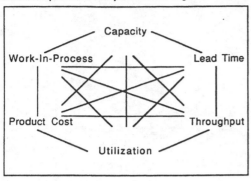

**Factory-Wide Relationships**
Exhibit 4

These variables are obviously interrelated; you cannot change one without affecting the others. As an example, a change in capacity will have an offsetting (although not necessarily equal) effect on both work-in-process inventory and lead time. Likewise, such a change will ultimately have an effect on the final cost of producing a product.

Once the network representation and values for key variables have been defined, new artificial intelligence and management science techniques can evaluate this information and provide expanded opportunities for detailed analysis.

Analyzing The Factory

The relationships described previously are identified pictorially in Exhibit 5. This exhibit displays the relationship between capacity and other key parameters such as lead time and work-in-process inventory. As an example, for a given level of demand and product mix, with sufficient capacity, lead times for producing the product will be relatively short. As capacity is reduced (while maintaining the same level of demand and product mix), lead time will increase. This increase occurs because lead time is now composed not only of processing time but also of wait, or queue, time. A similar relationship exists between capacity and work-in-process inventories.

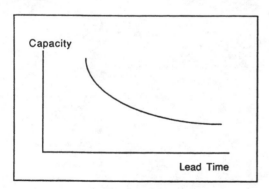

**Trade-off Curve**
Exhibit 5

These relationships, which we will refer to as trade-off curves, form the basis for the new approach to capacity management. These trade-off curves identify the key relationships between the critical parameters discussed earlier. Once the parameters have been defined and their relationships identified, assessing the effect of changes in one parameter on the other parameters becomes straightforward.

This evaluation is done most effectively by creating a set of heuristics (a set of relationships stated in the form of a set of formulas which define these relationships). Heuristics take into consideration different situations, analyze them, and quickly assess the impact of any changes. When these trade-off curves are developed for every product family and every work center, the impact of changes in one product family on other product families can be quickly identified. (We have already established that all of these parameters are interrelated; a change in one product family will affect other product families just as a change in capacity at one work center will affect the flow of product at other work centers.)

Reallocating Existing Capacity

Once existing conditions have been analyzed and the appropriate trade-off curves developed, you can start to ask questions such as "Is there a way that I can utilize my existing capacity more effectively?" In other words, without adding any overall capacity, but simply by shifting existing capacity from one work center to another, can I accomplish a goal such as reducing lead time or minimizing work-in-process inventory? Using a set of trade-off curves derived using a Greedy heuristic, you can assess where relatively small increments in capacity at one work center, and offsetting decrements in capacity at another work center, will have a positive overall effect on your factory.

By looking at these situations and asking these questions, you will be better able to effectively manage your operations. Artificial intelligence techniques make this possible.

Meeting Competitive Pressures

Sometimes doing the best you can with your existing capacity isn't good enough. Situations arise where you have a real need to meet a competitive situation (such as a 3 week lead time) or a corporate goal (such as reducing work-in-process inventory by 20%.) Specific goals are set, and simply reducing lead time or work-in-process inventory as much as possible is not sufficient.

Once again, using artificial intelligence techniques and analyzing the appropriate trade-off curves can help you evaluate the feasibility and impact of specific objectives, such as reducing lead time for a particular product family from 4.5 to 3 weeks. Using trade-off curves and a Greedy heuristic to identify where the greatest benefit will be realized from relatively small additions to capacity, this approach will provide significant immediate access to the critical "what if" capabilities desired by managers.

**CONCLUSION**

Even though the expert system approach to capacity planning is in many ways unique and a significant step forward in the science of managing capacity, the basis for what works and what doesn't really has not changed. Capacity planning can't stand alone. It is dependent on many other factors, including good systems for material planning, production planning, and master scheduling. Of course, without capacity management, these other systems provide at best a stop-gap solution to the problems of the modern manufacturer. However, given that the proper foundation is in place, using AI techniques combines the best traits of human instinct, knowledge, and experience with the power, speed, and consistency of the computer in order to make the tough business decisions and trade-offs that are essential if manufacturers are to survive in today's changing world.

**REFERENCES**

Bitran, G.R. and D. Tirupati, "Tradeoff Curves, Targeting, and Balancing in Queueing Networks," Department of Management working paper 86/87 - 4 - 9, University of Texas at Austin, 1986.

Goddard, Walter E., "Practical Principles of Capacity Planning", APICS 128th Annual International Conference Proceedings, p. 81.

Jasany, Leslie C. and Koelsch, James R., "Artificial Intelligence: facts and fantasies", Production Engineering, November 1986, p. 67.

## BIOGRAPHIES

Mary E. Cross is the Product Marketing Manager for Palladian Software, Inc. Palladian is the leading developer of expert systems applications. At Palladian, she is responsible for product marketing and product definition for the Operations Advisor, a capacity management expert system. Prior to joining Palladian, she was the Senior Product Manager at Distribution Management Systems, Inc. where she was responsible for DMS's Forecasting and Distribution Resource Planning efforts. Ms. Cross was also a manager at the consulting firm of Pittiglio, Rabin, Todd and McGrath where she specialized in consulting to high technology companies in the areas of operations and systems planning, selection, and implementation. While at PRTM, Ms. Cross did extensive work throughout the electronics industry in manufacturing and MIS.

Mary holds a B.S. degree in Computer Science and Mathematics from Vanderbilt University and a S.M. degree in Management from MIT. She has spoken at regional, national, and international conferences for APICS and The Council of Logistics Management and has guest lectured operations courses at the Massachusetts Institute of Technology.

Barbara J. Perrier is an Associate and Chief Financial Officer with New Enterprise Associates, a venture capital firm. In this capacity, she serves as a resource in the areas of financial control and manufacturing systems to the over 100 companies that are current investments of NEA. She also serves as an industry specialist in software - including AI and MRP systems. Before joining NEA, Ms. Perrier was the worldwide corporate Controller and Chief Financial Officer of Katalistiks, International, a subsidiary of Union Carbide. Katalistiks is a world-wide manufacturer of fluid cracking catalysts used in oil-refining. In this position, she was responsible for implementing manufacturing systems at plants in Savannah, GA and Delfzijl, the Netherlands. Prior to Katalistiks, Ms. Perrier was the Corporate Controller for the Kemp Manufacturing companies. At Kemp, she was a member of the project team that implemented an MRPII system, including capacity planning at four locations.

Barbara has undergraduate degrees in Economics and Accounting from Towson State University and an MBA from Loyola College and is a CPA and a CPIM. She serves on the national steering committee for the Process Industries Special Interest Group and is the author of the APICS publication - "Software Requirements Checklist for Process Industries."

Reprinted from *Production and Inventory Management*, Vol. 25, No. 2, 1984

# THE EVILS OF LOT SIZING IN MRP

Ralph St. John, DBA, CPIM,* CDP
*Arizona State University      Tempe, AZ*

Looking back on the last two years of published articles in the field of production and inventory control, particularly with regard to MRP, it is quite remarkable that we continue to be inundated by the subject of lot sizing. Wagner-Whitin, part period balancing, EOQ, period order quantity, least unit cost, Silver-Meal (and its many derivatives) still seem to be "hot" topics in our attempts to optimize the production and inventory planning functions of MRP. And how inappropriate is this passion for lot size evaluation when the creation of cycle inventories is the very antithesis of the society's Zero Inventory Crusade! Lot sizing *creates* inventory, it does not eliminate inventory.

This article summarizes the reasons why the marginal value of one more lot-sizing comparison study is virtually worthless to the P&IC practitioner, and to plead with authors, researchers, software companies, and practitioners alike to direct their attention to subjects that really need attention. There are some significant payoffs to be achieved in other areas that are going unexplored while some of the most brilliant minds in our profession continue to pollute the literature with more and more lot-sizing studies.

## MISAPPLICATION OF LOT SIZING

Let's first clear the air of a major misconception in the evaluation of lot-size techniques. Most articles that are written about lot sizing purport to apply to MRP systems, yet approximately nine out of ten treat the lot-size question with regard to a single item—the so-called single-stage case. Any analysis that examines a single item at a time cannot possibly be considered relevant to a multistage MRP system. [Ed. note: see the article by Nandakumar, this issue.]

The entire philosophy of MRP deals with the interdependencies that exist between parts—both vertical dependencies that are evidenced by bill-of-material structures and horizontal dependencies which result when many components on the same structural level must be made available at the same time in order to release a parent assembly order. Furthermore, MRP focuses on products rather than individual parts. How, then, can lot sizing of a single item be adequately evaluated without accounting for the effects on all other parts in the system?

The majority of lot-size studies, of course, don't really apply to MRP at all regardless of whether or not they say they do; they apply to independent inventory items that happen to have a discontinuous demand pattern, and this is the realm of time-phased order point. At the very least, if it is necessary to study lot sizing at all, let's correctly identify the application of such rules as time-phased order point rather than MRP. In fact, the studies that have correctly considered the dependent relationships in an MRP context have concluded that lot-sizing rules should be considered only in terms of the overall system impact. (See Biggs, *et al.* [1], Collier [2], McLaren [3], and New [5].)

## THE EFFECT ON AGGREGATE INVENTORY LEVELS

Although alternative lot-sizing methods are generally *evaluated* on the basis of a few selected items treated independently, the final decision on the "best" method is often *applied* en masse to either all items or to major groupings of items. In addition to the method, the significant determining factors—namely the inventory carrying cost and the order (or setup) cost assumptions—are often applied universally. The effects on the total level of inventory from a *change* in lot-sizing method or cost-factor variable can be ruinous. Bursting warehouses and serious depletion of cash reserves are common results of the blind application of new "optimum" lot-sizing rules.

MRP software packages are often the unwitting villains with regard to aggregate inventory levels when implementation of such systems is not accompanied by sufficient knowledge, education, and precautionary measures. Nearly every package program for MRP includes a half dozen or so choices of lot-size techniques which can be selected by just checking off a box on a customization document. (Many offerers, in fact, seem to pride themselves, through their advertising, on having many options to choose from.) It makes the decision seem almost routine. Yet one of the first rules when implementing a new MRP system should be to *retain pre-MRP lot sizes* until the system is up and running successfully. Subsequent experimentation with lot sizing (if you feel you must) should be conducted with a few selected items at a time and with a thorough evaluation and understanding of the effects of such changes on overall inventory levels.

## LOT SIZING AS A SOURCE OF NERVOUSNESS

Lot sizing rules can be classified into two types—static rules, which employ a constant lot size, and dynamic rules, where lot size is recalculated each order period. Actually, there is only one truly static rule, and that is a fixed-order quantity that is always applied regardless of actual period-by-period net requirements. Such a rule is not generally even considered in most lot-sizing studies because it is non-optimum-seeking and will result in "remnants"—parts which are in excess of known present needs but, at the same time, are inadequate to cover known future needs. Of course the fixed-order quantity may be determined by applying a dynamic rule, such as the EOQ, once every year or two, but ordering that quantity consistently during the intervening period of time.

The dynamic rules evaluate an optimum or near-optimum lot size every time the materials plan is regenerated or, for net change systems, whenever a part record is rebalanced. The insidious part of applying dynamic lot-sizing rules is that the pattern of net requirements is changing regularly with each replanning cycle—both in terms of quantity and in terms of timing. And every time the pattern of net requirements changes, the corresponding planned orders are likely to change also, often materially, when subjected to a dynamic lot-sizing rule. When the planned order for a parent item is so revised, then the gross requirements for the components are also revised, even when those requirements may already be committed for coverage by *open* factory or purchase orders. Steele [8] cites an example where *cancellation* of a high-level requirement results in *expediting* a lower-level open order, entirely due to the effects of dynamic lot sizing. (This also serves to illustrate the point made above that independent lot-size decisions where items are, in fact, interdependent constitutes a serious oversight.) Perhaps the most frequent use of the firm planned order technique in MRP systems, where human intervention is invoked to override the normal MRP logic, is in response to the need for protection against dynamic lot-sizing methods.

In a recent survey conducted by Wemmerlöv [10] of several MRP users, the fixed order quantity method together with a "new" technique called PDL (planner-determined lot size) were found to be used by over half the respondents. The next two most popular lot-size methods were the simple period order quantity and lot-for-lot, which denotes the absence of lot sizing altogether. The more elaborate dynamic methods which are often proven "superior" in comparative studies were seldom used. What an odd "coincidence" it is that the results from the most thoroughly researched characteristic of MRP systems—lot-size rules—seem to be largely ignored in practice.

A special note regarding the lot-for-lot method of order quantity determination is in order. Lot-for-lot ordering is not only a truly *dynamic* lot-size method but is more subject to system nervousness than any other technique. And yet it is the *only* method that is completely compatible with a "zero inventory" or "just in time" philosophy. It is foolish, however, to attempt to solve the problem of system nervousness by applying dynamic lot-sizing rules that themselves are a source of nervousness. The problem must be solved by achieving short lead times, discipline in master scheduling, and good execution of sound production plans.

## SOURCE OF UNBALANCED WORKLOADS

The lumpy demand patterns that are so prevalent among the dependent component items handled by MRP systems are largely the result of lot sizing at the higher levels of the product structure. It is this lumpy, irregular occurrence of requirements that has given rise to the "science" of lot sizing in lieu of the straightforward and simple EOQ formula. The lumpy demands also result in lumpy orders—both factory orders and purchase orders—which result in very uneven workloads on both the shop and on suppliers.

Much attention has been devoted in recent years to the subject of rough-cut resource requirements planning as a means to derive a Master Production Schedule (MPS) that is feasible in terms of capacity needs. Batching, or lot sizing, at the *master schedule* level is therefore accounted for in terms of key resources. Capacity Requirements Planning (CRP) represents the more detailed intermediate-range capacity plan which follows MRP to fine-tune the schedule of order releases in order to ensure relatively balanced loads in each work center. As we become more adept at balancing workloads at the MPS level, some writers have even suggested that we may eventually do away with the need for CRP.

However, any lot sizing that occurs below the top level of the product structure during the explosion process of MRP completely invalidates the rough-cut capacity plan except on a cumulative basis over the entire planning horizon. Even though capacity may be adequate to cover the planned workload *in total*, the effects of lot sizing are to batch, shift, and clump production needs into extremely unbalanced load patterns. CRP becomes a load-leveling technique to solve *major* capacity imbalances rather than a "fine-tuning" process. The dysfunctional effects of lot sizing on workload balance have been shown by Biggs, Hahn, and Pinto [1], Collier [2], and St. John [6] in multistage MRP simulation studies.

It is very sad that the demanding data requirements of CRP—standard routings and time estimates for both operation and interoperation times—make it one of the last applications of a complete production control system to be implemented. We hear of many MRP systems which fail to achieve their potential and usually place the blame on such things as lack of top management support, inaccurate inventory or bill of material records, lack of user commitment, insufficient education, and poor master schedule practices. Perhaps we should add to this list of implementation faults the indiscriminate use of lot-sizing rules *without* the workload balancing methods of CRP to compensate for the imbalances created by lot sizing.

## ERRONEOUS CALCULATION METHODS

Every exotic lot-sizing method basically attempts to balance inventory carrying costs with order or setup costs in one way or another. Yet the usual means for describing these major cost factors are frequently incorrect. A good case can be made for the fact that the only relevant costs to the lot-size decision are the *marginal* costs of ordering one more unit into inventory versus placing one more purchase order or performing one more setup.

Carrying cost, for example, is most often considered to be an opportunity cost—the percentage return given up by investing in inventory instead of the best possible alternative investment—*plus* the cost of having inventory at all. The cost of having inventory, in addition to the opportunity cost, includes handling, moving, storage, counting, insuring, taxes, and risks of obsolescence, spoilage, and shrinkage. From a marginal cost point of view this usual method of calculation is very nearly correct, since the largest element of carrying cost is the very legitimate opportunity cost, though the other cost elements, such as storage and moving costs, might well be challenged by the marginalist. The resulting marginal cost to carry would still be close to today's most frequent estimates—in the range of 30 to 40% annually of the value of an item.

What does it cost to place one additional purchase order? An answer along the conventional lines of the total purchasing and receiving department's budget dollars divided by the number of orders placed would be incorrect. That kind of calculation yields an *average* cost, not a marginal cost. The marginal cost to place one more order should be an extremely small value relative to average cost. The justification for this view is that your present personnel are being paid their salaries, the office furniture is there, and the space is allocated whether you place one more order or not. These are sunk costs and are simply not relevant to the lot-sizing decision. The cost of the purchase order form itself, of course, should be considered, but not the time to prepare it, because the preparer will be there, on salary, anyway.

A similar argument can be made for the cost of one more equipment setup. The chances are that one more setup could be accommodated without hiring any more workers or even incurring any overtime. Of course, eventually you would have to hire another setup person, putting you at a higher cost base, but then you will have many more "free" setups available as the additional worker's time gets used up. The allocation of fixed costs is a convenient accounting technique but has no place in decision making—including the determination of lot sizes.

Now let us consider the effects of applying lot-sizing rules using marginal costs. We can even use the single independent item approach without a loss of generality, though we have previously shown it to be inappropriate for evaluation in MRP systems. If the marginal cost to carry inventory is very high and the marginal cost to order is very low, what should we expect the result to be when applied to a lot-size algorithm? The answer: *very* small lot sizes *or* the actual amount of the net requirement, whichever is larger. In short, we would be almost guaranteed to adopt a lot-for-lot ordering policy.

## DIVERSION FROM REAL RESEARCH OPPORTUNITIES

Consider for a moment one more example of the opportunity cost concept. There is an opportunity cost associated with the time, effort, and thinking that go into lot-size methodology research. It is simply the value we are *not* realizing had the same degree of time, effort, and thinking been applied to subjects that are more worthwhile. Let us ponder just a few such subjects that have a high payoff potential, are consistent with the zero inventory theme, and have not been adequately studied—group technology, reducing setup time, and reducing work-in-process queues (and the excessive lead times that accompany large queues).

In a recent article by Nakane and Hall [4], the subject of stockless production (Japanese style) was thoroughly described. One of the first steps recommended by the authors is the conversion, wherever possible, of job shop methods into flow shop methods. Group technology is an approach that is consistent with this goal. With group technology, production parts are grouped based on common routings through various work centers. Where a sufficient volume of grouped items exists, the equipment is physically rearranged to create a new work center in a flow process layout to which all parts in the group are routed. The result is to provide assembly line "islands" within the job shop. Not only is scheduling and status reporting made easier, but substantial reductions in queue size and lead time are likely outcomes. Although some literature currently exists on the subject of group technology, it has not been adequately analyzed nor the benefits properly quantified.

In the same article, the use of automated setup machinery which drastically reduces setup time is also described as a necessary condition for production in very small batch sizes. Of course, the design of special machinery or technical methods improvement is primarily an engineering activity. But management is not likely to provide resources for such a program unless the benefits to be derived can be demonstrated. Surely there is an opportunity for formal research and case study reports in this area to quantify the operating cost/profit results from reduced setup times.

It is interesting to note how reduced setup times would affect lot-size decisions even when assuming average costs. As average setup costs decrease, lot sizes would also decrease. Even though this cause-and-effect relationship is intuitively obvious to anyone who has ever seen an EOQ formula, we will surely be subjected to the inevitable study which will show the degree of lot-size reduction for each conceivable method relative to the other methods when setup times are reduced.

The subjects of queue size and lead times, which are naturally interrelated, have been attacked consistently in the literature. Interoperation times that constitute 90 to 95% of total job time are frequently cited as both prevalent and excessive. Yet most of the criticism leveled at excessive queues seems to stem from "expert opinion" rather than from formal studies that attempt to quantify the associated costs (see, however, St. John [7]). And what is strange about the queue size/lead time problem is that it has been recognized for so long and yet there is very little evidence that anything is being done about it.

Let's examine a single illustration which will place a proper perspective on the benefits derived from lot-size research compared to one of the alternatives. Figure 1 shows two cost lines derived from an MRP simulation study. The solid cost line represents a lot-for-lot ordering policy, while the dashed cost line depicts the use of part period balancing as a lot-sizing method.

## FIGURE 1

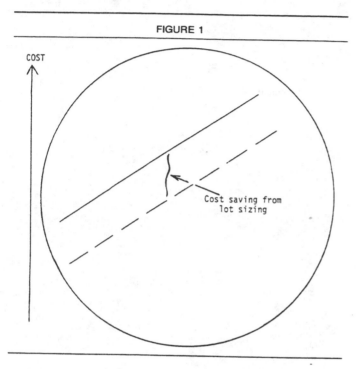

Obviously, since cost is measured on the vertical axis, the use of lot sizing provides a lower cost alternative than lot-for-lot. The saving is represented by the vertical difference between the two cost curves. A typical thorough evaluation would also plot the Silver-Meal, EOQ, Wagner-Whitin, and other methods in an attempt to show the best possible technique which would maximize the difference between the two cost lines.

Why, you should be asking, are the two cost lines in Figure 1 diagonal instead of horizontal? The explanation lies in the fact that Figure 1 represents a very small microcosm extracted from a larger computer-drawn graphic plot created using regression analysis. Figure 2 shows the more complete result, with the source of Figure 1 circled to show its origin (St. John [6]). As in Figure 1, cost is shown on the vertical axis of the plot, but what about the horizontal axis? The horizontal axis of Figure 2 depicts the amount of slack (wait) time which is included in the planned lead-time estimates used by the MRP process. The values range from zero slack (a pure assembly line process) on the left up to a maximum slack value which represents 95% wait time (or queue time) in the schedule.

This example suggests that there is a *fairly* good likelihood that there is more benefit to be gained from the study of lead-time allowances than from alternative lot size methods. In fact, if we had just one reported study in the areas of lead-time reduction, queue reduction, setup reduction, or group technology applications for every five studies of lot-sizing techniques that have been printed in the last ten years, we would be a quantum jump ahead in achieving manufacturing improvements that are scarcely dreamed possible.

## THE NATURE OF MARKETS AND PRODUCTION PROCESSES

We are in the midst of a revolutionary period with regard to manufacturing philosophies. We are being driven to achieve shorter lead times, more efficient production processes, more variety in the products we make, and faster response to the needs of our customers. The end result of this progression will demand that we drive lot-size thinking *out* of our production planning activities. Our competition, particularly from overseas, is forcing such an approach on us at the present time.

In addition, there is an irresistible market presence that is driving us to this same conclusion. Toffler [9] suggests that mankind is on the threshold of an entire new civilization which he calls the Third Wave. Toffler characterizes manufacturing in this new era as moving beyond mass production into an environment of short-run partially or completely customized products. And he indicates that the trend is in the direction of one-of-a-kind products customized for each user. Whether or not you completely agree with Toffler's future scenario, or its timing, there is evidence today which supports his ideas in terms of the proliferation of product options, colors, and features. The significant shift to a service-based economy in recent years is also indicative of the demands for uniqueness from users of goods and services.

The important point relative to lot sizing is that these present directions are inconsistent with a large-batch philosophy. The economies of scale that have for so long justified our purchase, transport, and production of goods in large quantities for the sake of efficiency need to be reconsidered in view of modern technology and market demands. There is certainly a strong suggestion that our historic approach involving the trade-off of order costs and setup costs to determine optimum lot sizes may have to give way to other, more subjective factors that may result in near-elimination of lot size concepts.

## CONCLUSION

It could easily be interpreted from the foregoing discussion that lot-size studies are worthless. This is not true. Recalling the statements introducing this article, it was suggested that the *marginal value* of discovering new optimal solutions and the consequent comparative analysis with existing lot-size methods is so miniscule that it is virtually worthless. (And this same statement could easily have been made with equal validity five or more years ago.) We simply have sufficient knowledge in this area, and to pursue it further is akin to beating a dead horse.

The kind of lot-size studies that do continue to be justified are those that show the *effects* of lot sizing, of any kind, in multistage MRP systems, which highlight the interlocking relationships of production and purchase orders as indicated previously. The few studies of this nature that have been reported up to the present time often reveal dysfunctional consequences from lot sizing—system nervousness, unbalanced workloads, and excess inventories—rather than positive benefits.

The time has come to lay the lot-sizing issue in MRP systems to rest and move on to bigger and better research opportunities. Why not preface every future lot size comparison article and every MRP computer software packaged program with the following adaptation of a well-known saying:

WARNING: It has been determined that lot-sizing methods are dangerous to the health of your MRP system.

FIGURE 2

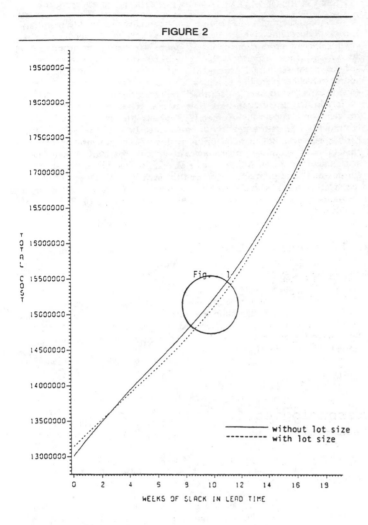

## REFERENCES

1. Biggs, Joseph R., Hahn, Chan K., and Pinto, Peter A., "Performance of Lot-sizing Rules in an MRP System with Different Operating Conditions," *Academy of Management Review*, Vol. 5, January 1980, pp. 89–96.
2. Collier, David A., "A Comparison of MRP Lot Sizing Methods Considering Capacity Change Costs," *Journal of Operations Management*, Vol. 1, February 1981, pp. 23–29.
3. McLaren, Bruce J., "Joint Lot Sizing Algorithms for Multi-Component Products," *AIDS Proceedings*, November 1975, pp. 36–38.
4. Nakane, Jinichiro and Hall, R. W., "Management Specs for Stockless Production," *Harvard Business Review*, Vol. 61, May–June 1983, pp. 84–91.
5. New, Christopher C., "Lot sizing in Multi-level Requirements Planning Systems," *Production and Inventory Management*, Vol. 15, 4th Quarter 1974, pp. 57–72.
6. St. John, Ralph E., "The Cost Effects of Inflated Planned Manufacturing Lead Times in Material Requirements Planning Systems," unpublished doctoral dissertation, Arizona State University, 1983.
7. St. John, Ralph E., "Inflated Planned Lead Times: What is the Cost?" *26th Conference Proceedings of APICS*, 1983.
8. Steele, Daniel C., "The Nervous MRP System: How to do Battle, *Production and Inventory Management*, Vol. 16, 4th Quarter 1975, pp. 83–89.
9. Toffler, Alvin, *The Third Wave*, Wm. Morrow & Co., NY, 1980.
10. Wemmerlöv, Urban, "Interviews with Thirteen American Companies with Experience of MRP," Report #3001, Lund Institute of Technology, 1977.

**About the Author—**

*RALPH ST. JOHN* is an instructor in the Decision and Information Systems Department at Arizona State University. He has taught production, purchasing, and computer systems classes at ASU for the past seven years and prior to that time was employed by IBM as a manufacturing industry specialist. Dr. St. John has also been an active APICS member for 10 years, serving varied positions at the chapter, regional, and national levels of the society. He is currently serving the society as chairman of the Curricula and Certification Council.

**CPIM Reprints**

**Evaluation Form**

APICS is interested in your comments so that we can provide you with an educational tool from which to prepare for the CPIM certification examinations. As APICS keeps the material up-to-date, we ask for your comments regarding this material. Please respond by completing this form and sending it to:

CPIM Reprints Evaluation
APICS
500 West Annandale Road
Falls Church, VA 22046-4274

Please circle reprint: Inventory Management
Just-in-Time
Master Planning
Material and Capacity Requirements Planning
Production Activity Control
Systems and Technologies

If you have questions concerning the selection of articles or have suggestions for the inclusion of material in future editions, please provide below.

_____
_____
_____
_____
_____
_____
_____
_____
_____
_____

Thank you for participating in the quality improvement process that will help APICS ensure we are providing our customers with complete educational material.